Archetypes and Motifs
in Folklore and Literature

Archetypes and Motifs in Folklore and Literature

A HANDBOOK

Jane Garry and Hasan El-Shamy, Editors

M.E.Sharpe
Armonk, New York
London, England

The EuroSlavic fonts used to create this work are © 1986–2002 Payne Loving Trust.
EuroSlavic is available from Linguist's Software, Inc.,
www.linguistsoftware.com, P.O. Box 580, Edmonds, WA 98020-0580 USA
tel (425) 775-1130.

Library of Congress Cataloging-in-Publication Data

Archetypes and motifs in folklore and literature : a handbook / edited by Jane Garry and
Hasan El-Shamy.
   p. cm.
 Includes bibliographical references and index.
 ISBN 0-7656-1260-7 (hardcover : alk. paper)
 1. Folklore—Classification. 2. Folk literature—Themes, motives. I. Garry, Jane.
II. El-Shamy, Hasan M., 1938–GR72.56.A73 2004
398'.012—dc22   2004009103

Printed in the United States of America

The paper used in this publication meets the minimum requirements of
American National Standard for Information Sciences
Permanence of Paper for Printed Library Materials,
ANSI Z 39.48-1984.

∞

MV (c) 10   9   8   7   6   5   4   3   2   1

Contents

B. Mythical Animals

C. Tabu

D. Magic

K. Deceptions

L. Reversal of Fortune

M. Ordaining the Future

N. Chance and Fate

P. Society

Q. Rewards and Punishments

R. Captives and Fugitives

Illustrations

Preface

This book was conceived with two goals in mind: to serve as an introduction for those who may not be familiar with Stith Thompson's great *Motif-Index of Folk Literature,* and to present in-depth essays on a few of the many thousands of motifs that his work classifies. Although we have had to limit our selection we have striven to include those we judged to be of primary significance.

Thompson's *Motif-Index* is one of the most important works in folklore studies produced in the twentieth century. Some may view it merely as a taxonomic endeavor, but as Thompson stated, "Before it can become an object of serious and well-considered study, every branch of knowledge needs to be classified. There was a time when geology and botany consisted of random collections of facts and hastily constructed theories. It was only when this anecdotal stage gave way to systematic classification that real progress was made toward a thorough method of study" (1977, 413). Although others before Thompson had noted the need to classify narrative elements of folklore (see Introduction on page 15), his work was unique in that it was the first to go beyond mere alphabetical listings of terms, and it differentiated between motifs and folktale types. The *Motif-Index* and its companion, *The Types of the Folktale* by Antti Aarne, which Thompson translated and enlarged, have greatly facilitated comparative work in folklore that is ongoing today.

We present in this work sixty-six essays covering numerous motifs and archetypes. Although Thompson eschewed classification based on psychological principles, Jungian approaches to folklore study are found in many of the essays here, and we have chosen to elaborate upon the concept of the archetype. We hope that in addition to serving as an introduction to the *Motif-Index* and the endlessly fascinating subject of folklore, this collection may also provide a few hours of pleasurable reading and evoke some of the wonder and delight felt on first hearing the old stories.

Introduction

This book contains essays on some of the most important motifs and archetypes found in folklore and literature throughout the world. The book is keyed to Stith Thompson's *Motif-Index of Folk Literature* (1932–1936; second edition 1955–1958).

Simply defined, a motif is a small narrative unit recurrent in folk literature. In his introduction, Thompson writes, "Certain items in narrative keep on being used by storytellers; they are the stuff of which tales are made . . . there must be something of particular interest to make an item important enough to be remembered, something not quite commonplace."

In a later essay, Thompson famously defines a motif by saying:

> A mother as such is not a motif. A cruel mother becomes one because she is at least thought to be unusual. The ordinary processes of life are not motifs. To say that "John dressed and walked to town" is not to give a single motif worth remembering; but to say that the hero put on his cap of invisibility, mounted his magic carpet, and went to the land east of the sun and west of the moon is to include at least four motifs—the cap, the carpet, the magic air journey, and the marvelous land. (1972, 753)

Although a mother "as such" may not be a motif, *mother* is such a basic experience of human existence that it may be considered an archetype. What is the difference between a motif and an archetype? While a motif is a unit of interest in a tale or some other genre such as a proverb, joke, ballad, or riddle, an archetype is a pattern of primary significance with deep psychic resonance that also occurs in various literary genres.

MOTIFS AND ARCHETYPES IN LITERATURE

Mircea Eliade observes that the nineteenth-century novel is "the great repository of degraded myths," and, amplifying this statement, Harry Levin remarks, "thus the novels of Dickens could be regarded as fairy tales about the babes in the wood encountering wicked witches in protean disguises, while the focal point of Balzac's work would be the motif of the youngest son who sets out to seek his worldly fortune" (Levin 1974, 242). In fact, we know that Dickens was very aware of fairy tales as he wrote his novels and that he consciously employed fairy tale motifs in his work (Grob 1966, 246). Many writers have mined the troves of traditional myth and tales: Homer's *Odyssey* and the works of Chaucer, Shakespeare, Cervantes, Milton, and Hardy are just a few examples of literary masterpieces that contain elements from folklore. The profound resonance that these works have for us can be at least partially explained by the presence of the ancient motifs they contain. As Gilbert Murray writes: "The things that thrill and amaze us in *Hamlet* . . . are not any historical particulars about medieval Elsinore . . . but things belonging to the old stories and the old magic rites, which stirred and thrilled our forefathers five and six thousand years ago" (1927, 236). When the ghost of Hamlet's father appears on the battlements of Elsinore castle to urge Hamlet to avenge his murder, that is the old story of the "Return from the dead to reveal murder" (Motif E231). The motifs in the *Odyssey* include Polyphemus (G100; AT 1137), the harpies (B52), the sirens (B53), the enchantress Circe, who transforms men (G263.1), the journey to the world of the dead (F81), the successive transformations of Proteus (G311), and the lotus flower that causes Odysseus's companions to forget the homeward way (D1365.1.1) (Thompson 1977, 278–279).

The concept of the archetype was appropriated from the work of the Swiss psychoanalyst C.G. Jung and applied to literary theory in two related fields, archetypal theory and mythological theory. The idea of the archetype is linked with Jung's concept of the collective unconscious, in which dwell "archaic or—I would say—primordial types, that is, with universal images that have existed since the remotest times" (Jung 1981, 5). Although his primary focus was psychological, specifically dreams, Jung was interested in manifestations of the archetype in myth and fairy tale, believing that "myths are first and foremost psychic phenomena that reveal the nature of the soul" (1981, 6).

While many scholars disagree with Jung's premises and conclusions regarding archetypes, especially that there is a biological basis for them in the human psyche, there is no doubt that some of the figures he identifies are recurrent characters in mythology, folklore, and literature. Some of the chief archetypes with which Jung is concerned are "the *shadow,* the *wise old man,* the *child* (including the child hero), the *mother* . . . and her counterpart the *maiden,* and lastly the *anima* in man and the *animus* in woman" (Jung 1969, 4). Additional archetypes identified by Jung include the trickster and the hero.

Maud Bodkin, one of the first scholars to apply Jung's ideas to literature, rejects the notion that archetypes are "stamped upon the physical organism" or "inherited in the structure of the brain," but interprets them instead as persistent cultural symbols that are passed down through generations via folklore and literature. She states, "I shall use the term 'archetypal pattern' to refer to that within us which, in Gilbert Murray's phrase, 'leaps in response' to the effective presentation . . . of an ancient theme" (Bodkin 1934, 4).

The critic Northrup Frye did much to apply Jung's ideas of the archetype to literature, although he dissociated the concept of the archetype from depth psychology. Numerous scholars—including James Hillman, Bettina Knapp, and Martin Bickman—have worked with archetypes, with varying degrees of emphasis on the original psychological nature of Jung's work. In 1997, Carol Rupprecht pronounced archetypal theory "a fledgling and much misconstrued field of inquiry with significant but still unrealized potential for the study of literature and of aesthetics in general" (122). Similarly, mythological theory retains a powerful appeal.

CROSS-CULTURAL STUDIES OF MOTIFS

In studying the distributions of motifs, one finds that the same object in different cultures may hold vastly different meanings. For example, snakes are found in the mythology and folktales of many cultures. While in Judeo-Christian tradition the snake usually symbolizes evil, in India it is a sacred creature that plays "a major role in folklore and in many Buddhist, Jaina, and Hindu legends. . . . In southern India, especially on the west coast, many houses have a snake shrine or a snake grove in a corner of the garden, where offerings, especially of milk, are made to the snakes" (Dallapiccola 2002, 139–140). In European folklore the dragon is a guardian of remote, dark regions and often a beast to whom humans must be sacrificed, but in many Asian cultures dragons are helpers of human beings and bring good luck.

The enthusiasm for folklore that blossomed in Europe in the eighteenth century has been called "a predictable preoccupation of romantic scholarship" (Feldman and Richardson 1972, 443). Initially restricted to curiosities of European "peasant" cultures, folklore gained a cross-cultural dimension after ethnology revealed the existence of what were perceived to be analogous materials among non-Europeans. It was through the study of folklore that philosophical issues and questions were initially raised in anthropology that are still debated by anthropologists. For example, what are cultural universals, and do they exist at all? Although later scholars have been more cautious regarding universals, nineteenth-century folklore was predicated upon their existence, and scholars such as Thomas Keightley, Edward B. Tylor, Adolf Bastian, Andrew Lang, Robert R. Marett, and James G. Frazer pointed to the psychic unity of man to explain them (although some scholars, notably

Lang, expressed a belief in the role of diffusion as well). The error of the nineteenth-century folklorists was not that they focused on similarities, but that their methods for alleging such similarities were not always sound. Much of what they did involved picking and choosing arbitrarily among inadequate ethnological data and inferring similarity where in many cases it did not exist.

But with over a century of subsequent fieldwork to draw on, today both anthropologists and folklorists are in a better position to make cross-cultural comparisons than were the early folklorists. According to Dundes, studies in the distribution of myths reveal that while there is no myth that is truly universal, so is there no myth that has ever been found to be limited to a single culture (1984, 270). Elsewhere he concludes: "Mythology must be studied in cultural context in order to determine which individual mythological elements reflect and which refract the culture. But, more than this, the cultural relative approach must not preclude the recognition and identification of transcultural similarities and potential universalities" (1962, 1048).

With regard to the *Motif-Index,* certain limitations must be addressed. For example, it has been well documented (and acknowledged by Thompson himself) that his coverage of motifs for areas such as Central Africa, North American, and Oceania is inadequate. This was in large part because published sources for materials from these areas were inadequate. As just one example of the differences encountered in cross-cultural analysis, African tales differ from European in one noteworthy sense: they are heavily dominated by animal protagonists. Thompson assigns only 299 numbers for animal tales. Moreover, a universal feature of the animals in African tales is their ability to speak, which they do in almost every story. Therefore, Thompson's list of motifs for talking animals is virtually meaningless for African stories. Also, Thompson's treatment of trickster tales, another prominent type of African tale, is insufficient (Pierson 1971, 210). What little coverage Thompson gives to trickster figures is focused on human tricksters rather than animal tricksters.

THE HISTORY OF THE CLASSIFICATION OF TALES AND MOTIFS

Thompson was not the first scholar to work on identifying and listing motifs; the need for classifying narrative elements was seen in the nineteenth century. The first system was an attempt at ordering folktales, done by Johann Georg von Hahn in 1864, in the notes to his *Griechische und albanesische Märchen.* In 1908, R.H. Lowie published a brief article in the *Journal of American Folklore* called "Catch-words for Mythological Motives," which built on two recent articles in German by Paul Ehrenreich. Lowie says, "The advantages of a uniform terminology—of brief, unequivocal designations for widespread elements which are constantly referred to in mythological discussions—are obvious" (1908, 24). These and other early endeavors were flawed in several respects, but the biggest problem was that they were alphabetical lists and they did not distinguish between the tale type and the separate motifs of which the tale type is composed.

Finnish Folklore and the Historical-Geographical Method

Folklore had been collected in Europe before the eighteenth century, but its study gathered momentum in the latter half of that century from the currents of nationalism and romanticism that were predominant in the British Isles and on the Continent. The work on classification that led directly to the *Motif-Index* was carried out in Finland at the end of the nineteenth century, although there had been a number of tale type indexes published elsewhere, including, for example, von Hahn's *Griechische und albanesische Märchen* (Leipzig 1864), and Joseph Jacobs's "The Science of Folktales and the Problems of Diffusion" in *Papers and Transactions of the International Folklore Congress, 1891* (Azzolina 1987, xxvi–xxvii). The first collections of folklore in Finland consisted of magic songs (runes) and proverbs. The popularity that these publications generated rapidly developed into a national movement to document other literary aspects of folklore. From this campaign came a vast collection of folk songs, runes, epic poetry, myths, legends, folktales, proverbs, and riddles, and the scope and visibility this gave to the country's cultural heritage ultimately led to folklore becoming the focus of Finnish national identity.

Among the Finnish folklorists who were instrumental in bringing order to the national collection was Julius Krohn (1835–1888), who developed the historical-geographical method to compare versions of the epic songs of the *Kalevala*. He broke the songs down into small units and studied their distributions, attempting to determine the place of origin and the geographical distribution of each song. Refining and expanding the concept of his father's historical-geographical method, Kaarle Krohn (1863–1933) applied the method to folktales. Starting with tales in the Finnish tradition, he was instrumental in encouraging scholars to collect tales all over the world for comparative and historical study.

Tale Types and the Tale Type Index

Krohn's student, Antti Aarne (1867–1925), adopted the historical-geographical method in his study of tales and devised a system to catalog and sort them by type, publishing his *Verzeichnis der Märchentypen* (*Tale Type Index*) in 1910. In his introduction, Aarne anticipated that an index of motifs might be created, and Thompson undertook that monumental task while he translated and expanded Aarne's tale type index, which appeared in English as *The Types of the Folktale* (first revision 1928 and second revision 1961. As the present work goes to press, the third revision (by Hans-Jörg Uther) is forthcoming).

While the type-index implies that all versions of a type have a genetic relationship, the motif-index makes no such assumption (Thompson 1977, 416). The *Motif-Index* was a more ambitious work than *The Types of the Folk Tale* because it endeavored to cover not only folktales, but "ballads, myths, fables, medieval romances, exempla, fabliaux, jest-books, and local legends." Although the scope of coverage was greater, Thompson was working with a smaller unit of study, the most basic thematic elements of folklore. Most oral tales incorporate a single or a limited number of tale types; however, a tale may contain dozens of motifs.

Tale types are prefaced by "AT" for Aarne-Thompson, or simply "Type": for example, AT 310 or Type 310. A tale type may end with an alphabetical letter to indicate that it is a subtype or a variation on a cardinal tale type (e.g., AT 510A). A number of tale types have been the subject of monographs, most written in German, and many written by Antti Aarne.

STRUCTURE OF THE *MOTIF-INDEX*

The classification system of the *Motif-Index* has been likened to the Dewey decimal system of library classification, in that the numbering scheme uses decimal points for virtually unlimited expansion, and these numbers are arranged under broad subject headings which are assigned letters, as follows: A Mythological Motifs; B Mythical Animals; C Tabu; D Magic; E The Dead; F Marvels; G Ogres; H Tests; J The Wise and the Foolish; K Deceptions; L Reversal of Fortune, M Ordaining the Future; N Chance and Fate; P Society; Q Rewards and Punishments; R Captives and Fugitives; S Unnatural Cruelty; T Sex; U Nature of Life; V Religion; X Humor; Z Miscellaneous. Therefore, a motif is designated by an alphabetical letter indicating its general nature within Thompson's schema followed by a digital number, for example, E324, "Dead mother's return to aid persecuted children." In this example, the organization is as follows: (the numerous motifs that fall under all these headings are not included because of space considerations):

E. THE DEAD

E0–E199.	Resuscitation
E200–E599.	Ghosts and other revenants
E200–E299.	Malevolent return from the dead
E300–E399.	Friendly return from the dead
E324.	Dead child's friendly return to parents, frequently to stop weeping.

The *Motif-Index* also contains a bibliographic list giving citations where examples of this motif may be found from Irish, English, American,

Lithuanian, Spanish, Chinese, North American Indian (Pawnee), and Eskimo (Greenland) sources.

Thompson states that the classification system "makes no assumption that items listed next to each other have any genetic relationship, but only that they belong in neighboring logical categories. The classification is for the practical purpose of arranging and assorting narrative material so that it can be easily found" (1977, 423–424).

CRITICISM OF THE *MOTIF-INDEX*

In a work of such scope and detail, it is not surprising to find some problems and omissions. In addition to its concentration on European material, Thompson chose not to consider psychological aspects of motifs, claiming that they "are not, I think, of much practical help toward the orderly arrangement of stories and myths of a people." One of us (El-Shamy 1997) argues that psychological principles can and should be used as indexing devices. Thompson's definition of motif has been criticized for being both vague and ambiguous since "it variously refers to theme, plot (tale type), actor, item (object), or descriptive element. A precise application of the term requires that it refers to only one kind of unit" (Apo 1997).

Summarizing and addressing criticisms of both the *Motif-Index* and the *Tale Type Index,* the late Alan Dundes affirmed that the *Motif-Index* remains a monumental work of scholarship and a central tool in folklore and literary studies (1997, 195).

New Motifs and Tale Types

The symbol "§" at the end of a motif number designates a new motif, for example W251§, "Beliefs (theories) about composition of character (personality)"; W256§, "Stereotyping: generalization of a trait of character, from person to group (and vice versa) (El-Shamy 1995, xv). Like motifs, new tale types are also indicated with the symbol "§." These new motifs and types have been developed by later scholars, and no attempt has been made to collate them within the existing classifications. El-Shamy gives 8,700 newly developed motifs in *Types of the Folktale in the Arab World: A Demographically Oriented Approach* (2004).

New Work

As mentioned above, a number of scholars have augmented Thompson's work by publishing lists of supplementary motifs and types, which are distinguished with the addition of the symbol "§." Numerous indexes devoted to areas of the world that Thompson did not adequately cover may be found in a reference book devoted to them (Azzolina 1987). In 1992, Alan Dundes wrote, "Some day when (and if) comprehensive tale type indices have been completed for the entire world, there can then be an attempt to put together one master tale type index for all the world's folktales" (xxi).

REFERENCES

Aarne, Antti, and Stith Thompson. 1961. *The Types of the Folktale: A Classification and Bibliography.* FFC no. 74. Helsinki: Folklore Fellows Communications.

Apo, Satu. 1997. "Motif." In *Folklore: An Encyclopedia,* ed. Thomas Green. Santa Barbara, CA: ABC-CLIO.

Azzolina, David. 1987. *Tale Type and Motif Indexes: An Annotated Bibliography.* New York: Garland.

Bascom, William. 1992. *African Folktales in the New World.* Bloomington: Indiana University Press.

Bodkin, Maud. 1934. *Archetypal Patterns in Poetry.* London: Oxford University Press.

Dallapiccola, Anna L. 2002. *Dictionary of Hindu Lore and Legend.* London: Thames and Hudson.

Dundes, Alan. 1962. "Earth-Diver: Creation of the Mythopoeic Male." *American Anthropologist* 64 (5:1): 1032–1051.

———, ed. 1984. *Sacred Narrative: Readings in the Theory of Myth.* Berkeley: University of California Press.

———. 1992. Series Editor's Preface. In *African Folktales with Foreign Analogues,* by May Klipple. New York: Garland.

———. 1997. "The *Motif-Index* and the *Tale Type Index*: A Critique." *Journal of Folklore Research* 34 (3): 195–202.

El-Shamy, Hasan M. 1995. *Folk Traditions of the Arab World: A Guide to Motif Classification.* 2 vols. Bloomington: Indiana University Press.

———. 1997. "Psychologically-based Criteria for Classification by Motif and Tale Type." *Journal of Folklore Research* 34 (3): 233–243.

———. 2004. *Types of the Folktale in the Arab World: A Demographically Oriented Approach.* Bloomington: Indiana University Press.

Feldman, Burton, and Robert D. Richardson. 1972. *The Rise of Modern Mythology, 1680–1860.* Bloomington: Indiana University Press.

Finnegan, Ruth. 1970. *Oral Literature in Africa.* Oxford: Oxford University Press.

Georges, Robert A. 1997. "The Centrality in Folkloristics of Motif and Tale Type." *Journal of Folklore Research* 34 (3): 203–208.

Grob, Shirley. 1966. "Dickens and Some Motifs of the Folktale." In *Myth and Literature: Contemporary Theory and Practice,* ed. John B. Vickery. Lincoln: University of Nebraska Press.

Jung, C.G. 1981 [1969]. *Collected Works of C.G. Jung,* Vol. 9 (Part 1): *Archetypes and the Collective Unconscious.* Ed. and trans. Gerhard Adler and R.F.C. Hull. Princeton, NJ: Princeton University Press.

Levin, Harry. 1974. "Motif." In *Dictionary of the History of Ideas,* ed. Philip P. Wiener, 235–244. New York: Scribner.

Lowie, R.H. 1908. "Catch-words for Mythological Motives." *Journal of American Folklore* 21 (80): 24–27.

Murray, Gilbert. 1927. *The Classical Tradition in Poetry.* Cambridge, MA: Harvard University Press.

Piersen, William D. 1971. "An African Background for American Negro Folktales?" *Journal of American Folklore* 84 (332): 204–214.

Rupprecht, Carol Schreier. 1997. "Archetypal Theory and Criticism." In *The Johns Hopkins Guide to Literary Theory and Criticism.* Baltimore: Johns Hopkins University Press.

Thompson, Stith. 1972. "Motif." In *Funk and Wagnalls Standard Dictionary of Folklore, Mythology, and Legend,* ed. Maria Leach and Jerome Fried, 753. New York: Funk and Wagnalls. First ed. 1949.

———. 1973. *The Types of the Folk-Tale: A Classification and Bibliography.* Antti Aarne's *Verzeichnis der Märchentypen* translated and enlarged by Stith Thompson. FFC no. 184. Helsinki: Folklore Fellows Communications. Second revision.

———. 1977. *The Folktale.* Berkeley: University of California Press. Orig. ed. New York: Holt, Rinehart, and Winston, 1946.

How to Use This Book

The organization of this book follows that of the *Motif-Index*. Specific topics are found under the broad subject heading letters. Most of the entries included here are for "umbrella" motifs; more specific motifs are discussed within these entries and listed alphabetically in the index.

Following are the broad subject headings, with Thompson's descriptions, taken from the introduction to the *Motif-Index,* which we have amplified (he did not provide descriptions for Q, R, S; we have added these, as well as elaborated on some of his descriptions).

A. Mythological Motifs [and related beliefs]

Motifs having to do with creation and with the nature of the world: creators, gods, and demigods; the creation and nature of the universe, and especially of the earth; the beginnings of life; the creation and establishment of the animal and vegetable world.

B. Mythical Animals

Not all tales in which animals figure are placed here, for most frequently it is the action and not the particular actor that is significant in such stories. Here appear, on the contrary, animals that are in some way remarkable as such: mythical animals like the dragon, magic animals like the truth-telling bird, animals with human traits, animal kingdoms, weddings, and the like. Then there are the many helpful or grateful beasts, marriages of animals to human beings, and other fanciful ideas about animals.

C. Tabu

Motifs here are based upon the primitive idea of tabu. Forbidden things of all kinds are listed here, as well as the opposite of that concept, the unique compulsion. Thus, the chapter consists largely of incidents based on certain principles of conduct that are rooted in archaic fears of the supernatural.

D. Magic [and similar supernatural occurrences]

This is the most extensive group, and truly constitutes the stuff of folk and fairy tales, with divisions for all kinds of magical transformation (such as from a person to a different person, an animal, or object) and disenchantment; magic objects (such as food, clothing, weapons, conveyances, and instruments); magic powers (strength, knowledge, love induced by magic, immortality, forgetfulness, bewitching) and other manifestations.

E. The Dead

These motifs concern ideas about the dead—resuscitation, ghosts, and reincarnation—as well as ideas concerning the nature of the soul. There is a tremendous amount of material on "Ghosts and other revenants," E200–E599, indicative of just how powerful the idea of some kind of visitation from the dead, both malevolent and friendly, has been in cultures around the world.

F. Marvels

Motifs here include journeys to other worlds; extraordinary creatures such as fairies, spirits, and demons; wondrous places, such as castles in the sea; and marvelous persons and events. Heroes in myth, legend, and folktale throughout the world have journeyed to three main types of otherworld: the upper world (F10), lower world (F80), and earthly paradise (F111).

G. Ogres [and Satan]

Dreadful beings such as ogres, witches, and the like are contained here. It will be seen that there is naturally much relation between E, F, and G; for example, between ogres and evil spirits, or between fairies and witches or ghosts. These relationships are noted by means of cross-references.

H. Tests

All motifs here are comprehended under the term "Tests," although they were originally broken down into three sections—Recognition, Riddles, and Tasks and Quests. However, tales of recognition are really tests of identity; riddles and the like, tests of cleverness; and tasks and quests, tests of prowess. In addition are to be found sundry tests of character and other qualities.

J. The Wise and the Foolish

This section was likewise originally three chapters—Wisdom, Cleverness, Foolishness. Their fundamental unity is apparent: the motivation is always mental. The first part (wisdom) consists in large part of fable material. The tales of cleverness and stupidity come in large measure from jest-books.

K. Deceptions

In the motifs of the previous section the attention is directed primarily to the mental quality of the character. In K, on the contrary, primary importance is given to action. A very large part of narrative literature deals with deceptions. The work of thieves and rascals, deceptive captures and escapes, seductions, adultery, disguises, and illusions constitute one of the most extensive chapters in the classification.

L. Reversal of Fortune

Here appear reversals of fortune including motifs commonly associated with rags-to-riches stories, such as L50, "Victorious youngest daughter," also the basis of tale types 361, 425, 431, 440, 480, 510, 511, 707, 901, and 923, which are variants of the Cinderella tale. Other reversals of fortune include the sections L200–L299, "Modesty rewarded"; L300–L399, "Triumph of the weak"; and L400–L499, "Pride brought low."

M. Ordaining the Future

Deals with such definite ordaining of the future as irrevocable judgments, bargains, promises, and oaths.

N. Chance and Fate

The large part that luck plays in narrative (and life) is shown. The capriciousness of luck and the personifications of fate are covered. Included are tales of gambling as well as lucky and unlucky accidents and encounters.

P. Society

Here are motifs concerned with the social system. Not all tales about kings and princes belong here, but only such motifs as rest upon some feature of the social order: customs concerning kings, or the relation of the social ranks and the professions, or anything noteworthy in the administration of such activities as law or war. A great number of cross-references appear in this chapter. This chapter is the least developed area of the *Motif-Index*.

Q. Rewards and Punishments

Stories illustrating consequences of different actions and behaviors, for example "Murder punished," Q211; "Killing an animal revenged," Q211.6; "Piety rewarded," Q20. Also, "The nature of rewards," Q100, and "Kinds of punishment," Q400, are elaborated.

R. Captives and Fugitives

Here are stories dealing with abductions, captivity, and chases (often by supernatural creatures such as monsters).

S. Unnatural Cruelty

Here are found motifs dealing with various methods of murder and mutilation, some quite grisly ("Murder by tearing out heart," S139.6). Many of the stories deal with cruel relatives ("Cruel father," S11; "Cruel mother," S12; "Cruel children and grandchildren," S20), with themes involving the "Cruel stepmother," S31, particularly common. Also prominent is the motif of "Abandoned or murdered children," S300.

T. Sex

Here are motifs dealing with sex, although there are, of course, many other parts of the index where such motifs are also of interest. Here particularly come wooing, marriage, married life, and the birth of children, as well as sundry types of sexual relations.

U. The Nature of Life

Here are gathered a small number of motifs, mostly from fable literature, of a homiletic tendency. A tale is told with the sole purpose of showing the nature of life. "Thus goes the world" is the text of such tales.

V. Religion [and religious services]

Motifs making up incidents depending upon religious differences or upon certain objects of religious worship are found here.

W. Traits of Character

Stories designed to illustrate traits of character, both favorable ("Man speaks no evil," W24; "Patience," W26) and unfavorable ("Greed," W151; "Stinginess," W152; "Jealousy," W181).

X. Humor

This category contains incidents whose purpose is entirely humorous. Many cross-references to merry tales listed elsewhere are given.

Z. Miscellaneous Groups of Motifs [and symbolism]

Topics that do not have a formal entry in the *Motif-Index* are listed here. Of particular importance for our present treatment of archetypes and motifs is the subdivision of Symbolism (Z100–Z199). Yet this is another underdeveloped area of the *Motif-Index*.

ABBREVIATIONS AND STYLE EMPLOYED IN THIS VOLUME

AT Designates a tale type found in Aarne-Thompson, *The Types of the Folktale.* It is followed by a number and an italicized title, for example, AT 425A, *The Search for the Lost Husband.* A type number may be followed by a letter indicating a standard variation on the general narrative theme. For example AT 425A, *The Monster (Animal) as Bridegroom*; AT 425B, *The Disenchanted Husband: The Witch's Task*; AT 425C, *Beauty and the Beast*, and so on constitute subtypes of the main tale type.

Tale types may also be prefaced merely by the word "Type," for example Type 425B.

When Thompson expanded Aarne's original work in 1928 he indicated new types by the use of asterisks. These types were listed in a separate appendix. Many had been found rarely or only in a single country. In the 1961 revision of the *Type Index* they were integrated into the main body of the work, but set in smaller type and with an asterisk or asterisks appended. In a few cases where fieldwork revealed more ubiquity of a type it was changed to a regular type, and so noted.

KHM Designates a story from Grimms's *Kinder- und Hausmärchen* (*Children's and Household Tales*). It is followed by a title in quotation marks.

For example, KHM 14, "The Three Spinning Women." In some cases, titles of stories from KHM are the same or similar to the titles of the tale type of which they are a version; for example, KHM 44, "Godfather Death" ("Der Herr Gevatter" in the original), is also known as AT 332, *Godfather Death*. However, KHM 49, "The Six Swans," is known by a different tale type name: AT 451, *The Maiden Who Seeks Her Brothers*.

Motif Designates an entry in Thompson's *Motif-Index*. Motifs are classified by a letter and number, and titles are enclosed by quotation marks. For example, Motif B122, "Bird with magic wisdom." Sometimes the number includes a decimal, for example, D861.7, "Magic object carried off by bird."

About the Editors and Contributors

EDITORS

Jane Garry, freelance editor and researcher, is a library researcher at Yale University libraries for the *Oxford English Dictionary*. She has coedited *Trial and Error: An Oxford Anthology of Legal Stories* (1998) and *Facts About the World's Languages: An Encyclopedia of the World's Languages, Past and Present* (2001).

Hasan El-Shamy is a professor of folklore in the Departments of Folklore and of Near Eastern Languages and Cultures at Indiana University. His recent publications include *Types of the Folktale in the Arab World: A Demographically Oriented Approach* (2004). He is currently working on *A Motif Index for 'Alf Layla wa Laylah (The Thousand Nights and a Night)*.

CONTRIBUTORS

D.L. Ashliman taught folklore, mythology, German, and comparative literature at the University of Pittsburgh for thirty-three years and was named emeritus in 2000. He also served as a guest professor in the Departments of Comparative Literature and of Folklore at the University of Augsburg, Germany. His recent publications include an edition of *Aesop's Fables* (2003) and *Folk and Fairy Tales: A Handbook* (2004).

Karen Bamford is an associate professor of English at Mount Allison University, New Brunswick, Canada. She is the author of *Sexual Violence in Jacobean Drama* (2000) and with Alexander Leggatt, coeditor of *Approaches to Teaching English Renaissance Drama* (2002).

Betty J. Belanus is folklorist and education specialist at the Smithsonian Center for Folklife and Cultural Heritage. In 2002 she published, with John Major, *Caravan to America: Living Arts of the Silk Road,* as well as *Seasonal,* a novel.

Susan M. Bernardo is an associate professor of English at Wagner College. She recently coedited *Gender Reconstructions: Pornography and Perversions in Literature and Culture.*

Hande A. Birkalan is an assistant professor of anthropology at Yeditepe University in Istanbul, Turkey. Her recent publications include "Gecekondu Re-Visited: A Critical Essay," in *European Journal of Turkish Studies* (2004), and "The Arabian Nights in Turkish: Translations, Reception, Issues in Turkish Literature," *Fabula* (2004).

John P. Brennan is an associate professor of English at Indiana University–Purdue University Fort Wayne. He is the author of, most recently, "The Nightingale's Forum: A Privy Council," in *Chaucer Review* (2004).

Esther Clinton has completed her course work for the Ph.D. in folklore at Indiana University and is currently writing her dissertation. She also works with Literacy Volunteers of America, helping English-as-a-second-language students.

Peter L. De Rose, attorney-at-law, is a member of the College of the State Bar of Texas. Formerly assistant professor of English at Lamar University, he is the author of *Jane Austen and Samuel Johnson* and editor of the three-volume *Concordance to the Works of Jane Austen.*

Anne E. Duggan is an assistant professor in the Department of Romance Languages and Literatures, Wayne State University. She has written on early modern French women writers as well as the fairy tale. Her recent publications include "Women and Absolutism in French Opera and Fairy Tale," *French Review* (December 2004) as well as a forthcoming book called *Salonnières, Furies, and Fairies: The Politics of Gender and Cultural Change in Absolutist France.* She is associate editor for *Marvels & Tales.*

el-Sayed el-Aswad is a professor of anthropology and chair of the Department of Sociology, Tanta University, Tanta, Egypt. He has held teaching and research positions at the University of Michigan and Wayne State University and taught at the United Arab Emirates University, where he founded and served as head of the Unit of Anthropological and Folkloric Resources. His most recent publications include "Islam in Contemporary Arab Countries: The United Arab Emirates," in *Worldmark Encyclopedia of Religious Practices,* ed. Thomas Riggs (forthcoming), and "Applied Anthropology in Egypt: Practicing Anthropology within Local and Global Contexts" in *The Global Practice of Anthropology* (2004).

Elizabeth Wylie Ernst wrote her dissertation on historic representations of the Grimms' *Frau Holle* and regularly teaches the very popular large-enrollment courses Indo-European Folktale and Germanic Myths, Legends and Sagas at the University of Pittsburgh. She is currently working on an article on Viking survivals in the Orkneys. The author also serves as German program coordinator, and is responsible for curricular planning and development for many aspects of the German language program, including phonetics, graduate student reading courses, professional German, first-year language courses, and summer exchange student tutorials.

Deanna Delmar Evans, a professor of English at Bemidji State University, Minnesota has published articles in several journals, including *Studies in Scottish Literature, Neophilologus, Medieval Feminist Newsletter, Medieval Association of the Midwest Journal,* and *Minnesota English Journal.* She edited "The Babees Book" in *Medieval Literature for Children* (2003) and wrote entries for *Dictionary of Medieval Biography, Medieval Folklore, Catholic Women Writers,* and *The Rise of the Medieval World: 500–1300.*

Christine Goldberg specializes in comparative research on international tale types. She was a staff member of Hans-Jörg Uther's project to revise *The Types of the Folktale* and writes for the *Enzyklopädie des Märchens.* Recently, she has edited a reissue of William A. Clouston's *Popular Tales and Fictions* (2002) and published a series of articles about tales in which a child outwits an ogre.

Janet L. Langlois is an associate professor of English at Wayne State University. She coedited *Sexism and Stereotypes in Modern Society: The Gender Science of Janet Taylor Spence.* Current projects include a study of horror film as ethnographic critique, work on narratives of racial passing, and personal experience narratives of angelic encounters.

Millicent Lenz is professor emerita and adjunct research associate at the University at Albany, State University of New York. She has authored *Nuclear Literature for Youth: The Quest for a Life-Affirming Ethic* (1990) and, with Peter Hunt, *Alternative Worlds in Fantasy Fiction* (2001), plus numerous articles.

Deeksha Nagar is a professor of folklore, cultural anthropology, and multiculturalism at the University of Northern Colorado and is affiliated with the urban education program there. She divides her time between Colorado and Lucknow, India, in order to run an organization called Sanchit Smriti, devoted to expanding research and archival projects of literary and cultural significance there. She is currently researching the lives and lore of the migrant Nagar community, residing in the state of Uttar Pradesh in India.

Kimberly A. Nance is an associate professor of foreign languages at Illinois State University. Her recent publications include "The Dynamic of Folklore in Lorca's Early Poetics: Opening Libro de Poemas and Unfolding 'Pajarita de papel,'" *Anales de la Literatura Española Contemporánea.*

Judith Neaman is professor emerita of English at Yeshiva University. She is the author of *Suggestion of the Devil,* a study of madness in the Middle Ages, and coauthor with Carole G. Silver of *Kind Words: A Thesaurus of Euphemisms.* She has written numerous articles, and portions of her recent work on medieval optics appear in "The Mystery of the Ghent Bird and the Invention of Spectacles," *Viator* (1993), and in the translations and notes dealing with optical materials in *Life of Margaret of Ypres,* edited by Margot King (2000).

Joan Peternel is an independent scholar who publishes in several genres. She has just completed a book-length manuscript entitled *Doubles: The Hero-Bride and the Heroine Bridegroom in Four Modern Novels and Other Works.* Peternel has recently published an essay-memoir in *The Abiko Annual,* a short story in *James Joyce Finnegans Wake Studies* (2003), and several poems in *Iambs & Trochees* (2003).

Gregory Schrempp is an associate professor of folklore and codirector of the Program in Mythology Studies at Indiana University. His most recent work is an anthology on theory of myth, coedited with William Hansen: *Myth: A New Symposium* (2002).

Carole G. Silver is a professor of English at Yeshiva University and chair of the university-wide Humanities Division. Beginning with *The Romance of William Morris* (1982), she has written widely on Victorian Pre-Raphaelite literature and painting. Her recent work has been in literature and folklore, including *Strange and Secret Peoples: Fairies and Victorian Consciousness* (1999) and a forthcoming article on the fairy-faith in nineteenth-century America. She has also been researching and writing on colonial South African women writers.

Ruth Stotter is the former director of the Dominican University Storytelling Program, past convener of the Folk Narrative Section for the American Folklore Society, and the recipient of the 2004 Reading the World Award. She served four years as a judge for the Aesop Prize Committee, sponsored by the

Children's Folklore Section of the American Folklore Society. In 2001 she conducted a workshop on symbolism in fairy tales at the National Storytelling Conference. Her most recent publication is *More About Story* (2001).

Elizabeth Tucker is a member of the English Department at Binghamton University, where she teaches folklore and fantasy literature. She is the author of *Campus Legends* (forthcoming 2005) and has recently written folklore articles for *Midwestern Folklore, Children's Folklore Review,* and *Voices: The Journal of New York Folklore* as well as memoir pieces and poetry for *Long Shot* and the *Paterson Literary Review.*

Natalie M. Underberg is assistant professor of film and folklore at the University of Central Florida. She taught folklore and anthropology at Indiana University before coming to UCF to help develop the UCF Heritage Alliance, which seeks to bring the Central Florida community together by celebrating the region's rich diversity through education, technology-based heritage projects, folklife research, preservation, and network-building. Her research interests include narrative, ethnographic methodology, and folklore and technology. Underberg is the president of the Florida Folklore Society. Her recent publications include "Peru" in *Worldmark Encyclopedia of World Religious Practices* (2004) and "Sor Juana's Villancicos: Context, Gender and Genre," *Western Folklore* (2002).

❀ A ❀

Mythological Motifs

Nature of the Creator

Motif A10

❀

Although the precise nature and characteristics of the creator deity may differ from one culture to another, specific archetypal qualities of the creator can be discerned.

The creator often integrates opposites and contraries into one unity, being simultaneously male and female, visible and invisible, first and last, creator and destroyer, very near and very remote. In various creation myths, the creator is depicted as a hermaphroditic deity. The creator is half man and half woman or is thought of as both male and female (Motif A12, "Hermaphroditic creator"). In ancient Egyptian texts, Atum was portrayed as a bisexual god and was sometimes called the "Great He-She." He was alone in the world and had to produce offspring without a mate (Ions 1968, 26). "God of double sex carries within him seed of gods" (Motif A111.3.0.1). In Genesis (1:27), God created "in his own image," "male and female," before Eve was created from Adam's body. As Freeman (1988, 52) indicates, well-known versions of the creation from Greek mythology also represent an androgynous deity in the union of Father Sky and Mother Earth or Father-Mother God. As shown in Hindu mythology, before the existence of husband and wife there was a being incorporating masculine and feminine features together. Hindu documents known as Upanishads, dating back to 800 BCE, state that in the beginning there was "Self" alone, in the shape of a person (*purusha*). He was as large as man and wife together. He looked around and saw nothing but his Self. Because he felt no delight, he wished for a second. "He then made his Self to fall in two and thence arose husband and wife" (Watts 1963, 83). In another version of Hindu mythology, Brahma the Creator and Shiva the Destroyer are "synthesized" in Vishnu the Preserver. But he, too, is of double aspect, male and female (Watts 1963, 88, 101). However, this does not negate other archetypes of deity found in different cultures or myths in which the deity is depicted either as a male, implying fatherhood, masculinity, and aggressiveness, or as a female, implying motherhood, tenderness, and nurturing.

The deity is self-created (A118) and the first being in existence prior to any other entity. The creator is tired of solitude and therefore inaugurates the creation (A73). Creation myth is intended to show that one objective of creative action is to bring into being humans or entities that can mirror basic features or qualities of the creator. It is said that we are created in the image of God. In this context, there is a resemblance between the creator and the created.

The creator is involved in such activities as creating, healing, redeeming, nurturing, and governing. The giver of life creates the universe and other beings through his love, mercy, and reasoning. Reason "has to do with finding the ground of being and the fundamental structuring of the order of the universe" (Campbell with Moyers 1988, 29). Various interpretations of Islamic tradition, for instance, refer to the perfected order of nature as a "sign," or paradigm for the adoration due the creator (el-Aswad 1994, 2002; Burkhalter 1985). Archetypal examples of creators known for their wisdom are the Egyptian god Ptah, the Persian god Ahura Mazda, and the Hindu god Brahma. However, the creator is not just theoretically wise but is also practical and involved in the actual practices of creation. The creator is conceived of as a handyman, fashioner, molder, or maker. The Egyptian god Ptah, also known as the Divine Artificer, was depicted as a skilled engineer, stonemason, and metalworker. He was also patron of the fine arts (Ions 1968).

The creator is able to emanate himself from a single principle or idea. Because the creator deity exists prior to his creation of the world, his actions seem arbitrary and beyond human understanding. The creator is distinguished by his well-determined will or volition. For instance, Atum was depicted as the "complete one" and "Universal God" because he created himself out of water by his own effort or will (Ions 1968, 40). In order to exercise his will on the universe, the creator must be omnipotent. The universe itself expresses the power, freedom, and wisdom of the creator. After the completion of his creative act, the deity often deserts his creatures and does not concern himself with them except in critical times of calamity.

The creator from above (A21) or the supreme god as creator (A101.1) is associated with sacred space, namely the sky or heaven, which symbolizes might, remoteness, height, and perfection. The "most high" spontaneously becomes an attribute of divinity. However, the creator goes beyond mere identification with the sky because he has created the entire cosmos. Many of the supreme gods of traditional peoples are called by names designating height,

From Francis Cleyn, *Ovid's Metamorphosis English'd, Mythologiz'd, and Represented in Figures* (1632).

the celestial vault, or meteorological phenomena. The supreme divinity of the Maori, for example, is named Iho, meaning elevated or up high. The supreme god of the Akposo Negroes, Uwoluwu, also signifies what is high or in the upper regions. To the Kachaw of Micronesian society, the creator is known simply as the Owner or Dweller of the Sky (Goodenough 1986), and to the Ainu, he is known as the Divine Chief of the Sky, the Sky God, and the Divine Creator of the World (Eliade 1959, 118–120). Among the Dinka, the divinity is "in the above" though that place is distinct from the "physical" sky (Lienhardt 1961, 32). These attributes, however, are not necessarily related to the idea of the creator as a supernatural being. Though the word *nhialic* among the Dinka, for example, connotes a personal and masculine reference to God, it is not identical with the concept of God as supernatural being as used in Western culture. Rather, it refers to "Creator," "God the creator," "God (my) father," "Being," a personal "Supreme Being," "Power," and "Divinity" devoid of supernatural implications (Lienhardt 1961, 28–31). Anthropomorphism renders the creator human, and not solely a supernatural being. In Egyptian creation myth, Ptah was represented as a living man wearing horns, a solar disk, and plumes (Ions 1968, 106). Also, the high gods of Babylon "were conceived to be human in their bodily shape, human in their passions, and human in their fate; for like men they were born into the world, and like men they loved and fought and died" (Frazer 1951, 309).

In other creation myths, however, god is invisible (Motif A11, Motif A102.9). In ancient Egyptian creation mythology, especially Theban cosmogony, the god Amon was associated with air as an invisible, dynamic force. He was identified with the power of the supreme and invisible creator (Ions 1968, 37). However, being an "immaterial archetype," god has been associated with "archetypal light" (Jung 1990, 3). Among the Desana of the Tukano Indians (in the Colombian Northwest Amazon), the Sun Creator is not the sun that illuminates the earth, but rather a creative principle that, although continuing in existence, is invisible and can be known only by the beneficial influence that emanates from it. The Sun Creator sent the visible sun that people see in the sky as his eternal representative. It is through this sun that the Creator Sun exercises his power, giving his creation light, heat, protection and, above all, fertility (Reichel-Dolmatoff 1971, 41–42). Among the Dakota Indians, the creator, Wakanda, is the omnipresent, invisible life force represented in seven divine names: the Above, the Below, Darkness, Sun, Moon, Morning Star, and Thunder (Underhill 1965, 202).

The archetype of the "One" or the "All" represents a perfect state of being that contains the opposites and which is therefore self-sufficient, content, and independent (Freeman 1988, 50). In various creation myths, the creator is depicted as being the first and the last as well as the creator and destroyer without any sense of contradiction. In Hindu myths, Krishna says, "I am the self existing in the hearts of all beings. I am the beginning, the middle and also the end of beings" (Watts 1963, 79). The ten-armed Shiva (Motif A123.5.1), the Destroyer, is simply the opposite face of Brahma, the Creator. In Islamic tradition, Allah "is the First and the Last, and the Visible and Invisible" (Qur'an 57:3). About himself, allah says that he was a hidden treasure and desired to be known; therefore he created the creation in order to be known (Chittick 1989, 67; Maclagan 1977, 23).

The creator deity combines the attributes of visibility and invisibility simultaneously. However, his invisibility is more significant than his visibility. In ancient Egyptian creation myth, the sun god Ra was both visible and invisible. Although the sun emerged from the chaos, its original form was invisible and not known. It came into being out of itself. The unique deity, however, was not the *visible* sun, although it was omnipresent and the entire earth lived, rejoiced, and flourished in its light (el-Aswad 1997, 70–80; Sourouzian 1987, 28–29). Degrees of visibility as well as of light and heat were connected to the movements of the sun, whose different names and forms reflected that spectrum. Atum meant the sun in the evening twilight or "he who is not" during the night. Khepri meant "he who becomes," describing an aspect of the rising sun. The name Khepri is related to the verb *kheper,* meaning "to come into being," as well as to the noun *kheperer,* which refers to the scarab beetle. The name Ra meant the sun reigning in the zenith (Moret 1972, 370). Moreover, the god Ra manifested himself in multiple visible forms, symbols, and archetypal images. He appeared as "a falcon or a ram or in anthropomorphic form with the falcon's or a ram's head, and so forth. These are all merely visible effigies, conceived as hieroglyphs, intended to allow recognition throughout his numerous characteristics and attributes" (Sourouzian 1987, 26).

Elite Literature

The archetype of the creator, god or human, is reflected in numerous forms of literature in different periods of time. In most mythological and religious literature, the nature of the divinity is mirrored in the creatures. In Genesis, Adam and Eve, the progenitors of all humankind, are created by God in his own image. Thus, man is defined as fundamentally a (created) creator and maker, as Sir Philip Sidney recognized in his essay *A Defense of Poetry* and as John Milton portrayed in the poem *Paradise Lost* (Berman 1981). The story of Eve being created from Adam's rib is obviously one of Blake's sources for the Los-Enitharmon episode (Cantor 1984, 49). In the *Book of Urizen* and within his understanding of the Bible's "In the beginning was the Word," Blake depicted Urizen as a creator whose creative activities began when he first uttered words and named things (Cantor 1984, 38).

Man's sense of self-fulfillment is thus inextricably bound up with being true to his "creatorness," which is his God-given nature. As "human creator" (Motif A15), man shares and participates in creating the world (Foster 1988, 177). In *Frankenstein,* a novel Mary Shelley wrote in 1818, Victor Frankenstein, a young German student of philosophy, desires to be a creator of life. This young man realizes that he himself is the creator as well as the center of his own universe. He does God's work in creating a man, but has the devil's motives: pride and the will to power (Cantor 1984, 105; Foster 1988, 183). Thus the creature is truly made in the image of his creator. Frankenstein and the monster are mirror images of each other. They are the same being, viewed in different aspects, as creator and as creature (Cantor 1984, 106).

el-Sayed el-Aswad

REFERENCES

Berman, Morris. 1981. *The Reenchantment of the World.* Ithaca: Cornell University Press.

Burkhalter, Sheryl L. 1985. "Completion in Continuity: Cosmogony and Ethics in Islam." In *Cosmogony and Ethical Order: New Studies in Comparative Ethics,* ed. Robin W. Lovin and Frank E. Reynolds, 225–250. Chicago: University of Chicago Press.

Campbell, Joseph, with Bill Moyers. 1988. *The Power of Myth.* New York: Doubleday.

Cantor, Paul. 1984. *Creature and Creator: Myth-making and English Romanticism.* Cambridge: Cambridge University Press.

Chittick, William C. 1989. *The Sufi Path of Knowledge: In al-'Arabi's Metaphysics of Imagination.* Albany: State University of New York Press.

el-Aswad, el-Sayed. 1994. "The Cosmological Belief System of Egyptian Peasants." *Anthropos* 89: 359–377.

———. 1997. "Archaic Egyptian Cosmology." *Anthropos* 92: 69–81.

———. 2002. *Religion and Folk Cosmology: Scenarios of the Visible and Invisible in Rural Egypt.* Westport, CT: Praeger.

Eliade, Mircea. 1959. *Cosmos and History: The Myth of Eternal Return.* New York: Harper and Row.

El Shamy, Hasan, M. 1995. *Folk Traditions of the Arab World: A Guide to Motif Classification.* 2 vols. Bloomington: Indiana University Press.

———. 1997. "Archetype." In *Folklore: An Encyclopedia of Forms, Methods, and History,* ed. Thomas A. Green. Santa Barbara, CA: ABC-CLIO.

Foster, Leslie D. 1988. "Birth of the Hero." In *Dictionary of Literary Themes and Motifs,* ed. Jean-Charles Seigneuret. Westport, CT: Greenwood Press.

Frazer, James George. 1951. *The Golden Bough: A Study in Magic and Religion.* New York: Macmillan.

Freeman, Alma S. 1988. "Androgyny." In *Dictionary of Literary Themes and Motifs,* ed. Jean-Charles Seigneuret. Westport, CT: Greenwood Press.

Goodenough, W.H. 1986. "Sky World and This World: The Place of Kachaw in Micronesian Cosmology." *American Anthropologist* 88 (3): 551–568.

Ions, Veronica. 1968. *Egyptian Mythology.* Middlesex: Hamlyn.

Jung, C.G. 1990 [1959]. *The Archetypes and the Collective Unconscious.* Bollingen Series 20. Princeton, NJ: Princeton University Press.

Lienhardt, Godfrey. 1961. *Divinity and Experience: The Religion of the Dinka.* Oxford: Oxford University Press.

Maclagan, David. 1977. *Creation Myths: Men's Introduction to the World.* London: Thames and Hudson.

Moret, Alexandre. 1972. *The Nile and Egyptian Civilization.* Trans. M.R. Dobie. London: Routledge and Kegan Paul.

Reichel-Dolmatoff, Gerardo. 1971. *Amazonian Cosmos: The Sexual and Religious Symbolism of the Tukano Indians.* Chicago: University of Chicago Press.

Sourouzian, Hourig. 1987. "Egyptian Religion." In *The Egyptian Museum Cairo Official Catalogue,* ed. Mohamed Saleh and Hourig Sourouzian. Mainz, Germany: Verlag Philipp von Zabern.

Underhill, Ruth. 1965. *Red Man's Religion: Beliefs and Practices of the Indians North of Mexico.* Chicago: Chicago University Press.

War Craft II: Battle.net Edition. 1999. Irvine, CA: Blizzard Entertainment.

Watts, Alan W. 1963. *The Two Hands of God: The Myths of Polarity.* New York: George Braziller.

The Hero Cycle

Various Motifs in A

❁

The essential parts of the hero cycle center around the three main rites of passage: birth, initiation, and death (Raglan 1965; van Gennep 1960). The culture hero's story begins with his miraculous or in some other way unusual birth; he may be the offspring of a god, a man who is not his mother's husband, a virgin mother, or a brother-sister or other incestuous pair. He is usually then abandoned or an attempt may be made on his life. His story typically picks up again after he reaches puberty, at which time a sign or event marks him as special and destined for greatness. The culture hero then undertakes a series of adventures, quests, and/or tests during which he may slay monsters or search for something of value. His death, like his birth, is cloaked in mysterious circumstances, often involving a heroic death or his own sacrifice. The culture hero may then make a journey to the underworld, and a suggestion that he will one day return to his people often lingers (Burrows, Lapides, and Shawcross 1973; Daemmrich and Daemmrich 1987; Raglan 1965).

Burrows, Lapides, and Shawcross (1973) note that the hero quest is "ultimately the activity of finding the Self, to unite the conscious with the unconscious . . . [and is] the goal of the hero" (460). In archetypal theory, the adventures of the hero represent the overcoming of unconscious desires, often manifested in various creatures and objects (Burrows, Lapides, and Showcross 1973). A hero's descent into the netherworld also represents an important step in his development. Afterward, he often returns to the world of the living. Charlotte Spivack discusses the Jungian implications of this journey: "By psychological extension the descent to the underworld may also be construed as a descent to the dark realm of the unconscious" (1988, 363).

UNIVERSAL PATTERNS

Scholars have tried to devise the quintessential list that would account for the major points of the hero pattern. Otto Rank's *The Myth of the Birth of the Hero* (1959), Lord Raglan's *The Hero: A Study in Tradition, Myth, and Drama* (1956), and Joseph Campbell's *The Hero with a Thousand Faces* (1956) provide several such examples. Raglan's "The Hero of Tradition" sets out twenty-two points of the hero cycle:

1. His mother is a royal virgin.
2. His father is a king, and
3. Often a near relative of his mother, but
4. The circumstances of his conception are unusual, and
5. He is also reputed to be the son of a god.
6. At birth an attempt is made, often by his father, to kill him, but
7. He is spirited away, and
8. Reared by foster parents in a far country.
9. We are told nothing of his childhood, but
10. On reaching manhood he returns or goes to his future kingdom.
11. After a victory over the king and/or a giant, dragon, or wild beast,
12. He marries a princess, often the daughter of his predecessor, and
13. Becomes king.
14. For a time he reigns uneventfully, and
15. Prescribes laws, but
16. Later he loses favor with the gods and/or his subjects, and
17. Is driven from the throne and city.
18. He meets with a mysterious death,
19. Often at the top of a hill.
20. His children, if any, do not succeed him.
21. His body is not buried, but nevertheless
22. He has one or more holy sepulchers. (Raglan 1965, 145)

According to this scheme, then, a number of mythical, legendary, and historical figures can be scored. For example, Oedipus receives twenty points, Heracles receives seventeen points, Moses receives twenty-one points, and King Arthur receives sixteen points (Aarne and Thompson 1987). Dundes (1980) applied the "hero pattern" to the story of Jesus Christ and found he scored seventeen points.

The unusual circumstances of the culture hero's birth can take many forms. He may be the son of a god (A512.3), like Heracles in Greek myth and Jesus in Christianity, or of the creator (A512.2), as in South American tales of the Guaraní. His mother may be a virgin (A511.1.3; A511.1.3.3), as in Roman Catholic and Buddhist tradition. This miraculous conception motif may extend back a generation or two (in Roman Catholic hagiography, Saint Anne, the mother of the Virgin Mary, is said to have been barren and conceived only after fervent prayer). Such elaborations bolster the extraordinary pedigree of a culture hero. When the conception involves rape, incest, trickery, or magic, "[t]he underlying implication may be that the abnormality of the act and the overwhelming passion which inspires it create or liberate a powerful magic force with which the hero is imbued and which drives him to transcend normal human limitations" (Cavendish 1982, 239). Thompson traces the hero cycle in Native American mythology and legend, noting that the motif of the hero's miraculous birth is found over most of the continent, but involves different circumstances. For example, in the Southwest the hero is conceived through rain falling on his mother, while the theme of a pregnancy resulting from consuming something is spread among most other tribes (Thompson 1977).

The cycle usually continues at this point with the abandonment (A511.2.1, "Abandonment of culture hero at birth") or attempted elimination of the hero (A511.2.3, "Culture hero hidden in order to escape enemies"). This may be accomplished in a number of ways. In the Old Testament, Moses is set afloat in a basket in order to escape massacre; this ruse leads to his adoption and upbringing by foster parents (A511.3.1, "Culture hero reared in seclusion"). Oedipus is abandoned by his father in an attempt to escape fulfillment of an oracle. The stories of Krishna (an incarnation of Vishnu) and Jesus both include an evil figure who orders the massacre of innocent children in order to destroy the hero as a babe (Krishna is threatened by Kansan, Jesus by Herod). Similarly, some African myths make fairly clear the father's anxiety over being overthrown by his own son. In an Azande tale, the father uses magic to eliminate an incestuous son (Kluckhohn 1965). In the realm of *Märchen,* in Type 410, *Sleeping Beauty,* the heroine is cared for by foster parents in order to avert a prophecy foretelling her lapse into a death-like sleep (Aarne and Thompson 1987).

RITES OF PASSAGE

The culture hero's story frequently omits much mention of the rest of his childhood until he reaches adolescence. Arthurian legend picks up when the hero removes the sword from the stone; Jesus does not appear in public after his birth until his encounter with the wise men at the temple at the age of twelve. As Raglan put it so memorably decades ago, "The most surprising things happen to our hero at birth; the most surprising things happen to him as soon as he reaches manhood, but in the meanwhile nothing happens to him at all" (1965, 152). What to make of this strange omission? If we consider that the hero cycle is, at its core, really the story of a culture hero's transition through the rites of passage, then we can understand that "the story of the hero of tradition . . . is the story of his ritual progress" (Raglan 1965, 152). In Native American myth and legend, the hero's short childhood—he often grows up in just a few days—is a widespread concept (this is related to Motif A527.1, "Culture hero precocious"). The truncated childhood of the hero means that little is narrated about the boyhood period—which links the Native American hero cycle to that of Indo-European/Semitic tradition (Thompson 1977).

Once he comes of age, then, the hero sets out on his adventures—in search of something or committed to overcoming a threat to his people. In the ancient Mesopotamian *Epic of Gilgamesh* (circa 2000 BCE) the hero, accompanied by his faithful companion Enkidu, slays a monster and, after his companion is killed, embarks on an ill-fated quest for immortality. The Arthurian cycle (including Wolfram von Eschenbach's *Parzival,* thirteenth century) set the pattern for medieval romances about "knights errant" (although Daemmrich and Daemmrich [1987] dates the appearance of the quest for the Holy Grail and the adventures of Sir Lancelot and the other knights of the Round Table to Thomas Malory's 1485 work *Morte d'Arthur*).

An element of many hero cycle stories is the temptation of the hero by the personification of evil. Here it is not an external monster that needs to be slain; rather, the hero must spiritually overcome an adversary and thus establish his moral claim to greatness. These temptations, to some extent, revolve around similar themes: worldly power and escape from hunger, to name two (Conway 1881). In Buddhism, for example, Mara, the personification of evil, tempts the Buddha to give up his quest for enlightenment (Carus 1969), while Christ is tempted by Satan to accept his gift of worldly power in exchange for paying homage to him.

QUEST FOR THE FATHER

One widespread theme in the hero's adventures is the father quest. Peter Barta describes the three possible forms the search for the father may take: the son does not know his father but has a token making him recognizable to his father; the son and the father fight—but they do not know each other when they begin the fight; the son is raised away from his father but is drawn to him because he is rejected by those around him (Barta 1988). Ancient Greek epic uses the theme of the father-quest with some frequency, including the incident of an often fatal battle between father and son, most famously Oedipus's unwitting murder of his own father in a fight. In the European *Märchen,* it is the hero's departure from his natal home "to seek his fortune" in the wider world that often sets the tale in motion. Seen in this way, the magic tale is an elaboration of the middle part of the hero cycle—a recounting of the adventures and quests that led to his rise to prominence. Type 300, *The Dragon Slayer,* for example, is a prototypical story of the hero's quest (and strikingly similar to the story of Perseus) (Aarne and Thompson 1987; Dundes 1980, 1968).

Outside of the Indo-European/Semitic tradition, the hero's adventures also play an important part in the hero cycle. For instance, Thompson (1977) discusses Manabozho, the culture hero of the Central Woodland Native Americans. As part of the myth, Manabozho dives for earth in floodwaters (A812, "Earth Diver"), but, unlike other creation myths, this activity is one of the culture hero's many adventures rather than a central creation act. Much of Manabozho's story concerns two common culture hero activities: vanquishing monsters (A531, "Culture hero (demigod) overcomes monsters") and bringing culture to the people (A541, "Culture hero teaches arts and crafts"). Kluckhohn (1965) notes that the "slaying of monsters" theme appears in thirty-seven out of the fifty cultures he studied: "here the distribution approaches equality save for a slightly greater frequency in North America and the Insular Pacific. . . . Thus in Bantu Africa (and beyond) a hero is born to a woman who survives after a monster has eaten her spouse (and everyone else). The son immediately turns into a man, slays a monster or monsters, restores his people—but not his father—and becomes chief" (163).

DESCENT INTO THE UNDERWORLD

Death, descent into the underworld, and resurrection are widespread in the world's tale traditions (Zolla 1981). A few examples are given below.

In Sumerian and Babylonian myth the goddess Inanna/Ishtar ventures to the underworld to see her lover Dumuzi/Tammuz. The great Greek hero Odysseus must go to the land of the dead in order to learn the predictions of the prophet Tiresias, recounted in Book Eleven of the *Odyssey.* Aeneas in Virgil's *Aeneid* visits the land of the dead to hear the prophecies of the Sibyl, who tells him to take the golden bough from a particular tree so that he can communicate with his dead father and thus succeed in his perilous journey (Spivack 1988). The Norse hero Vainamoinen journeys to the underworld of Tuonela in order to learn a magic formula. In the Catholic tradition, the Apostle's Creed states that Christ "suffered under Pontius Pilate, was crucified, died, and was buried. He descended into Hell; the third day he rose again from the dead." During this "harrowing of hell" Jesus is believed to have freed the souls held captive in the afterworld.

Dante's *Divine Comedy* (c. 1320) contains a famous descent into hell in the first book, the *Inferno,* timed "to parallel Jesus' harrowing expedition between Good Friday and Easter Sunday" (Spivak 1988, 367). With the shade of Virgil as his guide, the poet explores the nine circles of hell. "Dante begins his journey at age thirty-five, the mid-point of his life, when he suddenly finds himself lost in a dark wood" (Spivak 1988, 367). Modern readings of this work as well as more ancient depictions of underworld journeys stress the inward journey that they symbolize. Spivak remarks that "the descent into hell is a necessary stage not only for the hero but for everyone's psychological and spiritual development" (1988, 368) and Campbell states that "the really creative acts are represented as those deriving from some sort of dying to the world" (1968, 35).

THE HERO'S RETURN

The hero cycle motif of the expected return of the hero has most notably entered the realm of written literature in the Arthurian legends, where it is prophesied that the king will once again return to help his people (A580, "Culture hero's (divinity's) expected return"). Similarly, in Christianity and Hinduism, Jesus Christ and Vishnu, respectively, are expected to return one day to reward the good and punish the bad (Carus 1969). In addition, Thompson notes that the theme of the hero leaving for the west, as well as the hero's anticipated return, is also found in many areas of North America (1977).

In a provocative study titled *Custer and the Epic of Defeat* (1974), Bruce Rosenberg demonstrates the recurrence of the hero pattern in popular and literary narrative over many centuries, focusing particularly on the theme of heroic defeat. Elsewhere he writes:

> All of these distributional and integrative elements occur repeatedly because of the way our culture has decided, collectively, over several millennia, that certain stories must be told. If a warrior is to be heroic and held in esteem . . . he cannot have led a larger force to its defeat at the hands of a small but skillfully superior enemy. And so on; all the elements in this narrative type reflect the way our culture believes that heroes are defeated and the way their defeat must be related—if they are to be considered heroes. (1991, 247)

The hero cycle thus tells the life history of an extraordinary person who is marked for greatness at birth, accomplishes significant deeds, and yet dies a mysterious death. Scholars have debated whether the discovery of this "hero pattern" effectively disproves the historicity of its subject. Today, most scholars versed in folklore theory realize that the existence of formulaic elements in a narrative neither proves nor disproves the actual existence of an individual; rather, they frame the story of a hero in such a way that tellers and listeners can appreciate, figuratively and allegorically, the esteem in which he is held.

For an excellent discussion of the hero cycle, see Archer Taylor's (1964) classic "The Biographical Pattern in Traditional Narrative."

Natalie M. Underberg

See also: Death or Departure of the Gods and Return.

REFERENCES

Aarne, Antti, and Stith Thompson. 1987. *The Types of the Folktale.* Helsinki: Suomalainen Tiedeakatemia.

Barta, Peter. 1988. "Search for Father." In *Dictionary of Literary Themes and Motifs,* ed. Jean-Charles Seigneuret, 1141–1148. Westport, CT: Greenwood Press.

Burrows, David, Frederick Lapides, and John T. Shawcross. 1973. *Myths and Motifs in Literature.* New York: Free Press.

Campbell, Joseph. 1968 [1956]. *The Hero with a Thousand Faces.* New York: Meridian.

Carus, Paul. 1969. *The History of the Devil and the Idea of Evil.* New York: Land's End Press.

Cavendish, Richard, ed. 1982. *Legends of the World.* New York: Schocken Books.

Conway, Moncare. 1881. *Demonology and Devil-Lore.* Rev. ed. 2 vols. New York: Holt.

Daemmrich, Horst, and Ingrid Daemmrich. 1987. *Themes and Motifs in Western Literature.* Tübingen: Francke.

Dundes, Alan. 1968. "Introduction to the Second Edition." In Vladimir Propp, *Morphology of the Folktale.* Austin: University of Texas Press.

———. 1980. "The Hero Pattern and the Life of Jesus." In *Interpreting Folklore,* 223–261. Bloomington: Indiana University Press.

Kluckhohn, Clyde. 1965. "Recurrent Themes in Myths and Mythmaking." In *The Study of Folklore,* ed. Alan Dundes, 158–168. Englewood Cliffs, NJ: Prentice Hall.

Raglan, Lord. 1956. *The Hero: A Study in Tradition, Myth, and Drama.* New York: Vintage.

———. 1965. "The Hero of Tradition." In *The Study of Folklore,* ed. Alan Dundes, 142–157. Englewood Cliffs, NJ: Prentice Hall.

Rank, Otto. 1959. *The Myth of the Birth of the Hero.* New York: Vintage.

Rosenberg, Bruce. 1974. *Custer and the Epic of Defeat.* University Park: Penn State Press.

———. 1991. "What is Natural Narrative?" In *Folklore and Literature: Rival Siblings,* 236–251. Knoxville: University of Tennessee Press.

Spivack, Charlotte. 1988. "Descent Into Hell." In *Dictionary of Literary Themes and Motifs,* ed. Jean-Charles Seigneuret, 363–372. Westport, CT: Greenwood Press.

Taylor, Archer. 1964. "The Biographical Pattern in Traditional Narrative." *Journal of the Folklore Institute* 1: 114–129.

Thompson, Stith. 1977. *The Folktale.* Berkeley: University of California Press.

van Gennep, Arnold. 1960. *The Rites of Passage.* Chicago: University of Chicago Press.

Zolla, Elémire. 1981. *Archetypes.* London: George Allen and Unwin.

Death or Departure of the Gods

Motif A192, and Return, Motif A193

❀

In *The Golden Bough* (1914), Sir James Frazer observes that because people have created gods in their own likeness, the issue of mortality has been a central concern in mythology. Many of the gods in world mythologies are immortal, but some die or go away.

The dying god motif (A192) figures prominently in Norse mythology. After the gentle and sweet-natured god Balder has a disquieting dream, his mother, the goddess Frigg, exacts an oath from all living and nonliving things that they will never harm her son. Only the mistletoe does not swear, for Frigg thinks it too small and insignificant (McLeish 1996, 83). Balder's supposed invulnerability is the source of great amusement among the Aesir gods, who, believing that no harm can befall him, hurl axes and spears at him for sport. The mischief maker Loki, however, gives Balder's blind half brother Hoder a sprig of mistletoe to throw and Balder is slain by it (Lindow 2001, 66). The other gods light a great pyre on a ship on which they lay Balder's body (Littleton 2002, 319). As the ship sails out to sea (A192.2.2, "Divinity departs in boat over sea"), it is engulfed in flames (A192.2.4, "Divinity departs in column of flame"). Racked by grief, Odin, chief of the Aesir family of gods, instructs the messenger Hermoth to seek Balder's release from Hel's kingdom of the dead. Hel is willing to comply with Odin's request only if all living things shed tears of sorrow for Balder (Jordan 1993, 103). Everyone complies except a giantess (Loki in disguise), and Balder remains in Hel's kingdom.

The death of Balder leads directly to what the poetic *Edda* calls *ragna rok,* the "fate or doom of the gods," which is a central incident in the larger Teutonic myth of the destruction of the world (MacCulloch 1964, 336–337). Dramatizing the destruction variously by an all-consuming fire, by a mighty winter, and by the world itself sinking into the sea, the *Voluspa* shows that "as the gods are not eternal, *a parte ante,* so their life at last comes to an end" (A196.1, "Fate controls gods") (MacCulloch 1964, 337). Although Odin and Thor and many other gods are all killed, their sons survive and "the end of the world contained the germ of a new beginning" (Littleton 2002, 325).

In the Aztec mythology of Central America, Quetzalcoatl is the god of the spirit of life, "teacher of the arts, originator of the calendar, and the giver of maize" (Campbell 1973, 358). As monarch of the ancient city of Tollan, he is the helper and benefactor of humanity and is permanently at war with Tezcatlipoca, the god of darkness and sorcery (McLeish 1996, 511). Using trickery to defeat Quetzalcoatl, Tezcatlipoca tempts him into carnality and drunkenness and then shows him his own reflection in a mirror. Horrified at the sensual image that he sees, Quetzalcoatl buries his treasures, burns his palace, and abandons the city of Tollan (Cotterell 1997, 224). Dressing himself in his finest robes and wearing his insignia of feathers, he walks into the flames of a funeral pyre at the seashore. At his immolation, a flock of birds arise from his ashes and fly toward the sun (McLeish 1996, 511). Some say his soul (Campbell 1973, 359) and others his heart (Jobes 1961, 1313; Littleton 2002, 560) ascends to heaven (A192.2.1, "Deity departs for heaven (skies)") and becomes the morning star. According to another tradition, after Quetzalcoatl arrives at the sea, he sails eastward on a raft of serpents (A192.2.2, "Divinity departs in boat over sea").

In Hawaiian mythology, deities die or depart the world in a variety of imaginative ways. Most of the Pahulu gods of sorcery on the island of Lanai are killed by the prophet Lanikaula and the rest are banished (Beckwith 1970, 110). Some deities depart for heaven or the skies (A192.2.1, "Deity departs for heaven (skies)").

Oa-tabou-te-ra'i, child of the war god Oro and the beautiful mortal Vairaumati, becomes a great chief, and at his death he ascends to the heavens (Beckwith 1970, 38). His father had previously left the earth in a column of flame (A192.2.4). Kane, who is the leading deity among the Hawaiians and who is responsible for the creation of man and woman, lives on earth with his creatures. After humans break his laws, they become subject to death, and Kane ascends to heaven to live (Beckwith 1970, 42–43). Hina, the goddess of darkness and death, comes from the heavens to be the wife of an industrious Maui chief. Weary of laboring over her children, however, she leaps to the moon (A192.2.1.1, "Deity departs for moon"). Her husband leaps to catch her, but her leg breaks off in his hand, and there she hangs in the moon to this day. A variant of the Hina tradition holds that she "started by the rainbow path to the sun, but, finding it too warm, she climbed instead to the moon" (Beckwith 1970, 241–242, 221).

For other Hawaiian gods, departure from this world is by boat over the sea (A192.2.2). The keeper of the god Kaili, for instance, makes a canoe and places Kaili in it, together with food, kava, and tapa cloth. After weeping over the god, the keeper sets Kaili adrift on the ocean, and by the mana of the god the canoe sails onward and is never seen again (Beckwith 1970, 29). Similarly, the god Lono—who descends from heaven on a rainbow, marries the beautiful Ka-iki-lani, and then beats her to death for suspected infidelity—builds a canoe "such as mortal eyes have never seen since" and sails forth alone with a promise to the people that some day he will return in another form (Beckwith 1970, 37).

In the form of a handsome man, the pig god Kamapua'a woos Pele, the goddess of fire (Cotterell 1997, 276). Pele at first refuses his advances, calling him "a pig and the son of a pig" (Beckwith 1970, 205), although the two ultimately have a child, who is the ancestor of the chiefs and commoners of Hawaii. Kamapua'a leaves Hawaii and draws up a new home from the ocean depths (A192.2.3, "Divinity departs to submarine home"), where he establishes a family.

In Japanese mythology, Izanami, sister-wife of the god Izanagi, creates the lesser deities and the natural world, including the Japanese islands (Carlyon 1981, 105). But Izanami dies of a terrible fever in giving birth to the god of fire. She descends to *yomotsu-kuni,* the land of gloom (Cotterell 1997, 116; Leeming 1997, 345). There Izanagi follows in order to retrieve her (F81.1, "Orpheus. Journey to land of dead to bring back person from the dead"), but he flees in horror at the appearance of her decomposition.

DYING AND RISING GODS

Some gods who die return to life (A193, "Resurrection of gods"), and this motif is often associated with rituals celebrating the life cycle of vegetation. Frazer was the first modern scholar to write about the dying and rising god in the ancient world: "[u]nder the names of Osiris, Tammuz, Adonis, and Attis, the peoples of Egypt and Western Asia represented the yearly decay and revival of life, especially of vegetable life, which they personified as a god who annually died and rose again from the dead" (quoted in Mettinger 2001, 18). The dying and rising god has been debated in the scholarly literature throughout the twentieth century (for a summary, see Mettinger 2001, 15–39). By the end of the century, the consensus was that most of the gods identified as dying and rising died, but there was no return or resurrection. In his 1987 article on mystery religions, for example, Kurt Rudolph claims that the oft-made connection between the mystery religions and the idea of dying and rising divinities is defective. However, in 2001 Tryggve Mettinger affirms that many of the gods of the mystery religions die (often violently), descend to the underworld, are lamented and retrieved by a woman (usually a fertility or earth goddess), and are restored to life, for at least part of each year. Reviewing the critical literature along with primary sources and some important material that was not seen until recently, Mettinger concludes, "The world of ancient Near Eastern religions actually knew a number of deities that may be properly described as dying and rising" (217), although he adds that "One should not hypostasize these gods into a specific type '*the* dying and rising god.' On the contrary, the gods mentioned are of very different types, although we have found tendencies to association and syncretism" (218).

Mystery Religions

Beginning about three thousand years ago and lasting into the early days of Christianity in the Mediterranean world, there were a number of mystery religions, so-called because devotees had to be initiated and were sworn to secrecy not to divulge the rites (C423.5, "Tabu: revealing sacred mysteries"). Many of these mystery religions seem to have been based on indigenous fertility festivals and involved the gods mentioned by Frazer (above) as well as others, such as Cybele, Dionysus, Orpheus, Mithra, and Demeter and Persephone. Rudolf says that the mysteries may have been concerned with themes of loss, search, and recovery, (apparent) death and return to life, the passing of tests, and transformations (1987, 237). A few stories about these gods are given below.

The best-known deities connected with mystery religions in Greece were Demeter and Persephone, who were worshipped in the yearly rituals at Eleusis. We know comparatively more detail about the Eleusinian mysteries than others. The ritual is bound up with the myth of the abduction of Persephone by the god of the underworld. Persephone, daughter of Demeter, Greek goddess of the earth and crops, is picking flowers one day when the god of the underworld arises, grabs her, and takes her down to Hades as the earth closes in behind them. Demeter searches for her daughter and in her grief allows the crops to die, and only when Zeus compels Hades to release Persephone for part of each year does Demeter allow the earth to bloom again. About the annual rituals held at Eleusis, one scholar says, "whatever went on at Eleusis dealt with the mystery of life and regeneration as well as with the impenetrable secret of death and the hope for some ray of light in the tenebrous underworld" (Athanassakis 1976, 73).

In ancient Egyptian mythology, Osiris is king and judge of the dead and lord of the flood and vegetation, identified with the rising and falling of the

Nile (Cotterell 1997, 40). He is believed to be the wise pharaoh who showed the Egyptians how to use grain for bread. His civilizing reign as pharaoh is brought to an end by his jealous brother Seth, who announces at a festive banquet that he will give a jeweled golden sarcophagus to whoever fits perfectly in it (Leeming 1997, 241). As soon as Osiris lies in it, Seth closes and seals the coffin shut and has it thrown into the Nile, from which it is carried out to sea and then to the Phoenician shore, where a tamarisk tree springs up around it. When Seth learns of the attempt to revive Osiris by the god's sister and consort Isis, Seth cuts the corpse of Osiris into pieces and disperses them throughout Egypt. The scattering of his body was allegorized later with the winnowing and scattering of grain in the fields (Jordan 1993, 196). Isis carefully reassembles all the pieces of Osiris's body and revives him long enough to conceive the child Horus. Annually, Osiris is reincarnated in the sacred black bull Apis, but he always returns to the underworld after the growing season (Jobes 1961, 109). The cult of Isis spread to Greece and then to Rome, becoming "one of the most widely disseminated Oriental religions of late antiquity, especially from the second century BCE on" (Rudolph 1987, 235).

Dionysus, god of wine, son of Zeus and the Theban princess Semele, was also not among the deathless Olympian gods (Hamilton 1942, 64). Although different versions of the Dionysus myth exist, he is believed to have died a violent death and to have been resurrected in the annual renewal of the grapes of the vine. The rites associated with his cult were ecstatic and sexual.

Dumuzi/Tammuz was originally a god of shepherding, but "eventually he developed links with gods of vegetation (Ningishzida, Damu) and was presumably a god of vegetation from the Late Bronze Age on" (Mettinger 2001, 218). In the Sumerian myth about him, *Inanna's Descent* (ca. 2000 BCE), Dumuzi is chosen to spend half the year in the underworld, alternating with his sister, Geshtinanna. "The concept of the alternation of the two deities in the Netherworld was to a large degree based upon the alternation of the barley and wine-growing seasons: Dumuzi embodied the grain, Geshtinanna the vine" (Mettinger 2001, 190). Mettinger finds possible proof that there was ritual activity connected with Dumuzi in a recently discovered letter written by one Yaminite king to another, in which he compares his own difficult circumstances to those of Dumuzi: having escaped death during an uprising, he writes, "Why, now, [am I not] like Dumuzi? They kill him . . . he always comes back to the temple" (201).

HEROES

It is not only gods that people have been loath to let die; one of the distinguishing characteristics of the hero is that he can make the journey to the land of the dead and return (A580, "Culture hero's (divinity's) expected return. Divinity or hero is expected to return at the proper time and rescue his people from their misfortunes"). For example, the Northeastern Woodland Native American groups tell stories of their hero, Glooscap, who leaves for the west and goes to another world, preparing for "the great battle" on the final day (Thompson 1977, 306). The Central Woodland culture hero Manabozho, after taming monsters (A531) and bringing culture to his people (A541), eventually leaves for the west (A561, "Divinity's departure for west"), but "there is sometimes a hint that he may eventually return" (Thompson 1977, 308).

In Britain, the earliest writings about King Arthur—Gildas's *Liber quernlus de excidio Britanniae* (*The ruin of Britain*)—date to before 547 CE, and Loomis says that belief in Arthur's survival began by 1113 (1979, 64). Geoffrey of Monmouth's famous *Historia Regum Britanniae* (*History of the Kings of Britain*, ca. 1136) drew on many sources, some now lost. He wrote that after the battle of Camlan, "the renowned king Arthur was mortally wounded and was borne thence to the Isle of Avalon for his wounds to be healed" (Barber 1972, 125). (E481.4.1, "Avalon, Happy otherworld where dead are healed"; A571.2, "Culture hero still alive on mysterious island"). Even when the grave of Arthur was supposedly identified around 1190, the idea of his return persisted; Malory wrote in the fifteenth century, "And many men say that there ys written upon the tumbe thus: *hic iacet Arthurus, rex quondam rexque futurus* (Here lies Arthur, once king, who shall be king again)" (Barber 1972, 133). Barber notes that the idea of the returning hero is common in the medieval world and that there were legends to that effect about Charlemagne and Frederick Barbarossa (1972, 122).

The motif of the dying god is a powerful one that continues to resonate to this day. In her study *Dying Gods in Twentieth-Century Fiction* (1990), K.J. Phillips describes its use by modern writers:

> The dying gods have to be reckoned a major modern motif. In fact, most of the principal modernists know and elaborately adapt the stories of these gods . . . including Conrad, Kafka, Forster, Lawrence, Hemingway, Woolf, Faulkner, Mann, and Welty. Even after the modernists, when the first flush of enthusiasm for Frazer had faded, allusions to dying deities do not slacken off. Authors after 1950 are as steeped in such myths as their elders: Beckett, O'Connor, Bellow, Malamud, García Márquez, Konwicki, and Oates. (14–15)

Peter L. De Rose and Jane Garry

REFERENCES

Athanassakis, Apostolos N. 1976. *Homeric Hymns*. Baltimore: Johns Hopkins University Press.
Barber, Richard. 1972. *The Figure of Arthur.* London: Longman.
Beckwith, Martha. 1970. *Hawaiian Mythology.* Honolulu: University of Hawaii Press.

Campbell, Joseph. 1973 [1949]. *The Hero with a Thousand Faces.* 2nd ed. Princeton: Princeton University Press.

Carlyon, Richard. 1981. *A Guide to the Gods.* New York: William Morrow.

Cotterell, Arthur. 1997. *A Dictionary of World Mythology.* New York: Oxford University Press.

Frazer, Sir James George. 1996 [1914]. *The Golden Bough.* New York: Simon and Schuster.

Hamilton, Edith. 1998 [1942]. *Mythology.* Boston: Little, Brown.

Jobes, Gertrude. 1961. *Dictionary of Mythology, Folklore, and Symbols.* 3 vols. New York: Scarecrow Press.

Jordan, Michael. 1993. *Encyclopedia of Gods.* New York: Facts on File.

———.1993. *Myths of the World.* London: Kyle Cathie.

Leeming, David Adams, ed. 1997. *Storytelling Encyclopedia: Historical, Cultural and Multiethnic Approaches to Oral Traditions Around the World.* Phoenix, AZ: Oryx Press.

Lindow, John. 2001. *Norse Mythology: A Guide to the Gods, Heroes, Rituals, and Beliefs.* New York: Oxford University Press.

Littleton, C. Scott. 2002. *Mythology.* London: Duncan Baird.

Loomis, Roger Sherman. 1979 [1959]. "The Legend of Arthur's Survival." In *Arthurian Literature in the Middle Ages.* Oxford: Oxford University Press.

MacCulloch, John Arnott. 1964. *Eddic.* Vol. 2 of *The Mythology of All Races.* New York: Cooper Square.

McLeish, Kenneth. 1996. *Myth: Myths and Legends of the World Explored.* London: Bloomsbury.

Mettinger, Tryggve. N. 2001. *The Riddle of Resurrection: "Dying and Rising Gods" in the Ancient Near East.* Stockholm: Almqvist and Wiksell.

Phillips, K.J. 1990. *Dying Gods in Twentieth-Century Fiction.* Lewisburg, PA: Bucknell University Press.

Rudolph, Kurt. 1987. "Mystery Religions." In *The Encyclopedia of Religion,* ed. Mircea Eliade, 10: 230–239. New York: Macmillan.

Thompson, Stith M. 1977. *The Folktale.* Berkeley: University of California Press.

Creation Myth: Cosmogony and Cosmology

Motifs A600–A899

❀

As a primordial archetype, the myth of creation explains the origin of the universe, describing how the world and its animate and inanimate entities were created, and visible and invisible forces brought into being. It provides explanations of the total cosmos, including the primal order of the heavens and the earth, the entities therein, and the origins and hierarchies of human beings and their gods. As such, it concerns the "establishment of natural order" (A1100–A1199) and "ordering of human life" (A1200–A1699). Being a prototype, creation myth establishes an exemplary model of human experience. In brief, creation myth is a symbolic and sacred narrative concerning the origin of the world as conceptually constructed by a particular community or group of people.

The myriad number of creation myths can be understood by concentrating on some of their basic commonalities that can be defined as "motifs" or "universal images that have existed since the remotest times" (Jung 1990, 3). Simultaneously, various themes can be found in one creation myth. These themes are concerned not only with the origin of the universe and the means by which it was created, but also with the dominant cultural paradigms and archetypal images found among different groups of people in widely dispersed places and times (Stephens 1983).

Creation myths accentuate patterns of transformation from nothingness to full existence, from chaos to order, from dark to light, and from meaninglessness to meaningfulness. These patterns of creation become possible through elements such as the thought, volition, and action of the creator. A significant aspect of the term *archetype* designates the God-image in man (Jung 1990, 3).

Though worlds in creation myths are depicted as having different qualities from those of the ordinary world, divine modes of creative acts are strikingly comparable to those of human beings and include fashioning, molding, carving, weaving, earth-diving, and uttering or speaking among the means of creation (A640, "Other means of creating the universe"). For example, in some versions of ancient Egyptian myths, the creator Khnum is depicted as a potter who creates men from clay and fashions them on a potter's wheel (Ions 1968, 38).

One of the dominant themes in creation myth is the establishment of order in the face of an overwhelming threat of chaos and fatal disruption. In contrast to a primordial universe consisting of some undifferentiated matter, nearly all of the great creation myths share a pattern in which the ordered universe is either brought out of chaotic disorder or created from nothingness. Chaos "is the state in which everything is, but so undifferentiated that nothing can be manifest in particular; it is pure entropy, an even, indifferent distribution of energy" (Maclagan 1977, 14). According to the Heliopolitan cosmology based on the earliest Egyptian mythologies that go back to the Old Kingdom (2700 BCE), there existed Nun, the primordial ocean in which the germ cells of all things floated. Nun is unorganized chaos, nothingness, or a formless mass without structure. It is the creator Atum who conquers chaos through the creation of the universe. By effort of his will, Atum "stood up out of Nun and rose above the water; thereupon the Sun came into being, the Light was, and Atum, duplicated and made external to the primordial Water, took the name of Ra" (Moret 1972, 374). This divine creative act injects order into preexisting chaos. It is worth noting that after the creation is completed, all chaotic factors and negative forces retreat to the marginal zones of the ordered universe (Grimal 1992, 41). As the lord of the universe, Ra lives in the heavens and is responsible for maintaining order in all aspects of life. Each morning he is reborn in the east and travels across the sky in a boat called the Bark of Millions of Years, accompanied by a number of gods who act as his crew.

If Egyptian creation myth depicts chaos as a primeval ocean containing the germs of all things, traditional Chinese creation myth represents it as an immense, formless cosmic egg encompassing all the elements of a featureless universe, intermingled and mixed together. According to the Chinese myth, P'an-ku, the Cosmic Man or first living entity, unfolds inside that chaotic cosmic egg and creates humans. He establishes order in the universe by separating opposing elements such as male and female, yang (sky) and yin (earth), light and dark, and dry and wet (Christie 1968, 43).

In Babylonian creation myth, chaos is perceived as an enemy to life and order. In an effort to establish order in the universe, Marduk destroys Tiamat, the primordial mother of the ocean, representing a liquid chaos, and divides her body into two cosmic halves: the sky and the earth (Eliade 1959, 54). In

Greek creation myths and their Roman counterparts, darkness and the featureless state of the universe constitutes the initial chaotic condition from which order emerges. In this void there is only the bird, Nyx, that lays a golden egg from which Eros, the god of love, is born. The shell splits into two halves; one half becomes the Sky or Uranus, and the other becomes Earth or Gaia. However, with the aid of Eros, the two halves are reunited (Stapleton 1978), establishing unity and order in the universe.

Creation myth shows how the universe is created by command of the creator (A611, "*Fiat creation.* Universe is created at command of creator") and how the creator's thought materializes (A612, "Creation: materialization of creator's thinking. Creator 'thinks outward in space' and thus produces the universe") and is transformed into reality. This myth explains that the whole universe in some mythical and religious traditions is created by the verbal command of God: "Be!"—it became (A611.0.1, "Creator uses particular formula (letters) to create universe"). In the Bible we read, "In the beginning was the Word" (John 1:1). "Word" is the Greek *logos* or "reason," signifying order in both man and universe (Foster 1988). We see further that the Arabic word *al-kaun,* "cosmos" or "universe," is derived from the root *k-u-n,* which means "to be, to exist, to take place, to happen" (el-Aswad 2002, 165). It refers to the dynamic process of being and becoming as exclusively exercised by God, who "when He intends a thing, His command is, 'Be,' and it is!" (Qur'an 30:82). In ancient Egypt, the great God Ptah creates all creatures through his uttered thought or spoken word (Frankfort 1948, 20; Ions 1968, 34). Also, in some versions of ancient Egyptian creation myth, Atum, known also as Ra, creates himself out of Nun by an effort of thought or will as well as by uttering his own name. The secret of Ra's power is derived from and depends on his hidden name (Sourouzian 1987, 26, el-Aswad 1997, 70–71). It is "the thought which came into the heart of a god and the commanding utterance which brought that thought into reality. This creation by thought conception and speech delivery has its experiential background in human life: the authority of a ruler to create by command" (Wilson 1946, 65).

Another theme found in several creation myths is that significant components of the universe are made of the bodily substance of the primordial being or creator. The Egyptian god Atum creates the world from his own substance through masturbation (Ions 1968, 26). However, in some versions of archaic Egyptian creation myths Ra, having no female or wife, creates out of himself a divine pair of offspring. One is male, called Shu (air), the lord of dryness, and the other is female, known as Tefnet, the goddess of humidity or moisture. Ra is called the "father of the gods" and of all other living creatures, which are thought to have grown from his sweat and tears (Ions 1968, 41). In the Persian creation myth, the first man is born from the sweat of the creator,

Ahura Mazda. Meanwhile, in Babylonian creation myth, Marduk creates the cosmos from a fragment of Tiamat's torn body and creates man "from the blood of the demon Kingu, to whom Tiamat had entrusted the Tablets of Destiny" (Eliade 1959, 55). Creation takes place in Hindu creation myth when a cosmic lotus emerges from the navel of Vishnu (A123.9). When the lotus blossoms, the creator Brahma appears from inside the lotus and carries on the creative process by fashioning a multitude of worlds, including the world in which we live (Kinsley 1982, 66). In Norse creation mythology, Ymir, the progenitor of the giants and the first being in the world, is killed by three creators, Oden, Vili, and Ve, who fashion the earth from his body, the sea from his blood, the mountains from his bones, and the heavens from his skull (Gabriel 1975, 275–278).

Chinese creation myth also indicates that the cosmos is created from the bodily parts or remains of a primordial being or deity. After his death, P'an-Ku's body becomes the substance from which significant parts of the cosmos, including the sky and earth, are made. The sun and moon are made from his eyes, the wind from his breath, thunder from his voice, and rain from his sweat (von Franz 1968, 213–14; Maclagan 1977, 25). In some creation myths, parts of the universe are created not directly from the body of the primordial god, but rather from one of his descendants. In Maori creation mythology, Vatea and Tangaroa argue about the first-born of Papa's children. To settle the dispute, Papa cuts the child into two halves and distributes them to the two gods. Vatea throws his portion to the heaven where it turns into the sun. Meanwhile, after keeping his part for a while, Tangaroa casts it to the sky, where it becomes the moon (Alpers 1966).

Some creation myths involve several levels or stages of creation, indicating the ceaseless processes of continuous creation of the universe through to the end of time. This means that the universe or parts of the cosmos are gradually created. The biblical narrative shows the order of creation as occurring successively in six days and describes the occurrences of each day. In both biblical and Islamic cosmogonies, God, after creating the heavens and some of its creatures, creates man or Adam from potter's clay (Burkhalter 1985, 224–226). Eve is then created out of Adam's rib. Creation myths involve the creation of man by deities or other entities at various stages. Among the Desana group of the Tukano Indians, the sun is called the Sun Father because it created the universe by the power of its yellow light, giving life and nourishment to the whole universe. The Sun Father creates the earth with its animals and plants, but there are still no people. The Sun Father, however, fashions a man who serves as a creator of people. The man creates various beings in such a way that they would represent him (Reichel-Dolmatoff 1971, 23–25). Through this creative action, a hierarchical structure in the universe, in which human beings are situated between deities and animals, is established. Continuous creation also implies repetition and regeneration in the sense that the creation of the world can be repeated and reproduced. "Allah is He who effects the creation, hence He repeats it" (Qur'an 10:3). This eternal repetition of the cosmic act "permits the return of the dead to life, and maintains the hope of the faithful in the resurrection of the body" (Eliade 1959, 62).

As primordial god creates part of the universe, other agents, such as his offspring, create and differentiate further parts from each other. This process implies hierarchy as well as competition and conflict between genealogies and generations of gods. Atum or Ra creates his eldest children Shu (air) and Tefnet (moisture), from whose union another two deities, Geb (earth) and Nut (sky), are born. Nut is represented as a woman stretching her naked body over the earth. The lord Shu (air), however, holds up the sky, separating her from her husband Geb (earth). Four deities, opposed in pairs, are born from the union of the earth and sky. These four deities, Osiris and Isis, and Seth and Nephthys, are integrated in the Great Ennead of Heliopolis, forming what can be called a social cosmology (el-Aswad 1997). Hierarchical order establishes the cosmic order or cosmic state (Wilson 1946, 139), in which dominant forces of the universe are ordered based on rank (Ricoeur 1967, 176).

God exists yet is invisible and his creations or actions that affect the natural world are perceived in myths as evidence of his hidden nature. Put differently, many creation myths imply that there is an invisible world that underlies the world of created entities. For instance, the Iroquois believed that "every thing on earth had an 'elder brother' in the sky realm" (Maclagan 1977, 24). The invisible quality as the underlying principle or theme of the creation act is repeatedly stressed in various forms of narratives. In official doctrines of the Twelfth Dynasty, Osiris is "the soul of Ra, his great hidden Name which resides in him" (Moret 1972, 385). The name of Osiris is enough to turn a dead man into a god (Moret 1972, 260). Also, Isis painstakingly attempts to seize Ra's secret or hidden name to empower herself.

ELITE LITERATURE

Archetypal patterns implicit in creation myths are not restricted to archaic or folk cultures. They are found in modern elite literature and science fiction. All forms of literature—plays, short stories, novels, and motion pictures— reveal the recurrent themes or archetypes, indicating how a contemporary artist has adapted an ancient myth to the values and aspirations of modern culture (Knapp 1984). The search for authentic mythic archetypes can begin with William Blake's *Book of Urizen*. Blake introduces the character of Urizen, an old man with a white beard representing the being men worship under the name of Jehovah, as doing the work of the creator, "establishing time and space and thus creating the world as we know it" (Cantor 1984, 30). As a creator Urizen does not bring the world out of nothingness, but rather establishes a cosmic order by "staking out boundaries in what had been an undifferentiated unity" (Cantor 1984, 31).

A striking example of the impact of traditional mythic patterns on science fiction is Mary Shelley's *Frankenstein* (1818), in which as "the creator of a man Frankenstein plays the role of God" (Cantor 1984, 103). In the story, the creature or man is created in the image of his creator in such a way that both of them are mirror images of each other. This homology between the creator and the created indicates that human lives have significance for people on the whole who follow these stories. Frankenstein creates a being because he wants someone to worship him with complete devotion: "A new species would bless me as its creator and source; many happy and excellent natures would owe their being to me. No father could claim the gratitude of his child so completely as I should deserve theirs" (quoted in Cantor 1984, 110). However, as original as the Frankenstein myth was, much of the power of Shelley's novel can be traced to the ways she found of drawing upon traditional mythic patterns (Cantor 1984, 103).

The archetype of creating beings is also mirrored in popular children's literature. In Carlo Collodi's story, *Pinocchio,* Geppetto, the woodcarver, creates a special puppet and wishes it were a real boy. The Blue Fairy touches the puppet gently, bringing it to life and advising proper and moral behavior. Pinocchio, however, does not follow her advice and as a result begins to transform into a donkey. Recognizing his errors, Pinocchio changes his behavior and demonstrates noble actions, especially toward his father, Geppetto, whom he rescues from the sea and for whom he was about to lose his life. Finally the Blue Fairy reappears and brings him into life as a real boy (Collodi 2001).

Another well-known example is the *Star Wars* film trilogy, in which the cosmic battle between natural humans and machine creations constitutes a profound theme. As Ferrell (2000) and Roemer (1998) note, George Lucas, the writer, producer, and director of the films, engaged Joseph Campbell as an adviser to create a modern myth that connects to audiences of all ages. The force or power, a dominant theme in *Star Wars,* not only creates distinct and powerful beings or humans but also re-creates or changes them dramatically into machines. For instance, Anakin Skywalker is a child conceived by the will of the Force (or God). He has extreme force potential, as evidenced by a record number of certain elements in his bloodstream that render him undefeatable. Though he is a humble and innocent character in his childhood, when he lives in slavery, Anakin shows great power that attracts Obi-Wan Kenobi, a Jedi Knight, to train him to become a Jedi. However, Anakin, later, falls to the destructive zone of the force and abandons his past and his humanity. He becomes the destructive machine Darth Vader, Dark Lord of the Sith, representing the dark side of the force. The monster mask of Darth Vader represents the soulless or monster force in the modern world. Darth Vader is a robot or "a bureaucrat, living not in terms of himself but in terms of an imposed system" (Campbell with Moyers 1988, 1440). As the *Star Wars* trilogy shows, when a successful reworking of myth takes place the novel, play, or film achieves merit and classic status.

el-Sayed el-Aswad

See also: Nature of the Creator.

REFERENCES

Alpers, Antony. 1966. *Maori Myths and Tribal Legends.* Boston: Houghton Mifflin.

Burkhalter, Sheryl L. 1985. "Completion in Continuity: Cosmogony and Ethics in Islam." In *Cosmogony and Ethical Order: New Studies in Comparative Ethics,* ed. Robin W. Lovin and Frank E. Reynolds, 225–250. Chicago: University of Chicago Press.

Campbell, Joseph, with Bill Moyers. 1988. *The Power of Myth.* New York: Doubleday.

Cantor, Paul. 1984. *Creature and Creator: Myth-making and English Romanticism.* Cambridge: Cambridge University Press.

Christie, Anthony. 1968. *Chinese Mythology.* London: Hamlyn.

Collodi, Carlo. 2001 [1882]. *Pinocchio.* Compiled by Cooper Edens. San Francisco, CA: Chronicle Books.

el-Aswad, el-Sayed. 1997. "Archaic Egyptian Cosmology." *Anthropos* 92: 69–81.

———. 2002. *Religion and Folk Cosmology: Scenarios of the Visible and Invisible in Rural Egypt.* Westport, CT: Praeger.

Eliade, Mircea. 1959. *Cosmos and History: The Myth of Eternal Return.* New York: Harper and Row.

Ferrell, William K. 2000. *Literature and Film as Modern Mythology.* Westport, CT: Praeger.

Foster, Leslie D. 1988. "Birth of the Hero." In *Dictionary of Literary Themes and Motifs,* ed. Jean-Charles Seigneuret. Westport, CT: Greenwood Press.

Frankfort, Henri. 1948. *Ancient Egyptian Religion: An Interpretation.* New York: Harper Torch Books.

Gabriel, E.O. 1975. *Myth and Religion of the North.* Westport, CT: Greenwood.

Grimal, Nicolas. 1992. *A History of Ancient Egypt.* Trans. Ian Shaw. Oxford: Blackwell.

Ions, Veronica. 1968. *Egyptian Mythology.* Middlesex, UK: Hamlyn.

Jung, C.G. 1990. *The Archetypes and the Collective Unconscious.* Bollingen Series 20. Princeton, NJ: Princeton University Press.

Kinsley, David R. 1982. *Hinduism: A Cultural Perspective.* Englewood Cliffs, NJ: Prentice Hall.

Knapp, Bettina L. 1984. *A Jungian Approach to Literature.* Carbondale: Southern Illinois University.

Maclagan, David. 1977. *Creation Myths: Men's Introduction to the World.* London: Thames and Hudson.

Moret, Alexandre. 1972. *The Nile and Egyptian Civilization.* Trans. M.R. Dobie. London: Routledge and Kegan Paul.

Reichel-Dolmatoff, Gerardo. 1971. *Amazonian Cosmos: The Sexual and Religious Symbolism of the Tukano Indians.* Chicago: University of Chicago Press.

Ricoeur, Paul. 1967. *The Symbolism of Evil.* Boston: Beacon Press.

Roemer, Danielle M. 1998. "Campbell, Joseph (1904–1987)." In *Encyclopedia of Folklore and Literature,* ed. Mary Ellen Brown and Bruce A. Rosenberg. Santa Barbara, CA: ABC-CLIO.

Sourouzian, Hourig. 1987. "Egyptian Religion." In Mohamed Saleh and Hourig Sourouzian, *The Egyptian Museum Cairo Official Catalogue.* Mainz, Germany: Verlag Philipp von Zabern.

Stephens, Anthony. 1983. *Archetypes: A Natural History of the Self.* New York: Quill.

von Franz, Marie-Louise. 1968. "The Process of Individuation." In *Man and His Symbols,* ed. Carl Young et al., 158–229. Garden City, NY: Doubleday.

Wilson, John A. 1946. "Egypt: The Nature of the Universe." In *The Intellectual Adventure of Ancient Man,* ed. H. and H.A. Frankfort, J. Wilson, and Thorkild Jacobsen, 39–70. Chicago: University of Chicago Press.

Fight of the Gods and Giants

Motif A 162.1

❀

Webster's Dictionary (1983) defines *giant* as a "legendary manlike being of great stature and strength" and does not assign any negative attributes. In world mythologies, however, giants are generally colossal figures of evil disposition, enemies of gods and mortals, and frequently exhibiting an unusual trait such as breathing fire, having multiple heads, or engaging in cannibalism.

GIANTS AND GODS

Giants have a complicated relationship with gods. Sometimes giants have given birth to gods, for example, the god Loki, the evil trickster in Norse mythology, whose parents were both giants. Alternatively, gods have given birth to giants, for example, Diti, granddaughter of Brahma, and mother of Daityas or giants. Gods have also created and installed giants as guardians of a particular place, person, or thing, such as in Sumerian mythology when Enlil, the divine ruler of earth (George 1999, 223), makes Humbaba the guardian of the great cedar forest.

Both gods and giants are apt at transforming themselves into any creature of their choice and sometimes manipulating their own body parts. For example, in Chinese mythology, when the god Huang Di decapitates the nameless giant, the giant rises up again as Xing Tian, the Headless One (F531.1.2.1, "Headless giant"). Using his nipples as eyes and his navel as his mouth, he takes up arms again in search of his head (Walls and Walls 1988, 48).

In some cases, a god assumes the form of a giant to conquer evil (Vishnu), and sometimes giants assume human or animal form to bully mortals and divinities (Shurpanakha and Marichi) (D630, "Transformation and disenchantment at will") (Menon 2001, 175, 187–197).

FIGHT BETWEEN GODS AND GIANTS

Particularly in Norse, Greek, and Indian mythologies, there are important contests between gods and giants.

The Giants at War with Olympian Gods

The war between the giants and the Olympian gods, the *Gigantomachia,* is presented as one of the fiercest of all battles in Greek mythology. It is first mentioned by Xenophanes (ca. 535–500 BCE), and the writings of Apollodorus contain numerous references to it.

The giants, often regarded as the fourth race of monsters (Hamilton 1942, 80), are born from the blood of Uranus (Sky), the father of the Titans. Often described as a race of reptilian creatures (F531.1.8.2, "Giant as serpent") (Leeming 1976, 55), giants receive a boon from their mother, Gaea (Earth), that makes them impervious to the weapons of the gods. However, they do not have immunity from the weapons of men.

When Zeus overthrows his father, Cronus, and establishes the dynasty of the Olympian gods, he faces severe, continuous opposition from Titans and other children of Gaea. During this war, Porphyrion, the king of the giants, attempts to seize Zeus's wife Hera (R11.3, "Abduction by giants"), and Alcyoneous, the most powerful of all giants, hurls rocks at the Olympian gods (F531.3.2, "Giant throws a great rock").

When the gods are not able to prevail against the giants, they invite mortals, product of their creation, to defeat those with whom the gods share blood ties. With the aid of the mighty Herakles (Hercules), weapons of men, and the stratagems of commanding the sun and the moon not to shine and cutting down the herb that "furnished the giants with a charm against wounds" (F531.6.5.3, "Giant has wound-healing balm") (Murray 1935, 44), Zeus is able to launch a powerful campaign against the giants (A165.7, "Army of the gods").

The Frost Giants and the Creation of Earth and Giants at the End

According to the Norse *Edda,* in the beginning of the world there was nothing except an empty space, bordered by the region of mist, ice, and snow on the northern side. The "warm breaths" from the "sun-land" cause the ice to melt and topple over. From this frozen wreckage springs Ymir, the first frost giant (F531.1.9), who feeds on the milk of the cow who in turn lives by licking the ice-blocks, "from which, in consequence of the licking, was produced Bori, the fashioner of the world" (Murray 1935, 357–358).

In the combat between the children of Bori and Ymir, Ymir is killed (F531.6.12, "Disappearance or death of giants") and the dynasty of the frost giants is ended (F531.6.1.7, "Giants as sons of Ymir or Aurgelmir"). The victors devise creative uses for Ymir's body parts. Thus, "the flesh of the Ymir became the earth; his blood the sea; his bones, the mountains; his teeth, cliffs and crags; his skull, the heavens, wherein his brains float in the form of clouds" (Murray 1935, 358). It is the killing of Ymir and the other frost giants and the accomplishment of creation that gives Bori's sons a divine position in Norse mythology

Orchard says that the primary characteristic of the giants is their "essential hostility to gods and men" (1997, 55). In the apocalyptic final battle, known as Ragnarok, it was believed that the world would come to an end. Many factions would meet on the battlefield of Vigrond, including the giants, who would fight against both gods and men.

The Suras and the Asuras: In Quest for Immortality

Although the Sanskrit word *asura* and its synonyms *daitya, danava,* and *rakshasa* are generally translated as "demon" in English, in terms of iconography, attributes, and literal meaning for certain types of *asuras* the term "giant" is more suitable. (Mohan and Kapoor 1990, 350, 366).

According to Vedic mythology, as recounted in the epic *Mahabharata,* at the beginning of the universe both the *suras* (gods) and the *asuras* (giants) are equal in strength. Over time, the giants improve their skills and become adept at defeating gods and conquering heaven. The only thing that replenishes the energy of gods and helps them reconquer heaven is *amrit,* the drink of immortality. However, in one of the periodic cycles of the creation of the universe, *amrit* and other precious things fail to reappear. The only way to recover them is by churning the *Ksheer Sagar* or the ocean of milk.

The gods need the strength of the giants to recover *amrit* from the depths of the great ocean, so they seek collaboration with them by promising them a share of the drink of immortality for their help. However, as soon as the pot of *amrit* emerges, the gods and the giants start quarrelling about who should drink it first. Vishnu then takes the form of a beautiful maiden called Mohini and lures the giants into handing her the pot. Failing to recognize the true identity of Mohini, the giants ask her to distribute *amrit* to everyone. However, as soon as Mohini finishes distributing *amrit* to the gods, she disappears. When the giants realize that the gods have cheated them of their rightful share, they become violent and a fierce battle ensues. But this time, having consumed the drink of immortality, the gods successfully subdue the giants and take control of heaven.

Soon the *asuras* realize that without *amrit* they are neither strong nor immortal. The only way to regain their former powers is to please the mightiest of deities and obtain their protection. They diligently devote themselves either to Brahma, the Creator, or to Vishnu, the Preserver, or to Shiva, the Destroyer, and succeed in attaining divine boons that grant them immunity from death in an extraordinary way. For example, Hiranyakashyapu asks Brahma:

> Let me never be killed by these means: the striking and throwing weapons of my enemies, thunderbolts, dried tree trunks, high mountains, by water or fire. Let me be free from the threat of death from gods, Daityas, seers, Siddhas and whatever other beings you have created. But why go on? Let me not be slain in heaven, on earth, in the daytime, at night, from neither above or below." (Dimmitt and van Buitenen 1978, 77)

At another time it is Ravana, the villain in the epic *Ramayana,* who asks Shiva for strength that makes him invincible and then asks Brahma for immunity against death: "Bless me that I never find death at the hands of a deva, danava, daitya, asura, rakshasa, gandharva, kinnara, charana, siddha, or any of the divine and demonic beings of heaven and earth" (Menon 2001, xviii) Ravana excludes men from his list because he doubts if anyone from the "puny race of men" could ever possess the strength to hold weapon against him (Menon 2001, xviii).

However, once the wish of *asuras* is granted, as a general rule, they renounce their austerities and became tyrants. Often they become the masters of the entire three worlds, inflict cruelty upon their citizens, and force men to worship them instead of gods. During this period of oppression, the gods hold several councils to eliminate the threat, and frequently Vishnu, the Preserver of the world, takes incarnations, visits the three worlds, vanquishes the evil, and restores the order of the universe.

Since a god who has granted the wish of his devotee, regardless of whether the devotee is a human or an *asura,* is also his or her lifelong protector, the god cannot take away the boon he has given due to the power of his divine word. However, he can allow another god to take the initiative and end the calamity his protégé has brought upon the universe. Generally, the god punishing the *asura* devises a strategy that will not conflict with the boon granted by a deity. In the case of Hiranyakashyapu, for example, Vishnu brings an end to his life by taking incarnation as Narsimha, a giant who is half man and half lion (A122, "God half mortal half immortal") and therefore not a man, animal, god, demon, or product of the creation of Brahma, against whom the *asura* had obtained immunity. Vishnu kills Hiranyakshapu at dusk (which is neither day nor night), hoisting the *asura* on his thigh (so that he is neither in earth nor in sky) and using his claws instead of a weapon.

Another path for achieving immortality and divinity is by accumulating merit. The *asuras* know that anyone who attains one hundred merits in accordance with the Vedas can become Indra, the king of heaven and therefore divine. When King Bali, a *daitya* (giant), conquers the three worlds with his austerities, gods lose control over heaven. Eventually, Vishnu decides to take incarnation as a Brahmin (learned man) and reinstate gods in heaven. When Bali organizes a religious sacrifice to honor the Brahmins of his kingdom, Vishnu in the form of a Vaman (dwarf) asks him for as much land as he can cover in three paces. The moment Bali grants his wish, the Vaman assumes the form of an enormous giant (A 133.2.1, "Giant god goes with three steps through the world"). In the first step he covers the heaven, in the second the earth (F531.3.5.2, "Giant's mighty stride spans earth's width"), restoring the kingdom of gods to them; he relinquishes his right to a third pace by granting King Bali the dominion of Patala, the nether regions (Ions 1967, 51). This example illustrates that the conflict between gods and giants does not consist of war alone. Sometimes there are contests like these through which gods can inflict a crushing defeat over giants by sheer strategy.

INDIVIDUAL COMBATS BETWEEN GIANTS AND GODS

Individual combats between gods and giants are unusually thrilling and full of suspense. In Brahmanical mythology, even though in their incarnations as humans gods may possess the ability to distinguish a giant from a human, they may still be quite vulnerable. For example, when a giantess named Putna assumes the form of a beautiful woman (D55.2.3, "Giant changes to normal size") and comes to kill baby Krishna, the latter is able to recognize her true form right away. Although as an infant he can do very little to protect himself, when Putna tries to poison him by pretending to nurse him under the cover of her dress, Krishna sucks so hard at her breast that he kills her.

Although one may assume that gods are all-knowing, in their human forms they are often oblivious to future events. Rama, an incarnation of lord Vishnu, is unaware that his chase after the golden deer is a ploy to remove him from the scene so that Ravana can kidnap his wife, Sita. Rama also struggles hard and long to kill Ravana. Since the latter is blessed with ten heads and twenty arms, each time Rama cuts one head, another appears in its place (D1602.12, "Self-returning head. When head is cut off it returns to proper place without harm to owner"). Finally, Ravana's brother Vibhishana informs Rama that he should aim at the *asura*'s navel to kill him.

The analysis of various motifs depicting the fights of the gods and giants shows that often the two share familial ties and similar aspirations and ambitions. Most of their fights are directed toward gaining control over the universe. Giants do not have any allies. They primarily rely on their own resources and often possess superior strength to gods. Gods, on the other hand, may seek assistance from mortals, including their own incarnations, to defeat giants. Such combats are usually violent and result in the victory of gods. In certain circumstances when gods fear defeat in war, they employ stratagems to achieve victory.

The motif of the fight of gods and giants functions at a symbolic level, with gods representing good and giants evil. The war between good and evil is a bitter one and there are occasions when even gods must suffer and struggle and, in Norse mythology, die. But in spite of all obstacles, as guardians of order and justice, gods (and those allied with gods) must strive to defeat and remove giants, symbols of chaos and unrest, in order to safeguard the beauty and order of their creation.

Deeksha Nagar

REFERENCES

Dimmitt, Cornelia, and J.A.B. van Buitenen, eds. 1978. *Classical Hindu Mythology: A Reader in Sanskrit Puranas.* Philadelphia: Temple University Press.

George, Andrew, trans. 1999. *The Epic of Gilgamesh: A New Translation.* New York: Penguin Classics.

Hamilton, Edith. 1942. *Mythology.* Boston: Little, Brown.

Ions, Veronica. 1967. *Indian Mythology.* London: Paul Hamlyn.

Leeming, David. 1976. *Mythology.* New York: Newsweek Books.

Menon, Ramesh. 2001. *The Ramayana: A Modern Retelling of the Great Indian Epic.* New York: North Point Press.

Mohan, B., and B.N. Kapoor, eds. 1990. *Meenakshi Hindi-English Dictionary.* Meerut, India: Meenakshi Prakashan.

Murray, Alexander. 1935. *Manual of Mythology.* New York: Tudor.

Orchard, Andy, ed. 1997. *Dictionary of Norse Myth and Legend.* London: Cassell.

Walls, Jan, and Yvonne Walls. 1988. *Classical Chinese Myths.* Hong Kong: Joint Publishing Group.

Webster's Ninth New Collegiate Dictionary. 1983. Springfield: Merriam-Webster.

Doomsday (Day of Judgment)

Motif A1002

❀

Doomsday (from Old English *doom*) is the Day of Judgment when Jesus will come again to judge the living and the dead, determining who will be saved and who will be damned. The names Doomsday and Judgment Day are also used more generally to refer to the events leading to and including the end of this world, as we know it. The belief that the world will end on a predetermined date is a concept as universal as that of Creation (A1000, "World catastrophe. The world is destroyed. The incidents are usually the same whether a final destruction is thought of or a destruction which may be overcome by a renewal of the earth").

The events leading to the Christian doomsday are described in greatest and most authoritative detail in the Apocalypse (in English, Revelation). *Apocalypse,* the Greek word for "uncover" or "reveal," is the title of the last book of the New Testament. The Apocalypse purports to be St. John the Apostle's vision of the end of the world, a vision that he received from God through an angel on the Isle of Patmos. The book dates from about 96 CE. This book is neither the first nor the only version of the end of the world, although not all apocalypses contain a final Day of Judgment (which is the crowning moment of Christian eschatology, the study of last things, and the science of salvation). The closest analogues of the Apocalypse appear in such Old Testament canonical works as the books of Daniel, written about 165 CE (McGinn 1979, 6), Ezekiel, Joel, Zechariah, Jeremiah, and Isaiah. Noncanonical Old Testament passages containing doomsday images (the names used in the Old Testament is Last Days or Day of the Lord, not Judgment Day (McGinn 1992, 8) appear in Esdras, Enoch, Tobit, Maccabees, and Baruch. In the New

Testament, four passages are commonly known as "the little Apocalypse": Matthew 24:3–25, Luke 21:5–13, I Corinthians 15, and I Thessalonians 4:13–5:33 (McGinn 1992, 9). Numerous noncanonical or apocryphal apocalypses associated with the New Testament include The Apocalypse of Peter, The Apocalypse of Paul, The Apocalypse of Thomas, The Apocalypse of the Virgin, and The Revelation of St. Stephen.

Both the Old and New Testament apocalyptic images and themes have sources or analogues in such earlier cultures and systems of belief as the Babylonian, the Persian, the Zoroastrian, the Gnostic, the Stoic, and the Epicurean (Daniels 1999, 19–47). Among the elements generally considered definitive of apocalyptic tone and thought are a final predetermined flood (A1010, "Deluge. Inundation of whole world") or conflagration (A1030, "World-fire. A conflagration destroys the earth"), a last battle between the forces of good and evil (A1080, "Battle at end of world. Armageddon.—Revelations"), a sequence of signs and portents that marks the approach of the end, often including the rise of a treacherous adversary (the Antichrist in Christianity) (Rusconi 1999, 287–235), the coming of a messiah, a reign of peace, a last judgment that separates the good souls from the evil, and, finally, a joyous proclamation of a new and different world (A1006, "Renewal of world after world calamity"). Apocalyptic books or passages of books and the accompanying belief in predetermined last days are common not only to the major Western religions, Judaism, Christianity, and Islam, but also to Zoroastrianism and Baha'i, and the major Eastern religions and philosophies of Buddhism, Hinduism, Confucianism, and Taoism. The end of time appears in such widely diverse sites as North and South American Indian religions, African tribal religions, and Indonesian, Maori, Polynesian, Melanesian, and Micronesian religious myth and lore (*World Scripture* 1991, 783; Daniels 1999, 19–47).

Although by no means a universal source for all of the apocalyptic views, Christian Book of Revelation is the definitive text for all Western apocalypses. Its imagery and motifs are sufficiently archetypal to make its general outline crucial to understanding the meaning of doomsday. The narrator, John, describes himself as "in the spirit on the Lord's day" and says, "I heard . . . a great voice as of a trumpet, saying, 'What thou seest write in a book and send to the seven churches'" (Apocalypse 1:10–11). John obediently records "the revelation of Jesus Christ which God gave him [through His angel] to make known to his servants the things that may shortly come to pass." These are the events that will signify the end of the Old World and the beginning of a "new heaven and a new earth" (Apocalypse 21:1).

Doomsday is supposed to occur at the end of time after the sounding of seven trumpets, the appearance of seven signs, and the lifting of the seven seals of the closed book, which reveals the mysteries they concealed. The natural signs of the end include earthquakes, oceans filled with blood, floods, fire, falling stars, the darkening of the sun and the moon, various plagues, and other catastrophes (A1002.2. "Signs before the Day of Judgment"). These disasters herald a war in heaven and a final battle called Armageddon, in which good triumphs over evil. The dragon, Satan, will be bound for a thousand years, during which there will be a reign of peace. From this thousand-year reign of peace that precedes the end of the world comes the term "millenarianism" (or chiliasm), used to characterize apocalyptic faith and tone (McIver 1999, 4; McGinn 1992, 17). After a thousand years, Satan will be loosed. Disguising himself as Christ, this Antichrist will deceive the nations by performing miracles in order to win converts who will worship him instead of God (A1075, "End of world heralded by coming of Antichrist"). Finally, the Antichrist will be defeated and the divine Christ will come again on Doomsday to judge the living and the dead. These events and scenes are considered significant warnings for which those of an apocalyptic bent are always on the alert. Among the most familiar and most often cited scenes in John's book are the trumpets of judgment, the adoration of the lamb, and the 144,000 virgins in the procession of Christ, the bridegroom, past the jeweled walls and through the streets of the Heavenly Jerusalem (McIver 1999, 11–13). Among the best-known characters in the tale are Christ (called "the son of man"), the woman clothed with the sun and the moon, the seven-headed beast, the Whore of Babylon, and the Great Beast who is the Antichrist. Among the most popular symbols are the seven-branched candelabrum, the Four Horsemen of the Apocalypse, the twenty-four elders with their cups and harps, and Christ in a cloud of glory, sometimes holding the Great Book of the beginning and the end. In it are inscribed Alpha and Omega, from Christ's words, "I am Alpha and Omega, the beginning and the end" (Apocalypse 1:8).

Commentators on the Apocalypse have naturally been concerned to know the exact date of Doomsday. A long tradition of numerical calculations and comparisons of natural, political, social, and religious events with those described in the text has produced a series of predicted dates of the end of the world, some of which are now past. The majority, though by no means all, of the predicted dates of Doomsday have been millennial. Thus, the year 1000 was considered by many a likely time for the world to end. Great debate has surrounded the question of whether the number of Romanesque churches built around the year 1000 was due to millenarian terror and its relief (Focillon 1969, 50 et passim; Alexander 2000, 45, 46). At the time of the next great millennium in 2000, the world feared that chaos, caused by computer malfunction over the number of the year, would cause a complete breakdown of society. This "Y2K" phenomenon was a technologically imagined form of

Doomsday. Since apocalyptic thoughts and words seem to increase in times of political, social, physical, and even technological change and instability, it is not surprising that millenarianism persists today. In 1997, an Associated Press poll found that "nearly 25% of adult Christians—more than 26 million people [in the United States alone]—believe that Jesus Christ will return to earth in their lifetimes and set in motion the horrific events laid out in the biblical books of Revelation and Daniel." By 2000, the director of the Millennium Watch Institute had over 1,200 cults in his database ("Apocalypse Really Soon" 1999).

An American tradition of apocalypticism has flourished since the founding of this country. It appeared in the eighteenth-century hellfire and brimstone imagery of such divines as Cotton Mather and Jonathan Edwards, and in the establishment of nineteenth-century Utopian communities such as the Oneida Community, the Ephrata Community, New Harmony, Bethel, and Aurora (Lamy 1996, 27). A few of the many well-known millennialist sects are the Shakers, the Mennonites, the Jehovah's Witnesses, the Mormons, and the Seventh-Day Adventists.

DOOMSDAY TODAY

Since the 1960s, millennialist movements have mushroomed. These range in orientation from UFOlogy to the survivalism of such groups as the Montana Freemen and the Wisconsin Posse (Daniels 1999, 127–224). Such groups are well represented by *Soldier of Fortune* magazine, in which an advertisement for Sally's Survival Outfitters promised, "We'll supply you til Doomsday" (Lamy 1996, 79). Prominent millennialist groups of the late twentieth century have included The Unification Church of Sun Myung Moon; the Hare Krishnas; the People's Temple, of Jonestown fame; the Branch Davidians, whose leader, David Koresh, died in a standoff in Waco, Texas, in 1993; and Heaven's Gate, thirty-nine of whose members committed suicide in 1997 (Daniels 1999, 224–233).

Currently, one of the most popular themes among many Christian sects is the Rapture, an event based, but never explicitly named, in both Old and New Testament Apocalypses. It refers to an ecstatic moment at "the end of time, [when] the born-again will be snatched up to meet the Lord in the air" (Alexander 2000, 72). Of course, this short list gives a too-scant idea of both the long history and present popularity of such an emphasis not only in America but also throughout the world. Millennialism has appeared, not only in religious and technological forms, but also in such varied areas as philosophy, art, economics, politics, cosmology, ecology, and literature (Bynum and Freedman 2000, passim; Landes 2000, 129–131). Altizer might have been speaking of many of these disciplines when he wrote, "It is extraordinarily difficult, if not impossible to discover a truly major work of twentieth-century literature that is not apocalyptic" (1999, 3: 347). If apocalyptic determinism does flourish in times of stress and upheaval, twenty-first-century citizens can expect many predictions that Doomsday is at hand.

Judith Neaman

See also: Origin of Pentecost.

REFERENCES

Alexander, Jonathan. 2000. "The Last Things: Representing the Unrepresentable." In *The Apocalypse and the Shape of Things to Come,* ed. Frances Carey, 43–64. London: British Museum Press.

Altizer, Thomas J.J. 1999. "Modern Thought and Apocalypticism." In *The Encyclopedia of Apocalypticism,* ed. Bernard McGinn, John Collins, and Stephen J. Stein, 3: 325–359. New York: Continuum.

"Apocalypse Really Soon." 1999. ABC News.com. Cults Focus on the Year 2000. January 5, http://more abcnews.co.com/sections/world/Daily News/cults 980105 html.

The Apocrypha of the Old Testament. Revised Standard Version. 1957. New York: Thomas Nelson.

Bynum, Caroline Walker, and Paul Freedman, eds. 2000. *Last Things: Death and Apocalypse in the Middle Ages.* Philadelphia: University of Pennsylvania Press.

Daniels, Ted, ed. 1999. *A Doomsday Reader.* New York: New York University Press.

Focillon, Henri. 1969. *The Year 1000.* Trans. Paul D. Wieck. New York: Frederick Ungar.

Lamy, Philip. 1996. *Millennium Rage: Survivalists, White Supremacists, and the Doomsday Prophecy.* New York: Plenum Press.

Landes, Richard Allen. 2000. *Encyclopedia of Millennialism and Millennial Movements.* New York: Routledge.

McGinn, Bernard. 1979. *Visions of the End: Apocalyptic Traditions in the Middle Ages.* New York: Columbia University Press.

———. 1992. "John's Apocalypse and the Apocalyptic Mentality." In *The Apocalypse in the Middle Ages,* ed. Richard Emmerson and Bernard McGinn, 3–19. Ithaca: Cornell University Press.

McIver, Tom. 1999. *The End of the World: An Annotated Bibliography.* Jefferson, NC: McFarland.

Rusconi, Robert. 1999. "Antichrist and Antichrists." In *The Encyclopedia of Apocalypticism,* ed. Bernard McGinn, 2: 287–325. New York: Continuum.

World Scripture: A Comparative Anthology of Sacred Text. 1991. Andrew Wilson, ed. New York: Paragon.

Confusion of Tongues

Motif A1333

❀

The loss of a common language is a motif found in a number of creation myths that describe how the ancients lost their ability to understand each other's speech when one language was replaced by many. The golden age when all peoples could communicate freely with each other and live in peace was succeeded by the babble of tongues and strife among nations.

The main motif is listed as A1333, "Confusion of tongues. Originally all men speak same language. Because of a sin they come to speak different languages." However, the sin is not made explicit in any of the examples known, although in the most famous version, the Tower of Babel (C771.1, "Tabu: building too high a tower (Tower of Babel))" and F772.1, "Tower of Babel: Remarkably tall tower designed to reach sky"), it can be inferred that God destroyed the tower and confounded the language because of man's hubris. The story of the Tower of Babel appears in the Old Testament, Genesis 11, when "the whole earth had one language and few words." The people of Babylon built a tower,

> And the Lord came down to see the city and the tower, which the sons of men had built. And the Lord said, "Behold, they are one people, and they have all one language; and this is only the beginning of what they will do; and nothing that they propose to do will now be impossible for them. Come, let us go down, and there confuse their language, that they may not understand one another's speech." So the Lord scattered them abroad from there over the face of all the earth, and they left off building the city. Therefore its name was called Babel, because there the Lord confused the language of all the earth; and from there the Lord scattered them abroad over the face of all the earth (Genesis 11:5–9).

Although it has been impossible to prove archaeologically, scholars speculate that there may have been a specific ziggurat at Babylon that inspired this story. Kramer (1968, 108) confirms and corroborates the earlier work of E.A. Speiser, who pointed to a Sumerian source in the epic tale "Enmerkar and the Lord of Aratta," contained on tablets written during the Third Dynasty of Ur (about 2130–2021 BCE). The tale evokes a golden age—

> Once upon a time there was no snake, there
> was no scorpion,
> There was no hyena, there was no lion,
> There was no wild dog, no wolf,
> There was no fear, no terror . . .

—and goes on to tell how "the whole universe . . . to Enlil [one of the primary deities of the Sumerian pantheon] in one tongue spoke" (Kramer 1968, 109). Later, the god of wisdom, Enki, "changed the speech in their mouths / Brought contention into it, / Into the speech of man that until then / had been one" (110). The text does not explain why Enki confounded the people's speech, but Kramer speculates that he might have been jealous of their devotion to Enlil. Kramer also says that the Biblical story implying man's hubris is "undoubtedly a product of Hebrew religious imagination and moralistic temperament" (111).

In addition to Jewish myth, the *Motif-Index* lists the confusion of tongues motif as being found in India, Ireland, Indochina (Burma), North America, and Central America. Thompson remarks that the motif is quite prevalent among North American Indians, especially in the West, and to a lesser extent in the Northeast (1977, 317). It is also found in Africa in tales from the Kaffir (South Africa), Lamba (Zambia), and Ziba (Tanzania) people (Klipple 1992, 357). The frequency with which this motif occurs in North American Indian mythology is probably a result of the efforts of missionaries who promulgated stories from the Bible. "Not surprisingly, the range of recorded Indian Bible stories corresponds very closely to the range of stories the early missionaries say they emphasized: the Creation and its immediate aftermath, especially the creation of Adam and Eve and their temptation and fall; the Flood and Noah's survival; the Tower of Babel and the Confusion of Tongues; the Dispersal of the Tribes; Jonah and the Whale; the Red Sea Crossing" (Ramsey 1977, 447). The same explanation may account for its presence in Burma, Central America, Africa, and India.

However, of the many citations Thompson gives for this motif in *Tales of the North American Indians* (1929), he lists only one version (Choctaw) as similar to the Tower of Babel. In this story, the people marvel at the sky and determine to build a mound to reach the heavens, but every night while they sleep the winds scatter their rocks, and one morning they find they cannot understand each other, so they scatter. The Chins of Burma tell a Babel-like tale of their ancestors building a tower so they could reach the moon to do away with its phases. Their action angered the spirit of the moon, who wrecked the tower, scattering the people (Scott 1918, 266).

There are also versions of the confusion of tongues motif without the secondary motif of the tower-building. In the Kono creation myth from Guinea (Africa), the children of the god Alatangana all speak different languages. The god Sa caused this confusion of tongues because Alatangana eloped with Sa's daughter without his permission (Leeming and Leeming 1994, 163–164). From the Crow, a Plains Indians group, we have the story of Little Coyote, a trickster double of the creator Old Man Coyote. Little Coyote suggests to Old Man that he give the people different languages so that they will misunderstand each other and use their weapons in wars (Leeming and Leeming 1994, 64). Thus, in these two stories, people lose their universal tongue not as punishment for striving heavenward, but on the whim of an angry father-in-law in the first case and a troublemaking trickster in the second.

Jane Garry

REFERENCES

Klipple, May Augusta. 1992. *African Folktales with Foreign Analogues.* New York: Garland (The Garland Folklore Library, 3). Reprint of 1938 dissertation.

Kramer, Samuel Noah. 1968. "The Babel of Tongues: A Sumerian Version." *Journal of the American Oriental Society* 88 (1): 108–111.

Leeming, David, and Margaret Leeming. 1994. *Dictionary of Creation Myths.* New York: Oxford University Press.

Ramsey, Jarold. 1977. "The Bible in Western Indian Mythology." *Journal of American Folklore* 90 (358): 442–454.

Scott, James George. 1918. *Indo-Chinese Myth.* Vol. 12 of *Mythology of All Races.* Boston: Marshall Jones.

Thompson, Stith. 1929. *Tales of the North American Indians.* Cambridge, MA: Harvard University Press.

_____. 1977. *The Folktale.* Berkeley: University of California Press. Orig. ed. New York: Holt, Rinehart, and Winston, 1946.

Origin of Pentecost

Motif A1541.6

✿

Pentecost, meaning "fiftieth" in Greek, is a holiday that takes its name from its calendrical position on the fiftieth day after Easter. The Greek name Pentecost was first used in the Book of Tobit (Cabié 1965, 16; Gunstone 1967, 13). The Hebrew name of the holiday, Shavuos, means "seven weeks," because it falls seven weeks or fifty days after Passover and is sometimes known as the Festival of Weeks. It was originally an ancient Jewish festival that celebrated the wheat harvest in Israel. Exodus 23.16 proclaims, "you will observe the feast of the harvest, of first fruits of what the fields have produced from your sowing." It was one of the three "feasts of pilgrimage and sanctuary" during which pilgrims came to the temple to "offer the first fruits" of the three harvests: barley at Passover, wheat at Pentecost, and fruit at Succos (Potin 1971, 118). Only later did this feast come to be associated with the renewal of the covenant when the law was given to Moses on Mount Sinai (Potin 1971, 123).

The Essenes considered Pentecost a very important holiday, one on which to celebrate the entrance of new members into the community as well as the renewal of the covenant. Thus, the holiday that began as a harvest and pilgrimage festival devoted to offerings of the first agricultural fruits later came to be associated with spiritual first fruits, the conversion of new souls, and a community of the spirit. This tone marks the first New Testament record of Pentecost when the now dead Christ appears to the multitudes of all nations who are assembled "in one place." The moment, described in Acts 2.1–21, involves the thunderous sounds and tongues of flame associated with the theophany on Mount Sinai. At this Pentecost, the Word of God was understood in as many tongues as God created during the presumptuous building of the Tower of Babel, for which the Pentecostal descent of the Holy Spirit speaking in tongues was a remedy.

And when the days of Pentecost were drawing to
a close, they were all together in one place.
And suddenly there came a sound from heaven, as of a violent wind
blowing, and it filled the whole house where they were sitting.
Appeared to them parted tongues as of fire, which settled
upon each of them.
And they were all filled with the Holy Spirit and
began to speak in foreign tongues, even as the
Holy Spirit prompted them to speak.
Now there were staying at Jerusalem devout
Jews from every nation under heaven.
And when this sound was heard, the multitude
gathered and were bewildered in mind because
each heard them speaking in his own language.
But they were all amazed and marveled,
. . . .
[and all the people of the many nations gathered there said]
we have heard them speaking in our
own languages of the wonderful works of God.

In Christianity, as in Judaism, Pentecost is one of the three most important feasts of the year, ranking beside Christmas and Easter. In Acts 2, Jesus is understood as the Word and the ultimate fulfillment of God's covenant with those who are born again in spirit when the Holy Spirit communicates to the people of all nations, unifying them by the words intelligible to all in tongues of flame. While this is the biblical and religious underpinning of the holiday, these texts and doctrines alone do not begin to encompass either the rich associations or the long celebratory history of the holiday. Pentecostal traditions and customs are linked with pagan festivities, with ecclesiastical rites and sacraments, with civil celebrations, and, naturally, with folklore.

In the early church, Pentecost was the favored time for ordinations and entries of novices into orders and of converts into the faith (Burns and Fagin 1964, 52). Second only to Easter, it was the holiday favored for baptism, since the Pentecostal verses actually contain the passage "Now they who received his word were baptized" (Acts 2.41). No doubt its associations with baptism were partially responsible for the fact that Pentecost came to be understood as the day of the founding of the church. Still later, it was the day favored for knighting and coronations. Throughout Christendom, the time from Easter through Pentecost became the primary season for pilgrimage. Its English name was Whitsuntide, from White Sunday, so called because of the many baptismal robes in church on that day.

Domestic and royal celebrations of the day included hearty eating, drinking, and dance. Whitsun ale festivals accompanied by "ludicrous gestures and

acts of foolery and buffoonery" (Brand and Hazelett 1870, I:156) testify that
Pentecost was by no means universally celebrated in a manner consonant
with its pious origins. In England, ale brewed especially for the day and known
as either Whitsun or lamb ale was the subject of "A Serious Dissuasive Against
Whitsun Ales" as late as 1736 (Brand and Hazlett 1870, I:157). It is clear that,
even in the New World, many of the early harvest festival associations with
the day survived. Pentecost was a May feast. Occurring much later than May
Day, the holiday became so standard an occasion for legendary Arthurian
feasts and spring festivals in literature that it is now associated with the convention or *topos* of spring settings for medieval romances. These literary settings of the holiday celebrate Pentecost as the most joyous spring holiday
after Easter, observed in many pagan festivals that survived after their meanings had been lost to the celebrants. Both before and after the fiftieth day,
spring customs like Maypole dances and the crowning of a May King and
Queen were observed. Robin Hood and Maid Marian are often considered
late literary survivals of the May King and Queen.

While Pentecost has remained a major holy day in both Judaism and Christianity. it has recently seen a growing popularity and increasing influence in
the form of Pentecostalism. Pentecostalism is a religious movement that seems
to have first appeared in the nineteenth century, but has gathered its most
dramatic number of adherents in the twentieth century. In the United States, it
is sometimes colloquially designated as "born-again Christianity." The phenomenon is worldwide, however, and the numbers of Pentecostals are smaller
in America, the country where it originated, than in Latin America (Goff 1988,
4, 6, 8). The movement is now gaining great numbers of converts in Africa,
Asia, and Oceania. The *Harper Collins Dictionary of Religion* calls it "probably the fastest growing Christian religious movement during the twentieth
century" and cites the "worldwide membership in Pentecostal denominations
in the 1980s [as] estimated at 175,000,000—6.7 million in the United States
with millions more identifying with various charismatic movements" (Smith
1992, 836). Since that time, the numbers throughout the world have increased
exponentially. The movement began in the Protestant denominations and certainly by the 1970s included not only many of such traditional Protestant
groups as "Episcopalians, Presbyterians, Lutherans, Methodists, and Baptists,"
but also Roman Catholics (Goff 1988, 4).

Pentecostals are frequently classified into three groups: those calling themselves "classical Pentecostals," who trace their beginnings to the Pentecostal
revival in the United States about 1907; those who call themselves
"charismatics," who date from the 1960s in the United States; and those, largely
nonwhite, African, Latin American, and Asian, who believe in the fundamental traits and rites of the other two groups, but are rarely accepted by the

charismatics and classical Pentecostals "because some of their beliefs are considered heretical or non-Christian" (Anderson 1987, 11:230). The history of Pentecostalism is complex and sometimes ambiguous. It started in the United States in "the radical separatist wing of the Holiness movement" of the late nineteenth century (Anderson 1987, 11:232). It first appeared in Europe in 1907 and continues to develop there. Its beginnings in Asia and Africa are generally linked to the mission activity of other Pentecostal groups from the 1950s to the 1960s, and again in the 1980s.

Common to the various forms of Pentecostalism are millennialism, fundamentalism, the belief in spirit baptism, and spiritual healing. The majority of American Pentecostals "believe that the 'initial evidence' of spirit baptism is always glossolalia, or speaking in tongues." But other Pentecostals think that spirit baptism can be "evidenced by any one of the other charismata" or gifts of the spirit that appear in I Corinthians 12–14 (Anderson 1987, 232). They include "the manifestation of the spirit," "gifts of healing, services of help, power of administration and the speaking of various tongues" (I Corinthians 12.28). In general, Pentecostalism has been recognized as a "ritual prolongation of the original Pentecostal event" (Shaull and Cesar 2000, 92) in Acts 2 when the Holy Spirit descends on the multitudes of various nations.

Judith Neaman

REFERENCES

Anderson, John. 1987. "Pentecostal and Charismatic Christianity." In *Encyclopedia of Religion,* ed. Mircea Eliade and Charles Adams, 11: 229–239. New York: Macmillan.

Brand, John, and I.W. Carew Hazlett, eds. 1870. *Popular Antiquities of Great Britain.* 3 vols. London: John Russell Smith.

Burns, J. Patout, and Gerald M. Fagin, S.J. 1964. *The Holy Spirit Message of the Fathers of the Church.* 3 vols. Wilmington, DE: Michael Glazier.

Cabié, Robert. 1965. *La Pentecôte: L'evolution de la Cinquantaine pascale au cours des cinq premiers siècles.* La Bibliothèque de Liturgie. Tournai: Desclée.

Goff, James R., Jr. 1988. *Fields White Unto Harvest: Charles F. Parkham and the Missionary Origins of Pentecostalism.* Fayetteville: University of Arkansas Press.

Gunstone, John. 1967. *The Feast of Pentecost.* London: Faith Press.

The Holy Bible. Douay Rheims Confraternity Version.

Potin, Jean. 1971. *La fête juive de la Pentecôte: Étude du textes.* 2 vols. Paris: Editions du Cerf.

Shaull, Richard, and Waldo Cesar. 2000. *Pentacostalism and the Future of the Christian Churches: Promises, Limitations, Challenges.* Grand Rapids, MI: Eerdmans.

Smith, Jonathan Z., ed. 1992. *The Harper Collins Dictionary of Religion.* San Francisco, CA: Harper San Francisco.

Origins of Inequality

Motifs A1600–A1699

A principal function of myths in all cultures is to explain and justify the existence of observable things and phenomena. Among these are differences in human language, physical appearance, perceived abilities, and social position. The resulting stories extend across a wide spectrum of style and purpose. Some are presented with scriptural dignity, demanding belief and adherence, while others are told as frivolous jokes with any serious intent hidden behind a cloak of irony and paradox. And some combine the sublime with the ridiculous, casting gods, saints, and shamans in humorous roles.

One such story is the account of the Norse god Heimdall, as recorded in the "Rigsthula" (lay of Rig), one of the most engaging stories in the *Poetic Edda.* As the tale unfolds, Heimdall, who has assumed the name Rig, journeys incognito from farmstead to farmstead and, in keeping with ancient hospitality traditions, is offered not only food and shelter, but also a place to sleep next to the host's wife. The meal in the first house is coarse bran bread with broth. The boy conceived during this stay grows into a swarthy lad named Thrall, with dull eyes, wrinkled skin, gnarled knuckles, and a hulking back. His offspring are slaves and servants (A1657, "Origin of slaves"). At the next house, Rig is served boiled calf-meat and other delicacies. The boy conceived here is named Karl, and from this ruddy-skinned, bright-eyed lad come common folk, but free: yeomen, craftsmen, and farmers (A1655, "Origin of peasantry"). At the third house, Rig receives white bread, bacon, roasted fowl, and wine. The boy conceived here is named Earl, and this handsome lad becomes the progenitor of nobles and kings (A1656, "Origin of noblemen"). One of Earl's sons is given particular notice, a boy named Kon, whose name means "king" and who becomes a master of runic lore. Thus the main social divisions derive from one god's extramarital cohabitation in various human households.

A widespread story within the Judeo-Christian tradition offering similar explanations is "Eve's Unequal Children" (AT 758; Motif A1650.1), exemplified by the Grimms' version (KHM 180). Here God announces that he himself will inspect Adam and Eve's household. Eve, ashamed of her less attractive children, hides them in various nooks and crannies, putting only her good-looking offspring on display. God blesses the attractive children with a progeny of kings, princes, counts, knights, nobles, burghers, merchants, and scholars. The ugly, hidden children, however, are promised offspring of peasants, fishermen, smiths, tanners, weavers, shoemakers, tailors, potters, teamsters, sailors, messengers, and household servants. When Eve complains about the Lord's unequal blessings, he replies, "Eve, you do not understand. It is right and necessary that the entire world should be served by your children. If they were all princes and lords, who would plant grain, thresh it, grind and bake it? Who would forge iron, weave cloth, build houses, plant crops, dig ditches, and cut out and sew clothing? Each shall stay in his own place, so that one shall support the other, and all shall be fed like the parts of a body." Thus a rigid class structure is explained and given a pseudo-biblical validation.

In a Tagalog analogue, "The Creation Story" (Cole 1916, 187–188), the first man and woman on earth have many children, "and from them came all the different races of people." However, their house soon becomes so overcrowded that the father, in desperation, begins beating the children with a stick, causing them to flee in all directions. Those who take refuge in rooms within the house become chiefs. Those who conceal themselves inside the walls become slaves. Those who hide in the fireplace become black people. Those who run outside become free people. Those who flee to the sea disappear, coming back many years later as white people. Here, unlike in the Grimms' version, social position has a racial component.

Type 758 stories are also told with an alternate ending, for example as in the Icelandic tale "The Genesis of the Hid-Folk" (Arnason 1864, 19–20). Here, instead of Eve's hidden children producing the lower social classes, their offspring lose their humanity altogether, turning into trolls, elves, fairies, and other such "hidden people" (F251.4).

A less playful mythological explanation of a racial foundation for social inequality comes from two enigmatic passages in Genesis. One tells of the mark placed on Cain to prevent vigilantes from killing him after his murder of Abel (4:15). Although the mark is not described and is characterized as a mark of protection, not a curse, many generations of segregationist theologians have equated it with dark skin, claiming that the descendants of Cain, so marked, are spiritually inferior to those who trace their ancestry through Seth, a son born to Adam and Eve after the fratricide.

Other traditions are even more extreme. For example, in *Beowulf* (lines 102–114), we learn that the wicked monster Grendel is one of the "kinsmen of Cain." Those with whom he shares this ancestry are an evil lot: "From him [Cain] sprang every misbegotten thing, monsters and elves and the walking dead, and also those giants who fought against God time and again." Another example of Cain's descendants' grotesque appearance comes from the Jewish folktale "The Man with Two Heads" (Sadeh 1989, 56–58), where we are told that Cain's descendants now constitute a two-headed race that lives at the center of the earth.

Another biblical event traditionally used to explain and justify race-based segregation and slavery is the curse of Ham and Canaan (Genesis 9:18–27). This account, recorded with ambiguous brevity, relates how Noah is seen drunken and naked in his tent by his son Ham. He reports this to his brothers Shem and Japheth, who walk backward into the tent to avoid seeing their father and cover him. Upon learning what Ham has done, Noah pronounces a curse on Ham's son Canaan: "Cursed be Canaan; a servant of servants shall he be unto his brethren." A Jewish folkloric explanation of Canaan's curse is that Noah, in a drunken state, threatenes to marry again and establish a new race. To prevent this from happening, his grandson Canaan "did him a horrible bodily injury," upon which Noah curses him and all his descendants with permanent servitude (Hanauer 1935, 17).

According to long-standing tradition, Shem, Ham, and Japheth are the progenitors of the earth's three principal races, with Ham's offspring, through Canaan, being dark-skinned people, predestined by Noah's curse to be servants forever (A1614.1, "Negroes as curse on Ham for laughing at Noah's nakedness"). For many generations the shameful exploitation of these views, still alive in some circles, has provided religious validation for race-based slavery, inequality, and segregation.

There are many nonbiblical explanations for physical and social differences based on race. For example, according to a Seminole legend (Reaver 1987, no. 22; Motif A1631), in the beginning people emerged from a mountain. Indians came out first. A black man came out last. "He stayed in the mud so long that when he emerged he was coal black."

According to Joel Chandler Harris's Uncle Remus in "Why the Negro Is Black" (1880, no. 33), "way back yander" all humans were black. But then a pond is discovered whose water can wash a person white. There is a great rush to the pond, and the first people to arrive wash themselves white, using up much of the water. A second group, now with much less water, washed themselves to the shades of mulattoes, Chinese, and Indians. When the slowest group arrive, the water is nearly all gone, so they can only patter about in the puddles with the palms of their hands and the soles of their feet, and they remain black on the rest of their bodies (A1614.2, "Races dark-skinned from bathing after white men"). There is a general consensus that Harris's Uncle Remus stories, especially the early ones, were based on authentic African-American oral folklore current in nineteenth-century rural Georgia (Brookes 1950).

A pseudo-mythological explanation for hard menial labor falling dispro-portionately to blacks is offered in the frequently collected African-American folktale "Why Black People Work." A Creole version from Louisiana titled "An Old Black Man and an Old White Man Had a Race" is typical (Lindahl, Owens, and Harvison 1997, no. 35; Motif A1671.1). A black man and a white man engage in a race, and the winner is to select as his prize one of two closed sacks, a large one and a small one. The black man wins the race and chooses the large sack. Inside are plows, hoes, and other such heavy tools. The white man's smaller sack contains a book and a pencil. Thus the white man learns to read and write, and the black man has to work in the fields and is miserable all his life. This story is told as a joke, but serious, ironic contemplation lies behind its humor. For additional tales explaining or reflecting the social dif-ferences between blacks and other ethnic and racial groups—including whites, Jews, Mexicans, and Chinese—see Dorson (1967, 171–186) and Dance (1977, 1985, 3–8).

Other disadvantaged groups have similar explanations for their own situa-tions, and again the question arises whether such tales express an inferiority complex or a sardonic gallows humor, allowing a victim to gain a psychologi-cal advantage over his oppressors by laughing at his own predicament. For example, according to a Yaruro Indian myth from Venezuela (Karlinger and Pögl 1995, no. 28), soon after the creation of the earth the Yaruro people are given horses, but are afraid of them because of their great size. The whites are not afraid of the horses. The Yaruro are also given giant maize and tobacco plants and banana trees. In harvesting their first crop, they cut down the plants, unwittingly allowing the tops, which contain all the seeds, to fall onto the land of the whites. Thus the whites now have horses and plantations with bananas, maize, and tobacco, while the Yaruro have none of these.

Gypsy etiological legends offer similar examples. According to one such tale from Spain (Tong 1989, 178–179), before peopling the earth the Lord announce an assembly for the purpose of assigning positions in life. "Who-ever gets there too late won't get any," he warns. The two Gypsies invited are very lazy and do not arrive at the meeting until after all the destinies have been assigned to others, so the Lord says to them, "You can get on any way you can." Thus Gypsies must live by their wits, having no assigned place in the world (A1611.2, "Origin of Gypsies"). Additional tales told by Gypsies themselves explain why their people are scattered about the earth (Tong 1989, 34–35), how they became musicians (102–103), and why they do not have an alphabet (169).

Of course, not all origin legends are first-person accounts. They are often told by competing clans, and in such cases they are rarely benevolent. A legend about the origin of the Turks, current in Egypt as late as 1970 (El-Shamy 1980, no. 24; Motif A1611.6) and told as "fact, not story," tells how Alexander the Great walls in the evil people of Gog and Magog, except for a few who escape because they are away herding their animals. The offspring of these herders are the Turks, whose name, according to folk etymology, means "those who were left out."

Similarly, cultures with slave or untouchable castes often have legends describing their origins. In one such account from Sri Lanka, "How the Rodiya Caste Was Born" (Ratnatunga 1991, no. 22), a king discovers that a tribe of hunters is providing human flesh to his royal kitchen and that his daughter knows their gruesome secret but has said nothing, having herself acquired a taste for such meat. The king decrees that she and the hunters should be an untouchable caste, from generation to generation. And, as the story concludes, "to this day they are the wandering tribe of the island. They beg by dancing and singing or performing tricks. They are hardly ever employed."

The existence of a slave caste in ancient Hawaii is explained by the consequences of the strained marital relationship between two of Polynesia's most important deities. According to tradition, Wakea and his wife Papa have a daughter, Ho'ohoku who matures into a beautiful woman. Wakea was attracted to his daughter sexually, but sees no way to consummate his desires without arousing Papa's jealousy. A priest instructs Wakea to tell Papa that certain tabu nights have been decreed when husband and wife are not to sleep together. Papa accepts the tabu, thus giving her husband freedom to sleep with Ho'ohoku. In spite of Wakea's precautions, however, Papa discovers the deception, and the two separate. Wakea then flaunts his relationship with his daughter, and the spurned Papa seeks revenge by entering into a liaison with one of her former husband's slaves. This union produces a son named Kekeu, and from him comes a caste of slaves so strictly defined that if a member of any class should have a child by an offspring of Kekeu, this child too would become a slave (Beckwith 1970, 296–301).

Myths and legends that justify and codify inherited class inequality are supplemented by a large body of folktales suggesting that poverty is not necessarily a bad thing. A prominent example of such rationalization is the widespread tale "A Happy Man's Shirt" (AT 844), in which a king or other wealthy individual takes ill and is told that he will be cured only if he puts on the shirt of a truly happy man. After a long search, the king finds such a man, only to learn that this truly happy man has no possessions, not even a shirt. Similarly, in the Greek folktale "The Poor Man and the Money" (Megas 1965, no. 64; AT 754; Motif J1085.1, "The happy friar becomes unhappier as he receives ever more and more money. Gets rid of money and is happy as before"), a poor but happy man is given a sum of money by a rich neighbor, but the riches bring their new owner only worry and conflict. Recognizing the source of his woes, he returns the gift and thus regains his former happiness.

The Indian tale "Less Inequality Than Men Deem" (Frere 1881, no. 8) summarizes, both in its title and in its plot, the apologetic philosophy of the folklore in this section. Here a rajah complains that he is often ill, whereas a poor shepherd of his acquaintance always appears to be healthy, in spite of his constant exposure to wet and cold. As an experiment, the rajah transplants the shepherd into his palace, where he is protected from every discomfort. After some months of such coddling, the shepherd gets his feet a little wet, catches cold, and dies. The rajah's vizier concludes, "You see now to what dangers we are exposed from which the poor are exempt. It is thus that nature equalizes her best gifts; wealth and opulence tend too frequently to destroy health and shorten life, though they may give much enjoyment to it whilst it lasts."

D.L. Ashliman

See also: Justice and Injustice.

REFERENCES

Arnason, Jón. 1864. *Icelandic Legends.* Trans. George E.J. Powell and Eiríkur Magnússon. London: Richard Bentley.

Beckwith, Martha. 1970 [1940]. *Hawaiian Mythology.* Honolulu: University of Hawaii Press.

Beowulf: A Dual-Language Edition. 1977. Trans. Howell D. Chickering Jr. New York: Doubleday.

Brookes, Stella Brewer. 1950. *Joel Chandler Harris—Folklorist.* Athens: University of Georgia Press.

Cole, Mabel Cook. 1916. *Philippine Folk Tales.* Chicago: A.C. McClurg.

Dance, Daryl C. 1977. "In the Beginning: A New Look at Black American Etiological Tales." *Southern Folklore Quarterly* 41: 53–64.

———. 1985. *Folklore from Contemporary Jamaicans.* Knoxville: University of Tennessee Press.

Dorson, Richard M. 1967. *American Negro Folktales.* Greenwich, CT: Fawcett.

El-Shamy, Hasan M. 1980. *Folktales of Egypt.* Chicago: University of Chicago Press.

Frere, Mary. 1881. *Old Deccan Days; or, Hindoo Fairy Legends Current in Southern India.* 3d ed. London: John Murray.

Hanauer, J.E. 1935 [1907]. *Folk-Lore of the Holy Land: Moslem, Christian, and Jewish.* London: Sheldon Press.

Harris, Joel Chandler. 1880. *Uncle Remus: His Songs and His Sayings.* New York: D. Appleton.

Karlinger, Felix, and Johannes Pögl. 1995. *Märchen aus der Karibik.* Munich: Eugen Diederichs Verlag.

Lindahl, Carl, Maida Owens, and C. Renée Harvison. 1997. *Swapping Stories: Folktales from Louisiana.* Jackson: University of Mississippi Press.

Megas, Georgios A. 1965. *Griechische Volksmärchen.* Düsseldorf: Eugen Diederichs Verlag.

Poetic Edda, The. 1962. Trans. Lee M. Hollander. Austin: University of Texas Press.

Ratnatunga, Manel. 1991. *Folk Tales of Sri Lanka.* New Delhi: Sterling Publishers.

Reaver, J. Russell, ed. 1987. *Florida Folktales.* Gainesville: University Presses of Florida.

Sadeh, Pinhas. 1989. *Jewish Folktales.* Trans. Hillel Halkin. New York: Anchor Books.

Tong, Diane. 1989. *Gypsy Folktales.* New York: Harcourt Brace Jovanovich.

Hermaphroditism

❀

Hermaphroditism and androgyny are terms that designate the female's birth-giving capacity within a male or—less frequently—the male's inseminating capability within a female (also known as gynandry). In the context of combining the procreative functions of both sexes, this aspect of being bisexual is to be differentiated from sexual practices that may be labeled homosexuality and/or heterosexuality. It has been pointed out that a more expanded definition of the concept of "androgyny" suggests a spirit of reconciliation and cooperation between the male (the rational) and the female (the intuitive) aspects of the human psyche, between socially imposed traits and modes of behavior for the male and female sexes, or between the masculine (analytical) and the feminine (synthetic) approaches to reality (Freeman 1988, 49).

Jung describes the concept of an androgynous being as a projection of unconscious wholeness that archetypally refers back to a primordial state of mind (collective unconscious) in which procreation and sex differences are either totally fused or largely undifferentiated. This archetype, or stream of feelings, has become a unifying symbol, or a symbol of the creative union of opposites (Jung 1958, 139). Eliade and O'Flaherty point out that androgynes may be divided into two groups: separate male and female beings fused into one, and one fused being splitting into male and female parts, the splitting androgyne being far more common (1988, 281).

In folklore studies, hermaphroditism per se was not identified nor assigned a specific motif in the *Motif-Index* nor does it constitute a tale type. Yet incidents of its recurrence in folk literature have been encountered and designated as detail motifs elaborating on other acts or characters. These elaborations include A12, "Hermaphroditic creator: The creator is half man and half woman or is thought of as both male and female" (cited from Greek, Egyptian, Hindu, and Aztec sources); F547.2, "Hermaphrodite: Person with both male and female sexual organs" (cited from Greek and North American Navaho sources); T578, "Pregnant man" (cited from Irish, Icelandic, Eskimo [Greenland], North American Indian, and African [Basuto] sources); and T578.2, "Man transformed to female (human or animal) bears offspring," reported from "Irish myth" (see discussion of Type 705B§, below).

HERMAPHRODITISM IN ANCIENT CREATION MYTHS

In ancient mythologies, hermaphroditism plays a major role in accounting for the emergence of life in the act of creation by a creator. In ancient Egypt, bisexuality is associated with the earliest phases of creation: Nun (or Nu) is chaos—or the primordial waste of waters in which all creation is immanent—and is guarded by four bisexual frog- and serpent-headed deities (Ions 1968, 38). More explicitly, the god Atum seems to have been regarded as a bisexual deity who was sometimes called the "Great He-She." The Egyptians, conceiving of creation only in terms of sexual generation, were able through this concept to present Atum as an intensely powerful creative force owing nothing to the agency of another (Ions 1968, 26, 40). Similarly, the goddess Mut was perceived in a gynandrous context: despite being the consort of Amon, with whom she forms one of four divine couples as creators (A2.8.1), she is also said to be bisexual. This belief is seen by some scholars as a way of reinforcing Mut's position as mother of all living things (Ions 1968, 103).

Another form for the expression of this concept is the highly salient motif of male pregnancy due to eating or drinking; it is found in the ancient Egyptian account of the conflict between Horus and Seth for the rule. Seth—who had made homosexual advances toward Horus—is tricked by Horus's mother, Isis, into eating lettuce which has Horus's semen on it; he becomes pregnant and gives birth to moon (El-Shamy 1984).

Related to these concepts and beliefs are depictions of androgynous pairs seeking to be fused with each other. The Egyptian Nut (Sky) and Geb (Earth) as brother and sister separated by Shu (atmosphere) seek to be reunited into their former entity as one (Ions 1968, 46). As Alma S. Freeman (1988) shows, this archetypal theme exists in other cultures. In Greek mythology, well-known versions of the creation also represent an androgynous, or hermaphroditic, deity in the union of Mother Earth and Father Sky—a union responsible for all the duality and multiplicity in the universe. Likewise, in Hindu mythology, both the Purnas (compiled ca. fourth to eleventh centuries CE) and the Upanishads (ca. tenth to seventh centuries BCE) contain accounts of the separation of the originally androgynous godhead.

Freeman also points out that Taoism, the system of beliefs through which the ancient Chinese sought to explain the world, embodies a clear expression of androgyny. The Tao (male)—the undivided unity lying behind all earthly phenomena—gives rise to the yin (female) and yang (male) principles that signify the duality of nature. According to ancient Chinese thought, the harmonious interaction of yin and yang in the universe and in human beings resolves all the conflicts of nature and brings prosperity to the world (Freeman 1988, 52–53).

In Genesis (1:27), God creates man in his own image, "male and female," before Eve is taken from Adam's body; thus Adam and the Judeo-Christian God are androgynous. Similarly, the supreme being in American Indian creation mythology represents an androgynous whole from which male and female are created. The Cheyenne creation myth "How the World Was Made," for example, describes Maheo, the All Spirit, who fashions man from a rib taken out of his right side and woman from a rib taken out of his left side. Not only do ancient stories of the creation reveal a separation of the originally androgynous one into two, but many also describe the halves as thereafter striving unceasingly to reunite, to restore the primal state of wholeness.

HERMAPHRODITISM IN FOLKLORE

In contemporary lore, expressions of hermaphroditic beliefs seem to occur predominantly in two spheres: in folk elaborations on established religious beliefs (especially Semitic: in Judaism, Christianity, and Islam), and in ordinary folktales.

In the first sphere, or what may be labeled "religion among the folk," is the incongruent fact that only one male Satan (Lucifer, Eblis) was cast out of Paradise, yet multitudes of Satan's descendants are believed to populate the universe. This incongruity is explained in terms of "Hermaphroditic Eblis (Satan) begets he-satans and she-satans" (Motif A2924§); a related elaboration states that "Sex-organs [were] added to Eblis: penis on the right thigh, and vagina in the left thigh" (Motif A2924.0.1.1§; Damrīrī 1963, 1:209). A variation on this theme is that Satan had sexual intercourse with himself and laid four eggs, out of which came his offspring (cf. Motif T512.6, "Conception from drinking sperm"; El-Shamy 1984).

A related belief narrative from Moslem traditions reports how a "Man transformed to female (human or animal) bears offspring" (Motif T578.2; Type 705B§). The story is given as a personal experience narrative (i.e., told by its protagonist, named "Khurfah"—i.e., "Myth"). His report may be summed up as follows:

> I set out [from my home town] in flight. I suffered from strong thirst. I got to a well and went down into it to drink. A supernatural voice shouted at me

from the inside of the well: "Halt!" But I drank anyway. Then, the voice from within the well said: "If he happened to be a man, may God turn him into a woman; and if he happened to be a woman, may God turn her into a man!" Lo and behold: I became a woman. I came to the town, a man married me, and I bore from him two boys. Then I longed for returning to my hometown. On my way back, I drank from the same well. The voice said, "If he happened to be a man, may God turn him into a woman; and if he happened to be a woman, may God turn her into a man!" I turned into a man as I was before. I reached the town in which I lived, I married some woman; she bore for me two boys.

The account is concluded: "Thus: [as a man,] I have two sons from my loins; and two sons [born earlier] from my 'womb'!" (cited in El-Shamy 1995, 169–171. Although associated with a curse, this is clearly a story about androgyny.

Pregnant Man

In ordinary folktales, one of the most overt expressions of this archetype is the theme of "Pregnant man" (T578) and his offspring. In AT 705, *Born from a Fish,* a story known only from Scandinavia, a man eats a fish that he is supposed to feed to his wife and he becomes pregnant. A sequel to the tale elaborates on the experiences of the offspring of that male pregnancy. The tale (Type 705B§) may be summarized as follows:

> A man disobeys his wife's instructions and eats magic food (usually a fruit) intended to make her pregnant; he becomes pregnant. When the time comes for him to give birth, his wife instructs him to go to the woods (or desert), and to bring the baby home if it is a boy, and to abandon it, if it is a girl. Via an unusual part of his body (e.g., knee, calf, etc.), he brings forth a baby girl and abandons her as his wife had ordered. The infant is raised by a wild bird (usually a falcon or eagle) on top of a tree. A prince sees her (reflection on water, or as she attends a circumcision event) and falls in love with her but cannot reach her. An old woman tricks the maiden into descending; she is captured and married to the prince. (See El-Shamy 1984 and 1999, no. 5).

Varying versions of the male pregnancy theme have been reported from the Scandinavian Peninsula and other parts of Europe, Asia Minor, the Iberian Peninsula (and its cultural extensions in South America), North Africa and the Middle East—particularly in the Nile Valley area (and Somalia)—and various regions of sub-Saharan Africa. The sub-Saharan narrative seems to be, or to have been until recently, a belief account (i.e., sacred narrative, myth, belief legend, etc.), often with etiological functions.

A man (usually a hunter) gives birth to a number of children through his knee. He places them on top of a tree and warns them not to lower a rope with which someone can climb up to their abode, except for him. An ogre (or a wolf or a similar predator or adversary) tricks one of the children into lowering the rope. The ogre climbs the tree and devours the children. When the father returns and learns what happened, he challenges the ogre to a duel and splits its belly (or toe). The children come out alive. They become the forefathers of the various tribes in that region. (See El-Shamy 1984)

There are other African variants from the Kikuyu, Akamba, and Masai. The story has also been reported from Southern Africa (Basuto), West Africa (Yoruba), and Central Africa.

LITERATURE AND POPULAR CULTURE

Manifestations of this archetype have permeated a wide spectrum of formal and popular literary forms throughout the world. One of its latest manifestations is, perhaps, a film titled *Junior* (1994). In this Hollywood production, a powerful popular-culture heroic figure—cast in roles akin to those of mythological legendary characters of the ancient world—conceives and delivers a human infant. In this respect, the modern actor (Arnold Schwarzenegger) seems to have been cast in the archetypal stream of emotions that fashioned such mythological characters as Atum, Seth, and Zeus, who precede him in the hermaphroditic, or androgynous, act of a pregnant male bringing forth a child.

With reference to elite literature, the androgyny theme is perceived in broad terms that tend to be dependent on interpretation. An example of such perception is Freeman's view that during the Renaissance, William Shakespeare emerged as the chief exponent of "the androgynous vision." That vision is delineated in terms of androgynous roles in which Shakespeare, like the Greek writers, is argued to have portrayed certain characters. One such character is "the lively little sprite Ariel, who defies final gender/sexual identification" in *The Tempest.* Freeman also asserts that Shakespeare skillfully exploited the Renaissance tradition of depicting girls disguised as boys and boys disguised as girls in plays such as *The Two Gentlemen of Verona* and *As You Like It.* Freeman concludes that "disguise for Shakespeare is not always falsification." Rather, it "may be another indication of the wide spectrum of roles possible to individuals if they can but find the convenient trappings of another persona." Shakespeare's dramas—like the Greek tragedies—also embody an interplay between the masculine and feminine opposites. They further demonstrate the necessity for a proper balance between these two opposing principles if chaos and destruction are to be averted (Freeman 1988, 53–54).

Other powerful female characters in Shakespeare's works can be shown to derive from folk tradition of that period; these include Katherine in *The Taming of the Shrew* (ca. 1593), (Type 901, same title), and Portia in *The Merchant of Venice* (ca. 1596), (Type 890, *A Pound of Flesh*). In many Arab variants of Type 890, the "pound of flesh" contract (J1161.2) is between a girl's (Shakespeare's Portia) father and her future husband; disguised as a male judge or ruler, the girl frees her husband from the ghoulish contract with her own father. In the words of several female narrators of tales belonging to the victorious female theme, "A woman needs to be a man" (Motif P149.0.1§, "Manly woman, or girl [. . .]: resolute, serious, business-like (no-nonsense gal)").

Throughout the ages and across the globe, the themes of "Disguise of man in woman's dress" (K1836) and "Disguise of woman in man's clothes" (K1837), along with their narrative correlates, have been recurrent. They appear in reports intended as fact as well as ones that are manifestly fiction. Thus, this ever-present theme may owe its impetus to its archetypal nature and the fact that it incorporates three of Jung's four fundamental archetypes,

> the persona, the anima, the animus, and the *shadow*. The persona (or outermost aspect of personality) conceals the true self; it is the mask that an individual wears publicly and is comparable to the concept of role-playing. The anima is the feminine characteristics in the male. The animus is the masculine characteristics in the female. The shadow (or darker self) is the inferior, animal-like part of the personality; it is something primitive in our human nature." (El-Shamy 1997, 38)

There are numerous tale types revolving around the character of the victorious female-as-male (K1837, "Disguise of woman in man's clothes"). Companion motifs—such as "Test of sex: to discover person masking as of other sex" (H1578)—provide narrative pattern elaboration.

The tale types in the cycle include the following: *Search in Men's Clothing* (Type 425K)—a subtype of *The Search for the Lost Husband* (Type 425); *The Forsaken Fiancée: Service [in Man's Clothing] as Menial* (Type 884); *The Girl Disguised as Man is Wooed by the Queen* (Type 884A); *The Girl as Soldier* (Type 884B); *Girl Dressed as a Man Deceives the King* (Type 884B*); and the new tale types: *Girl Raised as Boy Falls in Love with the Boy to Whom She Should Have Been Betrothed (Play-mate)* (Type 884G§); and *Girl Wins Against Boy (Usually, Her Eldest Paternal-cousin) in a Contest of Worth—Typically, She Masks as Man* (Type 923C§; see El-Shamy 1999, no. 9).

In conclusion, it may be pointed out that Jung saw utilitarian functions for the hermaphroditism archetype. With reference to the role of hermaphroditism (and androgyny, its companion) in culture and society, Jung asserted, "Notwithstanding its monstrosity, the hermaphrodite has gradually turned into a subduer of conflicts and a bringer of healing, and it acquired this meaning in relatively early phases of civilization" (Jung 1958, 139–140). The data designated as new Type 953B§, cited above—according to which a hermaphrodite's experiences help in "freeing" a human captive—seem to lend support to Jung's assertion.

Hasan El-Shamy

REFERENCES

Aarne, Antti, and Stith Thompson. 1964. *The Types of the Folktale: A Classification and Bibliography.* Helsinki: Suomalainen Tiedeakatemia.

Damrīrī, Muhammad ibn Mūsa. 1963. Hayāt al-bayawān al-lenbrá [The Greater Life of Animals]. Cairo: 1963 (2 vols.)

Eliade, Mircea, and Wendy Doniger O'Flaherty. 1988. "Androgynes." 761–281. In *Encyclopedia of Religion,* ed. Mircea Eliade, 6: 761–281. New York: Macmillan.

El-Shamy, Hasan. 1981. "Emotionskomponente." In *Enzyklopädie des Märchens* (4–5): 1391–1395. Berlin; New York: W. deGruyter.

———. 1984. "Vom Fisch geboren (AaTh 705)." In *Enzyklopädie des Märchens* (4–5): 1211–1218. Berlin; New York: W. deGruyter.

———. 1995. *Folk Traditions of the Arab World: A Guide to Motif Classification.* 2 vols. Bloomington: Indiana University Press.

———. 1997. "Archetype." In Thomas A. Green, ed., *Folklore: An Encyclopedia of Forms, Methods, and History.* Santa Barbara, CA: ABC-CLIO

———, ed. and trans. 1999. *Tales Arab Women Tell: And the Behavioral Patterns They Portray.* Bloomington: Indiana University Press.

Freeman, Alma S. 1988. "Androgyny." In *Dictionary of Literary Themes and Motifs,* ed. Jean-Charles Seigneuret. Westport, CT: Greenwood.

Ions, Veronica. 1968. *Egyptian Mythology.* Middlesex: Hamlyn.

Jung, C.G. 1958. "The Special Phenomenology of the Child Archetype." In *Psyche and Symbol: A Selection from the Writings of C.G. Jung,* ed. Violet S. de Laszlo, 132–147. Garden City, NY: Doubleday Anchor.

❀ B ❀

Mythical Animals

Mythical Animals

Motifs B0—B99

❀

Stith Thompson's nearly exhaustive taxonomy of mythical animals in his *Motif-Index* lists nine sometimes overlapping categories. The largest of these, "Mythical beasts and hybrids" (Motif B10–B19.11), embraces the dragon, the basilisk, the unicorn, the chimera, animals with unusual limbs like the hydra, devastating animals such as the Erymanthian boar, hostile animals, the behemoth, and other mythical beasts. The class of "Beast-men" includes centaurs, satyrs, man-dogs, the lamia, and other combinations. Among "Mythical birds" (B30–B39.1), the roc and the phoenix are the most familiar. Counted among "Bird-beasts" (B40–B49.3) are the winged horse, the flying horse, the griffin, and the air-going elephant. Leviathan (B61) is the most famous of the "Mythical fish" (B60–B68). (Not detailed below is a small class of "Fish-beasts" (B70–B73).) "Other mythical animals" (B90–B99.2, also not discussed here) include the plumed serpent, the horned snake, the sea-serpent, and other reptiles and exotic forms. Celebrated examples in the "Bird-men" category (B50–B57) are in fact part women: the sphinx, the harpy, and the siren, as the most popular form of "Fish-men" (B80–B83) is the mermaid.

The dragon (B11–B11.12.7) is a nearly universal motif, a reptilian or snake-like hybrid or compound animal, covered with the scales of a fish and sometimes endowed with claws and wings and the head of an eagle, falcon, or hawk. Of tremendous size, the dragon often devastates the land or guards a treasure such as the Golden Fleece, which was stolen by Jason and the Argonauts. Famous dragon-slayers in the West include Perseus, Saint George, and the Arthurian knights. Unlike its Western cousin, the Eastern dragon, particularly in China and Japan, benefits, rather than terrorizes, people (Lum n.d., 111).

Another hybrid, the basilisk (B12–B12.3) is a mythical lizard or serpent whose hissing drives other serpents away. In ancient and medieval times, the basilisk was considered to have a lethal glance and fiery breath that consumed animals and foliage alike. Because the animal was decimating his troops, Alexander the Great is believed to have disposed of the basilisk by inducing it to look into a mirror (Rowland 1973, 28). The Parson in *The Canterbury Tales* relies upon a long medieval tradition when he compares a lustful glance to the deadly attention of the basilisk (Rowland 1973, 30).

The fabulous unicorn (B13) is an animal in the form of a horse or a goat whose one horn has magical and curative powers. Although by legend only virgins may capture unicorns, the hero in the Grimms' tale "The Brave Little Tailor" rises to the king's challenge of capturing a mischievous unicorn that is damaging the forest; only then can the tailor marry the king's daughter (Grimm and Grimm 1992, 85). In the West, the unicorn can symbolize courage, nobility, and purity as well as pride, wrath, and destructive forces (Leeming 1997, 474). The resemblance between the unicorn of Europe and the proud but gentle Ki-lin of China—like a large deer with the tail of an ox, horse's hooves, and a single short horn—suggests a possible common origin in some real or legendary creature (Lum n.d., 60–61).

Another hybrid, the chimera (B14.1), is described by Homer as "a foaming monster . . . / of ghastly and inhuman origin, / her forepart lionish, her tail a snake's, / a she-goat in between. . . . [which] exhaled / in jets a rolling fire" (*Iliad* 6, 154–158). Although Aeneas encounters fire-breathing chimeras, along with hissing hydras, and other monsters in the infernal regions (Bulfinch 1979, 267), the chimera plays a key role in only one myth—that of Bellerophon, who kills the creature in a dangerous challenge established to avenge the alleged seduction of King Iobates's daughter Anteia (Leeming 1997, 112). Because of the grotesqueness of its composition, the chimera has become over time synonymous with anything so improbable that it must be imaginary (McLeish 1996, 117).

The hydra (B15.1.2.8.1), a nine-headed water-serpent or serpentlike monster living in the swamps of Lerna, may be counted among those animals with unusual limbs or members (Grant and Hazel 1993, 163). One of the twelve labors of Heracles is to destroy the beast, but he has great trouble killing it because whenever he cuts off one of its heads, two grow in its place. Also in the class of animals with unusual limbs or members is Cerberus (B15.7.1), the monstrous hound with three heads, a serpent's tail, and a tangle of snakes writhing from his body. Cerberus is the watchdog that lives on the infernal side of the river Styx. He guards the entrance to the lower world and prevents the shades from leaving Hades. While he greets in a friendly manner the souls of the dead that are ferried across by the aged boatman Charon, Cerberus disapproves of living mortals attempting to enter the underworld. To get past him, Orpheus has to charm him with sweet music, and the Sibyl of Cumae, guiding Aeneas, throws him some cake soaked in drugged wine (hence, the expression "a sop to Cerberus") (Grant and Hazel 1993, 81).

Devastating animals (B16–B16.6.5) include many drawn from domestic species: monster cats, hounds, man-eating mares, swine, monster bulls, and destructive sheep. Among the wild animals are foxes, tigers, lions, wolves, bears, elephants, boars, deer, mice, bison, birds, reptiles, insects, and fish. The great Leviathan and the Erymanthian boar, which is slain by Heracles in his fourth of twelve labors (Fox 1964, 82), are examples of the latter class.

Hostile animals (B17–B17.2.4.1) include the griffin and the behemoth. The largest of all creatures except perhaps the Leviathan, the behemoth is described in the Talmud as "an oxlike animal some seven miles in length who daily grazes over a thousand miles of grass in paradise and will eventually be slain by the Jewish Messiah" (Lum n.d., 199).

Thompson's second major category of mythical animals is "Beast-men" (B20–B29.9), combining bestial and human form. The two major types of human-animal creatures are those with a human head and an animal body and those with an animal head and a human body. The centaurs (B21), for example, are a race of creatures with the trunk and head of a man and the body of a horse; they live on Mount Pelion in Thessaly. Most centaurs are lustful, savage, and licentious, and several myths associated with them concern their war with a neighboring nation (Grant and Hazel 1993, 78). Chiron, however, was one centaur reputed to be wise and good. His most famous pupil is Asclepius, the Greek god of healing (Leeming 1997, 103).

Unlike the centaur, the Minotaur (B23.1)—offspring of King Minos's wife Pasiphae and an unusually beautiful bull (Hamilton 1998, 212)—has the body of a man and the head of a bull. The siring bull was given to Minos to be sacrificed to Poseidon, but Minos keeps it for himself. As a punishment, Poseidon makes Pasiphae fall passionately in love with the bull, and she conceives the Minotaur. Minos has the architect and inventor Daedalus build a great labyrinth to confine the fierce monster, but Theseus, one of the fourteen Athenian youths to be sacrificed to the Minotaur, wrestles it to the ground and kills it (Hamilton 1998, 215).

Part goat and part man, the satyrs (B24–B24.1), of whom Pan is the chief divinity, are generative demons of the flocks and herds. Pictorial representations of the satyrs reveal two general periods of development: in the first, the human element is prominent, and they are regularly seen as "possessing the heads and bodies of men and the members of animals, such as horns, tail, pointed ears, shaggy hair, and the legs of goats or of horses" or as "beautiful youths bearing here and there upon their persons mere hints of the semi-bestial nature" (Fox 1964, 268–269). In the second period, the animal elements predominate, and Pan, the god of the pastures, is usually seen with "goat's legs and a leering, sensual countenance, while the flute of reed, the goatherd's staff, and the goatskin are his common attributes" (Fox 1964, 269).

Lamias (B29.1) are "sharp-clawed sphinx-like creatures with a woman's upper body who attacked men and boys and sucked their blood" (Gilmore 2003, 41). In some versions of Isaiah 13.22, a lamia, along with other evil creatures, is said to haunt the city of Babylon, laid waste by Jehovah (Rowland 1973, 115). Keats immortalizes the lamia in his poem, "Lambia," about a Corinthian youth who is seduced by a serpent woman described as "a gordian shape of dazzling hue,/Vermillion-spotted, golden, green and blue" (lines 47–48).

MYTHICAL BIRDS AND FISH

Among the most fabulous of "Mythical birds" (B31.1–B31.1.2) is the roc, a giant bird that can carry off people and elephants in its claws. Probably originating in Arabia and China, it is best known in the West from its appearance in the *Arabian Nights* and *The Travels of Marco Polo* (McMillan 1987, 75). The roc of myth may be based on a real bird such as the eagle, which in several European folktales exhibits similar prowess. In the Grimms' "Foundling," for example, a young boy is carried off by a giant bird, and in "Snow White and Rose Red," a little man is held in the talons of an eagle (1992, 189, 520–521). In "The Attack on the Giant Elk," an American Indian tale of the Southwest, the hero is carried by an eagle to the giant bird's nest (Thompson 1977, 339). In Hawaiian mythology, too, a great seabird carries the first man of creation, Kumu-honua, and his wife, Lalo-honua, off into the jungle (Beckwith 1970, 44–45).

Larger than an eagle and more graceful, the phoenix (B32–B32.1.1) is a bird that is consumed in fire, with a new phoenix arising from its ashes. It appears in the iconography and texts of ancient Egyptian, Greek, Indian, Arab, Russian, and Judaic traditions (Leeming 1997, 363). Although the myth of the phoenix came to be understood in Christian literature as an allegory of Christ's resurrection, the phoenix has been used in more secular contexts as an emblem of creative living (McMillan 1987, 75).

"Bird-beasts" (B40–B49.3) include the winged horse, the flying horse, and the griffin. According to Hesiod and Pindar, the winged horse Pegasus springs from the gorgon Medusa's blood when Perseus severs the monster's neck (Hamilton 1998, 184–185). The young Corinthian Bellerophon tries one day to ride Pegasus to Olympus, but Zeus sends a fly to sting the horse, and

Bellerophon falls crashing back to earth. Later Zeus harnesses Pegasus in his chariot team, to pull him across the sky as he hurls thunderbolts (McLeish 1996, 472). In Norse mythology, the flying, eight-legged steed Sleipnir carries Odin through the sea and air. When Odin's son Balder is killed, Hermod rides Sleipnir to Hel to offer a ransom (MacCulloch 1964, 43). Half lion and half eagle, the fierce and cunning griffin is the legendary guardian of vast gold mines in India and Sythia (Lum n.d., 47). Often associated with rulers of earth and sky, the griffin appears in heraldry, in manuscripts, and on cathedral walls (Bartscht 1987, 85–87).

The sphinx, the harpy, and the siren are the most familiar of the "Bird-men" (B50–B57). The sphinx (B51) has the face of a woman, the body and tail of a lion, and the wings of a bird. A frightful monster who lies in wait for travelers along the roads to Thebes, she propounds to those whom she seizes a riddle to be answered on pain of death: "What animal walks on four feet in the morning, two feet at noon, and three feet in the evening?" (Hamilton 1998, 376). Only the courageous and intelligent Oedipus is able to respond that she describes the three stages of human life. The harpies (B52) are loathsome birds with the arms and breasts of women. A vivid account of their repulsive behavior occurs in the tale of Jason and the Argonauts, who drive them away from tormenting the blind old seer Phineus (Fox 1964, 111). Aeneas, too, gives a horrifying description of his men's encounter with the harpies: "They tear the banquet to pieces, filthying all with their bestial touch. Hideous the sounds, nauseous the stench about us" (*Aeneid* 3, 227–228). The siren (B53–B53.4) is a bird with a woman's head (sometimes in mermaid form [B53.0.1]). By their sweet song the sirens in Greek mythology entice seamen to forgetfulness and death by hunger. Odysseus escapes their terror by filling his companions' ears with wax and lashing himself to the mast of his ship (*Odyssey* 2).

"Mythical fish" (B60–B68), as might be expected, abound in Hawaiian, Tahitian, and Tongan mythology. Ancestral sharks, for example, were celebrated among the fishing people as family guardians who were fed daily and were believed to drive fish into the nets, to save fishermen from death if their canoe capsized, and to ward off danger in other ways (Beckwith 1970, 128–132). The fish Uhu-makai-kai was considered to be the parent of all the fishes (Beckwith 1970, 24). In the Biblical tradition, the giant fish Leviathan, great adversary of God, may or may not have been a whale, and different descriptions of the huge sea animal may be found in Psalms 74:14 and 104:26, Job 41, and Isaiah 27:1 (South 1987, 360–361).

The "Mermaid" (B81–B81.13.12), a woman with the tail of a fish who lives in the sea, is the most common of the "Fish-men" category (B80–B83). Like the sirens, mermaids are fair to look upon (Thompson 1977, 244). Although specific tales about mermaids are not numerous, they have nevertheless furnished subjects for art, perhaps the most famous of which is the bronze statue in the harbor of Copenhagen. The statue commemorates the best-known of mermaid stories, Hans Christian Andersen's "The Little Mermaid," in which the creature is willing to trade her voice for legs in order to marry a prince (Andersen 1983, 57–76). The merman (B82–82.7), male of the species, never mates with a mermaid, but rather, like the creature in Matthew Arnold's "The Forsaken Merman," lures a human spouse into his cold sea-cave home only to be abandoned by her at the sound of church bells on shore (Thompson 1977, 244).

Peter L. De Rose

See also: Dragon; Leviathan; Mythical Birds.

REFERENCES

Andersen, Hans Christian. 1983 [1872]. *The Complete Fairy Tales and Stories.* Trans. Erik Christian Haugaard. New York: Random House.

Bartscht, Waltraud. 1987. "The Griffon." In *Mythical and Fabulous Creatures: A Source Book and Research Guide,* ed. Malcolm South, 85–101. New York: Greenwood Press.

Beckwith, Martha. 1970. *Hawaiian Mythology.* Honolulu: University of Hawaii Press.

Bulfinch, Thomas. 1979. *Bulfinch's Mythology.* New York: Gramercy Books.

Fox, William Sherwood. 1964. *Greek and Roman.* Vol. 1 of *The Mythology of All Races.* 13 vols. New York: Cooper Square.

Gilmore, David D. 2003. *Monsters: Evil Beings, Mythical Beasts, and All Manner of Imaginary Terrors.* Philadelphia: University of Pennsylvania Press.

Grant, Michael, and John Hazel. 1993 [1973]. *Who's Who in Classical Mythology.* New York: Oxford University Press.

Grimm, Jacob, and Wilhelm Grimm. [1812] 1992. *Kinder- und Hausmärchen.* Trans. and Introduction by Jack Zipes under title *The Complete Fairy Tales of the Brothers Grimm.* New York: Bantam.

Hamilton, Edith. 1998 [1942]. *Mythology.* Boston: Little, Brown.

Keats, John. 1999. *The Poems.* Introduction by David Bromwich. New York: Knopf/Everyman's Library.

Leeming, David Adams, ed. 1997. *Storytelling Encyclopedia: Historical, Cultural and Multiethnic Approaches to Oral Traditions Around the World.* Phoenix, AZ: Oryx Press.

Lum, Peter. n.d. *Fabulous Beasts.* London: Thames and Hudson.

MacCulloch, John Arnott. 1964. *Eddic.* Vol. 2 of *The Mythology of All Races.* 13 vols. New York: Cooper Square.

McLeish, Kenneth. 1996. *Myth: Myths and Legends of the World Explored.* London: Bloomsbury.

McMillan, Douglas J. 1987. "The Roc." In *Mythical and Fabulous Creatures: A Source Book and Research Guide,* ed. Malcolm South, 75–83. Westport, CT: Greenwood Press.

Rowland, Beryl. 1973. *Animals with Human Faces.* Knoxville: University of Tennessee Press.

South, Malcolm. 1987. "A Miscellany." In *Mythical and Fabulous Creatures: A Source Book and Research Guide,* ed. Malcolm South, 351–370. New York: Greenwood Press.

Thompson, Stith. 1977. *The Folktale.* New York: AMS Press. Orig. edition, New York: Holt, Rinehart, and Winston, 1946.

Mythical Animals: Dragon

Motif B11

❁

Dragons are imaginary and composite creatures (B11.2.1, "Dragon as compound animal"). Although they vary in detail, they are reptilian monsters, often represented with wings, huge claws, and fiery breath (Eberhart 1983, 9) (B11.2.11, "Fire-breathing dragon"). *Funk and Wagnalls Dictionary of Mythology and Folklore* describes the dragon, usually a male figure, as a composite of a snake and crocodile, its body covered with scales (Leach and Fried 1972, 325). While female dragons appear to be a rarity, the *Motif-Index* refers to a "she-dragon" motif in Irish myth and legend (B11.2.0.1.).

The dragon's forehands and head might be those of a lion, eagle, or hawk. Smith describes the dragon as a modified serpent, lizard, fish, shellfish, toad, elephant, horse, ram, deer, or another animal (1919, 77–78). Therefore, unless there are contemporaneous illustrations, it is difficult to know if some of the earliest literature is truly describing creatures we think of as dragons, or some other kind of monster.

Further complicating the definition of dragons is the fact that in some cultures they are benevolent—for example, in China, they have traditionally been regarded as symbols of good fortune—while in others they are malevolent. In the European tradition, where they are commonly viewed as inhabitants of remote or underground realms, they are an "amalgamation of indigenous Germanic and Celtic motifs with Christian biblical theological symbolism laid on a foundation of Middle Eastern, Anatolian, and Illyrian cosmogonic and mythographic concepts" (Evans 2000, 235)

Evans, in his discussion of the dragon in medieval folklore and literature, explains that the dragon's ubiquity in European legend was a result of biblical associations of it with the arch-figure of diabolical evil (B11.9, "Dragon as power of evil. So considered everywhere except in the East, where are also found beneficent dragons"). But this association of the dragon with evil came about through mistranslations of various Hebrew words as "dragon." "By the end of the Middle Ages well over 100 saints had been credited with critical encounters with diabolical foes manifest in the form of a dragon or monstrous serpent" (Evans 2000, 235).

MYTHOLOGY

The dragon figures prominently in the mythology of various Asian countries. Early dragon stories center around creation and an attempt to preserve creation from chaos. Leeming characterizes the dragon as the most important of Chinese mythological beasts, "a positive expression of *yang,* the male principle, balanced by the female *yin,* represented by the phoenix" (2001, 52). In Chinese mythology, Gun created new land after the god Tiandi covered the earth with floods in retaliation for human wickedness. Gun's action angered Tiandi, who struck him with a sword. Out of the wound sprung Gun's son, Yu, who stemmed the flood and became a yellow dragon who lived in the waters thereafter (Leeming 2001, 39, 206)

The earliest dragon story in Sumerian myth, from about 5000 BCE, tells of a dragon named Zu, the Sumerian storm god, also known as Anzu. This myth tells how Zu steals the Tablets of Law, which set out the laws of the Universe, from the god Enlil. Enlil sends the sun god Ninurta to retrieve the tablets and kill Zu. Ninurta and Marduk are sometimes interchanged in this myth (Röhrich 1981, 788; Lieck 1991, 53–54).

Another ancient dragon story is contained in the Babylonian creation myth, the *Enuma Elish.* In this story, Tiamet, the watery chaos, becomes a huge monster, perhaps a dragon, that is defeated by the god Marduk. In Egyptian mythology, a sea dragon named Apophis tries to overcome Ra, the Egyptian sun god. He is slain by Seth (Röhrich 1981, 788).

In Greek mythology, there is a race of gigantic toothed serpents, called *drakones,* some with multiple heads, wings, and/or poisonous venom that could kill at the touch. The females (*drakainai*) have the upper bodies of beautiful young women, but the long coiling tails of *drakones* in place of legs.

The *Motif-Index* lists "fight with dragon" as a motif (B.11.11). It is also a major tale type (AT 300). Here, the conflict between the hero and the dragon symbolizes the conflict between life and death, good and evil, and right and wrong (El-Shamy 1997, 38). There are many famous dragon slayers in myth and literature, including Perseus, Marduk, Apollo, Siegfried, Saint Michael, Saint George, Beowulf, Arthur, and Tristan (Leach and Fried 1972, 324).

Jason, with the help of the sorceress-princess Medea, sets out on a quest for the Golden Fleece, which is held by King Ares of Colchis and guarded by the Kholkian Drakon. Apollonius (1997) writes in the *Argonautika* (third century BCE):

> [T]hen did the monster undulate its enormous coils with their protective armor of hard dry scales. . . . Jason followed behind [Medea] in terror; but already the dragon, charmed by her spells, was relaxing the long spine of its sinuous earthborn frame, spreading out its countless coils, as some dark wave, stealthy and noiseless, rolls over a sluggish expanse of ocean. (4:141–153)

This story is Type AT 313, *Girl as Helper.*

Herakles's eleventh labor is to fetch the apples of the Hesperides, which are guarded by a hundred-headed dragon or serpent named Ladon (*drakon ladon*) on Mount Atlas. Herakles slays the dragon, as Apollonius writes in the *Argonautika,* but "now the snake, struck down by Herakles, lay by the trunk of the apple-tree. Only the tip of his tail was still twitching; from the head down, his dark spine showed not a sign of life" (4:1390f). Herakles also vanquishes the Hydra Lernaia, a gigantic water *drakon* with nine heads, and Skylla, a *drakaina.*

Perseus saves Andromeda from another type of serpent-monster, a *ketos,* which, in a depiction from a contemporary vase, looks like a dragon. Andromeda was being sacrificed to this monster, which had been sent by Poseidon to punish Andromeda's mother for boasting that she was more beautiful than the Nereides. Perseus falls in love with Andromeda and marries her (R111.1.4, "Rescue of princess (maiden) from dragon"; T68.1, "Princess offered as prize to rescuer"; AT 300, 301, 302, 303, 304, 506, 653).

FOLKTALES

The widespread European folktale theme of a princess being saved from a dragon by a young hero may not stem directly from the story of Perseus and Andromeda, but it certainly is analogous (Thompson 1977, 279).

The Dragon Slayer (AT 300) is a central folktale type in Europe. *The Two Brothers* (AT 303) is a related type that contains the dragon-slaying story of AT 300. Thompson says that in *Die zwei Brüder* (1934), Kurt Ranke cites about 1,100 examples of both tales, taken together. They are among the oldest stories in the European tradition and probably arose in France (1977, 24–31).

The folklore of the pagan tribes of northern Europe contained dragons, and various references are made to the dragon's serpentine nature (Lindahl, McNamara, and Lindau 2000, 236–237). In the *Nibelungenlied,* Siegfried kills a dragon, and the last creature faced by Beowulf is referred to as a dragon and described in a fair amount of detail (Heaney 1999). Other north European dragon stories are found in Germany's *Thidrek's Saga,* Old Norse narrative *Poetic Edda,* and Norwegian *Heimskringla* (Lindahl, McNamara, and Lindau 2000, 236–237).

The best-known dragon slayer of Christianity is Saint George, the patron saint of England, and an important saint in the Eastern Orthodox Church. While George was apparently a real person in the third century who was an early convert to Christianity, the dragon slayer element again harkens back to the Greek myth of Perseus and Andromeda. An early version of the story appears in *The Golden Legend; or, Lives of the Saints,* compiled by Jacobus de Voragine, Archbishop of Genoa, in 1275. The legend relates how a Libyan king's daughter was saved from a dragon by Saint George, and in gratitude the king's subjects were baptized. Tales and ballads about Saint George are found throughout European folklore, including in Poland, Germany, Russia, and England. There is an English ballad about Saint George in Richard Johnson's *Seven Champions of Christendome* (1597).

Dragon stories are also widespread in Eastern traditions and lore. "Dragon-King" stories (B11.12.5; D812.7, "Magic object received from the king") are noted by Eberhard (no. 65, "Wishing Stone") (Eberhard 1965). A dragon slayer, Hsu Sun, in Chinese mythology, is instrumental in killing two dragons in a boat (Werner 1922, 222–223). The dragon appears in Turkish folktale tradition under Type TTV 107, *Der Drache.* For example, in the collection of *Billur Kösk,* the tale "Zümrüd-ü Anka" (TTV Type 72) brings in the motif of dragon slayer: the young prince kills the dragon in order to rescue the princess held hostage in the well and marries the princess at the end of the tale (Alangu 1961, 109–111).

ELITE LITERATURE AND POPULAR CULTURE

Zohak, also known as Zahak or Zohhak, is the serpent king in the Persian epic *Shahnama,* the Book of Kings, written and compiled by the Persian poet Firdawsi in the late tenth to early eleventh centuries. King Zohak is kissed by Satan, who takes him into his web of evil. Two serpent heads grow out of the king's shoulders and this creature has to be fed human brains. Kawanah the blacksmith kills Zohak, after feeding him all Zohak's sons except for the last one (B11.8, "Sacrifice of human being to a dragon"; B11.2.7, "Snakes issue from dragon's shoulder").

In the writings of J.R.R. Tolkien, the dragons of Middle Earth are evil creatures, enormous in size and awesome in strength. There are three species: the first are the great serpents that crawl over the ground, second are the reptiles with limbs, and the third sort have wings like a bat that enable them to fly and to create storms on the land over which they fly. Because they are made

One of many depictions of Saint George, the most famous dragon slayer in European folklore. From Baptista Spagnuoli, *Lyfe of Saynt George* **(1515?).**

with magic, they keep themselves far from water and prefer the darkness above light, even starlight (Rahn 2000, 525–526). Bilbo Baggins of *The Hobbit* is a middle-aged hobbit of Middle Earth who finds himself on a journey with a group of young dwarfs to recover the ancestral treasure from the dragon of the Lonely Mountain. The expected outcome of folklore with the hero slaying the dragon is subverted, and instead a minor character kills the beast. He takes a small portion of the treasure (Rahn 2000, 525).

There are other legends about sea serpents that are variously described as looking like dragons (eyewitnesses describe them as having horselike heads atop serpentine necks), such as Chessie in Maryland and Virginia, the Loch Ness sea monster in Scotland, and Storsjöodjuret in the great lake at Ostersund in central Sweden (B11.3.1.1. "Dragon lives in lake") (Meurger and Gagnon 1988, 42–43).

A 2001 film, *Shrek,* puts a twist on the dragon-slayer type, with the ogre (Shrek) taking up the role of the prince who is supposed to slay the dragon and rescuing the young princess from the castle.

Hande A. Birkalan and Jane Garry

REFERENCES

Aarne, Antti, and Stith Thompson. 1964 [1961]. *The Types of the Folktale: A Classification and Bibliography* Helsinki: Suomalainen Tiedeakatemia.

Alangu, Tahir. 1961. *Billûr Kösk.* Istanbul: Remzi Kitabevi.

Apollonius, Rhodius. 1997. *The Argonantika.* Trans., intro., commentary, glosssary Peter Green. Berkeley: University of California Press.

Boratav, Pertev Naili, and Wolfram Eberhard. 1953. *Typen der Türkischen Voksmärchen.* Wiesbaden: Franz Steiner.

Cooper, J.C. 1992. *Symbolic and Mythological Animals.* London: Aquarian/Thorsons.

Dixon-Kennedy, Mike. 1997. *European Myth and Legend: An A-Z of People and Places.* London: Blanford.

Eberhart, George M. 1983. *Monsters: A Guide to Information on Unaccounted for Creatures, Including Bigfoot, Many Water Monsters, and Other Irregular Animals.* New York: Garland.

Eberhard, Wolfram. 1965. *Folktales of China.* Chicago: University of Chicago Press.

El-Shamy, Hasan M. 1997. "Archetype." In *Folklore: An Encyclopedia of Beliefs, Customs, Tales, Music, and Art,* ed. Thomas Green 1:36–39. Santa Barbara, CA: ABC-CLIO.

Evans, Jonathan D. 2000. "Dragon." In *Medieval Folklore: An Encyclopedia of Myths, Legends, Tales, Beliefs, and Customs,* ed. Carl Lindahl, John McNamara, and John Lindow (2 vols.) 1: 233–240. Santa Barbara, CA: ABC-CLIO.

Hansen, William. 2002. *Ariadne's Triad: A Guide to International Folktales Found in Classical Literature.* Ithaca, NY: Cornell University Press.

Heaney, Seamus, trans. 1999. *Beowulf.* London: Faber.

Leach, Maria, and Jerome Fried, eds., 1972. *Funk and Wagnalls Standard Dictionary of Mythology and Folklore.* New York: Funk and Wagnalls.

Leeming, David. 2001. *Dictionary of Asian Mythology.* New York: Oxford University Press.

Lieck, Gwendolyn. 1991. *A Dictionary of Ancient Near Eastern Mythology.* New York: Routledge.

Lindahl, Carl, John McNamara, and John Lindau, eds. 2000. *Medieval Folklore: An Encyclopedia of Myths, Legends, Tales, Beliefs, and Customs.* Santa Barbara, CA: ABC-CLIO.

Meurger, Michael, and Claude Gagnon. 1988. *Lake Monster Traditions: A Cross-Cultural Analysis.* London: Fortean Times.

Rahn, Suzanne. 2000. "Tolkien, J.R.R." In *The Oxford Companion to Fairy Tales,* ed. Jack Zipes, 525–526. Oxford: Oxford University Press.

Röhrich, Lutz. 1975. "Drache, Drachenkampf, Drachentöter." In *Enzyklopädie des Märchens,* 3:787–820. Berlin: DeGruyter.

Smith, G. Elliot. 1919. *Evolution of Dragon.* Manchester: University Press.

Thompson, Stith. 1977. *The Folktale.* Berkeley: University of California Press. Orig. ed. New York: Holt, Rinehart, and Winston, 1946.

Werner, Edward Theodore Chalmers. 1922. *Myths and Legends of China.* London: George and Harrap.

Zipes, Jack, ed. 2000. *The Oxford Companion to Fairy Tales.* Oxford: Oxford University Press.

Mythical Birds

Motif B30

❀

Many cultures deemed birds important in their mythology, legend, and folktale tradition, believing that they posses powers of prophecy and associating them with gods. The roc, phoenix, and griffin are examples of such birds (Bies 2002, 1022). They are seen to possess the ability to talk, offering guidance to humans, guarding treasures, and sending messages to gods (Jones 1995, 67; Ingersoll 1923, 20–28). Stories of these fabulous birds have parallels with stories of the *garuda* of India, the *simorgh* of Persia, the anka of Arabia and Turkey, the *feng-huang* of China, and the *bennu* of Egypt.

The *garuda,* probably the oldest of the great birds, is capable of blocking out the sun with its body and picking up elephants in its talons. It is depicted with a white face, an eagle's beak, and scarlet wings attached to a golden human's body. It was also called the bird of life, as it was thought to be the incarnation of fire (Ingersoll 1923, 206–207; Bies 2002, 1028).

The simorgh, the wise old bird of Persian folklore, is said to have lived on the Mountain Kaf for thousands of years. By some accounts it is immortal and is said to have a nest in the Tree of Knowledge (B31.5) (Lindahl, McNamara, and Lindau 2000, 449). The name means "thirty birds," and it is said that the simorgh is so old that it has seen the destruction of the world three times over (Ingersoll 1923, 205). It is known to take children into its nest to nurse them or foster them. A bird with the same name, which had orange metallic feathers, a silver head, a human face, four wings, a vulture's talons and a long peacock's tail, was an attendant to the Queen of Sheba (Bies 2002, 1027–1028). Carnoy notes that in Mazdean mythology the most celebrated bird is Saena, a bird similar to the Persian Simorg. Its open wings are like a wide cloud and fall of water crowning the mountains (Carnoy 1917, 289–290).

In Middle Eastern traditions, the *anka* is depicted as a bird of huge size, large enough to carry an elephant. It has a long life span, approximately 1,700 years. At the end of its life, it burns itself and rises again. The Arabs believed that it was a creation of God, originally a perfect bird, but that, over time, these birds devoured all the animals on earth and started carrying off children. People appealed to God, who prevented the *anka* from multiplying; thus it eventually became extinct.

THE ROC

There are four stories about the roc in the *The Thousand and One Nights,* two involving Abd al-Rahman and two involving Sinbad (Dawood 1973) (B31.1, "Roc. A giant bird which carries off men in its claws"). Sinbad sails on a commercial venture from his home in Basra, and the ship stops at a very pleasant island. Sinbad goes ashore, wanders in the lovely woods, falls asleep, and awakes to find that the ship is gone and that he is the only person on the island. He is carried to a better place by the *rukh* (B.552, "Man carried by bird") (Ingersoll 1923, 200–201). In the other Sinbad story and in one of the Abd al-Rahman stories, rocs destroy ships by dropping rocks on them (Marzolph 1997, 639).

In Turkish folklore, the marvelous bird *zümrüd-u anka*, of Indian or Persian origin, is found in different collections of tales. *Billur Kösk* is a collection of printed folktales widespread in the tradition in Turkey (Alangu 1961, 5–7). In the tale "Zümrüd ü Anka," the young prince walks toward the mountains and sleeps in a huge tree, which happens to be the nest of the *anka*. The nest is full of little *ankas,* whose mother is away. The little birds are approached by a snake that intends to kill them, but the young prince kills the snake. Upon her return, the *anka* finds out about the events and treats the hero well. She opens one of her wings to shade the prince. She also carries him to a faraway land. On the way, after they consume their food and drink stocks, the prince feeds the bird with pieces of his own flesh. But the bird does not eat them and she thinks of the prince as a hero. Since the *anka* is a holy bird, he is among the holy saints. With her great blessings, the bird cures the leg of the prince (B322.1, "Hero feeds his own flesh to the animal") (Alangu 1961, 114–115). Other tales with the *anka* motif have been collected by Pertev Naili Boratav and appear in *Typen der Türkischen Voksmärchen* (Eberhard and Boratav 1953).

Marco Polo describes seeing rocs in Madagascar, and envoys from Madagascar present the great Khan of Cathay with a roc feather. In fact, Madagascar was the home of a gigantic bird, the *Aepyornis maximus* or elephant bird, undoubtedly what Polo saw. This bird may not have become extinct until the sixteenth century. While huge like the roc, it could not fly (Ingersoll 1923, 201; Bies 2002, 1030).

The roc was thought of as a gigantic bird, here depicted carrying elephants. From "The Second Voyage of Sinbad the Sailor" in *Thousand and One Nights: or, The Arabian Nights' Entertainments,* translated by E.W. Lane; illustrated by William Harvey (1850).

The Arabic authors of the Middle Ages had much to say of the *anka,* also known as *al-rukh,* which supposedly lived in the Mountain Kaf, believed to be the mother of all the mountains. No one knows where the mountain is and what lies behind it. Ibn Battuta, an Arab traveler, encountered the stories of the roc (Nigg 1995, 53). Marzolph argues that a huge ostrich-like bird might have existed in historical times. The New Zealand moa bird, which became extinct in the fourteenth century, might have contributed to the genesis of the *rukh* (Marzolph 1995, 595).

THE GRIFFIN

Griffins (B42, "Griffin. Half lion, half eagle") are portrayed with a lion's body and an eagle's head, wings, and claws. The griffin is symbolically significant for its domination of both the earth and the sky because of its lion's body and eagle's head and wings (Franklyn 1967, 43–44).

In Greece, the griffin was a symbol of vigilant strength and an embodiment of Nemesis, the goddess of retribution (Bies 2002, 1027). In medieval times, the griffin was an agent of destruction, as in the German epic *Gudrun,* but later the bird had a more positive character. Griffins are frequently found in Eastern European tales symbolizing the unknown. They are found in the *The*

A griffin is created by rearranging the top flap in a "turn-up" book. From
Metamorphosis; or, a Transformation of Pictures, with Poetical Explanations, for
the Amusement of Young Persons **(1814).**

Two Brothers (AT 303); in the variants of *Amor and Psyche* (AT 425); and
also in motifs H1233.4.3, "Griffin as helper on quest"; A2232.4, "Griffin dis-
dains to go on ark; drowned: hence extinct"; N575, "Griffin as guardian of
treasure"; and B17.2.2, "Hostile griffin" (Bies 2002, 1026, 1029).

The Grimms' tale of the griffin tells of the son of a farmer who goes to the
griffin, because "it knows everything." He wants to get a feather from the
griffin's tail. But no Christian can talk to the griffin, because it would eat him.
Only when the bird is asleep can he pluck out the feather from the griffin's tail
says the wife of the griffin (Zipes 2002, 488–493). The same motif, about a
feather from the griffin's tail being used to cure the rich man's daughter who
is sick, appears in Celtic folklore as well (Danaher 1970, 81–91).

THE PHOENIX

A mythical bird of gorgeous plumage about the size of an eagle, the phoenix
was fabled to live in the desert of Arabia with a lifespan of 500 years. At the

close of this period, known as the phoenix "period" or "cycle," it "makes a nest of spices, sings a melodious dirge, flaps its wings to set fire to the pile, burns itself to ashes and comes forth with new life" (*Brewer's Dictionary* 1999, 906). Restored to youth, it lives for another 500 years, when the cycle is repeated. Thus, the phoenix is linked generally to concepts of resurrection, immortality, and cyclic resurgence (Chevalier and Gheerbrant 1969, 597–598).

Van den Broek's monumental treatise, *The Myth of the Phoenix According to Classical and Early Christian Traditions* (1972), lists hundreds of occurrences in Biblical, Greek and Latin, and Egyptian, Coptic, Syriac, and other Oriental texts. The phoenix has many analogues in different cultures, including the *anka* of Arabic lore and the *garuda* of Hindu mythology (Leach 1972, 869), the Taoist's *oiseau de cinabre* (*tan-niao*), the Chinese *feng-huang* (or *-hwang*), and the Siva of Hindu mythology. Cirlot traces connections to the Persian *simorgh* and the Turkish *kerkes* (1962, 253). Other counterparts are the Japanese *ho-ho* and the Russian firebird (Nigg 1995, 17–18). Many scholars connect the phoenix to the sacred Egyptian bird, the *bennu,* a bird similar to the stork or heron, which was believed to have been "the first creature to alight on the hill that came into being out of the primordial ooze" (Biederman 1994, 264). The *bennu* symbolized the Egyptian gods Ra and Osiris and was a hieroglyph for the sun. In the Egyptian Book of the Dead is recorded: "I am bennu, that which is in Heliopolis. I am keeper of the book that which is and of that which shall be."

In tracing the history of the phoenix, Van den Broek begins by noting "the widespread oriental conception of the bird of the sun" (1972, 397) and outlines a genealogy of the sun bird, from the Semitic world via Phoenicia to the Mycenaean culture and then on throughout the Greek world, where its Greek name became established. His extensive research leads him to proclaim that it is "probable that the Classical phoenix myth is a purely Greek product, i.e., the Greek variant of the mythical conception of the bird of the sun found in various cultures of the Near, Middle, and Far East" (398 and 398n). Classical writers who wrote about the phoenix include the Greeks Hesiod (eighth century BCE), and Herodotus (in his account of Egypt, ca. 430 BCE) and the Romans Ovid (in *Metamorphoses,* first century CE), Pliny the Elder (*Natural History,* (77 CE), and Tacitus (*Annals,* 109 CE). A key change in the phoenix legend came with the writings of Lactantius (Lucius Caecilius Firmanus), who wrote of the bird's fiery death. Although it was Clement of Rome (late first, early second century) who first reworked the phoenix myth as a Christian symbol of the Resurrection of Christ, Lactantius's Christian reinterpretation is the foremost example of the "apologetic method—the re-expression of fundamental Christian truths in a form that would be palatable to educated Roman pagans who might otherwise be appalled by a religion that venerated a crucified malefactor" (McGucken in Lactantius 1995).

The phoenix and related birds of youth figure in folk and fairy tales. The Irish story of Mael Dùin (tenth century), the immediate source of the famous *Navigatio Brendani,* was very influential in the Middle Ages and served as an impetus for voyages of discovery that led eastward to India and west to the New World (Dillon 1948, 124). In one episode, a huge phoenix-like bird eats of a fruit that, when cast into a lake, gives the water the power to renew the youth of those who bathe in it (129). A French-Canadian fairy tale features the golden phoenix, whose voice has youth-granting power: "Whoever lives within the sound of its voice will never grow old" (Barbeau 1958, 20). The Chinese phoenix, *feng-huang* or *feng-hwang,* differs from the phoenix of Western mythology in being a pair of birds, the male (feng) and the female (huang). The male symbolizes fire; the female is the sign of the empress. A bird of good omen, it is not seen in times of war. Music-loving, it may appear when it hears the flute. "The bird's song is said to be the source of the Chinese musical scale" (Nigg 1995, 16). With its unity that transcends duality, the *feng-huang* is "a powerful symbol of conjugal unity" (Biederman 1994, 264). It does not die and undergo rebirth, although it is immortal.

Poets and writers of fantasy have for centuries seized on the metaphorical potential of the magical bird, and psychologists find it an apt symbol "d'une irréfragable volonté de survie" (Chevalier and Gheerbrant 1969, 598). It can be viewed psychologically as the "phoenix" within ourselves, "enabling us to live out every moment and to overcome each and every partial death which we call a 'dream' or 'change'" (O. Wirth in Cirlot 1962, 253–254). Such symbolic significance transcends time. As just one example, Milton's poem *Samson Agonistes* (1671) speaks of the "self-begott'n bird" from the Arabian woods as the emblem of Samson's reconstitution of heroic fortitude and animal vitality (Wilkenfeld 1965, 166).

Van den Broek remarks that "it can only be concluded that the phoenix fulfilled an important function with respect to the meaning of human existence. . . . The phoenix could symbolize renewal in general as well as the sun, time, the empire, metempsychosis, consecration, resurrection, life in the heavenly paradise, Christ, Mary, virginity, the exceptional man, and certain aspects of the Christian life" (1972, 9).

In modern times there have been imaginative portrayals of the phoenix in literature for young readers. Carolyn Wells, in *Folly and the Forest* (1902), tells of a little girl who is flown by Pegasus to the nest of Phoenix, who relates his history to her. Described as the "biggest and most beautiful bird that ever lived," he dwells in paradisiacal surroundings, inhabits an aromatic nest, has a musical voice, and is kind and intelligent. His motive for self-immolation is nothing more than boredom and loneliness, and burning "does me more good than a Turkish bath." He is ecstatic to feel "so young and gay and frisky" on arising from the ashes. The only unpleasant aspect of the wonderful transformation is the smell of burning feathers (61–64). In the story "The Phoenix," by Sylvia Townsend Warner, "the phoenix is caged in a zoo and subjected to all sorts of abuse by scheming profiteers until it finally bursts into flames, destroying the zoo and killing everyone in the area" (*Storytelling Encyclopedia* 1997, 364). J.K. Rowling, in her Harry Potter fantasy series, portrays a magic phoenix, Fawkes, who belongs to the sage Dumbledore. Phoenix tail feathers are at the core of the wands of both Harry Potter and his nemesis, Lord Voldemort, suggesting the moral ambiguity of magic and the tenuous line between good and evil. The fifth book in the series is titled *Harry Potter and the Order of the Phoenix* (2003).

Hande A. Birkalan (roc and griffin) *and Millicent Lenz* (phoenix)

REFERENCES

Alangu, Tahir. 1961. *Billur Kösk masallari*. Istanbul: Renzi Kitabovi.

Barbeau, Marius. 1958. *The Golden Phoenix and Other French-Canadian Fairy Tales,* retold by Michael Hornyansky. New York: H.Z. Walck.

Biederman, Hans. 1994. *Dictionary of Symbolism: Cultural Icons and the Meanings Behind Them.* Trans. James Hulbert. New York: Meridian/Penguin.

———. 2002. *Knaurus Lexikon der Symbole*. München: Drömer Knaur Verlag.

Bies, Werner. 2002. "Phönix." In *Enzyklopädie des Märchens,* 10:1022–1035. New York: Walter De Gruyter.

Brewer's Dictionary of Phrase and Fable. 1999. 16th ed. By Adrian Room. New York: Harper Resource.

Carnoy, Albert. 1917. *Iranian Mythology*. Boston: Marshall Jones.

Chevalier, Jean, and Alain Gheerbrant. 1969. *Dictionnaire des symbols: mythes, reves, coutumes, gestes, formes, figures, couleurs, nombres.* Paris: LaFont.

Cirlot, J.E. 1962. *Dictionary of Symbols*. Trans. Jack Sage. New York: Philosophical Library.

Danaher, Kevin. 1970. *Folktales of the Irish Countryside*. Cork, Ireland: Mercier Pr.

Dawood, N.J. 1973. *Tales from the Thousand and One Nights*. New York: Penguin.

Dillon, Myles. 1948. *Early Irish Literature*. Chicago: University of Chicago Press.

Eberhard, Wolfram, and Pertev Naili Boratav. 1953. *Typen der türkischer Volksmärchen.* Wiesbaden: Franz Steiner Verlag GbmH.

Franklyn, Julian. 1967. *Shield and Crest: An Account of the Art and Science of Heraldry.* London: Mac Gibbon and Kee.

Ingersoll, Ernest. 1923. *Birds in Legend, Fable and Folklore*. New York: Longmans, Green.

Jones, Allison. 1995. *Laronsse Dictionary of World Folklore*. New York: Laronsse.

Lactantius. 1995. *The Phoenix* (De Ave Phoenice). Trans. E. Flintoff ; intro. John McGuckin. Bath: Old School Press.

Lindahl, Carl, John McNamara, John Lindow, eds. 2000. *Medieval Folklore: An Encyclopedia of Myths, Legends, Tales, Beliefs, and Customs.* Santa Barbara, CA: ABC-CLIO.

Marzolph, Ulrich. 1995. "Al- Rukhkh." In *Encyclopedia of Islam,* vol. 8, no.: 139–140: 595.

———. 1997. "Sindbad" (the sailor). In *Encyclopedia of Islam,* vol. 9, no.: 158: 638–640.

Nigg, Joe. 1995. *Wonder Beasts: Tales and Lore of the Phoenix, the Griffin, the Unicorn, and the Dragon.* Englewood, CO: Libraries Unlimited.

Storytelling Encyclopedia: Historical, Cultural, and Multiethnic Approaches to and Traditions Around the World. 1997. Ed. David Leemenz and Marion Sader. Phoenix, AZ: Oryx Press.

Van den Broek, R. 1972. *The Myth of the Phoenix According to Classical and Early Christian Traditions.* Trans. I. Seeger. Leiden: Brill.

Wells, Carolyn. 1902. *Folly in the Forest.* Philadelphia: H. Altemus.

Wilkenfeld, Roger B. 1965. "Act and Emblem: The Conclusion of Samson Agonistes." *ELH* 32, no. 2 (June): 160–168.

Zipes, Jack. 2002. *The Complete Fairy Tales of the Brothers Grimm.* New York: Bantam Books.

Leviathan

Motif B61

❀

Leviathan is a primeval sea monster—a giant fish, crocodile, or whale—of Hebrew folklore mentioned in five Old Testament poetic passages (Job 3:8; Job 41:1; Psalms 74:13–14; Psalms 104:26; Isaiah 27:1) and described and alluded to in others and also in the Apocrypha. Leviathan is said to cause a cataclysm by striking the earth with its tale (B16.4.1.1) and to cast up gorge that spreads disease (B16.4.1). The *Motif-Index* cross-references under Leviathan "Giant Fish" (B874), "Giant Whale" (874.3), and "Jonah. Fish (or water monster) swallows a man" (F911.4), the latter motif appearing in Irish, Italian, Babylonian, Indian, Melanesian, Indonesian, Hawaiian, and South American Indian folklore.

Yassif states that when myth is used in the Bible, it functions in "two common, classical forms: a narrative of the world of the gods, detailing their struggles with primal forces and their relationship with the human world; and the myth as an account of the origin of things and the various phenomena of the world (the 'etiological' myth')" (Yassif 1999, 10). While most of the fragments of the Leviathan myth within the Bible function in the former sense, there is also evidence of Leviathan as an etiological myth, for it explains the border between land and sea (Yassif 1999, 19). There is reason to believe that the biblical writers and redactors, in their use of mythic fragments, were afraid of giving godlike status to Leviathan. It has been suggested that "the special reference to God's creation of Leviathan in *Psalms* 104, 25–26 was probably intended to eliminate any doubt that this dragon-like creature was in any way an independent deity in biblical theology" (Werblowsky and Wigoder 1997, 415).

Scholars have attempted to reconstruct the Leviathan myth by drawing upon parallels within similar myths of the ancient Near East (Yassif 1999, 10). From such reconstructions, it is apparent that Leviathan stems from an ancient tradition of the dragon and the sea (Day 1985, 1). Many scholars have noted that the linguistic roots of the creature's Hebrew name *lewyatan* or *livyatan* (meaning "great serpent") suggest its mythic origin (e.g., Hartman 1963, 1330); the Hebrew consonants LWY are related to the Hebrew word for "coiled, twisted, writhed." Day, in fact, argues on linguistic grounds that the Hebrew name derives from the name of the dragon in the Ugaritic "Baal cycle" (Day 1985, 4–5).

Biblical scholars began to note similarities between the biblical myth and a creature similar to Leviathan in ancient near Eastern mythologies at the end of the nineteenth century. The "the divine conflict" of dragon and the sea in the Old Testament was the subject of a book published by H. Gunkel in 1895, and the American scholar G.A. Barton had given some attention to the topic two years earlier (Day 1985, 1–2). Day writes that Gunkel noted "the mythical character of various passages in the Old Testament which speak of a conflict between Yahweh and the sea and a dragon or dragons . . . and saw these as being an Israelite appropriation of the Babylonian myth of Marduk's victory over Tiamat at the time of creation recounted in the *Enuma elish*" (Day 1985, 1–2). In 1911, Frazer, in a section of *The Golden Bough* called "the slaughter of the dragon," also linked Leviathan with the "Babylonian" myth and with creation: the myth relates "how in the beginning the mighty god Marduk fought and killed the great dragon Tiamat, an embodiment of the primaeval watery chaos, and how after his victory he created the present heaven and earth by splitting the huge carcass of the monster into halves and setting one of them up to form the sky, while the other half apparently he used to fashion the earth" (Frazer 1966, 105–106).

In his extensive study of the biblical myth of Leviathan, Day believes that a causal relationship between Leviathan and the Creation myth exists. Where Day differs with the early scholars is in his contention that the imagery of the conflict is Canaanite and not Babylonian in origin (Day 1985, 1); thus the motif of Leviathan may be considerably older than the earlier scholars thought. Unlike Gunkel and Frazer, Day has the advantage of the Ugaritic texts, one of the great archaeological discoveries of the twentieth century.

In 1929, clay tablets dating from the fourteenth or fifteenth centuries BCE and written in cuneiform script in the Ugaritic language were discovered at the mound of Ras Shamra on the Syrian coast; they contain, among many other writings, a literary text known as "the Baal Cycle," a group of myths about the deity Baal, "the central god in the Ugaritic pantheon" (Rainey

1965, 102; Coogan 1987, 3:46–47). Translations of these tablets reveal several literary parallels with the Leviathan myth (Hartman, 1963, 1330). They tell how Baal, the "champion of the gods," vanquishes "Leviathan, the fleeing serpent . . . the crooked serpent, the tyrant of the seven heads (UT 67:I, 1–3)" (quoted by Rainey 1965, 120). Although Leviathan is never described as having seven heads in the Old Testament, a multiheaded creature is spoken of in Psalms 74:13–14—"[Y]ou broke the heads of the dragons in the water. / You crushed the heads of Leviathan; you gave him as food for the creatures of the wilderness"—and the "great red dragon" of Revelation 12:3 is said to have seven heads.

As the sea monster of chaos, Leviathan sparked the imagination of apocalyptic writers as well as later rabbinic writers. Biblical writers in later periods, both Jewish and Christian, used the processes of historicization and eschatologization to transform the creature into the Apocalyptic dragon (Day 1985, Chs. 3 and 4). Evidence of such transformation is evident in the Old Testament in Isaiah 27:1: "On that day the LORD with his cruel and great and strong sword will punish Leviathan the fleeing serpent, Leviathan the twisting serpent, and he will kill the dragon that is in the sea." According to Day, Leviathan in that passage most probably denotes Egypt "though it might refer to Babylon or Persia" (Day 1985, 177). Through an intertextual argument based on various Hebrew usage of the words for "serpent," Philips links Leviathan with the "crafty" serpent in the garden of Eden (Genesis 3:1) and also with the dragon of Revelation (Revelations 12:3); she notes that "in the Hebrew bible it [Leviathan] lacks the definitive identification as the adversary and the devil that appears in the extra canonical literature" (Philips 2000, 233, 236–245). These examples illustrate two additional motifs listed in the *Motif- Index:* "God battles Leviathan at the end of the world" (A1082.4) and "God conquers Satan at the end of the world" (A1082).

In the postbiblical Jewish literature written before the conquest of Palestine by the Arabs (632 CE—the date seen as the end of the "rabbinic period") (Yassif 1999, 70), Leviathan takes on some additional meanings in Jewish literature, often with eschatological nuances. Wigoder notes that aggadic sources indicate that both Leviathan and Behemoth are being kept alive to "provide a banquet for the righteous in the after life"; at a preordained time, the Lord will slaughter both beasts, "serve their meat at the 'eschatological feast,' make a tent from Leviathan's skin and supply the righteous banqueters with 'wine stored since Creation.' (Leviticus R. 13.3; Baba Bathra 746–65A; 4 Esdras 7,51; Apocalypse Bar 29,4)" (Wigoder 1989, 433; see also Hartman 1963, 1331). In the Talmud (B. B. 74b), Leviathan is killed by the Lord because he was "plotting to destroy the world"; in that text, Leviathan symbolizes "the forces of chaos and evil defeated by the power of good"

(Werblowsky and Wigoder 1997, 415). In medieval Jewish culture, "the kabbalists found esoteric significance in the story of Leviathan, identifying the male and female of the species with Samael and Lilith," and the great medieval Jewish philosopher, Maimonides (1135–1204), suggested that the Leviathan legends were "veiled prophecies referring to future events" (Werblowsky and Wigoder 1997, 415). Yassif indicates that "Jewish myths join the typical features of the international tall tale as an integral part of rabbinic tall tales," adding that "these myths deal primarily with the world to come" (Yassif 1999,188). Among such "tall tales" are "travelers' and seafarers' face-to-face encounters with the basic themes of Jewish mythology," providing "proof of their existence": Leviathan is one such "mythic" creature encountered (Yassif 1999, 189). Leviathan appears in a tale first in the Midrash of the Ten Commandments but "is copied and retold in other medieval sources," including the story cycle in the midrash Ecclesiastes Rabbah (Yassif 1999, 260), where Leviathan is showed in a positive light. Some of the mythic aura of Leviathan as mighty serpent of the sea survives; however, the links with the chaos monster, God's enemy, have been lost.

A giant fish or whale appears in the "First Voyage of Sinbad," one of the tales of the *Arabian Nights* (of Persian, Indian, and Arabic origin), when the ship in which Sinbad is sailing stops at what the sailors thought was an island, but which is really "a great fish stationary a-middlemost of the sea, whereon the sand hath settled and trees have sprung up of old time, so that it is become like unto an island" (Burton 2001, 334). The men unfortunately start a fire (J1761.1, "Whale thought to be island. Sailors light a fire on his back"), and, Sinbad says, "suddenly the island shook and sank into the abysses of the deep, with all that were thereon, and the dashing sea surged over it with clashing waves. I sank with the others down, down into the deep, but Almighty Allah preserved me from drowning and threw in my way a great wooden tub . . . I gripped it for the sweetness of life and, bestriding it like one riding, paddled with my feet like oars, whilst the waves tossed me as in sport right and left" (Burton 2001, 335). This encounter with a "great fish" is echoed in the nineteenth-century American novel, *Moby-Dick,* in which the narrator, cast into the sea after the whale destroys his ship, survives by clinging to a coffin that bobs to the surface of the sea.

Deanna Delmar Evans

REFERENCES

Ausubel, Nathan, ed. 1948. *A Treasury of Jewish Folklore: Stories, Traditions, Legends, Humor, Wisdom and Folk Songs of the Jewish People.* New York: Crown.

"The Book of Job." In *The Interpreter's Bible*. 1954. Ed. George Arthur Buttrick et al. New York: Abingdon.

Burton, Sir Richard F., trans. 2001 [1885–1888]. *The Arabian Nights: Tales from a Thousand and One Nights*. New York: Modern Library.

Coogan, Michael David. 1987. "Canaanite Religion: The Literature." In *The Encyclopedia of Religion*, ed. Mircea Eliade, 3:35–45. 3. New York: Macmillan.

Day, John. 1985. *God's Conflict with the Dragon and the Sea: Echoes of a Canaanite Myth in the Old Testament*. Cambridge: Cambridge University Press.

Frazer, James George. 1966 [1911]. *The Golden Bongh: A Study in Magic and Religion*. 3rd ed. London, NY: Macmillan, St. Martin's.

Ginsberg, H.L. 1945. "Ugaritic Studies and the Bible." *Biblical Archaeologist* 8:41–48.

Hartman, Louis F. 1963. *Encyclopedic Dictionary of the Bible: A Translation and Adaptation of A. vanden Born's Bijbels Woordenboek*, 2nd rev. ed., 1954–1957. New York: McGraw Hill.

Holy Bible. *New Revised Standard Version With Apocrypha*. 1989. New York: Oxford University Press.

International Bible Dictionary: Illustrated. 1977 [1859]. Ed. W.W. Rand. Plainfield, NJ: Logos International.

Perdue, Leo G. 1994. *Wisdom and Creation: The Theology of Wisdom Literature*. Nashville: Abingdon.

Phillips, Elaine. 2000. "Serpent Intertexts: Tantalizing Twists in the Tales." *Bulletin for Biblical Research* 10: 233–245.

Rainey, Anson F. 1965. "The Kingdom of Ugarit." *Biblical Archaeologist* 28:102–125.

Werblowsky, R.J. Zwi, and Geoffrey Wigoder, eds. 1997. *The Oxford Dictionary of the Jewish Religion*. New York: Oxford University Press.

Wigoder, Geoffrey, ed. 1989. *The Encyclopedia of Judaism*, 443. New York: Macmillan.

Wolfers, David. 1995. *Deep Things Out of Darkness: The Book of Job: Essays and a New English Translation*. Grand Rapids, MI: William B. Eerdmans.

Yassif, Eli. 1999. *The Hebrew Folktale: History, Genre, Meaning*. Trans. Jacqueline S. Teitelbaum. Bloomington: Indiana University Press.

Zuckerman, Bruce. 1991. *Job the Silent: A Study in Historical Counterpoint*. New York: Oxford University Press.

Animal Brides and Grooms:
Marriage of Person to Animal

Motif B600, and Animal Paramour, Motif B610

❀

The marriage and/or love between a human and one whose form is that of a magical or enchanted animal is a motif used from earliest times in the mythology and folklore of peoples from every part of the world. Thompson notes that Motif B600 is "extremely common." Among the many animal paramours and spouses are birds of all sorts (usually these are female), dogs, goats, bears, horses, bulls, fish, crocodiles, and snakes (Leach and Fried 1949, 1:61).

Some commentators argue that there is a difference between the tales of marriage between humans and animals and tales of humans having animal lovers (Leach and Fried 1949, 1:61). Tales of marriage between humans and animals are often *Märchen,* focus on transformation, and have happy endings, in which the animal metamorphoses into a princess or prince. The Grimms' tale of "The Frog Prince" and Madame de Beaumont's "Beauty and the Beast" (1757) are classic examples of this pattern. Animal paramour tales, on the other hand, are sometimes etiological or moralistic and often end with the slaying of the animal lover or the desertion of the human partner. The lines between the two categories are often blurred, however, and there are numerous tales of mermaid, seal, or swan brides, who, when they recover their caps (in the case of mermaids) or their skins, quickly desert their human husbands.

THE MARRIAGE PATTERN

The Search for the Lost Husband is Type 425 in Aarne-Thompson's classification, and Apuleius's telling of the myth of Cupid and Psyche, dating from the second century CE, is an example of 425A, *The Monster (Animal) as Bridegroom,* as is "East of the Sun and West of the Moon," from Norway. The familiar fairy tale "Beauty and the Beast" is Type 425C, *The Girl as the Bear's Wife.* In these stories, a girl marries or goes to live with what she thinks is a beast or animal who is really a god or an enchanted prince. These stories include some sort of prohibition made by the husband often against looking at him at a specific time, which the girl disobeys, resulting in the husband's leaving her and her setting out to search for him (C32.1, "Tabu: looking at a supernatural husband").

Often the animal groom is depicted as an especially noxious or unpleasant beast. He is a swine in Straparola's "Pig King," a snake in Basile's "Serpent," a "snotty goat" in a Russian folktale, and a crocodile in a Bantu legend. The grooms in many arranged marriages must have been perceived this way by their brides, who, full of anxieties about wedding, are taught the lessons of their culture about the self-sacrifice of female desires and/or the transformative power of love (Bettelheim 1977). Clearly, in many of these stories of animal husbands, the emphasis is on a young woman's acceptance of male sexuality, which she may find initially frightening, and on her growing to love a husband she finds initially unattractive. Older versions of the "beauty and beast" motif stress the civilizing value of women's virtue, the triumph of female gentleness over brute desire (Tatar 1999, 29). More recent versions, like the tales in Angela Carter's *Bloody Chamber* (1979), stress the values and virtues of the beast. As Marina Warner suggests, the passion, wildness, and defiance of the beast, his rebellion against the evils of civilization, are now perceived as good (Warner 1994, 307).

Tales of animal brides are strikingly similar, despite local coloration and variation. When not a bird or fish, the bride is often a small animal; she is a frog in Burma, Russia, Austria and Italy; a dog in India, Germany, and among American Indians; a mouse in Sri Lanka; and a tortoise in an account from *The Thousand and One Nights.* An ancient Japanese tale dating from 713 CE called "Urashima the Fisherman" depicts the bride as a turtle who vanishes forever when her husband calls her name. In general, even the gentlest animal brides bring with them an element of fear or distrust. That women could be half human and half animal, that they had ties to nature and could call up forces with which civilized beings had lost touch, made them threatening. Their animal nature reinforced the suggestion that women needed control. Significantly, while animal grooms are often revealed as handsome princes in disguise, female animals, though masked in human beauty, are frequently exposed as monsters (Leavy 1994, 121). In all, tales of animal brides may serve many functions. They may embody women's desires for autonomy and equality in marriage; they may reflect men's fantasies of captured and domesticated power; and they may also reflect male anxiety about desertion or abandonment by women. Interestingly, relatively few tales in the modern world utilize the idea that a husband must love and accept a "beastly" or animal wife.

In *The Folktale,* Thompson devotes a chapter to "Animal Wives and Husbands" (1977, 353–358) focusing on their occurrence in American Indian and Eskimo tales. He says they are most popular among the Plains Indians and the Eskimos of the North Pacific coast. In this latter area, as well as in Siberia and Japan, the tale of the fox woman is prevalent. Here, a mysterious housekeeper, who is sometimes a woman and sometimes a fox, is finally wed by the man with whom she lives. They are happy until he mentions her origins, at which point she leaves him in anger. Similar is the Plains Indians' tale of the "Piqued Buffalo Wife." A man weds a buffalo cow who becomes human and bears him a child. Harassed by the man's mortal wife, the buffalo woman and her child retransform themselves and return to the herd. The husband searches for them and is told by the buffalo leader that he may have them back if he can identify them. Helped by his child, he recovers them.

There are numerous tales among Eskimos from Greenland to Siberia of young girls wedding eagle or whale husbands. In these cases, the maidens wish for animal mates but are unhappy when their wishes are granted; they are rescued by mortal men—often their brothers. The tales of dog husbands are also somewhat frequent. In these, a woman is visited by a lover who is a man by night and a dog by day. The birth of dog children leads to her disgrace and banishment from the tribe. In most cases, she disenchants the children by throwing away their dog skins and all ends happily. In these tales, the dog is the legitimate husband, but in other tales of women's interactions with animal lovers, the relations are clandestine and lead to the punishment of those perceived as an adulterous pair. Among the most popular of these stories are tales of women's clandestine relations with snakes. In most cases, the angry husband kills the snake, and in many, he punishes or kills the wife as well (Thompson 1977, 356–357).

The Swan Maiden

One of the most popular and widespread versions of the animal bride is *The swan maid* (AT400*) (D361.1, "Swan Maiden"; F302.4.2, "Fairy comes into man's power when he steals her wings (clothes)"), an ancient motif that occurs throughout the world. "Elements of it are to be found in a story from the Indian *Rig Veda,* recorded 3000 years ago" (Poignant 1967, 82). In this abduction tale, a youth steals the feather dress of a swan maiden as she bathes and thus makes it impossible for her to fly away to her fairy or heavenly

The Snake Prince visits his wife

"The Snake Prince" from India is a variant of AT 425A, *The Monster (Animal) as Bridegroom.* The motif of the animal spouse is often coupled with a tabu against looking or speaking/naming. From Andrew Lang, *The Olive Fairy Book;* illustrated by H.J. Ford (1907).

world. He weds her in a "marriage by capture" (perhaps based on actual practice or ritual in early societies) and domesticates her until either she finds her feather dress or he beats her, strikes her with iron, or breaks a tabu—questioning her or speaking her name or looking at her at a specific time or place or something else he was told not to. Then she vanishes, sometimes forever. Poignant gives several examples from Oceania, including "The Porpoise Girl," popular in Micronesia. In these stories, a man steals the tail of a porpoise girl who comes ashore to watch men dance.

> The man married her and hid the package which contained her tail in the rafters. After a while she had two children and seemed content. Then one day, bugs falling from the rafters directed her attention to the parcel. She opened it, and finding her tail put it on. Before returning to the sea she warned her children that they must never eat porpoise meat. (Poignant 1967, 82)

Poignant notes that the swan bride motif has a widespread distribution in Oceania (82).

In Victorian Europe, the swan bride was a source of fascination. In *The Earthly Paradise* of 1868–1870, William Morris tells the tale in verse of the swan maiden captured by a young man who steals her plumage. Morris drew much of his material from the Scandinavian folktales that had been translated and presented to an eager public by Benjamin Thorpe and George Dasent. Nineteenth-century British folklorists became fascinated with this version of the animal bride motif; Sabine Baring-Gould devoted a chapter to swan maidens in *Curious Myths of the Middle Ages* (1866–1868), providing examples ranging from the Sanskrit to the Irish and reading the tales as solar myths, while Edwin Sidney Hartland devoted two lengthy chapters to them in *The Science of Fairy Tales* (1891). John Stuart Stuart-Glennie gained attention with his theory that swan maidens were feather-clothed but superior women of an archaic white race, wedded to men of color beneath them in level of civilization (Silver 1999, 97–98). By the end of the century, Tchaikovsky's *Swan Lake* ballet immortalized the motif of the swan maiden in dance.

Brides from the Deep

The most famous serpent bride is Melusine from medieval French legend, who, as a lamia, reverts to her serpent form one day a week while she bathes. The tale describes her metamorphosis into a snake when her husband, breaking the prohibition, enters her bathing room; it also renders her genealogically important as the mother of the Counts of Lusignan. Vernon Lee's late Victorian tale "Prince Alberic and the Snake Lady" depicts a lamia or serpent woman as an innocent victim of human cruelty. The title character of John Keats's "Lamia," a poem based on a tale in Burton's *Anatomy of Melancholy,* is less innocent but becomes a figure for imagination or perhaps delusion.

Among the most popular tales of animal/human pairing are those of seal maidens (selkies) from Celtic and Scandinavian folklore. These tales reveal much about the attitude toward and treatment of women in the places and eras in which they were told. Selkie brides (there are selkie grooms as well) are popular figures in the folklore of Scotland and Ireland, depicted, for example, in tales such as "The Daughter of the King of the Land of the Waves" (Campbell 1889–1895, 15–17). Euhemerists (those who believe that myth and folklore accounts are based on actual historical persons and occurrences) argue that selkies are derived from folk memories of actual women. David MacRitchie believes that early settlers in Scotland and the Shetland Islands probably encountered and even married Finnish and Lapp women who, because of their sealskin clothing and use of skin kayaks, had been misidentified as selkies (MacRitchie 1890, 4). Selkies have made occasional appearances in literature as well, especially in collections of tales partially based on folklore such as those of Fiona Macleod/William Sharp.

In "The Sin Eater" (1895), Macleod deals with the bestiality inherent in the source material by suggesting that seal brides could actually be female seals. Indeed, several of the tales are of the MacCodrum clan of the Outer Hebrides, known as "the MacCodrums of the Seals" because they claimed to be the offspring of a union between a selkie and a fisherman. A hereditary horny growth between their fingers made their hands resemble flippers. One Baubi Irqhart of the Shetland Islands claimed in 1895 to have a selkie as her great-great-grandmother (Silver 1999, 111–112).

Mermaid brides, more glamorous than seal women, had a special vogue in the Victorian era. They were made famous in such songs as "Married to a Mermaid" (1860s) and in romance novels such as H.G. Wells's *The Sea Lady.* Seafaring families all over the British Isles claimed descent from them. The most famous mermaid is, of course, the heroine of Hans Christian Andersen's "Little Mermaid," a softened, Christianized, and domesticated figure. The Irish and Scottish folklore accounts of mermaid wives are considerably less sentimental; several, like Thomas Crofton Croker's account of a "merrow" captured by an Irish fisherman, stress the hard life and domestic bondage of the captured animal bride. Croker's Merrow is an ideal wife, mother, and housekeeper until she finds her mermaid's cap and deserts both her husband and her children by him (Croker 1825, 1:247). The Lady of the Van Pool or Lady of the Van, in the Welsh version of the tale, leaves her spouse when he strikes her three times without cause. Having warned him against so doing, she immediately abandons him and their offspring.

NONMARITAL RELATIONS WITH ANIMALS

Among the best-known animal lovers is the Greek god Zeus, who often takes various animal forms when he wishes to make love to human females (A120.1, "God as shape-shifter"). He approaches Leda in the form of a swan, and Hera in the form of a cuckoo. He takes the form of a bull with Europa and Io. He visits Olympias, mother of Alexander the Great, in the form of a serpent.

Thompson remarks that in European tales "the animal actor is not really an animal" but a transformed or enchanted human (or god). "In tales of American Indians, however, and, indeed of primitive peoples everywhere, the marriage of human beings to actual animals is of very frequent occurrence" (1977, 353).

Thompson describes the story of the dog husband that has parallels to the story of Cupid and Psyche. He says this story is remarkably popular both on the North Pacific coast and among the Eskimo. "In all the stories, a girl is visited by an unknown lover who has the form of a dog by day and a man by night (D621.1, "Animal by day; man by night"). When, in due time, she gives birth to dog children, the tribe feels itself disgraced and deserts her. She is befriended by Crow, who hides some fire for her in a clam shell" (Thompson 1977, 355). She later spies on her pups, whom she sees in human form, with their dog skins hanging up, and these she destroys in order to keep them in human form (D721.3, "Disenchantment by destroying skin"). The story ends happily when she and her children prosper and the tribe, which has fallen on hard times, welcomes them back.

Thompson remarks that the sexual relationship between the girl and the dog is only incidental to this story, while "a considerable group of stories, known over the entire American Indian area, but especially popular among Plains tribes, finds its chief interest in the clandestine sexual relations of a woman with some animal" (1977, 356). In the story of "The Rolling Head,"

> A husband discovers that his wife has been leaving the camp to commit adultery with a snake. He kills the snake and punishes the wife. In some versions he serves the snake or the snake's privates to the wife, so that she eats it unawares. In other versions, particularly those of the Plains, he also kills the wife and cuts off her head. The head rolls after the man and his family, and they escape only with the greatest difficulty. (Thompson 1977, 356)

A similar story among the Plains tribes is "The Bear-Woman," in which a woman has a bear lover, whom her husband kills, and the woman turns into a bear and attacks her family.

Carole G. Silver

See also: Seduction; Quest for Vanished Husband/Lover; Tabu: Looking; Tabu: Speaking.

REFERENCES

Bettelheim, Bruno. 1977. *The Uses of Enchantment: The Meaning and Importance of Fairy Tales.* New York: Random House.

Campbell, Archibald. 1889–1895. *Waifs and Strays of Celtic Tradition.* Argylshire series 1–5. London: David Nutt.

Croker, Thomas Crofton. 1825. *Fairy Legends and Traditions of the South of Ireland.* Ed. Thomas Wright. London: William Tegg.

Leach, Maria, and Jerome Fried, ed. 1949. *Funk and Wagnalls Standard Dictionary of Folklore, Mythology and Legend.* 2 vols. New York: Funk and Wagnalls.

Leavy, Barbara Fass. 1994. *In Search of Swan-Maidens.* New York: New York University Press.

MacRitchie, David. 1890. *The Testimony of Tradition*. London: Kegan Paul.

Poignant, Roslyn. 1967. *Oceanic Mythology: The Myths of Polynesia, Micronesia, Melanesia, Australia*. London: Hamlyn.

Silver, Carole G. 1999. *Strange and Secret Peoples: Fairies and Victorian Consciousness*. New York: Oxford University Press.

Tatar, Maria, ed. 1999. *Classic Fairy Tales*. New York: W.W. Norton.

Thompson, Stith. 1977. *The Folktale*. Berkeley: University of California Press. Orig. ed., New York: Holt, Rinehart, and Winston, 1946.

Warner, Marina. 1994. *From the Beast to the Blonde: On Fairy Tales and Their Tellers*. New York: Farrar Strauss.

❀ C ❀

Tabu

Tabu: Eating and Drinking

Motifs C200–C299

❀

There are numerous tabus concerning eating and drinking; these include tabus against eating in a certain place (C210), eating certain things (C220), and eating at certain times (C230) (there are separate motifs for drinking in all these instances). Many of these tabus are found in cultural practice and are not merely literary devices, especially the tabus against specific foods, such as pork (C221.1.1.5, "Tabu: eating pork") and beef (C221.1.1.1.3, "Tabu: killing and cooking sacred cow").

One of the most famous eating tabus occurs in the Old Testament, in which Adam and Eve are expressly told not to eat of the Tree of Knowledge. Tempted by a serpent, Eve eats and entices Adam to do so, and God expels them from the Garden (A1331.1, "Paradise lost because of forbidden fruit (drink)").

In AT 310, *The Maiden in the Tower,* a witch confronts a man in her garden and demands as recompense his child when it is born. In the most well-known version, "Rapunzel" (KHM 12), the man's wife repeatedly asked for and ate greens from the witch's garden (C242, "Tabu: eating food of witch (demon)").

This chapter focuses on the tabus against eating food (C211) and drinking (C262) in the otherworld, which are seemingly universal.

EATING AND DRINKING IN THE OTHERWORLD

Dating from earliest times, the tabu against eating in the otherworld is present in the myth and folklore of many groups and is still accepted in several cultures.

In the earliest stories, the locale is the lower world, or land of the dead (C211.2, "Tabu: eating in lower world"); later stories tend to be set in a more vague otherworld, such as fairyland.

The etiological myth of Persephone, told in numerous versions from the Homeric "Hymn to Demeter" down through the Latin poets, describes Persephone or Kore as a virgin goddess protected by her mother, Demeter, the goddess of grain. Desired by Hades, the god of the underworld, Persephone is kidnapped as she gathers flowers. In her grief over her lost daughter, Demeter curses fertility and prevents all earthly creatures from propagating and all foods from growing or maturing. Finally, Zeus sends Hermes to ask Hades to allow Persephone to return to her mother. Hades assents, but secretly gives Persephone a seed of pomegranate which he urges her to eat, resulting in her having to return to the underworld for part of every year (C225.1, "Tabu: eating pomegranate seed"). "But," her mother tells her, "when the earth blooms with all kinds of sweet-smelling flowers in springtime, you will come up again from the kingdom of shadows."

Adapa, son of Ea, the god of wisdom in Babylonian mythology, proves wiser than Persephone. He refuses to partake even of bread and water during his visit to a subaquatic otherworld ("the house of the fish") and thus, while sacrificing immortality, can and does return to earth (Leach and Fried 1949, 9–10). So too Vainamoinen, the wise old hero of the Finnish *Kalevala,* who refuses the foaming beer offered to him in Tuonela, the land of the dead, and hence may return to the land of the living (Leach and Fried 1949, 1:410). The Japanese goddess Izanami is less fortunate. She dies giving birth to a fire god and descends to the underworld. When her husband tries to reclaim her, she warns him that she has eaten food in this realm and thus may not return to earth. Instead, she becomes a goddess of the underworld. A New Zealand Maori tale tells of a maiden who dies for love and whose lover begs the gods to let him visit her in Reinga, the Maori underworld. The lover is granted permission to visit, but is warned to eat nothing offered to him.

This prohibition against eating or drinking the food of the dead or that of the otherworld is found in North America among the Haida, Tsimshian, and Kwakiutl peoples as well as the Pawnee and Cherokee tribes (Leach and Fried 1949, 1:410). One Apache tale tells of two boys who eat the food of ga'ns (underground fairylike spirits) and can return to earth, but are never again able to eat the food of mortals. In some groups—the Tlingit, Tsimshian, and Kwakiutl—it is believed that people who have drowned have in actuality eaten the food of the fairylike land otters and can thus never return to normal life.

The people of New Caledonia believe that a newly dead person, arriving in the spirit world, is offered a feast of bananas. If the person partakes of it, he or she cannot return; if the person refuses, there is a chance of being restored to earth. The Melanesians warn living people who would visit Panoi (their underworld) not to touch any food in that place or they must stay there.

In British folklore, fairyland is often the otherworld in which no food may be eaten and the tempters are often fairies (C211.1, "Tabu: eating in fairyland"). Lewis Spence argues that there is no essential difference between the taboo that "forbids a mortal to partake of the food of the elves and that which prohibits him from eating food proffered him in the land of the dead" (Spence 1946, 79), and numerous folklorists see the fairies and their world as realms of the dead. In much lore from the British Isles, it is a dead friend or neighbor who warns the protagonist against eating fairy food. Many versions of a single tale are told all over the British Isles; the best-known version, called "The Fairy Dwelling on Selena Moor" (retold by K.M. Briggs), illustrates both belief in the fairies as the pagan dead and the dangers of tasting food in fairyland:

> When Mr. Noy, a local farmer, loses his way and wanders into a fairy realm, he finds that he is very thirsty and asks for a drink. But he is signalled by a young maiden dressed in white whom he recognizes as a former sweetheart, thought to have died some three or four years earlier. Though she carries ale, she denies him a drink and warns him against eating a fruit or plucking a flower if he wished ever to reach his home again. "Eating a tempting plum in this enchanted orchard was my undoing," she warns him. The fruit that enslaved her dissolved into "bitter water" in her mouth. Like all else in fairyland, fairy food is a snare and delusion: "What appear like ruddy apples and other delicious fruit are only sloes, hoggins [haws] and blackberries." Mr. Noy did escape, but, we are told, like other visitors to Fairyland, he pined and lost his thirst for normal life after his adventure. (Briggs 1977, 142–143)

In the medieval romance *Thomas of Erceldoun,* the Queen of Elfin warns the poet against eating fairy fruit; in the romance of *Ogier the Dane,* the hero is nearly destroyed by eating an apple from the fairy garden of the enchantress, Morgan La Fay. Conla, of the Third Fenian cycle of Irish legend, eats the apple given him by the beautiful Sidhe (fairy woman) and is thus compelled to follow her to Tir-na-nog, the Celtic otherworld, never to return to ordinary earth.

Lady Wilde tells two Irish tales parallel to "Selena Moor," though not as fully developed. In one, a young woman enticed into a fairy dance and then led to a banquet is warned by an unidentified man to "eat no food, and drink no wine, or you will never reach your home" (Briggs 1977, 65). Almost forced to drink, she is rescued by a redheaded man who gives her a magic plant to help her escape. In the other tale, "The Legend of Innis Sark" (Briggs 1977, 14–15), a young man transported asleep to fairyland first witnesses a horrible scene in a fairy kitchen—as an old woman is chopped up and boiled for food—and is soon after offered a share of a delicious-looking royal fairy banquet. He wisely refuses, arguing that he cannot eat since no priest is present to bless the food. He does drink some fairy wine and, as a result, the palace vanishes and he wakes. He, too, soon pines and dies, the fate common to those who break the prohibition.

Interestingly, in the Celtic enclaves from which many of these tales derive, food was left out for people thought to be kidnapped or "away" (i.e., comatose, paralyzed, or simply absent), so they would not be forced to eat fairy food, which would bind them to fairyland forever (Silver 1999).

YOU ARE WHAT YOU EAT

The concepts behind these varied tales are strikingly similar. All suggest that "we are what we eat." To eat the food of a spirit is to partake of the spirit's nature. Thus one gains kinship with those in the spirit world but at a price—that is, the renunciation of human nature. To eat fairy food endows one with a fairy nature and sometimes with power, but may prevent one from ever eating mortal food again. The knight in John Keats's famous "La Belle Dame sans Merci" has tasted fairy food in an "elfin grot" but is returned to earth dying amid visions of "starved lips." Partaking of food or drink in the land of the dead makes the visitor kin to or one with the dwellers in that land and thus unable to leave or to return to the land of the living. In this case, the fear of "pollution" by the dead or contact with them may play a significant role (Simons 1994). For behind the concept that we are or become what we eat is a law of contact and contagion. When one has contact with something or someone more powerful than humans or of another order of being, one takes on its essence.

Among other related manifestations of this tabu is the belief that some food is not to be eaten—in the underworld, otherworld, or anywhere else—because it is itself transmigrated souls (Latham 1987, 4:393). Vegetarianism is sometimes based upon this premise; according to Ovid's *Metamorphoses,* Pythagorus used this argument. Another similar belief is that since the food of the otherworld may make mortals immortal (as with Greek Psyche, below), otherworldly creatures must avoid human food lest it make them mortal (Latham 1987, 393). A Scandinavian tale tells of an elf-maiden who eats mortal food in order to stay with her lover; there are Celtic tales of Sidhe (fairy maidens) who renounce their fairy lives and become mortal by eating human food (Leach and Fried 1949, 1:410). There are also numerous tales of food that, if eaten, confers immortality upon those who eat it. Psyche, given the ambrosia of the gods, becomes a goddess; Gilgamesh, in the great Mesopotamean epic, fails at a chance to renew his youth because the magic plant he was to eat is stolen by a serpent. In Taoist belief, a peach from a paradisiacal fairyland ruled by His Wang Mu, the Chinese Queen Mother of the West, can make one immortal (Latham 1987, 4:392). Nevertheless, myths, tales, and popular wisdom remind us that even when there is a reward, the price is high. For as Tithonus, made immortal by ambrosia yet deprived of youth and vigor, learns, the gods themselves cannot take back their gifts; to eat the food of the divine is to lose one's human nature.

Carole G. Silver

REFERENCES

Briggs, K.M. 1977. *A Dictionary of Fairies: Hobgoblins, Brownies, Bogies, and Other Super-natural Creatures.* Harmondsworth: Penguin.

Latham, James E. 1987. "Food" in *The Encyclopedia of Religion.* Vol. 4. Ed. Mircea Eliade. New York: Macmillan.

Leach, Maria, and Jerome Fried, ed. 1949. *Funk and Wagnalls Standard Dictionary of Folklore, Mythology, and Legend.* 2 vols. New York: Funk and Wagnalls.

Rose, Herbert J. 1991. *A Handbook of Greek Mythology.* New York: E.P. Dutton.

Silver, Carole G. 1999. *Strange and Secret Peoples: Fairies and Victorian Consciousness.* New York: Oxford University Press.

Simons, Frederick J. 1994. *"Eat Not This Flesh": Food Avoidances from Prehistory to the Present.* 2d ed. Madison: University of Wisconsin Press.

Spence, Lewis. 1946. *British Fairy Origins.* London: Watts.

Tabu: Looking

Motifs C300–C399

❀

The tabu against looking at a certain person or thing (C310) is widespread in folklore, and the list of persons or things that must not be viewed includes a deity, a heavenly body, a rainbow, copulating snakes, and various supernatural creatures, including ghosts, fairies, a supernatural husband or wife, and supernatural helpers. This is only a partial list.

The looking tabu has three main scenarios: (1) A person voluntarily avoids the sight of the tabu object because it is too fearful to behold; (2) a person is warned not to look at a specific person or thing and ignores the warning at great cost to himself or herself, often breaking a magic spell; (3) the viewer receives no warning beforehand not to look at the tabu object, sees it, and suffers a bad fate.

In a prime example of the first instance, when God appears before Moses in the form of a burning bush, "Moses hid his face, because he was afraid to look at God" (Exodus 3:6) (C311.1.8, "Tabu: looking at deity"). In an example from Greek myth illustrating the second scenario, Zeus warns his mortal lover Semele that she must not see him in his godly manifestation, but she insists, and the sight destroys her.

There are a number of tales in Africa that tell of the origin of death as a consequence of looking at a forbidden thing, especially a specific act. A tale from the Chaga tells how people used to have the ability to live forever by shedding their skins like snakes. A god had warned that no one should observe anyone in this act, which must be performed alone, but a girl sees her grandfather shedding his skin and then death comes to the people (Feldmann 1963, 120).

LOOKING INTO RECEPTACLES

The Greeks had a story to explain the existence of suffering in the world, which Hesiod tells in *Works and Days* (seventh century BCE.). In retribution for Prometheus having stolen fire and given it to mortals, Zeus has Hephaestos fashion a beautiful woman, Pandora, whom Zeus sends to earth, and she opens the lid of a jar from which escaped all the evils that are now in the world (C321, "Tabu: looking into box (Pandora)"). Thompson notes that this motif is found in tales of several North American Indian groups.

A story from Java involves a man and his supernatural wife, a winged maiden whom he had tricked into marrying him by stealing her wings while she was bathing (D361.1, "Swan Maiden"; F302.4.2, "Fairy comes into man's power when he steals her wings (clothes). She leaves when she finds them"). One day the wife goes to the river to wash clothes and warns her husband not to look into the pot in which their dinner was cooking (C320, "Tabu: looking into certain receptacle"). He is curious about her cooking since she has always provided abundant meals even though he gives her only one measure of rice. No sooner has she left than he goes straight to the fire and lifts off the cover of the pot and peers in, to find only one grain of rice in boiling water. When his wife returns and sees the single grain of rice in the pot, she knows that her husband has looked in, destroying the magic power by which she had been able to produce food. She then finds her wings and flies off (Dixon 1916, 208).

LOOKING BACK

The unfortunate consequences of looking back (C331, "Tabu: looking back") are chronicled in many sources around the world. The *Motif-Index* lists occurrences in Greek, Jewish, Indian, French Canadian, Lithuanian, Chinese, Eskimo, Polynesian (Tonga Islanders), Hawaiian, South American, and African (Fang, Luba) folklore.

In the Old Testament, the Lord decides to destroy the city of Sodom because it has been overrun by wickedness, and he sends two angels to Lot and his wife to tell them to flee the city, warning them not to look back. "But his wife looked back from behind him, and she became a pillar of salt" (Genesis 19:26) (C961.1, "Transformation to pillar of salt because of breaking tabu").

The Greek myth of Orpheus is one of the most famous variants of the tabu against looking back, involving a journey to the underworld in order to fetch a dead loved one (F81.1, "Orpheus. Journey to land of dead to bring back person from the dead"). Thompson (1977) lists four components of the story: (1) journey to the land of the dead to bring back a wife (sweetheart, etc.); (2) permission obtained; (3) prohibition against looking at wife on way out (or other tabu); (4) tabu broken and wife lost.

Orpheus, a great musician, charms the guardians of the underworld with his music in order to plead with Hades to allow his dead wife, Eurydice, to return to the world of the living with him. Hades grants his request, with the stipulation that Orpheus not look back at Eurydice until they reach the upper realms. Orpheus is unable to resist one look back at her as they approach the light, and Eurydice vanishes back to the lower world and is lost to him. Thompson lists variants from Ireland, England, Norway, Babylonia, Siberia, India, China, Japan, Indonesia, New Zealand, Hawaii, Samoa, New Hebrides, Banks Islands (South Pacific), New Guinea, Africa, and Latin America. He states that parallels to the classical story occur in North America, especially on both coasts. "Out of some forty versions, only three tell of the successful return of the wife" (Thompson 1977, 351).

SUPERNATURAL HUSBAND OR WIFE

In the story of Cupid and Psyche, a Greek myth written down by Apuleius in the second century, Psyche is married to the god Cupid, who she believes is a monster. He has told her she may not look at him, and he only stays with her during the night, fleeing before dawn. Finally resolving, at the urging of her sisters, to look at her husband, Psyche lights a lamp in the middle of the night. As she leans over Cupid, he wakes up and immediately takes flight (C32.1, "Tabu: looking at supernatural husband"). Psyche then begins an arduous search for him. This story is the prototype of a number of tales under the heading *The Search for the Lost Husband* (AT 425). "East of the Sun and West of the Moon" and "Beauty and the Beast" are two well-known examples in the European tradition.

The tale of Melusine, or Melusina, a water fairy who has a serpent's tail that is manifest only one day of the week, was written in numerous sources between 1475 and 1577 in France, Germany, and Spain (Baring-Gould 1978) When she marries, she makes her husband promise that he will never look upon her on a specific day of the week. For years he obeys this injunction, but finally his curiosity gets the better of him and he spies on her while she is in her bath on the forbidden day. When she realizes that he has seen her, she flies off (C31.1.2, "Tabu: looking at supernatural wife on certain occasion (Mélusine). The husband must not see the wife when she is transformed to an animal").

NAKED WOMEN

The tabu against looking at a naked woman is embodied in a well-known legend attached to the city of Coventry in England, first written down in the late twelfth or early thirteenth century by Roger of Wendover. The townspeople

Melusine reverts to her serpent form one day a week, and her husband has been enjoined never to look upon her on that day. But eventually curiosity gets the better of him, and after he enters her bathing room she will vanish forever. From Jean d'Arras, *Mélusine* **(fifteenth century).**

of Coventry are suffering under a heavy tax, and Lady Godiva asks her husband to lessen their burden. He agrees on the condition that she ride the full length of the town nude, clothed only in her long hair. She does so, and the citizens are all commanded to shut their windows and stay indoors. All obey except one (C312.1.2, "Tabu: Looking at nude woman riding through town"). Peeping Tom is stricken with blindness because of his disobedience (C943, "Loss of sight for breaking tabu") (Thompson 1977, 265). The motif of Peeping Tom was not added to this legend until the seventeenth century.

In Greek myth, Actaeon, too, looks upon a naked woman, although he comes upon her by accident one day while he is hunting. She is not a mere woman but the goddess Artemis, and although Actaeon has not been fore-warned not to look at her, he too suffers a terrible fate for seeing her: she immediately turns him into a stag, and he is torn apart by his dogs (C312.1.1, "Tabu: man looking at nude goddess").

MISCELLANEOUS

From the Amazon comes a story about a young man who follows a beautiful star up a magic palm tree to the sky world. When he hears sounds of festivity and music, she warns him not to go see the dancing (C311.1.1, "Tabu: look-ing at ghosts"). But as soon as she leaves, he cannot repress his curiosity and goes toward the sound.

> What he saw was fearful! It was a sort of dance of the dead! A crowd of skeletons whirled around, weird and shapeless, their putrid flesh hanging from their bones and their eyes dried up in their sunken orbits. The air was heavy with their foul odor. The young man ran away in horror. On his way he met the star who blamed him for his disobedience and made him take a bath to cleanse him of the pollution. But he could no longer endure the sky world, but ran to the spot where the leaves were tied to the sky and jumped on to the palm tree, which immediately began to shrink back toward the earth: "You run away in vain, you shall soon return," the star called after him; and so indeed it was, for he had barely time to tell his kindred of his adventure before he died. (Alexander 1920, 307–308)

Another dance that is tabu to see is performed by Yu, the Chinese culture hero. In the shape of a bear, Yu performs a dance upon the stones of Houan-yuan pass in order to allow floods to flow through, and his wife is forbidden to see it. Yu tells his wife that when he wants food brought to him he will beat on his drum. One day he accidentally strikes the drum and his wife, bringing food, sees Yu perform the magical dance. She is turned to stone (C961.2, "Transformation to stone for breaking tabu") (Holden 2000, 155).

In a story collected by the Grimms, a poor shoemaker and his wife awaken one morning to find some beautifully made shoes. This happens for several days, and finally they decide to hide and watch during the night. They dis-cover that the shoes are being made by two naked little men, and they resolve to make some clothes for them. When the elves return one night and find the clothing laid out for them, they put it on and run off, never to reappear (C51.4.3, "Tabu: spying on secret help of fairies"). While the shoemaker and his wife do not suffer a terrible fate from seeing the elves, the elves do leave as soon as they know they have been observed (F361.3.1, "Fairies leave work unfinished when overseen"). A similar motif, albeit in a much more powerful form, is found in the ancient Greek *Hymn to Demeter,* when the goddess Demeter, posing as a nursemaid, is seen by her charge's mother in her nightly ritual of immortalizing the baby by anointing him with ambrosia and putting him in the fire. Demeter then angrily throws the baby down and abandons him. Another tale from the Grimms' collection illustrating the dangers of seeing what should not be seen is the story of Frau Trude. A headstrong little girl goes into the forest to see an old woman named Frau Trude, although her parents expressly forbid her to go. When she looks through Frau Trude's window, the girl sees the crone in her true witch form, with a head of fire. Frau Trude then turns the girl into a block of wood and throws her into the fire (C311.1.6, "Tabu: seeing witch in her true form").

According to Greek myth, Tiresias while walking in the woods sees two snakes copulating and is transformed into a woman (D513.1, "Man looks at copulating snakes: transformed to woman"). He does not regain his male identity until seven years later when he again beholds a pair of mating snakes.

There are taboos against looking in certain directions (C330); in North America the looking down taboo occurs sporadically in folktales from the Southwest to the Aleutian Islands (Demetracopoulou 1933, 116).

There is a tabu against looking up a chimney (C337. "Tabu: looking up chimney") and in some versions of AT 480 (*Kind and Unkind*) a girl is threatened with death for looking into a fireplace.

See also: Quest for the Vanished Husband.

Jane Garry

REFERENCES

Alexander, Hartley B. 1920. *Latin American Mythology.* Vol. 11 of *The Mythology of All Races.* Boston: Archaeological Institute of America.

Baring-Gould. 1978 [1868]. *Curious Myths of the Middle Ages.* Oxford: Oxford University Press.

Demetracopoulou, D. 1933. "The Loon Woman Myth: A Study in Synthesis." *Journal of the American Folklore Society* 46 (180): 101–128.

Dixon, Roland B. 1916. "Oceanic Mythology." Vol. 9 of *The Mythology of All Races.* Boston: Archaeological Institute of America.

Feldmann, Susan, ed. 1963. *African Myths and Tales.* New York: Dell.

Holden, Lynn. 2000. "Looking or Seeing." In *Encyclopedia of Taboos,* 154–155. Oxford: ABC-CLIO.

Thompson, Stith. 1977. *The Folktale.* Berkeley: University of California Press. Orig. ed. New York: Holt, Rinehart, and Winston, 1946.

Tabu: Speaking

Motifs C400–C499

❊

The entire Chapter C of the *Motif-Index* is devoted to tabus, obedience to which results in actions of avoidance as well as compulsion. The *Motif-Index* lists various examples of speaking tabus, including speaking during a certain time (C401), before a certain time (C402), asking questions (C410), speaking to strangers (C492), cursing (C494), using obscene language (C496), and uttering the name of a person or thing (C430) or god or gods (C431).

SPEAKING DURING A CERTAIN TIME

The Grimms' *Kinder- und Hausmärchen* collection includes three tales exemplifying C401. In "The Twelve Brothers" (KHM 9), a sister who has unwittingly plucked twelve flowers that caused her brothers to be transformed into ravens is told by an old woman that the only way to disenchant them is to remain dumb for a period of seven years "and if thou speakest one single word, and only an hour of the seven years is wanting, all is in vain, and thy brothers will be killed by the one word." The girl is later married to a king, but does not speak or laugh. The king's mother convinces him that his wife is evil and he finally condemns her to be burnt at the stake just as the seven years are up. As the fire is burning, twelve ravens come flying to the spot, transform back into her brothers, and she is able to tell her story. "The Six Swans" (KHM 49) has a similar story line. "The Three Black Princesses" (KHM 137) is a very different story, but incorporates the same motif in that the hero is told by three enchanted princesses whose castle he has entered that he might disenchant them if he stays a year and does not speak to them or look at them

Guessing the name of a supernatural creature gives power over it (Motif C432.1). From "Tom Tit Tot," an example of the folktale type AT 500, in Joseph Jacobs, *English Fairy Tales;* illustrated by John Batten (1890).

in that period (thus this story also includes the tabu against looking at a certain person or thing, Motif C310).

NAMING

Anthropologists have noted that the belief that one's existence is bound up in one's name is widespread, and this is reflected in folklore. Ernst Cassirer says, "He who gains possession of the name and knows how to make use of it has gained power over the object itself; he has made it his own with all its energies" (1957, 117). In the Danish ballad "The Sword of Vengeance," the owner of a magical sword is able to make it stop slaughtering only by calling to it by name (Wimberly 1965, 89–90).

Child lists numerous examples from Scandinavian ballads in which warriors either lose their strength or receive their death blow if anyone calls out their name during a battle contrary to their injunction not to name them in front of their adversary (1965, 1:489)

In the *Odyssey,* Odysseus craftily tells the Cyclops Polyphemos, who has asked his name, that it is "Noman." Not revealing his name saves Odysseus from certain death later when he mortally wounds Polyphemos and other ogres, coming to the entrance of the cave in response to Polyphemos's screams, ask if anyone is trying to kill him. When he responds that Noman is trying to kill him, they retreat.

An old proverb, "Talk of the devil and he will appear," explains motif C433, "Tabu: uttering name of malevolent creature (Eumenides). To avoid the evil results of naming these creatures other names are substituted." In Greek mythology, there are two, and later three, avenging deities, the horrific-looking daughters of night, who punish wrongdoers both in this world and after death. The Romans called them the Furies. The Greeks originally called them the Erinyes; "the form Eumenides, which signifies 'the well-meaning,' or 'soothed goddesses,' is a euphemism, because people dreaded to call these goddesses by their real name" (Smith 1958, 120). It has been remarked upon that the word *bear* among Slav nations has been displaced for fear that uttering the name will bring the creature. In Bulgarian, the bear is literally "honey-eater." "We find [this circumlocution] in Czech, Slovak, Russian, Serbo-Croat; only the Poles among the Slavonic peoples have created their own circumlocution *niedzwiedz;* in German the bear is often called *der Braune*" (Adler 1978, 59).

In AT 444B*, *Guessing the Girls' Names,* a sorcerer kidnaps two beautiful princesses, takes them to a distant country, and offers them in marriage to anyone, including animals, who can guess their names. Many men try without success. A toad and a turtle overhear the princesses talking, learn their names, and win them in marriage (N475, "Secret name overheard by eavesdropper"). When the girls, angry at the animals, throw them against the wall, they are disenchanted and become princes.

The tabu against uttering the name of a malevolent creature also has its reverse in folklore, in that naming the devil will cause him to go away (C432.1, "Guessing name of supernatural creature gives power over him"). Exorcising a demon by naming him is the climax of one version of the British ballad "Riddles Wisely Expounded," in which an "unco" (uncouth) knight comes to the home of a widow and her three daughters, says that the youngest must lie with him that night, and if she can answer ten riddles he will marry her. She answers all of them, including the last—What is worse than a woman?"—by replying "Clootie" (a name for the devil), and the ballad concludes, "As soon as she the fiend did name, / He flew away in a blazing flame" (Child 1965, 1:5).

The Name of the Helper (AT 500) is a widespread folktale type found in Europe (Thompson 1977, 48). The story appears in the Grimms' *Kinder- und Hausmärchen* as "Rumpelstiltskin," in which a little man helps a girl spin straw into gold but makes her promise to give him her firstborn child in return. When he comes to collect the baby, she balks, and he tells her she may keep the child if she can guess his name within three days. This would be an impossible task since he does not have a conventional name, except that on the last night he is overheard intoning his name while dancing around a fire, and the next day she is able to name him, causing him to disappear in a fury (C432.1, "Guessing name of supernatural creature gives power over him").

In a story from the Kru of Africa's Ivory Coast, a young girl goes to the land of the dead and is given refuge by an old woman. Death discovers her and withholds food from her unless she can tell him his name. She is able to do this with the help of a bird (Werner 1925, 177–178).

Puccini's opera *Turandot,* based on the 1762 play of the same name by Carlo Gozzi and said to derive from a Chinese tale, contains the motif of naming. Princess Turandot has renounced men and says she will only marry the man who can answer three riddles successfully; those who fail will die. Calaf succeeds, and Turnadot is so distraught that Calaf offers to forgo the marriage (and forfeit his life) if she can guess his name by morning. She decrees that no one shall sleep until his name is discovered. In the end, however, she overcomes her aversion to the idea of marriage, and the opera has a happy ending.

Jane Garry

REFERENCES

Adler, Max K. 1978. *Naming and Addressing: A Sociolinguistic Study.* Hamburg: Buske.

Cassirer, Ernst. 1957. *Language: Vol. 1 of The Philosophy of Symbolic Forms.* New Haven, CT: Yale University Press.

Child, Francis James. 1965. *The English and Scottish Popular Ballads.* Vol. 1. New York: Dover. Orig. ed. Boston: Houghton, Mifflin, 1882–1898.

Smith, Sir William. 1958. *Smaller Classical Dictionary,* revised by E.H. Blakeney and John Warrington. New York: E.P. Dutton.

Thompson, Stith. 1977. *The Folktale.* Berkeley: University of California Press. Original ed. New York: Holt, Rinehart, and Winston, 1946.

Werner, Alice. 1925. "African Mythology." Vol. 7 of *Mythology of All Nations.* Boston: Archaeological Institute of America.

Wimberly, Lowry Charles. 1965. *Folklore in the English and Scottish Ballads.* New York: Dover. Orig. ed. Chicago: University of Chicago Press, 1928.

Tabu: Forbidden Chambers

Motif C611

❈

The widespread tabus against entering one forbidden place (C610, "The one forbidden place"), or more specifically a forbidden chamber (C611, "Forbidden chamber. Person allowed to enter all chambers of house except one"), derive from two distinct kinds of social restrictions. First, cautionary tabus warn against physical and perceived spiritual dangers in such natural sites as woods, mountaintops, or bodies of water, as well as places controlled or frequented by potential adversaries. Second, tabus also impart awe to and protect sacred areas accessible only to consecrated individuals, for example, the Holy of Holies section in the ancient Temple of Jerusalem.

Both types of restrictions are reflected in folktales and myths. The forbidden chamber motif, in particular, is found in many types of tales, and in some types it is the nucleus of the stereotypical formulation. For instance, "Mary's Child" from the Grimms' *Children's and Household Tales* (KHM 3, AT 710, *Our Lady's Child*) exemplifies folktales using the forbidden chamber motif as a religious interdiction. This story, told throughout the Catholic world and popular even in Protestant Europe, tells how a poverty-stricken man and woman give their daughter to the Virgin Mary for foster care. Mary takes the child to heaven. When the girl is fourteen years old, Mary gives her keys to the thirteen doors of the kingdom, warning her, however, not to open the thirteenth door. The girl cannot resist the temptation and opens the forbidden door, behind which she sees the Holy Trinity seated in fire and splendor. From her contact with this brilliance, one of her fingers turns to gold, so Mary knows that the girl has been in the forbidden room. The girl denies her transgression and is cast from heaven. After much travail and suffering, the heroine confesses her disobedience and is forgiven.

In some Type 710 tales, the prohibition comes not from a saint but from a demon. For example, in the Swedish tale "Gray Cape" (Blecher and Blecher 1993, 231–234), a princess is captured by a female troll. The captive is treated well and has full access to the troll's castle, except for one forbidden door. Again, the heroine, unable to resist the temptation, opens the door, only to find the troll herself on the other side. Like the heroine in the Grimms' tale, she is given a chance to redeem herself with a simple confession, but she refuses and is cast out. And again, after much suffering, she confesses her transgression and in the end is rewarded with marriage to a handsome prince.

The best-known European folktales featuring forbidden doors are those of Types 311 and 312, *Three Sisters Rescued*. Type 311 tales seem to be the older and more widespread of these two. Again, the Grimm brothers provide an exemplary rendition. Their "Fitcher's Bird" (KHM 46) opens with a sorcerer abducting a young woman and installing her as a de facto bride in his house in the woods, where she is treated well, albeit with specific restrictions. First, she must carry an egg at all times, with its obvious symbolism of femininity, fertility, and fragility. (In other versions she is given an apple or a flower, items with similar symbolic possibilities.) Her second restriction is the prohibition against opening a specific door, although she is given a full set of keys to the house. Predictably, she opens the forbidden door, behind which she discovers an execution chamber filled with body parts and gore. Horrified, she drops the egg into the gore, staining it. When her husband returns, he knows from the stained egg that she has violated his prohibition, and he forthwith drags her back to the forbidden room and cuts off her head, then hacks her body to pieces. Next he abducts the dead woman's sister, and the entire process repeats itself.

The sorcerer then captures the youngest of the three sisters, giving her the same freedoms and restrictions. As soon as he is out of sight she sets the egg aside for safekeeping and enters the forbidden room. She puts her mutilated sisters back together and restores them to life. The man returns home and finds no evidence that the heroine has disobeyed him. Inexplicably, the former power structure of the household now reverses itself. Henceforth she gives the orders, and he must obey. She requires him to carry a basketful of goods to her impoverished parents. Hidden in the basket are the two resuscitated sisters. While he is struggling under this burden, she disguises herself as a giant bird (again the symbolism is obvious) and walks away from captivity. Later she sends her relatives back to the sorcerer's house, and they set it on fire, burning up the villain in the process.

In some versions of this story, for example, "How the Devil Married Three Sisters," from Italy (Crane 1885, no. 16), the malefactor is no less an evildoer than Satan himself, and the forbidden door is the entrance to hell. Here the item to be carried by the bride is a flower, which is singed when she opens the door to hell, and her husband then casts her into the fiery abyss. The episode repeats itself with a second sister, then threatens to do so with a third, but this last sister puts her flower in a safe place before opening the fateful door, thus enabling her to rescue her sisters and to effect her own escape.

Type 312 folktales, which also feature an execution chamber behind a forbidden door, differ from their Type 311 counterparts in that here the heroine does not magically restore her sisters to life and then bring about her own escape, but instead she is rescued in a heroic (but thoroughly nonmagical) attack by her brothers on her captor's castle. The stereotypical formulation of this tale is Perrault's "Blue Beard" (1697). Perrault's heroine is not abducted, but willingly marries the sinister-looking Blue Beard. She too is treated well, but prohibited from opening one specific door. Again, she violates the tabu and discovers a chamber filled with corpses and blood, then drops the key into the gore. No amount of scrubbing will remove the stain from the key, and when Blue Beard sees it he prepares to execute his disobedient wife. However, before he can carry out the murder, her brothers storm the castle and kill the wicked husband.

A male counterpart to the forbidden-chamber motifs discussed above can be found in the extremely widespread folktales of Type 303, known generically as *The Blood Brothers*. The concluding episode of these stories features a forbidden place that lures the hero to his apparent death, but in the end he is miraculously rescued by a younger brother. "The Castle of No Return" from Spain is a typical rendition (Thompson 1974, no. 5). Here the older of twin brothers leaves home, arranging a magic sign that will summon his brother should he need help. The adventurer kills a dragon and marries a princess, but his domestic bliss is short-lived. A castle in the distance rouses his curiosity. His wife warns him that this is the "castle of no return," but his restlessness drives him forth to investigate. In other versions of this tale, the forbidden place is a forest, a road, or a city. Once in the forbidden place, the young husband encounters a witch (possibly a symbol for the generic "other woman") who turns him to stone. At this point the prearranged signal alerts the younger twin of his brother's danger. He seeks out his petrified twin, overcomes the witch, and reverses the enchantment. Thus here, as in virtually all folktales featuring a forbidden-place motif, the transgression serves as a learning experience rather than as an irreversibly fatal act.

D.L. Ashliman

REFERENCES

Blecher, Lone Thygesen, and George Blecher. 1993. *Swedish Folktales and Legends*. New York: Pantheon Books.

Crane, Thomas Frederick. 1885. *Italian Popular Tales*. Boston: Houghton, Mifflin.

Grimm, Jacob and Wilhelm. 1980. *Kinder- und Hausmärchen [KHM]*. 3 vols. Ed. Heinz Rölleke. Stuttgart: Reclam. Based on the edition of 1857.

Perrault, Charles. 1697. *Histoires, ou contes du temps passé, avec des moralitez*. Paris: Claude Barbin.

Thompson, Stith. 1974. *One Hundred Favorite Folktales*. Bloomington: Indiana University Press.

❀ D ❀

Magic

Transformation

Motifs D0–D699

❀

The very broad category of transformation is one of the most fundamental motifs in storytelling. A basic impulse in telling and listening to stories is a desire for escape from the everyday world, and stories involving magical transformations, while providing imaginative escape for the audience, often involve literal escape of the characters, as when someone changes from one form into another to avoid being caught by a pursuer (D671, "Transformation flight"). In the case of voluntary transformation, the process is called shape-shifting; when one is transformed by another, it is called enchantment or bewitchment.

In tales the world over, people shape-shift into the opposite sex (D10), a higher or lower station in life (D20), a different race (D30), a different size (D55), into the likeness of another person (D40), into an older person (D56.1) or a child (D55.2.5). A handsome man can become hideous (D52.1) and an ugly man can become handsome (D52.2). In addition, people transform into various animals (D100–D199) and objects (D200–D299). The *Motif-Index* also covers animals transforming into people (D300–D399), other forms of transformation (D400–D499), the means of transformation (D500–D599), and miscellaneous transformation incidents (D600–D699).

Thompson points out that transformation and reincarnation are related. "A person or animal or object changes its form and appears in a new guise, and we call that transformation; but if the living being dies between the two stages, we have reincarnation. Yet in spite of this clear theoretical distinction, we have a great interchange of motifs between these two categories" (1977, 258).

In the *Motif-Index* Thompson lists a motif for "Enchanted person" (D5), remarking, "No real difference seems to exist between transformation and enchantment. Unlike a transformed person, however, a bewitched or enchanted person may retain his original physical form, but may be affected mentally or morally."

Examples of transformations in folklore and literature are so numerous that this essay can mention only a fraction of them.

The motif of a person being transformed by a witch or other malevolent figure into an animal is a familiar one to all readers of European fairy tales. In "The Frog Prince" (AT 440), a prince is changed into a frog; in "Snow White and Rose Red," a prince is changed into a bear; in "Beauty and the Beast" (AT 425C), a prince is changed into an unidentified animal. In the *Odyssey,* the enchantress Circe transforms Odysseus's men into pigs, but changes them back into men again when Odysseus requests it (Book 10).

In Islamic folklore, the jinn were shape-shifters, thought of as supernatural creatures with bodies of flame, often traveling about as whirlwinds (Irwin 1994, 203–204). An *Ifrit* (powerful jinni) who suspects the narrator of "The Second Kalandar's Tale" in the *Arabian Nights* of cuckolding him asks his victim to choose "into what shape I shall bewitch thee; wilt thou be a dog, or an ass or an ape?" The narrator declines to choose, and the Ifrit "set me down on a mountain, and taking a little dust, over which he muttered some magical words, sprinkled me therewith saying, 'Quit that shape and take thou the shape of an ape!'"

Popular characters in Hawaiian folklore are the *kupua,* nonhuman creatures who have extraordinary powers, including the ability to take human shape and "transform themselves, stretch or shrink themselves, fly through the air, take giant strides over the land and perform great feats of strength" (Poignant 1967, 53).

REPEATED TRANSFORMATION

In one of the most spectacular instances of transformation, a person rapidly transforms into one form after another (D610, "Repeated transformation"). This striking image occurs in the *Odyssey* when Proteus, the Old Man of the Sea, changes into a lion, a serpent, a leopard, a boar, running water, and a tree as Menelaos and his men hold him, demanding to know how they are to find their way home. The goddess Eidothea tells Menelaos:

> As soon as you see him [Proteus] lying down, you must all summon up your strength and courage and hold him fast there despite his struggles and his endeavours to elude you. He will seek to foil you by taking the shape of every creature that moves on earth, and of water and of portentous fire; but

you must hold him unflinchingly and you must press the harder. When at length he puts away all disguise and questions you in the shape he had when you saw him resting, then cease from your constraint; then, O king, let the ancient sage go free and ask him which of the gods is thwarting you and how you are to reach home again over the teeming ocean. (Book 4)

Another Old Man of the Sea in Greek mythology, Nereus, also shape-shifts when the hero Herakles holds him fast and asks him the way to the Garden of the Hesperides.

An example of repeated transformation is found in the British ballad "Tam Lin" (Child 39), in which Tam Lin, held captive by the fairies, enlists the aid of a mortal lover to disenchant him by holding him fast while he undergoes rapid repeated transformations (D757, "Disenchantment by holding enchanted person during successive transformations"). In version A, he tells the girl that he shall be turned into "an esk [newt], adder, bear, lion, red hot gaud [bead] of iron, and finally a burning gleed," which she must throw into the well, and he will regain his human form (Child 1965, 342). Child gives an example of repeated transformation in a Greek tale that was taken down from the recitation of an old Cretan peasant between 1820 and 1830, which echoes the myth of Thetis and Peleus. A peasant who falls in love with one of the Nereids asks an old woman how he can win her and is told he should seize her by the hair and hold on, without fear, while she metamorphoses into various shapes. The instant he touches her, she changes shape, becoming a dog, a snake, a camel, and fire. The repeated transformation motif also occurs in folktales known as *The Magician and His Pupil* (AT 325), originally from India and found in Europe as well as North Africa (Thompson 1977, 69).

Repeated transformation is sometimes combined with the transformation flight motif (D671); these examples involve a girl taking successive shapes in order to flee from a suitor, but the suitor changes shape to follow and he catches her. An early example appears in the Indian *Brihadaranyaka-Upanishad*. In the beginning is self, in the shape of a person. He says, "'I am,' but felt no pleasure. Wishing for a second being, he caused himself to separate into two pieces, male and female. He approached his mate, but she transformed herself into a cow, but he became a bull and united with her, thus cows were born. She became a mare, and he a stallion, and thus horses were born. She became a ewe, and he a ram, and thus sheep were born. In like manner he created everything that exists in pairs, down to the ants" (*Upanishads* 1897, vol. 2, Adhyaya 1, Brahmana 4, stanzas 1–4).

Child cites examples of songs with the transformation flight motif from France, Greece, Romania, Moravia, Poland, and Serbia (1965, 399–403). He gives the text for one version from Scotland, *The Twa Magicians* (no. 44), in

which the girl becomes a dove, and her suitor follows her as another dove;
then she becomes an eel and he becomes a trout; then she becomes a duck,
and he a drake; she becomes a hare, and he a hound; she becomes a mare, and
he a saddle. Finally she becomes a silken plaid, "And stretched upon a bed, /
And he became a green covering, / And gaind her maidenhead."

COMBAT TRANSFORMATION

Sometimes combatants will change form while engaged in battle (D615,
"Transformation combat. Fight between contestants who strive to outdo each
other in successive transformations"). A vivid example occurs in "The Second Kalandar's Tale" from the *Arabian Nights* in the battle between the *Ifrit*
and the king's daughter Sitt al-Husn. She undertakes to disenchant a young
man who has been transformed into an ape, by fighting the *Ifrit,* who first
changes into a lion.

> Then said he, "Take what thou hast brought on thyself;" and the lion opened
> his jaws and rushed upon her; but she was too quick for him; and, plucking
> a hair from her head, waved it in the air muttering over it the while; and the
> hair straightway became a trenchant sword-blade, wherewith she smote the
> lion and cut him in twain. Then the two halves flew away in air and the head
> changed to a scorpion and the Princess became a huge serpent and set upon
> the accursed scorpion, and the two fought, coiling and uncoiling, a stiff fight
> for an hour at least. Then the scorpion changed to a vulture and the serpent
> became an eagle which set upon the vulture, and hunted him for an hour's
> time, till he became a black tom-cat, which miauled and grinned and spat.
> Thereupon the eagle changed into a piebald wolf and these two battled in the
> palace for a long time, when the cat, seeing himself overcome, changed into
> a worm and crept into a huge red pomegranate, which lay beside the jetting
> fountain in the midst of the palace hall. Whereupon the pomegranate swelled
> to the size of a watermelon in air; and, falling upon the marble pavement of
> the palace, broke to pieces, and all the grains fell out and were scattered
> about till they covered the whole floor. Then the wolf shook himself and
> became a snow-white cock, which fell to picking up the grains purposing
> not to leave one; but by doom of destiny one seed rolled to the fountain-edge
> and there lay hid. The cock fell to crowing and clapping his wings and sign-
> ing to us with his beak as if to ask, "Are any grains left?" . . . Then he ran
> over all the floor till he saw the grain which had rolled to the fountain edge,
> and rushed eagerly to pick it up when behold, it sprang into the midst of the
> water and became a fish and dived to the bottom of the basin. Thereupon the
> cock changed to a big fish, and plunged in after the other, and the two disap-
> peared for a while and lo! We heard loud shrieks and cries of pain which
> made us tremble. After this the ifrit rose out of the water, and he was as a
> burning flame; casting fire and smoke from his mouth and eyes and nostrils.

And immediately the Princess likewise came forth from the basin and she was one live coal of flaming lowe [a blaze]; and these two, she and he, battled for the space of an hour, until their fires entirely compassed them about and their thick smoke filled the palace. (Burton 2001, 83–84)

An example from ancient Egyptian myth involves the son of Ra, Horus, who defends his father against plotters seeking to overthrow him. Horus changes into a winged sun disk and flies at the enemy, routing them.

The enemy were, however, not yet defeated, for they changed themselves into crocodiles and hippopotami and attacked the boat of Ra himself. Again, Horus and his followers routed them, harpooning them from the boat. Once more assuming the form of a winged sundisk and setting himself at the prow of the boat, Horus pursued the survivors throughout Upper and Lower Egypt inflicting terrible defeats upon them. (Ions 1968, 68).

When Herakles wrestles Akhelous, Akhelous shape-shifts into a bull, but Herakles knocks off one of his horns and defeats him. In the Finnish *Kalevala,* Lemminkainen changes into an eagle:

Thereupon young Lemminkainen,
Handsome Islander and hero,
Changing both his form and features,
Clad himself in other raiment,
Changing to another body,
Quick became a mighty eagle,
Soared aloft on wings of magic. (Rune 28)

THE TRANSFORMATIVE BEDTRICK

In the area of seduction, myth and folktale are filled with examples of gods and mortals changing shape in order to make love to the object of their desire (D658.2, "Transformation to husband's (lover's) form to seduce woman"; D659.7, "Transformation: wife to mistress. Transformed wife substitutes for husband's mistress"). Wendy Doniger explains what a "bedtrick" is: "You go to bed with someone you think you know, and when you wake up you discover that it was someone else—another man or another woman, or a man instead of a woman, or a woman instead of a man, or a god, or a snake, or a foreigner or alien, or a complete stranger, or your own wife or husband, or your mother or father" (2001, 1). An example from Hindu mythology involves the goddess Parvati, who transforms herself on occasion in order to trick her husband, the god Shiva. "Often she transforms herself into, or disguises herself as, a seductive foreign woman, a woman of low class, or an Outcaste woman" (2001, 17).

LOATHLY LADIES

The motif of the loathly lady (D732, "Man disenchants loathsome woman by embracing her") was popular in medieval Europe; a version was immortalized by Chaucer in "The Wife of Bath's Tale." A knight who is under penalty of death unless he finds the answer to the question "What do women most desire?" meets an old hag who says she knows the answer and will tell him, if he will marry her. He agrees; she gives him the answer: "to have mastery over their husbands." He reluctantly goes to bed with her, and she gives him a choice: to have her as she is, "a true, humble wife," or to have her young and fair and "take your aventure of the repair that shall be to your house by cause of me." The distracted knight tells her to choose and thus, by giving her mastery, breaks the spell she was under, and she transforms back to her original young and beautiful form. (In Chaucer's *The Wedding of Sir Gawain and Dame Ragnell* and in John Gower's *Tale of Florent,* the choice is different: whether to have a wife ugly by day and fair by night, or vice versa (D621.3, "Ugly by day, fair by night").

Other stories involve a woman being disenchanted from an animal form if a man will kiss her three times, each time when she is in the form of a different terrifying animal (D735.2, "The three kisses") (Thompson 1977, 259). There is also the motif of the loathly bridegroom (D733). Cross-referenced is the motif of magic beautification (D1860), the transformation of a plain person into one of great splendor, as in the Cinderella tales.

NORTH AMERICA AND AFRICA

Thompson lists the following transformation motifs occurring in North American tales: D531, "Transformation by putting on skin"; D641, "Transformation to reach difficult place"; D642, "Transformation (miscellaneous) to escape death"; D275, "Transformation to snake for easy traveling"; D642, "Transformation to feather to escape death"; D550, "Transformation by eating or drinking"; D611, "Protean beggar"; D615, "Transformation combat"; D651, "Transformation to kill enemies" (1929).

As for transformation motifs in Africa, Schmidt remarks:

> In European tales innocent persons frequently are transformed by evil forces into animals or objects, and one of the main topics is how heroes contrive their disenchantment. Enchantment and disenchantment are comparatively

rare in African magic tales. Every now and then heroes as well as their antagonists can change their form. When the young hunter flees from the supernatural elephants he turns himself into various animals and the warthog who wants to have a human wife becomes a handsome young man. But it is exceptional that like in European tales a wicked person enchants heroes or heroines. (2001, 266)

Schmidt goes on to speculate that compared to African tales, in which the heroes tend to be killed outright by their adversaries, enchantment in European tales may be a metaphor for death, with the heroes returning to life by being turned back into their human form, while the African must grow back whole after part of his body is put into a calabash (266–267).

LITERATURE

Metamorphoses, written by Ovid in the first century CE, is a long work whose many stories all involve some sort of transformation. There are numerous stories from Greek myth involving shape-shifting gods, or mortals being changed into objects such as trees or rocks or spiders. While the colorful tales from myth are entertaining, there seems to be a more serious side to the theme of metamorphosis. In the last section, Ovid relates the teachings of Pythagoras, who speaks of different and ongoing kinds of change in the world, including geological ("For my part, I would have thought that nothing lasts for long with the same appearance. So the ages changed from gold to iron, and so the fortunes of places have altered. I have seen myself what was once firm land, become the sea: I have seen earth made from the waters: and seashells lie far away from the ocean, and an ancient anchor has been found on a mountaintop") and political ("So we see times change, and these nations acquiring power and those declining") (Book XV).

Apuleius's *The Golden Ass* (ca. 150) also deals with metamorphosis; when Lucius, the protagonist, sees a witch transform herself into a bird by taking a potion, and he tries to copy her, but becomes a donkey instead. The book has other references to metamorphosis as Lucius strives to turn back into a man.

Transformation is the primary theme of Shakespeare's comedy *A Midsummer Night's Dream* (1595).

A statue comes to life in the Don Juan legends of European folklore, first appearing in literature in Tirso de Molina's 1616 play, *El Burlador de Sevilla.* The statue is that of the commander of Seville, which animates in order to punish his daughter's seducer. Molière's play *Don Juan, ou le Festin de Pierre* (1665) and Mozart's opera *Don Giovanni* (1787) also use this theme (D435.1.1, "Transformation: statue comes to life").

George Bernard Shaw wrote the play *Pygmalion* (1912) based on the Greek myth of the sculptor of the same name who falls in love with his statue, which is transformed to a living woman by the goddess Aphrodite in response to Pygmalion's prayers. The play, which features the transformation of a Cockney flower girl into a refined, polished young woman, was adapted as a musical, *My Fair Lady* (1956) by Frederick Loewe and Alan Jay Lerner.

In the coming-of-age novel or *Bildungsroman*—for example, Dickens's *David Copperfield*—we see young people undergoing the metamorphosis into adults. In Dickens's fairy tale–like *A Christmas Carol,* the elderly Scrooge is transformed from a selfish, unsociable miser into an engaged, caring member of society after being taken on fantastic journeys into the past, present, and future by a series of divine tutors.

As Edinger remarks, "Almost any long or complex work of literature deals with time and change, which are themes strongly associated with metamorphosis" (1988, 843). And Campbell states that in looking back on our lives we find in the end that we have experienced "a series of standard metamorphoses" common to all human beings (1968, 13).

Jane Garry

See also: Bewitching; Entrance into Girl's (Man's) Room (Bed) by Trick Flight (Magic).

REFERENCES

Burton, Sir Richard F. 2001. *The Arabian Nights. Tales from A Thousand and One Nights.* Trans. with preface and notes by Sir Richard F. Burton. New York: Modern Library.

Campbell, Joseph. 1968 [1949]. *The Hero with a Thousand Faces.* Princeton, NJ: Princeton University Press.

Child, Francis James. 1965 [1882–1898]. *The English and Scottish Popular Ballads.* New York: Dover. Orig. ed. Houghton Mifflin.

Doniger, Wendy. 2001. *The Bedtrick: Tales of Sex and Masquerade.* Chicago: University of Chicago Press.

Edinger, Harry. 1988. Metamorphosis. In *Dictionary of Literary Themes and Motifs.* Ed. Jean-Charles Seigneuret, 842–850. Westport, CT: Greenwood Press.

Ions, Veronica. 1968. *Egyptian Mythology.* Middlesex: Hamlyn.

Irwin, Robert. 1994. *The Arabian Nights: A Companion.* London: Allen Lane, Penguin Press.

Poignant, Roslyn. 1967. *Oceanic Mythology: The Myths of Polynesia, Micronesia, Melanesia, Australia.* London: Paul Hamlyn.

Schmidt, Sigrid. 2001. *Tricksters, Monsters, and Clever Girls: African Folktales—Texts and Discussions.* Köln: Rüdiger Köppe.

Thompson, Stith. 1929. *Tales of the North American Indians.* Cambridge: Harvard University Press.

———. 1977. *The Folktale.* Berkeley: University of California Press.

The Upanishads. 1897. Trans. Max Müller. New York: Christian Literature.

Flight (Magic)

Motifs D670–D674

❀

Carl Jung suggests that the flight motif is a kind of inversion of the heroic quest theme, although both lead to the same end: "Instead of the quest we have flight, which nonetheless appears to win the same reward as adventurers valiantly sought, for in the end the hero marries the king's daughter" (Jung 1968, 229). Marie-Louise von Franz sees the magic flight motif as representing an attempt to escape from the unconscious so as not to be consumed by it (von Franz 1982).

The magic flight motif (D670) usually appears in two main forms: the "Transformation flight" (D671) and the "Obstacle flight" (D672). In the transformation flight, those being pursued (usually by an ogre or other monsterlike figure) shape-shift into another form in order to avoid being caught. In the obstacle flight, the fleeing persons toss behind them objects that delay the chaser. AT 313, *The Girl as Helper in the Hero's Flight,* is a very common tale type that involves flight by the hero and his helper, during which they may both transform themselves and throw obstacles.

THE TRANSFORMATION FLIGHT

The transformation flight motif is extremely widespread. Thompson cites it in Irish, English, Greek, Jewish, Indian, Japanese, Philippine, Eskimo, North American, South American, and African collections. The motif has several subtypes. In the first (D671.0.1, "Fugitive transforms self to stone. Thrown to safety by pursuer"), the fleer transforms into stone in order to escape and is consequently thrown to safety by the chaser. It appears to be an African redaction and has been collected from the Zulu, Bechuana, Gan, and in Northern Rhodesia. In the second (D671.0.2, "Fugitive transformed by helper to escape detection"), a helper transforms the fugitive in order to ensure escape.

Ancient Greek mythology offers some of the earliest recorded instances of the transformation flight motif. Daphne's flight from Apollo represents a celebrated example of a transformation associated with the act of fleeing. When the nymph attempts to escape from the advances of the god Apollo (who became obsessed with Daphne after being struck by Cupid's arrow), she prays to her father, a minor god, to preserve her chastity. He responds by turning her into a laurel tree. Among others, the Roman Ovid's epic *Metamorphoses* (ca. 2–17 CE) and Giovanni Boccaccio's idyll *Il ninfale fiesolano* (fourteenth century) have included this episode. Ovid's work in particular includes a number of stories in which a male god pursues a female mortal (or one of lower status, at any rate). Other pursuit-transformation tales include the following: Syrinx seeks refuge in a river from the god Pan and turns into a reed, the nymph Arethusa is transformed into a fountain while trying to flee from the river god Alpheus, Picus changes into a bird while attempting to resist Circe's advances, and Artemis becomes a hind to evade Otus and Ephialtes (Daemmrich and Daemmrich 1987; Drabble 1995; Edinger 1988; Elkhadem 1981).

THE OBSTACLE FLIGHT

The obstacle flight (D672) is, according to Thompson, "one of the most widely distributed motifs in folk-lore" (1929, 333); indeed, it "is literally world-wide" (1977, 60). For example, the obstacle flight motif appears in Native American tradition "not only in European borrowings, but in tales . . . where it seems to be quite free from such influences. It is known both in Siberia and in South America, and the theory seems not unreasonable that it came to America from Asia a long time ago" (Thompson 1977, 349).

The story of Jason and Medea, an example of AT 313, *The Girl as Helper in the Hero's Flight,* includes a grisly kind of obstacle flight: the body parts of Medea's brother Apsyrtos are thrown into the sea. In an ancient Egyptian tale, "The Two Brothers," Anup is married, while his brother Batu is not. When Anup's wife accuses Batu of trying to seduce her (actually she tried to seduce him), Batu's cow warns him to flee. Batu calls for help to the sun god, who creates a stream full of crocodiles to impede Arup's pursuit (Thompson 1977). In a story from Halmahera, Indonesia, a giant's son and his companions, in fleeing from his father, throw salt behind them, which becomes an ocean that delays the giant, though finally he drinks it up. When he again comes after them, they throw ashes behind them, blinding the giant. He continues to pursue and they continue to throw a variety of objects (Dixon 1916, 236–237). In a Chinese tale called "The Bank of the Celestial Stream," a swan maiden tale (D361.1, "Swan Maiden"; F302.4.2, "Fairy comes into man's power when he steals her wings"), a version that is dated to the second century BCE tells of a fleeing wife who uses a golden hairpin to draw a line in the sky which becomes a long, celestial river (Eberhard 1965, 43–44).

Atalanta

Listed under Captives and Fugitives (Escapes and Pursuits) is Motif R231, "Obstacle flight—Atalanta type. Objects are thrown back which the pursuer stops to pick up while the fugitive escapes." In these cases, the objects become not obstacles but tempting distractions. In the myth of Atalanta, the person throwing the objects (Melanion) is not being pursued but is engaged in a footrace with the beautiful Atalanta. She has pledged to remain a virgin and will only marry the man who can defeat her in a race. When Melanion prays to Aphrodite to help him win the race, the goddess gives him three golden apples to throw during the race. Atalanta picks them up and losses time, enabling Melanion to win (H331.5.1.1, "Apple thrown in race with bride. Distracts girl's attention, and as she stops to pick it up, suitor passes her").

Other manifestations of the Atalanta-type obstacle flight occur in the arrow chain stories of Coastal and Plateau tribes of North America. For example, in a Tlingit tale ("The Arrow Chain"), a hero makes an arrow chain to ascend to heaven; he rescues his friend and leaves a magic spruce cone to answer for him while they escape. To delay the moon's pursuit, the hero tosses a piece of devil's club (a shrub) that turns into a big patch of devil's club, a rose bush becomes a huge thicket of roses, and a grindstone becomes a large cliff. In a Greenland Eskimo tale, "The Eagle and Whale Husbands," a girl who weds a whale is rescued by her brothers who arrive in a boat; during the flight she throws first her outer, then her inner, and finally her long jacket in the whale's path. These maneuvers detain him so that they safely reach the shore. In a Blackfoot Plains Indian tale, "The Bear-Woman," an enraged woman transforms herself into a bear and pursues several children who delay her first by sprinkling a handful of water, which becomes a great lake, and then by throwing a porcupine tail (a hairbrush), which turns into a large thicket (Thompson 1929, 1977).

THE GIRL AS HELPER IN THE HERO'S FLIGHT

The magic flight also figures in the plotline of several *Märchen*. As mentioned above, Type 313, *The Girl as Helper in the Hero's Flight,* typically begins with the hero somehow coming to the ogre's home, where he is assigned impossible tasks (such as planting, growing, and harvesting a vast crop of grapes that must be made into wine by dinnertime) that he is able to complete with the supernatural assistance of the ogre's daughter. It is the hero's and the daughter's decision to flee from the ogre that introduces episode III (The Flight). They may leave behind magic objects that answer for them and during their flight transform into various people and things in an effort to evade the ogre's pursuit (D671, "Transformation flight"), or they may toss behind them magic objects that become obstacles in the ogre's path (D672, "Obstacle flight") while they escape via a magic bridge. This folktale appears in the German Grimm and Russian Afanasiev folktale collections. It has been collected from a great many countries, but the most versions have been collected from Ireland—515 versions, according to Aarne and Thompson (1987). There are a number of subtypes of this tale, and the magic flight motifs figure in all but one (313J, *The Sorceress and the Sunshine Fairy,* in which the hero is saved by two figures, but apparently without means of a magic flight). Subtypes A, B, and C follow the same basic plot but with different introductory or closing episodes. In the other subtypes, the magic flight is followed by additional means of escape; for example, in 313D and E, the magic flight is followed by transformation into a bird—both these subtypes have a specifically Central-Eastern European distribution. In 313F and G, the characters escape in part due to the help of an animal; in 313F, *Escape by Help of Sheep,* a Polish variant, the character is aided by a sheep, while in 313G, *Three Brothers Search for Stolen Cow,* an Icelandic variant, an owl and the hair of a cow aid the escape. Type 313H, *Flight from the Witch,* includes both transformation and obstacle flights and appears in German and Russian tale collections (Aarne and Thompson 1987).

Thompson discusses the variety of ruses the fleeing couple can adopt in Type 313 to evade the ogre's pursuit: "He sometimes finds only a rose and a thornbush, or a priest and a church. . . . [Or] they may throw behind themselves magic objects such as a comb, a stone, or a flint which become obstacles—a forest, a mountain, or a fire" (Thompson 1977, 89). This tale is immensely widespread and sometimes it is difficult to discern when a tale is really of this type or a parallel, because stories involving a supernatural woman, impossible tasks, and magic flight can be found in many disparate parts of the world without necessarily being derived from European sources. For example, a similar tale is found in the *Ocean of Story,* a nineteenth-century translation of an eleventh century tale collection in Sanskrit. Thompson traces the appearance of this tale as unmistakably belonging to this type to the Renaissance, when it appeared in such collections as Giovanni Basile's *Il Pentamerone* (1634) (Aarne and Thompson 1987).

James Taggart sees the magic flight motif (in Spanish versions of Type

313) as expressing a woman's efforts to break away from her natal family and transfer her loyalty to her new husband. He writes: "Ursula [the heroine's name in this version] escapes from her father by casting away items that represent her former identity as a daughter as she develops her new identity as a wife. She leaves her spittle and casts away her comb, which becomes a thick fog blocking her father's pursuit. She changes form, becoming a hermitage, and she makes Joaquín [the hero's name in this version] the priest" (1990, 185).

THE MAGICIAN AND HIS PUPIL

In Type 325, *The Magician and His Pupil,* a father enrolls his son in a sorcerer's school where the son learns magic secretly, allowing him to flee under various guises or by recourse to magic obstacles. Episode II (Magic Flight) is composed solely of the two main magic flight motifs: D671, "Transformation flight," and D672, "Obstacle flight." This folktale appears in the German Grimm (KHM 68), Danish Grundtvig (number 56), and Russian Afanasiev tale collections and has been collected in the most versions from Irish (189 versions) and Lithuanian (72 versions) tale-tellers (Aarne and Thompson 1987). Thompson calls it one of the most popular of the European *Märchen* (1977).

OTHER TALES

Type 327, *The Children and the Ogre,* tells about children being abandoned by their parents in the woods. The children wander until they come to a witch's gingerbread house (the children may end up at the house of the ogre-figure through some other means as well). The witch then tries to fatten the children so they can be eaten. Somehow the children escape, whether it be by burning the witch in her own oven or by means of a magic flight. In episode III (Escape), the children may escape via a transformation flight (D671) or an obstacle flight (D672) (Aarne and Thompson 1987).

In Type 314, *The Youth Transformed to a Horse,* a youth flees from the devil on an enchanted horse and throws magic objects behind him to impede the devil's pursuit. Episode IV (Obstacle Flight) of this tale is composed of the obstacle flight motif (D672). Type 502, *The Wild Man,* is about a prince (aided by his faithful servant) who, by way of a special horse, wins the hand of a princess. Episode II (Escape from the Wild Man) may include the obstacle flight motif (D672).

Klipple lists a tale called "Rasoazanakomby et sa Mère" in a French collection of tales from Madagascar, in which a girl running away with a suitor scatters seeds along the way to detain her pursuing mother (1992, 415; Motif R231).

OTHER FLIGHT MOTIFS

In addition, Thompson lists three more magic flight motifs: "Reversed obstacle flight" (D673), in which magical obstacles appear to impede the fugitive's flight (from Arabic tradition); "Magic flight with the help of a he-goat" (D674), in which the animal saves a girl that has been pledged to the devil (from Lithuanian tradition); and "Sea turns to ice to permit flight" (D675, from Eskimo tradition). The reversed obstacle flight figures in stories from Plateau (Nez Percé, Wasco, and Twana), Northern Pacific (Tsimshian), Plains (Pawnee), and Southeast (Cherokee) Native American groups (Thompson 1929).

In general, the magic flight motif can be employed whenever a pursuer must be evaded or at least delayed. Among its many uses, it can serve as a boon offered by the gods in a time of trouble or provide a means of establishing one's own identity during a process of individuation.

Natalie M. Underberg

REFERENCES

Aarne, Antti, and Stith Thompson. 1987. *The Types of the Folktale.* Helsinki: Suomalainen Tiedeakatemia.

Daemmrich, Horst, and Ingrid Daemmrich. 1987. *Themes and Motifs in Western Literature.* Tübingen: Francke.

Dixon, Roland B. 1916. "Oceanic Mythology." Vol. 9 of *The Mythology of All Races.* Boston: Archaeological Institute of America.

Drabble, Margaret, ed. 1995. *The Oxford Companion to English Literature.* Oxford: Oxford University Press.

Eberhard, Wolfram. 1965. *Folktales of China.* Chicago: University of Chicago Press.

Edinger, Harry. 1988. "Metamorphoses." In *Dictionary of Literary Themes and Motifs,* ed. Jean-Charles Seigneuret, 842–850. New York: Greenwood Press.

Elkhadem, Saad. 1981. *The York Companion to Themes and Motifs of World Literature: Mythology, History, and Folklore.* Fredericton, NB: York Press.

Jung, C.G. 1968. [1955] *Aion: Researches into the Phenomenology of the Staff.* Princeton, NJ: Princeton University Press.

Klipple, May Augusta. 1992. *African Folktales with Foreign Analogues.* New York: Garland (Garland Folklore Library, 3). Reprint of 1938 dissertation.

Taggart, James. 1990. *Enchanted Maidens: Gender Relations in Spanish Folktales of Courtship and Marriage.* Princeton, NJ: Princeton University Press.

Thompson, Stith. 1929. *Tales of the North American Indians.* Cambridge: Harvard University Press.

———. 1977 [1946]. *The Folktale.* Berkeley: University of California Press. Orig. ed. New York: H.H. Rinehart and Winston.

von Franz, Marie-Louise. 1982. *An Introduction to the Interpretation of Fairy-tales.* Dallas: Spring Publications.

Magic Bodily Members:
Human Eye and Hand

Motif D990

❀

Throughout the ages, human bodily members have played significant roles in people's cosmological and magical belief systems and daily lives. Of the human magic bodily members, the eye and the hand have been among the most widely spread motifs to disclose opposing power. The hand and the eye are thought to be imbued with cosmic, magical, and psychic forces that can be transmitted to human beings and other entities. Their widespread popularity is based on common experience people share when they become sensitive to their vitality and energetic power. In some contemporary cultures, particularly Arab societies, the hand and the eye represent archetypal notions of grace (*baraka*) and envy *(hasad),* respectively (el-Aswad 2002).

   Both the hand and the eye play a critical role in people's everyday social interactions. They are vital parts of a person's body that physically and symbolically connect him or her with the outside world. Though they are used differently, the eye and the hand, through glance and touch respectively, are crucial means of communication. The hand, as associated with touch, is an important means for establishing good relationships with others. In both traditional and modern societies, people clasp, shake, or wave their hands to salute each other. The hand is also used to express helpfulness; to "extend, lend, or give a hand" is to offer assistance, applause, or appreciation. Similarly, in specific social contexts, the eye is used idiomatically to express love and affection—"to be in one's eye—endearment" (Z66.1) or to be the "apple of one's eye." Though eye contact is very important in the process of communication, cultures have been observed to differ in the signaling of communicative intent by eye gaze (Argyle 2000). People in contemporary Arab cultures, for example, tend to make very short eye contacts rather than gazing or staring at each other since the hidden feelings of jealousy one might have toward another person are reflected in the eye (el-Aswad 2002).

THE EYE

As an omnipotent and all-seeing power, the image of the human eye has been regarded in many archaic cultures as an archetypal representation of deity as well as of the entire cosmos. In ancient Egypt, for example, the universe was portrayed as having two eyes, the sun and the moon, whose power could never be challenged by malevolent forces (Hocart 1942, 388). There were multiple eyes in ancient Egypt, including the Eye of Atum, the Eye of Ra, the Eye of Horus, and the Great Goddess Eye. According to one version of the Egyptian creation myth, Atum sends his Eye, *udjat,* in search of Shu, the god of air, and Tefnet, the goddess of humidity. While the Eye is away, Atum replaces it with another, much brighter Eye. The first Eye, identified as a deity, is enraged at having been replaced and becomes a "vengeful and evil" Eye (A128.2.1.1). Ra appeases the eye by placing it on his brow in the form of the uraeus, the serpent, to govern the whole universe (Ions 1968, 27, 41). A variant of this myth tells that the Eye of Ra (a form of Atum) separates and, having its own mind, fails to return. Consequently, Shu and Tefnet are sent to bring it back. While resisting, the Eye sheds the tears from which humans are created. Humans, then, were born from the creator's eye (A1211.4).

The Egyptian Eye, also a symbol for the Great Goddess, is identified as the Daughter of the High God and referred to as the Mother Goddess since all of mankind had come from her tears. This Egyptian Eye is also a source of danger, as represented in the myth of Osiris when Isis kills the son of the king of Byblus by a glance of her eye. As a destructive force, the eye of the High God is depicted as the Great Goddess of the universe in her terrible aspect (Clark 1959, 220). In early Indian mythology, the mother goddess, Shahti, the source of all energy in the universe, appears in a variety of incarnations. As Sati and Parvati, she is loving and caring, but as the warrior goddesses Kali, she is most terrifying. As Kali, she "was portrayed as a black-skinned hag with pendulous breasts and a necklace of skulls or severed heads. Like Shiva, she had an all-seeing third eye in her forehead. Her male victims, made impotent without the goddess' activating energy, had no way of resisting her attack" (Kinsley 1982, 150). In Japanese mythology, Amaterasu, the sun goddess, is born from the left eye of the primeval being Izanagi (Lurker 2000, 19–20).

As a representation of justice, might and good, the Eye of Horus had a special meaning to the ancients. Called the *wadjet* or *udjat* eye, it was ultimately worn as an amulet for magical protection. Horus is a symbol of the divine spirit as victor, so his fighting power is believed to come from the eye of the High God. In Egyptian mythology, the right eye is the original eye of the creator and the striking power of the High God in all his manifestations. The Eye of Horus, which gives life to Osiris, is called the "Slaughterer of the enemies of Horus." Strictly it is Horus, the son of Isis and archetype of the pharaohs, who restores justice by overthrowing Set, the archetype of evil and injustice. Set "had red eyes and red hair, red being the colour of evil to the Egyptians" (Ions 1968, 63). During the fierce battle between Horus and his uncle Set, Horus castrates the latter, yet loses his left or weak eye (Ions 1968, 65), which becomes a symbol of sacrificial offering. It is interesting to note that in mythological contexts a "wound to the head or eye marks those who are sovereign (by virtue of royalty, sacrality, knowledge, magic, and/or righteousness) . . . and wounds to the lower body mark low-ranking persons, whose appetites for food or wealth may be perceived as ignoble or dangerous and who are reduced to positions of servile captivity" (Lincoln 1999, 131). One further wonders if this mythical event in which Horus loses his left eye provides a clue to the common belief among contemporary Egyptian folk that seeing a person with a blinded left eye, *a'awar shamal,* is a sign of *shu'm,* or a bad omen.

The eye has magical power that is simultaneously connected to psychological, natural, and cosmological spheres (el-Aswad 2002). The belief in the evil eye, the evil look, or the magic eye maintains that certain creatures, including men, animals, and other living (visible or invisible) entities, possess the magical power to cause negative, harmful, or bewitching effects by means of a glance (D2071, "evil eye"), including killing (D2071.2, "Person kills with evil eye").

The evil eye is a power that has driven man to invent and use magic. The evil eye, also called the envious eye, is the source of a sickness transmitted by someone who is envious, even without intention. As related to the negative effect of the evil eye, envy is defined as the wish for a blessing to be removed from someone without any gain or benefit to oneself, as opposed to the wish for a blessing to be transferred from the other to oneself. Elworthy (1895) suggests that the evil eye is a sort of "animal magnetism" representing one of the hereditary and instinctive convictions of mankind.

It is common for people of the Middle East and other parts of the world to hang small plates and other round objects on the doors of their houses to distract the attention of envious people and prevent the negative effect of their eye. By distracting the glancer's attention, a person averts the evil eye (D2071.1.2.1). Round or eye-shaped objects, including the Arabic number five, *khamsah* (connoting the five fingers of the hand), are taken to be symbols of good luck, protection, and group solidarity. In some cultures attuned to the evil eye belief, a person who praises a child immediately reduces the threat by touching or spitting on the child or uttering some phrases for the purpose of protection. The evil eye is averted by spitting (D207.1.1). In other cultures, children taken to public places are smeared with dirt. Sometimes the mother says something negative about her child to avert any possibility of envy. On happy occasions, such as weddings, salt is thrown into the air or on the gathering to avert the evil eye. Salt also acts as a guard against the evil eye (D2071.1.4.3). In contemporary rural Egypt, the presence of the magical and psychic force of the malicious self is mediated through the indexicality of the eye, *al-'ain,* or the inhaled breath of air or gasp, *shahqa.* Women and children are believed to be vulnerable to the other's dangerous self. To avoid the effect of the wicked self or the envious person, *al-hasud,* women deliberately cover themselves and their children or neglect their children's appearance.

The concept of the evil eye reflects competition and conflict among members of a society. Usually those who are socially privileged are the main targets of the evil eye. Believing oneself to be the target of the evil eye, therefore, promotes self-esteem. Through an envious eye, however, a person can destroy himself as well as his assets as the returning glance of the evil eye blights the original glancer (D2071.1.5). In the Middle Eastern context, people use the simile "money (assets) is not to be envied by anybody but its owners." Though the notion of envy reflects unhealthy relationships between members of the community, the envious eye as a negative psychic force goes beyond the social reality and imposes itself as an existing phenomenon. In contemporary rural Egyptian culture, two types of the eye are associated with states of both the cosmos and the person. On the one hand, there is the cool eye, *'ain barda,* which is harmless, and, on the other, there is the hot eye, *'ain harra,* which is evil or destructive, *'ain radiyya.* To display good intentions when admiring someone, a person utters "may my eye be cool and cause you no harm," *'ainy 'alaik barda.* The envious eye is depicted as either the blue eye or the yellow eye, *'ain safrah.* In the Arab culture, the color yellow denotes sickness, weakness, dryness, and impurity and is colloquially used to mean excrement (el-Aswad 2002).

Blue symbolizes protection and is cosmologically associated with the heavens. In this connection, people in various parts of the world use blue amulets to protect themselves and their property from the envious eye. Blue, then, is used as a guard against the evil eye (D2071.1.4.1§, "Blue as guard against evil eye"). In addition to blue bead eye-charms, numerous other eye-design and hand-design amulets are used to repel the evil eye and counteract the malevolent, invisible psychic forces dispersed in the cosmos. The varied combinations of the iconographic elements include the eye, the hand, or both, such as the eye-in-the-hand. The eye is believed to watch not only the visible world as defined by culture, but also the invisible world that exists beyond human control. For example, the "all-seeing eye" located above the pyramid shown on the reverse side of the U.S. one-dollar bill suggests the importance of divine guidance in American society. It also means "the eye of God" (Campbell with Moyers 1988, 25).

THE HAND

Parts or products of the human body can cure disease (D1500). Miracles of physical healing by the hand of messiah are mentioned in the Bible. The hand is also seen an embodied symbol of the benevolent, invisible (cosmic-heavenly) force, displaying itself through touch. The hand is a symbol of strength and power, and a picture of it has been regarded as a representation of God, or the Invisible Hand (H986). As a symbol of unseen protective power and blessing, the hand is used as an amulet for warding off the envious eye. The hand charm, known as *al-kaff* or the hand of Fatima (daughter of the prophet Muhammad), is used among Arabs for protective purposes. Pictures, paintings, and drawings of the hand are made by villagers to protect themselves and their property from the envious eye.

In religious ceremonies, people seek above all to communicate with sacred powers in order to maintain and increase connection with them. Only the right hand, as imbued with grace, is fit for these beneficial relations since it participates in the nature of things and beings on which the rites are to act. The magic power of the right hand is used for good (D996.0.1.1§); thus sacred offerings are presented to the gods with the right hand. It is the right hand that receives favors from heaven and that transmits them in benediction (Hertz 1973, 15). In Arab culture, it is common to see a blessed man using his right hand to rub the bodies of sick people in order to heal them. The right hand here represents the blessed person as a whole and is believed to have a curative effect on the sick (el-Aswad 2002). For Muslims, the healing hand of the pious people of *baraka* (blessing) is called the white hand (recounting the miracle of the prophet Moses when he displayed his hand, which had turned as white as light, when he removed it from his garment), signifying purity, goodness, and health. The saint's hand is said to illuminate darkness (D1478.1). While the right hand is associated with ideas of sacred power, purity, and benevolence, the left hand is associated with that which is profane, impure, and malevolent. "The preponderance of the right hand is obligatory, imposed by coercion, and guaranteed by sanctions; contrarily, a veritable prohibition weighs on the left hand and paralyzes it" (Hertz 1973, 6–12).

If the left hand is despised and humiliated in the world of the gods and of the living, it has its domain where it commands and from which the right hand is excluded, but this is a dark and ill-famed region (D996.0.2.1§, "Magic power of left hand for evil"). The power of the left hand is always somewhat occult and illegitimate; it inspires terror and revulsion. Thus the belief in a profound disparity between the two hands sometimes goes so far as to produce a visible bodily asymmetry. Even if it is not betrayed by its appearance, the hand of sorcery is always the cursed hand.

Metaphorically, the hand is classified according to its color (white or black), its position as related to the body (right or left), its condition (open or closed), and its moral connotation (blessing or cursing). In southern India, Shiva is portrayed as Nataraja, King of the Dance, with multiple hands. The upper left hand holds a flame, symbol of creative dissolution and purgation. The upper right holds a drum, because the world is a manifestation of rhythm and vibration. The lower left hand points to the raised left foot, which, seeming to float above the ground, represents liberation. The lower right hand is in the gesture of *abhaya,* "Fear not." The right foot presses down upon the demon (Watts 1963, 245–246).

There is contagious magic by touch (D1789§). The Nubas of eastern Africa believe that they would die if they enter the house of their priestly king. Also, among the Cazembes of Angola, the king is regarded as so holy that no one can touch him without being killed by the magical power pervading the king's sacred person. The common practice people have devised to rescue the person who violates this tabu relies on a ritualistic manipulation of the hands: the sinner, kneeling down before the king, "touches the back of the royal hand with the back of his own, then snaps his fingers; afterwards he lays the palm of his hand on the palm of king's hand, then snaps his fingers again. This ceremony is repeated four or five times, and averts the immanent danger of death" (Frazer 1951, 235–236).

In Egypt, devotees visiting the shrines of saints "pass their hands over the rails which enclose the tomb, then stroke themselves and their children as if they were collecting and dispensing an emanation from the saint himself. In the same way the ancient are to be seen in the bas-reliefs transmitting with their hands the vital principle represented by the *'ankh* symbol" (Hocart 1942, 370; italics in original). Also, in the Bible, the raising of the hand to a god is regarded as an act of worship (Budge 1978, 467).

The belief in the mystical effectiveness of the hand and the evil eye is not confined to traditional people. Literate people participate in this belief, yet are unable to explain how bodily members exercise their magical power and produce fortune or misfortune.

ELITE LITERATURE

Direct and indirect references and allusions to magic bodily members are found throughout literature, including the works of Francis Bacon, William Shakespeare, and Edward Bulwer-Lytton. Shakespeare recognized the powerful image of the eye. Using the Egyptian symbol of the eye, he conjures up the image of the dawning sun:

> Full many a glorious morning have I seen
> Flatter the mountain tops with sovereign eye.
> (quoted in Clark 1959, 220).

In literature, the eye is depicted as the source of vision for poets and creative writers. The eye, Bettina Knapp points out,

> is not to be compared with the brash intellectual/rational illumination of earthly humans. Rather, it may be likened to Siva's divine eye or the eye depicted on sarcophagi in ancient Egypt: the eye within which a blackened pupil stares into the distance—sees the human in all of his conditions and states—follows him around the universe. The eye is the gateway leading to the source—the All: the omniscient and omnipotent essence of divine existence. (1989, 179)

In one of his novels, Ignazio Silone uses belief in the evil eye to account for an Italian peasant's worldview. Anthony Mancini makes it the focal point of a detective story (Georges 1998, 194).

In the literature of contemporary interactive computer software, one finds the healing hand and Holy Vision of the Paladin and the powerful and all-seeing Eye of Kilrogg among other features related to bodily members, whether attached to or detached from the body. For example, the "Ogre-Mage creates a free-floating apparition in the form of a disembodied Eye that he can then direct through the air to look down upon enemy forces and encampments . . . [t]his ever vigilant eye transmits its view to the caster giving him the knowledge of both the lands it wanders and those creatures who live there" (*War Craft II* 1999, 76).

el-Sayed el-Aswad

REFERENCES

Argyle, Michael. 2000. "The Laws of Looking." In *Conformity and Conflict: Readings in Cultural Anthropology,* ed. James Spradley and David W. McCurdy, 61–69. Needham Heights, MA: Allyn and Bacon.

Budge, E.A. Wallis. 1978. *Amulets and Superstitions.* New York: Dover.

Campbell, Joseph with Bill Moyers. 1988. *The Power of Myth.* New York: Doubleday.

Clark, R.T. Rundle. 1959. *Myth and Symbol in Ancient Egypt.* London: Thomas and Hudson.

el-Aswad, el-Sayed. 2002. *Religion and Folk Cosmology: Scenarios of the Visible and Invisible in Rural Egypt.* Westport, CT: Praeger.

El-Shamy, Hasan M. 1995. *Folk Traditions of the Arab World: A Guide to Motif Classification.* 2 vols. Bloomington: Indiana University Press.

Elworthy, Frederick Thomas. 1895. *The Evil Eye: An Account of This Ancient and Widespread Superstition.* London: J. Murray.

Frazer, James George. 1951 [1911–1915]. *The Golden Bough: Studies in Myth and Religion.* New York: Macmillan.

Georges, Robert A. 1998. "Evil Eye." In *Encyclopedia of Folklore and Literature,* ed. Mary Ellen Brown and Bruce A. Rosenberg, 193–194, Santa Barbara, CA: ABC-CLIO.

Hertz, Robert. 1973. "The Pre-eminence of the Right Hand: A Study in Religious Polarity." In *Right and Left: Essays on Dual Symbolic Classification,* ed. by Rodney Needham, 3–31. Chicago: University Chicago Press.

Hocart, A.M. 1942. "The Legacy to Modern Egypt." In *The Legacy of Egypt,* ed. A.M. Hocart, 369–469. London: Oxford University Press.

Ions, Veronica. 1968. *Egyptian Mythology.* Middlesex: Hamlyn.

Jung, Carl G. 1964. "Approaching the Unconscious." In *Man and His Symbols,* ed. Carl Jung, M.L. von Franz, Joseph. Henderson, Jolande Jacobi, and Aniela Jaffe, 18–103. Garden City, NY: Doubleday.

Kinsley, David R. 1982. *Hinduism: A Cultural Perspective.* Englewood Cliffs, NJ: Prentice Hall.

Knapp, Bettina L. 1989. *A Jungian Approach to Literature.* Carbondale: Southern Illinois University.

Lincoln, Bruce. 1999. *Theorizing Myth: Narrative, Ideology, and Scholarship.* Chicago: Chicago University Press.

Lurker, Manfred. 2000. *Dictionary of Gods and Goddesses, Devils and Demons.* Trans. G.L. Campbell. London: Routledge and Kegan.

War Craft II: Battle.net Edition. 1999. Irvine, CA: Blizzard Entertainment.

Watts, Alan W. 1963. *The Two Hands of God: The Myths of Polarity.* New York: George Braziller.

Soothsayer (Diviner, Oracle, Etc.)

Motif D1712

❀

Soothsayers (prophets, fortune-tellers, etc.) are generally involved in foretelling the future or determining answers to questions through supernatural means. The word *prophet* comes from the Greek, meaning "speaker for." Prophets thus, in this sense, are people who speak for another, usually the gods, and reveal their will (Fiske 1911; Weber 1999). An oracle, especially in the ancient Greek sense, is "an answer given by a god to a question asked by a human. The answers were delivered through a priest or priestess, or by means of signs and dreams. The shrines in which these answers were delivered were also known as oracles" (Elkhadem 1981, 156).

An archetypal connection to the diviner can be seen in the figure of the alchemist. In medieval Europe, the alchemist stood as a symbol for the productive melding of science and mysticism. Nathan Cervo traces the provenience of the alchemist's practice: "The alchemists of the Middle Ages learned their art from the Arabs in Spain and southern Italy, who in turn had adopted it from the Greeks, who again had developed it on Egyptian soil in the fourth century BCE" (Cervo 1988, 19). Another archetypal figure related to the diviner is the divine tutor. Joseph Alfred identifies the figure of the divine tutor as a "divine or superhuman being who undertakes to educate a youth—usually a young man—to prepare him for some purpose or role" (Alfred 1988, 395). Biblical prophets offer a good example; they "relate to God as pupils receiving instruction for the people. . . . Their tutors—angels or other marvelous figures—explain to them the meaning of visions or experiences so that their instruction becomes ordered and unified" (Alfred 1988, 397).

Soothsayers and diviners, however, can also take on the archetypal connotations of the scapegoat and become victims of the concept of killing the messenger. Weidhorn explains: "The bearer of bad tidings is in some irrational, primitive way associated with the evil events he tells about and is punished . . . as if he has become the scapegoat and as if 'killing the messenger' will somehow make the adverse events vanish as well" (Weidhorn 1988, 1109). Thus, a prophet, a figure at times not at the center of social life and who sometimes delivers prophecies that will not be well received, can be in danger of becoming a scapegoat.

Soothsayers, diviners, and oracles play an important role in early mythology. The blind Tiresias (D1712.2, "Blind man as soothsayer"), a Theban soothsayer, is himself father of the female Manto, who in turn is mother of the prophetic Mopsus. Tiresias prophesies perhaps most famously in Sophocles' tragedy *Oedipus Rex* (AT Type 931) (ca. 428 BCE). Cassandra is another prominent prophet in Greek antiquity, with the dubious distinction of having her pronouncements perpetually disregarded (M301.01, "Prophet destined never to be believed.") The ten Sibyls are mythic female prophets in Greco-Roman mythology. Perhaps the best known is the Cumanean Sibyl, who inscribes her predictions on leaves and deposits them at the entrance of her dwelling to be consulted before being blown away by the wind (M301.21) The Sibyls appear in Vergil's *Aeneid* and Ovid's *Metamorphoses* (Elkhadem 1981). The ancient Sibylline tradition eventually found expression in a parallel Judeo-Christian one: the *Sybylline Oracles.* Their prophecies were incorporated into the works of the early church fathers Theophilus of Antioch and Clement of Alexandria and, later, Saint Augustine. Later in European history, elements of the *Sybylline Oracles* reappeared in popular texts such as the fourteenth-century *Erlösung* and the sixteenth-century *Luzerner Antichristspiel* by Zacharias Bletz (Frey 1998).

Among the most famous oracles for contemporary readers are those in Sophocles' *Oedipus Rex*. The first tells Laius that his newborn son Oedipus will one day kill him. Later in the story, Oedipus himself receives a prophecy from the Delphic oracle that he will murder his father and marry his own mother. In good Greek fashion, of course, he flees from what he believes to be his natal parents only to unwittingly kill his true father and marry his birth mother upon arrival in Thebes (M343, "Parricide prophecy"; M344, "Mother-incest prophecy"; M370.1, "Prophecy of death fulfilled") (Elkhadem 1981).

The ancient Israelite priests, meanwhile, were diviners; later on they came to adopt a role more like that of a teacher and received the title *prophets*. Samuel, the ancient prophet who appointed King Saul as leader, was, according to Fiske (1911), originally more a diviner or seer in the old sense than a teacher in the more recent sense, but came to be transformed in later texts into the newer incarnation of Israelite prophet. The early Israelite diviner-priests, called *Levis,* cast predictions by consulting an ephod featuring the image of a calf or bull. Like later prophets, too, they also credited prophecies to predictions received from angels (M301.10, "Angels as prophet") (Fiske 1911). Their ancient oracles produced answers through the use of dice (to elicit "yes" or "no" answers) as well as through inducement of ecstatic states on the part of the diviner. M.F.C. Bourdillon writes: "We find references to the use of oracles soon after the Hebrews settled in Palestine in the twelfth to eleventh centuries BCE" (Bourdillon 1977, 128). But the later prophets condemned these acts, and the book of Deuteronomy explicitly forbids divination and soothsaying (Bourdillon 1977).

The sayings of the prophets thus became the more important type of oracle toward the end of the sixth century (M301.7, "Biblical worthy as prophet"). Bourdillon notes:

> Rather than relying for their position on any particular events, wonders, or signs, the greater prophets and their schools appeared to acquire recognition from the stand they took in the history of the people; they were steadfastly loyal to the cult of Yaweh and the moral standards associated with it. . . . Prophets are frequently cited as denouncing the popular adoration of foreign cults, especially in the early days of the fertility cult of Baal. (Bourdillon 1977, 131)

The case of Elijah demonstrates the way that the pronouncements of prophets served a function of regulating social behavior. He foretold the destruction of King Ahab's line (in the first book of Kings), including that of his successor when he committed idolatry through use of a foreign oracle (in the second book of Kings) (M342, "Prophecy of downfall of kingdom") (Bourdillon 1977).

In addition, hagiography provides a rich source for the pronouncements of prophecies in early Christianity (M301.5, "Saints [holy men] as prophets," and M364, "Various prophecies connected with saints [or holy men]"). In *Prophecies, Miracles and Visions of St. Columba (Columcille),* by the sixth-century Saint Adamnan, the various prophecies of the Irish saint are described. For example, Adamnan relates the legend of how Saint Columba supposedly made a posthumous appearance to the Saxon king Oswald to foretell his triumph over the enemy (M356.1, "Prophecies concerning outcome of war," and M356.1.2, "Prophecies concerning heroes in battle") (Adamnan 1895; Thompson 1955–1958).

One of the most famous diviner-magicians in European legendry is Merlin (related to Motifs D1712.01, "Astrologer-Magician," and M301.3, "Druids as prophet"). The wizard plays a seminal, albeit background, role in the Arthurian legend cycle, in which he uses his gift of foretelling the future to assist King Arthur in his battles. Merlin's legend makes an early appearance in *Nennius's Historia Britonum* (ca. 800) (Elkhadem 1981). Horst and Ingrid Daemmrich trace the introduction of Merlin as prophet-magician in literature to Geoffrey of Monmouth's *Prophetia Merlini* (1134), offering this description of the scene in which his career is inaugurated: "Merlin is consulted by Aurelius, king of the Britons, in order to solve the problem of the tower whose construction is mysteriously disturbed each night. His revelation of the existence of two dragons beneath the tower and his explanation of their allegorical meaning for the Britons launched the motif of Merlin as prophet-consultant" (Daemmrich and Daemmrich 1987, 179). Throughout the Middle Ages and into the Renaissance, Merlin appears as a prophet-consultant regarding battles and political matters. For example, motifs M356.5, "Prophecy: end of Round Table for Arthur's knights," and M361.1, "Prophecy: certain hero to achieve Holy Grail," appear in Thomas Malory's 1485 work *Morte d'Arthur*. In some versions of his legend, Merlin is reputed to be the son of the devil, but born to a human mother. While having inherited some of his father's magical abilities such as that of transformation, he uses his power for good, especially as adviser to King Arthur. Later, in Sir Walter Scott's *Minstrelsy of the Scottish Border* (1802–1803), Merlin makes the leap into Scottish legendry as a forest-dwelling prophet (Daemmrich and Daemmrich 1987; Thompson 1955–1958).

In sixteenth- and seventeenth-century Europe, soothsayers like astrologers and alchemists were considered scientists, relying on visions and the movements of the stars to make their predictions. Paracelsus and his teacher Tritemius were examples of this type of soothsayer (D1712.01, "Astrologer-Magician"). Also at this time, chapbooks and almanacs provided popular prophecies and astrological readings. For example, the prophecies of Nostradamus remain widely known even today. Weber explains that prophecy as a pseudo-scientific practice was widely accepted in the seventeenth century and in fact continued as a respectable activity into the nineteenth century (Weber 1999). Somewhat similarly, the Welsh believed in so-called inspired people, or *Awenyddion*. They employed spirit possession to deliver cryptic responses to questions that were then interpreted for clients by a third party (Lewes 1911).

In the Scottish Highlands there were reputed to exist certain individuals believed to possess "second sight." The so-called Warlock of the Glen, for example, divined by peering through a hole in a round white stone (Motif D1712.1, "Soothsayer at work by various means of divination"). One of his pronouncements so displeased a powerful member of the Mackenzie clan that she had him hanged for it (a particularly dramatic example of the prophet as scapegoat). Sir Walter Scott, who was steeped in the manners and customs of Scotland and used them for dramatic effect in his fiction, has a character foretell a murder through second sight in his story "The Two Drovers" (1827). An old woman sees her nephew's hand and dirk (a short knife) covered with blood and begs him not to take the weapon on the journey he is about to undertake. He refuses to leave the knife, but compromises by giving it to a comrade to hold, but later takes it back, with tragic consequences (D1825.1, "Second sight. Power to see future happenings"). The motif of second sight appears also in Scottish, Irish, Icelandic, Indian, and North American folklore.

In the genre of European *Märchen,* AT Type 516, *Faithful John,* contains Motif M302.1, "Prophesying through knowledge of animal languages." The story tells of a prince who falls in love with a princess by seeing her picture or dreaming about her. His faithful servant overhears a conversation of birds (or ghosts) foretelling the perils to come to the newlyweds and tries to prevent them (M352, "Prophecy of particular perils to prince on wedding journey"). This folktale appears in a number of tale collections, such as Giambattista Basile's *Il Pentamerone* (1634–1336) and the Grimms' *Kinder- und Hausmärchen* (KHM 6), and seems to have been especially popular in Ireland (Thompson 1977).

Outside of Indo-European tradition, Mayan priest-prophets were called *chilam,* meaning "mouthpiece" or "interpreter of gods" (Peterson 1990, 16). These prophets relied on books and visions induced by drugs such as peyote and hallucinogenic mushrooms to produce their prophecies, which frequently played a role in the political sphere. The prophet would lie on his back at home and receive his prophecies from a god or spirit believed to be perched on his roof (related to Motif M301.11, "Spirit as prophet"). Chilam Balam was a famous priest-prophet among the ancient Mayans who lived at the end of the fifteenth and the start of the sixteenth centuries. His final prediction refers to the Itzas, a Mayan group, and has traditionally been interpreted as foretelling the arrival of the Europeans. Among the ancient Aztecs, the astrologer-priests conducted the divining (D1712.01, "Astrologer-Magician"). One of their main functions was to determine if a child was born on an auspicious or an inauspicious date. To do this, they consulted the *tonalamatl,* or "book of the days and destinies" (Peterson 1990, 39).

In Arab Islamic tradition, it is believed that God has placed "the Veil" between the heavenly and earthly realms. Because humans and jinn (popularly known as "genies" in European and United States culture) are generally limited to the "other side" of this Veil, they are believed to be blocked from the "boon of clairvoyance." But certain humans, including prophets and saints, *can* divine in Islamic cosmology (M301.5, "Saints (holy men) as prophets," and M301.7, "Biblical worthy as prophet"). These people can be granted clairvoyance by God on the basis of their piety, and they therefore are able to read from the "tablet of destiny" (which is believed to lie on the other side of "the Veil"). Prophets are characterized as possessing the power of prophecy and the power of miracles to validate their prophecies. Solomon, for example, is believed to command the jinn and the wind, as well as having the power to understand the language of animals (M302.1, "Prophesying through knowledge of animal languages"). In addition, prophets and certain saints are said to know the time and place of their own deaths (M341.0.6§, "Person knows place of own death"). While jinn cannot divine in the sense of foretelling the future, they can be called on to report on the past and present. Jinn, then, can determine the causes of past events and diagnose illnesses. While in an Islamic worldview the power of prophecy is believed to come from God, in folk Islam there are also believed to be those who conduct sacrilegious forms of divination. These practitioners are called *sahir* and are distinguished from *shaikh* (or shamans) who practice divination by sacred means. Thus, it is the source from which diviners obtain their power that marks them as "good" or "bad" (El-Shamy 1995).

In many societies, such as the Shona of Africa and the Berbers of Morocco, diviners play a role in politics, healing, and even cursing. But they often have to rely on their ability to keep their prophecies in line with the popular will. In other words, the "credibility of oracles depends on their apparent wisdom, and apparent wisdom is defined by the beliefs and opinions of those to whom it must appear as wisdom" (Bourdillon 1977, 126). Soothsayers, diviners, and oracles are with us yet today. Farmer's almanacs and newspaper horoscopes can still be consulted. Prophets have continued to exert an influence on custom and belief well into the modern age. One example is the case of Wovoka, a famous (or infamous) Native American prophet who claimed to have experienced a vision from God foretelling the disappearance of the whites. In order to keep up the pretense, however, he became increasingly corrupt and ultimately incited the so-called Last Indian War. In addition, the American prophet Joseph Smith believed that he received a visit from the Angel of God in 1823 and subsequently founded the Mormon Church (Peterson 1990).

Natalie M. Underberg

REFERENCES

Adamnan, Saint 1895. *Prophecies, Miracles and Visions of St. Columba (Columcille)*. London: Henry Frowde.

Alfred, Joseph. 1988. "Divine Tutor." In *Dictionary of Literary Themes and Motifs*, ed. Jean-Charles Seigneuret, 395–400. Westport, CT: Greenwood.

Bourdillon, M.F.C. 1977. "Oracles and Politics in Ancient Israel." *Man* 12: 124–140.

Cervo, Nathan. 1988. "Alchemy." In *Dictionary of Literary Themes and Motifs*, ed. Jean-Charles Seigneuret, 18–31. Westport, CT: Greenwood.

Daemmrich, Horst, and Ingrid Daemmrich. 1987. *Themes and Motifs in Western Literature*. Tübingen: Francke.

Elkhadem, Saad. 1981. *The York Companion to Themes and Motifs of World Literature: Mythology, History, and Folklore*. Fredericton, NB: York Press.

El-Shamy, Hasan. 1995. *Folk Traditions of the Arab World: A Guide to Motif Classification.* 2 vols. Bloomington: Indiana University Press.

Fiske, Amos. 1911. *The Great Epic of Israel: The Web of Myth, Legend, History, Law, Oracle, Wisdom and Poetry of the Ancient Hebrews.* New York: Sturgis and Walton.

Frey, Winifred. 1998. "Sibylla Led Astray: Sibyls in Medieval Literature." In *Demons: Mediators Between This World and the Other: Essays on Demonic Beings from the Middle Ages to the Present*, ed. Ruth Petzoldt and Paul Neubauer, 51–64. Frankfurt am Main: P. Lang.

Lewes, Mary. 1911. *Stranger Than Fiction: Being Tales from the Byways of Ghosts and Folklore.* London: W. Rider and Son.

Peterson, Scott. 1990. *Native American Prophecies.* New York: Paragon House.

———. 1997. *Religion Among the Folk in Egypt: A Cognitive Structural Analysis of the Supernatural Belief-Practice System in the Contemporary Egyptian Arab Folk Cultures.* Bloomington: Indiana University Press.

———. 1977. *The Folktale.* Berkeley: University of California Press.

Weber, Eugen. 1999. *Apocalypses: Prophecies, Cults, and Millennial Beliefs Through the Ages.* Cambridge, MA: Harvard University Press.

Weidhorn, Manfred. 1988. "Scapegoat." In *Dictionary of Literary Themes and Motifs*, ed. Jean-Charles Seigneuret, 1109–1117. Westport, CT: Greenwood.

Magic Invulnerability

Motif D1840

❀

MAGIC STRENGTH

People around the word, from ancient times to the era of mass culture that produced Superman, ascribe magic invulnerability to their heroes. This supernatural protection is often paired with superhuman strength (F610, "Remarkably strong man"). Folktales of types AT 590 (*The Prince and the Armbands*) and 650A (*Strong John*) offer many examples. In the Norwegian folktale "The Blue Belt" (Asbjørnsen and Moe 1983, 2:196–210; AT 590), the hero receives extraordinary strength by means of a magic belt (D1344, "Magic object gives invulnerability"), by which he also is protected from stones rolled on him by a troll, attacks by lions, and more. In the Grimms' "The Young Giant" (KHM 90; AT 650A), a small boy, nursed on a male giant's milk, becomes superhumanly strong, and he uses his strength both offensively and defensively. In one episode he is sent into a well to do some work, and his overseer attempts to kill him by dropping a millstone on him. The boy at the bottom shouts back, "Shoo the chickens away from the well. They are scratching sand into my eyes." He then emerges wearing the would-be fatal millstone around his neck like a collar. In a Swiss variant, "The Hairy Boy" (Sutermeister 1873, no. 52), the title hero is attacked by 500 soldiers with firearms, but "the hairy boy calmly plucks the bullets from his body and throws them back at the soldiers, killing them all." And finally, in the Irish folktale "Adventures of Gilla na Chreck an Gour" (the fellow with the goat-skin), the title hero, another superhumanly strong lad, overpowers a three-headed giant and takes from him "a bottle of green ointment, that wouldn't let you be burned, nor scalded, nor wounded" (Kennedy 1891, 21–28).

ACHILLES' HEEL

Like the Grimms' young giant mentioned above, the Greek hero Achilles may have derived his great strength, and with it a degree of invulnerability, from his childhood diet, which consisted of the entrails of lions and wild boars plus the marrow of bears (Apollodorus 1975, 3:172). However, an account by the Latin poet Statius (1957, 2:269) gives another explanation of the hero's invulnerability: Achilles' mother, Thetis, a sea nymph, dips him when an infant into the River Styx, holding him by his right heel. The magic waters do not penetrate her grip, and he is left vulnerable in that one spot (Z311, "Achilles heel. Invulnerability except in one spot"), the proverbial Achilles' heel. In the end, he is brought down by a poisoned arrow guided by Apollo to this one fateful spot.

Another hero from Greek mythology who was protected by an impenetrable skin is Caeneus, who—as Ovid tells the story in his *Metamorphoses* (1950)—is born female (book 12, lines 180–216). Caenis, as she was known in her early years, was raped by Neptune (Poseidon to the Greeks), and as a reward to her for the pleasure he had taken at her expense, the sea god granted her any wish. To prevent such a wrong from happening to her again, Caenis asked to become a man. This wish was granted, and Neptune added an additional blessing: magic protection against all weapons.

Siegfried (Sigurd) is a northern hero sharing many attributes of Achilles and Caeneus, leading some to theorize that these stories evolved from common Indo-European myths. As recorded in the Middle High German epic *Der Nibelunge Not* (*The Nibelungenlied*) (1947), Siegfried, too, has one vulnerable spot on his otherwise impenetrable horn skin (D1361.3.2.), a patch between his shoulder blades where a leaf had fallen while he was bathing in the blood of a freshly slain dragon (verses 100, 898–902). Jealous Brunhild conspires with Hagen to discover from Siegfried's wife, Kriemhild, her husband's one weakness; then Hagen literally stabs the great hero in the back (verse 981).

The most famous invulnerable being in Norse mythology is the beloved god Balder. As the story is recorded in the *Prose Edda* (Snorri 1954, 80–81), Balder the Good dreams that something threatened his life. To set him at ease, Frigg, the wife of Odin, "exacted an oath from fire and water, iron and all kinds of metals, stones, earth, trees, ailments, beasts, birds, poison, and serpents, that they would not harm Balder." However, thinking that the little bush called mistletoe is too young to be a threat, she does not get the oath from it, thus unwittingly leaving the one thing that proves fatal to him (Z312, "Unique deadly weapon. Only one thing will kill a certain man"). After Frigg's intervention, the Aesir (partheon of Norse gods) take great sport in throwing things at Balder, knowing that it is all harmless fun—harmless, that is, until the evil trickster Loki, who knows of the one gap in Balder's magic shield, makes a dart from mistletoe and gives it to one of the Aesir, who guilelessly throws it at Balder, killing him instantly. And, in the words of Snorri, "this was the greatest misfortune ever to befall gods and man."

SAINTS' LEGENDS

Belief in invulnerability against specific threats, including fire, poison, and weapons, has a religious basis in many cultures. The ancient Hebrews Shadrach, Meshach, and Abednego, having refused to bow down to a pagan idol, survive being cast into a fiery furnace (Daniel 3; Motif D1841.3.2.1, "Fiery furnace as a mean of torture for a saint remains ineffective"). Similarly, the prophet Daniel, accused of making a petition to Jehovah instead of to the secular king, is thrown into a lions' den, but escapes unharmed (Daniel 6). And in the New Testament (Mark 16:37–38), believers are promised that "they shall take up serpents; and if they drink any deadly thing, it shall not hurt them."

Christian saints' legends abound in accounts of such divine protection (D1840.1, "Magic invulnerability of saints"). Saint George, probably the best known of all nonbiblical Christian saints, exemplifies a number of the protections promised to the faithful. According to *The Golden Legend* (1900, vol. 3, ch. 58), he is forced to drink strong venom, but it does not harm him. Then he is placed between two wheels covered with swords, but the wheels break, and the saint escapes unscathed. Finally Saint George is thrown into a cauldron of molten lead, where he appears to his tormentors to be having a leisurely bath. These miracles brought about many conversions to Christianity, but Saint George's invulnerability is limited, and in the end he suffers a martyr's death by beheading.

TRIAL BY ORDEAL

Such beliefs have led, and not only in the Judeo-Christian tradition, to the acceptance of ordeals as proofs of innocence (H220, "Ordeals. Guilt or innocence thus established"). The great Indian epic *Ramayana* (1870–1874, book 6, cantos 117–120) records how Rama's wife Sita is abducted by the ogre Ravana, remains chaste during her imprisonment, and following her rescue proves her purity by walking unharmed into a blazing pyre (H221, "Ordeal by fire. Suspected person must pass through or jump over fire to determine guilt or innocence"). Walking through fire or carrying a red-hot iron (H221.2, "Ordeal by hot iron") is mentioned as a lie-detector test in Sophocles' *Antigone* (lines 260–268). The Grimms' *German Legends* (*Deutsche Sagen*, 1816–1818) contains three accounts (DS 465, 480, 482) of wives who submit to fire ordeals in order to prove their own or a husband's innocence: one woman allows herself to be set afire while wearing a dress made of wax, another carries a red-hot iron, and a third walks barefoot across glowing plowshares. All are miraculously spared any injury.

The ordeal of the hot iron is given a wonderfully ironic treatment in Gottfried von Strassburg's medieval epic *Tristan* (1980, lines 15047–15764). Isolde, entangled in an adulterous affair with Tristan, agrees to undergo the ordeal of the red-hot iron to prove her innocence. Just before the ordeal, she contrives to fall into the arms of Tristan, disguised as a pilgrim. Then she swears before God that she has never lain with any man, except for her husband King Mark and the holy pilgrim. Because her oath is literally true, God protects Isolde, and she carries the red-hot iron without injury. One interpretation of this episode, which proves, in Gottfried's words, that Christ is as "pliant as a wind-blown sleeve," is that the poet is thus ridiculing a test of innocence that, whether officially accepted by the church or not, was nonetheless still widely believed. For a summary of medieval Christian attitudes, policies, and practices concerning trials by ordeal, see Leitmaier (1953).

Although the red-hot iron ordeal and its companion, the boiling water ordeal were codified into law throughout medieval Europe, their use was controversial. For example, Heinrich Kraemer and Johann Sprenger, in their infamous *Malleus Maleficarum,* written about 1486 under the authority of Pope Innocent VIII, theorize at some length as to the legality of requiring or allowing accused witches to attempt to prove their innocence by carrying a red-hot iron (1928, part 3, question 17). Their conclusion is that to do so would be counterproductive, given witches' demonic invulnerability (G229.4, "Invulnerability of witches"). They end their discussion with the account of "a notorious witch" who was seized by a count: "When she was being tortured and questioned, wishing to escape from their hands, she appealed to the trial by red-hot iron; and the count, being young and inexperienced, allowed it. And she then carried the red-hot iron not only for the stipulated three paces, but for six, and offered to carry it even farther. . . . She was released from her chains and lives to the present time, not without grave scandal to the Faith in those part." (Kraemer and Sprenger 1928, 234).

Demonic invulnerability, to some degree, protects ogres and supernatural fiends throughout the world. For example, the ten-headed, twenty-armed ogre Ravana in the *Ramayana* immediately grows a new head or a new arm to replace one that has been cut off, although he too, like Achilles and Siegfried, has one vulnerable spot, and in the end Rama brings him down with an arrow to the heart (1870–1874, book 6, cantos 109–110). And in *Beowulf* neither the best iron nor the sharpest blade can harm Grendel, for through a spell he has made himself invulnerable against all weapons (1977, lines 800–805; Motif

D1841.5). Beowulf, with apparent foreknowledge of Grendel's magic, attacks the monster with his bare hands and mortally wounds him by pulling off his arm.

SILVER BULLETS

In spite of the relative invulnerability of ogres, countless legends relate how they are defeated by heroes, often ordinary people, who take advantage of some unique deadly weapon (Z312). The most famous such device in northern Europe is the proverbial silver bullet, often prescribed against trolls, witches, werewolves, and other such creatures. However, it should be noted that to be fully effective the bullet must be made of *inherited* silver (Haas 1903, 98–99). Additional shields and weapons against supernatural foes include iron, calling the enemy by name, exposure to sunlight, Christian artifacts, specific herbs, incantations, inscribed runes, and of course the legendary wooden stake driven through the heart of a vampire. Throughout the world, local legends abound that tell how a seemingly invulnerable foe was overcome by a single well-chosen weapon. In such instances, the shaman with knowledge is infinitely more powerful than the warrior with conventional weapons.

If knowledge is power, then Odin is indisputably the most powerful of the Norse gods, for he is a master of runes, those mysterious chanted incantations and carved symbols that promise their users many things, but nothing more prominently than protection from foes. In the "Hávamál," a proverb collection attributed to Odin and included in the *Poetic Edda,* the god claims to know runes and spells that can dull the swords of one's foes, break the chains of the fettered, stop a spear in midflight, reverse another person's curse, extinguish a burning building, guard a ship in a gale, frighten away witches, and even bring a dead person back to life (1962, nos. 148–157)—in short, provide magic invulnerability to the knowledgeable.

D.L. Ashliman

See also: Tests.

REFERENCES

Apollodorus. 1975. *The Library of Greek Mythology.* Trans. Keith Aldrich. Lawrence, Kansas: Coronado Press.

Asbjørnsen, Peter Christen, and Jørgen Engebretsen Moe. 1983 [1852]. *Norske Folkeeventyr.* 2 vols. Oslo: Den Norske Bokklubben.

Beowulf: A Dual-Language Edition. 1977. Trans. Howell D. Chickering Jr. New York: Doubleday.

The Golden Legend, or Lives of the Saints [Legenda aurea]. 1900. Compiled by Jacobus de Voragine 1275. Trans. William Caxton, ed. F.S. Ellis. London: Temple Classics.

Grimm, Jacob, and Wilhelm Grimm. 1972 [1816–1818]. *Deutsche Sagen [DS].* 2 vols. Darmstadt: Wissenschaftliche Buchgesellschaft.

———. 1980. *Kinder- und Hausmärchen [KHM].* 3 vols. Ed. Heinz Rölleke. Stuttgart: Reclam. Based on the edition of 1857.

Haas, Alfred. 1903. *Rügensche Sagen und Märchen.* Stettin: Johs. Burmeister's Buchhandlung.

Kennedy, Patrick. 1891. *Legendary Fictions of the Irish Celts.* London: Macmillan.

Kramer [Kraemer], Heinrich, and James [Johann] Sprenger. 1928. *Malleus Maleficarum.* Trans. Montague Summers. London: John Rodker.

Leitmaier, Charlotte. 1953. *Die Kirche und die Gottesurteile: Eine rechtshistorische Studie.* Vienna: Herold.

Der Nibelunge Not [The Nibelungenlied]. 1947. Leipzig: Insel Verlag.

Ovid. 1950. *Metamorphoses.* Trans. Mary M. Innes. London. Penguin Books.

The Poetic Edda. 1962. Trans. Lee M. Hollander. Austin: University of Texas Press.

The Rámáyan [Ramayana] of Válmíki. 1870–1874. Trans. Ralph T.H. Griffith. 5 vols. London: Trübner.

Snorri Sturluson. 1954. *The Prose Edda of Snorri Sturluson: Tales from Norse Mythology.* Trans. Jean I. Young. Berkeley: University of California Press.

Statius 1955–1957. *Statius, with an English Translation by J.H. Mozley.* 2 vols. London: W. Heinemann.

Sutermeister, Ott. 1873. *Kinder-und Hausmärchen aus der Schweiz.* Aaráu, Switzerland: Sauerländer.

von Strassburg, Gottfried. 1980. *Tristan. Nach dem Text von Friedrich Ranke.* Edited by Rüdiger Krohn. Stuttgart: Reclam.

Magic Invisibility

Motif D1980

❀

Magic invisibility has fascinated people since ancient times. The *Motif-Index* lists fifty subcategories of magic invisibility, including many objects that make invisibility possible.

An invisible person can go wherever he or she wants to go, unfettered by society's rules and restrictions. The absence of a visible body brings freedom to take what one wants, to experiment sexually, and to have adventures without risking sanctions and disapproval. This behavior fits Jung's archetype of the trickster: the bold, daring rule-breaker who puts his or her own desires above society's dictates. Jung views the trickster as the "unsocialized, infantile, and unacceptable aspects of the self" (Russo 1997, 242). The trickster archetype overlaps to some extent with the archetype of the Shadow, which represents aspects of the psyche perceived by society as dangerous, negative, and antisocial.

Invisibility sometimes suggests that a person is overlooked or disregarded. While many folktale characters that become invisible are dynamic and powerful, some are quiet. In contemporary times, invisibility has become a metaphor for the effects of oppression and marginalization, especially in relation to ethnic groups.

MYTHOLOGY AND EPIC

In ancient Rome, Discordia, goddess of strife, owns a ring that makes her invisible (D1361.1.17). Her Greek counterpart, Eris, is the instigator of the Trojan War. Perseus, son of Zeus, receives a cap of invisibility (D1361.15) for his battle with Medusa; Pluto, god of the underworld, owns a helmet of invisibility.

In Homer's *Iliad* and *Odyssey,* gods appear and disappear at will; Homer uses a special term for the materialization of invisible gods. Sometimes gods in *The Iliad* protect themselves and their favorites from sight with a cloud of mist (D1361.1.1). Unlike gods, human beings usually require an object to become invisible. In his story "The Ring of Gyges," Plato tells of a shepherd who takes a gold ring from a corpse that he finds in a cave. Discovering that the ring makes him invisible, the shepherd uses it to seduce the queen of the realm, murder the king, and become king himself. The corruptive power of the ring, which offers invisibility as a means to gain power, is irresistible (Plato 2000, 39–40).

Invisibility is also important in the corpus of folk literature that composes the epic of King Arthur. The mantle of Arthur and the ring of the moon goddess Luned, both of which grant invisibility, are among the thirteen most precious things of Britain (Bradley 1894, 517). Avalon, the enchanted isle to which Arthur is taken after death, is sometimes described as being rendered invisible by a magic mist (D1361.1). The motif of the magic mist is also found in North American tradition, among the Shuswap, Salish, and Pawnee (Thompson 1929, 339).

FOLKLORE

In tales, legends, customs, and beliefs, many objects have been given credit for causing invisibility; one of the most picturesque of these is fern seed (D1361.5.1). According to legend, the fern "bursts into fiery blossoms which disappear almost instantaneously, for evil spirits swarm thickly around them and carry them off" (Cox 1893, 517). Frazer explains that fern blossoms may appear on St. John's Eve in midsummer or on Christmas night; in Switzerland, a ritual of sitting beside a fern on St. John's Eve is connected to the legend of the devil bringing treasure to those who wait (1950, 816–817). Both Ben Jonson and Shakespeare were familiar with fern seed's potential for this kind of magic. In Shakespeare's *The First Part of King Henry IV,* can be found the line "We have the receipt of fern-seed, we walk invisible" (1960, 43). Apparently this means of becoming invisible was commonly known in Elizabethan times.

The Magic Cloak of Invisibility

One of the most popular objects for conferring invisibility is the magic cloak (D1361.12), featured in folktales of England, Ireland, Germany, the United

States, China, Japan, and the Philippines, among other areas. Thompson says the motif of the cloak of invisibility is found among the Ute and Micmac in North America (Thompson 1929, 339).

Perhaps the best-loved tale involving a cloak of invisibility is the Grimms' "The Worn-Out Dancing Slippers." A poor soldier, wishing to find out where the king's daughters go at night, receives a cloak from an old woman who says "When you put this on, you'll be invisible and can then stalk the twelve maidens" (Magoun and Krappe 1960, 475). Wearing the cloak, the soldier follows the princesses down to an underground kingdom, where he collects branches with silver, golden, and diamond leaves as tokens to show the king. As a reward, he is given the hand of the eldest princess in marriage, as well as the eventual inheritance of the kingdom. The hero of this folktale exemplifies the archetype of the trickster who gets what he wants through stealth. On the other hand, if the reader sees the underground kingdom as a source of evil and seduction, the poor soldier is the princesses' savior.

In the folktale "Cinderella," variants of which are known throughout the world, invisibility is one indication of the dead mother's protection of her daughter. In a Czechoslovakian variant, "The Princess with the Gold Star on Her Brow," the princess's mother appears to her in a dream, giving the gift of a white veil woven of mist that will make the wearer invisible (Waldau 1860, 502–518). In a Danish variant published in 1884, the ill-treated heroine receives magic dresses and a chariot from a tree that opens on command. A bagful of mist thrown in front of and behind the chariot makes the heroine "vanish like a shooting star into mist" (Cox 1893, 517). In this tale, the heroine is both a trickster and a virtuous young woman in need of aid.

Often a magic formula makes magic transformation possible. In the Disney movie *Cinderella* (1950), the fairy godmother repeatedly says "Bibbety bobbety boo," a nonsense rhyme that echoes serious incantations from the past. Cross refers to magic formulas for invisibility in Irish folk literature (1952). Sometimes invisibility can be induced by reading a magic formula backwards (D1985.2).

The magic wand (D1361.25) and the magic staff (D1361.25.1) are well-known objects for inducing invisibility. Both of these objects are associated with the magician or wizard, a powerful figure that fits Jung's archetype of the Wise Old Man. By waving his wand or staff, the wizard can cause invisibility and countless other magical effects. The magic cap of invisibility (D1361.15) that Perseus had also appears in a Chinese tale called *The Wang-liang's Magic Cap:* a poor man confronts an ogre and forces him to hand over his straw hat, which makes its wearer invisible (Eberhard 1965, 95) The cap of invisibility occurs in North American tradition among the Omaha and the Zuni (Thompson 1929, 339). Among the many other objects that facilitate invisibility are a magic flower (D1361.6), a magic calabash (D1361.4), and a magic tiger's hair (D1361.35). A dragon may have the power of invisibility (B11.5.2); so may a pig (B184.3.2.1). The related motif F241.3.1, "Fairy-swine," reinforces the idea that pigs have a predilection for enchantment. This concept can be found in the *Mabinogion,* interpreted for children in Lloyd Alexander's *The Book of Three* (1969).

Magic stones are also thought to have great power. Sometimes this power comes from an especially virtuous person, as in the Irish tale of the saint who banishes sorrow by blessing a stone (D1359.3.4, "Stone blessed by saint banishes sorrow"). According to Pliny, the precious stone heliotrope could make someone who carried it invisible (Cox 1893, 517). Stones that cause invisibility are often associated with evil personages. In Kittredge's study of witchcraft, a magic stone is credited with causing invisibility (1958, 176; Motif D1361.2).

Some folk beliefs about invisibility suggest occult practices, as in D1361.8, "Heart of unborn child renders person invisible." The most gruesome motif of this sort is D1361.7, the "Hand of Glory," a charm made of a dead man's hand that confers invisibility upon its owner. The name "Hand of Glory" is derived from the French *mandragore* or mandrake, a plant that is said to grow under the gallows. Sometimes a candle made from the fat of a man who has been hanged is part of the magic charm. Since fingers from unborn children were thought to be especially desirable providers of candles, some thieves in seventeenth-century Germany murdered pregnant women to obtain what they desired. A burning finger placed upon a table would show the thief that he could remain free from discovery until his work was done (Leach 1949, 477).

ELITE LITERATURE

The folkloric dimensions of magic invisibility have appealed to many authors. In J.R.R. Tolkien's *The Hobbit* (1937), Bilbo Baggins discovers a magic ring that, in rendering him invisible, allows him to escape from the threatening Gollum. Bilbo's cousin Frodo becomes the ring-bearer in Tolkien's *Fellowship of the Ring* (1955). Frodo finds that the ring makes him feel weak and overwhelmed; the ring functions as a metaphor for the corruptive power of evil. In C.S. Lewis's *Voyage of the Dawn Treader* (1952), the Dufflepuds recite a spell of invisibility to protect themselves from a spell that has made them look ugly. In contrast to these works in which invisibility is linked to negative behavior or influences, Eloise McGraw's *The Moor Child* (1996) presents invisibility as one of many skills necessary for fairies' survival. Young Moql, who does not have the talent to become invisible, must find another way to live happily in a realm where survival skills are crucial.

The popular magic cloak motif is featured in the best seller *Harry Potter and the Sorcerer's Stone* (Rowling 1997). In his first year of study at Hogwarts School of Witchcraft and Wizardry, young Harry Potter receives a cloak of invisibility as a Christmas present. Having once belonged to Harry's father, the cloak symbolizes fatherly protection. It allows Harry and his friend Ron to glide through the halls at night, searching for answers they are eager to learn. In the second book of the series, *Harry Potter and the Chamber of Secrets* (1999), a magic device renders Ron's car invisible. As Ron and Harry fly through the air in their magic car, the car suddenly vanishes.

Invisible places have also appealed to the imaginations of a number of writers. Marion Zimmer Bradley's *The Mists of Avalon* (1984) tells of the magic isle of Avalon, visible only to those who have the power to raise the mists. Authors of children's books have also written about places that are invisible to the eyes of most people. Julia Sauer's *Fog Magic* (1986) tells of a town that becomes visible only when a heavy fog has come down; at that point, certain children have the privilege of visiting the town to learn important lessons that will guide them toward adulthood.

Invisibility through scientific experiments is presented in H.G. Wells's *Invisible Man* (1897), in which chemicals render a scientist invisible. While science is the primary center of interest here, invisibility also seems to have magical connotations. This observation can also be applied to the recent film *Hollow Man* (2000), in which a scientist injects himself with a potent mixture of chemicals in order to become invisible. Although the injection comes from the world of science, its effects—including personality change and trickster-like behavior—come from the folklore of invisibility.

While literal invisibility has interested people for many years, metaphoric invisibility has been important in literature. In Ralph Ellison's *Invisible Man* (1952), the black central character's invisibility denotes powerlessness, oppression, and effacement from society. Similarly, in works by authors representing various ethnicities and gay/lesbian sexuality, invisibility has signified powerlessness. Through characters' personalities and voices, invisibility is transformed into vibrant visibility.

Elizabeth Tucker

See also: The Trickster.

REFERENCES

Alexander, Lloyd. 1969. *The Book of Three.* New York: Ballantine.
Bradley, Marion Zimmer. 1984. *The Mists of Avalon.* New York: Random House.

Cox, Marian R. 1893. *Cinderella.* London: Publications of the Folk-Lore Society.

Cross, Tom Peete. 1952. *Motif-Index of Early Irish Literature.* Bloomington: Indiana University Press.

Eberhard, Wolfram. 1965. *Folktales of China.* Chicago: University of Chicago Press.

Ellison, Ralph. 1952. *Invisible Man.* New York: Random House.

Frazer, Sir James. 1950. *The Golden Bough.* New York: Macmillan.

Homer, 1995. *The Iliad.* Trans. Samuel Butler. New York: Barnes and Noble.

———. 1997. *The Odyssey.* Trans. Robert Fagles. New York: Penguin.

Kittredge, George L. 1958. *Witchcraft in Old and New England.* New York: Russell and Russell.

Leach, Maria. 1949. *Standard Dictionary of Folklore, Mythology and Legend,* Vol. 1. New York: Funk and Wagnalls.

Lewis, C.S. 1952. *Voyage of the Dawn Treader.* New York: Harper Trophy.

Mabinogion. 1991. Ed. Thomas Jones. New York: Charles E. Tuttle.

Magoun, Francis P., Jr., and Alexander H. Krappe. 1960. *The Grimms' German Folk Tales.* Carbondale: Southern Illinois University Press.

McGraw, Eloise. 1996. *The Moor Child.* New York: Simon and Schuster.

Plato. 2000. *The Republic.* Ed. G.R.F. Ferrari. New York: Cambridge University Press.

Rowling, J.K. 1997. *Harry Potter and the Sorcerer's Stone.* New York: Scholastic.

———. 1999. *Harry Potter and the Chamber of Secrets.* New York: Scholastic.

Russo, Joseph. 1997. "A Jungian Analysis of Homer's Odysseus." In *The Cambridge Companion to Jung,* ed. Polly Young-Eisendrath and Terence Dawson, 240–254. Cambridge: Cambridge University Press.

Sauer, Julia. 1986. *Fog Magic.* New York: Penguin.

Shakespeare, William. 1960. *The First Part of King Henry IV.* London: Methuen.

Tolkien, J.R.R. 1937. *The Hobbit.* New York: Ballantine.

———. 1955. *The Fellowship of the Ring.* New York: Ballantine.

Thompson, Stith. 1929. *Tales of the North American Indians.* Cambridge: Harvard University Press.

Waldau, Alfred. 1860. *Böhmisches Märchenbuch.* Prague: K. Gerzabek.

Wells, H.G. 1983 [1897]. *The Invisible Man: A Grotesque Romance.* New York: Bantam.

Bewitching

Motif D2020

❀

Bewitching occurs when someone with magic power enchants or transforms a person, animal, or thing. Most bewitching has a negative effect; people die or suffer injuries (D2060, "Death or bodily injury by magic"); animals are paralyzed (D2072.0.2, "Animal rendered immovable"); cows give curdled milk (D2083.3); beer is magically kept from brewing (D2084.1); and swords are magically dulled (D2086.1). The person who bewitches, in folklore and literature from ancient times to the present, is usually a woman.

These *maleficia*, acts of malice, fit the stereotype of the evil witch in the Middle Ages. The *Malleus Maleficarum* of 1486 offers many details of witches' nefarious deeds: murder of infants, castration of men, and corruption of food, among other horrors. As Jeffrey Burton Russell explains in *Witchcraft in the Middle Ages* (1972), *maleficia* constituted a form of "low magic" feared by rural folk, while divination, "high magic," was the province of philosophers and alchemists.

According to the *Malleus Maleficarum,* written by two Dominican priests, "All witchcraft comes from carnal lust, which is in women insatiable" (Summers 1968, 29). Many more women than men were identified as witches by clerics in the Middle Ages. This focus on women can be explained by the prevalence of the Great Mother archetype, which has, as Erich Neumann explains, both positive and negative poles. The positive elementary character, which is creative, loving, and nurturing, derives from the mother-child relationship, while the negative elementary character arises from "anguish, horror, and fear of danger" in the unconscious (1955, 147). Kali, the Indian goddess of death, is one embodiment of the Great Mother's negative side. The witch figure, with its emphasis on death, injury, and destruction, is another.

MYTHOLOGY AND EPIC

In Homer's *Odyssey,* the enchantress Circe transforms Odysseus's men into swine (G263.1, "Witch transforms person to animal"). Only Odysseus himself, protected by the herb moly, is able to avoid transformation. He persuades Circe to change his men back into human form and spends a year on her island, learning how to respond to dangers he will encounter later in his voyage. Circe, both dangerous and kind, represents both sides of the Great Mother archetype.

In contrast to Circe, the Gorgon Medusa of Greek mythology has no redeeming qualities. With serpent hair, golden wings, and bronze claws, Medusa can turn human beings to stone if her eyes meet theirs (D581, "Petrification by glance"). In the legend of Perseus, the hero avoids this fate by looking at Medusa in a shield or mirror.

Another powerful female figure is Morgan Le Fay of the Arthurian cycle. In some versions of King Arthur's story, Morgan uses her skill with herbal medicine to try to heal the wounded King Arthur. Late medieval narratives of King Arthur's death describe Morgan as an abhorrent sorceress; this approach dominates the film *Excalibur* (1981). In Malory's *Morte Darthur,* Morgan plans for Arthur's downfall (1982). Records from pagan times link Morgan with the Irish goddess Morrigan and mermaids of the Breton coast (Loomis 1950, 747).

In Jewish lore related to the book of Genesis in the Bible, Lilith, Adam's first wife, is a demonic figure who threatens the lives of newborn infants. Girls are endangered by Lilith until their third week of life. Some amulets of protection against Lilith bear the names of the three angels who tried to bring Lilith back to Adam: Sanvi, Sansanvi, and Semangelaf. In *The Book of Lilith* (1996), Jungian Barbara Black Koltuv analyzes Lilith's archetypal features, explaining the importance of integrating her powerful energy into the psyche.

SYMPATHETIC MAGIC

Sympathetic magic (D2061.2.2) is another means of bewitchment. The abuse or destruction of an object or animal may cause someone's murder (D2061.2.2; Kittredge 1958, 73). In Irish mythology, piercing a person's shadow with a spear may cause the person to fall down dead (D2061.2.2.1; Cross 1952) In Great Britain and the United States, many people believe that the destruction of a person's picture leads to death (D2061.2.2.3). Similarly, the burning of a person's hair may cause death or serious illness (D2061.2.2.4.1). In one picturesque form of sympathetic magic noted in England, boiling a person's gloves is a good way to make sure that the person will never need gloves again (D2061.2.2.5.1).

In the southern United States, a magic hair-ball facilitates bewitching (D2070.1; Hand 1964, 668). Witches' balls of opaque glass have been sold in American mail-order catalogs in the recent past, suggesting that people are still interested in traditional modes of enchantment.

Among the Azande of Zaire, witchcraft is caused by a substance inside the witch's body. After the witch's death, this substance can be discovered and removed. Male and female witches consume the souls of their victims, who fall ill and waste away (Parrinder 1958, 133). Like Azande witches, Ewe witches of Dahomey and Togo steal souls; they also suck people's blood. Female Ewe witches stay inside during the day and wander around at night; their feet are pointed backwards, and their favorite mode of locomotion is walking on their hands (Parrinder 1958, 135).

According to Native American folklore, which has been influenced to some extent by European beliefs, witches can be either women or men. The Navajo belief in skinwalkers—witches who wear the skin of wolves, mountain lions, and other animals—has created many narratives. Among Eastern Woodlands Indians, witch bundles made of sticks, cloth, and other materials are believed to injure and kill people. Each year, the witch bundles must be fed with human flesh, preferably the flesh of the witches' own family members (Metraux 1950, 1179). In the movie *The Blair Witch Project* (1999), witch bundles frighten the young filmmakers and lead them astray; one of the most horrifying scenes in the movie shows a piece of human flesh caught inside the witch bundle's folds.

THE EVIL EYE

How do witches enchant their victims? Folklore from Europe, India, and North America heavily emphasizes the evil eye (D2071, "Evil Eye. Bewitching by means of a glance"). In Irish folklore, the evil eye develops because of exposure to a magic concoction (D2071.0.2.; Cross 1952).

The evil eye can cause sickness (D2064.4) or insanity (D2065.5). A magic glance can be so powerful that it reduces a tree to ashes (D2082.1). According to British folklore, someone with the power of the evil eye cannot look at any living thing before breaking fast in the morning without causing the living thing to wither and die (Baughman 1966). Animals are especially vulnerable to this menace; even a brief glance can cause farm animals to sicken and die (D2071.2.1).

Just as amulets of protection can fend off Lilith, certain magic ornaments can keep the evil eye at bay (D2071.1). One popular method for averting the evil eye is spitting (D2071.1.1); another involves swinging a cat over a child's cradle (D2071.1.2). Dressing a child in clothes appropriate for the opposite sex may confound the evil eye so that it misses its mark (D2071.1.3). According to Indian folklore, returning the glance of the evil eye can seriously injure the giver (D2071.1.5).

TALES AND BALLADS

Bewitchment is an important event in many folktales. In *Sleeping Beauty,* AT 410, a witch or evil fairy, excluded from the princess's christening, places a curse upon the princess. When the girl reaches maturity, she pricks her finger upon a spindle or another sharp object and falls into an enchanted sleep. In the Grimms' version of the story, "Dornroschen," it is not just the princess who is enchanted; all of the people and animals at the king's court fall asleep for one hundred years (D1960.3, "Sleeping Beauty. Magic sleep for definite period (e.g., a hundred years"; Magoun and Krappe 1960, 183–184). The Disney movie *Sleeping Beauty* (1959) portrays the evil Maleficent as a powerful, determined woman who can irresistibly draw the princess toward her preordained enchantment.

In "Beauty and the Beast," a version of *The Monster (Animal) as Bridegroom* (AT 425A), a young woman goes to live with a hideous beast who was once a handsome prince. Because of a spell that has been placed upon him, he can regain his true form only if someone loves him unconditionally. Once the young woman has proved her devotion, he becomes a handsome prince once more (Opie and Opie 1974, 182–195). Similarly, in *The Frog King* (AT 440), the first story in the Grimms' collection, a witch has deprived a young man of his rightful appearance; only true love will free him from his enchantment (Magoun and Krappe 1960, 3–6). The movie *Shrek* (2001) reverses the usual direction of transformation: instead of choosing to become beautiful by traditional standards, the young woman who has been enchanted decides to keep her ogrelike appearance.

Various folk ballads feature enchantments. One of the most colorful ballads is "Allison Gross" (Child 1965, 35), in which "the ugliest witch in the North Country" unsuccessfully attempts to seduce a young man. When he resists her advances, she turns him into a "laily worm" and makes him "toddle about the tree." Fortunately, the Queen of the Fairies comes by on Halloween and reverses the spell. This ballad is unusual in that a fairy reverses the spell of a witch. Another ballad involving a spell is "Kemp Owyne" (Child 34), in which three kisses break the spell placed on a girl by her cruel stepmother; the girl has become a fierce sea monster, and only true love can restore her to her original form (D735.2, "Three redeeming kisses").

Some enchantments result in magic love-sickness (D2064.0.1). Attraction by magic (D2074) can leave the victim weak with longing for the spell-maker.

According to one specific prescription, a girl's heart magically removed and fed to a man draws her to him (D1905.1). Some contemporary witches in New York State have said that if a man eats a steak marinated in a witch's menstrual blood, he will feel irresistibly attracted to the witch who prepared his dinner.

ELITE LITERATURE

Among Shakespeare's characters who can bewitch others are the three cauldron-stirring sisters in *Macbeth* (G201, "Three witch sisters") and the mischievous fairies in *A Midsummer Night's Dream. Macbeth* reflects the medieval stereotype of the evil-minded witch, while *Midsummer Night's Dream* includes love magic that represents widespread folk belief.

In Charlotte Brontë's 1846 novel *Jane Eyre,* Mr. Rochester tells Jane that she has the look of another world: "When you came on me in Hay Lane last night, I thought unaccountably of fairy tales, and had half a mind to demand whether you had bewitched my horse: I am not sure yet" (127).

Arthur Miller's play *The Crucible* (1952) explores accusations of bewitchment in Salem, Massachusetts, showing how the slave Tituba's magical practices led others to fear widespread occult influence.

Novels of the mid- to late twentieth century and early twenty-first century have moved from depiction of Satanic witchcraft, as in Ira Levin's *Rosemary's Baby* (1967), to playful portraits of beautiful women with magic power, as in John Updike's *The Witches of Eastwick* (1984). Both of these books were made into motion pictures, and there was a popular television series in the 1960s and 1970s, *Bewitched,* about a benign modern witch.

Two books for children that sympathetically portray young women suspected of practicing witchcraft are Elizabeth George Speare's *The Witch of Blackbird Pond* (1958) and Monica Furlong's *Wise Child* (1989). In J.K. Rowling's *Harry Potter and the Sorcerer's Stone* (1997), female witches and male wizards teach students to become expert in using magic power. Talented students like Harry learn to use their powers well; "Muggles" (ordinary humans) with no magic power are regarded with contempt.

Literary interest in Native American witchcraft has increased. Louise Erdrich's *Tracks* (1989) tells of Fleur Pillager, who bewitches men in unusual ways. In Tony Hillerman's detective novel *Skinwalkers* (1990), Navajo witches create a puzzle that is almost impossible to unravel; only a detective of Native American descent can find the answer that eludes others.

Elizabeth Tucker

REFERENCES

Baughman, Ernest. 1966. *Type and Motif-Index of the Folktales of England and North America*. The Hague: Mouton.

Brontë, Charlotte. 1998 [1846]. *Jane Eyre*. Oxford: Oxford University Press.

Child, Francis James. 1965 [1882]. *The English and Scottish Popular Ballads*. 5 vols. New York: Dover.

Cross, Tom Peete. 1952. *Motif-Index of Early Irish Literature*. Bloomington: Indiana University Press.

Erdrich, Louise. 1989. *Tracks*. New York: Harper and Row.

Furlong, Monica. 1989. *Wise Child*. New York: Mass Market.

Hand, Wayland D., ed. 1964. *The Frank C. Brown Collection of North Carolina Folklore*. Durham, NC: Duke University Press.

Hillerman, Tony. 1990. *Skinwalkers*. New York: HarperCollins.

Homer. 1997. The Odyssey, trans. Robert Fagles. New York: Penguin.

Kittredge, George Lyman. 1958. *Witchcraft in Old and New England*. New York: Russell and Russell.

Koltuv, Barbara Black. 1996. *The Book of Lilith*. New York: Nicholas Hays.

Levin, Ira. 1967. *Rosemary's Baby*. New York: Random House.

Loomis, Roger. 1950. "Morgan LeFay." In *Standard Dictionary of Folklore, Mythology and Legend*, ed. Maria Leach, Vol. 2. New York: Funk and Wagnalls.

Magoun, Francis P., Jr., and Alexander H. Krappe. 1960. *The Grimms' German Folk Tales*. Carbondale: Southern Illinois University Press.

Malory, Sir Thomas. 1982. *Le Morte Darthur*, ed. R.M. Lumiansky. New York: Scribner.

Metraux, Alfred. 1950. "Witchcraft." In *Standard Dictionary of Folklore, Mythology and Legend*, ed. Maria Leach, Vol. 2. New York: Funk and Wagnalls.

Miller, Arthur. 1952. *The Crucible*. New York: Viking.

Neumann, Erich. 1955. *The Great Mother*. Princeton: Princeton University Press.

Opie, Iona, and Peter Opie. 1974. *The Classic Fairy Tales*. New York: Oxford University Press.

Parrinder, Geoffrey. 1958. *Witchcraft: European and African*. London: Faber and Faber.

Rowling, J.K. 1997. *Harry Potter and the Sorcerer's Stone*. New York: Scholastic.

Russell, Jeffrey Burton. 1972. *Witchcraft in the Middle Ages*. Ithaca: Cornell University Press.

Shakespeare, William. 1969 [1673]. *Macbeth*. London: Cornmarket Press.

———. 1999. *A Midsummer Night's Dream*. New Brunswick, NJ: Transaction.

Speare, Elizabeth George. 1958. *The Witch of Blackbird Pond*. New York: Dell.

Summers, Montague, trans. 1968. *Malleus Maleficarum*. London: Folio Society.

Updike, John. 1984. *The Witches of Eastwick*. New York: Knopf.

Wishes

Various Motifs

❀

"In olden times, when wishing still did some good . . ." This opening phrase of the Grimms' "Frog King" (KHM 1; AT 440, *The Frog King or Iron Henry*) serves as a motto for their entire collection of *Children's and Household Tales*. Because a principal function of fairy tales (more precisely, magic or wonder tales) is fantasy wish fulfillment, it could be argued that most such stories are about wishing, both the explicit wants verbally expressed by the characters and the unspoken (sometimes unconscious) desires of the storytellers and their listeners. Persecuted heroines escape kitchen drudgery by marrying into royalty (AT 510A, *Cinderella*). Poverty-stricken, abandoned children discover great wealth, then legally and justifiably kill the adults who are abusing them (AT 327A, *Hansel and Gretel*). Soldiers too old and too severely wounded to remain in service become rich and powerful by marrying beautiful princesses (AT 562, *The Spirit in the Blue Light*). Young brides turn life-threatening ar- ranged marriages into happily-ever-after romances (AT 425C, *The Girl as the Bear's Wife*). The list could be extended endlessly.

The antiquity of the wishes motif in folktales is attested by the presence of stories in Ovid's *Metamorphoses* (first century CE) and a fifth-century Hindu collection, the *Panchatantra* (known in English as the *Fables of Bidpai*), de- scribed below.

There is no better example of the tales featuring explicitly formulated wishes than the widespread story of the simpleton whose wishes always come true (AT 675, *The Lazy Boy*). One of Europe's oldest recorded magic tales, this story is found both in the pioneering collections of Straparola (1989, 3:1) and Basile (1932, 1:3), as well as in nineteenth- and twentieth-century collections from most European countries. The Grimms' version, "Hans Dumb," is one of the most concise formulations extant, but they included it only in the first edition of their *Children's and Household Tales* (1812, no. 54). The story begins when a misshapen village idiot gets a princess pregnant by merely thinking about her (T513, "Conception from wish"). Through a magic paternity test, the king discovers who the father of his grandson is, then sets father, mother, and newborn adrift at sea. The simpleton, now faced with the most extreme challenges of fatherhood, wishes his young family safely ashore, with a castle for their new home. He then wishes himself into a good-looking and intelligent prince, and they settle into a happy married life. Thus at every turn the simpleton hero changes his life through magic wishes. In some versions of the tale, the lad's extraordinary power is explained (a fairy's gift or a reward from an enchanted fish, caught and then released), but in others, for example the Grimms', no explanation is offered. It is as though the power of fantasy, properly approached, can change anyone's life, with no special intercession from outsiders required.

WISHES GRANTED BY MAGIC OBJECTS

Magic wish-granting items abound in folklore and mythology: rings (D1076), lamps (D1162.1), bottles (D1171.8), carpets (D1155), horses (B181), snuff boxes, tinder boxes, mirrors (D1163), orbs, staffs (D1254), cloaks (D1053), boots (1065.1), purses (D1192), weapons (D1080), books (D1266), stones (D931), sacks (D1193), tables (D1153), amulets (D1274), and talismans (D1734.1). Some are single-purpose items with the power to render the users invisible, carry them to a distant place, serve food, assure victory in combat, impart information, or provide endless wealth; whereas others grant their owners any wish (D1470.1). The most famous such all-purpose, wish-fulfilling magic object is Aladdin's enchanted lamp, and as was the case with the Type 675 tales discussed above, there is no obvious moral logic behind fate's selection of the person blessed with the magic lamp. In fact, Aladdin, like Hans Dumb, is not the virtuous, deserving lad that one might expect, but rather is introduced as "a headstrong and incorrigible good-for-nothing" (*Tales from The Thousand and One Nights* 1973, 165). A large number of Aladdin-inspired European tales (Types 560–595) follow a similar pattern, with their heroes more often coming from the ranks of simpletons and rogues than from any other group. This feature has made it all the easier for generations of ordinary people with no special virtues or gifts to vicariously enjoy, if only in their fantasies, the wish fulfillment around which these tales are constructed.

No single folktale group better exemplifies the granting of wishes to individuals of questionable character than does type 330A, *The Smith and the*

Devil. A Gypsy version from the Indian subcontinent, "How the Gypsy Went to Heaven" is typical. In return for hospitality, God grants a Gypsy black-smith four wishes. The smith's enigmatic response is that no person can de-scend from his apple tree without his permission, no one can get off his horse blanket without being released, no one can escape from a certain iron box without his permission, and he can never be separated from his turban. Years later, when the angel of death comes, the smith tricks him into the apple tree and will not release him until the angel promises him another twenty years of life. The same thing happens with the horse blanket and the iron box, but finally the smith dies and reports to heaven. God responds, "No, I don't want him here," but he does agree to let the smith look inside. God opens the door a crack, and the smith throws his turban in and sits down on it. No one can remove him from his turban, and that is how the Gypsy goes to heaven (Tong 1989, 15–17; Motif K2371.1.1, "Heaven entered by trick: permission to pick up cap. Trickster throws a cap or leather apron inside the gate").

At first look, the smith's wishes seem to be absurd, but there is method in his madness. In other instances, the opposite is true. A wish appears, at least superficially, to be beneficial but turns out to be catastrophic. The most fa-mous example of such a shortsighted wish is "Midas's Golden Touch" (AT 775; Motif J2072.1). As Ovid tells the story, Silenus, a tutor and companion of Bacchus (Dionysus), is captured by a band of peasants and taken to their king, Midas. The king, recognizing the importance of his captive, receives him with honor and then returns him to Bacchus. The god of wine and revelry rewards Midas by promising him any wish. The greedy king asks that every-thing he touches would turn to gold. His pleasure with this new source of wealth is short-lived, for he nearly starves to death when all his food and drink turns to gold. His prayers for release are finally answered when Bacchus instructs him how to divest himself of the magic touch by bathing in the Pactolus River (1950, book 11).

FOOLISH AND RECKLESS WISHES

Other folkloric wishes are so grotesquely absurd that only a fool would re-quest them, and therein lies the appeal of the stories featuring them. The sim-plest everyman can take pleasure in comparing himself with these characters. An excellent example is found in "Slow, the Weaver" from book five of the *Panchatantra,* dating to the fifth century CE. When a weaver named Slow receives one magic wish from a fairy, he consults with his wife before making his decision. She theorizes that if he had a second head and a second pair of arms, he would be able to operate two looms and thus double their meager income. Seeing the logic of her theory, he so wishes, but he is unable to put his new head and limbs to the test, for when his fellow villagers see him they take him for a demon and stone him to death (1964, 449–453; Motif J2070, "Absurd wishes").

"Slow, the Weaver" belongs to the tale type 750A, titled simply *The Wishes*. Most commonly the number of wishes granted is three. In the usual formula, the first wish is squandered on a trifle, the second is uttered in reckless revenge with disastrous results, and the third must be used to undo the consequences of the first two. "The Sausage" from Sweden is typical. A woman performs a service for a fairy and is granted three wishes. While fantasizing about what she might request, she remembers that her husband is expected home for dinner soon, so she wishes for a big sausage, which magically appears. When her husband learns that she has thus squandered a wish, he angrily wishes the sausage onto her nose, and immediately it attaches itself. They have to use the final wish to free her from this unnatural appendage (Djurklou 1901, 27–32; J2071, "Three foolish wishes. Three wishes will be granted: used up foolishly"). Essentially the same story is also told with reversed gender roles, for example, "The Three Wishes" from England (Jacobs n.d., 107–109).

A ribald version that follows the above formula is found in the *Thousand and One Nights*. Allah grants three wishes to a certain man, who consults his wife before executing them. Her advice, in the florid translation of Richard Burton (1885–1888), is, "The perfection of man and his delight is in his prickle; therefore do thou pray Allah to greaten thy yard and magnify it." He follows her advice, and his member immediately grows so large that "he could neither sit nor stand nor move about." He forthwith prays to Allah that he be freed of the monstrosity, only to find himself "pegless as a eunuch." They now find no other recourse but to wish him back to his original state (6:180–181).

This writer heard a similar joke in southern Utah in 2001: A cowboy spares a snake's life, and the snake grants him three wishes. "Make me as strong as Arnold Schwarzenegger, as good-looking as Robert Redford, and as well hung as the horse I'm riding," responds the cowboy. Arriving home, he looks in the mirror and admires his handsome face and rippling muscles, but then screams out, "Oh no! I forgot that I was riding a mare!" The same story—almost verbatim, but with Joe Louis and Clark Gable as the icons of popular culture—was collected in the early 1950s in Michigan by Richard M. Dorson (1967, no. 206).

In a subcategory of type 750A tales, one wish is granted to two different people with positive results for one and negative for the other. The playful pseudo-etiological legend "Origin of the Island Hiddensee" is typical. During heathen times, the story goes, the island was a peninsula attached to the large island of Rügen in the Baltic Sea. A Christian missionary seeking shelter is turned away by one woman, but hospitably received by her neighbor. The generous woman's reward is the magic gift to continue all day her first activity of the morning (J2073.1, "Wise and foolish wish: keep doing all day what you begin"), which in her case is to measure a piece of linen that she has woven. She continues to measure all day, filling her house with valuable cloth. Envying this good fortune, the selfish neighbor now invites the missionary to lodge with her. The next morning, the guest departs after granting her the same wish that had benefited her neighbor. She decides to count the money she has saved in a jar. However, first of all she has to go outside to answer an unexpected call of nature. Suddenly the holy man's blessing takes effect, and with such force that the land is flooded and becomes separated from Rügen (Haas 1903, no. 201).

The above tales forcefully illustrate that care must be exercised in making wishes; we may well get what we ask for. This cautionary note is scattered through folktales of many types, as illustrated in the following examples, five from the Grimm brothers and one from Hungary. A queen wishes, "If only I had a child as white as snow, as red as blood, and as black as ebony," and soon afterward she has a baby girl as white as snow, with lips as red as blood, and with hair as black as ebony (KHM 53; AT 709, *Snow White*). A childless woman wishes for a baby, "even if it were ever so small—no larger than a thumb," and seven months later she gives birth to a perfectly formed baby, no larger than a thumb (KHM 37; AT 700, *Tom Thumb*). A childless man exclaims, "I will have a child, even if it is a hedgehog," and his wife gives birth to a half-human, half-hedgehog baby (KHM 108; AT 441, *Hans My Hedgehog*). A husband and wife with seven sons finally have a baby girl, but she is sickly, so the father sends her brothers for water to perform an emergency baptism. The boys are slow in returning, and, fearing that the girl will die without being baptized, the father cries out in anger, "I wish that those boys would all turn into ravens." They turn into ravens and fly away (KHM 25; AT 451, *The Maiden Who Seeks Her Brother*). A mother, irritated at a misbehaving daughter, says, "I wish that you would turn into a raven and fly away," and the girl turns into a raven and flies away (KHM 93; AT 401, *The Princess Transformed into Deer*). An unmarried woman says to herself, "I wish God would give me a sweetheart, even if one of the devils he were," and a young lad comes to court her, who turns out to be the devil himself (Dégh 1965, no. 4).

An important variation on the reckless-wish theme is the Grimms' cautionary tale "The Fisherman and His Wife." A magic fish grants a fisherman a series of wishes, each one demanded by his greedy wife. She asks for a better house, then a mansion, then to be king (not queen!), then emperor, and then pope. All wishes are fulfilled, until the dissatisfied woman violates a tabu by finally asking to become "like God," at which point a violent storm erupts, and the fisherman and his wife find themselves back in the filthy shack where they started (KHM 19; AT 555, *The Fisher and His Wife;* Motif C773.1, "Tabu: making unreasonable requests. Given power of fulfilling all wishes, person oversteps moderation and is punished"). In a Japanese version, "The Stonecutter," the recipient of magic wishes does not violate a tabu, but goes full circle following his own desire to become ever more powerful. The beneficiary of a mountain spirit, the stonecutter first asks to become a rich man, then a prince, then the sun, then a cloud, then a cliff, and finally a stonecutter (Brauns 1885, 87–90). No single wish is deemed foolish or excessive. No punishment is meted out. In the end, the stonecutter wishes himself back where he started, and all is well.

D.L. Ashliman

REFERENCES

Basile, Giambattista. 1932. *The Pentamerone.* Trans. from the Italian of Benedetto Croce. Edited by N.M. Penzer. 2 vols. New York: Dutton. First pub. 1634–1636 as *Lo Cunto de li Cunti* (The tale of tales).

Brauns, David. 1885. *Japanische Märchen und Sagen.* Leipzig: Verlag von Wilhelm Friedrich.

Burton, Richard F., trans. 1885–1888. *The Book of the Thousand Nights and a Night: A Plain and Literal Translation of the Arabian Nights Entertainments.* 10 vols. plus 6 supplemental vols. Privately printed by the Burton Club.

Dégh, Linda. 1965. *Folktales of Hungary.* Trans. Judit Halász. Chicago: University of Chicago Press.

Djurklou, Gabriel. 1901. *Fairy Tales from the Swedish.* Trans. H.L. Bækstad. Philadelphia: J.B. Lippincott.

Dorson, Richard M. 1967. *American Negro Folktales.* Greenwich, CT: Fawcett.

Grimm, Jacob, and Wilhelm Grimm. 1812–1815. *Kinder- und Hausmärchen: Gesammelt durch die Brüder Grimm.* 2 vols. Berlin: Realschulbuchhandlung.

———. 1980. *Kinder- und Hausmärchen* [KHM]. Ed. Heinz Rölleke. 3 vols. Stuttgart: Reclam. Based on the ed. of 1857.

Haas, A. 1903. *Rügensche Sagen und Märchen.* Stettin: Johs. Burmeister's Buchhandlung.

Jacobs, Joseph. n.d. *More English Fairy Tales.* New York: G.P. Putnam's Sons. First published 1894.

Ovid. 1950. *Metamorphoses.* Trans. Mary M. Innes. London: Penguin Books.

The Panchatantra. 1964. Trans. Arthur W. Ryder. Chicago: University of Chicago Press.

Straparola, Giovanni Francesco. 1898. *The Facetious Nights.* Trans. W.G. Waters. 4 vols. London: Privately printed for members of the Society of Bibliophiles. First published as *Le piacevoli notti,* 2 vols., 1550–1553.

Tales from the Thousand and One Nights. 1973. Trans. N.J. Dawood. Hammondsworth: Penguin.

Tong, Diane. 1989. *Gypsy Folktales.* New York: Harcourt Brace Jovanovich.

❀ E ❀

The Dead

Ghosts and Other Revenants

Motifs E200–E599

❀

Thompson devotes an entire chapter (E) to the subject of the dead. Most of the chapter is taken up by motifs dealing with "Ghosts and other revenants" (E200–599); other divisions are "Resuscitation" (E0–199), "Reincarnation" (E600–699), and "The soul" (E700–799).

The belief in ghosts is nearly universal. It has been suggested that there is a correlation between the nature of child-rearing practices within a specific society and the character of that society's supernatural beings, including ghosts (studies cited by Ember and Ember 1999, 426). Commonly, however, ghosts or ancestor spirits in any one culture can be both menacing and benevolent, and most often ghosts who appear to the living are relatives or lovers as opposed to strangers. The revenant will return for a variety of reasons, reflected in the divisions "Malevolent return from the dead" (E200–299) and "Friendly return from the dead" (E300–399).

MALEVOLENT RETURN FROM THE DEAD

Sometimes the revenant returns to inflict punishment; this is particularly true if the person was murdered, when the principal motive is to out the murderer (E231, "Return from the dead to reveal murder"). In the ballad "Young Benjie," (Child 86), the brothers of a girl who drowned keep watch over her corpse in an effort to discover who caused her death.

> About the middle o the night
> The cocks began to craw,
> And at the dead hour o the night
> The corpse began to thraw [twist]. (Child 1965, 2:283)

The girl's ghost informs them that her lover Benjie pushed her into the water, and they then ask her what kind of punishment they should inflict.

One of the most famous ghosts of literature is Hamlet, King of Denmark, who returns to walk the battlements of his castle and urge to his son, Prince Hamlet, to avenge his murder (*Hamlet*, 1.5).

The Dead Carry Off the Living

The fear that the dead will somehow pull the living after them down into the grave is a common motif (E266, "Dead carry off living"). Often this is accomplished through a kiss (E217, "Fatal kiss from dead"). For example, "Sweet William's Ghost" (Child 77) has numerous variants in which the story line diverges somewhat, but the basic story is that the ghost of a man who died just before he was to wed appears to his lover to ask her to return his love token (E311, "Return from dead to return and ask back love tokens"). Not realizing that he is dead, the girl asks her lover to come in and kiss her. He replies that he is "no earthly man" and that if he kisses her "Thy days will not be lang" (E217, "Fatal kiss from dead") (Child 1965, 1:229, version A). When she realizes he is dead, she complies with his request and returns his token, but follows him to the graveyard, where in some versions she asks if she can accompany him into the grave (he says no) and then dies.

In his notes to "The Suffolk Miracle" (272), Child writes, "A tale of a dead man coming on horseback to his inconsolable love, and carrying her to his grave, is widely spread among the Slavic people (with whom it seems to have originated) and the Austrian Germans . . . and has lately been recovered in the Netherlands, Denmark, Iceland, and Brittany" (1965, 5:60). Child pronounces "The Suffolk Miracle" a degraded version of "one of the most remarkable tales and one of the most impressive and beautiful ballads of the European continent." The motif in question is E215, "The Dead Rider (Lenore). Dead lover returns and takes sweetheart with him on horseback. She is sometimes saved at the grave by the crowing of the cock, though the experience is usually fatal." The motif also constitutes a tale type, AT 365, *The Dead Bridegroom Carries Off his Bride,* with Finnish, Finnish-Swedish, Estonian, Livonian, Lithuanian, Lappish, Norwegian, Danish, Icelandic, Irish, French, Dutch, Flemish, German, Italian, Romanian, Slovenian, Serbo-Croatian, Hungarian, Czech, Polish, and Russian versions. In 1773, the German poet Göttfried August Bürger wrote *Lenore* in ballad style; it was extremely popular and widely translated, including an English translation by Dante Gabriel Rossetti.

Another Child ballad—"Fair Margaret and Sweet William" (74)—contains an example of motif E211, "Dead sweetheart haunts faithless lover." Margaret sitting in her bower window combing her hair, sees her lover with his new bride. "Down she cast her iv'ry comb, / And up she tossd her hair, / She went out from her bowr alive,/ But never no more came there" (Child 1965, 2:201, version B). The ballad continues:

> When day was gone, and night was come,
> All people were asleep,
> In glided Margaret's grimly ghost,
> And stood at William's feet.

The ghost asks William how he likes his bride and he replies that he likes her well, but better he likes "that fair lady / That stands at my bed's feet." In the morning his bride tells him she had a foreboding dream "that our bowr was lin'd with white swine, / And our bride-chamber full of blood" (D1812.5.1.2, "Bad dream as evil omen"). William goes to Margaret, finds that she is dead, kisses her corpse (E217, "Fatal kiss from dead"), and dies.

An African tale tells of a ghost who tricks a woman into going into a pit and jumps down after her and they both disappear (Krug 1912, 109). This is an example of a malevolent stranger ghost, not the spirit of a person she knew in life.

Bloodthirsty Revenants

Thompson remarks that there are many tales about the wandering and malicious dead. "They frequently make unprovoked attacks on travelers in the dark (E261), or they haunt buildings and molest those bold enough to stay in them overnight" (E282–284; Type 326) (1977, 257). The most horrific return from the dead involves those who come from the grave at night to suck the blood of the living (E251, "Vampire"). The vampire his ancient roots perhaps in Egyptian and Tibetan religious beliefs that the living must perform extensive burial rituals in order to seal the dead off from the living, whom the dead would bring into their own state. Later, the idea of the corpse thirsting for the blood of the living became the dominant theme of the vampire, and Green remarks on the significance of Christ commanding his disciples to drink the wine (a symbol of his blood) during the Last Supper: "Here, within this very cornerstone of Christianity, is located the pervasive spirit of evil in the vampire's literal interpretation of Christ's admonition; it drinks the blood for eternal life" (Green 1988, 1375)

Although it is widely believed that the folklore of the vampire became prominent in Slavic countries, particularly in the region of Transylvania, some scholars suggest that the theme trickled down from European literature. Early works featuring the female vampire include Goethe's ballad *The Bride of Corinth* (1797), Keats's poem *Lamia* (1820), Poe's stories "The Fall of the House of Usher" (1839), "Ligeia" (1840), and especially "Berenice" (1840), and Le Fanu's "Carmilla" (1872). The male vampire appears in Stagg's ballad *The Vampyre* (1810), Polidori's *The Vampyre: A Tale* (1819), and Prest's *Varney the Vampire, or The Feast of Blood* (1847). The culmination of the male vampire is, of course, Bram Stoker's *Dracula* (1897) (Green 1988, 1375–1380).

In societies that honor the dead, failing to do so will result in the ghost returning. Motif E246, "Ghosts punish failure to sacrifice to them" can be found in ancient Greek, South American Indian (Brazil), and African tales. A similar motif is E245, "Ghosts punish failure to provide for their wants. Haunt man because he does not leave food and drink for them."

Motif E238, "Dinner with the dead" (also a tale type, AT 470, *Friends in Life and Death*), is extremely widespread throughout Europe. A man invites a dead friend to dinner, who then takes his host back to the land of the dead. During the journey through the otherworld they see many strange sights, and when the host finally returns to the world he finds he has been away many centuries, and he dies the next day. This motif also is prominent in the Don Juan legend, of Spanish folklore, which has been used in literary and operatic works.

FRIENDLY RETURN FROM THE DEAD

Seeing ghosts of the recently dead as relatively benign appears in anthropologist Bronislaw Malinowski's work with the Trobriand Islanders in Melanesia off the coast of Papua New Guinea:

> The *kosi,* the ghost of the dead man, may be met on a road near the village, or be seen in his garden, or heard knocking at the houses of his friends and relatives, for a few days after death. People are distinctly afraid of meeting the *kosi,* and are always on the lookout for him, but they are not in really deep terror of him. (Malinowski 1954, 151)

Return of the Dead Mother

A mother's drive to protect her children is so strong that she can come back from the grave to suckle (E323.1.1, "Dead mother returns to suckle child"). This motif is particularly strong in Japanese death legends in oral, print, artistic, and film representations. A cluster of stories around the *ubume*—a mother who dies—explores the complex relationship of a mother, who has often died in childbirth, and her living child. Folklorists Michiko Iwasaka and Barre

Toelken note that the legends reveal ambivalence because the surviving child can be seen as causing the mother's death. "At the same time," they note, "a mother has a solid obligation to defend or nurture her child even in death; thus, not only does the child nurse at the breast, but it receives sweets or rice cakes which the mother's ghost provides at considerable expenditure of energy" (1994, 60–79).

The mother can return to help her children in other ways (E323.2, "Dead mother returns to aid persecuted children"). This motif as well as E366, "Return from dead to give counsel," is prominent in some versions of the Cinderella cycle (AT 510, *Cinderella and Cap o' Rushes;* AT 510A, *Cinderella;* AT 923, *Love Like Salt*), stories that are found virtually around the globe and go back thousands of years. The dead return to give counsel in tales from many cultures, including Irish, Icelandic, Italian, Finnish-Swedish, Jewish, Indian, Chinese, Korean, North American Indian (Iroquois, Onondaga), South American Indian (Brazilian), and African (Jaunde, Fang).

British folklorist Gillian Bennett (1999) notes that the British women whom she interviewed in her study of contemporary personal experience narratives of the supernatural, or *memorates,* distinguished between what they called "ghosts," who are malevolent (E280) and more kindly presences that she labeled "witnesses," often deceased family members, who comforted grieving relatives in some way (E366). In one interview, a woman told Bennett about the return of her deceased mother to forewarn and so prepare her children for a death in the family.

The Unquiet Grave

There is a large body of material involving the dead being unable to rest because of prolonged mourning by their survivors (C762.2, "Tabu: too much weeping for dead"), which prompts the ghost to return to ask them to cease weeping (E361). Sometimes the ghost returns to a lover, as in the ballad "The Unquiet Grave" (Child 78):

> A twelvemonth and a day being past,
> His ghost did rise and speak,
> "What makes you mourn all on my grave
> For you will not let me sleep?"
> (Child 1965, 2:237, version B)

Frequently the ghost is a child returning to its parents (E324, "Child's friendly return to parents"). This motif is particularly widespread, occurring in British, Lithuanian, Spanish, Chinese, North American Indian (Pawnee), and Eskimo (Greenland) sources.

THE GRATEFUL DEAD

The motif of the grateful dead (E341) appears in a cluster of tales, AT 505–508, falling under the heading *The Grateful Dead.* In all these tales, the hero, who at the outset of his quest has spent his last penny to pay off creditors of a dead man so that the corpse can be buried, is later aided by a mysterious helper who turns out to be the ghost of that dead man. He appears sometimes as an old man, a servant, or a fox. According to Thompson the motif is ancient and probably originated in Hebrew literature in the story of Tobit (1977, 53). These tales were the subject of early monograph studies by Gerould (2000) and by Liljeblad (1927).

THE VANISHING HITCHHIKER

Most folklorists agree that the urban legend known as "the vanishing hitchhiker" (E332.3.3.1) is unique in being the only one concerned with the supernatural (Brunvand 2001), although Linda Dégh, disagreeing with Brunvand, argues that many urban legends and contemporary supernatural stories intersect (Dégh 2001). In this tale, a driver stops to pick up a young woman hitchhiker, drives her to her home, and finds that she has vanished from the car, except for leaving a scarf or sweater behind. Upon inquiring at the house about her, the driver finds that she has been dead for some time. Often the ghost has made similar attempts to return, usually on the anniversary of her death in an automobile accident.

WHY THOSE WHO DIE DO NOT RETURN TO LIFE

The dangers of speaking to the dead are illustrated in an African tale from the Bakongo. A girl whose family was dead goes one day to the market of the dead and sees the ghosts of her family members. When she tries to talk to them, they do not answer, and vanish (C497, "Tabu: speaking to the dead"). On subsequent days she repeatedly tries to talk to them until, finally, her grandmother relents. Then the ghosts warn the girl that she must not tell anyone that she has seen or talked with them. But the girl tells a friend, who, insisting on seeing for herself, accompanies her to the market the next day. The ghosts are angry and say that the friend may not leave. But when the girl leaves, her friend follows her down the road. One of the ghosts then decapitates the friend. The girl tells them to kill her too. Meanwhile, at home, when people cannot find the girls, they whistle for them. "But they heard nothing. That is how it happens that, to this day, when one is once dead, he is never seen again. Before that, if you whistled, you saw

them. It is the girl who did that by going to the market of the dead"
(Feldmann 1963, 178–79).

Jane Garry and Janet L. Langlois

REFERENCES

Bennett, Gillian. 1999. *Alas, Poor Ghost! Traditions of Belief in Story and Discourse.* Rev. ed. of *Traditions and Belief: Women and the Supernatural.* Logan: Utah State University Press.

Brunvand, Jan Harold. 2001. *Encyclopedia of Urban Legends.* Santa Monica, CA: ABC-CLIO.

Child, Francis James. 1965 [1882–1898]. *The English and Scottish Popular Ballads.* 5 vols. New York: Dover. Orig. edition, Houghton Mifflin. Dégh, Linda. 2001. *Legend and Belief: Dialectics of a Folklore Genre.* Bloomington: Indiana University Press.

Ember, Carol R., and Melvin Ember. 1999. *Anthropology.* Upper Saddle River, NJ: Prentice Hall.

Feldmann, Susan. 1963. *African Myths and Tales.* New York: Dell.

Gerould, Gordon Hall. 2000 [1908]. *The Grateful Dead: The History of a Folk Story.* Urbana: University of Illinois Press.

Green, Gary L. 1988. "Vampirism." In *Dictionary of Literary Themes and Motifs*, ed. Jean-Charles Seigneuret, 1373–1382. Westport, CT: Greenwood.

Iwasaka, Michiko, and Barre Toelken. 1994. *Ghosts and the Japanese: Cultural Experience in Japanese Death Legends.* Logan: Utah State University Press.

Krug, Adolph N. 1912. "Bulu Tales from Kamerun, West Africa." In *Journal of American Folklore* 25 (96): 106–124.

Liljeblad, Sven. 1927. *Die Tobiasgeschichte und Andere Märchen mit toten Helfern.* Lund, Sweden: P. Lindstedts Univ.-Bokhandel.

Malinowski, Bronislaw. 1954. *Magic, Science and Religion.* Introduction Robert Redfield. Garden City, NY: Doubleday Anchor.

Thompson, Stith. 1977 [1946]. *The Folktale.* Berkeley: University of California Press. Orig. ed. New York: Holt, Rinehart, and Winston.

❀ F ❀

Marvels

Otherworld Journeys

Motifs F0–F199

❀

There are generally three otherworlds to which heroes in myth, legend, and folktale journey: the upper world (F10), the lower world (F80), and the earthly paradise (F111), although these are not always clearly distinguished from one another, and as Thompson remarks, sometimes the direction in which the journey to the otherworld is made is very vaguely indicated (1977, 147). But the vagueness only adds to the sense of wonder in a journey to a world beyond the quotidian one; indeed, these journeys are classified under Chapter F, "Marvels."

THE UPPER WORLD

The nature of the upper world varies. It may be conceptualized as heaven (A661, "Heaven. A blissful upper world"), or it may be a place of peril or unhappiness, such as the star-world (F15, "Visit to star-world"), the land of the moon (F16, "Visit to land of moon"), or the land of the sun (F17, "Visit to land of the sun"). These worlds are accessed by ladder (F52), tree (F54), plant (F54.2), or a sky-window (F56). Transportation to or from the upper world can be by a cloud (F61.1), a feather (F61.2), smoke (F61.3.1), or by being carried by a bird (F62), a deity (F63), heavenly maidens (F63.1), or an angel (F63.2).

An example of a journey to an upper world is contained in "The Star Husband Tale," one of the most prevalent tales in North America. There are several versions, and in all of them a girl travels to the star-world (F15, "Visit to star-world") and usually marries a star (Thompson 1966, 126–130). In some versions, this upper world is reached by climbing a tree (F54, "Tree to upper world"). While the girl lives in the upper world, often there is a tabu against digging (C523, "Digging tabu"), and when she ignores it and digs, the girl finds that she is able to see down to her home on earth. She then plans to escape, with varying degrees of success. Sometimes escape is possible by being lowered down in a big basket (F51, "Sky rope").

In the English folktale "Jack and the Beanstalk" (AT 328A, AT 555, AT 852), Jack plants some beans that grow overnight into a gigantic beanstalk, which he climbs to the upper world (F54.2, "Plant grows to sky"). He comes to a giant's castle where his adventures continue for three days. When the giant chases him, Jack descends the beanstalk and cuts it down, and the giant falls to earth and is killed.

There are also folktales in which the upper world is clearly the Christian Heaven, for example, *The Smith and the Devil* (AT 330), *The Tailor in Heaven* (AT 800), and *Master Pfriem* (AT 801). These stories originated in the jestbooks of the Renaissance and were taken over by storytellers (Thompson 1977, 149).

THE LOWER WORLD

Access to the lower world can be through a door or gate (F91), a pit, hole, spring, or cavern (F92), a mountain (F92.4), cave (F92.6), well (F93.0.2.1), or path (F95). Sometimes a person is swallowed up by the earth and taken to the lower world (F92.2). In folktales the lower world tends to be a nebulous place located vaguely under the earth and inhabited by unusual denizens, but it will not be a frightful place of death.

An example of this kind of otherworld is found in the well-known tale type, AT 480, *The Spinners by the Well*. In the version collected by the Grimms, "Frau Holle,"

> the despised younger daughter sits spinning by a well and loses her shuttle in the water. Being scolded by her mother, she jumps into the well to recover it. She loses her senses and awakes in the lower world. In reply to various appeals, she milks a cow, shakes an apple tree, takes bread out of an oven, and the like. At last she takes service with a witch, and she is so industrious that she pleases the witch. (Thompson 1977, 125)

The girl eventually returns home with a reward and her sister jumps into the well to claim hers, but being unkind and haughty, she refuses to do any work and is punished.

A tale told by the Chaga of Africa also has the motif of entering the underworld through water. A girl and her brother are tending a field to keep monkeys away. They leave briefly to get a drink at a pool and the monkeys come and eat everything. The girl, in despair of her parents' anger, jumps into the pool. She sinks down until she comes to the underworld, where she finds an old woman living in a hut, with whom she lives and works for a long time, but eventually she wishes to return home. The old woman grants permission and asks a mysterious question: whether the girl would prefer the hot or the cold. The girl chooses the cold, dips her arms and legs into a cold pot, and instantly her limbs are covered with gold bangles. The story diverges from the pattern of AT 480 at this point, since her brother does not also go to the underworld upon her return. The story does, however, include jealousy of her riches by neighbors, but in typical fairy-tale fashion the girl finds a husband and lives happily ever after (Parrinder 1967, 64–65).

The Chaga also have a story about a little girl who goes out to cut grass, steps in a quagmire, and sinks down to a lower world, singing "The spirits have taken me." Attempts to retrieve her are unsuccessful, but after a time a tree grows up from the spot where she disappeared, until it reaches the sky (F54, "Tree to upper world"). Some boys climb the tree, saying that they are going to the world above. They too are never seen again, but the tree remains, and the people call it *Mdi Msumu,* the story-tree (Scheub 2000, 2).

The Land of the Dead

Vivid descriptions of the underworld as the land of the dead, which is forbidden to mortals, are found in the myths, legends, and epics of many different cultures (F81, "Descent to the lower world of death"). The motif of the descent to the lower world of the dead evolved quite early into a vehicle for philosophical and theological speculation.

In its basic form, the descent to the underworld serves merely as a means of describing an exotic world not known directly by the living, or as a test of the hero's mettle. Used in more complex fashion, the hero's descent is a means of gaining knowledge or power and represents anxiety about death and what might happen after life. Many journeys to the underworld are either an actual or a symbolic death of the hero, who usually returns to his people.

The related motif of a journey to the land of the dead to rescue a beloved or important person addresses even more clearly anxiety about death and the desire to conquer or overcome death's awesome power. "A test of strength between love and death is at the base of the legends and myths in which one left behind in this world follows the beloved or relative to the land of no return" (Siikala 1987, 303). The myth of Orpheus, who journeys to the underworld to rescue his wife Eurydice and bring her back to life, epitomizes this motif (F81.1, "Orpheus. Journey to land of dead to bring back person from the dead"). After gaining permission to leave the underworld with Eurydice,

Orpheus ultimately fails in his mission because he disobeys the injunction of the god of the underworld, Hades, not to look back at her as they make their way to the upper world. The story is extremely widespread in folklore around the world and has been used in elite literature as well. Other examples of rescue from the underworld in Greek myth are Dionysus rescuing his mother, Semele, and Herakles rescuing Theseus and Ascalaphus during his twelfth labor, which is to seize Cerberus, bring him up to Eurystheus, and then return him to the underworld. Unlike the case of Orpheus, these rescues are successful, as is the one recounted in a Chinese tale called "Husband and Wife in This Life and in the Life to Come," in which a man goes on a journey in search of his dead wife. Stopping at an inn to inquire the way to the land of the dead, the husband is told to wait for his wife at the well. After some time, he does indeed see her shade approach. In time they are able to flee the underworld, and, after his wife is reincarnated as the baby daughter of a couple in whose house they stop, he is able to be reunited with her again on earth (Eberhard 1965, 31–33). In Maori tales, heroes are successful in rescuing their loved ones by deceiving the guardians of the underworld and escaping (Siikala 1987, 303).

The oldest recorded example of F81.1 is probably contained in the Sumerian texts relating to Inanna (she is Ishtar in later Babylonian texts). Although she is queen of heaven and earth, Inanna becomes jealous of her sister Ereshkigal's role as queen of the dead and the underworld (Wolkstein and Kramer 1983, 61). Dressed in her sovereign finery, she sets out on "the road from which no traveler returns" (55) and makes her way to Ereshkigal's palace. Forced to surrender her garments in seven stages, Inanna places herself unwittingly in the power of the angered Ereshkigal and is turned into "a piece of rotting meat . . . hung from a hook on the wall" (60). When the great gods intervene, Ereshkigal is forced to relent, with the proviso that Inanna must find a substitute to take her place among the dead, and she returns to the upper world accompanied by demons who will take the substitute back to the underworld. After she pleads with the demons not to take several of her associates, she notices that Dumuzi, her consort, is not properly dressed for mourning, and she angrily instructs the demons to take him. After some farcical shape-shifting in which he escapes several times, Dumuzi is finally struck dead by the demons and whisked off to the underworld (71–84). Becoming remorseful, Inanna laments her decision, and a bargain is finally struck in which Dumuzi will spend half of each year in the underworld with Ereshkigal and half with Inanna on earth (85–89).

While many commentators regard the story of Dumuzi's cyclical departure and return as a form of vegetation myth, the Sumerian texts offer no clear indication that the original audience would have viewed them as such. The natural cycle interpretation seems much better suited to the story of Demeter and her daughter Persephone, retold in a number of Greek and Latin texts, most notably the Homeric *Hymn to Demeter* and Claudian's *De raptu Proserpinae.* The motif is F92.2.1, "Girl gathering flowers swallowed up by earth and taken to lower world." Persephone's underworld journey is, like Dumuzi's, involuntary, since she is abducted by Hades. Demeter is a cereal goddess, and when she is in mourning for the loss of her daughter she halts fertility not only in the fields but also among humans and animals, something Inanna is unable or unwilling to do. Finally Zeus intercedes and Persephone is restored to Demeter for two-thirds of the year, upon which Demeter renews the crops and thereafter they die only during the period of each year when Persephone is in the underworld. It is known that this myth was connected with an ancient fertility ritual held every autumn in Eleusis, near Athens. Persephone epitomizes the descent to the lower world and the return, signifying the cyclical nature of life in the yearly rebirth of vegetation.

In the Babylonian epic *Gilgamesh,* derived from older Sumerian myth from the second millennium BCE, the hero undertakes a difficult journey after the death of his beloved comrade Enkidu, hoping to discover the secret of eternal life from his ancestor Utnapishtim, who dwells not in the underworld but in a blessed isle beyond the waters and the mountains. The arduousness of Gilgamesh's journey to this otherworld is characteristic of the journey to the underworld, and there are some parallels with the latter, particularly the crossing of a body of water with the help of a boatman. Gilgamesh ultimately fails in his quest for immortality, returning with the knowledge that one cannot cheat death and that one must make the most of the life the fates have decreed. He has also worked through his grief, so his emotional and intellectual equilibrium are both restored (Foster 2001, 72–95). Gilgamesh's journey is described in more detail below in the section on the earthly paradise.

One of the most elaborate examples of the F81 motif is found in the great Quiche Mayan epic *Popol Vuh.* The heroes, a pair of twins named Hunahpu and Xbalanque, not only restore their father and uncle Hun Hunahpu and Vucub Hunahpu (also twins) from death, but assert the control of the living over the dead. Hun Hunahpu and Vucub Hunahpu had annoyed the death gods by constantly playing ball on a court that was the entrance to Xibalba, the underworld. The death gods lured them into the world below and sacrificed them. Eventually the next generation, Hunahpu and Xbalanque, take up handball and in their turn arouse the ire of the death gods. Summoned like their father and uncle to Xibalba, the twins deal much more cleverly with the underworld lords and learn their names (C432.1, "Guessing name of supernatural creature gives power over him"). After many trials, the young twins gain control of Xibalba and resurrect the remains of their father and uncle, who are then raised into the heavens to become the sun and the moon (Taube 1993, 56–62).

One of the best-known examples of the journey to the underworld is found in book 11 of the *Odyssey* of Homer. The ostensible reason for Odysseus's visit to Hades is to consult the prophet Tiresias about the rest of the journey home, but since Circe pretty much tells Odysseus beforehand what he will learn from the seer, the episode serves mainly to underline the hero's extraordinary qualities. (The phantom-shade of Herakles actually makes this point when he asks Odysseus what he will do to top this exploit.) While in the underworld, Odysseus's interviews with the shades of his mother, Anticlea, Agamemnon, and Achilles connect the narrative with the broader Trojan legend. Odysseus tells the grieving shade of Achilles, the great hero of the Trojan War, that their comrades have honored him as a god, and that even in death he has great authority over the dead. Achilles replies "O Shining Odysseus, never try to console me for dying. I would rather follow the plow as thrall to another man . . . than be a king over all the perished dead." (Lattimore 1975, 180). In the Finnish *Kalevala,* the culture hero Vainamoinen is one of several who make the arduous three-week journey to the dark territory of Tuonela, the Finno-Ugric nether world, but the only one who returns unharmed. The purpose of his journey is to learn the magic verbal formula that will allow him to complete the ship that will take him on his mysterious final journey. While he wisely refuses to drink the worm-infested beer offered him by Tuonetar, queen of the dead, he does fall asleep. The son of Tuoni, king of the dead, then entraps him in an iron net, but Vainamoinen takes on the form of a serpent and makes his escape, having learned what he needs (Guirand 1977, 305–306).

Werner notes that there are many stories throughout Bantu Africa of hunters pursuing animals into a burrow or hole that leads them to the abode of the dead (F92, "Pit entrance to lower world. Entrance through pit, hole, spring, or cavern") (Werner 1925, 184).

Fairyland as Land of the Dead

There are some striking similarities between fairyland and the land of the dead. For example, the eating and drinking tabu applies to both places (C211.1, "Tabu: eating in fairyland"; C211.2., "Tabu: eating in lower world"), and Lewis Spence (1946) has argued that fairyland may in fact be a metaphor for the land of the dead since it is often located underground (F211, "Fairyland under a hollow knoll ([prehistoric burial] mound, hill, síd"). Some of the same rituals and prohibitions govern relations between mortals and fairies and mortals and the dead. For example, both fairies and the dead vanish or retreat at daybreak; both groups lure mortals to them and both may be placated in the same way with gifts or offerings. Similarly, both fairyland and the world of the dead are marked by distorted time or timelessness (Silver 1999, 41–42). In the Scottish ballad *Tam Lin,* the mortal Tam Lin is abducted by the Queen of Fairies. Although he describes fairyland as "a pleasant place," he says that every seven years the fairies make a sacrifice to hell, and he fears he will be the one sacrificed. He therefore enlists the aid of a mortal lover to pull him down from his horse when he rides in the fairy procession at midnight on Halloween and to hold him fast through various transformations until the spell he is under is broken and he can return to the everyday world.

THE EARTHLY PARADISE

The concept of an earthly paradise as a pleasant place, or *locus amoenus* (Curtius 1953, 192, 195)—sometimes a forest or valley but most often a garden—long predates Christianity and is found in virtually all mythologies and religions. It is also prominent in secular adventure or love tales and in the letters and diaries of explorers centuries later than Columbus, who was only one of many seeking a shorter route to the Indies, sometimes a half-conscious synonym for paradise. Even today there are individuals and groups who believe there is an earthly paradise. Current travel advertising exploits the desires and superstitions of skeptical customers by using terms like "tropical paradise."

The definition, location, and topography of the earthly paradise have been subjects of debate for more than three millennia. Delumeau maintains that the word *paradise,* when used alone, originally "almost always meant the earthly paradise. For nearly three millennia, first the Jews and then Christians, with only a few exceptions, did not doubt the historical character of the story in Genesis about the wonderful garden that God caused to appear in Eden" (1995, 3). Religious texts, epics, romances, vision literature, apocalypses, and travel literature all describe journeys to an earthly paradise. The Old Testament, however, does not describe a journey to the earthly paradise; instead, Adam is placed there by God at Creation. The earthly paradise, a garden made at Creation as a residence and responsibility for Adam and Eve, is mentioned in Ezekiel 28 as having been lost through disobedience. Thus, the first biblical passages about the earthly paradise focus on man's loss of it.

Although the distinctions between celestial and terrestrial paradises have become increasingly confused during four thousand years of tradition, the earthly paradise is not heaven, but another world, reachable by either mystical or mysterious physical means. The mystic modes are primarily prophetic or ecstatic visions or dream visions. The physical modes allow deserving people in an appropriately receptive state of soul (whether that state is induced by penitential or ecstatic feelings, psychological or spiritual need, prayer, or meditation) to fly, walk, ride, or sail to paradise while they are still alive.

The Ubiquitous Garden

The original word for paradise is the Persian *apiri-Daeza,* which means a walled orchard or garden (Delumeau 1995, 4). Kramer writes that the very idea of a paradise, a garden of the gods, is likely of Sumerian origin:

> The Sumerian paradise is located . . . in Dilmun. It is in this same Dilmun where later, the Babylonians, the Semitic people who conquered the Sumerians, located their "land of the living," the home of their immortals. And there is good indication that the Biblical paradise, too, which is described as a garden planted *eastward* in Eden, from whose waters flow the four world rivers including the Tigris and Euphrates, may have been originally identical with Dilmun, the Sumerian paradise-land. (Kramer 1961, 102)

The journey of Gilgamesh, described above, may be the first recorded account of a journey to the earthly paradise. Gilgamesh undertakes a quest to find Utnapishtim, the only man who ever gained immortality. Gilgamesh travels into the mountains that guard the rising and setting of the sun and must walk through a dark tunnel under a mountain and cross "the waters of death" to reach Dilmun. Dilmun has traits that typify many earthly paradises. It is a garden filled with fruits and jewels where nothing ages or dies. It is an island at the confluence of two rivers. The Sumerian tale of *Enki and Ninhursag* calls Dilmun a land or island east of Sumer and describes it as "pure and bright" ("Paradise" 1973, 13.81). The Eden of Genesis is also a garden from which four rivers flow, and it is rich with plants and animals. The tree of life and the tree of the knowledge of good and evil are present only in Genesis. The paradise God describes to Ezekiel (28:13 ff.) as one now lost to man is called Eden, "the garden of God." Perched on "the mountain of the lord," this garden is filled with the precious stones later repeated in Revelation as those adorning the walls of the heavenly Jerusalem.

Greek models of paradise originate in Hesiod's *Works and Days* (seventh century BCE) in the description of the golden age of Chronos. When the golden age was lost, only Arcadia remained as a beautiful, bucolic place. Arcadia endured in European literature through the Renaissance.

The loss of paradise is a common motif in myth and literature (A1331, "Paradise lost"), as is nostalgia for the lost paradise. Daemmrich writes, "Delumeau (153–66) connects the 'nostalgia for the lost paradise' to the abandonment of the search for the original earthly paradise during the sixteenth and seventeenth centuries, precisely the time of the rise of scientific inquiry" (Daemmrich 1997, 210).

In Greek and Roman culture, the physical site of paradise on earth was usually called either the Plains or Fields of Elysium or the Isles of the Blessed. Sometimes it was located in the mythic land of the Hyperboreans, which lay beyond Boreas, the North Wind. The Zoroastrian paradise is one of the multiple worlds typical of the metaphysical topography of the religion. Common to all of these paradises is luxuriant growth, prosperity and plenty, a harmonious coexistence between man and beast, as well as perpetual youth, spring, and fruitfulness.

Christian Visions of the Earthly Paradise

Two periods are probably richer in accounts of journeys to the earthly paradise than any others. The first is the period between the third century BCE and the second century CE. This was a time of turmoil, when such Old and New Testament visions as those of Enoch, Elijah, Baruch, the Apocalypses of Peter and Paul (caught up in body and/or soul into the third heaven), and the Apocalypse itself (Delumeau 1995, 23–26) were written. The second period is the twelfth century (Haas 1999, 455), when such influential visions as Tundale's *Vision* and mystical journeys as Saint Brendan's *Voyage* describe two modes of transport to the earthly paradise. While asleep, Tundale is led to seven otherworlds (Haas 1999, 456) by an angel. Saint Brendan's *Voyage,* one of the Irish journeys that belong to the seafaring tradition, may actually have been written first as early as the sixth century, but was reproduced and varied many times in the twelfth. It recounts the story of a group of monks who sail to the land of the Saints (Haas 1999, 460).

"Nonfiction" Accounts

Several types of accounts or stories about the earthly paradise supported popular belief in it. One is the literature about Alexander. In the imperial Roman tradition of apotheosis, he took a journey to paradise in one fourth-century work. Another example was the famous twelfth-century hoax of the letter from a so-called Prester John, who claimed to be a Christian king in a paradisiacal land in Asia and summoned all Christians to come to his nation, a religious, political, and agricultural paradise on earth. Yet a third example was the encyclopedic tradition of geography found in much revered and reproduced sources like Isidore of Seville's seventh-century *Etymologiae* and Vincent of Beauvais's thirteenth-century *Speculum maius*. Finally, there was a body of travel literature, ranging from the accounts of Marco Polo to those of Sir John Mandeville, which located paradisiacal lands in the East, or in the Tigris and Euphrates area, or even, in the case of Irish folk tradition, in the west where the fairies lived. A belief in the reality of the earthly paradise was further bolstered by its appearance on medieval maps, where it sometimes appeared not too far from the center of the world map, Jerusalem.

Sometimes, the traveler arrives at the earthly paradise without any physical means of locomotion, as in the fourteenth-century English dream vision poem, *Pearl*. The narrator, mourning for a lost "child," falls asleep on her tomb and wakens to find himself confronting her in the form of a pearl maiden who appears on crystal cliffs separated from him by a jewel-strewn river. The writer seems to have been influenced by the most important dream vision in literature, Dante's *Divine Comedy*, written less than a century earlier. The vision motif (Patch 1950, 81 ff.) found in Tundale's and others' visions is prevalent throughout the Middle Ages. However, the forms it takes become more varied as it ages. It is the format not only of such religious visions as St. Patrick's *Purgatory*, but also of secular, consolatory visions like Chaucer's *Book of the Duchess* and of love visions like *The Romance of the Rose*, in which the earthly paradise is a courtly love garden. The earthly paradise becomes a topos in many garden trysts and is even used ironically, as in Chaucer's "The Merchant's Tale." The earthly paradise is one of the major forerunners of the utopian tradition, at its zenith in the sixteenth century when Thomas More's *Utopia* gives its name to numerous ideal societies.

The nineteenth century, with its revolutionary industrial growth and its political, social, and scientific innovation, was a time for imagining social and economic paradises, of which William Morris's *The Earthly Paradise* and H.G. Wells's *Modern Utopia* were but two.

Earthly paradises continue to thrive in such current forms as accounts of near-death experiences, science fictions located on other planets, and spiritual or psychological searches for paradisiacal states of being. Whereas the travelers to the earthly paradise once walked, rode, sailed, or flew to these regions beyond their accustomed lands, they now tend to fly in planes or space vehicles, to meditate, to cogitate, or even to inject themselves into the terrestrial paradises of the twenty-first century.

OTHER OTHERWORLDS

Lewis Carroll's *Alice's Adventures in Wonderland* (1865) begins with Alice following the White Rabbit down the rabbit hole (F92, "Pit entrance to the lower world"). Alice emerges in Wonderland, a world where absurdity and surrealism govern. "Other world inside the body of the person" (F133.6§) was introduced as a new motif by El-Shamy, and it is found in medieval lore, especially in the writings of François Rabelais. "Submarine other world," F133, is illustrated by Hans Christian Andersen's famous tale "The Little Mermaid." The novel *Journey to the Center of the Earth* by Jules Verne (1871) is an example of an otherworld journey in the modern science fiction mode (F15, "Journey inside the earth"). L. Frank Baum's *The Wonderful Wizard of Oz*

(1899) includes a description of the otherworld to which Dorothy journeys from Kansas that reads very much like a description of an earthly paradise: "The cyclone had set the house down . . . in the midst of a country of marvelous beauty. There were lovely patches of green sward all about, with stately trees bearing rich and luscious fruits. Banks of gorgeous flowers were on every hand, and birds with rare and brilliant plumage sang and fluttered in the trees and bushes. A little way off was a small brook, rising and sparkling along between green banks" (Baum 1903, 20).

A brief medieval English lyric, despite naming a specific place, gives the impression of being an invitation to an otherworld.

> I am of Irelond,
> And of the holy lond
> Of Irelond.
> Gode sire, preye I thee,
> For-of Seint Charitee
> Come and daunce with me
> In Irelond.

Speirs remarks:

> The dancer from across the sea—from a sacred or magical other country—is still perhaps essentially a faery or otherworld visitant (or a human impersonator of such a character) in the performed dance. . . . This particular song, chiefly by means of its rhythms and repetitions of sound, suggests to the reader a trance-like or rapt condition in the dancer whose song it is; consequently, a supernaturally compelling or appealing power seems to emanate from the dancer. (Speirs 1957, 60)

Since life can be conceptualized as a journey, it is not surprising that journeys, including those to otherworlds, should be common in folklore and literature.

John P. Brennan and Jane Garry (upper and lower worlds); *Judith Neaman* (earthly paradise); *Hande A. Birkalan* (other otherworlds)

See also: Choice of Roads.

REFERENCES

Aarne, Antti, and Stith Thompson. 1964 [1961]. *The Types of the Folktale: A Classification and Bibliography.* Helsinki: Suomalainen Tiedeakatemia.

Baum, L. Frank. 1903. *The Wonderful Wizard of Oz.* Chicago: Bobbs Merrill.

Clark, Jerome. 2000. *Extraordinary Encounters: An Encyclopedia of Extraterrestial and Otherworldy Beings.* Santa Barbara, CA: ABC-CLIO.

Curtius, E.R. 1953. *European Literature and the Latin Middle Ages.* Trans. Willard R. Trask. New York: Pantheon Books.

Daemmrich, Ingrid G., ed. 1997. *Enigmatic Bliss: The Paradise Motif in Literature.* 1 vol. New York: Peter Lang.

Delumeau, Jean. 1995. *History of Paradise: The Garden of Eden in Myth and Tradition.* Trans. Matthew McConnell. New York: Continuum.

Dorson, Richard M., ed. 1975. *Folk Tales Told Around the World.* Chicago: University of Chicago Press.

Eberhard, Wolfram. 1915. *Folktales of China.* Chicago: University of Chicago Press.

Elkhadem, Saad. 1981. *The York Companion to Themes and Motifs of World Literature.* Fredericton, NB: York Press.

The Encyclopedia of Apocalypticism. 1999. Ed. Bernard McGinn, John J. Collins, and Stephen J. Stein. 3 vols. New York: Continuum.

Foster, Benjamin. 2001. *Epic of Gilgamesh.* New York: W.W. Norton.

Gaster, Theodore H. 1952. *The Oldest Stories in the World.* Boston: Beacon Press.

Gray, John. 1985 [1982]. *Near Eastern Mythology.* Rev. ed. New York: P. Bedrick Books.

Guirand, F. 1977. "Finno-Ugric Mythology." In *New Laronsse Encyclopedia of Mythology.* Trans. R. Aldington and D. Ames. London: Hamlyn.

Haas, Alois M. 1999. "Otherworldly Journeys in the Middle Ages." In *The Encyclopedia of Apocalypticism,* ed. Bernard McGinn, John J. Collins, and Stephen J. Stein, 3:442–466. New York: Continuum.

Kramer, Samuel Noah. 1961. *Mythologies of the Ancient World.* Chicago: Doubleday/Quadrangle Books.

Lattimore, Richmond. 1975 [1965]. *Odyssey of Homer.* New York: Harper Colophon.

Lieck, Gwendolyn. 1991. *A Dictionary of Ancient Near Eastern Mythology.* New York: Routledge.

Manuel, Frank E. and Fritzie P. 1979. *Utopian Thought in the Western World.* Cambridge, MA: Belknap Press.

"Paradise." 1973. *Encyclopedia Judaica.* 13:78–86. Jerusalem: Encyclopedia Judaica.

Parrinder, Geoffrey. 1967. *African Mythology.* London: Paul Hamlyn.

Patch, Howard Rollin. 1950. *The Other World According to Descriptions in Medieval Literature.* Cambridge, MA: Harvard University Press.

Pentikäinen, Juha Y. 1999. *Kalevala Mythology.* Trans. Ritva Poom. Bloomington: Indiana University Press.

Scheub, Harold. 2000. *Dictionary of African Mythology: The Mythmaker as Storyteller.* Oxford: Oxford University Press.

Siikala, Anna-Leena. 1987. "Descent into the Underworld." In *Encyclopaedia of Religion,* ed. Mircea Eliade, 4:300–304. 16 vols. New York: Macmillan.

Silver, Carole G. 1999. *Strange and Secret Peoples: Fairies and Victorian Consciousness.* New York: Oxford University Press.

Speirs, John. 1957. *Medieval English Poetry: The Non-Chaucerian Tradition.* London: Faber and Faber.

Spence, Lewis. 1946. *British Fairy Origins.* London: Watts.

Taube, Karl. 1993. *Aztec and Maya Myths.* Austin: University of Texas Press.

Thompson, Stith. 1966 [1929]. *Tales of the North American Indians.* Bloomington: Indiana University Press.

———. 1977 [1946]. *The Folktale.* Berkeley: University of California Press. Original ed. New York: Holt, Rinehart and Winston.

Werner, Alice. 1925. *African Mythology. Vol. 7 of the Mythology of All Races.* Boston: Archaeological Institute of America.

Wolkstein, Diane, and Samuel Noah Kramer. 1983. *Inanna, Queen of Heaven and Earth: Her Stories and Hymms from Sumer.* New York: Harper and Row.

Zaleski, Carol. 1987. *Otherworld Journeys: Accounts of Near-Death Experience in Medieval and Modern Times.* New York: Oxford University Press.

Fairies and Elves

Motifs F200–F399

❊

Although there are creatures in world folklore and literature that are similar to those known in English as fairies, fairies are uniquely European, prominent in the cultures of Western Europe, especially in Celtic areas such as Ireland, Scotland, Cornwall, and Brittany. In Germany and Scandinavia they are known as elves, *nisses, neks,* kobolds, and nixies. A few commentators identify the peris of Persian mythology and folklore with the fairies—mainly on the basis of false etymology (*peri = feerie*)—but they are not truly analogous. Originally beautiful female spirits, perceived as evil and held responsible for eclipses, droughts, and crop failures, peris later metamorphosed into benevolent figures whose special function was to guide human souls to paradise (Jones 1995, 345). In Islam and in pre-Islamic Arabia we find the jinn, supernatural beings but again not really like the fairies; for one thing, they are often invisible, formed from "smokeless fire." Thompson classifies Indian *bongas* (F201) under fairies, stating that they are "roughly equivalent to fairies. Generally malevolent, but often not." Eberhard's 1965 collection of Chinese folktales includes several tales containing creatures that he calls fairies.

The word *fairy* or, more directly, *fay* is from late Latin *fata* or *fatae,* earlier *fatum,* meaning "fate." The thirteen fairies who stood beside the cradle of the Sleeping Beauty in the "fairy tale" of that name are a direct link to their ancient foremothers, the Fates, who stood beside the cradle of Meleager in Greek mythology. These female beings were as powerful as the gods in presiding over human destiny.

In the European Middle Ages, the word *fairy* signified enchantment and the land where enchanted beings dwelt in addition to the inhabitants of this land (Leach 1949 1, 363). They were thought to live alongside mortals, often in subterranean dwellings (F210, "Fairyland"; F211, Fairyland under a hollow knoll (mound, hill, sĭd). A nineteenth-century commentator, Thomas Keightley, categorized fairies as "distinct from men and from the higher orders of divinities" (1850, 3). But whether they are called fays, *fées* (French), fairies, "the little people," "the good folk," or "the hidden people," they have certain traits in common. They are generally invisible; they have the power of "glamour" with which they enchant or hypnotize; they are ordinarily smaller than humans, ranging from four feet to a few inches tall. They may be helpful and benign, destructive and malevolent, or merely capricious and mischievous. Though they are thought to excel humans in power, knowledge, and longevity, they are not immortal.

Fairies range from the beautiful and godlike Tuatha De Danann of the Irish to the naked, long-nosed, crude, and hairy little creatures known as boggarts. Nevertheless, there is some consensus about fairy types and traits. The elfin peoples are often divided into two general categories, those that belong to a group, race, or nation (what K.M. Briggs calls "trooping fairies") and those that essentially dwell alone, "solitary" fairies (Briggs 1977, 131). Aristocratic groups and kingdoms appear to derive from Celtic sources, while the more common, homey dwarfs and household familiars seem to be part of England's Germanic heritage. However, Anglo-Saxon and Scandinavian elves and dwarfs must also be included among the trooping fairies alongside the Scottish "Seelie" and "Unseelie Courts," the Welsh Tylwyth Teg, and the Irish Sidhe or Tuatha De Danann. This last group, "the people of the hill" or "the children of the goddess Danu," are widely celebrated in epic and legend. Ruled over by a queen more often than by a king, the social organization of these groups is hierarchical and strikingly similar to folk-fantasies of human royal courts. This fairyland is often depicted as a world without change, decay, illness, or aging. Here, one fairy day may be a hundred mortal years, and these fairies spend their days in lavish feasting, music, song, and dance, often luring mortals to join them. Fairies possess jewels and silken robes, fine horses, dogs and even cattle, and their life is one of ease and pleasure.

Fairies give birth and, although long-lived, die, but they are not blessed with either fertility or ease in childbirth—which may explain their thefts of mortal infants and their need for human nurses and midwives. They ride out in elegant processions called "Fairy Rades" (rides), though their purpose is less noble than their appearance, for they come to abduct human children. In general, they "seem" beautiful, but their appearance may be fraudulent—an effect of their power of "glamour" or illusion.

Individual or solitary fairies are very different. They include the "household familiar" varieties, including brownies, boggarts, Pucks, lobs, and hobs.

A fairy dance. "The elf-queene, with hir joly compaignye, / Daunced ful ofte in many a grene mede" ("The Wife of Bath's Tale" by Geoffrey Chaucer, late fourteenth century). From "The Elfin-Grove" in Brothers Grimm, *German Popular Stories,* illustrated by George Cruikshank (1824–1826).

These, like the Roman Lars, are small, ancestral household deities who attach themselves to families and alternate between helpful services like sweeping and washing and mischievous thefts and pranks. Other solitaries, like the Irish leprechaun or fairy shoemaker, have specific tasks or trades; still others, like the Welsh Lady of the Van, are attached to specific places—lakes, rivers, trees, mines, and cairns. All vary in size, appearance, and behavior. They range from the human-sized, beautiful but evil Glaistig of the Highlands, a vampire who drinks human blood, to the small, grotesque brownie—hairy, naked, and ugly but essentially helpful.

Fairy character is best described as capricious and amoral. Fairies love and reward cleanliness and order, yet have no qualms about stealing from human beings. They are known to take the "goodness" or essence out of milk and other foods; they steal the peas from the pods and take human possessions as well. Yet they are generous too and will reward mortals who aid them. They are passionate about protecting their privacy and severely punish those who spy on them or visit uninvited, but they are also capable of great hospitality. They are often wanton and highly sexual in nature; they take mortal lovers at whim and, in the case of the *lhiannon-shee* (fairy mistress) of Ireland, literally destroy them with amorous attention. Capable of great kindness and goodness, they must be treated with politeness, respect, and, above all, with caution. At their worst, they are capable of powerful evil; they can paralyze with elf-shot or fairy-stroke and quite easily cause human suffering and death. Many of their actions, however, fall between these categories; fairies are mischievous, like the Cornish pixies who can playfully or dangerously lead travelers astray. They can be utterly capricious; in one frequently repeated tale, they remove the hump from one poor hunchback and place it on another human being.

Much of the folklore about fairies deals with their role as kidnappers (F320, "Fairies carry people away to fairyland"; F321, "Fairy steals child from cradle"). Other frequently told tales deal with the love between humans and fairies, usually in the form of the mortal man's passion for and marriage to a fairy-bride. These stories generally follow the same pattern: a man captures, falls in love with, and weds a beautiful fairy. He is prohibited from certain actions; striking her with iron, mentioning her name, or seeing her at certain times. When he breaks the tabu, she leaves him and he either loses her for good or succeeds in regaining her after many tests and trials. There are also tales of mortals visiting the fairy world and of fairies appearing in the mortal world to ask for and receive human aid. Such tales, some still half-believed, may suggest the human need to think that we are not entirely alone on earth.

There have been numerous ideas on the origin of fairies. As early as the Middle Ages these elfin creatures were seen as fallen angels. A minority argued that the fairies were devils, but most believers suggested that they were those undecided angels who lacked the strength to either stand with God or fall with Satan. Some fell into the sea, becoming the mer-creatures of the waters; some fell into the caverns of the earth and became goblins, kobolds, and other evil beings; some fell into woods and forests, becoming elves, pixies, and the like. Another similar idea made them the children of Adam and Eve whose existence the couple denied to God, or even the pre-Adamite inhabitants of earth. In short, this "religious view" depicted the elfin peoples as morally indeterminate, not good enough for heaven or bad enough for hell, but constituting a second race inhabiting this world.

Equally common was the idea that fairies were a special category of the dead, either those who had died before their appointed time or those who had died unbaptized. Some thought them the spirits of extinct races, of the ancient Druids, of those drowned in the biblical flood, and, generally, of the pagans who had died before Christ's dispensation. A more modern occultist explanation makes them the souls of the recent dead, locked in a transitional phase between lives, awaiting reincarnation or transportation to the astral plane. Lewis Spence in *British Fairy Origins* (1946) makes a good case for the belief in fairies stemming from a cult of the dead. Their small size may be correlated with the traditional depiction of the soul as smaller than the person from whom it issues; the dwellings of fairies and those of the dead (within barrows, hills, or other subterranean realms) are similar; the same stories are told of both groups, and many place persons believed dead in fairyland, coexisting with the fairies. Interestingly, the same rituals and prohibitions govern relations with fairies and the dead; both are night-creatures who must vanish or retreat at daybreak; both groups lure mortals to them and both may be placated in the same way with gifts or offerings. Similarly, both fairyland and the world of the dead are marked by distorted time or timelessness; in each, mortals are forbidden to taste food or drink (C211.1, "Tabu: eating in fairyland") (Silver 1999, 41–42).

Another premise, now less frequently maintained, holds that fairies are diminished forms or "trickled-down" versions of the ancient British, Celtic, and classical gods and goddesses. Gods and heroes, reduced in stature and importance as new faiths are substituted for belief in them, become the elfin tribes. Thus Queen Medb, a female hero of Irish epic, becomes Queen Mab of fairyland. Another view derives fairies from the nature spirits worshiped by humans in the early stages of civilization when "animism" prevailed, so that a local water-spirit would later be anthropomorphized into an undine or mermaid.

Some of the most interesting theories are euhemeristic, that is, speculations that myths and folk beliefs stem from actual historical persons and events. In this view, fairies derive from folk memories of earlier or aboriginal inhabitants of a given country. David MacRitchie popularized this idea in *The Testimony of Tradition* (1890), a book in which he argued for the existence of the fairies as memories of a small, primitive, pre-Celtic race forced into caves and mounds as well as into nocturnal habits, thefts, and rapid flight by their Celtic conquerors.

Modern spiritualists, theosophists, and Rosicrucians have added to the number and variety of origin theories by suggesting that fairies are the elementals of Paracelsus and seventeenth-century alchemists and magicians. The latter groups had argued that each element was ruled by a resident spirit: sylphs were made of air, gnomes of earth, salamanders of fire, and undines or nymphs of water. Mystics and occultists conflated the elementals with the fairies of folklore and believed them influential in séances, poltergeist occurrences, and other psychic phenomena. After Darwin, some believers argued that fairies were simply life-forms existing on another branch of the tree of evolution; though invisible to humans, they were fellow occupants of earth. Supporters of this theory, including Sir Arthur Conan Doyle, whose book *The Coming of the Fairies* (1922) widely publicized photographs of elfin creatures, thought them little nature-spirits whose special function was to fertilize and tend plants and flowers.

FAIRIES IN LITERATURE

Beginning with an ancient Anglo-Saxon charm against elf-shot, fairies have been chronicled in literature. They appear in Arthurian romance and in other medieval works, including *Sir Orfeo* and *Sir Huon of Bordeaux*. Some of these stories made their way into ballads and may be found in a number of the English and Scottish ballads in F.J. Child's collection, especially "King Orfeo," "The Elfin Knight," "Tam Lin," "The Wee Wee Man," "Thomas Rhymer, Thomas of Erceldoune," and "The Queen of Elfan's Nourice." In Chaucer's *Canterbury Tales* (late fourteenth century), the Wife of Bath, recounting a tale set in the time of King Arthur, remarks that, at that time, "Al was this land fulfild of fayerye. / The elf-queene, with hir joly compaignye, / Daunced ful ofte in many a grene mede." She goes on to acknowledge that "I speke of manye hundred yeres ago" and that because of the prevalence of Christianity, the elves and fairies have gone away. Nevertheless, "true" accounts of their actions may be found in the chronicles and histories of Ralph of Coggeshall, Gervase of Tilbury, and Walter Map, as well as in the later account, *The Secret Common-wealth of Elves, Fains, and Fairies* (1691), by the Reverend Robert Kirk of Aberfoyle (Briggs 1967). They appear in several of Shakespeare's plays, most notably in *A Midsummer Night's Dream,* but also in *Romeo and Juliet, The Merry Wives of Windsor* and *The Tempest*. Fairies are revivified in the poetry of the Romantics (especially in the work of John Keats) and in the paintings of the Victorian fairy-painters, including Richard Dadd, John Anster Fitzgerald, and Sir Joseph Noel Paton. The Victorians had a fascination with fairies arising from the nineteenth-century study of folklore, which especially attracted the Irish writers and folklorists of the Celtic revival, including William Butler Yeats, AE (George Russell), Patrick Kennedy, Lady Wilde, and Lady Gregory. In an 1898 article in the periodical *Nineteenth Century,* Yeats wrote that there is not a place outside of the large Irish towns "where they do not believe that the Fairies, the Tribes of the goddess Danu, are stealing their bodies and their souls" (Yeats 1976, 2:56). In Tolstoy's novel *War and Peace* (1869*),* as Natasha and her brother are driving home after a day in the countryside, Natasha says that she has been thinking in the darkness that they might arrive not at their home, but in fairyland (Book 7, Part 7). This little fantasy is poignant because Natasha is on the brink of marriage, perhaps not quite ready to give up her childhood. She also adds, "I know that I shall never again be as happy and tranquil as I am now," and, indeed, her life, and the lives of all the people of Russia, are soon to be turned upside down by war.

The fairies survive in contemporary literature, playing roles in books by such figures as Sylvia Townsend Warner, Angela Carter, and Tanith Lee, and they live on in contemporary life in their newest transformation—as the huge-eyed, small gray creatures visiting from other worlds in their UFOs.

Carole G. Silver

See also: Abductions.

REFERENCES

Briggs, K.M. 1967. *Fairies in English Tradition and Literature.* Chicago: University of Chicago Press.

———. 1970. "Fairies." *Man, Myth and Magic: An Illustrated Encyclopedia of the Supernatural,* 4:901–906. New York: Marshall Cavendish.

———. 1977. *A Dictionary of Fairies: Hobgoblins, Brownies, Bogies and Other Supernatural Creatures.* Harmondsworth: Penguin.

Doyle, Sir Arthur Conan. 1922. *The Coming of the Fairies.* London: Hodder and Stoughton.

Eberhard, Wolfram. 1965. *Folktales of China.* Chicago: University of Chicago Press.

Jones, Alison. 1995. *Larousse Dictionary of Wold Folklore.* Edinburgh: Larousse.

Keightley, Thomas. 1850 [1833]. *The Fairy Mythology: Illustrative of the Romance and Superstition of Various Countries.* Rev. ed. London: Whittaker, Treacher.

Leach, MacEdward. 1949. "Fairy." *Funk and Wagnalls Standard Dictionary of Folklore, Mythology and Legend.* 2 vols. New York: Funk and Wagnalls.

MacRitchie, David. 1890. *The Testimony of Tradition.* London: Kegan Paul.

Silver, Carole G. 1999. *Strange and Secret Peoples: Fairies and Victorian Consciousness.* New York: Oxford University Press.

Spence, Lewis. 1946. *British Fairy Origins.* London: Watts.

Yeats, William Butler. 1959. *Mythologies.* New York: Collier Books.

———. 1976. *Unpublished Prose by W.B. Yeats.* Ed. John P. Frayne and Colton Johnson. 2 vols. New York: Columbia University Press.

Water Spirits

Motif F420

❁

Traditional cultures everywhere associate water with supernatural beings, and understandably so, given the necessity of water for all life; the ever-changing appearance of rivers, lakes, and oceans; obvious but rarely predictable connections between water and weather; and the inability of humans to exist more than a few minutes submerged, while other living beings thrive under water. Furthermore, wells and springs are entryways (although virtually impassible by humans) into underground realms and to whatever secrets they might contain. Veneration and fear are not unreasonable responses to this mysterious medium and its inhabitants.

Although early Christian leaders protested against their converts' residual pagan beliefs, popular theology soon evolved to explain pre-Christian supernatural beings in Christian terms. *Beowulf,* essentially a heathen work, but with Christian trappings, provides a prominent example. In lines 102–114 we read that Grendel and other monsters and demons are "kinsmen of Cain." Grendel's principal domicile is, of course, beneath a mere, and Beowulf's dramatic battle with Grendel's even more ferocious mother takes place in this underwater realm.

Another popular explanation for the origin of fairy-like creatures derives from the biblical war in heaven. The following account from southeast Germany is typical of those found throughout Europe: "When God cast out the arrogant angels from heaven, they became the evil spirits that plague mankind. . . . Those who fell onto the earth became goblins, imps, dwarfs, thumblings, alps, noon-and-evening-ghosts, and will-o'-the-wisps. Those who fell into the forests became the wood-spirits who live there. . . . Finally, those who fell into the water became water spirits: water-men, mermaids, and merwomen" (Köhler 1886, 99).

An even more poetic Christian rationalization of heathen beliefs concerning water spirits comes from Wales. According to legend, Saint Patrick, a transplanted Welshman, returned to Wales for a visit. While he was walking along Crumlyn Lake, some Welsh people began to abuse him for migrating to Erin. Not willing to let the insult go unpunished, Saint Patrick transformed his accusers into water creatures, the males into fish and the females into water fairies. To this day, Crumlyn Lake is inhabited by their offspring (Sikes [1880], ch. 3).

One of the oldest and best documented manifestations of water worship is the belief in magic or holy wells and springs (D926). Although a worldwide phenomenon, such sites are especially important in Ireland and in Celtic Britain. In many instances, linguistic, archaeological, folkloric, and documentary evidence combines to map out a provenance that includes heathen mythology, fairy-lore, Christian veneration, and neopagan mysticism. One such place is Clootie Well near the village of Munlochy in Scotland. It is said that this well was originally the home of a fairy, who expected the gift of a piece of cloth (cloot) before allowing a mortal to drink of its magic water. Still today the bushes and trees surrounding the well are covered with pieces of cloth left behind by visitors who playfully or seriously continue to practice the ancient belief. Similar traditions are associated with healing wells and springs throughout the British Isles: the Chalice Well near Glastonbury, England (a mecca for latter-day mystics of all sorts), the Madron Holy Well in Cornwall, and Saint Brigid's Well in Kildare Town, Ireland, to name but a few. Offerings of cloth, pins, and coins are commonplace. In fact, the practice of throwing coins into a fountain for good luck, obviously a survival of ancient well worship, is a worldwide phenomenon, showing no sign of abatement.

Not all gifts made to water deities are as benign as cloth, pins, and coins. Legends from around the world describe animal and human sacrifices for the protection of buildings, especially those adjacent to water (F420.5.2.5, "Water-spirits interfere with building bridges, dams"). Typically, the victims are mortared alive within the foundation of a building or bridge (S261). The following legend from Germany exemplifies the type. The spillway of a mill on the Haun River is damaged by high water and ice. A drunkard assures the miller that burying a child alive within the foundation will prevent further damage. This is done, and shortly afterward the drunkard drowns in the river, and the miller dies of grief. Since then the miller's ghost has haunted the area, pushing one victim into the river each year (Wolf 1853, no. 218). This legend verifies the belief in foundation sacrifices while at the same time vilifying those who practice them. However, the legend still implies that some unnamed water spirit, even if it does not accept the sacrifice of an innocent child, nonetheless requires a victim on a regular basis. The belief that certain bodies of water demand one human death every year or so is widespread (F420.5.2.1.6, "Water-spirit claims a life every seven years"; F420.5.2.6.1, "Water-spirits take revenge if yearly tribute is not given").

The inherent and obvious danger of water has led to supernatural explanations for mishaps of all types. Some such supernatural explanations are nothing more than bugbears, fictitious creatures invented by adults to frighten children into avoiding dangerous places. These traditions are usually local, so the intimidating creatures' names and the descriptions of their misdeeds vary from region to region. Two such sinister beings, formerly promoted by parents in Yorkshire, England, are named Jenny Green-teeth and Peg-o'-the-Well (Parkinson 1888, 202–203).

Not all water monsters are fictions invented by protective parents. In addition to countless sea monsters observed by sailors, every region has its own apparitions domiciled in local rivers and lakes. A few examples must suffice. Water bulls (F420.1.3.4), fierce amphibious creatures that often caused the death of domestic cows, were reported on the Isle of Man and in Scotland and Norway well into the nineteenth century. The water kelpie (F420.1.3.3) was a horse-like creature in Scotland, feared for its propensity to lure a man to mount it, then carry him to his death in a river or lake. A similar creature, known as the *njugl,* was known in the Shetland Islands.

Scotland is still home to a famous water apparition, the Loch Ness Monster, which is in many ways a rationalization of ancient mystical beasts. Its defenders, instead of relying on fairy mythology or medieval theology to explain its existence, base their beliefs on evolutionary biology. Although Loch Ness is today the world's best-known searching ground for prehistoric monsters, several hundred additional lakes and rivers worldwide claim similar sightings. Lake Champlain is the best-known such site in North America. In Europe, monsters seen in Lake Seljordsvatnet, Norway, and Lake Storsjön, Sweden, are famous in their respective regions. Perhaps once feared, these leviathans are now actively promoted by tourism boards, and they have long since lost any threatening aspect.

Another sea creature once widely feared but now adored is the mermaid. The objects of countless sightings, mermaids, like their less familiar male counterparts mermen, are mysteriously attractive to members of the opposite sex, but the sighting of a mermaid usually augers bad luck, which for seamen means a shipwreck. Child gives several versions of the ballad "The Mermaid" (Child 289), in which the sailors spy a mermaid on a rock "with a comb and a glass in her hand," and shortly afterwards a storm comes up and sinks their ship (Child 1965, 5:148–152). Marriages between mermaids and land men

(B81.2), like those between swan maidens and humans, are seldom happy. "The Mermaid Wife" from Shetland, a typical legend (Douglas 1901, 153–155; AT4080), is parallel to numerous swan maiden stories. An inhabitant of Unst, the northernmost of the Shetland Islands, one night sees a number of mermen and mermaids dancing on a sandy beach, with several sealskins lying nearby. Seeing him, they seize their skins, regain the form of seals, and disappear into the sea. The Shetlander succeeds in snatching up one skin, which belongs to a beautiful maiden. Unable to return to the sea, she remains with him and becomes his wife. He carefully hides her sealskin. The couple live together several years, and she bears him several children. One day, one of the children finds the hidden sealskin and shows it to his mother. She receives it with joy, embraces her children, then races to the seashore, pursued by her earthly husband. Donning the skin, she dives into the waves, saying as she disappears, "Farewell. I loved you very well when I resided upon earth, but I always loved my first husband much better." Although identified in this legend as mermaids and mermen, these creatures who can alternate between seal and human form are called *selkies* or *silkies* elsewhere, especially in Ireland.

Female water creatures—whether called mermaids, nixies, nymphs, or sprites—often are dangerously seductive (F420.1.2.1, "Water-maidens are of unusual beauty"). The same can be said of their male counterparts, although there are relatively few legends depicting seductions of mortal women by water-men. An example is a Shetland ballad called "The Great Silkie of Sule Skerry" (Child 113) about a creature who is "a man upon the land and . . . a silkie in the sea" who begets a child upon a human woman (Child 1965, 2:494).

A typical legend of underwater seduction is "The Sea Nymph" from Sweden (Hofberg 1893, 75–76). One night a number of fishermen see a woman's wet hand reach in through the door of their hut. One of them, a newly married man from Kinnar, takes hold of the hand, only to be pulled out the door into the darkness. The next day his comrades search for him, but he has disappeared without a trace. After three years, his wife finally remarries. A mysterious stranger who resembles the bride's missing husband appears at the wedding celebration. He tells how a sea nymph had dragged him into an underwater realm (F420.5.2.1.1, "Water-maiden enamors man and draws him under water"). There he had forgotten his life on earth until that very morning, when the nymph stated that there was to be a wedding in Kinnar. His memory returned, and he asked for permission to see the bridal procession. The nymph agreed, under the stipulation that he not enter the house. However, he could not resist, and here he is. Just as he completes his story, a tempest comes up, blowing half the roof off the house. The man immediately falls ill and dies three days later.

One of Europe's best-known water sprites is Lorelei (also spelled Lore Lay), who haunts the base of a cliff on the Rhine River near the village of Bacharach. Her story is known both in folk legends and in ballads by Clemens Brentano, Heinrich Heine, and others. Lorelei, it is said, is a young woman who unintentionally causes men to fall in love with her. Suspecting her of witchcraft, a bishop summons her to his court. Weary of her destructive power over men, she begs for a death sentence. Instead, the bishop, moved by her beauty, pronounces her free of all guilt, then proposes that she dedicate herself to God. He calls three knights to accompany her to the convent. Their route takes them past a high cliff overlooking the Rhine. Standing at the edge of the precipice, Lorelei says, "See that boat on the Rhine. The boatman is my lover!" With no further warning, she jumps from the cliff into the Rhine. She still sits on a rock at a dangerous bend in the river, singing a seductive song and combing her golden hair (F420.5.3.1), thus luring incautious boatmen onto the rocks.

Another famous European water nymph is Undine (sometimes spelled Ondine), a being described and named by Paracelsus, the Swiss physician and alchemist. Although undines (the word can be both a personal name and a noun describing a type of spirit) have water as their natural home, they function on land and often marry, but they require utmost trust and fidelity from their husbands. Such spirits are featured in many European chapbooks written during the Reformation and Renaissance. The heroine is traditionally named Melusine or Melusina. The following account from the Harz Mountains of Germany is typical of the many local and regional legends about this being.

A knight, lost in the woods, finally comes upon a castle inhabited by a beautiful young woman. She gives him food and shelter, and he falls in love with her. She accepts his proposal of marriage under the condition that every Friday she would be free to go out and do whatever she wants, and that he would not try to follow her. This he promises, and they marry, living happily together for a long time. One Friday a stranger comes and is given lodging. The lady of the house makes no appearance. The husband explains his wife's weekly absence, whereupon the stranger says that nothing good can come from such behavior. This conversation so alarms the husband that he immediately sets out to find his wife. He finally discovers her in the cellar, half fish and half human, swimming in a small pond. Seeing her husband, she casts a sad glance at him and disappears. The husband dies soon afterward (F420.5.2.6.4, "Water-spirits avenge selves on mortal who fails to keep promise"). Now all that remains are the castle's ruins and the story (Ey 1862, 173–176).

Closely related to water-spirit legends are the countless tales of sunken bells that continue their ghostly tolling from beneath the water (F993, "Sunken bell sounds"). Told throughout Europe, these legends fall into two main categories. First are bells that were accidentally dropped into deep water while being transported—an example is the Kentsham bell that continues to toll off the coast of England (Burne 1884). Second, and more important, are bells associated with submerged towns (F725.2., "Submarine cities"). The most famous of these in Europe is the city of Ys, submerged beneath the Bay of Douarnenez in Brittany. The legend that its cathedral bells can still be heard from beneath the water inspired Claude Debussy's "La Cathédral engloutie" (The Sunken [or Engulfed] Cathedral).

Another musical piece prompted by sunken bells is the Welsh folksong "The Bells of Aberdovey," popular since the eighteenth century. Aberdovey is the town closest to the legendary port of Gwyddno, now submerged in Cardigan Bay. Writing in 1907, W. Jenkyn Thomas claimed, "The nearest town to the submerged realm of Gwyddno is Aberdovey. If you stand on the beach there, you will sometimes hear in the long twilight evening chimes and peals of bells. . . . The sounds come from the bells of one of Gwyddno's drowned churches, and these are 'The Bells of Aberdovey' that the song speaks about" ([1907], 41).

An account combining fairy mythology with science fiction tells of an underwater city at Langness, off the coast of the Isle of Man. Here, not only submerged church bells but also the barking of dogs and the bleating of sheep can be heard. "More than two hundred years ago," reported Sophia Morrison in 1911, a man descended to the underwater city in a diving bell. Through its windows he saw "great streets decorated with pillars of crystal glittering like diamonds, and beautiful buildings made of mother-of-pearl, with shells of every color set in it" (F420.2.1, "Water-spirits live in castles of crystal under water"). He also observed many handsome mermen and beautiful mermaids, but, fearing him, they quickly swam away. Back on dry land, the man longed to return to the "World-under-Sea" and stay there forever, and soon afterward he died of grief (182–185).

Sunken towns do not always stay submerged. Shannon City, beneath the estuary of Ireland's Shannon River, appears above water every seven years (something like the mythical town of Germelshausen in Germany that appears every hundred years, the model for the fictitious Brigadoon). However, any mortal who sees Shannon City above water will soon die (MacKillop 1998, 340).

In 2002 the present writer learned from a lifelong resident of Catchall, Cornwall, that nearby Mount's Bay was formerly dry ground, and when the ocean rose, for reasons unknown to my informant, seven parishes were flooded. Fishermen, I was assured, from time to time still hear the ringing of the underwater bells.

D.L. Ashliman

REFERENCES

Burne, Charlotte S. 1884. "Two Folk-Tales, Told by a Herefordshire Squire, 1845–6." *Folk-Lore Journal* 2: 20–22.

Child, Francis James. 1965. Reprint. *The English and Scottish Popular Ballads.* 5 vols. New York: Dover. Orig. ed. Boston: Houghton, Mifflin, 1882–1898.

Douglas, George. 1901. *Scottish Fairy and Folk Tales.* London: Walter Scott.

Ey, August. 1862. *Harzmärchenbuch; oder, Sagen und Märchen aus dem Oberharze.* Stade: Verlag von Fr. Steudel.

Gregor, Walter. 1881. *Notes on the Folk-Lore of the North-East of Scotland.* London: Folk-Lore Society.

Hofberg, Herman. 1893. *Swedish Fairy Tales.* Trans. W.H. Myers. Chicago: W.B. Conkey.

Köhler, Johann August Ernst. 1886. *Sagenbuch des Erzgebirges.* Schneeberg: Verlag und Druck von Carl Moritz Gärtner.

MacKillop, James. 1998. *Dictionary of Celtic Mythology.* Oxford: Oxford University Press.

Morrison, Sophia. 1911. *Manx Fairy Tales.* London: David Nutt.

Parkinson, Thomas. 1888. *Yorkshire Legends and Traditions.* London: Elliot Stock.

Sikes, Wirt. [1880]. *British Goblins: Welsh Folk-Lore, Fairy Mythology, Legends, and Traditions.* London: S. Low, Marston, Searle, and Rivington.

Thomas, W. Jenkyn. [1907]. *The Welsh Fairy Book.* London: T. Fisher Unwin.

Wolf, J.W. 1853. *Hessische Sagen.* Göttingen: Dieterichsche Buchhandlung.

Extraordinary Sky and Weather Phenomena

Motif F790

❀

Since the beginning of recorded history, human beings have gazed up at the sky to seek signs of what will happen next: good or bad weather, calamities, marvels, visions, and blessings. People have often associated celestial phenomena with religious beliefs and practices. In many religions, the sky is the home of a deity or deities and the place where people expect to go after their deaths. Sightings of extraterrestrial visitors have been documented by members of diverse cultures. Unidentified flying objects (UFOs), eclipses, comets, severe storms, and other unusual phenomena have found their place in both legends and elite literature, where they have tended to be viewed as determinants of future well-being and providers of important lessons.

During an interview at the Psychologische Gesellschaft in Basel in 1958, C.G. Jung said, "In our world miracles do not happen anymore, and we feel that something simply must happen which will provide an answer or show a way out. So now these UFOs are appearing in the skies" (F37§, "Inhabitants of another planet (extra-terrestrial) visit earth") (Jung 1977, 390).

According to Jung, extraordinary apparitions in the sky are not intrinsically meaningful; however, people tend to project their hopes and expectations upon these phenomena. Hope for a savior and fear of "ships of death," which may bring or dispose of souls, are significant archetypal ideas. Jung speaks of the fear that an atomic war will take souls away from the earth; he also speculates about the meaning of UFOs in individual cases, stating that this meaning "depends on the circumstances, on a dream, or on the person concerned" (1977: 390–391).

In late twentieth-century and early twenty-first-century folklore and popular movies, visions of unusual beings in the sky have been common. Since the 1950s there have been numerous legends of flying saucers or UFOs; one recurrent legend has insisted that the United States government is hiding evidence of alien invasion in Roswell, New Mexico. In the movie *Close Encounters of the Third Kind* (1977), a beautiful, shimmering spaceship, reminiscent of Gothic cathedrals, inspires quasi-religious awe. Later movies, such as *Men in Black* (1997), take a more jocular view of aliens' presence. The more serious fantasies of helpful and inspiring aliens support Jung's contention that an extraterrestrial savior's descent from the sky is an archetypal idea.

MYTHOLOGY

In Greek, Roman, Egyptian, and Norse mythology, celestial phenomena are personified by male deities. Helios, the Greek sun god, rides across the sky in a fiery chariot. The Egyptian sun god, Ra, was the inspiration for a namerons myths. Worship of the sun was prominent in the belief systems of the Aztecs and the Mayans of Central America as well. Zeus and Jupiter, supreme gods of the Greek and Roman pantheons, wield three thunderbolts that symbolize sovereignty as well as chance, destiny, and providence. Thor, the Norse god of thunder, dazzles human beings with his destructive force.

In Native American mythology, personification of the sun generally makes the sun male; only the Cherokee, the Inuit, and the Yuchi see the sun as female (Stirling 1945, 387–400). A Jicarilla Apache story tells of Holy Boy's theft of the sun as a small object from another deity, White Hactcin; the moon is stolen in the same way from Black Hactcin. Many Native American myths describe thunder as a male deity; for the Kato of California, Thunder is the creator of humankind. Among the Cherokee, thunder takes the form of twin boys, Wild Boy and Tame Boy, sons of Selu and Kanati (Corn Mother and Hunter), whose ball games in the sky cause thunderstorms. On the North Pacific coast and as far east as the Eastern Woodlands, thunderbirds produce thunder and lightning, wage war with snakes, and grant blessings.

The ancient Chinese deity P'an Ku creates the world through a series of dramatic weather phenomena. His breath makes the wind rise, his voice releases thunder, and his gaze brings flashes of lightning. Marie-Louise von Franz explains that P'an Ku, the "gigantic, symbolic human being who embraces and contains the whole cosmos," is an expression of the Self archetype (Jung 1964, 200). P'an Ku demonstrates the power of the Self through his control of the weather, which markedly changes the appearance of the cosmos.

Solar mythology, a theory proposed by the German folklorist Max Muller, suggests that the sun, at the center of early people's perception, significantly influenced myths and tales (1985). While this theory has little credence among folklorists today, it indicates the importance of celestial phenomena in storytelling patterns.

FOLKLORE

Early Irish folklore tells of many extraordinary creatures and objects in the sky. A flying dragon (B11.4.1) is commonly cited, as are death-bringing fire from heaven (F797), magic storms (D905), magic darkness (D908), and a magic mist caused by Druids (D902.1.1). Often the extraordinariness of a celestial event comes from the nature of the personage who caused it, not the nature of the event itself.

"Magic control of the elements" (D2140) is often attributed to magicians, saints, and witches in folklore of the Middle Ages in Great Britain and other parts of Western Europe. Saints can raise storms (D2141.0.9), often for benevolent purposes. For example, after his death on a warm day, Saint Frodobert makes the weather so cold and icy that mourners can walk across the ice to his funeral (D2145.1.1, "Local winter. Winter produced in one place while it is summer everywhere else"; Baring-Gould 1914). Witches are described in the *Malleus Maleficarum* of 1486 as dangerous creatures who can "raise and stir up hailstorms and tempests, and cause lightning to blast both men and beasts" (Summers 1968, 139). Magicians and witches frequently get credit for controlling the wind (D2142.0.1, "Magician controls winds").

The concept of evil forces manipulating the weather has persisted up to the present time. During the blizzard of 1994 in the northeastern United States, television evangelists speculated that evil was causing extreme weather, precipitating the arrival of the Day of Judgment. In the movie *Storm of the Century* (1999), based on Stephen King's book by the same name, an evil supernatural figure is found to be responsible for a threatening, unusual amount of snow (D2143.6, "Magic control of snow"). Perhaps this inclination to blame others for unusual weather comes from the Jungian archetype of the Shadow: the dark side of the human psyche that enacts troublesome and antisocial impulses. The Shadow takes many forms, but its need to cause unrest remains constant.

PREDICTING WEATHER

The desire to predict difficult or favorable weather has produced a large corpus of customs and beliefs that sometimes appear in myths and folktales. Rain, vital for the growth of crops, is the subject of many predictions. Extraordinary behavior of heavenly bodies (F961) includes a solar halo, which,

A hag raises storm and destruction, displaying magic control of the elements (Motif D2140). From Olaus Magnus, *Historia de gentibus septentrionalibus* (1555).

according to Illinois folklore, may show that rain will come before night; a sun dog (parhelic halo) south of the sun means rain will come from the southwest, while a sun dog north of the sun means that rain will come from the northwest. After a solar eclipse, five full days of rain can be expected. A New York proverb states, "When there's a ring around the moon, rain is coming soon"; another proverb explains, with reference to an upside-down Big Dipper, "If the stars are in a huddle, the world will be in a puddle" (Cutting 1952, 29–46).

Colors of the sky may indicate when rain is coming. One very popular proverb known to both farmers and mariners is "Red sky at night, sailors' delight. Red sky at morning, sailors take warning." In New England, rain can be expected if the horizon has a greenish tinge; a purple haze forecasts a return to fine weather. If clouds in the parallel bands make the pattern of a "mackerel sky," rain may be predicted: "Mackerel sky, mackerel sky, three days wet and three days dry" (Botkin 1947, 630–635).

Sometimes the colors of the sky reveal greater calamities than a temporary absence of rain. At the beginning of the Irish potato famine in 1845, a "thick blue fog" covered the sky; farmers who had never seen such a fog before feared that a dreadful calamity was about to happen. Some farmers blamed the color of the sky on fairies, who, they thought, were "battling over the potatoes" (Bartoletti 2001, 9). Just as witches were blamed for many mishaps in medieval European folklore, the fairies were held accountable for the onset of the disastrous famine. A magic fog is also prominent in the Finnish *Kalevala,* as well as in the Arthurian cycle in Great Britain.

Sometimes people attempt to change the weather by performing certain rituals. A belief in India states that a certain man must laugh in order for it to rain (D2143.1.11, "Certain man must laugh in order for it to rain"). According to Buddhist mythology, a white elephant can make rain fall (D2143.1.13). From Irish mythology comes the belief that rain can be produced by striking a rock (D2143.1.7). Folk belief in Ireland, India, and Africa, among other places, explains drought by the presence of magic (D2143.2). In late nineteenth-century Nebraska, professional rainmakers fired explosions from balloons; they also prepared gunpowder explosions on high mountains. People in various regions of the United States have said that Fourth of July fireworks bring rainstorms. Conversely, some Americans have maintained the belief that "preparation for rain scares it away" (Hyatt 1965, 32). Carrying an umbrella, for example, may be considered a good way to keep rain from falling at an inconvenient or perilous time. According to North Carolina folklore, rain or snow on a couple's wedding day means that the groom will die first. A rainy wedding day may be worrisome, but some newlyweds have contended that rain has brought them good luck.

Folklore of the sea, derived from ancient mariners' beliefs, emphasizes severe weather and wind patterns. Many customs and stories tell of buying the wind: throwing a coin or coins overboard to gain a favorable breeze (Dorson 1964). This ritual originates from human sacrifice to bring wind to a becalmed ship, as in Agamemnon's sacrifice of his daughter Iphigenia in Greek tragedy. A narrative from Texas tells of a man who bought a dollar's worth of wind because of greed. His boat turned over, and his wife and children drowned (Mullin 1978, 35–40).

In the Midwest and Southwest of the United States, narratives and folk beliefs about tornadoes are common. A popular liar's tale tells of a man riding a tornado (X1004.2, "Lie: man rides cyclone"). A greenish sky is said to predict a tornado's approach, as does the first clap of thunder after the last snow storm. Anyone who dares try to change a tornado's direction can drive an ax into the top of a stump, pointing the ax handle in the direction the tornado should turn. Deflection may not be necessary if one believes that a tornado cannot strike a town between mountains and hills or in a valley (Hendricks 1980, 147).

The magnitude of a tornado's destructive force has inspired popular movies, including *The Wizard of Oz* (1939) and *Twister* (1996). In *Twister,* the scientists who pursue and track tornados become folk heroes: the only individuals brave enough to deliberately place themselves in a tornado's path. Following Joseph Campbell's hero pattern, their "call to adventure" is the announcement that a tornado is on its way (Campbell 1949).

Lightning is another form of severe weather that people take pains to avoid. The proverb "Lightning never strikes twice in the same place" helps to explain why people may take shelter under burnt trees or logs. In Illinois, people may burn blessed palm leaves or throw an ax into a yard to deflect lightning; in Texas, they may cross their suspenders and cover mirrors. Sometimes lightning has the connotation of punishment (C984.5, "Disastrous lightning for breaking tabu"); for example, African-American folk belief states that lightning striking while a man is dying means the devil has come to fetch his soul. The phrase "May the Lord strike me dead!" takes on new meaning when a person is outdoors in a thunderstorm. Sometimes, however, lightning is viewed as a source of awe-inspiring power. In the movie *Powder* (1995), the hero who is struck by lightning gains extraordinary sensitivity and the ability to practice telekinesis. This innocent, pale-skinned hero resembles an angel (A285.0.1), but his association with fire and destruction makes him seem demonic as well.

LITERATURE

Shakespeare used vivid imagery of weather to reflect human affairs. In *Hamlet,* Horatio, musing on the significance of the appearance of the ghost of Hamlet's father, speaks of portents of disaster in the sky before Caesar's murder:

> As stars with trains of fire and dews of blood,
> Disasters in the sun; and the moist star,
> Upon whose influence Neptune's empire stands,
> Was sick almost to doomsday with eclipse. (1.1.117–120)

The three witches in *Macbeth* meet during thunder and lightning. When Macbeth addresses them later in the play, he asks them to tell him the truth:

> Though you untie the winds and let them fight / Against the churches; though the yesty waves / Confound and swallow navigation up. (4.1.52–54)

Later, the weather grows ominous as a reflection of the unnatural murder that has occurred: Lennox says:

> The night has been unruly. Where we lay, / Our chimneys were blown down.
> . . . / Some say, the earth / Was feverous and did shake. (2.3.56–57, 62–63)

Ross says still later:

> Thou seest the heavens, as troubled with man's act,
> Threatens his bloody stage. By th' clock 'tis day,
> And yet dark night strangles the traveling lamp. (2.4.5–7)

The last excerpt is a fine literary example of motif F961.1.1, "Sun refuses to shine when murder is done."

Countless literary works have reflected people's fascination with catastrophic storms, the natural forces of chaos and destruction. In Louise Erdrich's *Tales of Burning Love* (1997), a woman freezes to death in an Easter blizzard and four other women, all of whom are ex-wives of the same man, spend the night together in a car during another massive snowstorm. In *The Perfect Storm* (1997) by Sebastian Junger, an unusually dangerous hurricane takes the lives of fishermen trying to get home.

In fantasy literature, severe weather often portends magic or dramatic transition. The four children in C.S. Lewis's *Chronicles of Narnia* (1950) do not discover Narnia until the weather becomes stormy. Similarly, a violent thunderstorm leads to Meg Murry's meeting with three witches in Madeleine L'Engle's *A Wrinkle in Time* (1973). In J.R.R. Tolkien's *The Fellowship of the Ring* (1955), thick fog causes the hobbits to be captured by barrow-wights (K1886.2, "Mists which lead astray"). And in Julia Sauer's *Fog Magic* (1986), a little girl can find a village from the past only when fog blankets the area. Extreme weather of all kinds serves as a catalyst for magic, but fog, which can change the appearance of an entire area, works especially well.

Mark Twain writes of a solar eclipse in *A Connecticut Yankee in King Arthur's Court* (1889). Knowing that an eclipse will occur, the hero from modern times is able to impress King Arthur and his courtiers, becoming a powerful seer in their eyes. In this case, the hero has no command of magic; his scientific knowledge becomes a sign of extraordinary skill. In this novel, as in many other folkloric and literary contexts, mastery of the sky denotes power of the highest order.

Elizabeth Tucker

REFERENCES

Baring-Gould, Sabine. 1914. *Lives of the Saints.* Vol. 1. Edinburgh: J. Grant.

Bartoletti, Susan Campbell. 2001. *Black Potatoes.* New York: Scholastic Press.

Botkin, Ben. 1947. *A Treasury of New England Folklore.* New York: Crown.

Campbell, Joseph. 1949. *The Hero With a Thousand Faces.* New York: Bollingen.

Cross, Tom Peete. 1952. *Motif-Index of Early Irish Literature.* Bloomington: Indiana University Press.

Cutting, Edith. 1952. *Whistling Girls and Jumping Sheep.* Cooperstown: Farmers Museum and New York Folklore Society.

Dorson, Richard M. 1964. *Buying the Wind: Regional Folklore in the United States.* Chicago: University of Chicago Press.

Erdrich, Louise. 1997. *Tales of Burning Love.* New York: HarperCollins.

Hand, Wayland D., ed. 1964. *The Frank C. Brown Collection of North Carolina Folklore.* Vol. 7. Durham, NC: Duke University Press.

Hendricks, George D. 1980. *Roosters, Rhymes, and Railroad Tracks.* Dallas: Southern Methodist University Press.

Hyatt, Harry M. 1965. *Folklore from Adams County Illinois.* Hannibal, MO: Western Printing and Lithographing.

Jung, Carl G. 1964. *Man and his Symbols.* London: Aldus Books.

———. 1977. *C.G. Jung Speaking,* ed. William McGuire and R.F.C. Hull. Princeton: Princeton University Press.

Junger, Sebastian. 1997. *The Perfect Storm.* New York: Norton.

King, Stephen. 1999. *The Storm of the Century.* New York: Simon and Schuster.

L'Engle, Madeleine. 1973. *A Wrinkle in Time.* New York: Bantam.

Lewis, C.S. 1950. *The Lion, the Witch and the Wardrobe.* New York: HarperCollins.

Muller, Max. 1985. *Chips from a German Workshop: Essays on the Science of Religion.* New York: Scholars Press.

Mullin, Patrick B. 1978. *I Heard the Old Fishermen Say: Folklore of the Texas Gulf Coast.* Austin: University of Texas Press.

Pound, Louise. 1959. *Nebraska Folklore.* Lincoln: University of Nebraska Press.

Sauer, Julia. 1986. *Fog Magic.* New York: Penguin.

Stirling, M.W. 1945. "Concepts of the Sun Among American Indians." *Smithsonian Report for 1945.* Washington, DC: Smithsonian.

Summers, Montague, ed. 1968. *Malleus Maleficarum.* London: Folio Society.

Tolkien, J.R.R. 1955. *The Fellowship of the Ring.* Boston: Houghton Mifflin.

Twain, Mark. 1889. *A Connecticut Yankee in King Arthur's Court.* New York: Charles L. Webster.

Ogres

Cannibalism

Motif G10

❀

The eating of human flesh (anthropophagy) is to civilized people one of the most repellent events imaginable (C227, "Tabu: eating human flesh"). In their efforts to understand this practice, ethnologists have recognized many different forms of cannibalism: cultural vs. individual, ritual vs. gustatory vs. survival (G70.1, "Hungry seamen eat human flesh"; G78.1, "Cannibalism in time of famine"), endo- vs. exo- and even auto- (G51, "Person eats own flesh"), mortuary, and medical. In one or another of its forms, cannibalism is associated with the horrors of murder, human sacrifice, fear of the dead, human dismemberment, and starvation (Thomsen 1983). Sigmund Freud connected the fear of being eaten with castration anxiety, and psychologists and artists continue to link cannibalism with sexuality (Thomsen 1983, 110–144; Ranke 1973, 1977–, s.v. Freud). Recently, because of its connections with colonialism, cultural relativism, and human bodies, cannibalism has been popular in literary studies both as a subject and as a metaphor. In modern popular culture, it is most commonly encountered in horror films and in descriptions of Satanism.

Groups of disliked persons have long been accused of abhorrent acts, including cannibalism. In Europe, such groups have traditionally been characterized as anti-Christian: witches (G11.3, "Cannibal witch"), Satanists, and Jews (V361, "Christian child killed to furnish blood for Jewish rite"; Dundes 1991). The Western cliché of Africans as cannibal savages is complemented by corresponding African and African-American ideas of whites as cannibals (Turner 1993, 9–32). The prevalence of such usually unfounded accusations has made the extent of the actual practice of cannibalism very difficult to determine. In this connection, it is often noted that the Christian practice of

Holy Communion, eating bread and drinking wine as the symbolic or actual body and blood of Christ, strikes nonbelievers as cannibalistic.

Cannibals in folklore span a continuum from animals who devour people (e.g., the wolf in AT 333, *Little Red Riding Hood;* the cat in AT 2027, *The Fat Cat*) (Ranke 1977– , s.v. *Fressermärchen*) through more or less humanoid werewolves and monsters (the troll in AT 2028; the Chinese Grand-aunt Tiger in AT 123/333) (Dundes 1989, 21–63), through human strangers who eat people, to cannibalistic relatives. Folktales and legends from all parts of the world feature ogres who seem to belong to a subhuman race of creatures and who eat, or at least threaten to eat, people (Macculloch 1905, 279–305, chapter 10; Warner 1999, 1–183). Modern usage of the word ogre began in 1697 in French literary folktales; *ogress* was used in an early (1713) English translation of *The Thousand and One Nights.* Etymologically, these words come from Orcas, a name of Hades, the Roman god of the underworld. Like the closely-related *orca,* "whale," an ogre is something that swallows (Ranke 1977– , s.v. Ogre).

In a popular folktale pattern, one or more humans enter an ogre's dwelling and at least some of them escape by outwitting their adversary. The encounter with the Cyclops Polyphemus in Homer's *Odyssey* (book 9, lines 105–566; AT 1137) is an early example. In a stereotyped but nevertheless terrifying folktale scene, the hero (or heroine) arrives at an ogre's house and hides; the ogre returns home and exclaims "I smell human meat" (G84, "Fee-fi-fo-fum. Cannibal returning home smells human flesh and makes exclamation," and G532, "Hero hidden and ogre deceived by his wife (daughter) when he says that he smells human blood"), implying that he intends to eat the visitor. The ogre often sharpens his knife or his teeth (G83). In fairy tales, including several subtypes of AT 327, *The Children and the Ogre,* and AT 328, *The Boy [Girl] Steals the Giant's Treasures,* the hero escapes. In legends, however, he may not. In either genre, the ogre may eat other human characters (Ranke 1977– , s.v. *Menschenfleisch riechen*).

Eaters of corpses inhabit tales from many parts of the world. In the Middle East, ghouls, like ogres elsewhere, are often stupid and may rely on their sense of smell rather than on their sight. If the hero or heroine greets a ghoul or ghouleh (female) politely, the monster will help the suppliant. In particular, the interloper may suck the dangling breast of a ghouleh and thus become her foster child (Muhawi and Kanaana 1989, 415–416; Goldberg 1997, 126–130).

Tales of cannibals and cannibalism appear particularly frequently in Australia, New Zealand, Melanesia, Indonesia, and Africa. Géza Róheim says that cannibalism is the most outstanding feature of the narratives he collected in central Australia (1966, 27). Whaitari is a female cannibal deity in New

Zealand myth who comes down from the sky to capture men in a net. A tale from Mangaia in the South Pacific tells of a sky cannibal who lets down a basket in which he catches and hauls up his human prey; similar stories are told in Rotuma, a small island west of Samoa (Dixon 1916, 62–63) Schmidt says that in Africa ogre stories are extremely popular and lists three main groups of fiends that try to kill and eat humans: "supernatural animals, particularly lions and hyenas, all-swallowing monsters of sometimes apocalyptic dimensions, and the ogre in human shape" (2001, 277–278). The creatures in the latter group, however, usually have some physical characteristic that sets them apart from true humans. Among the Nama-speaking peoples, the ogre is called Khoe-oreb, meaning literally "man-eater": "Their standard attributes are the axe and the big pot in which they cook their victims. . . . Man-eaters are incredibly strong and fast, and like in nightmares persons cannot escape from them" (Schmidt 2001, 278–279). Eventually, however, they usually do escape, employing such motifs as the obstacle flight (D672, "Flight into the tree"); R251, "Flight on a tree, which ogre tries to cut down"), or rescue by faithful dogs (B524.1.1, "Dogs kill attacking cannibal (dragon)") (279).

In "The Fourth Voyage of Sinbad" in *The Arabian Nights,* Sinbad and his shipmates are shipwrecked and make their way to an island where they encounter cannibals. "All who came to their country or whoso they caught in their valleys on their roads . . . they slaughtered them by cutting their throats and roasted them for the King's eating; but, as for the savages themselves, they ate human flesh raw" (Burton 2001, 357).

The forbidden chamber—a room which the hero or heroine is forbidden to open (C611)—often turns out to contain bloody corpses and evidence of cannibalism. Similarly, in AT 955, *The Robber Bridegroom,* a young woman discovers that her husband-to-be is a murderer who butchers his victims. The witch's house in the horror tale AT 334, *The Witch's Household,* often contains evidence of man-eating in the form of human bones or cooking meat. Such gruesome details appear in Russian tales that feature the witch Baba Jaga.

The idea that a relative or trusted friend should have an appetite for human flesh has been developed in several popular tales. In AT 315A, *The Cannibal Sister,* a young girl lays waste to an entire village, eating livestock as well as humans. Like another African cannibal wife (G11.6, "Man-eating woman"), she is often vanquished by the hero's dogs (Goldberg 1998). Early versions of Sleeping Beauty (AT 410) include a sequel in which the mother of the prince schemes to eat her daughter-in-law and grandchildren. They are saved by a compassionate executioner who substitutes animal parts (K512.2.1, "Animal substituted for child served at meal").

Motif G72, "Unnatural parents eat children," is the most pitiful example of atrocities concerning parents and children. In AT 720, *My Mother Slew Me, My Father Ate Me,* a child is killed and cooked by his mother and served to his father for dinner. A tree grows from the child's bones, and a bird sings about the murder and cannibalism (Belgrader 1980). Often this account begins with a mother who eats the meat that should have been her family's dinner. She replaces it with part of her body, flesh from her leg or breast. From eating this meal, she and her husband develop a taste for human meat, and they decide to cook one of their children (G36, "Taste of human flesh leads to habitual cannibalism"). This introduction can lead instead into other tales in which the children, having overheard their parents' murderous plan, run away.

In several tales of persecuted women, AT 451, 652, 706, 707, 710, and 712, a new mother is falsely accused of having eaten her newborn child. The accusation is supported by "evidence" in the form of animal blood (K2116.1.1, "Innocent woman accused of eating her new-born children"). In a tale from India and Arab lands, children are actually eaten by their starving mothers. A queen who is really an ogress causes her co-wives to be imprisoned in a pit. There, they give birth, and all except one eat their children (AT 462, *The Outcast Queens and the Ogress Queen*). Only rarely do stories tell of children eating their parents. In Cinderella tales (AT 511 and 510A) in the Balkans, the mother is eaten by her children, either in her human form or after she has been turned into a cow (Xanthakou 1988; Rooth 1951, 213–215).

Origin myths include both infanticide and patricide, followed by eating the victim (Macculloch 1980, 208–209; Thomsen 1983, 24–28). According to Hesiod's *Theogony* (lines 453ff.), the Greek god Kronos, afraid that one of his children will supplant him, swallows them in succession, until, finally, his wife Rhea substitutes a stone for the infant Zeus. Zeus, when grown, forces Kronos to vomit up all the other children, who become the Olympian gods. In *Totem and Taboo* (1960), Sigmund Freud developed a modern myth in which an archetypal "primal horde" (a term borrowed from Charles Darwin) of brothers killed and ate their father. According to Freud, this event led to two pillars of culture, reverence for a totem animal and the prohibition of incest.

Unwitting cannibalism (G60, "Human flesh eaten unwittingly") emphasizes the horror of eating taboo (or contaminated) food more than the horror of being eaten. Rumors and legends often explain how the human flesh was accidentally or deliberately put into food, or how people happened to eat something not intended for consumption (X21, "Accidental cannibalism") (Ranke 1973; San Fernando Valley Folklore Society 2001). In Greek mythology, Tantalus cooks his son Pelops and serves him to the gods, in order to see whether they notice the difference between human and animal flesh. Pelops is resuscitated but, because Demeter ate part of his shoulder, that part of his body is replaced with ivory (Frazer 1921, 2:156–157; Motif E33,

"Resuscitation with missing member"). The eighteenth-century London barber-murderer Sweeney Todd, popularized in a 1979 musical production by Stephen Sondheim, is said to have disposed of the corpses of his victims by preparing and selling the meat as food (Thomsen 1983, 163–165).

Motif G61, "Relative's Flesh Eaten Unwittingly," a personalized form of G60, is amply documented in North America, Asia, Africa, and Europe. Since World War II, Motif G61 has circulated as an urban legend motivated only by ignorance or misunderstanding. Cremated remains of a relative are included in a package sent to family members overseas, and the recipients eat the ashes, believing them to be food (San Fernando Valley Folklore Society 2001).

The most extreme examples of G61 involve a person being tricked into eating his own relatives (cf. AT 1115–1162). Thus, in AT 327, *The Children and the Ogre,* where a clever person outwits an ogre, the ogre may be tricked into eating his own wife or daughter, thinking it is the human intruder who has been cooked (cf. Motif G512.3.2.1, "Ogre's wife (daughter) burned in his own oven"; Cosquin 1922, 366–372). At the end of tales with a substituted bride, the flesh of the imposter wife is preserved like meat and sent to the false bride's mother, who eats it (Goldberg 1997, 150–161 passim). The wolf may feed Little Red Riding Hood parts of her grandmother's body (Dundes 1989, 13–20). In an African development, a child recognizes the source of the food and exposes the murder and dismemberment (G 61.1, "Child recognizes relative's flesh when it is served to be eaten").

A horrific example of G61 occurs in the story of Pelops's son Atreus, who revenges himself on his brother Thyestes by serving him a meal consisting of Thyestes's own children. After Thyestes finishes eating, Atreus shows him the hands and feet of his children. In Shakespeare's gory play *Titus Andronicus* (1593/4), two villainous brothers are "baked in that pie; whereof their mother daintily hath fed" (5.3.60f.). In AT 992, *The Eaten Heart,* the same trick is played on a woman whose husband or father disapproves of her lover enough to have him killed and butchered. When she is told she has eaten her lover's heart, she kills herself. This story, which has been popular in European literary tradition since the Middle Ages, also appears in folktales from many parts of the world, including native North America (Ranke 1977– , s.v. *Herzmäre*).

Christine Goldberg

See also: Forbidden Chambers.

REFERENCES

Belgrader, Michael. 1980. *Das Märchen von dem Machandelboom.* Frankfurt: Peter Lang.
Burton, Sir Richard F., trans. 2001 [1885–1888]. *The Arabian Nights: Tales from a Thousand and One Nights.* New York: Modern Library.

Cosquin, Emmanuel. 1922. *Études folkloriques*. Paris: E. Champion.

Dixon, Roland B. 1916. *Oceanic Mythology*. Vol. 9 of *The Mythology of All Races*. Boston: Archaeological Institute of America.

Dundes, Alan, ed. 1989. *Little Red Riding Hood: A Casebook*. Madison: University of Wisconsin Press.

———. 1991. *The Blood Libel Legend. A Casebook in Anti-Semitic Folklore*. Madison: University of Wisconsin Press.

Frazer, James George, trans. and ed. 1921. *Apollodorus: The Library*. 2 vols. Loeb Classical Library. New York and London: Harvard University Press, William Heinemann.

Freud, Sigmund. 1960 [1913]. *Totem and Taboo*. London: Routledge and Kegan Paul.

Goldberg, Christine. 1997. *The Tale of the Three Oranges*. FFC no. 263. Helsinki: Suomalainen Tiedeakatemia.

———. 1998. "Dogs Rescue Master from Tree Refuge: An African Tale with World-Wide Analogs." *Western Folklore* 57: 44–61.

Macculloch, J.A. 1905. *The Childhood of Fiction: A Study of Folk Tales and Primitive Thought*. New York: E.P. Dutton.

———. 1980 [1908–1926]. "Cannibalism." In *Encyclopaedia of Religion and Ethics,* ed. James Hastings, 3:194–209. Edinburgh: T. and T. Clark.

Muhawi, Ibrahim, and Sharif Kanaana. 1989. *Speak, Bird, Speak Again: Palestinian Arab Folktales*. Berkeley: University of California Press.

Ranke, Kurt. 1973. "Zum Motiv 'Accidental Cannibalism' (Thompson X21)." In *Dona Ethnologica, Leopold Kretzenbacher zum 60. Geburtstag,* ed. Helge Gerndt and Georg R. Schroubek, 321–325. München: R. Oldenburger.

———, ed. 1977– . *Enzyklopädie des Märchens*. 11 vols. Berlin: W. de Gruyter, s.v. *Erzähltypen* (for tale type references); *Fressermärchen* (Marianne Rumpf); Freud, Sigmund (Elliot Oring); *Herzmäre* (Albert Gier), *Kannibalismus* (Birgitta Hauser-Schaublin); *Menschenfleisch reichen* (Christine Shojai-Kawan); Ogre (Thomas Geider).

Róheim, Géza. 1966. "Myth and Folktale." In *Myth and Literature: Contemporary Theory and Practice,* ed. John Vickery. Lincoln: University of Nebraska Press.

Rooth, Anna Birgitta. 1951. *The Cinderella Cycle*. Lund: C.W.K. Gleerup.

San Fernando Valley Folklore Society. 2001. Urban Legends Reference Pages. www.snopes.com/horrors.

Schmidt, Sigrid. 2001. *Tricksters, Monsters and Clever Girls: African Folktales; Texts and Discussions*. Köln: Rüdiger Köppe.

Thomsen, Christian W. 1983. *Menschenfresser in der Kunst und Literatur, in fernen Ländern, Mythen, Märchen und Satiren, in Dramen, Liedern, Epen und Romanen*. Wien: Christian Brandstätter.

Turner, Patricia. 1993. *I Heard It Through the Grapevine*. Berkeley: University of California Press.

Warner, Marina. 1999. *No Go the Bogeyman*. London: Chatto and Windus.

Xanthakou, Margarita. 1988. *Cendrillon et les soeurs cannibales*. Cahiers de l'homme N. S. 28. Paris: École des Hautes Études.

❀ H ❀

Tests

Identity Tests

Motifs H0–H199

❀

Thompson introduces the section on Recognition Tests in the *Motif-Index* by saying, "Elaborate means are employed in folk-literature for the recognition of persons even though they have been separated a very short time." In cases where people are not recognized by sight, identity must be proved through common knowledge (H10), such as telling a story known to both persons concerned (H11), telling one's life history (H11.1), ancestry (H11.1.4), singing a song (H12), or producing a token (H80). Sometimes recognition occurs when a person's conversation with objects or animals is overheard (AT 313, 533, 706, 870). There are, in addition, numerous other motifs of establishing identity and recognizing someone who has returned after an absence.

COMMON KNOWLEDGE

In *The Skillful Hunter* (AT 304), a hero who has killed giants who were menacing a castle lies with a princess sleeping there. He takes something from her when he leaves, either a handkerchief or a ring. After her child is born, she is condemned to stay at an inn where all guests must tell their life stories. In time the hero comes, tells his story, and produces his token (H80, "Identification by tokens"), and they marry (Thompson 1977, 34). This story thus combines two elements of recognition: telling one's life story and producing a token.

Recognition can come about by seeing a scar (H51; AT314) or birthmark (H51.1; AT 400, 850). An extremely famous example of the scar motif is in Book XIX of the *Odyssey,* when Odysseus returns home after twenty years and his old nurse, Eurycleia, washes his feet and sees the scar on his leg from the wound of a wild boar that he had hunted as a young man. The motif also occurs in the *Thousand and One Nights* and in Indonesian, Chinese, and North American (Ponka, Blackfoot, Eastern Cree) tales. In Book XXI, Odysseus is further able to prove his identity by bending his bow, which the suitors cannot do (H31.2., "Recognition by unique ability to bend bow"; D1651.1, "Only master able to bend bow").

In some cases a royal pedigree is recognized when a person is unable to sleep on a bed that has a pea under its dozen mattresses (H41.1, "Princess on the pea").

THE BROKEN TOKEN

A common theme of recognition is identification by matching parts of a divided token (H100), commonly a broken ring whose two parts fit together (H94.5, "Identification through broken ring. The two parts of the ring fit together"). In the ballad "Hind Horn" (Child 17), a man who has been away from the princess to whom he has been betrothed for seven years sees that the ring she gave him has turned pale, a sign that she has found another man. He returns home and arrives on her wedding day (N681, "Husband (lover) arrives home just as wife (mistress) is to marry another"). He disguises himself as a beggar and is unrecognized by the princess when he comes to the castle. She gives him a drink of wine and when he returns the cup to her he drops in the ring she had given him. She recognizes the ring and asks him where he got it. He tells her she herself gave it to him, and, recognizing him, she says she will follow him as a beggar. Child lists many analogues to this ballad, most having the motif of the ring, which is kept intact by the departing lover in some cases and broken in other cases, with each partner keeping one half. Versions occur in medieval stories (one written down in the first quarter of the thirteenth century) and romances from various parts of Europe including Russia and Greece (Child 1965, 187–208).

The broken token motif is also found in the tale of *Bearskin* (AT 361), an unusual example of a hero enlisting the aid of the devil (in most folktales the devil is an adversary). In exchange for living in a filthy bearskin for seven years, the devil provides the hero with an inexhaustible supply of money from a pocket in the bearskin. The hero helps an impoverished man with three daughters, two of whom treat him badly while the youngest is kind to him despite his appearance. At the end of seven years, the hero cleans himself, dresses in fine clothing, and goes back to the house of the three sisters, making himself known by the broken ring he had divided with the youngest. Thompson says this story "has been told frequently in literature since the seventeenth century, but a strong oral tradition has also preserved the story. It is extraordinarily popular in the folklore of the Baltic states, of Sweden, Denmark, and Germany; and it is known over all parts of Europe" (1977, 65–66).

In a Chinese story called "Husband and Wife in This Life and in the Life to Come," a man's dead wife is reincarnated in a baby (T589.5, "Newborn child reincarnation of recently deceased person"). The baby keeps her right hand tightly clutched until she is seventeen years old, when the husband opens it and finds half a coin which makes a perfect whole with his own half (Eberhard 1965, 31–33).

Related to identification by tokens is S334, "Tokens of royalty (nobility) left with exposed child." King Aegeus, the father of the Greek hero Theseus, leaves a sword and a pair of sandals under a rock as tokens, telling Aethra, the baby's mother, that when the boy is strong enough to lift the rock he should retrieve them and bring the tokens to him at Athens. When Theseus arrives years later, Aegeus's wife, Medea, convinces him to poison the young man, and only after Theseus draws his sword to cut his meat at dinner does Aegeus recognize him as his son.

AT 780, *The Princess Confined in the Mound,* contains motif H13.1.1, "Recognition by overheard conversation with horse." In this story, found predominantly in Scandinavia, a princess is confined in a mound by her father because of her obstinacy in wanting to marry a certain prince. She finally escapes after years of imprisonment and obtains a position as a maid in her beloved's castle. The prince is soon to be married, and his bride-to-be arranges for the heroine to take her place at the wedding, in order to conceal her pregnancy or her unattractiveness. The heroine agrees not to tell the prince, but she contrives to let him know by telling her story to a horse, a bridge (H13.2.1), or a stone (H13.2.2). The Grimms' tale "The Goose Girl" (KHM 89) is a variant of this story.

THE SLIPPER TEST

One of the most famous recognition tests is that of the slipper (H36.1). It is significant that the oldest recorded complete telling of a European Cinderella story (AT 510A, *Cinderella*), "The Cat Cinderella" from Basile's *Pentamerone,* written in 1634 (1932, 1:6), contains what has become the most memorable motif in the tale: the recognition of the true bride by the fit of her lost slipper (H36.1, "Slipper test. Identification by fitting of slipper"). However, strictly speaking, in Basile's tale the identifying item is not a slipper, but a cloglike piece of footwear called a patten, worn over the shoe. Although normally constructed with a high platform to protect the wearer from mud, the item lost by Basile's heroine is described as "the richest and prettiest patten you could imagine." Not only is it marked by fine workmanship and dainty size, but when put to the trial of discovering the runaway beauty, it darts forward to the heroine's foot, just as iron flies to a magnet, thus magically confirming that the true bride has been found.

The next version to be published was that of Charles Perrault, "Cinderella; or, the Little Glass Slipper," in his classic collection *Stories or Tales from Times Past, with Morals,* with the added frontispiece *Tales of Mother Goose* (1697). This story's defining motif, the slipper, is not only prominently featured in the tale's title, but is also given an otherworldly aspect by being made of glass. It is not true, as suggested by the 1911 *Encyclopaedia Britannica* and subsequent writers, that Perrault's glass slipper is a mistranslation into English of *pantoufle en vair* (fur slipper), mistaken for *en verre* (of glass). Nor are the claims entirely believable that Perrault himself understood *verre* when his oral informant used the word *vair.* These arguments, which have been substantially discredited by Paul Delarue (1982, 110–114), are based primarily on some modern critics' unwillingness to let fairy tales be fairy tales, imposing on them instead a utilitarian logic that storytellers have rarely adhered to. Of course, fur is a more practical material for slippers than is glass, but glass, crystal, diamonds, pearls, gold, feathers, and other symbolically rich substances are featured in magic tales of all epochs and from around the world in ways that violate everyday logic. Fairy tales thrive on unreality.

Two of the unique properties of glass are its transparency (purity) and its fragility, thus making it an appropriate symbol of virginity, as exemplified, for instance, in the bridegroom's breaking of a glass at a traditional Jewish wedding. This symbolic value notwithstanding, in most European versions of *The Cinderella Story,* including that of the Grimm brothers (KHM 21), the slipper is made of gold, also an impractical material for footwear, but one with rich symbolic traditions. In magic tales, anything can be made of gold: plants, animals, people, organs and limbs, castles, carriages, clothing. The word *gold* in essence becomes a synonym for "good," "desirable," "pure," or any other positive quality.

It has often been demonstrated that the shoe, in various folkloric contexts, serves well as a symbol of sexuality, especially female sexuality. This is true whether the shoe is made of fur, glass, gold, or more conventional materials such as leather or cloth. Any such symbolic value would be lost on younger listeners, but not on older members of the storyteller's audience. The Grimms' title *Children's and Household Tales* reflects the multiple levels of significance contained in most of the stories in their pioneering collection, an observation that would apply equally well to most classic folktale collections.

In Europe, the normal pattern is for the prince first to fall in love with the heroine and then to use the lost slipper to reclaim her. A number of explanations

Cinderella having fitted on the Glass Slipper produces it's fellow.

Elaborate means are employed in folk-literature for the recognition of persons even though they have been separated a very short time. The slipper test (Motif H36.1) is found in versions of Cinderella occurring all over the world. From "Cinderella and the Glass Slipper" in *The Fairy Library*, illustrated by George Cruikshank (1854).

are offered as to how she loses her slipper. Most often, as in Perrault's story, for example, the heroine, in her haste to leave a festive event, simply drops it. In other renditions, as in that of the Grimms, the prince purposefully sets a trap, catching the slipper in pitch or tar. In at least one version, a Gypsy tale from England titled "The Little Cinder-Girl" (Briggs 1970, 1:383–388), the trap seems to have been set by the heroine, using her shoe as bait. Her magic helper tells her explicitly, "Mark what thou shalt do now. Do as I bid thee. Go to church, and this time thou must leave still earlier; the prince will follow thee. One slipper will drop from thy foot, and he will come after thee and find it." In a few instances, such as the Irish "Fair, Brown, and Trembling" (Curtin 1890, 37–48) and the Romanian "The Bewitched Calf and the Wicked Step-Mother" (Gaster 1915, no. 89), the prince forcefully pulls the shoe off the fleeing heroine.

Once the prince has the slipper in hand, the bridal test is quite straightforward: If the shoe fits, marry her. No other qualities seem important. In a large number of versions, preeminently that of the Grimms, one or more of the heroine's sisters or stepsisters mutilate their feet in order to make the shoe fit (J2131.3.1). Inexplicably, the prince does not notice the false bride's wounds until he is on his way home with her. Typically, he discovers the fraud only after a bird tells him that his bride has blood in her shoe. The symbolic interpretation of this episode is obvious.

How the heroine's slipper is lost differs substantially in various tellings of the story, with each explanation symbolizing different motivations on the part of both the leading male and the leading female. A sparsely told tale from Scotland begins simply, "Lang lang syne, in some far awa' country ayont the sea, there was a grand prince, and he had a shoe made o' glass." The storyteller continues by stating that the prince decides to marry only the woman whose bonny wee foot would fit the slipper (Chambers 1870, 68–70). For a prince to fall in love with a woman he has never seen before just because of a shoe (T11.4.2) is especially common in Cinderella tales from the Middle East and the Orient, for example from Georgia (Wardrop 1894, 63–67), Iraq (Bushnaq 1986, 181–187), India (Frere 1881, no. 21), Vietnam (Thang and Lawson 1993, 75–89), and China (*Folk Tales from China* 1958, 6–22).

Of this group, the Vietnamese tale "Tam and Cam" is exemplary. Tam, dressed in elegant clothes magically supplied by a Buddha, is on her way to a festival. While crossing a stream, she loses one of her shoes. Sometime later, the king and his entourage arrive at the same spot. His elephants refuse to cross the water, leading to the discovery of the lost shoe, and the king forthwith proclaims that he will marry the girl whose foot fits the shoe.

In a Chinese tale (Eberhard 1965, no. 66), the heroine herself uses her lost shoe as a means of finding a bridegroom. While she is riding along in her magically obtained clothing, one of her embroidered shoes falls into a ditch. Unable to dismount and recover it, and unwilling to abandon it, she asks successive passersby to pick it up for her. Each one responds, "With great pleasure, if you will marry me." She rejects proposals from a fishmonger, a rice seller, and an oil merchant, but accepts the offer of a handsome scholar. He picks up the shoe and puts it on her foot, then takes her to his house and makes her his wife.

In a few instances, the shoe-fitting test fails. For example, in the Chilean tale "Maria Cinderella," the lost slipper perfectly fits both the heroine and her unworthy stepsister, but only Maria can produce the slipper's mate, so she still proves herself the true bride by means of a shoe (Pino-Saavedra 1968, no. 19). In at least one folktale, the expected gender roles are reversed. In "Sheepskin Boy" from Sweden, an anonymous and reticent hero drops one of his gold shoes, which is picked up by the princess, who then uses it to find her future bridegroom (Blecher and Blecher 1993, 118–123; AT 530).

Identifying a heroine by her shoe is not limited to Cinderella folktales, but is found in stories of other types as well. For example, in "A Lost Shoe of Gold" from Saudi Arabia, a sultan's daughter sees her tutor eating a dead horse and thus discovers that he is a ghoul. Terrified, she runs from his house, leaving one of her shoes behind. The ghoul, with the lost shoe as proof of her identity and of her presence in his house, cruelly harasses her, trying unsuccessfully to get her to admit what she saw. Enduring the persecution, she ultimately gains victory over the ghoul (Bushnaq 1986, 132–137; AT 894). In the Grimms' tale "The Trained Huntsman [Der gelernte Jäger, KHMIII]," the title hero kills three giants who threaten to attack a sleeping princess. He cuts out the giants' tongues and takes one of the princess's slippers. Later, an impostor claims to have killed the giants, but the huntsman shows the tongues and the slipper, thus gaining the hand of the princess in marriage (KHM 111, AT 304).

Shoes provide identification of a different kind in the Grimms' "The Blue Light" (KHM 116, AT 562, *The Spirit in the Blue Light*) and "The Shoes That Were Danced to Pieces" (KHM 133, AT 306, *The Danced-out Shoes*). In the first tale, a dismissed soldier spirits a princess into his room every night. The princess traps and identifies her abductor by hiding one of her shoes under his bed. In the second tale, twelve princesses mysteriously dance their shoes to pieces every night. Another dismissed soldier discovers how they nightly enter an underground realm to dance with enchanted partners. His reward for putting an end to this forbidden activity is the hand in marriage of one of the twelve. As in most of the shoe episodes discussed in this article, these tales suggest significant possibilities for symbolic interpretation.

D.L. Ashliman (slipper test) *and Jane Garry*

REFERENCES

Basile, Giambattista. 1932. *The Pentamerone.* New York: E.P. Dutton. Croce. Ed. N.M. Penzer. 2 vols. New York: Dutton. First published 1634–1636 as *Lo Cunto de li Cunti.*

Blecher, Lone Thygesen, and George Blecher. 1993. *Swedish Folktales and Legends.* New York: Pantheon Books.

Briggs, Katherine M. 1970. *A Dictionary of British Folk-Tales in the English Language.* Part A, Folk Narratives. 2 vols. London: Routledge and Kegan Paul.

Bushnaq, Iner. 1986. *Arab Folktales.* New York: Pantheon Books.

Chambers, Robert. 1870 [1841]. *Popular Rhymes of Scotland.* London: W. and R. Chambers.

Child, Francis James. 1965 [1882–1898]. *The English and Scottish Popular Ballads.* New York: Dover. Orig. ed., Houghton Mifflin.

Curtain, Jeremiah. 1890. *Myths and Folk-lore of Ireland.* Boston: Little, Brown.

Delarue, Paul. 1982 [1951]. "From Perrault to Walt Disney: The Slipper of Cinderella." In *Cinderella: A Casebook,* ed. Alan Dundes, 110–114. New York: Wildman Press.

Eberhard, Wolfram. 1965. *Folktales of China.* Chicago: University of Chicago Press.

Folk Tales from China. 1958. Fourth series. Peking: Foreign Languages Press.

Frere, Mary. 1881. *Old Deccan Days; or, Hindoo Fairy Legends Current in Southern India.* 3rd ed. London: John Murray.

Gaster, M. 1915. *Rumanian Bird and Beast Stories.* London: Folk-Lore Society.

Grimm, Jacob, and Wilhelm Grimm. 1980. *Kinder- und Hausmärchen* [KHM]. 3 vols. Ed. Heinz Rölleke. Stuttgart: Reclam. Based on the edition of 1857.

Perrault, Charles. 1697. *Histoires, ou contes du temps passé, avec des moralités.* Paris: Claude Barbin.

Pino Saavedra, Yolando. 1968. *Folktales of Chile.* Trans. Rockwell Gray. London: Routledge and Kegan Paul.

Thang, Vo Van, and Jim Lawson. 1993. *Song Ngu, Truyên Dân Gian Viêt Nam: Vietnamese Folktales.* Danang: Danang Publishing House. Vietnamese and English on facing pages.

Thompson, Stith. 1977 [1946]. *The Folktale.* Berkeley: University of California Press. Orig. ed. New York: Holt, Rinehart.

Wardrop, Marjory. 1894. *Georgian Folk Tales.* London: David Nutt.

Riddles

Motifs H530–H899

❀

It should come as no surprise that Thompson required twenty-six pages of the *Motif-Index* to list and classify riddle motifs in traditional narrative. Riddles are classified under Tests of Cleverness. The presence of riddles in folk narratives often functions as a test of the hero or protagonist.

Skill in propounding and solving riddles is highly prized in traditional cultures as a mark of intellectual agility, shrewdness, practical wisdom, and worldly knowledge: it is only logical that traditional narrative should recount the riddling exploits of noteworthy characters and exploit audience interest in verbal and intellectual play, an interest that appears early in the young and in some cultures is institutionally encouraged among adults.

The riddle is a verbal puzzle or cipher, at the heart of which is metaphor. Solving the riddle usually entails recognizing multiple connections between the riddle's vehicle (the metaphorical substitution) and its tenor (the meaning or solution to the riddle). Such multiple similarities extend and enlarge the metaphor, moving it in the direction of allegory, Spenser's "dark conceit," puzzle, or enigma. These qualities may be illustrated from the riddle posed by the Sphinx at Thebes and solved by Oedipus (AT 932, *Oedipus;* H761, "Riddle of the Sphinx: what is it that goes on four legs in the morning, on two at midday, and on three in the evening?"). The Sphinx has afflicted Thebes with plague, but she will lift the epidemic if anyone can answer her riddle. Oedipus, entering Thebes after having unknowingly killed his father Laius, the king of Thebes, on the road from Delphi, easily solves the riddle: man, who crawls in infancy, walks upright in maturity, and requires the assistance of a cane in old age. The solution depends upon recognizing three tropes: the metaphor that perceives the human life span in terms of a single day, and the metonymical associations of human arms with animal forelegs, and of the walking stick with the leg.

In the Oedipus example, the hero's ability to solve the riddle leads to his being made king of Thebes and given the widowed queen—his own mother—in marriage. While his success inadvertently fulfills the second part of the baleful prophecy that accompanied his birth and thus leads, years later, to his undoing, for the time being it characterizes him as a superior human being: even his father had failed the Sphinx's test, apparently, and was on his way to Delphi to seek oracular assistance when his fateful encounter with Oedipus took place.

There are a number of classes of riddle stories. One is the neck riddle, in which the answering of a riddle is the only way to avoid death. Another is the wager or contest riddle, in which a riddle is put to someone for large stakes; another is the suitor riddle, in which a wife can be won upon guessing a riddle; another is the clever girl riddle, in which a girl wins a husband by answering riddles. Sometimes the types overlap, as in the suitor riddle where the hero not only does not get the bride if he fails to answer the riddle, but loses his life as well.

THE NECK RIDDLE

The neck riddle occurs when a protagonist must either propound or expound a riddle or a series of riddles in order to avoid being killed. Some versions of the Oedipus legend say that the Sphinx kills those who try but cannot solve her riddle (H541.1.1, "Sphinx propounds riddle on pain of death"). Neck riddlers are alike in being highly motivated, but the riddles they pose or solve are quite various.

In Type 927, *Out-riddling the Judge,* a man is set free when the judge is unable to answer his riddles (H542, "Death sentence escaped by propounding riddle king (judge) cannot solve"). One riddle commonly propounded here is "What has seven tongues in one head?" Answer: a bird's nest with seven young in a horse's skull.

There are many variants of Type 812, *The Devil's Riddle* (H543, "Escape from devil by answering his riddles"). Aarne-Thompson lists examples from Scandinavia, the British Isles, France, Spain, Germany, Italy, Hungary, Slavic nations, and Greece. The Grimms collected a version, called "The Devil and His Grandmother" ("*Der Teufel und seine Großmutter,*" KHM 125), in which three soldiers who have deserted from the army are aided by the devil, who promises them untold riches as long as they can answer his riddles at the end of seven years. They lead a merry life for that period, but as the deadline approaches, they despair of their fate. An old woman inquires why they are so sad (N825.3, "Old woman helper"), and when they confide in her, she says that one of them must go into the forest and look for a little rock house that he must enter. It turns out to be the house of the devil's grandmother, who conceals the soldier so he can hear the devil give the answers to the riddles (N451, "Secrets overheard from animal [demon] conversation"). When the devil poses the riddles, they are easily answered, and the devil flies away with a loud cry.

In versions of Type 461, *Quest for Devil's Hairs,* a youth is sent on a quest to hell or must find the cleverest person in the world, and along the way various riddles are posed to him, such as why a certain tree does not flourish, why a spring has gone dry, where a lost key is, and so forth (H544, "Answers found in other world to riddles propounded on way"). The devil's wife hides the youth when he arrives in hell and helps him find the answers to the questions.

RIDDLE CONTESTS

Riddle contests (H548) are very ancient, and a notable one appears in the Old Testament where Samson propounds a riddle to the Philistines (Judges 14). Another example of the riddle contest is Type 922, *The Emperor and the Abbot.* This tale was the focus of one of the most exhaustive folktale studies in the historic-geographic method, by Walter Anderson (*Kaiser und Abt,* 1923). Child (1965) printed two ballad versions called "King John and the Bishop."

THE SUITOR RIDDLE

Aarne-Thompson lists numerous tale types which contain motif H551, "Princess offered to man who can out-riddle her," including Types 725 (*The Dream*), 851 (*The Princess Who Cannot Solve the Riddle*), and 900 (*King Thrushbeard*—although the version known from the Grimm collection does not contain the riddling element).

The medieval Latin legend of Apollonius King of Tyre, presumably based on a lost Greek romance, was translated into Old English and later into most other European vernaculars. The legend appears as Book 8 of John Gower's *Confessio Amantis* (ca. 1390); with a change of the hero's name it was the source for Shakespeare's tragicomic romance Pericles, *Prince of Tyre* (ca. 1607). In that version, Antiochus, king of Antioch, wards off potential suitors of his beautiful daughter by posing a riddle that they must solve on pain of death. The answer to the riddle contains the dark secret that the king and his daughter are lovers.

THE CLEVER GIRL RIDDLE

Motif H561.1, "Clever peasant girl asked riddles by king," is a component of Type 875, *The Clever Peasant Girl,* who in some versions answers riddles correctly and wins the king as her husband.

One of the best examples of this class is the ballad "Riddles Wisely Expounded" (Child 1). In this ballad a man beds a maiden and when she asks in the morning if they are to wed, he says they will wed only if she can answer his riddles. In some versions the man is a knight and upon her successfully guessing the riddles he marries her; in others, he is a "fiend" and flies away as soon as she names him (C432.1, "Guessing name of supernatural creature gives power over him").

In a discussion of Child 2, "The Elfin Knight," which contains "riddlecraft" in the form of impossible tasks, Wimberly says that "a maid escapes being carried off to the Otherworld by outwitting her dead lover. The impossible tasks set by him are met on her part by a proposal of tasks equally difficult" (1965, 305). The verses that follow are from Child's version G from 1810. The lover asks:

> "Can you make me a cambrick shirt,
> Parsley, sage, rosemary and thyme
> Without any seam or needle work?
> And you shall be a true lover of mine."
> "Can you wash it in yonder well,
> Where never sprung water nor rain ever fell?"
> "Can you dry it on yonder thorn,
> Which never bore blossom sine Adam was born?"

The girl replies:

> "Now you have asked me questions three,
> I hope you'll answer as many for me."
> "Can you find me an acre of land
> Between the salt water and the sea sand?"
> "Can you plow it with a ram's horn,
> And sow it all over with one pepper corn?" (Child 1965, I:18)

When the knight cannot do these things, the girl escapes having to follow him in death (E266, "Dead carry off living").

Klipple gives a précis of a Swahili story from the East African cattle area illustrating Motif H552, "Man marries girl who guesses his riddles." It involves being able to solve not only verbal riddles but symbolic ones as well

(AT 875A, *Girl's Riddling Answer Betrays a Theft*). This tale type as well as others involving riddles was the subject of a study by Jan DeVries that concluded that tales involving clever girls originated in Europe and spread to North Africa and the Near East, while those involving male riddle solvers (AT 920, *The Son of the King and the Son of the Smith* and AT 932, *The King and the Peasant's Son*) originated in India (Thompson 1977: 158–160).

Jane Garry and John Brennan

See also: Tabu: Speaking.

REFERENCES

Anderson, Walter. 1923. *Kaiser und Alt: die Geschichte eines Schwanks.* Helsinki: Suomalainen Tiedeakatemia, Academia Scientiarum Fernnica.

Child, Francis James. 1965. *The English and Scottish Popular Ballads.* New York: Dover. Original ed. Boston: Houghton, Mifflin, 1882–1898.

DeVries, Jan. 1928. "Die Märchen von Klugen Rätsellögern." *FF Communications* No. 73. Helsinki.

Klipple, May Augusta. 1992. *African Folktales with Foreign Analogues.* New York: Garland.

Thompson, Stith. 1977. *The Folktale.* Berkeley: University of California Press.

Wimberly, Lowry Charles. 1965. *Folklore in the English and Scottish Ballads.* New York: Dover. Orig. ed. Chicago: University of Chicago Press, 1928.

Quest

Motif H1200

❀

Thompson classified quests under Chapter H (Tests) as tests of prowess. The significance of the quest, however, goes far beyond its function as a test of the hero. As Leeming writes, "Life renewal is always the ultimate goal of the quest, and life renewal is both a spiritual and a physical process" (1987, 147). He stresses that a quest need not involve a physical journey because it is essentially a religious endeavor, so that the Buddha seeking enlightenment while sitting under a tree is on a quest just as much as is Jason, sailing to Argos in search of the Golden Fleece. Moreover,

> what heroes do in the old quest stories, flesh and blood human beings act out through the medium of religious ritual and related disciplines. The Muslim who journeys to Mecca is given the special title of *hajj* for having followed in the steps of the Prophet. The shaman . . . journeys ritually and psychically to the "other world" to confront the spirits who would deprive an individual or tribe of health or life. . . . Even the ordinary worshiper becomes a real quester. . . . [and] undertakes a re-creative journey in microcosm from the chaos of the world to the cosmos of ultimate reality or primal cause. . . . A modern secular version of this spiritual journey takes place on the psychiatrist's couch, where renewal involves a quest of self-discovery by means of a process of recalling— literally, remembering. (Leeming 1987, 147)

Scholars of comparative folklore, literature, and religion have long noted a universal pattern, known as the hero cycle, that holds cross-culturally. Heroes or religious deities are marked, called, and tested, events that correspond to birth, initiation, and death, the significant events in an individual's life that are ritually observed. The hero's birth and parentage are unusual and the test (quest) often involves symbolic or actual death and, sometimes, resurrection.

THE QUEST IN FOLKTALES

While the pattern is most transparent and whole in myth and epic, parts of it can be discerned in folktales. As Underberg notes in her essay on the Hero Cycle on page 10 in this volume, the magic tale is an elaboration of the middle part of that cycle, namely, the hero's quest.

In 1928, the Russian scholar Vladimir Propp analyzed the structure of some hundred Russian fairy tales that correspond to tale types in Aarne and Thompson's *Types of the Folktale* (AT 300–749) and noted that "the names of the dramatis personae change (as well as the attributes of each), but neither their actions nor functions change. From this we can draw the inference that a tale often attributes identical actions to various personages. This makes possible the study of the tale *according to the functions of its dramatis personae*" (emphasis in the original) (Propp 1971, 20). Propp identified thirty-one functions, and although not all are present in all tales, those that are present always occur in the same order unless the tales have been mangled. For example, function 11 is the departure of the hero or heroine from home, and function 20 is the return. Propp distinguishes between seeker-heroes and victim-heroes, noting that their departures are different: seeker-heroes proactively go off in search of something, while victim-heroes often are compelled to leave (39). Victim-heroes are often banished from home and may be ordered killed, but are saved by a compassionate person and then have adventures in the world; for example, Snow-White is ordered killed by her stepmother but the hunter spares her (AT 709). It is the seeker-heroes who typically go on a quest.

Other functions include testing and/or interrogation of the hero/heroine, which prepares the way for receiving either a magical agent or helper (function 12; Motif H1550–H1569, "Tests of character"; D1581, "Tasks performed by use of magic objects"; N810, "Supernatural helper"), and difficult tasks proposed to the hero/heroine (function 25; Motif H900, "Tasks imposed"). Again, these functions or motifs are typical of the quest in myth and epic, and Dundes remarks that Propp's functions 23 to 31 correspond very well with the last portion of the *Odyssey* (Propp 1971, xiv).

Thompson also classified tasks as tests of prowess (H900–H1199). Like quests, tasks function as tests of the hero, who must perform them in order to defeat evil, restore order, and/or achieve union with a woman (or man). Tasks may be impossible (H1010), contrary to the laws of nature (H1020), paradoxical (H1050), tedious (H1110), or superhuman (H1130), and they can be performed within the context of a quest or independently of it.

Tales such as *The Dragon Slayer* (AT 300) or *The Water of Life* (AT 551) are prime examples of folktales embodying the quest motif; in the former, the hero must rescue a princess from being sacrificed to a dragon that is the scourge of a kingdom; in the latter, he must find the healing waters to restore his father to health. Thompson writes that there are "some half a dozen" tales in which the quest is the central event (1977, 105). The two tales mentioned above are in this latter category, as is *The Bird, the Horse, and the Princess* (AT 550).

While the number of tales in which the quest is the major part of the story is small, Thompson states that there is a "very large number" of tales in which tasks and quests figure as a subordinate part of the story. He lists the following: *Jack the Giant Killer* (AT 328), *The Devil's Riddle* (AT 812), *Tom-Tit-Tot* (AT 500), *The Three Old Women Helpers* (AT 501), *The Monster's Bride* (AT 507A), *Ferdinand the Faithful and Ferdinand the Unfaithful* (AT 531), *The Devil as Advocate* (AT 821B), *The Healing Fruits* (AT 610), *The Gifts of the Dwarfs* (AT 611), *The Two Travelers* (AT 613), *The Three Oranges* (AT 408), *The Wolf* (AT 428), *The Prince and the Armbands* (AT 590), *The Spinning Women by the Spring* (AT 480), *The Journey to God to Receive Reward* (AT 460A), *The Journey in Search of Fortune* (AT 460B), *The Prophecy* (AT 930), *The Dream* (AT 725), *Three Hairs from the Devil's Beard* (AT 461), *The Clever Peasant Girl* (AT 875), *The Son of the King and of the Smith* (AT 920), and *The Master Thief* (AT 1525) (1977, 105).

As an example, in *Tom-Tit-Tot*—commonly known from the Grimms' version, "Rumpelstiltskin" (KHM 55)—a poor girl is given the task of spinning a roomful of straw into gold. The completion of this task, as extraordinary as it is, is but a prelude to the central motif of the story: learning the name of her supernatural helper, which releases her from the bargain he made with her to give up her first child to him in exchange for his help (C432.1, "Guessing name of supernatural creature gives power over him").

In *Three Hairs from the Devil's Beard,* the quest (for the tale involves a journey to the otherworld) is more crucial to the story. The hero is sent by a powerful person, often his prospective father-in-law who is a king, on a quest to hell to obtain three hairs from the devil's beard. "In all these stories, the other world is conceived of as lying beyond a great body of water" (F141, "Water barrier to otherworld"; Thompson 1977, 140). On his way, the hero is asked various questions by people he meets—why a certain tree does not flourish, how a sick princess can be cured, why a certain spring has gone dry. Finally, the man who ferries the hero across the water asks how he (the ferryman) can be relieved of his work (F93.0.1.1, "Ferryman to lower world"). When the hero arrives in hell, the devil's mother hides him and obtains for him not only the three hairs but the answers to the questions (G530.3, "Help from ogre's mother"). As he returns home, the hero provides the answers to the questions to those who asked them, gains a rich reward, and wins his wife. He coincidentally is rid of his prospective father-in-law, who greedily follows in the hero's wake in search of the gold, but does not succeed either in gaining the fortune or in returning home. Thompson may have considered this story's quest as subordinate because the tale is often combined with another tale, AT 930 *The Rich Man and His Son-in-Law,* which serves as an introduction to the action just outlined.

A TALE QUEST FROM NORTH AMERICA

"Mudjukiwis" is a Cree Indian tale that contains a quest for a lost wife (H1385.3, "Quest for vanished wife [mistress]").

> Ten brothers, the eldest of them being named Mudjikiwis, keep house together. When they return from the hunt, they find that their house has been mysteriously put in order (N831.1, "Mysterious housekeeper"). They take turns in remaining home to investigate the mystery. One of the brothers succeeds in finding a girl who has been hiding from them. He marries her, and she remains as housekeeper for the brothers. Mudjikiwis, the eldest brother, becomes jealous, and tries to win the girl from his brother. When she rejects him, he shoots her and goes back home. When her husband misses her and follows her, she tells him that she is supernatural and that after four days if he will come for her, he can find her. He becomes impatient and comes for her on the third day. She therefore disappears, leaving bloody tracks behind her. Her husband now undertakes a long quest to recover her. . . . He encounters a mysterious old woman helper . . . [who] informs him that his wife is one of ten daughters of the supernatural people in the sky. From this old woman he is sent on in turn to three others. . . . They give him magic objects to help him climb into the upper world. By means of these objects, and by the power of transformation which they give him, he succeeds in overcoming all the perils of the journey and reaching the upper world (H1260, "Quest to the upper world"). He finds that there is to be a contest to see who is to marry his wife. He wins the contest, and takes back not only his own wife, but her nine sisters for his nine brothers. (Thompson 1977, 350; 1929, 135–144)

THE QUEST IN MYTH, EPIC, AND LITERATURE

As stated above, the quest is an extremely important motif in myth and traditional epics of many cultures. While the epic has not been found in all cultures, it is extremely common around the world. It had been assumed that epic literature was unknown in Africa, but since the last third of the twentieth century intensive fieldwork has proven that assessment wrong. There is a rich mine of epics that runs across the Sahel and down into Central Africa, defined by William Johnson as the "African Epic Belt" (Johnson, Hale, and Belcher 1997, xv).

For example, Biebuyck (1969, 1978) has collected multiple variants of the Mwindo epic among the Nyanga in Zaire, which, he affirms, fit the standard definitions and characterization of epic literature (1978, 3). Some of the motifs in these versions are A511.1.3.3, "Immaculate conception of culture hero"; A511.2.1, "Abandonment of culture hero at birth"; A527.1, "Culture hero precocious"; H1270, "Quest to lower world"; F81.1, "Journey to land of dead to bring back person from the dead"; N831, "Girl as helper"; H900, "Tasks imposed"; D1581, "Tasks performed by use of magic objects"; and A566, " Culture hero returns to upper world"; A581, "Culture hero returns."

The quest has been a theme used by writers of literary epics, most notably by Dante in *Inferno,* the first book of *The Divine Comedy* (ca. 1320). Earlier, Virgil wrote of the quest of Aeneas to found a new civilization (Rome) in the *Aeneid* (19 BCE), which also involves a descent to the underworld. Medieval writers who elaborated Celtic and Christian themes produced the various works of the Arthurian legends, including the quest for the grail, which is undertaken by the Knights of the Round Table in order to heal the dying Fisher King and his kingdom's barren land.

Jane Garry

See also: Hero Cycle; Individuation; Otherworld Journeys; Quest for the Vanished Husband.

REFERENCES

Biebuyck, Daniel. 1978. *Hero and Chief: Epic Literature from the Banyanga, Zaire Republic.* Berkeley: University of California Press.

Biebuyck, Daniel, and Kahombo C. Mateene, eds. 1969. *The Mwindo Epic from the Bahyanga (Congo Republic).* Berkeley: University of California Press.

Johnson, William John, Thomas A. Hale, and Stephen Belcher. 1997. *Oral Epics from Africa: Vibrant Voices from a Vast Continent.* Bloomington: Indiana University Press.

Leeming, David. 1987. "Quest." In *Encyclopedia of Religion,* ed. Mircea Eliade. New York: Macmillan.

Propp, Vladimir. 1971 [1958]. *The Morphology of the Folktale.* Trans. Laurence Scott. 2d ed. Ed. Louis A. Wagner. Introd. Alan Dundes. Austin: University of Texas Press.

Thompson, Stith. 1929. *Tales of the North American Indians.* Cambridge, MA: Harvard University Press.

———. 1977. *The Folktale.* Berkeley: University of California Press. Orig. ed. New York: Holt, Rinehart, and Winston, 1946.

Quest for the Vanished Husband/Lover

Motifs H1385.4 and H1385.5

❀

In folklore, a woman's quest for her vanished husband or lover is the central motif in numerous tales named for these motifs (H1285.4 and H1385.5), AT 425 A-P, *The Search for the Vanished Husband*. That quest also appears in related tales (AT 430, 432, 441). One of the best documented and researched tale types, AT 425 has been the subject of monographs by Tegethoff (1922), Swahn (1955), and Megas (1971), as well as numerous articles. It may be summarized as follows: a girl is married or betrothed to a supernatural male, who may appear as a beast or monster by day and a man at night (D621.1). She violates a tabu—frequently an injunction to secrecy about his condition (C421)—and he vanishes. To regain him, she must typically perform a penitential search, overcoming apparently insuperable obstacles, such as climbing a glass hill, as in the Scottish "The Black Bull of Norroway" (Chambers 1847); or wearing out seven sets of iron clothes, seven pairs of iron shoes, and seven iron canes, as in the Afghani "Khastakhumar and Bibinagar" (Dorson 1975); or, as in the Italian "Filo d'Oro and Filomena" (Calvino 1980), crossing the River of Serpents, the River of Blood, the River of Bile, and scaling a mountain. The search usually entails the heroine's emotional and physical abjection; in "The Magic Box" from Armenia (Hoogasian-Villa 1966), the bride walks for so many years that her hair becomes pure white, symbolizing her loss of youth and beauty. In "The Snail *Choja*" from Japan, the bride wades through muddy fields seeking her snail spouse, "until her face was splattered . . . her beautiful kimono was completely covered in mud," and she is prepared to drown herself (Seiki 1963, 88). In some variants the wife is pregnant, and the labor of the quest mimics the labor of birth (according to

Christian tradition a punishment for Eve's sin): in "The Serpent and The Grape Grower's Daughter" from France, the abandoned wife "cried night and day and walked unceasingly; she was all the more afflicted and her wandering was all the more painful in that she was with child" (Delarue 1956, 180). Sometimes the actual birth precipitates the successful conclusion of the quest: thus, in "The Sun and His Wife" from Greece, the heroine gives birth to a boy, and "[w]hen the Sun's sister saw it, she cried, 'That is my brother's child, and this is his wife'" (Megas 1970, 60). Here the sister's recognition of her brother's paternity and the wife's status is sufficient to secure the happy ending: the Sun returns. The wife is frequently aided in her quest by three helpers (H1235, "Succession of helpers on quest")—often crones, sometimes her husband's relatives—who give her three valuable objects; they may also impose tasks, such as filling a bowl with tears. When she at last finds her husband—"east of the sun, and west of the moon," in the words of the well-known Norwegian version (Asbjørnsen 1953)—he is usually living in the home of a rival bride, and the first wife must undertake menial labor in or near their house. In the Kashmiri "Nágray and Hímal," a princess follows her snake husband to his home in a spring, where she becomes the servant and victim of his jealous serpent wives (Knowles 1977). In European versions, she frequently exchanges the objects given by the helpers for three nights in the same room as her husband; on the third night he finally recognizes her (D1978.4, "Hero wakened from magic sleep by wife who has purchased place in his bed from false bride"). His recognition usually ends the enchantment under which the husband has lived: rejecting the false bride and embracing the true one, he resumes his true identity. At the end of a Scottish variant, "The Hoodie-Crow," the husband declares, "That is my married wife . . . and no one else will I have," and "at that very moment the spells fell off him, and never more would he be a hoodie" (Lang 1910, 340). "The Camel Husband," from Palestine, lacks the rival bride but emphasizes the redemptive nature of the wife's search: her husband cries, "You have chased me into the land of the Djinn and crossed the boundary between the world above and the world beneath, you have opened the way for my return. From today I can live not as a camel but as a man" (Bushnaq 1986, 192–193).

More than 1,500 versions of this tale type have been recorded from Europe, Asia, parts of Africa, and the European traditions in North America (Noy 1963; Nicolaisen 1989; Anderson 2000). These, however, "are only a fragment of the mass of variants that could be accumulated from the living oral tradition" (Dorson 1975, 230): the tale "has achieved an acceptance through time and space and among peoples of the most diverse cultures as [has] no other magic tale" (Ward 1989, 119). It first appears in literature as the story of Cupid and Psyche (AT 425A, *The Monster [Animal] as Bridegroom*), an "old wives' tale" embedded in Apuleius's *The Golden Ass* (second century CE). However, scholars have traced its antecedents to Greek and Hittite mythology of the second millennium BCE (Anderson 2000). Megas (1971) shows that some of the oldest elements in the tale were not used by Apuleius, but remain current in modern European versions, evidence of an independent oral tradition.

INTERPRETATION

Early interpreters read the Cupid and Psyche story as a Neoplatonic allegory in which Psyche represents the human soul and Cupid represents the Divine Principle in humankind. Desiring the beauty of the Divine, the soul seeks it throughout the world, enduring affliction as a necessary purification (Wright 2000). Psyche's tasks are "images of the mighty toils and anxious cares which the soul must necessarily endure after her lapse, in order to atone for her guilt" and return to the world of essences (Apuleius 1795, xii–xiii). In the twentieth century, psychologists advanced influential interpretations. Thus Neumann (1956) views the story of Cupid and Psyche in Jungian terms as a myth of feminine psychic development. Psyche's disobedience in shedding light on her lover is a heroic act of individuation, a rebellion against the state of unconscious sensuality represented by the power of Aphrodite, the Great Mother:

> The embrace of Eros [Cupid] and Psyche in the darkness represents the elementary but unconscious attraction of opposites, which impersonally bestows life but is not yet human. But the coming of light makes Eros 'visible,' it manifests the phenomenon of psychic love . . . as the human and higher form of the archetype of relatedness. It is only the completion of Psyche's development, effected in the course of her search for the invisible Eros, that brings with it the highest manifestation of the archetype of relatedness: a divine Eros joined with a divine Psyche. (Neumann 1956, 109–110)

Psyche's tasks symbolize a feminine initiation that culminates in her redemption of Eros: "Through Psyche's sacrifice and [symbolic] death the divine lover is changed from a wounded boy to a man and savior, because in Psyche he finds . . . the feminine mystery of rebirth through love" (Neumann 1956, 125).

Bettelheim, from a Freudian perspective, interprets Psyche's quest as the attempt to unify sex, love, and life by overcoming sexual anxieties. He sees in Psyche a type of the modern woman:

> Despite all warnings about the dire consequences if she tries to find out, woman is not satisfied with remaining ignorant about sex and life. Comfortable as an existence in relative naïveté may be, it is an empty life which must not be accepted. Notwithstanding all the hardships woman has to suffer to

be reborn to full consciousness and humanity, the [animal-groom] stories leave no doubt that this is what she must do. Otherwise there would be no story: no fairy story worth telling, no worthwhile story to her life. (Bettelheim 1976, 295)

Propp (1949) suggests that the story of Cupid and Psyche has a basis in an ancient ritual of sexual initiation: Psyche represents the girl who encounters her lover in darkness; after the initiation, he leaves, forgets her, and starts a family. Rebelling against ritual law, the girl pursues and reclaims her lover. Calvino, noting the popularity of the AT 425 tale type throughout Italy, cites Propp's theory as an explanation of the story's persistent eroticism: "Although the customs of millennia are disregarded, the plot of the story still reflects the spirit of those laws and describes every love thwarted and forbidden by law, convention, or social disparity. That is why it has been possible, from prehistory to the present, to preserve . . . the sensuality so often underlying this love, evident in the ecstasy and frenzy of mysterious nocturnal embraces" (Calvino 1980, xxx). For Calvino, the story is a timeless tale of erotic love overcoming law or social custom; by contrast, Dawkins explains the perennial attraction of the story in its reflection of marital relations: "The loss of the mate through disobedience or by some misunderstanding, or lack of sympathy reflects the quarrels of lovers and their alienation. That the lost mate can indeed be won back, but only after toil and sacrifice, presents equally a human truth" (Dawkins 1953, 55).

Feminist scholars and critics have challenged ahistorical interpretations of the AT 425 tale, highlighting its gender ideology. The self-sacrifice and submission of the heroine, they argue, should be seen not as essential feminine qualities, but rather as aspects of a patriarchal script for women. Bacchilega argues that the story "repeatedly reenacts the patriarchal exchange of women, and affirms women's collusion with the system" (Bacchilega 1997, 76). She concludes that its "insidiously patriarchal appeal depends most on the active but self-effacing heroine—a protagonist with agency whose subjectivity is construed as absence and whose symbolic reward is giving rebirth to another" (78). Tatar compares the gender roles in AT 425 tales with those in AT 400 (*The Man on the Quest for His Lost Wife*). She observes that in the former the heroines are rewarded for the expression of emotion, while in the latter the heroes are rewarded for impassive stoicism.

No matter in what cultural context or epoch European tales about animal-brides and animal-grooms are told, they each present a surprisingly durable notion of female and male roles. Women, as a study of *The Search for the Lost Husband* reveals, are creatures of feeling. . . . The desire for greater intimacy and the overvaluation of family attachments always get these women in trouble, even as their surplus of emotion (passion or compassion) gets their grooms out of trouble. And finally, the desire to meet the needs of others . . . and to please their husbands . . . shows the extent to which these fairy-tale figures are invested in becoming connected and establishing relationships. (Tatar 1992, 160)

Recent fieldwork on the AT 425 tale by folklorists, who stress its local and historically specific meanings, provides support for a feminist analysis. Dégh studied the ethnic Hungarian version of the Cupid and Psyche tale, in which a girl is married to a snake prince; when she burns the snakeskin in an attempt to disenchant him, he abandons her angrily. To regain him, she must plant a grain of wheat and a walnut, and water them with her tears until she can bake a bread and a walnut cake. After seven years, she can start her voyage of another seven years with the token food to find him. Throughout her fourteen years of penitential labor and travel, she is pregnant but, bound with an iron hoop, unable to give birth until she finds her husband and wins him from a rival. According to Dégh, this story dramatizes the consummation of an arranged marriage and its consequences:

> The woman's domain is the home where she serves the husband and raises his sons; her procreative capability is her main worth. The man, on the other hand, is powerful and free of ties. He takes the reluctant girl by force, then, and for disobeying his orders leaves her and orders her to leave after him in pursuit while he also ties her with impregnation. She becomes his property for good but he has no obligation to her; he is free to establish new family ties. (Dégh 1995, 150)

Analyzing the performance of Spanish AT 425 variants, Taggart finds that older women use the stories to prepare younger women for the transition from courtship to marriage. Girls are encouraged to overcome sexual anxieties and schooled to assume the burden of emotional labor in marriage: the wife's love will humanize her husband and restore rifts in their relationship. Men retell the same stories, affirming this division of labor and their need for a woman's devotion. "The metaphorical description of the women's role in maintaining the marital bond appears in the 'Cupid and Psyche' stories told by women as well as men, in which heroines endure long and difficult ordeals to restore their relationships with lost husbands. The role of men in maintaining the marital tie is substantially less, judging from the stories circulating in oral tradition" (Taggart 1990, 164). Taggart contrasts Spanish oral tradition, in which lost husband tales are popular and lost wife tales (AT 400) scarce, with that in Nahuat and Mayan culture, where lost wife tales are more prominent: "'Lost Wife' tales undoubtedly express Mayan and Nahuat men's anxiety about losing the nurturance of women on whom they heavily depend, and they capture the actual experiences of many young husbands whose wives have returned to their parents after a family quarrel" (211). He suggests that lost wife tales are comparatively rare in Spanish oral tradition because a social structure in which women marry late promotes faith in the conjugal bond and the power of a woman's love for a man.

The story of Cupid and Psyche has appeared in numerous literary versions, including plays by Lope de Vega (*Psiques y Cupid,* 1608), Don Pedro Caldéron de la Barca (*Ni amor se libra de Amor,* 1669), and Molière (*Psyche,* 1671); poems by William Morris ("The Earthly Paradise," 1868) and Coventry Patmore ("To the Unknown Eros," 1877); and novels by Walter Pater (*Marius the Epicurean,* 1885), Sylvia Townsend Warner (*The True Heart,* 1929) and C.S. Lewis (*Till We Have Faces,* 1956). Since the eighteenth century, when Madame Le Prince de Beaumont published her influential version of AT 425 (subtype C), "Beauty and the Beast" stories have appeared widely in European literature (Hearne 1989; Ralph 1989; Warner 1994; Zipes 1994; Accardo 2002).

Karen Bamford

REFERENCES

Aarne, Antti. 1961. *The Types of the Folktale: A Classification and Bibliography.* Trans. and enlarged by Stith Thomson. FFC no. 3. 2d revision. Helsinki : Suomalainen Tiedeakatemia.

Accardo, Pasquale. 2002. *Metamorphosis of Apuleius.* Madison, NJ: Farleigh Dickinson University Press.

Anderson, Graham. 2000. *Fairytale in the Ancient World.* London: Routledge.

Apuleius. 1795. *The Metamorphosis, or the Golden Ass, and Philosophical Works, of Apuleius,* trans. Thomas Taylor. London: Sold by R. Triphook and T. Rodd.

Asbjørnsen, P.C. 1953. *East of the Sun and West of the Moon.* New York: Macmillan.

Bacchilega, Cristina. 1997. *Postmodern Fairy Tales: Gender and Narrative Strategies.* Philadelphia: University of Pennsylvania Press.

Bettleheim, Bruno. 1976. *The Uses of Enchantment: The Meaning and Importance of Fairy Tales.* New York: Knopf.

Bushnaq, Inea, trans. and ed. 1986. *Arab Folktales.* New York: Pantheon, 1986.

Calvino, Italo. 1980. *Italian Folktales.* Trans. George Martin. New York: Harcourt Brace Jovanovich.

Chambers, Robert. 1847. *Popular Rhymes of Scotland.* 3d ed. Edinburgh: Chambers.

Dawkins, Richard M. 1953. *Modern Greek Folktales.* Oxford: Clarendon.

Dégh, Linda. 1995. "How Do Storytellers Interpret the Snakeprince Tale?" *Narratives in Society: A Performer-Centered Study of Narration,* 137–151. FFC no. 255. Helsinki: Suomalainen Tiedeakatemia.

Delarue, Paul. 1956. *The Borzoi Book of French Folk Tales.* Trans. Austin E. Fife. New York: Knopf.

Dorson, Richard M., ed. 1975. *Folktales Told Around the World.* Chicago: University of Chicago Press.

Hearne, Betsy. 1989. *Beauty and the Beast: Visions and Revisions of an Old Tale.* With an essay by Larry DeVries. Chicago: University of Chicago Press, 1989.

Hoogasian-Villa, Susie, ed. 1966. *100 Armenian Tales and Their Folkloric Relevance.* Detroit: Wayne State University Press.

Knowles, J. Hinton. 1977. *Folk-Tales of Kashmir.* New York: Arno Press.

Lang, Andrew, ed. 1910. *The Lilac Fairy Book.* London: Longmans.

Megas, Georgios, ed. 1970. *Folktales of Greece.* Trans. Helen Coloclides. Chicago: University of Chicago Press.

———. 1971. *Das Märchen von Amor und Psyche in der griechischen Volksüberlieferung.* Athens: Athens Academy.

Neumann, Erich. 1956. *Amor and Psyche: The Psychic Development of the Feminine.* Trans. Ralph Manheim. Princeton, NJ: Princeton University Press.

Nicolaisen, W.F.H. 1989. "Foreword." *Midwestern Folklore* 15: 69–70.

Noy, Dov, ed. 1963. *Folktales of Israel.* Trans. Gene Baharan. Chicago: University of Chicago Press.

Philip, Neil, ed. 1992. *The Penguin Book of English Folktales.* Penguin: London.

Propp, Vladimir. 1949. *Le radici storiche dei racconti di fate.* Trans. Giuseppe Cocchiara. Turin: Einaudi.

Ralph, Phyllis C. 1989. *Victorian Transformations: Fairy Tales, Adolescence and the Novel of Female Development.* American University Studies: series 4, English Language and Literature, Vol. 96. New York: Peter Lang.

Seiki, Keigo, ed. 1963. *Folktales of Japan.* Trans. Robert J. Adams. Chicago: University of Chicago Press.

Swahn, Jan-Öjvind. 1955. *The Tale of Cupid and Psyche.* Lund: CWK Glerrup.

Taggert, James M. 1990. *Enchanted Maidens: Gender Relations in Spanish Tales of Courtship and Marriage.* Princeton: Princeton University Press.

Tatar, Maria. 1992. *Off With Their Heads: Fairytales and the Culture of Childhood.* Princeton, NJ: Princeton University Press.

Tegethoff, Ernst. 1922. *Studien zum Märchentypus von Amor und Psyche.* Bonn: K. Schroeder.

Ward, Donald. 1989. "'Beauty and the Beast': Fact and Fancy, Past and Present." *Midwestern Folklore* 15: 119–125.

Warner, Marina. 1994. *From the Beast to the Blonde.* London: Chatto and Windus.

Wright, Constance S. 2000. "The Metamorphosis of Cupid and Psyche in Plato, Apuleius, Origen, and Chaucer." In *Tales Within Tales: Apuleius Through Time,* ed. Constance S. Wright and Julia Bolton Holloway, 55–72. New York: AMS.

Zipes, Jack. 1994. "The Origins of the Fairy Tale." In *Fairy Tale as Myth: Myth as Fairy Tale,* 17–48. Lexington: University Press of Kentucky.

❀ J ❀

The Wise and the Foolish

Individuation

Motif J1030.1§

❀

Individuation is "the process whereby a part of a whole becomes progressively more distinct and independent" (English and English 1966, 258). Individuation plays a critical role in the development of the self and is one of the main archetypes in Jungian analytical psychology and a key to the understanding of the great world religions and philosophies (Progoff 1953, 144). Prefacing *Individuation in Fairy Tales,* Marie-Louise von Franz, one of C.G. Jung's closest associates and dedicated disciples, states, "individuation is a natural, ubiquitous phenomenon which has found innumerable symbolic descriptions in the folk tales of all countries. One can even say that the majority of folk tales deal with one or another aspect of this most meaningful basic life process in man" (1990, vii).

PSYCHOLOGICAL FACTORS AND THE *MOTIF-INDEX*

Relating the mystical yet pervasive concept of the self to the classificatory system of the *Motif-Index* requires a reconsideration of the *Index*'s basic schema. As pointed out by the present writer (El-Shamy 1995, I:15–16), Thompson eschewed treating psychological factors. Although the *Motif-Index* dedicates a whole section (W) to "Traits of Character" and addresses a few aspects of character under other headings (e.g., H1550, "Tests of character"; P12, "Character of kings"), the word *personality* does not appear at all in the *Motif-Index.* However, as pointed out by the present psychological (and sociological) concepts do appear in folk expressions as a matter of empirical observation by the folk, and they can be of significant classificatory (indexing) usefulness (El-Shamy 1995, I:15). For example, in *Folk Traditions of the Arab World: A Guide to Motif Classification,* key principles from cognitive psychological literature have been used as classificatory devices (El-Shamy 1995, I:xiii–xiv).

MATURITY GAINED BY LEAVING HOME

Jung's concept of the process of individuation and its effect on the individual is a theme that recurs repeatedly in lore, literature, and belief systems. From a general perspective, individuation may be viewed as the gaining of wisdom by a person; thus individuation may be classified as one of the motifs within the J chapter ("The wise and the foolish"). More specifically, individuation belongs to the category of "Acquisition and possession of wisdom (knowledge)," of which "Self-dependence" (J1030) is an aspect. A new motif that addresses individuation in general terms is designated as J1030.1§, "Maturity (growing up, independence, 'individuation') gained by leaving home."

Leaving home and gaining wisdom in the world independently of one's parents and other family members may be seen as part of the struggle between the individual and society. The individual seeks independence while society seeks to keep the individual within its fold (El-Shamy 1997, I:38). This dynamic tension constitutes the process of individuation.

One of the cases von Franz uses to illustrate this process is a tale from Spain titled "The White Parrot," which she treats without reference to available motif or tale type indexes (von Franz 1990, 219 n. 1; *Spanische Märchen* 1940, 155). The tale belongs to AT 707, *The Three Golden Sons.* She summarizes it: "The queen bears marvelous children. They are stolen away. The queen is banished. The [children's] quest for the speaking bird, the singing tree, and the water of life."

The Types of the Folktale outlines Type 707 as follows:

I. *Wishing for a Husband.* (a) Three girls make a boast that if they marry the king they will have triplets with golden hair, a chain around the neck, and a star on the forehead. (b) The king overhears the youngest and marries her.

II. *Calumniated Wife.* (a) The elder sisters substitute a dog for the new born children and accuse the wife of giving birth to the dog. (b) The children are thrown into a stream but rescued by a miller (or a fisher) (c) The wife is imprisoned.

III. *The Children's Adventures.* (a) After the children have grown up, the eldest son sets out to find his father or (b) to seek the speaking bird, the singing tree, and the water of life. (c) He and his brother, who goes for him, both fail and are transformed to marble columns. (d) The sister by courtesy and obedience to an old woman succeeds in rescuing them and bringing back the magic objects.

IV. *Restoration of Children.* (a) The attention of the king is drawn to the children and the magic objects. (b) The bird of truth reveals to him the whole history. (c) The children and the wife are restored; the sister-in-law is punished. (Aarne and Thompson 1964)

Despite the confining title that specifies the number of children and limits the children's gender to males, several variations and subtypes of the narrative are encountered. Typically, the tale's action involves castaway infants: one sister and her only brother (El-Shamy 1980, no. 9), one sister and her brothers who may be two or three in number, or brothers only and no sister (O'Sullivan 1966, no. 19; in sub-Saharan Africa), as the title of the tale type specifies. Often the children are twins.

This tale type is extremely widespread throughout the world, which may indicate the archetypal nature of its basic plot. In all its manifestations, the process of individuation can be seen as the central force around which the plot coheres. The tale is normally concluded with the children—regardless of their gender—surviving the dangers of the outside world and triumphantly returning to their original home to right social injustices. Justice is achieved by applying the benefits of some of their acquisitions during their forced sojourn and quests for treasured objects (i.e., self).

Because of the role that the bird plays in revealing the truth, von Franz views it as the "central motif" around which her Jungian interpretations are developed. The self, or the "hidden treasure," in tale type AT 707 is symbolically represented by a number of unique items. Of these we may mention the dancing plant (D1646, "Magic dancing object"; D1646.5§, "Magic dancing bamboo—reed"), the singing object (D1615, "Magic singing object"), and the truth-speaking bird (B0131, "Bird of truth"; B0131.2, "Bird reveals treachery"); also present are the acts of petrification (D231, "Transformation: man to stone. [(Petrification]") and disenchantment (D700, "Person disenchanted"; R159§, "Sister disenchants bewitched brother"; D700.1§, "Petrified person (community) disenchanted").

For Jung and his disciples, any of these objects or acts constitutes a hidden treasure that is part of the elusive self, which the person is trying to approach or comprehend. Von Franz equates the dangers the children face in acquiring these items with forces or agents guarding a treasure (or self) against looters-to-be. She states that wherever there is a treasure there is a snake wound around it, and wherever there is the water of life there is a lion guarding it. Thus, "you cannot get near the self and the meaning of life without being on the razor's edge of falling into greed, into darkness, and into the shadowy aspect of the personality" (von Franz 1990, 49). Hence, the acquisition by the castaway children of such treasures as the dancing bamboo, and the singing water may be seen as steps bringing the adventurer closer to the ultimate truth (self), which he or she will never be able to fully comprehend.

The final step in the process of individuation is the acquisition of the speaking "bird-of truth" (the white parrot in von Franz's Spanish version). The bird is a symbol for the mysterious truth that the unconscious speaks. That means that it is a "threshold" phenomenon: it conveys the wondrous thoughts of the unconscious in its speech. It is probably the paradox that it is a bird speaking in human language that makes it a very fitting symbol (von Franz 1990, 67) The bird tells the community (the children's father) the truth about life and his children, explaining that the substitute for the children (cat, dog) could not be his offspring because it is not human.

With the father and the community renouncing the old belief about the "children" and accepting the truth as presented by them (or by an indisputable source of truth acting on their behalf), a significant aspect of the process of individuation is accomplished.

PETRIFICATION AS A SYMBOL OF INABILITY TO DEVELOP

A recurrent trait of the talking bird is its magic ability to transform the person who seeks to possess it into stone (Motif D231, "Transformation: man to stone. [(Petrification)]"). This transformation occurs upon the seeker's breaking of a tabu imposed by the bird; in AT 707, the tabu is usually speaking or replying to the bird (Motif C406§, "Tabu: answering (responding to) call or question"). Frequently, the brother—like many others before him—becomes a marble column, a stone, a granule of sand, or the like. It is the sister who saves her male sibling from this oblivion. Petrification may be seen as a symbol of the inability to develop and, consequently, the inability to be in touch with the self (von Franz 1990, 68). To be disenchanted and rendered into human form once more is to continue to grow and attempt to approach and comprehend the mysterious self.

Another case in which individuation seems to be the cardinal theme is Motif H1376.2, "Quest: learning what fear is." The motif constitutes the driving force for tale type AT 326, *The Youth Who Wanted to Learn What Fear Is*. A Turkish rendition presented through the editorship of a Hungarian folklorist (Kunos 1913, 12–18) may be summarized as follows:

> I. A woman asked her son to close the door because she had fear. She could not explain what fear was. So he set out to find out what fear can be.
>
> II. He met forty fearsome robbers in the mountains but he was not afraid. One of them sent him to the cemetery to make pastry. A hand reached out from

the grave and asked for its share; he struck it with a spoon, thus causing it to disappear. Another robber sent him to a lonely building. He entered and saw on a raised platform a swing in which "a child was weeping." A "maiden" approached him and asked that he let her climb upon his shoulders to reach the child. "He consented and the girl mounted," but she pressed his neck with her feet until "he was in danger of strangulation." However, she jumped down and disappeared after dropping a bracelet. The youth took it and left. A Jew claimed that the bracelet was his. The two went to the judge, but neither could prove his claim. So the judge decided to impound it until either could produce its match as proof of ownership. At the coast, the boy saw a ship tossing to and fro and heard fearful cries. "He quickly divested himself of his clothes, sprang into the water, dived to the bottom of the sea," and found the Daughter-of-the-Sea shaking the vessel. "He fell upon her, flogged her soundly, and drove her away." As he walked he saw a garden in front of which there was a fountain. Three pigeons dived into the water; each was transformed into a maiden. They laid a table and drank a toast "to the health" of the youth who had shown no fear. These three maidens were the ones involved. The youth presented himself. "All three maidens hastened to embrace him." He told them about the case of the bracelet. "They took him to a cave where a number of stately halls that opened before him overwhelmed him with astonishment." They gave him the bracelet's match; he took it to the judge, won his case, and hastened back "to the cave." The maidens told him, "You part from us no more," but he "tore himself away" and left. He came to a spot where there was a crowd. He was informed that "the shah of the country was no more." A pigeon was to be set loose and he on whose head the bird should alight would be "declared heir to the throne." Three different pigeons chose the youth, but each time he refused the honor. "The widow of the late ruler" promised to "show him fear" if he would accept the "dignity for tonight at least." He consented. Soon he learned that "whoever was shah one day was dead the next." During the night he burned a "coffin" which was being prepared for him; then he slept soundly. In the morning the slaves carried the news that he had survived to the "sultana."

III. The sultana, thereupon, ordered the cook to place "a live sparrow in the soup-dish for supper." Evening came. "The young shah and the sultana sat down for supper." At the sultana's persuasive insistence, the reluctant "youth" lifted the lid off the soup-dish. "A bird flew out"; that incident gave him a momentary shock of fear. "Seest Thou!" cried the sultana. "That is fear."

IV. "Then the marriage feast was ordered [. . .]. The young shah had his mother brought to his palace and *they* lived happily ever after." (El-Shamy 1967; El-Shamy 1986).

In the text outlined above, a youth with no independent social identity seeks to wrest his place in society (represented by parental authority). He leaves home and experiences the struggle between life and death, represented by robbers, cemeteries, graves, drowning, and a coffin being prepared for him; he also experiences the struggle between good and evil, represented by helping a "maiden" with her child, disputing with a usurper, refusing erotic association with supernatural beauties, and saving ship passengers; and his final struggle as an individual is with societal authority represented by royalty. The youth triumphs over all of these struggles, which embody pairs of Jungian archetypes. In the case of the adversary from a different ethnic or religious group, the victory is through civility and legal means rather than violence. Finally, having been selected by a bird as the true successor to kingship, the boy succeeds in learning what he had set out from home to learn: what fear is. In learning this emotion, which is required for survival, the youth has approached his self. Also, he has gone through the process of individuation and can exercise his own authority over the community by becoming its ruler.

CHOICE OF ROADS AND INDIVIDUATION

Heroes and heroines on quests are usually faced with the need to make a momentous choice, such as choosing a certain road or direction from among others. Such a choice is represented by Motifs N122.0.1, "The choice of roads: at parting of three roads are equivocal inscriptions telling what will happen if each is chosen," and N122.0.2§, "The choice of roads: Road of Safety, Road of Sorrow, or Road of No-return."

A case that seems to be confined to the individuation of a young female in a male-dominated society occurs in a folktale that is widespread in the Middle East and that may be summarized as follows:

> There are two brothers: a rich one who has seven sons, and a poor one who has seven daughters. The father of the daughters addresses the father of the sons as "Father-of-Joys," but the father of the sons addresses the father of the daughters as: "Father-of-Sorrows" (or the like). The youngest daughter persuades her father to propose a trade-mission as a competition between the eldest son and the youngest daughter. The father of the sons ridicules the proposition, but agrees. The rich brother provides his son with capital and servants; the poor brother has no assets with which he would aid his daughter. She, however, manages to raise a little capital with the help of women neighbors.
>
> The trip begins with both competitors (paternal cousins) together on the road. They come to a parting of the road where three choices are given: "Road of Safety," "Road of Sorrow," "Road of No-return." The boy jumps ahead of the girl and takes the "Road of Safety"; she takes "The Road of He-Who-Goes-Doesn't-Return."
>
> Disguised as a man, she comes to a country where salt is exchanged for gold. She trades her salt for gold and becomes a prominent merchant (AT 1651A, *Fortune in Salt;* Motif N411.4, "Salt in saltless land sold for fortune"). The prince of the country falls in love with the new merchant (Motif

T463.0.1§, "Pseudo-homosexual (male) attraction: man falls in love with another man who turns out to be a woman in disguise"). She successfully eschews detection of her true gender and departs to her home with her legitimately earned wealth. By treachery, her male cousin claims that the wealth is his own and reports to the girl's father that his daughter has gone astray.

Truth is revealed before the town's judge and all its inhabitants. The prince (who had followed his guest after learning her actual identity) testifies to her honorable conduct. The cheating cousin and his father are put to shame. The heroine and her father are honored. She marries the prince. (El-Shamy 1999, no. 9, 1–9; cf. no. 30)

The tale is designated as new tale type 923C§, *Girl Wins Against Boy (usually, her Eldest Paternal-cousin) in a Contest of Worth* (El-Shamy 1995, I:429). Our text reflects a number of gender-oriented themes. Among these is the disadvantageous position (e.g., low communal esteem, raising capital, choice of roads) in which a girl—as a matter of course—is placed. Yet in spite of these shackles, the heroine emerges as the winner and succeeds in getting the community to view her in more positive terms. By taking a risk, choosing a hazardous road, and maintaining her gender-role, she comes closer to understanding her capabilities. The wealth that she brings home is comparable to the guarded treasure, or the self. Her triumphal homecoming symbolizes a completed process of individuation as a capable female.

INDIVIDUATION IN POPULAR CULTURE AND ELITE LITERATURE

Examples of the recurrence of the process of individuation in popular culture can be marshaled in droves. For example, in the motion picture *Home Alone* (1990), a small boy is left alone (abandoned, albeit inadvertently) by his entire family, who are traveling abroad. He is victimized by a pair of burglars. In his turn, he exacts a series of painful acts of revenge on them, climaxing in their arrest by the police. Upon their return from their trip, family members who had earlier slighted the boy accord him his due recognition and acclaim.

If we allow for different lifestyles and technological innovations, we will find that the plot sketched above occurs in an international tale type: AT 1538, *The Youth Cheated in Selling Oxen Avenges Himself.* Both the boy in the motion picture and the youth in the folktale avenge themselves on robbers through a series of acts of revenge including whipping, trapping, and tarring and feathering (or gluing and feathering). Motifs commonly found in both narratives include K2400§, "Deception for deception (tit for tat): deceived person gets even in a like manner (same ruse, strategy, trick, etc.)"; N262§, "Train of troubles from boy's (youth's) vengeance. In different disguises he punishes his cheaters (robbers) by repeated beatings"; and J18.1§, "Robber reformed by repeated beatings."

In elite literature, examples of individuation may be found in innumerable works, including Charles Dickens's *Oliver Twist* (1837–1839) and *David Copperfield* (1849–1850), and Mark Twain's *The Adventures of Tom Sawyer* (1876). In the latter, Twain describes the experiences of two runaway boys: Tom and Huck. The novel is brought to a close (Chapter XXXV) with the triumphal return of the runaways with plenty of cash (cf. treasure). In the Conclusion, Twain states that the boy who ran away from home and about whom he wrote is not the same one that returned. He writes: "So endeth this chronicle. It being strictly a history of a boy, it must stop here; the story could not go much further without becoming the history of a man." The story ends where folktales with corresponding subject matter normally end: the presumed completion of the process of individuation.

Hasan El-Shamy

See also: Choice of Roads and Crossroads; Sister and Brother.

REFERENCES

Aarne, Antti, and Stith Thompson. 1964. *The Types of the Folktale: A Classification and Bibliography.* FFC no. 184. Helsinki: Suomalainen Tiedeakatenia.

El-Shamy, Hasan. 1967. "al-lâshuʿûr al gamâʿî wa al-folklore (Collective Unconsciousness and Folklore) [2]." In *Al-Majallah* 126 (June): 21-29.

———. 1980. *Folktales of Egypt: Collected, Translated and Edited with Middle Eastern and African Parallels.* Chicago: University of Chicago Press.

———. 1985: "Sentiment, Genre, and Tale Typology: Meaning in Middle Eastern and African Tales." In *Papers III.* 8th Congress for the International Society for Folk Narrative Research, ed. R. Kvideland and T. Selberg, 255–283. Bergen, Norway: Etno-Folkloristisk Institut.

———. 1995. *Folk Traditions of the Arab World: A Guide to Motif Classification.* 2 vols. Bloomington: Indiana University Press.

———. 1997. "Archetype" and "Jungian Psychology." In *Folklore: An Encyclopedia of Forms, Methods, and History,* ed. Thomas A. Green. 2 vols. Santa Barbara, CA: ABC-CLIO.

———. 2004. *Types of the Folktale in the Arab World: A Demographically Oriented Tale-Type Approach.* Bloomington: Indiana University Press.

———, ed. and trans. 1999. *Tales Arab Women Tell and the Behavioral Patterns They Portray.* Bloomington: Indiana University Press.

English, Horace B., and Ava English. 1966. *A Comprehensive Dictionary of Psychological and Psychoanalytical Terms.* New York: David McCoy.

Kunos, Ignácz. 1913. *Forty-Four Turkish Fairy Tales.* London: Harrap.

O'Sullivan, Sean. ed. 1966. *Folktales of Ireland.* Chicago: University of Chicago Press.

Progoff, Ira. 1953. *Jung's Psychology and Its Social Meaning.* New York: Grove.

Spanische Märchen. 1940. In *Die Märchen der Weltliteratur.* Jena: Diederichs Verlag.

von Franz, Marie-Louise. 1990. *Individuation in Fairy Tales.* Boston: Shambhala.

❀ K ❀

Deceptions

Contest Won by Deception

Motifs K0–K99

❀

Athletic contests, especially those promoting skills useful in hunting and warfare, figure prominently in popular and folk cultures from earliest history and around the world. Monuments to this interest still exist, not only in the remains of ancient sports arenas, but in tales and legends of such contests. And, if the folkloric record even remotely reflects actual events, victory did not always go to the best runners, jumpers, and hurlers. Countless folktales contradict the moralizing proverb, "Cheaters never win, and winners never cheat."

The most basic of all athletic contests is the footrace, which has given rise to the largest number of folktales about sports deception. These are told both as animal fables and as jests featuring human actors. In animal fables, the contestants are grossly mismatched, such as a tortoise or hedgehog against a hare. The human jests typically feature an ordinary person pitted against a troll, giant, ogre, devil, or other ostensibly superhuman adversary.

In the famous Aesopic fable "The Tortoise and the Hare," the victory goes not to a trickster, but rather to a steady plodder (AT 275A, Motif K11.3, both titled *Hare and tortoise race: sleeping hare*). However, most tales in this cycle depict winning by trickery, not by honest persistence. One ploy is simply to hitch a ride (K11.2, "Race won by deception: riding on the back. One contestant rides on the other's back"). The Swiss tale "The Fox and the Snail" (Sutermeister 1873, no. 20; AT 275, *The Race of the Fox and the Crayfish*) is typical. The snail accepts the fox's challenge to race from Schwäg Meadow to St. Gallen. (Authentic place names give the fable at least a degree of realism.) The snail hides himself in the fox's bushy tail. Arriving at the finish line, the fox turns around to see how far behind him the snail is, and the snail jumps down from the tail and calls out, "I'm already here!" Thus, concludes the storyteller, "the proud fox had to admit that he had lost." Essentially the same fable is told around the world, with only the animals changing to better represent the native creatures in the various settings. Thus, in Russia, the contestants are a fox and a lobster; in northeast Africa, a lion and a turtle; among the Kootenai Indians, an antelope and a frog; among the Seneca Indians, a beaver and a turtle; in Japan, a cat and a crab; and in Tibet, a tiger and a frog.

An even more widespread variation of this tale cycle involves look-alike helpers substituting for the weaker runner at various points along the course (K11.1, "Race won by deception: relative helpers"). When the participants are animals, the tale is categorized as type 275A*. The Grimm brothers' version, "The Hare and the Hedgehog" (KHM 187) is exemplary. A hedgehog, tired of a neighboring hare's incessant belittling remarks, challenges the hare to a footrace. The hedgehog prepares for the contest by having his wife hide at the finish line. The two runners take off, but to the hare's great surprise, when he arrives at the goal a hedgehog (whom he takes for his opponent) is already there. The hare insists that they race back, only to find a hedgehog taunting him at the other end of the course. Unwilling to admit defeat, the hare runs back and forth between the two markers until he drops dead from exhaustion. In these tales facelessness and anonymity, normally marks of the weak and the poor, become weapons, not merely for survival, but also for victory, power, and revenge against indignities suffered in the past. Understandably, type 275A* tales are especially well represented in the folklore of minority cultures; in the United States, they are found abundantly in African-American folklore.

Similar stories are also told with human actors, in which case they are categorized as type 1074 (with the same title as Motif K11.1, above). With human contestants, the opponent is normally cast as an ogre, who by all expectations should be the more powerful player. This ogre is often identified as the devil. The Swedish tale "Old Nick and the Girl" (Djurklou 1901, 87–95) is typical. A girl who loves to dance accepts a pair of leather shoes from Old Nick (a euphemism for the devil), under the agreement that after using them for one year she will surrender herself to him. When he comes to get her, she complains that the shoes were inferior, so she should not have to pay for them. To prove their inferiority, she challenges the devil to a race. He is to wear the leather shoes in question, and she a pair of shoes made from bark. They will run from Fryksend to Frykstad and back again. (Authentic place names again give the tale an aura of credibility.) What the devil does not know is that the girl has a twin sister, whom she positions at one of the goals. Although he runs "much faster than one can ride on the railway," the girl he thinks is his legitimate opponent is waiting at the turning point and the finish line. He runs the full course three times, but in the end has to acknowledge himself beaten, thus losing his claim on the heroine.

The devil of these tales is not the scheming, wickedly clever, and nearly omnipotent Satan of traditional Judaism and Christianity, but rather an unsophisticated, selfish bully with very limited powers of both body and mind. Official theology may offer dire warnings against dealing with the devil (as evidenced, for example, in such cautionary tales as the *Faust* chapbook of 1587), but in these tales simple country folk make pacts with the devil and win! Perhaps the dupes of these jests are devils in name only, with their actual genealogies leading back to the trolls, ogres, giants, and even gods of mythologies discredited—but not entirely supplanted—by Christianity.

One such heathen deity-turned-demon is Odin or Wodan, who—soon after the conversion of northern Europe to Christianity—reappeared in folk belief as the Wild Huntsman. Encounters between him and mortals, recorded in innumerable local and regional legends, often include an athletic challenge. "Wod, the Wild Huntsman" (Colshorn and Colshorn 1854, 192–193) from northern Germany presents such an episode. A drunken peasant, returning home through the woods late one night, is accosted by a tall man on a white horse who suddenly bolts down from the clouds and demands, "How strong are you? Let's have a contest." He then gives the peasant one end of a chain and challenges him to a tug-of-war. The peasant secretly wraps his end around a tree, and the demonic rider loses (K22, "Deceptive tug-of-war. Small animal challenges two large animals to a tug-of-war. Arranges it so that they unwittingly pull against each other [or one end of rope is tied to a tree]"). The peasant's prize is the blood (which he must carry in his boot) and hindquarter of a recently killed stag. Safely at home, the peasant discovers that the meat has turned into a bag of silver and that his boot is filled with gold.

An even better-known deceptive athletic contest from Germanic mythology is the three-stage meet to which Brunhild subjects all suitors. She herself is both the challenger and the promised prize for victory, but death awaits all who fail. Gunther accepts her challenge and appears to defeat her in all three events: shot put, long jump, and javelin throw. However, unknown to the strong heroine, Gunther was aided in all three tasks by the great champion Siegfried, made invisible with a magic cape. Brunhild honors her pledge and marries Gunther, but she refuses to submit to his intimate advances, so Siegfried and his magic cape must come to Gunther's aid once again, this time in a bedroom wrestling match. Brunhild is forced into submission, and, as the anonymous poet who recorded this adventure in the thirteenth century so delicately put it, "at love's coming her vast strength fled so that she was now no stronger than any woman" (*Der Nibelungen Not* 1947, ch. 7, 10).

Multiple athletic contests are also described in jests, typically with a rather slow-witted giant repeatedly allowing himself to be tricked by an ordinary, but clever and opportunistic human. "The Brave Little Tailor" (AT 1640, of the same title), as told by the Grimm brothers (KHM 20) and many others, knits together one such episode after another. The tailor squeezes whey from cheese, claiming it is water from a stone (AT 1060, *Squeezing the [Supposed] Stone*). He throws a stone (actually a bird) so high that it never returns to earth (AT 1062, *Throwing the Stone*). The giant bends down a tree for the hero to pick some fruit. He lets go, and the tailor flies into the air, but then claims to have jumped over the tree on purpose (AT 1051, *Bending a Tree*). The giant cannot match any of these feats. Another contest often featured in this cycle of multi-event tales is a climbing match between the ogre and the hero's "little daughter," or so the dupe is given to believe, but the daughter turns out to be a squirrel (AT 1073, *Climbing Contest*). Or the ogre agrees to wrestle with the hero's "old grandfather" and is matched against a bear, who mauls him terribly (AT 1071, *Wrestling Contest [with Old Grandfather]*).

Some contests between man and ogre involve practical workaday skills, in contrast to the athletic matches featured above. A very widespread example is the contest in mowing hay or grain (AT 1090, *Mowing Contest*), typically with an ordinary peasant pitted against the devil. The hero uses one of two strategies to win. In some tales, he and the devil mow side by side around a large field, with the hero taking the inside (and thus shorter) swath. Other tales describe an even more devious tactic. The peasant prepares the devil's patch beforehand by driving iron rods into the ground among the grain stalks. These dull the devil's scythe so severely that he cannot possibly keep pace with the peasant.

Another race involving practical skills is the sewing contest between man and devil (AT 1096, *The Tailor and the Ogre in a Sewing Contest*), and here too the devil is unbelievably stupid. The mortal tailor threads both needles: his with a modest length of thread and the devil's with a piece a hundred yards long. It takes the devil so long to pull each stitch tight that the hero wins handily.

With a few exceptions, the athletic and occupational contests discussed above prove embarrassing to the heroes' victims, but they are not fatal, thus allowing a storyteller to tie together any number of episodes in a single tale. But even the most prolific storytellers must somewhere draw their yarns to a close. A much-used episode to achieve this end is the eating contest, typically with a troll or a giant (AT 1088, *Eating Contest*). Before the match commences, the hero hides a bag beneath his shirt; then, instead of stuffing his stomach, he stuffs the bag. The troll is amazed at the hero's capacity. To show the troll how one could eat still more, the hero pretends to cut open his belly by slitting the bag. The troll follows his example and kills himself.

D.L. Ashliman

REFERENCES

Blecher, Lone Thygesen, and George Blecher. 1993. *Swedish Folktales and Legends.* New York: Pantheon Books.

Colshorn, Carl, and Theodor Colshorn. 1854. *Märchen und Sagen aus Hannover.* Hannover: Carl Ruempler.

Djurklou, Gabriel. 1901. *Fairy Tales from the Swedish.* Trans. H.L. Brækstad. Philadelphia: J.B. Lippincott.

Grimm, Jacob, and Wilhelm Grimm. 1980. *Kinder- und Hausmärchen* [KHM]. 3 vols. Ed. Heinz Rölleke. Stuttgart: Reclam. Based on the edition of 1857.

Der Nibelungen Not [*Nibelungenlied*]. 1947. Leipzig: Insel Verlag.

Sutermeister, Otto. 1873. *Kinder- und Hausmärchen aus der Schweiz.* Aarau: Sauerländer.

Thief Escapes Detection

Motif K400

❀

Crime and detection have been staples in folklore and fiction throughout history, and in many instances the storyteller's sense of justice sides with the lawbreaker, especially when the latter is from an oppressed class and the victim is from a privileged group. The resulting tales delight in exploits of thievery (see, for example, AT 1525–1530, 1535, 1539–1544, 1548, 1551, 1556) and also in the tricks played by the perpetrators to avoid detection.

Possibly the world's oldest detective story is the account of King Rhampsinitus's treasure chamber (*Rhampsinitus,* AT 950). Herodotus (1909) recorded this tale about 425 BCE in his untitled history of the Greco-Persian wars (book 2, ch. 21). As Herodotus retells the story (he himself heard it from temple priests in the Egyptian city of Memphis), two brothers gain access to the royal treasury by means of a secret passage. Seeing his wealth diminish but unable to discover how the thieves are getting inside, the king sets a trap. On their next incursion into the treasury, one of the brothers is caught in the trap. Unable to free himself and knowing that his own life is lost, he asks his brother to cut off his head and take it with him, for only by so doing can the thieves' identity be kept hidden (K407.1, "Thief has companion cut off his head so that he may escape detection"). The free brother honors this wish.

After finding the headless thief in the trap and surmising what has happened, the king hangs the corpse outside the palace, instructing the guards to take notice of anyone who is seen lamenting nearby. But this plan fails, for the surviving brother gets the guards drunk and steals the body. The king then sets up his own daughter as bait, sending her to a brothel with instructions to give herself to any man who will confess to her the most outrageous thing he has ever done. The thief accepts the challenge, but, sensing a trap, he prepares himself by putting the arm from a dead man in his own sleeve. He boasts of his crime to the princess, who seizes him by the arm to capture him, but he leaves her holding the corpse's arm and makes his escape. When the king learns of this latest audacious trick, he is so impressed with the thief's cleverness and verve that he not only pardons him for his past crimes but gives him the princess in marriage as well.

A similar episode is contained in "Ali Baba and the Forty Thieves" from the *Thousand and One Nights* (Burton 1887, 13:219–246). The same tale, often with surprising adherence to details of plot, has made its way into international folklore and has been collected in a broad swath of countries from Iceland to the Philippines.

Most folkloric accounts of unpunished theft are more mundane than the burglary of a king's treasury. Many folktales describe a servant (or wife) stealing food from a master's kitchen, a commonplace act that many storytellers and their listeners could identify with. *The Priest's Guest and the Eaten Chickens* (AT 1741; Motif K2137, same title) circulated widely in European jestbooks from the thirteenth century onward. It is also found in the *Thousand and One Nights* (Burton 1888, 15:255–258) and as a folktale from India westward through the Arabic world, virtually all of Europe, the Caribbean Islands, and North America.

A version collected by Richard Erdoes and Alfonso Ortiz (1984, 339–341) on the Rosebud Sioux Reservation in South Dakota retains all the earthy humor of its old-world antecedents. Spider Man invites Coyote for dinner at his lodge. After instructing his wife to prepare two buffalo livers, Spider Man goes out. Spider Man's wife is angry that she will get only leftovers from the feast, but she proceeds with her task. The frying livers smell so good that she cannot resist tasting a little piece, then another, finally eating all of both livers. Coyote arrives, and Spider Man's wife warns him that "we always have the balls of our guests for dinner." Coyote runs off in a frenzy, just as Spider Man returns. His wife explains the guest's unexpected behavior: "He didn't want to share the two livers with you, so he ran off with both of them." Spider Man pursues his fleeing friend while shouting, "Leave me at least one!" but to no avail.

Most recent European versions are more genteel in that the thieving cook sets up her alibi by telling the guest that his ears are at risk, not his manhood. As in this Native American version, most—but not all—renditions of this material side with the cook (sometimes a wife, sometimes a hired servant), showing obvious delight at her ingenuity in shifting onto a guest the blame for her theft. Some stories' titles demonstrate this positive bias, for example "Clever Gretel" (Grimm 1980, KHM 77) and "Clever Mollie" (Young and Young 1989, no. 71). Or the storytellers may turn essentially the same plot into a cautionary tale, warning about the wiles of women, as in the Indian version "The Good Husband and the Bad Wife" (Kingscote and Sástrî 1890, no. 11).

The theft of food by an underling, who then evades punishment with a clever deception, was also a favorite subject for ancient fabulists. Fables, of course, have traditionally been a relatively safe medium for the exposure of human foibles, especially those likely to be displayed in a culture strictly differentiated by class. Servants have been eating their masters' food surreptitiously, then making wild excuses if caught, as long as there have been servants and masters. Traditional fables, by hiding the human actors behind masks of animals, provide a layer of safety for the expression of sentiments that could not be stated openly in an authoritarian environment.

"The Stag without a Heart" (AT 52, *The Ass Without a Heart*, Motif K402.3), one of the *Aesopic Fables* of Babrius (Perry 1984, 117–123), provides an excellent example. A sick lion, unable to hunt, asks his companion, the fox, to lure a stag to the lion's den. This the fox does by convincing the gullible stag that he has been chosen as the dying lion's successor as king of beasts. The stag enters the den, and the overeager lion sets upon him, clawing his ears, but otherwise leaving him unwounded. The stag dashes into the woods.

The lion bullies the fox into trying the ruse a second time. The fox approaches the stag again, claiming that the stag misinterpreted the lion's eagerness. "He only wanted to give you advice for your upcoming kingship," clarifies the duplicitous fox. The stag accepts this explanation and returns to the den, where he is struck dead by the lion. The lion gorges himself on the fresh kill with the hungry fox looking on. When the opportunity presents itself the stealthy fox steals the heart and devours it. Not finding the prized piece, the lion confronts the fox. "He had no heart," answers the crafty thief. "What kind of heart could he or any creature have who came a second time into a lion's den?" The lion finds no argument against this logic, and the fox's theft remains undetected.

Modern versions of this fable usually substitute "brains" for "heart," reflecting current views that the brain, not the heart—as believed in antiquity—is the seat of intelligence.

Essentially the same fable is told in *The Panchatantra* (1964, 395–399), with a lion, a jackal, and a donkey as actors. The story also works well with human actors, as shown by Flavius Avianus, a fourth-century Latin writer, in his "The Pig without a Heart" (Perry 1984, 533–534). Here a pig tramples his master's grain field and is punished by having an ear cut off. Learning nothing from the pain, the pig enters the field again, and the landowner cuts off another ear. Unrepentant, the beast tramples the crop a third time, so it is slaughtered and served at a banquet. The cook preparing the feast eats the pig's heart. The master looks for the missing delicacy and accosts the cook, who claims, "The pig had no heart. It showed this when it kept returning to the grain field, only to lose parts of its body." The master accepts this explanation, and the cook goes unpunished.

In another account of stolen food, "The Fowl with One Leg" (AT 785A, *The Goose with One Leg;* Motif K402.1, "The goose without a leg"), a thieving cook has an even more audacious explanation for the missing piece. Told in Boccaccio's *The Decameron* (day 6, tale 4), the story also appears as a folktale throughout Europe as well as in the Western Hemisphere.

A South Carolina story contains all the essential elements of its European forebears (Levine 1977, 128). A slave eats one leg of the chicken he is preparing for his master. When confronted, the slave explains, "It must be a one-legged chicken, sir. I have seen plenty of one-legged chickens." Later, master and slave come across some chickens standing on one leg and huddled together to keep warm. The slave draws his master's attention to these one-legged birds. The master responds by shouting "Sish!" and the chickens put down their raised legs and flutter off. "They all have two legs," admonishes the master, to which the slave replies, "Sir, if you had said 'Sish!' to the chicken on the table, it would have stuck out its other leg, too." Here the thief fails to escape detection, but upon being exposed, he saves himself from punishment with a clever response.

Cleverness and stupidity are often featured in the same tale, each quality being delineated through contrast with the other. One such tale, an exemplary account of a thief escaping detection by trickery, is "The Simpleton and the Sharper" from the *Thousand and One Nights* (Burton 1885, 5:3–85; AT 1529, *Thief Claims to Have Been Transformed into a Horse;* Motif K403, "Thief claims to have been transformed into an ass"). A man steals a donkey from a simpleton, gives it to an accomplice, then places himself in the missing animal's halter. When the victim sees a human in his donkey's halter, the trickster claims that Allah had transformed him into a donkey for drunkenness and for abusing his mother, but that miraculously the enchantment just now has been lifted. The dupe congratulates the trickster for the reversal of his punishment and lets him walk away. The jest has a second punch line: A short time later, the simpleton sees his former donkey for sale at a market, and, thinking that the man has again been placed under his former curse, he approaches the beast and says, "For shame, getting drunk and beating your mother again! I'll not buy you a second time."

Stories abound in folklore and in popular culture about confidence games based on the victims' own greed and dishonesty. Most often these trickster tales focus on the theft itself, but in some instances the emphasis is on the evasion of punishment.

One example, often attributed to the Turkish trickster Nasreddin Hodja (also written Nasrettin Hoca, as well as other spellings), is the tale of "The Cauldron That Died" (Nesin 1988, 59; AT 1592B, *The Pot Has a Child and Dies;* Motif J1531.3, same title). Nasreddin borrows a large cauldron from his neighbor and returns it with a small pot inside. "Your cauldron had a baby," says the trickster. The neighbor, happy to take advantage of Nasreddin's simplemindedness, accepts the explanation and both pots. Later, Nasreddin borrows the cauldron again, but never returns it. When questioned by the owner, Nasreddin claims that the cauldron died. "How could a cauldron die?" challenges the neighbor. Nasreddin responds, "You had no doubt that it gave birth, yet you doubt if it died!" And thus the trickster deprives his victim of any recourse.

D.L. Ashliman

REFERENCES

Burton, Richard F., trans. [1885–1888]. *The Book of the Thousand Nights and a Night: A Plain and Literal Translation of The Arabian Nights Entertainments.* 10 vols. plus 6 supplemental vols. [n.p.]: Privately printed by the Burton Club.

Erdoes, Richard, and Alfonso Ortiz. 1984. *American Indian Myths and Legends.* New York: Pantheon.

Grimm, Jacob, and Wilhelm Grimm. 1980. *Kinder- und Hausmärchen* [KHM]. 3 vols. Edited by Heinz Rölleke. Stuttgart: Reclam. Based on the edition of 1857.

Herodotus. [1909]. *The History of Herodotus.* Trans. George Rawlinson. 4 vols. New York: Tandy-Thomas.

Kingscote, Mrs. Howard [Georgiana Wolff], and Natêsá Sástrî. 1890. *Tales of the Sun; or, Folklore of Southern India.* London: W.H. Allen.

Levine, Lawrence W. 1977. *Black Culture and Black Consciousness: Afro-American Folk Thought from Slavery to Freedom.* Oxford: Oxford University Press.

Nesin, Aziz. 1988. *The Tales of Nasrettin Hoca.* Trans. Talat Halman. Istanbul: Dost Yayinlari.

The Panchatantra. 1964. Trans. Arthur W. Ryder. Chicago: University of Chicago Press.

Perry, Ben Edwin. 1984. *Babrius and Phaedrus: Newly Edited and Translated into English, Together with an Historical Introduction and a Comprehensive Survey of Greek and Latin Fables in the Aesopic Tradition.* Cambridge: Harvard University Press.

Young, Richard, and Judy Dockrey Young. 1989. *Ozark Tall Tales: Collected from the Oral Tradition.* Little Rock: August House.

Seduction or Deceptive Marriage

Motifs K1300–K1399

❀

In Stith Thompson's taxonomy, seduction or deceptive marriage is a subcategory of the larger theme of Deception (ch. K), and he remarks that "there has always been a greater interest in deceptions connected with sex conduct than any other" (Thompson 1977, 202). Motifs in the seduction category include the seduction of mortals by gods (K1301), seduction through disguise or substitution (K1310), tricking the object of the seduction into entering a room (K1330), entering a girl's (or man's) room (or bed) by trick (K1340), and persuading (or wooing) a woman by trick (K1350).

Current usage would categorize many of the tales that appear under the heading "seduction" as rape. William Little observes that "the semantic and social distinctions that separate seduction and rape were less significant in the Middle Ages than they are in the twentieth century" (Little 1988, 1162). In literature and popular culture, seduction also has meanings that are not explicitly sexual. Little states, "[t]hese uses refer to leading a person astray in conduct or belief, temptation, enticement, and beguiling in order to do something immoral," but among Little's first examples is an instance of literary seduction calculated not to produce immorality but to prevent it. In *Alf Layla wa-Layla (The Arabian Nights)* (eighth to seventeenth centuries), Scheherazade must convince her husband, the sultan, to discontinue his custom of serial murder and replacement of each new wife. While Little asserts that in literature seduction generally has involved "inducing a woman to surrender her chastity," and he numbers among its subthemes "abduction, rape, libertinism, lechery, the rake, and the philanderer" (Little 1988, 1159), literary seduction is hardly limited to men, and the case of Scheherazade suggests an even more general sense of the term—the employment of trickery and temptation to cause people to commit whatever acts they would normally resist, including acts of love and mercy.

MYTHOLOGY

Some form of seduction is a motive factor in many folktales and literary works, including the foundational narratives of a number of cultures, such as Satan's seduction of Eve (and by extension Adam) in the Old Testament. Wendy O'Flaherty states that one of the explanatory narratives for the linga cults of India holds that in the guise of a beggar Shiva seduced the wives of religious men who had not acknowledged his divinity. As punishment, they castrated the "beggar," but when his linga fell to the ground darkness fell over the earth, and they pleaded with Shiva to restore things as they were. His condition was that they worship the linga for all eternity (O'Flaherty 1992, 27).

At the top of the Greek pantheon, the case of Zeus offers multiple examples of seduction of mortal women by gods (K1301) and seduction by disguise or substitution (K1310), along with the related motifs of god as shapeshifter (A120.1), gods in relation to mortals (A180), and philandering god (A188.1). In the encounters with Semele, a Theban princess who later gives birth to Dionysus, and with Niobe, mother of Argos, Zeus appears in his own guise. Appearing to Alcmene in the form of her husband (K1311, "Seduction by masking as woman's husband"), Zeus fathers Heracles. In the form of a shower of gold, Zeus comes to Danäe, princess of Argos and mother of Perseus. As a white bull, he seduces Europa, mother of Minos, Rhadamanthys, and Sarpedon. To Leda, queen of Sparta, Zeus appears as a swan in a union that produces two eggs, which hatch to reveal Polydeuces (Pollux) and Helen of Troy (in other variants, two sets of twins are born: Castor and Polydeuces and Clytemnestra and Helen of Troy) (Elkhadem 1981, 193–194; Leadbetter 1995–2003).

The motifs of shape-shifting gods and seduction through disguise combine to different effect in some cautionary Latin American variants of the *llorona* (weeping woman) tale. A young man walking home after a night of carousing meets a beautiful woman who invites him to embrace her. When the man reaches for her, she reverts to her real appearance and her face becomes hideous, or she lures him into a lake, where she pulls him under the water (Pérez 1951, 24; Barakat 1969, 271). Another *llorona* variant warns poor women against seduction by upper-class men who will soon abandon them. Here the woman is mourning the loss of her children, whom she killed in despair when her wealthy suitor left her for another woman, or out of jealousy when he remained interested in the children but not in her (Kirtley 1960, 156–157;

Casias 1998). Cautionary tales regarding seduction also take the form of urban legends, in which those who succumb risk waking up to discover consequences that include intentional infection with HIV (the lover has left, and "Welcome to the world of AIDS" is scrawled in lipstick on the bathroom mirror) or loss of bodily organs (the seducee wakes up groggy and with a surgical scar; doctors later confirm that a kidney has been stolen for sale) (Mikkelson and Mikkelson 2000, 2002). Here the seduction itself is only an instrument in some other nefarious plot.

Somchintana Thongthew-Ratarasarn discusses a Thai folk practice of magical seduction. In a 1979 article, she explains that

> [l]ove magic is a current belief-in-practice in central Thailand. It is a complex system of magic that is designed to induce its victims to fall helplessly in love with a designated suitor. Love magic is used within a general Buddhist context, but the magic itself consists primarily of elements derived from animistic folk beliefs and the Brahmanistic tradition. (Thongthew-Ratarasarn 1979, 3–4)

She describes a variety of material objects that play a role in seduction, including sacred diagrams, sacralized cigarette smoke, and male and female dolls placed in a small bottle of perfume and carried in the man's pocket or else buried in the backyard of the desired woman.

> A male can cause a female to fall in love with him by sacralizing a cigarette, smoking it in her presence, and puffing the smoke so that it touches her. The smoke is more sacred and effective if it is from the traditional Thai cigarettes made of dried banana leaves or dried nipa palm leaves (Nipa fruticans), stuffed with prepared tobacco. (Thongthew-Ratarasarn 1979, 12)

In literature, the Don Juan figure has been a long-lived and remarkably versatile archetype of seduction, beginning with Tirso de Molina's *Burlador de Sevilla* (1620) and continuing with such works as Molière's *Don Juan* (1665), Byron's *Don Juan* (1819–1824), Grabbe's *Don Juan und Faust* (1829), Pushkin's *Kamennyi gost'* (1830), Dumas's *Don Juan de Maraña* (1836), Zorilla's *Don Juan Tenorio* (1844), Cesbron's *Don Juan en automne* (1975), and Leven's *Don Juan de Marco* (1995) (Little 1988, 1165, 1167). In the earliest literary version of Don Juan, *El Burlador de Sevilla,* the consummate unregenerate sinner constitutes an extreme case even among the sharply drawn characters that were customary in seventeenth-century Spanish drama. As Charles Presberg confirms, an "eschatological drama in which a main character is consigned to hell" is "an extreme rarity in the literature of the period" (Presberg 1995, 223). Tirso's Don Juan succeeds with women through a combination of deception, mistaken identity, aristocratic social standing, and promises of marriage, but the libertine behavior that becomes the character's hallmark in the popular culture is in this play somewhat overshadowed. This first Don Juan's fatal error lies not in being a *burlador* of women, but in counting on the time to repent for it later, and thus presuming against the theological virtue of hope, one of the "unpardonable sins against the Holy Spirit" (Presberg 1995, 223). To various reminders of the inevitability of death and judgment, Don Juan inveterately replies that there is plenty of time, thus perverting the virtue of hope of salvation to the sin of presuming it, and leading to the chilling scene of a graveyard banquet at which Don Juan mockingly takes the cold hand of a statue of a man he has murdered, the father of one of the women he has betrayed, and is dragged down into the pits of hell. This dramatic moment is, however, only the penultimate word, as at the end of the play the temporal order that Don Juan temporarily disrupted is reestablished with a series of suitable marriages.

In Zorilla's *Don Juan Tenorio* (1844), Don Juan is saved from damnation at the last moment, redeemed by the love of the virtuous Doña Inés. Zorilla's Don Juan actually falls in love with one of his conquests and this love leads him to virtue, although not until after that woman has died. In this play, it is Doña Inés who makes the fateful (and probably heretical) wager, linking her eternal soul with his and thus convincing him to believe in the possibility of mercy. At the last moment, it is she who takes Don Juan's hand in the graveyard, snatching him away from the pit. As Joaquín Casalduero points out, the theological core of Tirso's play has been reduced to little more than a plot device serving to intensify the romanticism of Zorilla's version (Casalduero 1975, 146–147).

Although Byron's *Don Juan* (1818–1825) remained unfinished, there is evidence that Byron had foreseen for his character his own version of Hell— perhaps in the form of an unhappy marriage (Marchand 1973, 8:77). Byron's ironic treatment strips the supernatural dimensions from the Don Juan myth, leaving a preternaturally attractive boy with unusual erotic opportunities, among them his twenty-three-year-old religion tutor, Doña Julia; Haidée, his true love, who revives him after he is shipwrecked on her isolated island; Gulbayez, the sultan's wife, who purchases Juan for her daytime pleasure, dressing him in drag and hiding him at night in the sultan's 1,500-woman harem; and a predatory Catherine the Great. Here it is always the women who have the initial designs on Juan, as well as the social power to realize them. This Don Juan is more obliging than seducing.

The rehabilitative tendency reaches its apotheosis with Jeremy Leven's late twentieth-century cinematic version of *Don Juan de Marco* (1995), a Don Juan who no longer has anything for which to atone. Quite the contrary,

The folk legend of Don Juan, the "Seducer of Seville," was updated in the film _Don Juan de Marco_ (1995). In it, Don Juan says, "I never take advantage of a woman. I give women pleasure, if they desire it." From Guillaume de Lorris and Jean de Meung, _Le roman de la rose_ (fifteenth century).

he himself becomes the instrument of salvation for others. When the woman in the first scene of the film asks "You seduce women?" Don Juan replies "No, I never take advantage of a woman. I give women pleasure, if they desire it." At the outset of the film, this contemporary Don Juan is on his way to commit suicide because of despair at the loss of the woman with whom he had hoped to spend "all eternity." The police arrive and send for a psychiatrist, who takes him to the hospital. As the story unfolds, developments in the institution confirm Don Juan's mystical attraction—not only are all of the women obviously smitten, but one of the male attendants learns to dance and moves to Spain. Don Juan has a similar effect on the marriage of the psychiatrist and his wife, as doctor and patient trade therapeutic roles. Not only is Don Juan de Marco devoid of any of the Satanic imagery that characterized Tirso's and Zorilla's plays, but an abundance of conventional religious signals points in the other direction. He draws the jaded psychiatrist into a virtual catechism of rhetorical questions: "What is sacred? Of what is the spirit made? What is worth living for? What is worth dying for?" Whereas earlier Don Juans had embodied the sins of presumption and decadence, this one personifies the virtues of sensual and spiritual loving. Like Scheherazade, this contemporary Don Juan employs seduction, much of it verbal, to persuade his objects to reject a rigid, destructive status quo.

Kimberly A. Nance

See also: Entrance into Girl's (Man's) Room (Bed) by Trick.

REFERENCES

Barakat, Robert A. 1969. "Wailing Women of Folklore." *Journal of American Folklore* 82, no. 325 (July–September): 270–272.

Casalduero, Joaquín. 1975. *Contribución al estudio del tema de Don Juan en el teatro español.* Madrid: Porrúa.

Casias, Stephanie. 1998. "La Llorona: A Chicano Folktale." February 23, http://web.nmsu.edu/~tomlynch/swlit.lallorona.html.

Don Juan de Marco. 1995. Screenplay by Jeremy Leven. Dir. Jeremy Leven. Prod. Francis Ford Coppola. Perf. Johnny Depp, Marlon Brando, Faye Dunaway. New Line Cinema.

Doniger, Wendy. 2000. *The Bedtrick: Tales of Sex and Masquerade.* Chicago: University of Chicago Press.

Elkhadem, Saad. 1981. *The York Companion to Themes and Motifs of World Literature: Mythology, History, and Folklore.* Fredericton, NB: York Press.

Kirtley, Bacil F. 1960. "'La Llorona' and Related Themes." *Western Folklore* 19: 156–157.

Leadbetter, Ron. 1995–2003. "Zeus." In *Encyclopedia Mythica,* ed. M.F. Lindemans, www.pantheon.org/articles/z/zeus.html.

Little, Charles. 1988. "Seduction." In *Dictionary of Literary Themes and Motifs,* ed. Jean-Charles Seigneuret, 1159–1171. New York: Greenwood Press.

Marchand, Leslie, ed. 1973–1981. *Byron's Letters and Journals.* Vol. 8. Cambridge, MA: Belknap Press of Harvard University Press.

Mikkelson, Barbara, and David P. Mikkelson. 2000. "AIDS Mary." In Urban Legends Reference Pages, September 27, www.snopes.com/horrors/madmen/aidsmary.htm.

———. 2002. "You've Got to be Kidneying." In Urban Legends Reference Pages, April 28, www.snopes.com/horrors/robbery/kidney.htm.

O'Flaherty, Wendy. 1992. "Hinduism." In *Mythology,* ed. Richard Cavendish, 14–34. London: Little, Brown.

Pérez, Soledad. 1951. "Mexican Folklore from Austin, Texas." In *The Healer of Los Olmos and Other Mexican Lore,* ed. Wilson M. Hudson. Publications of the Texas Folklore Society, 24. Dallas: Southern Methodist University Press.

Presberg, Charles. 1995. "El condenado por presumido: The Rhetoric of Death and Damnation in *El burlador de Sevilla y Convidado de piedra.*" *Bulletin of the Comediantes* 42, no. 2 (Winter 1995): 223–243.

Thompson, Stith. 1977 [1946]. *The Folktale.* Berkeley: University of California Press. Orig. ed. New York: Holt, Rinehart and Winston.

Thongthew-Ratarasarn, Somchintana. 1979. *The Socio-Cultural Setting of Love Magic in Central Thailand.* Madison: Center for Southeast Asian Studies, University of Wisconsin–Madison.

Entrance into Girl's (Man's) Room (Bed) by Trick

Motif K1340

❊

Trickster tales often display substantial ingenuity, describing confidence games that involve multiple complex steps. However, the tricks designed to gain entry into the bed or bedroom of a member of the opposite sex are usually quite straightforward, suggesting perhaps that the "victims" in such pranks are, in truth, willing participants or that, as Wendy Doniger remarks in *The Bedtrick,* "the victims lie to themselves as much as the tricksters lie to them. . . . The lying of the trickster is the obviously false element in a bedtrick, but the lying of the victim, though less obvious, is often what sustains the mythology" (2000, 8). The motif of the bedtrick is ancient and widespread, occurring in the Old Testament, the *Rig Veda* and ancient Indian storytelling tradition, Greek myth, the *Arabian Nights,* several of Shakespeare's plays, various operas, and even movies (Doniger provides an extensive filmography of bedtricks and related plots [567–576]).

In an appendix, Doniger lists motifs from the *Motif-Index* corresponding to plots of the bedtrick, noting that these motifs encompass "four possible permutations of gender and seeking/avoiding: women, avoiding or seeking; and men, avoiding or seeking" (Doniger 2000, 493).

MYTHOLOGY AND LEGEND

In myth and legend there are many stories of gods and heroes shape-shifting in order to bed women they desire. Greek mythology abounds in stories of

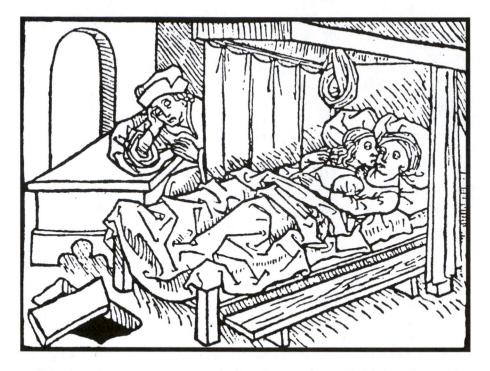

The motif of the bedtrick (K1340) is ancient and widespread, occurring in the Old Testament, the *Rig Veda* and ancient Indian storytelling tradition, Greek myth, the *Thousand and One Nights,* several of Shakespeare's plays, various operas, and modern films. From Brunns Aretinus, *De duobus amantibus* (1482).

Zeus seducing mortal women. In some cases, he accomplishes this by disguise or substitution (K1310, "Seduction by disguise or substitution"), sometimes by shape-shifting (A120.1, "God as shapeshifter"). He appears to Alcmene in the form of her husband (K1311, "Seduction by masking as woman's husband"; D658.2, "Transformation to husband's (lover's) form to seduce woman"), and fathers Herakles. To Danäe he appears as a shower of gold and fathers Perseus. He seduces Europea as a white bull and begets Minos, Rhadamanthys, and Sarpedon. To Leda Zeus appears as a swan in a union that produces either Polydeuces (Pollux) and Helen of Troy or, in other variants, two sets of twins: Castor and Polydeuces and Clytemnestra and Helen of Troy (Elkhadem 1981, 193–194)

Geoffrey of Monmouth relates how the wizard Merlin altered Uther's appearance to resemble the husband of Igraine, enabling Uther to lie with her (D658.2, "Transformation to husband's (lover's) form to seduce woman"; K1311, "Seduction by masking as woman's husband"). The future king Arthur is conceived that night.

FOLKTALES

There is a widespread group of tales called generically *The Princess Always Answers 'No'* (AT 853A; K1331). Although the setup varies, each story features a young woman instructed by her protective father (or in some instances her husband) always to say no to any proposal made to her by another man. Sensing the situation, the trickster asks a series of questions designed to elicit a desired response with a negative answer, such as: "Do you mind if I visit you tonight?" "Do you want me to stay outside in the cold?" "Do you want to sleep by yourself?" "Will you be angry if I . . . ?" The princess always answers no. The trickster gets what he wants, and—one suspects—his bed partner gets what she wants as well. Two examples of Type 853A tales, from opposite sides of Europe, are "No!" from Russia (Afanasyev 1966, 42–43) and "The Shepherd at Court" from Italy (Calvino 1980, no. 60).

Sometimes, as noted above, the sex-seeking trickster is a woman. A wickedly ironic tale featuring such a heroine is "A Wife Takes the Place of Her Husband's Lover" (AT 1379; K1843), popular in Renaissance jest-books. The basic plot is simple, but ingenious. A man repeatedly proposes an intimate rendezvous with a maid, who reports this indiscretion to his wife. Acting on the wife's orders, the maid accepts his proposal, but at the appointed time the wife herself goes to the dark meeting place, and thus the husband unwittingly has an affair with his own wife. Some versions include a second stinger. After satisfying himself, the husband decides to share the unseen woman with a friend, whom he sends into the dark room and whom the wife receives without objection.

Renaissance European examples of this tale include "An English Dyer Who Had an Adventure with His Wife" (Poggio Bracciolini 1928, no. 116) and "A Man, Having Lain with His Wife, Believing That He Was in Bed with His Servant, Sends His Friend to Do the Same Thing" (Margaret of Navarre 1922, 1:8). An American Indian tale with the same plot is "Iktome Sleeps with His Wife by Mistake" (Erdoes and Ortiz 1984, 372–374). One can only speculate how this European jest made its way into the repertory of a Sioux storyteller.

The Type 853A and K1379 tales discussed above are, as a rule, playful and lighthearted. No one gets hurt. Private space is violated, but—if one accepts the fiction of the stories—the ensuing encounters are mutually pleasurable.

The seductions featured in Type 900 tales are quite different, intended not for the sexual satisfaction of either party, but rather as a means of humiliating and subjugating a once-independent female. These tales, which belong to the taming of a shrewish wife cycle, have been reported throughout the world. An early literary version is "Pride Punished," from Basile's *Pentamerone* (1979, 1:10).

Type 900 tales open with a spirited (most storytellers use a negative adjective such as *haughty*) princess rejecting a suitor, who then disguises himself and returns to punish the offending woman. In most versions (although not in the Grimms' tale that gives the type its name, *King Thrushbeard*) the hero's revenge and subjugation process is set into motion with a seduction, enabling him—in the words of the proverb—to keep her barefoot and pregnant. This seduction usually begins when he tricks his way into her bedroom (K1341.1, "Entrance to woman's room in golden ram. Princess's curiosity aroused and the golden ram carried into the room. The youth is concealed inside").

The Norwegian folktale "Haaken Grizzlebeard" (Asbjørnsen and Moe 1983, 2:273–281) is typical. Disguised as a beggar, the rejected suitor offers the princess a golden spinning wheel in exchange for allowing him to sleep outside her bedroom door. She agrees, but during the night, claiming to be cold, he begins to chatter so loudly that she fears he will awaken her father, so to keep him quiet she lets him enter her room and sleep on the floor (K1361.3, "Seduction by begging into woman's room to get warm"). Another day he offers her another trinket, and he is allowed to sleep on her floor. On a third day he offers yet another item, in exchange for being permitted to sleep next to the princess's bed. Now trusting him, she agrees, but before the night is over, again to keep himself from freezing, he ends up in her bed. No further details are given, but some time later the princess has a baby, so she has no choice but to surrender herself to the man who made her pregnant.

An even simpler ruse is used in the Austrian folktale "The French Princess and the Turkish Emperor" (Reiffenstein 1979, no. 44). The rejected suitor disguises himself as a woman and thus gains access to the proud princess's bedroom, where he takes advantage of her innocence (K1321.1, "Man disguised as woman admitted to women's quarters: seduction"): "She did not know what he was doing with her, for she was still too naive, too young." Other tales describe additional tricks, none terribly ingenious. These episodes imply that no man should find it unduly difficult to gain access to a woman's bedroom, even if she is an independent-minded princess.

Many Type 900 tales also have a prejudicial national or ethnic subtext. These are not stories of magic. The narrators give no signals that they are set in a fantasy world, a realm of a different time and place than ours. In fact, in many instances the locale and sometimes even the principal characters are precisely identified. For example, in a Low German variant ("Fritz and the Princess," Wisser 1982, no. 44), the scorned suitor is King Fritz (Frederick the Great) of Prussia, who first seduces and then reforms a haughty Austrian princess. Similar tales from Germany ("The Three Balls," Kuhn 1859, 2:251–255), France ("The King of France," Karlinger and Gréciano 1974, no. 50), and Denmark ("Greyfoot," Bay 1899, 35) tell how German, French, and Danish kings seduce and tame sharp-tongued princesses from England. National pride and aggressive masculine values combine in these stories to identify the domineering king with the storyteller's own homeland, whereas the shrewish princess is said to come from a neighboring and competing country.

Another widespread family of tales depicting a mean-spirited man tricking his way into a woman's bedroom is Type 882, *The Wager on the Wife's Chastity.* Immortalized by its incorporation into Boccaccio's *Decameron* (2:9) and Shakespeare's *Cymbeline,* this tale also has made its way around the world in popular literature and oral folklore. In summary, it describes a wager between a trusting husband (call him Posthumus) and a rascally acquaintance (Iachimo), who bets that he can seduce Posthumus's wife Imogen. (The names are from Shakespeare.) Knowing that Imogen will never accept his advances, Iachimo has himself smuggled into her bedroom, hidden inside a chest, which Imogen naively has agreed to accept for temporary safekeeping. After Imogen is asleep, Iago slips out of the chest, observes details of the bedroom, takes note of a mole beneath the sleeping woman's breast, steals a ring from her night table, then returns to his hiding place. Soon afterward he claims victory by presenting evidence of an illicit rendezvous to Posthumus. The distraught husband orders his supposedly unfaithful wife killed, but she escapes. With time the truth comes out, husband and wife are reunited, and the trickster is exposed and punished.

A final tale type that often features a crafty entry into another person's bedroom is *The Search for the Lost Husband* (AT 425), a family of folktales with worldwide distribution. The Norwegian "East of the Sun and West of the Moon" (Asbjørnsen and Moe 1982, 1:230–242) is exemplary.

In the first part of this complicated story, the heroine marries a man who is a bear by day but a human by night. One night (acting on her mother's bad advice), she lights a candle to sneak a look at her sleeping husband. Drops of melted tallow awaken him (C916.1), and he angrily tells her that because of a spell cast on him by his stepmother, he will now have to go to a castle east of the sun and west of the moon and marry a woman with a nose three ells long. He then disappears.

Undaunted, his true wife sets out to find him. After much travail she arrives at his castle, but he does not recognize her. He is about to marry the long-nosed princess, who—as events make clear—already has access to and control over his bedroom. The heroine bribes the unworthy bride-to-be with three items that she has obtained on her way—a golden apple, a golden carding comb, and a golden spinning wheel, thus gaining access to her husband's bedroom for three successive nights (D2006.1.4, "Forgotten fiancée buys place in husband's bed and reawakens his memory"). There she hopes to bring him to a recognition of his former marriage, but the false bride gives him a sleeping potion each evening, so for the first two nights he sleeps through the heroine's entreaties. The third night, sensing that something is amiss, the prince only pretends to consume the drink offered to him by his fiancée, hears the heroine's pleas, comes to accept her as his only legitimate wife, and the two of them live happily ever after.

D.L. Ashliman

REFERENCES

Afanasyev, Aleksandr. 1966. *Russian Secret Tales: Bawdy Folktales of Old Russia.* New York: Brussel and Brussel.

Asbjørnsen, Peter Christen, and Jørgen Engebretsen Moe. 1982–1983 [1852]. *Norske Folkeeventyr.* 2 vols. Oslo: Den Norske Bokklubben.

Basile, Giambattista. 1979. *The Pentamerone.* 2 vols. Ed. N.M. Penzer. Westport, CT: Greenwood Press. First published 1634–1636 as *Lo Cunto de li Cunti.*

Bay, Jens Christian. 1899. *Danish Folk Tales.* New York: Harper and Brothers.

Calvino, Italo. 1980. *Italian Folktales.* New York: Pantheon Books.

Doniger, Wendy. 2000. *The Bedtrick.* Chicago: University of Chicago Press.

Elkhadem, Saad. 1981. *The York Companion to Themes and Motifs of World Literature: Mythology, History, and Folklore.* Fredericton, NB: York Press.

Erdoes, Richard, and Alfonso Ortiz. 1984. *American Indian Myths and Legends.* New York: Pantheon Books.

Karlinger, Felix, and Gertrude Gréciano. 1974. *Provenzalische Märchen.* Düsseldorf: Eugen Diederichs Verlag.

Kuhn, Adalbert. 1859. *Sagen, Gebräuche und Märchen aus Westfalen.* 2 vols. Leipzig: F.A. Brockhaus.

Margaret of Navarre. 1922. *The Heptameron of the Tales of Margaret, Queen of Navarre.* Trans. George Saintsbury. London: Privately printed for the Navarre Society Limited. First published 1558 under the title *Histoire des amans fortunez.* Published 1559 as *Heptaméréron des nouvelles.*

Poggio Bracciolini, Gian Francesco. 1928. *The Facetiae of Poggio and Other Medieval Story-Tellers.* Trans. Edward Storer. London: George Routledge and Sons.

Reiffenstein, Ingo. 1979. *Österreichische Märchen.* Düsseldorf: Eugen Diederichs Verlag.

Wisser, Wilhelm. 1982. *Plattdeutsche Märchen.* Düsseldorf: Eugen Diederichs Verlag.

❀ L ❀

Reversal of Fortune

Pride Brought Low

Motifs L400–L499

❀

In the *Motif-Index,* Pride Brought Low is a subdivision of Chapter L, Reversal of Fortune. The most direct and accessible phrase identifying this motif is "pride humbled," a condition often colloquially described in the United States as being "cut down to size" or "falling (or being knocked) off a high horse." The impressive number of idioms and images devoted to this theme over the past millennia may be attributed to the fact that numerous people and cultures are repelled by displays of vanity and gratified by any comeuppance visited upon the proud.

Sometimes, however, pride is considered a virtue, especially when it is pride in something or someone else, pride in a country or in a friend, for example. Vaunting one's own powers and feats was also considered an effective psychological weapon against adversaries in such cultures as the Anglo-Saxon, in which the gab or boast was part of a verbal display intended to intimidate the hero's opponent. Beowulf's account of the numerous monsters he slew during the days of his swimming match with Breca silences his detractor, Unferth. But even in those archaic societies that valued the efficacy of such verbal weapons, earnest (as opposed to pretended) pride earned a braggart the contempt of his fellows and punishment by either the gods or the force of fate. The same apparent paradox holds true today. Cheering squads at sporting events are expected to chant words that elevate their team and belittle their opponents. The victorious side is, nevertheless, expected to behave modestly and graciously at the end of the game.

The phrase "pride brought low" ignores the positive aspects of pride and hews to the more dominant tradition—that, since it is disproportionate vanity, it must be leveled. Pride is usually condemned by both Eastern and Western religions, principally because it mocks the ultimate superiority of a deity or deities and ignores the relative insignificance of their mortal worshipers. The major Western traditions, whether Christian, Islamic, or Jewish, have often called pride "the root of all evil." In one paradigmatic medieval illustration, there are "two trees, the tree of vices springing from the root of pride and the tree of the virtues, springing from the root of humility" (Bloomfield 1967, 84). Judeo-Christian ethics usually identify pride as the first fault of humanity, and the tree of pride is called the "vetus (old) Adam" (Bloomfield 1967, 84). Although some early Fathers of the Church saw other sins, such as concupiscence and avarice, as the cause of man's first alienation from God, most Christian theologians maintained, as they still do today, that pride impelled Adam and Eve to disobey God's commandment. Their punishments for falling from God's grace included expulsion from the Garden of Eden and, ultimately, mortality, but common to all the punishments was a lowering of the malefactors' condition.

In the later schemes of sins and virtues, pride's presumption is punished by humiliation. In fact, humility is the virtue that, in most systems of sin and virtue, remedies pride. Considering the scope and power of these beliefs, it is not surprising to find that the folk motif of the child overcoming the giant is found in innumerable cultures and societies. David's defeat of Goliath is the most famous biblical example.

The image evoked by the expression "pride brought low" depends upon a standard verbal and visual iconography of pride. Pride is always depicted as large in length and breadth. Words characterizing pride include "big," "too big," "overblown," "inflated," "puffed-up," "swollen," "high," "uppity." Expressions containing images of pride almost always depend upon forms of these words, so that a proud man may be "too big for his britches" or "full of himself," and a proud person was conventionally shown riding a "high horse."

The genealogy of pride is easily traceable in Western texts. Hubris, the name of a mysterious nymph in Greek myth (Payne 1951, 5–8) known as "Wantonness," mother of Pan (Rose 1959, 168), came to signify, first, excess or imbalance. Later, it "grew into a religious conception too: it now meant, the aggrandizement of man against God" (Jaeger 1945, I:168). First displayed by the titans, especially Prometheus, hubris was the tragic flaw that most often caused the downfall of the hero in Greek tragedy. It was the human presumption that a mortal either knew better than the gods or could avoid the obligations due to or the fate determined by the gods. Euripides wrote, "He who transgresses through overweening pride /or brings upon himself treasures unjustly acquired, / For him there comes a time of retribution. / All is taken from him" (*Eumenides* 553 in Payne 1951, 22). The fall of pride is graphically portrayed in the myth of Icarus, who flew so close to the sun that his wax wings melted and he fell to earth.

Among the images and sayings concerning the humbling of pride, the most familiar to Western readers are probably those in the Old and New Testaments. Isaiah 40:4, the major text of Handel's *Messiah,* proclaims the motif as the divine plan for the whole world as the Prophet promises, "Every valley shall be exalted and every mountain and hill shall be made low." Proverbs 29:23 assures the faithful that "a man's pride shall bring him low: but honour shall uphold the humble in spirit." A formative Christian image of pride appears in the *Psychomachia,* or Battle within the Soul, the allegorical account of a battle between the vices and the virtues by the early fifth-century Spanish writer, Prudentius. Prudentius's *Psychomachia,* which inspired many other literary battles between the vices and virtues, portrayed Pride as a woman:

> Galloping about, all puffed up on a mettled steed which she had covered with a lion's skin and from which she looked down on the columns with swelling disdain. High on her head she had piled a tower of braided hair to heighten her locks and make a lofty peak over her haughty brows.
>
> (Prudentius 1949–1953 I:291–293)

Pride's mantle "billows" and her large horse "champs" at the bit (293). Pride finally falls "headlong into a pit which cunning Deceit had dug across the field" (297). Thus, the allegorical figure Pride literally "goes before a fall" or, as Proverbs 16:18 says, "Pride goeth before destruction and an haughty spirit before a fall." The *Psychomachia* heavily influenced portraits of vices and virtues on later Romanesque and Gothic churches. Of course, Prudentius's portrait was not entirely original, for he encapsulated archetypal features of pride he had gleaned from the Bible, from Greek and Roman literature, and from early battle images in sculpture and relief. In each of these instances, Pride personified or a proud person is punished by being "brought low," the literal meaning of humbled. An image of pride, based perhaps on a church carving (see Katzenellenbogen 1964, passim), perhaps on Prudentius, but most likely on a by now stereotypic verbal portrait of the sin, appears in Villard de Honnecourt's twelfth-century sketchbook on a leaf containing an equally standard depiction of humility. Above the drawing of a male figure, caught in his voluminously swirling cloak as he loses his stirrups and begins to fall from his horse, appear the words "How Pride Stumbles" (Villard 1959, 13). Other stone renderings of pride as a man falling off a horse may be found in Chartres and Conques (Bloomfield 1967, 199). Depictions of Pride as a vice are featured in all the major literary masterpieces summarizing the history of Creation and the scheme of salvation. Dante's *Divine Comedy,* for example, includes a list of famous figures who fell because of their pride (*Purgatorio* 14,

70 ff.). John Bunyan's *Pilgrim's Progress* leads every Christian through "the Valley of Humiliation" where he learns that, "He that is down needs fear no fall, / He that is low no pride" (Bunyan 1986, 212). But the most widely known literary portrait of pride is undoubtedly Milton's Satan, "who was by the command of God driven out of Heaven with all his Crew into the great Deep" (*Paradise Lost* I, "The Argument"). Milton's Satan has a venerable lineage (Bloomfield 1967, 109), for believers have always asserted that his pride was the original sin, since his fall from heaven preceded Adam's fall from grace and was thus the first Judeo-Christian example of pride brought low.

A Hasidic commentator summarizes the significance of the motif and illustrates some of the ways in which it forms a continuum between folk culture and religion. "Said the Kotsker: 'The Lord brings the proud low, but the man of pride remains haughty even in his lower state; once more the Lord lowers him, and this continues until he is humbled to the very earth'" (Newman 1975, 355).

Judith Neaman

REFERENCES

Bloomfield, Morton W. 1967 [1952]. *The Seven Deadly Sins.* Lansing: Michigan State University Press.
Bunyan, John. 1986. *The Pilgrim's Progress.* Ed. Roger Sharrock. New York: Penguin.
The Holy Bible, Authorized King James Version. N.d. Grand Rapids, MI: Zondervan.
Jaeger, Werner. 1945. *Paideia: The Ideals of Greek Culture.* Trans. Gilbert Highet. 2d ed. 3 vols. New York: Oxford.
Katzenellenbogen, Adolf. 1964 [1939]. *Allegories of the Virtues and Vices in Medieval Art.* New York: W.W. Norton.
Newman, Louis I., ed. and trans. 1975. *The Hasidic Anthology: Tales and Teachings of the Hasidim.* New York: Schocken Books.
Payne, Robert. 1951. *Hubris: A Study of Pride.* New York: Harper Torchbooks.
Prudentius. 1949–1953. *Psychomachia: With an English Translation by H.J. Thomson.* Cambridge, MA: Harvard University Press.
Rose, H.J. 1959. *A Handbook of Greek Mythology.* New York: E.P. Dutton,
Villard, de Honnecourt. 1959. *The Sketchbook of Villard de Honnecourt.* Ed. Theodore Bowie. Bloomington: Indiana University Press.

❀ M ❀

Ordaining the Future

Bargain with Devil

Motif M210

❁

The theme of a bargain or binding contract with the devil can be traced back to the European Middle Ages. But the somewhat broader theme of the devil tempting human beings to imperil their souls in exchange for worldly riches or power is, according to several scholars, much older. Such a conception of the devil as exercising dominion over the worldly sphere is arguably rooted in a Judeo-Christian dualistic worldview. Thus, if the devil was in charge of the earthly realm, he could tempt humans to give up their souls (read: their allegiance to God in the heavenly realm) in order to enjoy more worldly pleasures (Conway 1881; Kelly 1985). Horst and Ingrid Daemmrich trace this theme back to "Enoch, the Talmud, and the Cabbala" (Daemmrich and Daemmrich 1987, 225), while Spivack (1988) sees its precursor in the Bible, first in the book of Job and later in the Gospels with Satan's temptation of Jesus Christ.

In archetypal terms, a bargain with the devil may be related to the figure of the shadow. Burrows, Lapides, and Shawcross define the shadow as the "negative double of the body, the image of evil, the alter ego of the soul" (1973, 461). Dimic characterizes the psychological significance of the shadow:

> It is taken to be instrumental in a child's development of a personal body image, and it is defined as one of the major human archetypes. . . . In contrast to the light of consciousness, the shadow is the darkness of the personal unconscious, the other, unfathomed side of the personality, its secret sharer. The shadow includes those sombre traits belonging to the same sex and is representative of the least-developed, inferior function of Jung's four types of consciousness (thinking, feeling, perceiving, and intuiting); the shadow is everything that the individual refuses to accept or understand in himself. . . .

> If not assumed and integrated, the shadow may become evil and destructive. In the collective unconscious, the shadow represents archetypal evil; referring to Gnostic and alchemic lore, Jung extends this analysis to God or Christ and Satan. (1988, 1208)

In folklore and literature, there exist two main variations on this theme: one focuses on the person's actual contract with the devil, while the other revolves around a person's attempt to (usually successfully) outwit the devil. The first is exemplified by the figure of Faust; the second, by the folktale cycle of the sharp-witted peasant and the rather stupid devil. These narratives often involve motif M211, "Man sells soul to devil."

FAUST

The Faust-cycle really encompasses a number of similar stories, beginning around the fourth and sixth centuries, with the diabolic contracts attributed to Saint Cyprian and Theophilus, respectively (Conway 1881; Elkhadem 1981; Spivack 1988). Spivack describes the standard form of this cycle:

> Represented as a formal and binding written document between the devil and a human, usually a professed magician who signs it with his blood, the pact offers renunciation of Christianity in exchange for demonic services to be rendered at the price of the signer's soul. This theme recurs in modern literature either as a conventional literal pact with a diabolic tempter or as an equivalent psychological experience. Both the motive for signing the pact and the outcome of the agreement vary. (1988, 941)

The legend of Saint Cyprian tells how he wagers his soul if the devil can make the beautiful Justina his. He is saved, however, because he becomes a Christian and dies alongside Saint Justina as a martyr (Conway 1881; Spivack 1988). Pedro de Calderón based his 1637 work *El mágico prodigioso* on this story. Theophilus, on the other hand, refuses election as bishop out of modesty but later regrets the decision. He strikes a bargain with Satan in exchange for restoration of his position in the church. He eventually repents, however, and is saved through the intercession of the Virgin Mary; this relates to motif M218.1, "Pacts with the devil sealed in blood made ineffective by a saint" (Elkhadem 1981). An early treatment of this story comes from Gautier de Coincy, who wrote *Le miracle de Théophile* around the year 1200. In addition, several other historical figures have had the bargain with the devil motif added to their legends: "Pope Joan," who is said to have sold her soul to Satan to secure election as supreme pontiff (Giovanni Boccaccio produced a literary work based on this legend); François Henry de Luxembourg, a ruthless French military leader during the time of Louis XIV (anonymous versions from the late seventeenth and early eighteenth century have been found); Paracelsus, the Swiss alchemist; Pope Sylvester II, who supposedly opened a school for sorcerers and attempted to cheat death by consulting either a magic oracular head or a familiar in the form of a black dog (he died anyway) (Elkhadem 1981). Paul Carus adds that the figure of Faust became a magnet for a number of other closely related older tales, such as those of Adelbertus Magnus, Johannes Teutonicus (Deutsch), Trithemius (Abbot of Sponheim), Agrippa of Nettesheim, Theophrastus, and Paracelsus (Carus 1969; see also Conway 1881). It seems likely that people have attached the motif of a contract with Satan to historical and legendary figures when a viable explanation for their extraordinary power, wealth, or cruelty was needed.

The essential structure of the Faust-cycle story involves a magician-doctor who makes a bargain to give his soul to the devil in exchange for a certain period of unlimited wish-fulfillment. In the German medieval legend the period of time is twenty-four years (Elkhadem 1981). In some versions, the individual is saved, usually through divine intervention or the undertaking of extreme penitential practices (Saint Cyprian, Theophilus, Johann Goethe's Faust); in others, the devil enforces the terms of the contract and drags him off to Hell (the 1587 Faust chapbook, Christopher Marlowe's *Faust*). The historical Faust is believed to have been a phony magician-philosopher who died in the early to mid-sixteenth century (Conway 1881; Spivack 1988). Trithemius, a medieval abbot, first mentions him in a 1507 letter (Conway 1881; Weber 1999). The first publication of the Faust-story appeared in 1587 in Germany as a chapbook titled *Das Volksbuch von Doktor Faust.* This Faust wants to be godlike in knowledge and power and is thus drawn to magic. The devil materializes as Mephistopheles and Faust signs, in blood, a twenty-four-year contract. Seeking fame and respect, he visits both Heaven and Hell and tours the world. He conjures Alexander the Great and Helen of Troy before the court of the Holy Roman Emperor and subsequently fathers a prophetic child with Helen. The tale ends in Faust's apparent damnation, suggested by the discovery of his mangled corpse (Carus 1969). In 1604, Christopher Marlowe published an English rendering of the tale, *The Tragicall History of Doctor Faustus,* which likewise includes what had come to be the essential elements of the Faust-cycle: the thirst for knowledge, the twenty-four-year contract, the signing of the contract in blood, and the protagonist's final damnation (Elkhadem 1981; Spivack 1988). Goethe's famous poem *Faust* (1808–1832), however, exhibits all these elements except for the ending—his Faust is saved because the devil is unable to fulfill his end of the bargain and satisfy Faust completely. As we will see shortly, Goethe's version almost seems a melding of the medieval form of the Faust story (as a morality tale) with the folktale representation of the devil as dupe outwitted by an impossible task.

FOLKTALES

More generally, in folklore the bargain with the devil motif (M210 and related motifs) is found in the traditions of many groups; it is related to a number of other motifs and figures in the plot of a host of folktales. In folktales, the devil figure may overlap with that of the ogre, giant, or even Death personified. The theme appears in medieval exempla and literature such as the *Legenda Aurea* (1270) and includes motifs such as M212, "Devil at gallows repudiates his bargain with robber," and M217, "Devil bargains to help man win woman" (Spivack 1988).

The contract with the devil (M211, "Man sells soul to devil)" serves as the initial situation in several folktales, such as Types 330, 360, 361, 756B, 810, and 812. For example, in Type 330, *The Smith Outwits the Devil,* a man agrees to surrender his soul to the devil after a certain period of time in return for being made a master smith. He is usually granted three wishes by a supernatural helper who provides him with objects he can use to entrap the devil (examples include a tree, chair, or bench to which the devil sticks and a bag or container in which the devil can be trapped). The smith uses these objects to overcome the snares of the devil—he gains more time or may be released from the contract. When the smith dies, however, neither Heaven nor Hell will accept him and he must instead wander the earth, emitting a spooky glow. This tale, according to Thompson (1977), is widespread in the world's traditions, including the *Kinder- und Hausmärchen* by the Brothers Grimm (tales 81 and 82) and in different areas of Europe as well as America. Fred Morgan (1968), for example, collected a version of this tale in the Uwharrie Mountains of North Carolina. The entrapped devil figure is more generally related to the theme of Death sticking to a bench or tree in Greek and Hebrew myth (Aarne and Thompson 1987; Thompson 1977).

In Type 360, *Bargain of the Three Brothers with the Devil,* brothers receive money in return for the devil's power over them (M211, "Man sells soul to devil"). An innkeeper commits a murder and the brothers are accused. They are rescued by the devil in the nick of time and the innkeeper is hanged instead. The devil is satisfied with the innkeeper's soul. This tale has been collected extensively, according to Aarne and Thompson, from Denmark and Germany in particular. Type 361, *Bear-Skin,* likewise involves a bargain with the devil in exchange for money. This time it is a soldier who agrees not to wash or comb himself for seven years; he ends up marrying the youngest sister in family and the two elder sisters hang themselves (Aarne and Thompson 1987). The devil tells him, "I got two; you one." This story has been collected somewhat recently by Taggart (1990) in the Cáceres region of Spain.

Type 765B, *The Devil's Contract,* is about a boy who goes to Hell to try to

A child who was sold or promised to the devil (Motif S211) is taken away from his parents. From Geoffrey de Latour Landry, *Der Ritter vom Turn* **(1493).**

retrieve a contract, signed before his birth, that promised him to the devil. He successfully retrieves his contract and thus evades the devil's power. This tale features motif M211, "Man sells soul to devil," along with related motifs about children being given to the devil (S211, "Child sold (promised) to devil (ogre)"). The most versions of this tale have been collected in Ireland, with a sizable number also coming from Germany and Lithuania (Aarne and Thompson 1987).

A number of folktales begin with the promise of children to the devil either by the parents or by the youths themselves. For example, Type 313A, a version of *The Girl as Helper in the Hero's Flight,* begins with motif S22.3, "Youth sells himself to an ogre in settlement of a gambling debt." Structurally, this strategy of opening a tale serves the function of setting the hero on his journey (away from his childhood home and out into the world). It thus sets the story in motion. Several other examples of stories set into motion by this cluster of related motifs are Type 310, *The Maiden in the Tower,* better known as *Rapunzel,* in which a man promises an offended witch his unborn child; Type 400, *The Man on a Quest for His Lost Wife,* in which a father unwittingly pledges his son to a monster; and Type 425C, *Beauty and the Beast,* in which a father may promise his daughter to the beast. The theme of a son promised to Satan appears in medieval romances like *Robert the Devil* and *Sir Gowther,* both of which end with the child's redemption. This theme is related to motif M219.1, "Bargain with the devil for an heir," and S223, "Childless couple promise child to devil if they may only have one" (Aarne and Thompson 1987; Thompson 1977).

In Type 810, *The Snares of the Evil One,* a man is protected from the devil by a priest who draws a magic circle around him. This story includes motif M211, "Man sells soul to devil," and appears in the Grimm (tale 92) and Svend Grundtvig (number 59) collections from Germany and Denmark, respectively. It appears to be especially popular in northern Europe and the Baltics. Type 812, *The Devil's Riddle,* concerns a man's success in outwitting the devil by solving riddles. This may involve guessing the true nature of enigmatic objects (examples include a gold cup that is really a cup of pitch and roast meat that is really a dead dog); answering seemingly impossible questions (such as What is sweeter than honey? or, What is whiter than white?); interpreting numbers symbolically; or performing impossible tasks. The man is successful because he eavesdrops on the devil or secures the help of the devil's grandmother or other supernatural helper. Again, this tale seems to be particularly prolific in northern Europe and the Baltics (Aarne and Thompson 1987). In addition, Polly Stewart notes that in some versions of the Child ballad "Riddles Wisely Expounded" (number 1), the heroine solves riddles in order to escape from the snares of the devil (Stewart 1993). Type 820 incorporates motif M213, "Devil as substitute for day laborer at mowing." The devil uses a magic sickle, but when the evil boss attempts the same feat, he dies of overexhaustion. This type has been collected mostly from northern Europe (Aarne and Thompson 1987).

It is in the more simple folktales, specifically Types 1170–1199, grouped under the heading *A Man Sells His Soul to the Devil,* that we see most clearly the representation of the devil as foolish and easily outmaneuvered. These tales share a common theme: the man saves his soul through trickery, usually by demanding that the devil perform impossible tasks. It is thus motif M211, "Man sells soul to devil," that sets these stories in motion. The devil is usually a buffoon. Thompson explains:

> Among the impossible tasks assigned the devil in stories of this kind are catching rabbits in nets set out in high trees (Type 1171), collecting all stones from the brook or field, making knots from drops of spilled brandy, making a rope from sand, straightening curly hair, catching a man's broken wind, pumping out water from the whole sea, or catching water in a sieve (Types

1171–1180). Other kinds of cheats are perpetrated on the devil. Having agreed to give the devil a part of his body, the man gives him a paring from his fingernail (Type 1181). Three other deceptive bargains are The Level Bushel, The Last Leaf, and The First Crop (Types 1182, 1184, and 1185). In the first, the student is to come into the devil's power if, at the end of a year, he does not at least return for the heaping bushel of gold a level one. The student immediately hands back the level bushel and keeps the surplus. In the second the man is to pay the devil when the last leaf falls from the tree. It is an oak tree, and the leaf never falls. The oak also figures in the third of these stories. The man is to pay the devil as soon as he harvests his first crop, but he plants acorns and the devil must wait long. These three tales are widely distributed and popular over most of Europe." (Thompson 1977, 44)

As a whole, these stories are especially popular in Scandinavia and the Baltics, although distributed throughout other areas of Europe (Thompson 1977).

Type 1186, *With His Whole Heart,* also known as *The Devil and the Advocate,* involves a declaration by the devil that he will not take anything not offered with one's whole heart. Someone curses the judge/advocate with such vehemence that the latter is taken off to Hell. This is motif M215, "With his whole heart: devil carries off judge." The story appears in Geoffrey Chaucer's "Friar's Tale" (*The Canterbury Tales,* 1478) and in English romances. It is a tale collected most frequently from northern and eastern Europe. Type 1187, *Meleager,* has as its basis the ancient Greek myth of Meleager, in which a person is permitted to live as long as a candle burns. This story has proliferated in Irish, Flemish, and French tradition. The remaining tales in this cycle involve bargains that turn on such stipulations as giving the devil the first thing driven over a bridge (Type 1191), singing a hymn (Type 1193), and saying the Lord's Prayer (Type 1199) (Aarne and Thompson 1987). In addition, Stewart points out that in "The Elfin Knight" (Child ballad no. 2), the tempter that the heroine attempts to evade by posing impossible tasks may in fact really be the devil (Stewart 1993).

Type 1191, *The Dog on the Bridge,* which seems especially characteristic of German folklore, may be associated with certain actual bridges in that country, the so-called Devil's Bridges. This type involves motif M211.2, "Man sells soul to devil in return for devil's building house (barn, etc.)." The builder may outwit the devil by having an animal (or animals) cross the bridge first, thus saving human souls (Aarne and Thompson 1987; Conway 1881).

If the theme of a bargain with the devil can be considered to include related figures such as a giant or Death personified, as suggested earlier, then such motifs figure in certain origin myths. For example, Denise Palume discusses several West African tales centering on the theme of the origin of death. In one, Death gives a hunter some meat and later returns for payment. The hunter gives Death one of his children. This tale, "Trading with Death," traveled from Africa to places like Jamaica and French Guiana. In another text, "The Two Brothers," Death demands that the spider say his name before he will give him meat. He then curses the spider's brother for having given him Death's name (Lebe). In the third text, a mother pretends to give her daughter to Death in exchange for meat, but tries to trick Death into letting her keep her daughter too. Another text, from the Kra, tells of a youth who agrees to serve a giant in exchange for some food. The giant lets him leave for a while if he will bring back another boy in his place (he brings his brother). The next time that the boy leaves, the giant demands a girl to marry (the boy brings his sister). Finally the boy asks again and the giant tells him to go into the giant's hut and take whatever he wants: he finds his sister's bones. Palume ties these stories to kinship structure, arguing that giving one's daughter to Death represents the loss of a female child through marriage to another lineage (Palume 1967).

Other variations on the theme of a bargain with the devil include M211.1, "Man unwittingly sells soul to devil," an element in medieval folktales. That for which the person sells his soul can vary tremendously (including seeing water turn into wine, visiting home in flying boat, magic power to escape capture, performing one specific job, granting of wishes, helping with robberies, assistance in reaching the priesthood, winning a woman, or securing an heir).

LATER LITERATURE

In elite literature, the bargain with the devil motif has been further developed. Adelbert von Chamisso's *Peter Schlemihls wundersame Geschichte* (1814) tells the story of a man who bargains away his shadow but subsequently finds himself so alienated from human company that he soon rues his decision (Elkhadem 1981; Dimic 1988). Oscar Wilde's character Lord Henry Wooten in *The Picture of Dorian Gray* (1891) is another example of a man selling his soul, in this case, for eternal youth. Stephen Vincent Benet's story "The Devil and Daniel Webster" (1937) takes place in New Hampshire, where a farmer named Jabez Stone sells his soul for ten years' worth of riches. He, like others, signs the contract with his blood. When the length of the contract expires, Jabez enlists Daniel Webster to take his case before an American jury and wins his freedom through invocation of the American self-image of individual liberty (Spivack 1988). In 1947 Thomas Mann published *Doktor Faustus,* in which the Faust character, Adrian Leverkühn, agrees to give up love for success. But here the devil only exists in Leverkühn's mind (Spivack 1988). Similarly, in modern movies, the theme continues to strike a chord with the popular psyche, ranging from comedies like *Bedazzled* (starring Elizabeth Hurley as a female devil) to the disturbing *Angel Heart* (in which an ostensible voodoo plot is framed by a man's ill-fated bargain with Satan).

Natalie M. Underberg

REFERENCES

Aarne, Antti, and Stith Thompson. 1987. *The Types of the Folktale.* Helsinki: Suomalainen Tiedeakatemia.

Burrows, David, Frederick Lapides, and John T. Shawcross. 1973. *Myths and Motifs in Literature.* New York: Free Press.

Carus, Paul. 1969. *The History of the Devil and the Idea of Evil.* San Francisco, CA: Land's End Press.

Conway, Moncare. 1881. *Demonology and Devil-Lore.* Rev. ed. 2 vols. New York: Holt.

Daemmrich, Horst, and Ingrid Daemmrich. 1987. *Themes and Motifs in Western Literature.* Tübingen: Francke.

Dimic, Milan. 1988. "Shadow." In *Dictionary of Literary Themes and Motifs,* ed. Jean-Charles Seigneuret, 1195–1210. Westport, CT: Greenwood Press.

Elkhadem, Saad. 1981. *The York Companion to Themes and Motifs of World Literature: Mythology, History, and Folklore.* Fredericton, NB: York Press.

Kelly, Henry. 1985. *The Devil at Baptism: Ritual, Theology, and Drama.* Ithaca: Cornell University Press.

Morgan, Fred. 1968. *Ghost Tales of the Uwharries.* Winston-Salem, NC: J.F. Blair.

Palume, Denise. 1967. "Two Themes on the Origin of Death in West Africa." *Man,* n.s., 2 (March 1967): 48–61.

Spivack, Charlotte. 1988. "Pact with the Devil." In *Dictionary of Literary Themes and Motifs,* ed. Jean-Charles Seigneuret, 941–948. Westport, CT: Greenwood Press.

Stewart, Polly. 1993. "Wishful Willful Wily Women: Verbal Strategies for Female Success in the Child Ballads." In *Feminist Messages: Coding in Women's Folk Culture,* ed. Joan Radner, 54–73. Urbana: University of Illinois Press.

Taggart, James. 1990. *Enchanted Maidens: Gender Relations in Spanish Folktales of Courtship and Marriage.* Princeton, NJ: Princeton University Press.

Thompson, Stith. 1977. *The Folktale.* Berkeley: University of California Press.

Weber, Eugen. 1999. *Apocalypses: Prophecies, Cults, and Millennial Beliefs Through the Ages.* Cambridge, MA: Harvard University.

Curses

Motifs M400–M462

❀

Cursing can be understood as an attempt to "call down evil upon God or creatures, rational or irrational, living or dead" (*Catholic Encyclopedia* 1999). Thompson classifies curses as a subsection under Chapter M, Ordaining the Future.

In early Christianity, Saint Thomas addressed cursing under the term *maledictio* (*Catholic Encyclopedia* 1999). Power traces the etymology of the word *curse* to the ancient Gaelic word *cúrsachadh,* which, in the ninth century, denoted "abuse." From this word and another one commonly used, *malediction,* we can derive two basic elements of cursing: abusing and speaking evil (Power 1974).

In the traditions of the ancient world, two well-known curses figure in the book of Genesis: first, when God drives Adam and Eve out of the Garden of Eden they and their progeny are cursed with the travails of human suffering; second, after killing his brother Abel, Cain is cursed by God and condemned to wander the earth. Curses appear a number of times throughout the Bible: "in various books of the Old Testament there are long lists of curses against transgressors of the Law [in Leviticus and Deuteronomy]. . . . So, too, in the New Testament, Christ curses the barren fig-tree [Mark] . . . pronounces his denunciation of woe against the incredulous cities [Matthew] . . . against the rich, the worldling, the scribes and the Pharisees, and foretells the awful malediction that is to come upon the damned [Matthew]" (*Catholic Encyclopedia* 1999).

A connection to an archetype may be made with the figure of the outcast, of which Cain is the prototypical figure. As Burrows, Lapides, and Shawcross explain, "The outcast is the alienated character, the outsider, the criminal. . . . the figures of Ishmael, the Wandering Jew, the Ancient Mariner, and the Flying Dutchman have been a part of our consciousness and unconsciousness" (1973, 357).

In ancient Greek mythology, Cassandra, famed as a seer, is cursed by Apollo so that no one will ever believe her predictions again after she broke a promise of love to him. Her prophecies thus go unheeded, to the peril of the city of Troy and of Agamemnon. The curse of Cassandra appears in Homer's *Iliad* and *Odyssey* as well as Vergil's *Aeneid* (ca. 30–19 BCE). Also in the *Aeneid,* when Aeneas leaves Dido, Queen of Carthage, she places a curse on him and his people before she commits suicide.

In Greek mythology, a curse placed on Labdacus (father of Laius and grandfather of Oedipus) and his progeny results in the ill fate of Laius, Oedipus, Antigone, and others (Elkhadem 1981, 58).

In Shakespeare's *Richard III* (1592–1593), Queen Margaret utters such a passionate curse against Richard and his allies that Buckingham says, "My hair doth stand on end to hear her curses" (1.3.303).

Two well-known condemnations, mentioned above in connection to archetypal theory, delivered as a punishment for blasphemy, can be considered curses. A sea captain, known as The Flying Dutchman, utters a blasphemous oath and for the rest of time he must sail around the Cape of Good Hope. The Wandering Jew (Aarne-Thompson Type 777), is condemned to walk the earth until the last day because he either uttered a blasphemous oath or struck Jesus Christ on his way to the crucifixion (Aarne and Thompson 1987; Elkhadem 1981).

Curse motifs (M400 and related motifs) are prolific in number and variety. One type of curse is the "cursing match," also known as flyting (M401). Hughes explains the custom as it existed in ancient Germanic society:

> The Old Norse root, *flyta,* seems initially to be restricted to a heroic ambience. In this brand of flyting, the insults are deliberately provocative, designed, to use another Northern word, to *egg* the opponent into action. . . . Skill in barbed insult, dexterity in the wounding phrase, is very much part of heroic language of the North, where the complexity of word-play reaches astonishing proportions in skaldic verse, which was delivered *ex tempore.* It is the verbal equivalent of virtuoso sword-play. (Hughes 1998, 47)

This was also a feature of Irish cursing in the early days of Christianity, which involved two individuals who uttered imprecations against each other in the form of a conversation. An important element in these cursing contests is the increasing vehemence of the curses from beginning to end, moving from insult to death wish (Power 1974).

The identity of the curser can range from a person cursing himself or herself (M411.0.1) to family members cursing other family members (for example, M411.1, "Curse by parent"). In the Child ballads, for example, jealous mothers curse sons and thereby destroy them and their new families. In "The Mother's Malison" (also known as "Clyde's Water," Child 216), the son refuses his mother's request to stay at home with her, intending instead to spend the night with his lady love. The mother utters this curse: "Clyde's water's wide and deep enough; / My malison drown thee!" (cited in Stewart 1993, 62). The son subsequently drowns trying to return home from his lady's house. In "Prince Robert" (Child 87), a mother curses her son's marriage and poisons him; later, his widow is cursed by the unremorseful mother and dies (Stewart 1993). Mothers can also utter curses unintentionally, with nonetheless disastrous results. For example, in Type 813A, *The Accursed Daughter,* a woman unwittingly curses her daughter to the devil through a careless statement (this tale appears in the Russian Afanasiev collection) (Aarne and Thompson 1987).

In addition, several outcast figures, including beggars (M411.2) and old women (M411.5), can also deliver damning imprecations. This can be seen quite clearly in the realm of Irish folklore. The so-called Tinker's Cant offers one example of a beggar's curse: "*That the midil may tasp you, you glodach crois ould beoir*" (in standard English, "That the devil may take you, you dirty old woman") (O'Farrell 1995). The widow's curse was, according to Power, among the most terrifying in Irish society: without a protector, without means of providing for herself, her wrath was still something to be avoided at all costs (Power 1974). In fact, wishing a widow's curse on someone is itself a curse: "*Mallacht na Bantrai ort*" ("The widow's curse on you") (O'Farrell 1995, 94). In Irish folklore, the theme of a widow pronouncing a curse on the executioner who hanged her son is widespread. For example, one well-known hereditary curse (intended to affect both the individual and his or her lineage into future generations) was attached to the Beresford family: when a member of this family hanged a widow's only son without justification, the widow cursed him and his lineage for seven generations (Power 1974).

Saints' legends are replete with the maledictions of holy men and women (M411.8, "Saint's (prophet's) curse"). Saint Patrick, for example, is credited with driving the snakes out of Ireland with a curse (Jacob 1967). Irish hagiography (called *facbala*) also tells of the pronouncement of hereditary curses. Again, Saint Patrick offers an example. According to legend, he once cursed a cruel slave owner who refused to reform. St. Patrick "fasted against him" (an important first step in pronouncing an Irish curse), then spat on a stone and uttered the curse that the man's family would never have a royal heir (Power 1974). Interestingly, one saints' method of cursing, that of ringing bells (M411.8.1), is reminiscent of the way that, historically, the Catholic

Church excommunicated members. This "cursing ritual" involved reading a sentence, ringing a bell, closing a book, and extinguishing a candle (Jacob 1967). Similarly, prophets could utter curses. The seventeenth-century curse of the Mackenzie clan offers an example. In 1609, Colin Mackenzie was named Earl of Seaforth. The third earl married another Mackenzie, Isabella, a woman with a fiery temper. As a consequence, the earl spent a good deal of time away from her. When she asked a local seer, named Kenneth Mackenzie but known as the Warlock of the Glenn, to use his divination skills to reveal where her husband was, the seer told her: in the arms of two other women. This so displeased the Lady Mackenzie that she had the warlock hanged. At the gallows, he once again consulted his divining-stone and foretold the end of the Seaforth Mackenzie line (Lewes 1911).

The priest's curse (M411.14; also M411.15, "Curse by monk"), however, was probably the single most feared type in traditional Irish society. Power hypothesizes that this was because the priest was considered a kind of religious virtuoso and so presumably had an ability to harness potentially destructive supernatural powers (Power 1974). Legends also attest to the existence of the priest's curse in England. One such curse from the sixteenth century was associated with the House of Cowdray. Sir Anthony Browne received an abbey from King Henry VIII as thanks for Browne's role in closing down the monasteries. At a banquet Browne threw to celebrate successfully turning the abbey into a personal residence, a monk pronounced a curse on him and his descendants, specifying that they would die through fire and water. In 1793, the last of the line drowned and the family castle was destroyed in a fire (Lockhart 1971).

The poet's curse (M411.18) also played an important role in traditional Irish society. In former times, poets were attributed mystical and even prophetic powers. The *glám dícenn* was a form of cursing ritual used by poets in ancient Ireland (Power 1974). In addition, curses can come from almost anyone, including a god (M411.4.1), a spirit (M411.7), an ogre (M411.10), a witch (M411.12), and an animal (M411.19).

The *Motif-Index* also categorizes curses by the occasions of their pronouncement (M412, "Time of giving curse"). Two mentioned in Thompson's index are M412.1, "Curse given at birth of child," and M412.2, "Curse given on wedding night." The former is part of Type 410, *Sleeping Beauty,* in which an offended fairy pronounces a death-curse on the newborn princess: she will die from pricking her finger on the spindle of a spinning wheel. Another fairy mitigates the curse from death to a hundred-year sleep (F316.1). This story has appeared in a number of well-known literary collections, including Giambattista Basile's *Il Pentamerone* (1634–1636) and Charles Perrault's *Contes de ma mere l'Oye* (1697). Also, Types 934E*, *False Prophecy,* and

934E**, *Daughter Cursed at Birth,* are related to this motif. In the former (a Greek subtype), a prophecy is made that at the age of sixteen a princess will ride around a public square on an ass—the prophecy is fulfilled when she is accused of theft. In subtype 934E**, a barren queen is granted a child but simultaneously cursed to see her only three times, and to lay a curse on her child each time (she does). This is an Icelandic variant (Aarne and Thompson 1987).

An important folk concept with regard to curses, seen especially in Irish culture, is that curses are more powerful if uttered from a hilltop or other elevated location. This idea is even incorporated into the text of one popular Irish curse—"Blast you from a height" (O'Farrell 1995, 113)—and is related to motif M413.1, "Curse given from a height. Will fall with full effect on objects at which it is aimed").

Additionally, the method of cursing can vary (M418). Thompson includes the following example from an Anglo-American folktale: M418.1, "Curse by 'building a fire of stones' in fireplace. The person who removes the stones is cursed." Generally, a form of sympathetic magic underlies many rituals associated with cursing. Imitative magic works according to the principle of "like produces like"—a voodoo doll is a good example. Contagious magic, on the other hand, operates on the idea that something that was once in contact with a person will continue to exert control over him or her even after it has been removed. Consequently, many curses require such objects as a lock of hair or nail clippings that once belonged to the cursee (Jacob 1967; Frazer 1955).

In Irish folklore, cursing stones were used. The so-called fire of stones presumably was brought by immigrants to the United States (hence its appearance in Thompson's *Motif-Index* as a part of Anglo-American tradition). A person would gather a heap of smooth stones and place them in a fire. Then, after kneeling to pronounce a curse, ending with a wish of ill-luck on the cursee until the stones were set afire, the curser would hide the rocks. Cursing-stones were usually associated with ancient churches and monasteries in Ireland. The ritual was specific: one fasted, prayed, then turned the stone counterclockwise while uttering a malediction on one's enemy. Another cursing ritual was called "sweeping Colm Cille's bed," referring to a large rock in Ireland that, according to legend, was used by Colin Cille, one of three patron saints of Ireland, as a bed. People who wished to place a curse would come to this crevice between sunset and sunrise and "sweep his bed" with a shirt or chemise (depending on the gender of the cursee) (Power 1974).

The types of curses that can be pronounced seem nearly limitless, but a number of them can be grouped into several main categories, including physical harm (M431), bad luck, curses on descendants, and death. Cursers can wish that, for example, the victim loses an eye (M431.1). This is an element of Type 1331, *The Covetous and the Envious,* in which an ostensible blessing is turned into a curse: a man is given any wish on the condition that his neighbor is given double (he wishes to lose one eye). This story appears, for example, in medieval Spanish exempla. Another bodily harm curse motif associated with a folktale is M431.2, "Curse: toads from mouth," which forms part of Type 403, *The Black and White Bride,* and Type 480, *The Kind and the Unkind Girls.* In the former, the story begins with a neglected stepdaughter coming into contact with a stranger (or strangers) able to grant wishes. Because she is kind, she is granted beauty and the boon of being able to produce gold or jewels from her mouth. Her sister, however, acts unkindly in the same situation and is made ugly and cursed with having toads drop from her mouth. This story appears in Giambattista Basile's *Il Pentamerone* (1634–1636) and has been especially popular in Danish, Finnish, German, and Irish folklore. Type 480, *The Kind and the Unkind Girls,* ends like Type 403 with the unkind girl being punished with frogs falling from her mouth. This tale also appeared in *Il Pentamerone,* as well as in the German Grimm (KHM 24), Danish Grundtvig (no. 37), and Russian Afanasiev collections. The most versions of this tale have been collected in Germany, Ireland, Russia, and Sweden (Aarne and Thompson 1987).

Misfortune constitutes another main category of curses. Irish and Yiddish curses offer pungent examples of these motifs. For example, an Irish curse declares, "That you may have forty-five ways of putting on your coat this harvest-time," a wish that a person would be so poor that his or her clothes would be ripped into rags (O'Farrell 1995, 93). In Yiddish folklore, wishing a bad year on someone is one of the most common kinds of curses, for example: "*Azá yor oyf im vi er hot mir farríkht di mashín.* ('May he have such a year as the way he fixed my car!')" (Matisoff 1979, 61). Such a curse reflects the Jewish conception of the importance of a "year's luck" (Matisoff 1979). Similarly, in an Icelandic variant of Type 556B*, *Curse and Countercurse,* a chess player is cursed by his female opponent with restlessness until he completes certain tasks (M455, "Curse: restlessness"). But the curse is countered by the help of a stepmother and grateful animals (Aarne and Thompson 1987.

One of the most common arenas of cursing in traditional societies concerns people's lineages. Cursing someone's descendants can be a type of group-curse (M460, "Curse on families"). Whole lineages are thus cursed—the wish being that the line will eventually fall to ruin (for example, M462, "Curse: race to lose sovereignty"). Max Lüthi argues that such curses are characteristic of legendry rather than of the folktale:

> In legendry a curse affects whole generations; it takes effect for centuries and burdens all progeny. . . . The folktale curse affects only figures who exist side by side; it never extends from early ancestors to later descendants. After

a curse is lifted, even people who have been bewitched for centuries do not hesitate to marry their young saviors, for savior and saved exist on the same level. . . . The otherworld of the folktale is not only a different dimension, but in it the past stands at ease side by side with the present. (Lüthi 1982, 22)

Scottish Highlander curses offer especially striking examples of family curses. Lockhart posits that most Highland families probably have had a curse in their history. He cites the "Curse of the M'Alisters" as an illustration of one such curse forecasting the end of a family line (Lockhart 1971). Similarly, among the Badaga (a South Indian group), the most serious curse is: "'*Ka:lu kedali* ('May you have no heirs!')" (Hockings 1988, 152).

Finally, the death-curse is the most damning of all (M451, "Curse: death" and related motifs). Again, Irish and Yiddish curses offer abundant examples that can exist both as part and independently of folk narrative. Such curses often reveal customs and beliefs on the part of the group that pronounces them. For example, "*Básna bpisín chugat!* 'The death of the kittens to you!'" refers to the custom of drowning unwanted cats in Ireland and is an example of motif M451.2, "Death by drowning" (Power 1974, 83). Another death curse that reveals an Irish custom is "Hungry grass grow around your grave" because this would prevent people from visiting the gravesite and thus saying prayers for the deceased (O'Farrell 1995, 76). Similarly, in Jewish tradition, wishing death on someone else is, not surprisingly, the most serious of all curses. However, one does not employ the word death (*shtarbn*) specifically—perhaps as a protection against being seized by it oneself. Rather, the burial-ground, the earth (*di erd*) is invoked. Such curses figure in short anecdotes such as one in which a man tells his friend that he and his wife get along wonderfully except for a certain "Agrarian Controversy." Asked for an explanation, he replies that he says *she* should lie in the earth, while she says *he* should (Matisoff 1979).

Scholars of curses seem to agree that there is something of an inverse relation between a group's amount of social power, on the one hand, and the proliferation of its cursing traditions, on the other. Power attributes the historical importance of curses among the Irish to their function as a "punishment-by-proxy"—people without real access to the means of power could achieve a sense of power through cursing (Power 1974). Similarly, Lockhart asserts that, in contrast to England, the curse in the Scottish Highlands was extremely common because it provided a means for the weak to confront the strong (Lockhart 1971). And Matisoff argues that, as with other traditions, Yiddish curses serve a therapeutic function, offering a "valve" to let off steam. This is because in traditional European Jewish society, uttering curses was one of the only ways to retaliate against oppression and prejudice (Matisoff 1979).

Natalie M. Underberg

REFERENCES

Aarne, Antti, and Stith Thompson. 1987. *The Types of the Folktale.* Helsinki: Suomalainen Tiedeakatemia.

Burrows, David, Frederick Lapides, and John T. Shawcross. 1973. *Myths and Motifs in Literature.* New York: Free Press.

Carus, Paul. 1969. *The History of the Devil and the Idea of Evil.* San Francisco, CA: Land's End Press.

The Catholic Encyclopedia. 1999. "Cursing," www.newadvent.org/cathen/04573d.htm.

Elkhadem, Saad. 1981. *The York Companion to Themes and Motifs of World Literature: Mythology, History, and Folklore.* Fredericton, NB: York Press.

Frazer, Sir James. 1955. *The Golden Bough: A Study in Magic and Religion.* 12 vols. New York: St. Martin's Press.

Hockings, Paul. 1988. *Counsel from the Ancients: A Study of Badaga Proverbs, Prayers, Omens and Curses.* Berlin: Mouton de Gruyter.

Hughes, Geoffrey. 1998. *Swearing: A Social History of Foul Language, Oaths and Profanity in English.* London: Penguin Books.

Jacob, Dorothy. 1967. *Cures and Curses.* New York: Taplinger.

Lewes, Mary. 1911. *Stranger Than Fiction: Being Tales from the Byways of Ghosts and Folklore.* London: W. Rider and Son.

Lockhart, John. 1971. *Curses, Lucks, and Talismans.* Detroit: Singing Tree Press.

Lüthi, Max. 1982. *The European Folktale: Form and Nature.* Trans. John D. Niles. Bloomington: Indiana University Press.

Matisoff, James. 1979. *Blessings, Curses, Hopes and Fears: Psycho-Ostensive Expressions in Yiddish.* Philadelphia: Institute for the Study of Human Issues.

O'Farrell, Padraic. 1995. *Before the Devil Knows You're Dead: Irish Toasts, Curses and Blessings.* New York: Sterling.

Power, Patrick. 1974. *The Book of Irish Curses.* Dublin: Mercier Press.

Stewart, Polly. 1993. "Wishful Willful Wily Women: Verbal Strategies for Female Success in the Child Ballads." In *Feminist Messages: Coding in Women's Folk Culture,* ed. Joan Radner, 54–73. Urbana: University of Illinois Press.

Thompson, Stith. 1977 [1946]. *The Folktale.* Berkeley: University of California Press. Orig. ed. New York: Holt, Rinehart, and Winston.

❀ N ❀

Chance and Fate

Chance and Fate

Motifs N0–N899

❀

Chapter N is concerned with the large part that luck plays in narrative (and life). Thompson covered wagers and gambling (N0–N99), the nature of luck and fate (N100–N299), unlucky accidents (N300–N399), lucky accidents (N400–N699), accidental encounters (N700–N799), and helpers—human, animal, and supernatural (N800–N899).

Belief in fate is founded in the universal apprehension that the world is governed by unseen forces and steered by unknowable laws. Interpretation of the mysterious workings of fate has formed the foundation for many of the world's religions as well as being one of the most commonly treated topics in folktales worldwide.

In the Norse religion, the power of the gods is subordinate to the impersonal power of fate, which dictates that most of them are to die during the "twilight of the gods" or Ragnarok, Doom or Destiny of the Gods.

The Norse god Odin and his wife, Frigga can see the future but are powerless to alter it. The Norse sagas also reflect the ability of select individuals to glimpse the workings of fate. Prophetic dreams figure in the *Laxerdael Saga,* while the title character in *Njal's Saga* is most significant for his ability to see into the future, and many characters are configured as "lucky" or "unlucky."

The Norse caste of shamans or predicted the future with the use of runes (*runä*), letters of the Norse alphabet and, when viewed individually, predictive devices (from Germanic *raunen,* "to whisper") thought by epigraphists to contain secret messages. They were believed to have been created by Odin, who achieved the ability to use them through ordeal. Each runic sign was believed to have its own property and to carry both a literal and a transcendant (predictive) meaning (Menninger 1992).

FATE PERSONIFIED

Fate in world folklore can be embodied in any number of ways (N110, "Luck and fate personified"). Often fate is seen as a human figure or figures, particularly female; one of the oldest personifications is Mammetum, the goddess of destiny, in Babylonian myth. Tyche was an early conception of fate, and fortune both good and bad, in Greek myth, assuming the guise of a minor goddess with the decline of the traditional gods (Hornblower and Spawford 2002). The Roman goddess of chance or luck was Fortuna, probably via Tyche. While Fortuna was at first considered a stable and generally beneficent deity, "with the increasing skepticism and loss of confidence of the later Empire . . . the stable goddess of Italian religious tradition gives way to a figure who, like the Greek concept of Tyche, represents instability and the power of unpredictable chance" (Kratz 1988, 540).

Other personifications of fate feature three goddesses (A463.1, "The Fates. Goddesses who preside over the fates of men"). These goddesses, who are often portrayed as spinning and cutting the skein of life, may be found in Greek, Norse, Indian, Lappish, and Irish myth. The Three Fates in Greek myth are known as Moirae (Parcae by the Romans): Clotho spun, Lachesis assigned to man his doom, and Atropos broke the thread. The Norse goddesses, called the Norns, were named Urd, Verdandi, and Skuld; they lived in the roots of the great ash tree Yggdrasil, the world tree. In the "Lay of Helgi" (*Poetic Edda),* the Norns spin a magical thread at the time of the hero's birth and then attach it to the heavens, marking with its ends the land over which Helgi would one day reign.

It has been suggested that such triune figures were originally inspired by the waxing, full, and waning phases of the moon (Dornseif 1925). (A more complex tableau is provided in Lithuanian folklore, where seven goddesses share the task of spinning, measuring, and cutting the woolen yarn that represents the span of a human life. The seventh washes the winding sheet they have created and gives it to the god of death.) Scottish and Irish folktales depict supernatural female fate figures as local spirits—the Banshees. They often comb their long hair, and their wailing signals that someone in the vicinity is about to die.

In the early French romance *Perceforest* (1300), direct survivals of the Three Fates are depicted: Lucida, Themis, and Venus. Later versions of AT 410, Sleeping Beauty, substitute fairies who carry out the traditional role of the fates by decreeing length of life to the newborn. An evil fairy who was not invited to the celebration puts a curse on the infant that she shall die of a spindle wound (M412.1, "Curse given at birth of child"). Another fairy mitigates the curse from death to a hundred-year sleep (F316.1, "Fairy's curse partially overcome by another fairy's amendment"). In many variants of the story, the child's parents attempt to escape the fate of the spindle by having all spinning wheels destroyed (M370, "Vain attempts to escape fulfillment of prophecy").

There may be a connection between the spinning Germanic figures Holle, Holla, Hulda, and Holda and the ancient triune goddess. These supernatural figures are often depicted as able to control the weather and affect human destiny. They reward mortals for industry in spinning and for altruism and punish them for selfishness and laziness.

Some ancient religions feature a male death-herald figure such as the Assyrio-Sumerian Namtar. In some folktales, fate is embodied by a death figure who comes to fetch people, as in the Hebrew folktale "Fate," in which a servant borrows his master's fastest horse only to meet Death while trying to escape him (Hanauer 1935), and "The Castle of Death," in which a clever man is able to cheat Death, thus changing his own fate during the encounter by asking to say a prayer and asking for fifty years to do it. In the Grimms' "Godfather Death" (KHM 44), Death shows his godson the candles that represent individual lives: "See," says Death, "these are the lights of men's lives. The large ones belong to children, the half-sized ones to married people in their prime, the little ones belong to old people; but children and young folks likewise have often only a tiny candle" (*Grimms' Household Tales*).

Folktales from predominantly Buddhist cultures often personify the fate figure in male form and can exhibit strong determinist tendencies. In "The Half-Man and the God of Fate" from Ceylon, a poor man goes to the god three times to complain of his fate and is given each time a half-man in a sack. Even Fate himself does not know what is in the sack. After the third visit, the poor man resigns himself to his destiny (Vedet 1992).

Boethius, writing his *Consolation of Philosophy* in the sixth century CE, gives us an early description of Fortune's wheel, perhaps inspired by the spindle of the ancient Fates:

> As thus she turns her wheel of chance with haughty hand, and presses on like the surge of Euripus's tides, fortune now tramples fiercely on a fearsome king, and now deceives no less a conquered man by raising from the ground his humbled face. She hears no wretch's cry, she heeds no tears, but wantonly she mocks the sorrow which her cruelty has made. This is her sport: thus she proves her power; if in the selfsame hour one man is raised to happiness, and cast down in despair, 'tis thus she shews her might. (ch. 2)

CHANGING ONE'S FATE

Folktales concerned with the theme of fate may be divided into two main groups, those treating the future as immutable and those in which protagonists are able to thwart or defy what fate has in store for them. In the story "Godfather Death," mentioned above, the godson, in his role as physician, tries to cheat Death, but Death takes him anyway, and he is horrified to see that his candle is tiny; Death will not give him a larger one, but instead snuffs it out.

One of the most compelling critical readings of the Greek myth of Oedipus (AT 931, *Oedipus*) sees it as the conflict of free will versus fate. Despite the precautions taken by Oedipus's parents and Oedipus himself to avoid the prophecies that he would kill his father (M343, "Parricide prophecy") and marry his mother (M344, "Mother-incest prophecy"), his fate is inexorable and all that was foretold comes to pass. It is questionable, however, whether the Greeks themselves saw the conflict between free will and fate as central to the story, since classical Greek does not even have a term for "free will."

An interesting example of a hero empowered to exercise free will is the African tale "Sleeping Fate" (Parrinder 1986), in which a poor traveler awakens fate after a twelve-year sleep, thereby improving the lot of others he meets along the way, as well as that of his own family. Other heroes who thwart their fate are those in the well-known German tale "The Bremen Town Musicians" and its Scottish variant "The White Pet," in which a group of aged animals threatened with destruction set out in the world to create an alternative society. Likewise in the Slavic tale "Why People Today Die Their Own Death," a community ends the practice of killing its old people when it is saved from starvation by the wisdom of the elderly protagonist.

As a further example, in "The Prince and the Three Fairies," a newborn prince is doomed to die at the age of twenty-one. At that age, he becomes engaged to the princess of a neighboring kingdom. They come to a river, and the prince falls in the water and drowns. In her grief, the bride asks the death fairy to take ten years of her life and give them to her husband. The fairy of death takes pity on her and it is done, but the prince has to die ten years later. In "The Sayings of the Moirs," a traveler overhears three women discussing the fate of a child just born to the innkeeper, it having been decided that she would marry no other than the traveler himself. The angry traveler throws the child out of a window and she is impaled on an arrow before being rescued by her mother. Years later, when going to bed with his wife, the man notices a deep scar in her side, the truth is revealed, and the couple agree that the pronouncements of the Moirs cannot be changed (Stamer 1990).

WAGERS AND GAMBLING

There are thousands of tales in which characters are shown taking chances and making wagers. One common type of wager is the competitive wager between, or about, prospective spouses. These tales may well have incestuous themes or overtones. Basile (1932) presents a common example in his tale "The Young Slave," in which the sister of the Baron Serva-scura is the only woman able to jump over a rose bush and thus must marry her brother.

The "silence wager" between husband and wife (AT 1351) is found in tales all over Europe as well as China, Turkey, Pakistan, Korea, and South America. Another common type of folktale involving spouses and wagering forms the basis for Shakespeare's play *The Merry Wives of Windsor* (ca. 1601). Some women strike a wager among themselves that the one who proves to have the most stupid, gullible, or least desirable husband should win a reward. Other types of folkloric wagers concerned with the fortunes of a marriage are exemplified by the ancient English tales that served as inspiration for Shakespeare's *Cymbeline* (ca. 1606). In these tales, a wager is made concerning the virtue of the wife, often with comic or negative results for the wagerer.

Foolish protagonists who trade away fortunes (AT 1415, *Lucky Hans*) appear in such tales as "Hans in Luck," "Gudbrand on the Hillside," and "What the Old Man Does Is Always Right." Non-Western examples of such tales are also plentiful. In "Old Man Ookhány," a Siberian tale, the protagonist makes one good trade after another, becoming rich by trading a shoulder blade. In the end, he is killed in revenge by his two young wives (Coxwell 1925). In such tales, two outcomes are consistent. In the first, the protagonist begins with something valuable (a horse, for example) and continues to trade with passersby for items of lesser value until he returns, happily, with something nearly worthless. In the second, the foolish character seems to be wagering or trading well but is in the end brought down by others he believes he has tricked.

In contrast to the fool who happily loses good fortune, the trickster figure proposes wagers, bargains, bets, or deals that will enable him (or her) to take advantage of other characters. Trickster figures exist in every culture for which records exist. These figures, usually mortal and outsiders to the communities in which they operate, are adept at manipulating the weaknesses of those around them and therefore altering their own destinies for the better.

People have been induced to take their chances on gambling for thousands of years. It is believed that both playing cards and dice arose from divinatory practices. The four suits of cards correspond to the four directions of the compass and were used in fortune telling; dice ("bones") were originally vertebrae or knucklebones of animals (Fried 1949, 436–437). In a folktale from India, dice are made from bones from a graveyard (N1.2.2). Folksongs contain many laments about gambling, a common one being "Jack O'Diamonds, Jack O'Diamonds, I know you of old, / You robbed my poor pockets of silver and gold."

Playing cards and dice may have originated in divinatory practices. In some tales, gamblers enlist supernatural aid in hopes of winning. From Meister Ingold, *Das goldene guldin Spiel* **(1472).**

Gamblers can enlist the aid of the supernatural, as for example D1407, "Magic object helps gambler win"; D1407.3, "Magic game board helps win"; and N6.1, "Luck in gambling from compact with devil." There are also tales of gambling with a supernatural adversary (N3), a god (N3.1), or the devil (N4).

Pushkin's short story "The Queen of Spades" (1833) is a haunting tale of gambling and the supernatural. During a long winter's evening of card playing, a young Russian nobleman, Tomsky, tells the story of his grandmother, who, as a young woman in Paris, was told a gambling secret that allowed her to pay back a tremendous debt she had incurred. One of the men at the table, Hermann, becomes obsessed with learning the old lady's secret and resolves to get to her by making love to her young ward. He does manage to gain access to the old countess's rooms, but frightens her to death without gaining the information he sought. The night after her funeral, the ghost of the countess appears in his bedroom and tells him the cards: "The three, the seven, and the ace will win for you if you play them in succession, provided that you do not stake more than one card in twenty-four hours and never play again as long as you live" (E366, "Return from dead to give counsel"; N221, "Man granted power of winning at cards"). Unfortunately, he does not heed the restrictions and the third time he plays he loses everything and goes out of his mind. Unlike poor Hermann, many protagonists in North American Indian tales are successful in gambling (N1.2, "Conquering gambler. Bankrupt gambler gets supernatural power and wins back his fortune"). The ultimate gamble, of course, is when one's life is at stake (N2.2, "Lives wagered"), and tales with this motif are found in Burma, India, Iceland, China, Hawaii, North America, and Africa.

UNLUCKY AND LUCKY ACCIDENTS

Thompson lists hundreds of accidental occurrences that propel the fortunes of the folktale hero or heroine. Primary among these are "Valuable secrets learned" (N440–N499). Many sources of crucial information for a hero or heroine come from overhearing the conversation of animals (N451, "Secrets overheard from animal (demon) conversation"). This motif, which occurs in Types 516, 517, 670, and 673, is known in Buddhist myth and Chinese, Japanese, and Korean sources.

Treasure Trove

The finding of buried treasure is one of the oldest and most common motifs in folklore. AT 676, *Open Sesame,* has variants all over the world, including Iceland, China, Tahiti, New Zealand, Samoa, and Africa; the most famous is the story of "Ali Baba and the Forty Thieves" from the *Arabian Nights.* Alarmed at the sight of a band of horsemen coming his way, Ali Baba hides by climbing a tree, from which he can see and hear everything (N455.3, "Secret formula for opening treasure mountain overheard from robbers"). A related tale, probably a variant, was collected by the Grimms ("Simeli Mountain" or "Simeliberg," KHM 142). The title character in AT 561, *Aladdin,* also from the *Arabian Nights,* is induced by a magician to go down into a treasure trove where, among other marvels, he sees trees that bear not fruit but precious gems, "such as emeralds and diamonds; rubies, spinels and balasses, pearls and similar gems astounding the mental vision of man" (Burton 2001, 587).

Accidental Encounters

Accidental encounters of all sorts, both lucky and unlucky, are the driving force of stories. Folksongs commonly open with the words "As I roved out one morning" or "As I was a-walking one midsummer's morning" and go on to describe a chance meeting, usually with a paramour (N710, "Accidental meeting of hero and heroine"; T30, "Lovers' meeting"). An English folksong called "The Game of Cards" or "The Game of All Fours," collected in numerous variants, combines the motif of such a meeting with the motif of card playing (a metaphor for another kind of play) and ends: "So I took up my hat and I bid her Good-morning / I said: You're the best that I know at this game / She answered: Young man, if you'll come back tomorrow / We'll play the game over and over again" (Kennedy 1975, 402–403).

In tales the world over, a hero or heroine meets up with one or more helpers who provide crucial services on a quest or journey. A prime example is "The Six Servants" ("Die sechs Diener," KHM 134), in which a king's son, setting out to win a princess whose father sets impossible tasks for her suitors, meets up with an extraordinary array of characters with amazing abilities that enable him to pass the tests and gain the hand of the princess.

SUPERNATURAL HELPERS

There are many supernatural helpers (N810), including giants or ogres (N812), monsters grateful to the hero for being spared (N812.5), genies or spirits (N813), angels (N814), and deities (N817). Some are ghosts (R163, "Rescue by grateful dead man"); the motif of the grateful dead is the basis for several tale types (AT 505–508).

In some stories, the helper is met not on a journey, but inside the home (N831.1, "Mysterious housekeeper. Men find their house mysteriously put in order. Discover that it is done by a girl (frequently an animal transformed into a girl)"; AT 709, *Snow-White*). The mysterious housekeeper is a recurrent motif among North American Indian traditions and occurs in Africa, China, Korea, Indonesia, Melanesia, and other areas as well as throughout Europe.

Other supernatural helpers include three odd-looking spinners (*The Three Old Women Helpers,* AT 501) and the strange little man ("Rumpelstiltskin") who saves a girl's life, enabling her to become queen, by helping her spin straw into gold (AT 500, *The Name of the Helper*).

HUMAN AND ANIMAL HELPERS

The girl as helper (N831) is an important motif that appears in many tales and constitutes two types, AT 311 (*Rescue by the Sister*) and AT 313 and its several subtypes (*The Girl as Helper in the Hero's Flight*). The latter is well known from the Greek myth telling of Jason's quest for the Golden Fleece and the help he receives from Medea. In many manifestations of this motif, the girl is able to raise up obstacles or change shape in order to facilitate escape from witches, ogres, or other pursuers.

Animals are helpers in numerous tales, especially in AT 553 (*Raven Helper*) and 559 (*Grateful Animals*). In these stories, the youngest of three brothers is kind to animals and in gratitude they tell him to call upon them should he need help. With their help, he successfully performs various seemingly impossible tasks (H982), such as sorting a large amount of grain in one night (B548.2.1) or recovering an object from the sea (H1132.1.1, "Fish recovers key [or ring, B548.2.2] from sea").

Elizabeth Ernst and Jane Garry

See also: Ghosts and Other Revenants; Flight (Magic).

REFERENCES

Ashliman, D.L. *Folklore and Mythology Electronic Texts*, www.pitt.edu/~dash/folktexts.html.
Basile, Giambattista. 1932. *Pentamerone.* London: E.P. Dutton.
Boethius. 1969. *The Consolation of Philosophy.* Trans. and intro. V.E. Watts. Harmondsworth: Penguin.
Burrows, David, Friederick Lapides, and John T. Shawcross. 1973. *Myths and Motifs in Literature.* New York: Free Press.
Burton, Sir Richard F. 2001. *The Arabian Nights: Tales from a Thousand and One Nights.* New York: Modern Library.
Carus, Paul. 1969. *The History of the Devil and the Idea of Evil.* New York: Land's End.
Coxwell, C.F., ed. 1925. *Siberian and Other Folk Tales: Primitive Literature of the Empire of the Tsars.* London: Dutton.
Coyle, T. Thorn. 1995. "Holda." *Folkvang Horg* 2.
Dornseif, Franz. 1925. *Das Alphabet in Mystik und Magie.* Leipzig: Teubner.
Ellis Davidson, H. 1993. *Lost Beliefs of Northern Europe.* New York: Routledge.
Erdoes, Richard, and Alphonso Ortiz. 1984. *American Indian Myths and Legends.* New York: Pantheon.
Fried, Jerome. 1949. "Games." In *Funk and Wagnalls Standard Dictionary of Folklore,* ed. Maria Leach and Jerome Fried. New York: Funk and Wagnalls.
Grimms' Household Tales. With the Authors' Notes. 1968 [1884]. Trans. Margaret Hunt. 2 vols. London: George Bell. Reprint. Detroit: Singing Tree.
Hamilton, Martha, and Mitch Weis. 2000. *Noodlehead Stories.* Little Rock, AR: August House.
Hanauer, J.E. 1935 [1907]. *Folk-Lore of the Holy Land: Moslem, Christian and Jewish.* London: Sheldon Press.
Hornblower, Simon, and Antony Spawford, eds. 2002. *Oxford Classical Dictionary.* New York: Oxford University Press.
Ions, Veronica. 1983. *Egyptian Mythology.* New York: Peter Bedrick Books.
Jones, Gwyn. 1984. *A History of the Vikings.* New York: Oxford University Press.
Kennedy, Peter, ed. 1975. *Folksongs of Britain and Ireland.* New York: Schirmer/Macmillan.
Kratz, Dennis M. 1988. "Fortune." In *Dictionary of Literary Themes and Motifs,* ed. Jean-Charles Seigneurer, 538–546. Westport, CT: Greenwood Press.

Menninger, Karl. 1992. *Number Words and Number Symbols: A Cultural History of Numbers.* Mineola. New York: Dover.

Parrinder, Geoffrey. 1986. *African Mythology.* New York: Harper and Row.

Pourrat, Henri. 1989. *French Folktales.* New York: Pantheon.

Pushkin, Alexander. 1968 [1833]. *The Queen of Spades and Other Stories.* Trans. Rosemary Edmonds. Harmondsworth: Penguin.

The Saga of Volsungs. 1990. Trans. Jesse L. Byock. Berkeley: University of California Press.

Snorri Sturluson's Edda. 1998. Trans. Anthony Faulkes. London: Everyman.

Stamer, Barbara, ed. 1990. *Types of Fate.* Frankfurt am Main: Fischer.

Stephenson, R. Rex. 2001. "The Three Old Women's Bet." In *The Jack Tale Players.* Schonburg, TX: I.E. Clark.

Verdet, Jean-Pierre. 1992. *The Sky: Mystery, Magic and Myth.* New York: Harry N. Abrams.

Choice of Roads

Motif N122.0.1, and Crossroads, Various Motifs

❦

The motif of "Choice of roads" appears under the broader motif heading, "Ways of luck and fate," N100–N299.

Throughout the world, the places where roads diverged or crossed have been regarded as unlucky or dangerous because of the presence of evil spirits, and in an effort to propitiate these spirits, deities have often been worshipped there. "We sacrifice . . . to the forkings of the highways and to the meeting of the roads" is a formula from the *Avesta,* the ancient scriptures of Zoroastrianism (MacCulloch 1981, 330). MacCulluch says, "Men always fear demons and spirits which they believe lurk on the edge of the forest path or rude roadway, ready to pounce upon the belated traveler, and in many cases roads are believed to be infested by them. . . . Hence they would be regarded as lurking at the intersection of roads, especially by night, when wayfarers were uncertain of the direction in which they ought to go" (1981, 332).

Crossroads have been invested with a sinister aura largely because, in numerous cultures (including ancient Greece and nineteenth-century England), they were the site of executions and/or burials. In addition, people must have felt great trepidation on reaching an unanticipated fork in an unmarked road, for much could be lost if they took the wrong road.

CHOICE OF ROADS

In many examples of folktales involving choice of roads, the decision of which road to take is randomly made, illustrating the old adage, "If you don't know where you're going, any road will take you there." Historically, divination was practiced in a variety of cultures when people were confronted with a choice of roads. An example is given by Macdonald in which the Machinga of Tanzania place a knife in a horizontal position and lay two roots against the blade: "The traveler then stands pointing to one of the roads and says 'Shall I take this one?' and if the roots remain still fixed he takes it, but if they fall to the ground he chooses the other path" (1969, I:215).

An early depiction of divination in choice of roads occurs in the Old Testament, when Ezekiel speaks of the two possible routes, either to Jerusalem or to Ammon, that the king of Babylon could have taken when he came to a fork in the road: "For the king of Babylon stood at the parting of the way, at the head of the two ways, to use divination. He shook the arrows to and fro, he consulted the teraphim, he looked in the liver" (Ezekiel 21:21) (D1311.17.2, "Divination by magic arrow").

In some tales animals choose which road to take (B151, "Animal determines road to be taken"). It may be an ass, bull, cow, elephant, fox, dog, or bird that shows the way.

THE QUEST

In stories of quests, the hero is often at the outset presented with a fork in the road, necessitating a decision as to which route to take in order to reach the object of the quest. Very often, such stories involve three brothers. An example is AT 550, *The Bird, the Horse, and the Princess*. The story has three brothers setting out to search for a golden bird that has been stealing golden apples from their father's garden. Thompson states, "As the brothers leave, they find a place where three roads part and where inscriptions on each tell what will happen if that road is chosen. Each brother chooses a different road" (1977, 107; N122.0.1). The story is extremely popular both in oral and literary tradition. Thompson notes that it is "quite as well known in Scandinavia as it is in Italy and Russia and the Baltic states, and, indeed all the rest of Europe. It is almost equally popular in western and southern Asia, where it appears in a number of versions in Armenia, India, Indonesia, and central Africa, and is told by the French in Missouri" (1977, 107).

The tale is commonly known in Russia as "The Firebird," which Boris Zvorykin translated into French, along with three other Russian tales, in the 1920s in a volume called *L'Oiseau de feu et d'autres contes populaires russes*. In that version, a column stands where the roads diverge, and the inscription on it reads: "He who travels from the column on the road straight ahead will be cold and hungry; he who travels to the right will be safe and sound, but his horse will be killed; and he who travels to the left will be killed, but his horse will be safe and sound" (Onassis 1978, 6, 14).

Other tale types involving choice of roads include AT 300, *The Dragon-Slayer,* and AT 303, *The Twins or Blood-Brothers* (N772, "Parting at crossroads to go on adventures"). These tale types are often combined. In his *Folktales of Germany,* Ranke gives a tale called "The Three Brothers," which is a combination of these two as well as Type 304, *The Hunter.* In it three brothers go off into the world together.

> After they had been walking along for some time, they came to a big tree where three paths separated. The eldest one said to the others, "Brothers, now we have to part, for we cannot stay together all the time," and the others agreed. Since Hans had nothing left in his knapsack, he was given a little by his brothers, and before separating, they all put their knives into the tree and they decided that he who first came back to this place should look at the knives. If he found one of the knives particularly rusty, he would know that its owner was in difficulty, and he was to go along that one's way in order to help him if he was still alive. When this was settled, the oldest brother went to the right, the second one took the middle path, and Hans went to the left. (Ranke 1966, 53)

Thompson gives as another example of the choice of roads motif a story from the Miao of China in which three brothers part at a "mountain pass." Although there is no literal crossroads or fork in the road, the brothers take different paths on a quest.

THE METAPHORICAL CHOICE OF ROADS

The metaphorical use of the choice of roads motif has a long literary tradition stretching back to the Sermon on the Mount: "Enter ye in at the strait gate: for wide is the gate, and broad is the way, that leadeth to destruction, and many there be which go in thereat: Because strait is the gate, and narrow is the way, which leadeth unto life, and few there be that find it" (Matthew 7:13–14). In his study *The Pilgrimage of Life*, Chew gives numerous examples of the motif in early Christian, medieval, and Tudor-Stuart sources. For example, in *Reson and Sensuallyte,* John Lydgate (ca. 1370–1450) dreams that Dame Nature offers him the choice between the Road of Reason and the Road of Sensuality (Chew 1962:176).

In the Puritan tract *Histrio-Mastix* (1633), William Prynne speaks of two roads leading to two very different destinations: "The road to heaven is too steep, too narrow, for men to dance in and keep revel rout. No way is large or smooth enough for kippling roisters; for jumping, skipping dancing dames, but that broad, beaten, pleasant road, that leads to hell" (F171.2, "Broad and narrow road in otherworld").

Emily Dickinson's poem (xxii) in *Poems, Second Series* (1891) uses the image of life as a journey, with coming to a fork in the road signaling impending death:

> Our journey had advanced;
> Our feet were almost come
> To that odd fork in Being's road,
> Eternity by term.

Robert Frost wrote "The Road Not Taken" in 1915, supposedly inspired by walks taken in Gloucestershire with his friend Edward Thomas, who, after taking one road, would often regret not having taken the other one.

> Two roads diverged in a yellow wood,
> And sorry I could not travel both
> And be one traveler, long I stood . . .

According to Lawrance Thompson (1964) and other scholars, Frost meant the poem to be gently ironic, although the irony was lost both on the general public and on Thomas himself. The poem may have been informed by an experience at a crossroads that Frost recounts in a letter of February 10, 1912:

> Two lonely cross-roads that themselves cross each other I have walked several times this winter without meeting or overtaking so much as a single person on foot or on runners. The practically unbroken condition of both for several days after a snow or a blow proves that neither is much travelled. Judge then how surprised I was the other evening as I came down one to see a man, who to my own unfamiliar eyes and in the dusk looked for all the world like myself, coming down the other, his approach to the point where our paths must intersect being so timed that unless one of us pulled up we must inevitably collide. I felt as if I was going to meet my own image in a slanting mirror. Or say I felt as we slowly converged on the same point with the same noiseless yet laborious stride as if we were two images about to float together with the uncrossing of someone's eyes. I verily expected to take up or absorb this other self and feel the stronger by the addition for the three-mile journey home. But I didn't go forward to the touch. I stood still in wonderment and let him pass by; and that, too, with the fatal omission of not trying to find out by a comparison of lives and immediate and remote interests what could have brought us by crossing paths to the same point in a wilderness at the same moment of nightfall. Some purpose I doubt not, if we could but have made out. (Sergeant 1960, 87–88)

CROSSROADS

Murder and Burial at Crossroads

Sophocles says in *Oedipus the King* (ca. 429 BCE) that it is at a place where three roads cross that Oedipus meets and slays a man he does not know, who is, in fact, his father. Only later, when Jocasta tells Oedipus that King Laius was murdered at the meeting of three roads near Delphi, does Oedipus suspect that he is the murderer of Laius; still later he learns that Laius was his father, and that in murdering him Oedipus has fulfilled the first part of the terrible prophecy that he will kill his father and marry his mother. Aeschylus, in telling the story of Oedipus in *The Seven Against Thebes* (467 BCE), places the murder in a different location, but still specifies that it was a spot "where three roads meet" (Gould 1970, 92, n. 716). Gould notes, "At *Laws* 9. 873b, Plato specifies that patricides, fratricides, and infanticides, when they have been put to death, must be thrown 'naked out of the city at a designated place where three roads meet' . . . the Laws are full of ancient customs only very slightly reordered, so Plato may be preserving an old custom" (1970, 92, n. 716; E431.17, "Criminals buried at crossroads to prevent walking").

Similarly, in England it was the custom until 1823 that suicides be buried at a crossroads, with a stake driven through the body (E431.16.3. "Suicide buried at crossroads"). Although this practice was nowhere stated as law (Stephen 1996, iii, 105), it was so ingrained that it took the passage of a statute (4 George IV, c. 52) to stop it ("it shall not be lawful for any Coroner . . . to issue any Warrant or other Process directing the Interment of the Remains of Persons, against whom a Finding of *Felo de se* shall be had, in any public Highway; but that such Coroner or other Officer shall give Directions for the private Interment of the Remains of such Body of such Person *Felo de se,* without any Stake being driven through the Body of such person").

In the previous year, 1822, Lord Londonderry, Viscount Castlereagh, leader of the House of Commons, committed suicide, and in order to bury him in Westminster Abbey the coroner's verdict stated that he was "under a grievous disease of mind" when he killed himself. Lord Byron wrote in the preface to cantos VI–VIII of *Don Juan,* "if a poor radical . . . had cut his throat, he would have been buried in a cross-road, with the usual appurtenances of the stake and mallet" (Gates 1988, 5). Indeed, the following year a young man who killed himself was rudely buried at the crossroads formed by Eaton Street, Grosvenor Place, and the King's Road, although a contemporary report notes that a stake was not driven through the body (Gates 1988, 6). It may well have been the juxtaposition of the radically different treatments of the two foregoing suicides that spurred the statute abolishing crossroads burials.

Writing after the abolishment of the custom, two novelists preserve the memory of it. Emily Brontë, in *Wuthering Heights* (1847; set in 1771–1803), has Heathcliff angrily say in regard to burial arrangements for Hindley Earnshaw that "correctly . . . that fool's body should be buried at the crossroads, without ceremony of any kind. . . . he has spent the night in drinking himself to death deliberately!" (cited in Gates 1988, 8). In Thomas Hardy's short story "The Grave at the Handpost" (1897), the members of a choir, walking out to sing just before midnight one night near Christmas, see men working at a newly dug grave and they immediately understand whose it is. "The choir knew no particulars—only that [Sergeant Holway] had shot himself in his apple closet on the previous Sunday. . . . The coroner's jury returned a verdict of *felo de se.*" Accordingly, he is buried at "the junction of the four ways, under the handpost" without a coffin and with a stake driven through him.

It appears that crossroads have generally served as a place of burial in many times and places; examples include ancient India, where a *dagoba* or stupa (a mound in which the bones and ashes were placed) was erected at crossroads; Uganda, where stillborn children and suicides were buried at crossroads; and Hungary, where persons believed to have succumbed to the malice of a witch or demon were sometimes buried at crossroads (MacCulloch 1981, 331).

Magic and Fairies at Crossroads

Besides divination, various other magical rites as well as supernatural creatures are associated with forkings and crossroads. For example, in an attempt to repel the demons and ghosts that were thought to exist at crossroads, divinities were sometimes worshipped there (D1786, "Magic power at crossroads").

In most of the versions of the ballad "Tam Lin" in Child's *English and Scottish Popular Ballads,* the disenchantment of Tam Lin, who is held captive by the fairies, must occur at "Miles Cross" or some other "Cross," which is likely a crossroads. Tam Lin asks his mistress to go there that night and pull him down from his horse as the fairy procession approaches (F217.3, "Fairies assemble at cross-roads") in order to free him from their spell.

> Gloomy, gloomy, was the night,
> And eerie was the way,
> As fair Janet, in her green mantle,
> To Miles Cross she did gae.
> About the dead hour o the night
> She heard the bridles ring,
> And Janet was as glad o that
> As any earthly thing.

Besides fairies, other supernatural creatures associated with crossroads include the jinn in Arabic cultures, vampires in Russia, and witches in various parts of Europe (MacCulloch 1981, 331).

Guardians of the Crossroads

The divinities associated with crossroads were almost always deities of darkness. Among the ancient Greeks, the goddess Hecate was commonly portrayed in triple form with faces turned in three directions. Representations of her, called Hecateia, were set up at the crossing of three roads, and these places were considered sacred to her (Jung and Kerenyi 1969, 112). Travelers asked for her protection and made offering to her at crossroads, especially since, in her darker aspects, she was associated with the underworld and with ghosts and demons and could presumably keep them at bay (MacCulloch 1981, 333). The god Hermes also was associated with roads and crossroads, as well as with travelers, thieves, merchants, and boundaries; he was also the escort of the souls of the dead to the underworld. Statues called herms were erected as mile and boundary and direction markers and here too travelers would make offerings. The herms were famously decorated with erect phalluses, "the sexual organs as warders-off of evil spirits" (MacCulloch 1981, 332). Similar phallic symbols, *chimata-no-kami,* or "road-fork gods," and *sahi-no-kami,* "preventive deities," were set up at crossroads in Japan (332).

The ubiquitous African trickster god known as Esu-Elegbara (Nigeria) and Legba (Benin) bears a striking resemblance to Hermes. He has spread throughout the African diaspora and appears in folklore of the Caribbean, South America, and the United States. He is the messenger of the gods, the guardian of the crossroads, "a phallic god of generation and fecundity" and "master of the elusive, mystical barrier that separates the divine world from the profane" (Gates 1988, 6).

The Devil at the Crossroads

Handbooks of magic from the Middle Ages mention crossroads as a place to conjure the devil and perform other rites. The antiquity of this location for magical operations is attested in Mathers's translation of several ancient Hebrew manuscripts of kabbalistic magic, called *The Key of Solomon.* While Mathers stresses that these works are not concerned with black magic, the following instructions occur:

> The places best fitted for exercising and accomplishing Magical Arts and Operations are those which are concealed, removed, and separated from the habitations of men. Wherefore desolate and uninhabited regions are most appropriate, such as the borders of lakes, forests, dark and obscure places, old and deserted houses, whither rarely and scarce ever men do come . . . but best of all are cross-roads, and where four roads meet, during the depth and silence of night. (Mathers 1889, 84)

The crossroads figures in the Faust myth, an elaboration of the very old motif of the "Bargain with the devil" (M211). The character of Faust, who sells his soul to the devil, seems to have been based on an actual person. A chapbook published in Frankfurt in 1587 called *Historia von D. Johann Fausten* tells of a scholar who mastered

> not only the Holy Scriptures, but also the sciences of medicine, mathematics, astrology, sorcery, prophesy, and necromancy.... These pursuits aroused in him a desire to commune with the Devil, so—having made the necessary evil preparations—he repaired one night to a crossroads in the Spesser Forest near Wittenberg. Between nine and ten o'clock he described certain circles with his staff and thus conjured up the Devil. (Ashliman 2001)

In Nathaniel Hawthorne's story "Young Goodman Brown" (1835), the protagonist sets out one evening on an unspecified but "evil purpose":

> He had taken a dreary road, darkened by all the gloomiest trees of the forest. ... It was all as lonely as could be, and there is this peculiarity in such a solitude, that the traveler knows not who may be concealed by the innumerable trunks and the thick boughs overhead; so that with lonely footsteps he may yet be passing through an unseen multitude.

Soon enough, "at a crook in the road" he meets a mysterious stranger whom we recognize as the devil.

In the American South, there was a superstition circulating among blues musicians in the first half of the twentieth century that some had sold their souls to the devil to play as well as they did. When Robert Johnson returned to his fellow musicians in Banks, Mississippi, in 1932 after having traveled deep into the Mississippi Delta, his guitar playing was so accomplished that Son House is said to have voiced the belief that he had struck the bargain. Another musician, named Tommy Johnson (no relation to Robert), told his brother how he himself became so proficient on the guitar:

> You take your guitar and you go to where a road crosses that way, where a crossroad is. Get there, be sure to get there just a little 'fore 12:00. ... You have your guitar and be playing a piece there by yourself. ... A big black man will walk up there and take your guitar, and he'll tune it. And then he'll play a piece and hand it back to you. That's the way I learned to play anything I want. (Guralnick 1989, 18)

There is a rich tradition of motifs regarding choice of roads and crossroads in both folklore and literature; for additional motifs on roads (for example, C614, "Forbidden road. All roads may be taken except one"), see the *Motif-Index*.

Jane Garry

See also: Individuation.

REFERENCES

Ashliman, D.L. 2001. "The Faust Legend," www.pitt.edu/~dash/faust.html.

Chew, Samuel. 1962. *The Pilgrimage of Life*. New Haven, CT: Yale University Press.

Gates, Barbara T. 1988 [1949]. *Victorian Suicide: Mad Crimes and Sad Histories*. Princeton, NJ: Princeton University Press.

Gould, Thomas. 1970. *Oedipus the King by Sophocles: A Translation with Commentary*. Englewood Cliffs, NJ: Prentice Hall.

Guralnick, Peter. 1989. *Searching for Robert Johnson*. New York: E.P. Dutton.

Jung, C.G., and Karl Kerenyi. 1969 [1949]. *Essays on a Science of Mythology*. Trans. R.F.C. Hall. Princeton, NJ: Princeton University Press.

MacCulloch, J.A. 1981 [1908–1922]. "Cross-roads." In *Encyclopaedia of Religion and Ethics*, ed. James Hastings. Reprint, Edinburgh: T&T Clark; New York: Scribners.

Macdonald, Duff. 1969 [1882]. *Africana*. 2 vols. London: Dawsons. Orig. ed., London: Simpkin Marshall; Edinburgh: John Menzies; Aberdeen: A. Brown.

Mathers, S. Liddell MacGregor. 1889. *The Key of Solomon the King (Clavicula Salomonis)*. London: George Redway.

Monteiro, George. 1988. *Robert Frost and the New England Renaissance*. Lexington: University Press of Kentucky.

Onassis, Jacqueline, ed. 1978. *The Firebird and Other Russian Fairy Tales*. New York: Viking.

Ranke, Kurt, ed. 1966. *Folktales of Germany*. Trans. Lotte Baumann. Chicago: University of Chicago Press.

Sergeant, Elizabeth Shepley. 1960. *Robert Frost: The Trial by Existence*. New York: Holt, Rinehart and Winston.

Stephen, Sir James Fitzjames. 1996 [1883]. *History of the Criminal Law of England*. 3 vols. London: Routledge. Original ed. London: Macmillan.

Thompson, Lawrance, ed. 1964. *Selected Letters of Robert Frost*. New York: Holt, Rinehart and Winston.

Thompson, Stith. 1977 [1946]. *The Folktale*. Berkeley: University of California Press. Orig. ed. New York: Holt, Rinehart, and Winston.

Wise Old Man/Woman

Various Motifs

꩜

Found in mythology, legend, folktales, and literature, the wise old man or woman is a protective figure who comes to the aid of the hero in his or her journey or quest. "For those who have not refused the call," writes Joseph Campbell, "the first encounter of the hero-journey is with a protective figure (often a little old crone or old man) who provides the adventurer with amulets against the dragon forces he is about to pass" (Campbell 1973, 69). The motifs are N825, "Old person as helper"; N825.2, "Old man helper" (a motif in Types 307, 329, 480, 512); N825.3, "Old woman helper" (motif in Types 316, 400, 480, 707); H1233.1, "Old person as helper on quest"; H1233.1.1, "Old woman helps on quest" (motif in Type 400, 425); and H1233.1.2, "Old man helps on quest."

Sometimes a wizard, hermit, teacher, shepherd, seer, priest, or crone, the wise old man or woman bestows wisdom, useful knowledge, or a charm that is beneficial to the hero (Leeming 1997, 493). In "The Phenomenology of Spirit in Fairytales," Jung defines the wise old man as a spiritual archetype in "the guise of a magician, doctor, priest, teacher, professor, grandfather, or any other person possessing authority," who always appears when "insight, understanding, good advice, determination, planning, etc., are needed but cannot be mustered on one's own resources" (Jung 1990, 216). Jung illustrates the concept with an Estonian fairy tale ("How an Orphan Boy Unexpectedly Found His Luck") in which an abused orphan who has let a cow escape meets a little old man with a long gray beard who advises him not to return home to further punishment and provides him with a burdock leaf that magically changes into a boat when he needs to cross water. Thus the old man, representing wisdom and insight, points the way for the youth.

"For those who have not refused the call," writes Joseph Campbell, "the first encounter of the hero-journey is with a protective figure (often a little old crone or old man) who provides the adventurer with amulets against the dragon forces he is about to pass" (Motif N825.3, "Old woman helper"). From *Märchenbuch* (1861); illustrated by Adrian Ludwig Richter.

Campbell gives an example of the wise old woman in the East African legend of Kyazimba, in which a desperately poor man is searching for the land where the sun rises. On his journey, he encounters a decrepit little woman who, on learning the nature of his quest, wraps her garment around him and magically soars, transporting him above the earth to the zenith of the sun. There she intercedes for Kyazimba with a brilliant chieftain who sits feasting with his retainers. After receiving a blessing from the chieftain, Kyazimba is sent home and thereafter lives in prosperity.

The protective figure in American Indian mythology of the Southwest is Spider Woman, an underground, grandmotherly personage friendly to humans (Jobes 1961, 1483). In the story of the twin Navajo war gods who journey to the house of their father the Sun, Spider Woman temporarily appears from a subterranean chamber with beneficial advice that enables the young heroes to meet their father's tests and thus be acknowledged as his children. She also provides magic weapons to protect them against enemy gods (Bierhorst 2002, 98). In many other North American Indian test and hero tales, an unnamed woman, usually referred to as "grandmother," advises the hero "how to kill monsters, escape from dangerous situations, what path to take, how to overcome obstacles on his way, etc." (Leach and Fried 1949, 819). Glooscap, the culture hero of the Northeast Woodland tribes, appears to the Indians with a woman "whom he ever addressed as Grandmother—a very general epithet for an old woman. She was not his wife, nor did he ever have a wife" (Thompson 1929, 5). This figure is an example of Motif A31, "Creator's (or culture hero's) grandmother," which is primarily an Algonquian motif but occurs sporadically in the American West (Thompson 1929, 275).

In mythology, the wise old man or woman is usually a god or goddess. In Homer's *Odyssey,* the young Telemachus is guided in the search for his long-absent father Odysseus by Mentor (actually Athena, the goddess of wisdom, disguised as the wise old teacher) and by the master charioteer King Nestor, who "in his wisdom . . . tell[s] . . . history and no lies" (1992, 3.23–24). In the Sanskrit epic the *Mahabharata,* the god Krishna assumes the guise of an old man to guide the hero, Arjuna.

The wise old man motif also exists independently of the quest. An ancient Assyrian story about King Asarhaddon's wise counselor Achikar, found in a papyrus text of about 420 BCE, illustrates Motif H561.5, "Wisdom of hidden old man saves kingdom." This motif appears in folktales (Type 981 of the same title) around the world, including much of Europe, in Turkey, India, and China (Aarne and Thompson 1961, 345). In these tales, the wise old man does not function as a guide to a younger man on a quest, although he does provide needed guidance. The story, in brief, is that all old men are ordered killed, but one young man hides his father. When everything goes wrong in the hands of the young rulers, the old man comes forward, performs assigned tasks, and rescues the kingdom through his wisdom. In a Japanese variant, a son hides his mother after the ruler decrees that all old people must be killed. Meanwhile, the ruler is overthrown by an enemy who will spare his life only if three seemingly impossible tasks are performed: making a coil of rope out of ashes (H1021.1, "Task: making a rope of sand"), running a single thread through the length of a crooked log (H506.4, "Test of resourcefulness: putting thread through coils of snail shell"), and making a drum sound without beating it. The hidden old mother cleverly provides the answers to these riddles, thereby saving the life of the ruler, who then rescinds the edict against the aged (MacDonald and Sturm 2001, 225).

In Biblical legend, as Stith Thompson notes, King Solomon's wisdom is illustrated by many stories of kingly wisdom accreting to the Solomon cycle (Thompson 1979, 266).

Medieval literature and legend provide other examples of the wisdom figure. In Arthurian legend, the wise enchanter or wizard Merlin uses magic and his knowledge of the past and future to help young Arthur defeat his enemies and establish the Round Table (Elkhadem 1981, 138). Perhaps Merlin was the model for the wizard Gandalf, who guides the hobbit Frodo on his perilous quest to deliver the magic ring to its source in J.R.R. Tolkien's *Lord of the Rings* (1954–1955).

Apart from wisdom, the old man or woman often embodies a moral dimension as well: he or she will test a character and then reward or punish that character. Kindness and charity are rewarded while churlishness and selfishness are punished. There are many tales of this type (AT 480, *The Spinning Women by the Spring. The Kind and the Unkind Girls*); one of the most well known is the Grimms' tale "Mother Holle" (KHM 24), and Thompson notes that variants are found "over nearly the whole world." (Thompson 1979, 126) Psychologically, the figure of the wise old man or woman in these tales represents the spiritual function of the personality welling up from the unconscious.

Peter L. De Rose

See also: The Kind and Unkind.

REFERENCES

Aarne, Antii, and Stith Thompson. 1961. *The Types of the Folktale.* Helsinki: Suomalainen Tiedeakatemia.
Bierhorst, John. 2002. *The Mythology of North America.* New York: Oxford University Press.
Campbell, Joseph. 1973. *The Hero with a Thousand Faces.* 2d ed. Princeton, NJ: Princeton University Press.
Elkhadem, Saad. 1981. *The York Companion to Themes and Motifs of World Literature: Mythology, History, and Folklore.* Fredericton, NB: York Press.
Hansen, William. 2002. *Ariadne's Thread: A Guide to International Tales Found in Classical Literature.* Ithaca: Cornell University Press.
Homer. *The Odyssey.* 1992. Trans. Robert Fitzgerald. Intro. Seamus Heaney. New York: Knopf.
Jobes, Gertrude. 1961. *Dictionary of Mythology, Folklore, and Symbols.* 3 vols. New York: Scarecrow Press.
Jung, C.G. 1990. *The Archetypes and the Collective Unconscious.* 2d ed. Princeton, NJ: Princeton University Press.
Leach, Maria, and Jerome Fried, eds. 1949. *Funk and Wagnalls Standard Dictionary of Folklore, Mythology, and Legend.* 2 vols. New York: Funk and Wagnalls.
Leeming, David Adams, ed. 1997. *Storytelling Encyclopedia: Historical, Cultural, and Multiethnic Approaches to Oral Traditions Around the World.* Phoenix, AZ: Oryx Press.
MacDonald, Margaret Reed, and Brian W. Sturm. 2001. *The Storyteller's Sourcebook: A Subject, Title, and Motif Index to Folklore Collections for Children, 1983–1999.* Farmington Hills, MI: Gale Group.
Thompson, Stith. 1929. *Tales of the North American Indians.* Cambridge, MA: Harvard University Press.
Thompson, Stith. 1979 [1946]. *The Folktale.* New York: AMS Press. Orig. ed.: New York: Holt, Rinehart and Winston.

❀ P ❀

Society

Sister and Brother

Motif P253

❀

The basic kinship unit of brother and sister constitutes a theme ranging from the mundane to the spectacular and from the licit to the illicit. The sibling relationship is not dependency-based but is a relationship between equals; for a brother or a sister the other is a friend, a colleague, a companion, and a source of love and affection (Kerényi 1975, 113). The network of social interactional patterns stemming from this basic kinship tie encompasses an expanding circle of relatives, especially the roles of a woman's brother as a maternal uncle to her child (P253.0.1, "Sister's son," and P297, "Nephew (Sister's son)"; (Gummere 1901; Bell 1922). Yet the significance of this theme cannot be inferred from the available folklore indexes of global coverage.

In his *Motif-Index,* Thompson assigns the sister and brother motif to AT 450, *Little Brother and Little Sister.* In AT 450, the siblings escape from home and live together in the wilderness; the brother disobeys his sister and is transformed into a deer (or like animal); the sister is taken as wife by the king, and her brother helps save her and her newborn child from a rival's plot. Similarly, *The Types of the Folktale* cites Motif P253 only in association with AT 450 and gives a derivative of the Motif—P253.3, "Brother chosen rather than husband or son"—as the basis for AT 985, which bears an identical title (Aarne and Thompson 1964).

In spite of this seemingly infrequent occurrence of Motif P253 as reported in the two standard indexes, the sister and brother theme appears with great frequency in folk traditions as well as in all other facets of culture and society. It is found in most of the twenty-three chapters of the *Motif-Index*'s classificatory schema. For example, in the Mythological chapter the following motifs appear: "Brother-sister marriage of the gods" (A164.1), "Demigod son of king's unmarried sister by her brother" (A511.1.3.2), "Sun-brother and moon-sister" (A736.1.2), "Paradise lost because of brother-sister incest" (A1331.2), and "Brother-sister marriage of children of first parents" (A1552.3); under Magic, the following intricate motif appears: "Girl exchanges form with sorceress in order to visit her brother and get a son by him" (D45.4); under Tests, the motif "Brother unwittingly qualifies as bridegroom of sister in test" appears (H310.2); and under The Wise and the Foolish, the following erotic motif is listed: "Boy strikes at a fly on his sister's breast: it turns into nipple and girl thinks it due to brother's caress" (J1833.1.1); under Chance and Fate, the following motif is cited: "Brother and sister unwittingly in love with each other" (N365.3.1); under Society, we encounter such motifs as "Sister faithful to transformed brother" (P253.2), "Clever sister saves life of brother" (P253.8), and "Woman dies of sorrow for death of brother" (P253.9); under Captives and Fugitives, we find "Sister escapes to the stars to avoid marrying brother" (R321.1); and under Sex, we find such motifs as "Brother-sister marriage" (T415.5) and "Man unwittingly ravishes his own sister" (T471.1).

The explicit listings of the presence of the brother-sister theme in the various units designated in Aarne and Thompson's (1964) *The Types of the Folktale* is incomplete. Numerous tale types carry indicative titles such as *Girl Flees from Brother Who Wants to Marry Her* (AT 313E*), *The Faithless Sister* (AT 315), *The Cannibal Sister* (AT 315A, Motif G348§, "Sister as devastating cannibal"), *Little Brother and Little Sister* (AT 450, cited above), *The Maiden Who Seeks Her Brothers* (AT 451), *The Sister Seeking Her Nine Brothers* (AT 451A), *Brother and Sister* (AT 872*), and the sketchily listed *Clever Girl Frees Her Brother from Prison* (AT 879C*). Yet other tale types revolving around brother and sister do not carry labels that indicate the presence of the theme, nor is the theme provided in the general alphabetical index of the *Types of the Folktale*. These unlisted tale types in which the brother-sister motif plays a major role include the following: *Hansel and Gretel* (AT 327A), in which the siblings face treacherous parents and a dangerous external world, and *Gregory on the Stone* (AT 933), in which a son who was born of brother-sister incest is abandoned and undergoes penance. Also, the incestuous nature of the plot of *Brother and Sister Heal the King* (AT 613C*), in which the siblings flee from their father who wants them to marry each other, is not indicated; nor is it compared to its thematic match in AT 313E* or to the equally incestuous AT 510B, *The Dress of Gold, of Silver, and of Stars* (girl flees from her father who wants to marry her).

In other tale types, the brother-sister theme is less overt; nonetheless, it plays a significant psychological role in the development of the narrative's plot. Such is the case with AT 1538*, *The Jester-bride,* and AT 1542, *"The*

Clever Boy. Peik with his fooling-sticks," in which a trickster, with his sister as confederate, seduces the daughters and/or wives of the rich and powerful in his community. Also, the brother-sister theme is underreported in *The Three Golden Sons* (AT 707, III, d) in which a sister rescues her brother(s) (e.g., Grimm, no. 96; El-Shamy 1980, no. 9).

The theme of unwitting incest between brother and sister occurs in early Egyptian mythology (see below). It also occurs in the *Thousand and One Nights* Motif N365.3.4§, ‡"Man meets a girl of unknown genealogy and marries her; she proves to be his sister" ("The story of the King Omar Ibn al-Nu¿mân and of his sons Sharkan and Dau' el-Makân"; see Chauvin 6:112, no. 277). Meanwhile, consensual brother-sister incest is the core of the story told by "The First Mendicant," in which a brother and sister escape to a tomb abode to live together as husband and wife: they are miraculously stricken dead with a thunderbolt (Chauvin Society 5:196, no. 115).

The actual commission of incest between brother and sister, wittingly or unwittingly, has been designated as a new tale type: 932§–933, *Brother-sister Incest: The Sethian Complex*. In addition to the Icelandic text given above, it appears frequently in Middle Eastern traditions dating back to ancient times and continuing to the present—932A§ (formerly 0932§), *The Sister Who Desires a Son Sired by Her Brother Achieves Her Goal: The Unsuspecting Brother,* and 932B§, *A Mother's Own Daughter as Her Daughter-in-Law: Bride Behaves as a Daughter-in-Law* (El-Shamy 1999, nos. 49 and 44 respectively).

Beside the manifest expression of sexual desires, the brother-sister incest theme may occur in less overt terms. In narrating a tale, a tale-teller may be confused about who is who among its personae, unwittingly revealing brother-sister incest. In its strongest form, this psychological mechanism of identification may be called identity transformation, whereby one person is simply recast in the role of another.

Another case of ambiguity and character transformation is found in Sudanese and Egyptian renditions of AT 313E*. The Sudanese tale illustrates a girl's flight to avoid the advances of her incestuous brother, who has become infatuated with physical attributes. Yet the separation between brother and sister is often temporary and/or the girl marries a person who may symbolically be equated with her brother (El-Shamy 1999, no. 46). This situation is most vividly illustrated in another Sudanese text titled "The Son of Nimêr," narrated by a fifty-year-old widow: "The son of Nimêr once took his horse to the river. There he found a lock of hair with which he could [have been able to] tie his horse. He said, 'I'll marry the girl to whom this lock of hair belongs even if she happened to be my sister, Fâtimah.'" The sister runs away and hides inside an old man's skin. She is captured in that disguise by "the son of Nimêr." They play a game and in the end "the son of Nimêr beat the old man and tore the garment of dry skin that Fâtimah had, and there was a beautiful girl. They . . . got married" (El-Shamy 1999, 320, no. 46). Although the assumption is that the two characters in the son of Nimêr are unrelated, the psychological implications are evident: the girl marries either her brother, after having been recast in a different context, or a brother-substitute.

The same unintentional (noncognitive) "error" is manifested in the Egyptian rendition of the tale. In that incomplete text, the brother persuades his fleeing sister to climb down from a tree in which she sought refuge. Yet the incestuous act is expressed through the use of the formulaic ending "And they lived in prosperity and stability and begot boys and girls," thus indicating the same affective implications involved in the Sudanese variant (El-Shamy 1999, no. 46–1).

The Russian fairytale titled "Prince Danila Govorila" (given here with motif identifications and minor deletions) may be classified as a combination of AT 313E*, AT 1121, and a theme comparable to tale type 872B§, *The Murdered Sister Is Reincarnated and Betrothed to her Brother: The Talking Bed* (El-Shamy 1995, 427).

> A young prince was given a magic ring by a witch, with the stipulation that he must marry none but the girl whose finger the ring fits (new Motif H361.1§, ‡"Girl whom ring (bracelet, ankle bracelet, etc.) would fit to be chosen as bride"). When he grows up he goes in search of a bride, but the ring fits no one. So he laments his fate to his sister, who asks to try on the ring. It fits perfectly (new Motif H367§, ‡"Sister unwittingly qualifies as bride of brother in test"; H310.2, "Brother unwittingly qualifies as bridegroom of sister in test"). Thereupon her brother wants to marry her, but she thinks it would be a sin and sits at the door of the house weeping (new Motif C162.5.1§, ‡"Tabu: brother-sister marriage"). Some old beggars (Motif N826, "Help from beggar") comfort her and advise her: "Make four dolls and put them in the four corners of the room. If your brother summons you to the wedding, go, but if he summons you to the bedchamber, do not hurry!"
>
> After the wedding her brother summons her to bed (new Motif P605.5.2§, ‡"A boy's (man's) sister in bed (scene, image)"; T59.1§, ‡"Lovers' play (foreplay): embracing, kissing, necking, etc."). Then the four dolls begin to sing (new Motif N681.3.0.2§, "Incest accidentally averted: talking furniture (bed, ornaments, etc.)"; N454, "Conversation of objects overheard"):

> > Cuckoo, Prince Danila
> > Cuckoo, Govorila,
> > Cuckoo, he takes his sister,
> > Cuckoo, for a wife,
> > Cuckoo, earth open wide,
> > Cuckoo, sister fall inside.

The earth opens and swallows her up (Motif R327, "Earth opens to rescue fugitive"; F942.3.1, "Earth opens at woman's bidding to enclose her"). . . . She goes along under the earth until she comes to the hut of Baba Yaga (the Russian arch-witch) whose daughter kindly shelters her and hides her from the witch (G530.2, "Help from ogre's daughter (son)").

The two girls seize the old woman and put her in the oven, thus escaping the witch's persecution (cf. AT 1121, *Ogre's Wife Burned in His Own Oven*). They reach the prince's castle, where the sister is recognized by her brother's servant. But her brother cannot tell the two girls apart, they are so alike (Motif H161.0.1, "Recognition of person among identical companions"). So the servant advises him to make a test: the prince is to fill a skin with blood and put it under his arm. The servant will then stab him in the side with a knife and the prince is to fall down as if dead (Motif K1875, "Deception by sham blood. [By stabbing bag of blood, trickster makes dupe think that he is bleeding]"). The sister will then surely betray herself (Motif H421, "Tests of true lover"; J1171, "Judging by testing love"; Type 926L§, *Test of Habitual Behavior (Love-Dependence, Hate-Avoidance)*. Usually between mother and child, husband and wife, owner and pet, etc.). The sister throws herself upon her brother with a great cry, whereupon the prince springs up and embraces her. But the magic ring also fits the finger of the witch's daughter (Motif T101.1.6.1.1§, "Bride (sweetheart) in the likeness of groom's sister"), so the prince marries her and gives his sister to a suitable husband.

(Jung 1966, 222–224)

According to Jung, the four dolls in the four corners of the room prevent the commission of incest by forming the marriage quaternion (an exchange marriage involving two pairs of cross-siblings). Thus, by putting four in place of two, the four dolls form a magic simulacrum that prevents the incest by removing the sister to the underworld, where she discovers her alter ego. It may also be argued that she goes through the process of individuation, emerging as an independent person.

Jung elaborates further that the incest constitutes an evil fate, motivated by "kinship libido." Thus, incest cannot easily be avoided. He also asserts that the practical solution is a lesser form of still endogamous marriage: "The best compromise is therefore a first cousin. There is no hint of this in our fairy-stories, but the marriage quaternio is clear enough" (Jung 1966, 224).

This endogamous arrangement is considered the preferred form of marriage among many groups, especially Arabs—regardless of religious persuasion.

Two tales from Yemen, one narrated by an elderly Jewish woman and the other by a young, Muslim female university student, project the same incestuous trend and conclude in a manner comparable to Jung's "marriage quaternio" (El-Shamy 1979, 28; 1999, 299–304, no. 39).

A brother and sister live alone. The brother marries; his wife doesn't like his sister. She gives the sister something to eat and the sister becomes pregnant. The brother discovers the pregnancy through his wife. The wife and the brother bury the sister alive. A palm tree grows where she was buried. The tree helps women with their laundry; but it humiliates the brother's wife. At the insistence of the wife the palm tree is cut down. The tree transforms itself into an egg. An old woman finds the egg, takes it, and the sister secretly comes out of it to help the old woman with housework, then returns into the egg. The old woman discovers her. Meanwhile the brother accuses his wife of killing his sister, kicks her out and wanders penniless around the world. He searches the city where his sister is. The brother works for the king. "The brother [. . . sees] his sister" and falls in love with her. He asks the king for the girl in marriage. The king arranges for the two to wed. An angel warns the sister that she is about to marry her brother; she requests a number of beds to be made of various materials. The brother is about to consummate the marriage with her and each bed says, "How can one marry his sister [. . .]" Finally the sister reveals her identity; they return to their old home. The sister marries another man and the brother marries a good wife. (El-Shamy 1979, 28; Noy 1963, 129–131)

In both Yemeni versions, the sister on the wedding night leads her brother coquettishly—fully cognizant of his identity—from one bed to another. The beds speak up and wonder: "How could marriage between a brother and his sister be legitimate!"—designated as Motif N681.3.0.2§, "Incest accidentally averted: talking furniture (bed, chair, ornament, etc.)." After this extended seductive act, the sister tells her brother the truth. He gives up his plans to marry his sister and both return to their paternal home where each marries someone else.

THE BROTHER-SISTER MOTIF IN MYTHOLOGY

Union between cross-siblings (opposite sex) seems to provide an archetypal answer to the dilemma of how human life multiplied after the creation by a creator of the first human pair (Motif A1270, "Primeval human pair"). Ancient Egyptian, Greek, Hebrew, Arab, and numerous other groups espoused sacred ideologies based on this "sinful" principle. More recently, some contemporary Christian writers seem to reconcile themselves to this notion (archetype).

In ancient Egypt, Geb-and-Nut, Osiris-and-Isis, and Set-and-Nephthys are examples of divine brother-sister marriages (Ions 1968). In certain cases, love between the twins is reported to have been prenatal (Motif A164.1.0.1§, "Twin sister and brother in love even when in mother's womb") (El-Shamy 1995). A contemporary folk theme that may date back to ancient times is "Twin infant sister and brother nourished by suckling each other's thumbs" (Motif

T611.1.2§); this motif recurs in many Egyptian renditions of AT 707 (El-Shamy 1980, 65, no. 9).

Ordinary mortals copied the practice of their deities and divine kings, whose universal custom in Egypt was for the brother to marry one of his sisters. The custom of these marriages, which to us appear incestuous, was so firmly seated that the Ptolemies eventually complied with it. The celebrated Cleopatra had her two brothers in succession as husbands.

In Greek mythology, Zeus, god of the sky and ruler of the Olympian gods, is also husband to his sister Hera, with whom he fathers Ares, the god of war; Hebe, the goddess of youth; Hephaestus, the god of fire; and Eileithvia, the goddess of childbirth. It is reported that Zeus and Hera had their first sexual experience together as youths while still living in their parents' abode; Zeus compares subsequent intercourse with Hera to that first encounter (Motif J10.1.1§, "Unforgettable first experience"; J10.1.1.2§, ‡"Unforgettable first intercourse"; El-Shamy 1995; 2004, 1088).

Other famous Greek brother-sister couples are Oceanus, who marries his sister Tethys, and Cronus, who is wed to his sister Rhea.

In *Metamorphoses,* the Roman poet Ovid (born in 43 BCE) presents a series of narratives about the history of the world. One of the myths is about Byblis and her twin brother Caunus. The cross-siblings are the children of Miletus and Tragasia, who live on Crete. Byblis falls into a consuming love for her brother Caunus. When her erotic love is not welcomed, she writes him a letter citing many gods who were siblings and together as husband and wife. The brother, disgusted with the idea of incest, flees to foreign lands. But the lovesick sister, in tears, pursues him across many countries. When she arrives in Phoenicia, her torrential tears dissolve her, and she turns into a spring. The city in which this transformation takes place is named Byblis after her (Ovid 1955, 215–221).

According to the Shinto creation myth, the islands of Japan are the "children" of the copulating brother-and-sister deities Izanagi and Izanami, who also give birth to the sun goddess Amateratsu, mythical progenitor of the Yamato line of emperors. These two siblings are descended from seven pairs of brothers and sisters who appeared after heaven and earth had separated out of chaos. A mighty bridge floats between the heavens and the primeval oceans; standing on this, Izanagi and Izanami stir the waters below with a jeweled spear to form the first land mass. Their union gives birth to the islands of Japan and to various deities.

What may now be termed "incestuous" cross-sibling unions account for the beginning of life among Jews, Christians, and Muslims. Religious texts say that Adam and Eve were the only human first pair that God created; they lived as man and wife and multiplied.

A mythical account of the origin of Satan (Eblis, Lucifer) as a failure to comply with a paternal command for brother-sister marriages appears in the *Thousand Nights and a Night.* So radically different is this account from the Qur'anic and biblical dogma that no oral rendition or other written counterparts of it have so far been reported. Moreover, it seems that virtually all literary commentators ignore the significance of its incestuous nature. The story is told by the mythical character Ṣakhr, the king of jinn, to a human seeker of the ultimate truth. This episode may be titled "Eblis: Disobedient Son Transformed":

> As for us [jinn, said Sakhr], the Almighty Maker created us of the fire; for the first that he made in Jahannam were two of His host, whom he called Khalit and Malit. Now Khalit was fashioned in the likeness of a lion, with a tail like a tortoise twenty years' journey in length and ending in a member masculine; while Malit was like a pied wolf whose tail was furnished with a member feminine. Then Almighty Allah commanded the tails to couple and copulate and do the deed of kind, and of them were born serpents and scorpions, whose dwelling is in the fire, that Allah may therewith torment those whom He casteth therein; and these increased and multiplied. Then Allah commanded the tails of Khalit and Malit to couple and copulate a second time, and the tail of Malit conceived by the tail of Khalit and bore fourteen children, seven male and seven female, who grew up and intermarried one with other. All were obedient to their sire, save one who disobeyed him and was changed into a worm which is Iblis. (Burton 1885–1888, 5:319)

Another curious aspect of this myth is that it endorses twin brother-sister marriage and metes out humiliating punishment for the one who opposes it (an example of Jung's "kinship libido"). In this respect, the myth contradicts earlier accounts of first marriages among the children of Adam and Eve. The Qur'an mentions only the incident of fratricide due to acceptance of an offering from one brother but not from the other (Qur'an 5:27). Yet parareligious literature argued that first marriages were deemed legitimate only between cross twins. The first murder was argued to have been a fratricide committed over tabooed marriage to one's own twin sister—Motif A1297.1§, "Cain killed Abel in order not to lose own twin sister as wife" (El-Shamy 1995).

Some evidence suggests that an East European (Hungarian) tale may have been derived from our present narrative-complex (or vice versa). The tale belongs to AT 613C*, *Brother and Sister Heal the King,* although *The Types of the Folktale* ignores the brother-sister incestuous theme and stresses the healing aspect. It may be presumed that characterizing this plot as a subtype of AT 613 was done on the basis of the shared theme of magic healing, rather than the flight of brother and sister to escape incest. Additionally, the classifier

(Thompson) perceived the female protagonist as a daughter to a father rather than as a sister to a brother. Consequently, this classification is nonsystemic. However, the description of the contents of AT 613C* provides evidence of its presumed link (or parallelism) to our present narrative-complex.

> A king with seven sons and seven daughters wants his sons to marry his daughters but the youngest son and daughter do not agree to this plan and leave. They sleep under a tree. The daughter has a dream about an ill king who could be healthy again if he takes a bath in the water coming from that tree." [The sister (daughter) masks as a man and, along with her brother, heals the king, who marries her afterward.] (Aarne and Thompson 1961/1964).

The tale type and the myth share the following pivotal themes: the number of brothers and sisters, the demand by the father, the rejection of the incestuous marriage by the children, and the healing of the king (which appears at the close of the *Thousand Nights and a Night* narrative-complex) (Burton 1885–1888, 5:389–394). However, the determination as to whether AT 615C* is actually related to our myth or whether the similarities are archetypal (coincidental) must await further research.

From the above, it may be concluded that the brother-sister theme is underrepresented in folkloristic theory and literature. This fact reflects a corresponding sketchy representation in psychological theory, especially the Freudian psychoanalytic and neopsychoanalytic approaches.

BROTHERS AND SISTERS IN LITERATURE

In literature, androgynous mergings often occur between male and female twins. As pointed out above, opposite-sex twins are a recurring symbol in literary works: "Throughout European literature, from the Greeks onward, the 'identity' of these twins has been continually stressed, as have in more outspoken periods, the incestuous impulses of the pair" (Freeman 1988, 55–56). In addition to Ovid's *Metamorphoses,* Freeman points out that in book 3 of the epic poem *The Faerie Queene* (1590–1596), Edmund Spenser describes opposite-sex twins enclosed in their mother's womb displaying an urge toward union with each other (Motif A164.1.0.1§, "Twin sister and brother in love even when in mother's womb"). Another literary work that portrays the strong attraction between opposite-sex twins is John Barth's novel *The Sot-Weed Factor,* in which Anna is driven toward fusion with her twin brother, Ebenezer. In a manner that recalls the love letter that the Roman Byblis of Crete wrote to her brother, Anna evokes a comparison from Burlingame (another character in the story) with Aristophanes' version of the ancient split of the whole into parts that eternally seek each other:

> Your sister is a driven and fragmented spirit, friend; the one half of her soul yearns but to fuse itself with yours, whilst the other half recoils at the thought. It's neither love nor lust she feels for you, but a prime and massy urge to coalescence. . . . As Aristophanes maintained that male and female are displaced moieties of an ancient whole, and wooing but their vain attempt at union, so Anna . . . repines willy-nilly for the dark identity that twins share in the womb, and for the well-nigh fetal closeness of their childhood. (Barth 1960, 117)

In a similar manner, the hero of Lord Byron's "Manfred" (1817) sees his own likeness in his twin sister, for whom he expresses a passionate love. And Thomas Mann's story "Wälsungenblut" ("Blood of the Walsung," 1921) depicts Siegmund and Sieglinde, a brother and sister from a rich family who find themselves in sexual embrace (Freeman 1988, 55–56).

Arabic literature is replete with expressions of affection and strong bonding between brother and sister. Perhaps one of the most celebrated examples is the work of the pre-Islamic (mid-seventh century CE) poet nicknamed al-Khansâ'. She lost her brother, Sakhr (no relation to Sakhr the king of jinn mentioned above) and spent the remainder of her life eulogizing him in heart-wrenching poems (Motif P253.9.1§, "Sister becomes insane due to death of brother. (The Khansâ' Syndrome)"; Type 971C§, *Insanity (Death) from Death of Beloved Sibling (Brother or Sister). (The Khansâ' Syndrome); El-Shamy, 2004, 1020).

Nagîb Mahfuz, the Egyptian Nobel-laureate for literature (1988), gives a modern example of the brother-sister bond. The setting is Cairo across three generations, starting in the 1910s and concluding with the 1950s. In his autobiographical trilogy, the novelist presents himself as the family's youngest child, Kamal; he has an awe-evoking father, a kind and loving mother, two brothers, and two sisters, Khadeejah and 'Aishah. Mahfuz describes Kamal's love for his sister 'Aishah, closest to him in age.

> Kamal's love and emotional attachment to 'Aishah were deep. . . . He responded to her love with love to the extent that he would not drink a swallow of water out of the water pot without inviting her to drink ahead of him so that he would place his lips on the spot which had been wetted by the moisture of her mouth. (El-Shamy 1976, 58–59)

POPULAR CULTURE

A Japanese motion picture, *The Profound Desire of the Gods* (1968), which takes place on a remote rural island of Japan, illustrates the centrality of the brother-sister theme in the native traditional culture. The prominent director

Shohei Imamura is reported to have used the Shinto creation myth (cited above) as an emotional backdrop for the film. The plot's protagonists include a brother and sister who are lovers; the sister is regarded as a shamaness by her tribe. In local legend, a similar union spawned the island's early population. Kim argues that in older times such an incestuous union would not have been seen as a serious violation of social mores. Currently, however, the spread of modern values makes the lovers' fellow tribal folk ashamed of their old customs. Consequently, they persecute the siblings for breaking the incest taboo.

In the motion picture trilogy *Star Wars, The Empire Strikes Back,* and *The Return of the Jedi* (1977, 1980, 1983), Princess Leia and Luke Skywalker seem to be falling in love. However, their love cannot be fulfilled for they prove to be brother and sister (Motif T415.4, "Two lovers give each other up when they learn that they are brother and sister").

In *The Shipping News* (2002), a sister exacts revenge against her brother who had raped her during their early youth (Motif T471.9.1§, ‡"Incestuous rape: brother (sober) rapes his sister"). She pours his cremated remains into a toilet and relieves herself on them (Motif E478.1§, ‡"Indignities to corpse (by living person)").

CONCLUSION

Ernest Jones argues that Freud's adherence to the Oedipal tale limited his vision into the abundant myths that told of the brother-sister marriage as well as the love and Eros between opposite-sex siblings (Jones 1949, 157–158). This psychoanalytic dominance has also been characteristic of the study of folklore, where the Oedipal school of interpretation allows for no alternate approaches.

It has been shown in sociocultural context from Ireland that certain family living conditions are conducive to the occurrence of actual incest. However, when compared to parent-child (Oedipal) incest, brother-sister incest proved to be "free of gross personality disorder, neurosis or psychosis" (Lukianowicz 1972, 309); this finding may also be extended to Egypt (El-Shamy 1981, 320). Therefore, Jung's archetypes related to the sister and brother theme, though developed independently of actual social interactional conditions, offer a more adaptive system for dealing with kinship in general and the brother-sister bond in particular.

Hasan El-Shamy

See also: Incest; Individuation; Hermaphroditism.

REFERENCES

Aarne, Antti, and Stith Thompson. 1964 [1961]. *The Types of the Folktale: A Classification and Bibliography.* 2d rev., FFC no. 74. Helsinki: Folklore Fellows Communications.

al-Tha¿labî, Ahmad Ibn Muhammad. n.d. *kitâb qisas al-'anbiyâ' al-musammâ bi al-¿arâ'is* (The Book of Prophets' Stories, Labeled: *al-¿arâ'is*). Cairo (no publisher).

Barth, John. 1960. *The Sot-weed Factor.* New York: Doubleday.

Bell, C.H. 1922. *The Sister's Son in the Mediaeval German Epic.* Berkeley: University of California Press.

Burton, Richard, trans. and ed. 1885–1888. *The Book of the Thousand Nights and a Night: A Plain and Literal Translation of The Arabian Nights Entertainments.* 10 vols. London: H.S. Nichols.

Chauvin, Victor. 1892–1922. *Bibliographie des ouvrages arabes ou relatifs aux Arabes: publiés dans l'Europe chrétienne de 1810 à 1885.* 12 vols. Liége: H. Vaillant-Carmanne.

Christian Answers Network. www.christiananswers.net/q-aig/aig-c004.html.

El Shamy, Hasan M. 1976. "The Traditional Structure of Sentiments in Mahfouz's Trilogy: A Behavioristic Text Analysis." In *Al-Arabiyya: Journal of the American Association of Teachers of Arabic* 9 (October): 53–74.

———. 1979. *Brother and Sister. Type 872: A Cognitive Behavioristic Analysis of a Middle Eastern Oikotype.* Folklore Monograph Series, No. 8. Bloomington: Indiana University Press.

———. 1980. *Folktales of Egypt: Collected, Translated and Annotated with Middle Eastern and African Parallels.* Chicago: University of Chicago Press.

———. 1981. "The Brother-Sister Syndrome in Arab Family Life: Socio-cultural Factors in Arab Psychiatry: A Critical Review." *International Journal of Sociology of the Family,* Special Issue, *The Family in the Middle East,* ed. Mark C. Kennedy. 11 (2): 313–323.

———. 1982: "Belief Characters as Anthropomorphic Psychosocial Realities." In *al-kitâb al-sanawî li-ᶜilm al-'igtimâᶜ* (Annual Review of Sociology) 3: 7–36; Arabic abstract, 389–393.

———. 1995. *Folk Traditions of the Arab World: A Guide to Motif Clarification.* Bloomington: Indiana University Press.

———. 1999. *Tales Arab Women Tell and the Behavioral Patterns They Portray.* Bloomington: Indiana University Press.

———. 2004. *Types of the Folktale in the Arab World: A Demographically Oriented Approach.* Bloomington: Indiana University Press.

Franz, Marie-Louise von. 1990. *Individuation in Fairy Tales.* Boston: Shambhala.

Freeman, Alma S. 1988. "Androgyny." In *Dictionary of Literary Themes and Motifs,* ed. Jean-Charles Seigneuret. Westport, CT: Greenwood.

Gummere, Francis B. 1901. *Sister's Son.* Oxford. "Offprint from an English Miscellany Presented to Dr. Farnwell."

Hamilton, Terrick, trans. 1981 [1819]. *Antar: A Bedoueen Romance.* Intro. Ben Harris McClary. Delmar, NY: Scholars' Facsimiles and Reprints.

Haykal, Muhammad Husayn. 1967 [1914]. *Zaynab: manâdhir wa 'akhlâq rîfiyyah* (Zaynab: Rural Scenes and Manners). 3d ed. Cairo: Maktabat al-Nahdah al-Mirīyah.

Ions, Veronica. 1968. *Egyptian Mythology.* Middlesex: Hamlyn.

Jones, Ernest. 1949. *Hamlet and Oedipus: The Oedipus Complex as an Exploration of Hamlet's Mystery.* New York: Doubleday.

Jung, C.G. 1966. *The Practice of Psychotherapy: Essays on the Psychology of the Transference and Other Subjects.* Trans. R.F.C. Hull. 2d ed. Bollingen Series XX. New York: Pantheon.

Kerényi, Karl. 1975. *Zeus and Hera: Archetypal Images of Father, Husband, Wife.* Trans. Christopher Holme. Princeton, NJ: Princeton University Press.

Kim, Nelson. 2003. www.sensesofcinema.com/contents/directors/03/imamura.html.

Lukianowicz, N. 1972. "Incest." *British Journal of Psychiatry* 120: 301–313.

Mahfûz, Nagîb. 1991, 2001 (Cairo trilogy): 1 (1991): *Palace of Desire* (Bayna al-Qasrayn). Trans. William Maynard Hutchins, Lorne M. Kenny, Olive E. Kenny. Egypt: American University in Cairo Press; 2 (1991): *Palace Walk* (Qasr al-Shawq). Trans. William Maynard Hutchins and Olive E. Kenny. New York: Anchor Books/Doubleday; 3 (2001): *Sugar Street* (al-Sukkariyyah). Trans. William Maynard Hutchins and Angele Botros Samaan. Egypt: American University in Cairo Press.

Noy, Dov. 1963. *Jefet Schwili Erzählt.* Berlin: W. de Gruyter.

Ovid. 1955. *Metamorphoses.* Trans. Mary M. Innes. London: Penguin.

Step Relatives

Motif P280

❀

"Stepmothers hate their husband's children." This proverbial statement from the Iraqi folktale "The Little Red Fish and the Clog of Gold" (Bushnaq 1986, 181; AT 510A, *Cinderella*) expresses a sentiment found in thousands of tales around the world. There are many reasons why fairy-tale villains are so often cast as stepmothers (P282, "Stepmother").

To begin with, mortality rates were very high in the preindustrial times when most traditional fairy tales were evolving. Economic pressure to remarry quickly following the death of a spouse led to many matrimonial mismatches, or at least the expectations of the twenty-first century would label them as such. Substantial differences in emotional makeup and age were common. For a child to have a stepparent was not unusual, and often the replacement parent would be quite unlike the deceased one. But why are the female stepparents, rather than their male counterparts, so often cast as villains by traditional storytellers? This familiar observation is at first view all the more puzzling when one considers that household stories were transmitted primarily by women. One explanation is socialization, for in a strongly patriarchal society no one, not even in a fantasy tale, would be comfortable laying too much blame on male characters. Further, by placing other mother figures in bad light, the female storytellers could make themselves look good by comparison. These tales of abusive females also serve as a warning to the man of the house, who—given the realities of mortality—soon might be looking for a new wife.

Moreover, these accounts may reflect the workings of a "selfish gene," to quote sociobiologist Richard Dawkins (1976), theorizing about an inherent tendency for all living things to promote their own genetic material to future generations. If true, such theories would explain a natural proclivity for a stepparent to favor his or her own offspring over those of a new spouse. Recent sociological studies indicate that this may be the case. See, for example, Daly and Wilson (1999), Case and Paxson (2000), and Case, McLanahan, and Lin (2000).

Whether or not the evil stepmothers of folklore reflect a past or present reality, they serve a number of important psychological functions, as pointed out by Bruno Bettelheim (1976, 66–73) and others. Fairy tales provide a socially acceptable outlet for the venting of pent-up aggressive feelings toward authority figures. Thus Hansel and Gretel (KHM 15; AT 327A, *Hansel and Gretel*) kill the witch who has both nurtured and terrorized them; then, upon returning home, they discover that their stepmother has died. In other tales, the previously victimized stepchildren directly witness (or perhaps even order) the execution of their stepmothers, and these are not gentle deaths, as illustrated by a few more examples from the Grimms' collection. Snow-White's stepmother is forced to dance herself to death wearing red-hot iron shoes (KHM 53; AT 709, *Snow-White*). Her counterpart in "Little Brother and Little Sister" (KHM 11; AT 450, same title) is burned to death. The murderous stepmother in "The Juniper Tree" (KHM 47; AT 720, *My Mother Slew Me, My Father Ate Me. The Juniper Tree*) is crushed by a millstone, dropped on her by a bird, a reincarnation of the stepson she killed earlier in the tale.

A stepmother's own daughter, whom she favors at the expense of the heroine, often shares the older woman's punishment. In the Grimms' "The White Bride and the Black Bride" (KHM 135; AT 403A, *The Wishes*), the evil stepmother and stepsister are stripped naked, placed in a barrel studded with nails, then pulled through the countryside by a horse. Two tales from the Orient are even more drastic. Both the Vietnamese "Tam and Cam" (Thang and Lawson 1993, 75–89; AT 510A, *Cinderella*) and the Indian "Teja and Teji" (Ramanujan 1991, 219–224; AT 511, *One-Eye, Two-Eyes, Three-Eyes*) end with the execution of the scheming stepsisters, whose flesh is then fed to their conspiracy partners, their own mothers.

In addition to providing graphic fantasies of revenge on authority figures, tales about wicked stepmothers also assist children in addressing their ambivalent feelings toward their closest parent, who is at once both nurturer and disciplinarian. By placing a hateful being in the revered office of motherhood, storytellers provide a character with two mutually contradictory parts, thus helping children cope with the often chaotic demands of growing up. This ambiguity is reflected in countless folktales and is especially obvious in some of the Grimms' best-known stories. Particularly revealing is their characterization of the woman who badgers her husband into abandoning Hansel and Gretel in the woods. In the Grimms' original version of this tale (1812), the shrewish woman is unambiguously identified as the children's mother, not their stepmother. However, in their final version (1856), they introduce her as a *Stiefmutter* (stepmother) but then proceed to call her *Mutter* (mother) twice in the text, and simply *Frau* (wife or woman) fourteen times.

Another infamous stepmother in the Grimms' collection also began her fairy-tale career as a mother. In the first edition of "Little Snow-White" (1812), the jealous queen who tries to kill the beautiful princess is clearly identified as the heroine's mother. In the second edition (1819), the Grimms added the explanation that Snow-White's mother died during childbirth and that the jealous queen was the father's second wife, hence Snow-White's stepmother. Yet another ambiguous mother-stepmother is found in the Grimms' "The Twelve Brothers" (KHM 9; AT 451, *The Maiden Who Seeks Her Brothers*). Here the evildoer is the heroine's mother-in-law, the king's mother. She is called "mother" until the end of the tale when her perfidy is revealed, and then, we read, "the wicked stepmother was brought before the court and placed in a barrel filled with boiling oil and poisonous snakes, and she died an evil death." It seems, in this story at least, that the word "stepmother" has been redefined as "unworthy mother." This extended definition is authenticated in the dictionaries of several European languages. For example, *Webster's Third New International Dictionary* (1966) lists among the definitions of *stepmother*, "one that fails to give proper care or attention." No corresponding negative definition for *stepfather* is given.

A child's ambivalent feelings toward maternal authority are further demonstrated when one compares different versions of the same tale where storytellers have assigned the same role to different mother figures. Three Type 511 stories, all with essentially the same plot, illustrate this point. In the Grimms' "One-Eyes, Two-Eyes, and Three-Eyes" (KHM 130), the villain is the heroine's mother. In "The Wicked Stepmother" from Kashmir (Knowles 1893, 127–129), she is, as the title indicates, the stepmother. And in "Teja and Teji" from India (Ramanujan 1991, 219–224), the villain is the father's elder wife in a polygynous marriage.

Almost every tale featuring an abusive stepmother asks implicitly, "Why does the abused child's father permit this mistreatment?" But this question is rarely posed directly, much less answered. The German proverb, "Whoever has a stepmother also has a stepfather" (Wander 1867, 4, col. 854) refers to a perceived inability or unwillingness of fathers to curb stepmothers' cruelty, a major subtext in fairy tales, and one that for the most part remains unmentioned. In too many tales to enumerate, the widowed father, having taken a new wife, simply disappears from the storyteller's view, and the conflict between the new mistress of the house and her stepchildren unfolds apparently without his knowledge and certainly without his intervention. One notable exception is the Russian tale "Baba Yaga" (Afanas'ev 1975, 363–365, AT 313H*; *Flight From the Witch*), where the heroine's father, after establishing his wife's guilt, shoots her to death.

A curious detail in many folktales about wicked stepmothers is the matchmaking role of the father's daughter, thus laying part of the guilt for future abuse on the victim herself. An extreme example is found in "The Cat Cinderella" from Basile's *Pentamerone* (1932) (1:6; AT 510A). As the story opens, the heroine kills her cruel stepmother, hoping afterward to make a match between her father and a more affable woman. But her second stepmother turns out to be even more abusive than was the first, and to make matters worse, she brings into the marriage six daughters of her own that she had kept in hiding until then.

A number of tales, including the Grimms' "Three Little Men in the Woods" (KHM 13; AT 403B, 480), begin with the depiction of two girlfriends, one the daughter of a widow, the other the daughter of a widower. The widow approaches the man's daughter with the straightforward proposal, "Tell your father that I would like to marry him, and then you shall wash yourself in milk every morning and drink wine, but my own daughter shall wash herself in water and drink water." The heroine convinces her father, who is at first very reluctant, to marry the widow. Predictably, the stepmother keeps none of her promises, instead viciously turning against her stepdaughter, while favoring her own daughter at every turn. Also predictably, the stepmother's and stepdaughter's cruelty is repaid in kind. At the story's end, the king (who in the meantime has married the heroine) places the two evil ones into a barrel pierced with nails and rolls them down a hill into water.

In keeping with the "selfish gene" theory mentioned above, the cruelty of fairy-tale stepmothers is not entirely arbitrary. Typically a stepmother's abuse is motivated by her attempts to promote the welfare of her own offspring, usually one or more daughters, the heroine's stepsisters (P284). In her mind, and probably rightly so, her own daughters are in competition with their stepsister for limited rewards, typically a wealthy and powerful husband. Most Cinderella stories (AT 510A), the world's most popular folktale, center around such a competition between stepsisters. Most versions of "The Black and the White Bride" (AT 403, 403A, 403B) and "Little Brother and Little Sister" (AT 450) also feature stepsisters competing for a husband. In each of these tale types, the evil stepsister (with the help of her mother) is willing to kill her virtuous counterpart, but the murdered heroine is miraculously brought back to life, and her stepsister and stepmother are duly punished. Another tale type featuring the competition between stepsisters is "The Kind and the Unkind Girls" (AT 480), but here the competition is more for wealth than for marriage, with the reward, as one would expect, going to the kind and generous girl, rather than to her unkind and selfish stepsister.

In preindustrial households, competition among male children must have been just as fierce as that among their female counterparts. There are a great many international folktales depicting fraternal rivalry, but the antagonists are virtually always identified as brothers, not stepbrothers (P283). Similarly, stepfathers (P282) play a much smaller role in traditional folktales than do stepmothers. One notable exception is the Gypsy tale "The Little Bull-Calf" from England (Jacobs n.d., 186–191; AT 511A, 300), which begins when the hero's father dies, "and his mother got married again to a man that turned out to be a very vicious stepfather, who couldn't abide the little boy." At the story's end, the hero marries a princess and takes over the kingdom, and "then his stepfather came and wanted to own him, but the young king didn't know such a man." Extrapolating from this and previously discussed tales, one might conclude that vicious fairy-tale stepmothers are tortured to death, whereas their male counterparts are merely disowned.

D.L. Ashliman

REFERENCES

Afanas'ev, Aleksandr. 1975. *Russian Fairy Tales.* New York: Pantheon Books.

Basile, Giambattista. 1932. *The Pentamerone.* Translated from the Italian of Benedetto Croce. Ed. N.M. Penzer. 2 vols. New York: Dutton. First published 1634–1636 as *Lo Cunto de li Cunti.*

Bettelheim, Bruno. 1976. *The Uses of Enchantment: The Meaning and Importance of Fairy Tales.* New York: Alfred A. Knopf.

Bushnaq, Inea, ed. and trans. 1986. *Arab Folktales.* New York: Pantheon.

Case, Anne, Sara McLanahan, and I-Fen Lin. 2000. "How Hungry Is the Selfish Gene?" Cited in *Princeton University Research Notes,* September, www.princeton.edu/pr/news/notes/00/09-september.htm.

Case, Anne, and Christina Paxson. 2000. "Mothers and Others: Who Invests in Children's Health?" Cited in *Princeton University Research Notes,* September, www.princeton.edu/pr/news/notes/00/09-september.htm.

Daly, Martin, and Margo Wilson. 1999. *The Truth about Cinderella: A Darwinian View of Parental Love.* New Haven: Yale University Press.

Dawkins, Richard. 1976. *The Selfish Gene.* Oxford: Oxford University Press.

Jacobs, Joseph. n.d. *English Fairy Tales.* New York: A.L. Burt.

Knowles, J. Hinton. 1893. *Folk-Tales of Kashmir.* London: Kegan Paul, Trench, Trübner.

Ralston, W.R.S. 1873. *Russian Folk-Tales.* London: Smith, Elder.

Ramanujan, A.K. 1991. *Folktales from India: A Selection of Oral Tales from Twenty-two Languages.* New York: Pantheon Books.

Steel, Flora Annie. 1894. *Tales of the Punjab: Told by the People.* London: Macmillan.

Thang, Vo Van, and Jim Lawson. 1993. *Song Ngu, Truyên Dân Gian Viêt Nam: Vietnamese Folktales.* Danang: Danang Publishing House. Vietnamese and English on facing pages.

Wander, Karl Friedrich Wilhelm. 1867. *Sprichwörter-Lexikon: Ein Hausschatz für das deutsche Volk.* 5 vols. Leipzig: F.A. Brockhaus.

Webster's Third New International Dictionary of the English Language. 1966. Springfield, MA: G. and C. Merriam.

❀ Q ❀

Rewards and Punishments

The Kind and Unkind

Motif Q2

❈

The motif of the kind and the unkind (Q2, "Churlish person disregards requests of old person (animal) and is punished. Courteous person (often youngest brother or sister) complies and is rewarded") is also found in multiple tale types, the most famous being AT 480, *The Spinning Woman at the Well.* Thompson notes that "a cursory examination of appropriate bibliographical works shows nearly six hundred versions" of this tale type (1977, 126). While addressing uncomfortable family problems such as parent-child hostility and sibling rivalry, this folktale tests the hero or heroine's character (H1550, "Tests of character")—specifically, kindness (Q40, "Kindness rewarded"), generosity (Q42, "Generosity rewarded"), and politeness (Q41, "Politeness rewarded").

Tales about kind and unkind girls follow a typical plotline. A stepmother mistreats her good stepdaughter and dotes upon her selfish, impolite, and usually ugly daughter (S31, "Cruel stepmother"; B848.2.1, "Stepmother mistreats girl"). The good daughter is kind and polite to a supernatural being. Rewarded with a gift for her kindness, the good girl returns home and sparks her stepmother's jealousy. In order to acquire the same riches for her own daughter, the stepmother sends her to meet the being. The girl is selfish and uncooperative and instead of being rewarded she is punished.

The heroes or heroines who are found to be kind are rewarded with gifts that are a symbolic representation of their inner character (Q111, "Wealth as a reward"). These may take the form of a physical transformation (D1860, "Magic beautification"), jewels falling from the mouth when speaking (D1454.2, "Treasure falls from mouth"), or some similar boon (F545.2.1, "Gold star on forehead"). The heroes or heroines who fail the test (Q280,

"Unkindness punished"; Q291, "Hard heartedness punished"; Q276, "Stinginess punished"; Q321, "Laziness punished") are swiftly punished with a gift that is a symbolic representation of their inner nature, such as receiving a box or basket containing bees, toads, or snakes or being similarly physically transformed; frogs and snakes falling from the mouth when they speak (M431.2, "Curse: toads from mouth"), a donkey tail appearing on their forehead, or being dipped in pitch (Q475.2, "Shower of pitch as punishment"). The rewards and punishments are always in clear opposition, mirroring the opposing character traits of the two protagonists who are tested.

The story may begin with the parent thrusting the innocent protagonist out into the dangerous world, where he or she overcomes adversity. The heroine may be commanded to spin by the well (as in the German "Mother Holle") or in an isolated hut in the forest (S143, "Abandonment in forest"), as in the Russian tale "Blindman's Bluff"; sent outside in winter inappropriately dressed for cold weather with instructions not to return unless she brings back violets or strawberries (H1023.3, "Task: bringing berries (fruit, flowers) in winter"); or commanded to remain in a snowfield all night (the Russian "King Frost"). In an African (Ashanti) tale, "Anansi and His Son" it is a father who drives his son away, saying, "I don't want to see you again."

In many AT 480 tales, the bad parent, as well as the bad child, is punished. For example, the mother dies of grief in "King Frost" and "Blindman's Bluff" (Q411, "Death as punishment"). In the Grimms' tale "Three Little Men in the Woods," when the king asks, "What punishment does a person deserve who drowns another?" the mother replies, "For an evil deed like that, no better fate than to be put in a barrel lined with sharp nails and rolled down a hill" (Q581, "Villain nemesis. Person condemned to punishment he has suggested for others"). Unable to bear her misfortune of losing her favorite daughter, the mother kills herself in "Humility Rewarded and Pride Punished" (Bengal, India). The mother becomes "black of heart" and dies in "Black of Heart" (Hausa, Africa). In "The Three Heads of the Well" (England), the queen mother hangs herself when she learns that her favorite daughter has married a cobbler.

The magic or fairytale component in this story is derived from the otherworldly, supernatural, and potentially dangerous figure that the two children meet, who, unlike the biased parent, bestows rewards and punishments fairly, based on the hero or heroine's inner qualities. Reinforcing the good mother–bad mother archetypal pattern, this figure is often portrayed as an elderly woman, especially when the main characters are young girls. In other variants, this figure is the Virgin Mary, Saint Nicholas, Saint Christopher, angels, God, and Jesus—religious figures that often function as parent substitutes in prayers and dreams. They also suggest quasi-divine, spiritual essence. Other figures doing the testing include Jack Frost (Russia), cats (Spain), a

The story of a girl, mistreated and cast out, who emerges in an otherworld where she is tested (Motif H1550, "Tests of character") and rewarded (Q40, "Kindness rewarded"; Q42, "Generosity rewarded"; Q41, "Politeness rewarded"), is found all over the world and is classified as AT 480, *The Spinning Woman at the Well.* From "The Two Caskets" in Andrew Lang, *The Orange Fairy Book;* illustrated by H.J. Ford (1906).

sparrow (China and Japan), a troll (Norway), a bear (Russia and southwest American Indian), fairies (Spain), a mermaid (Brittany), the twelve months (Greece and Italy), little men in the woods (Germany and Chile), three heads in a well (England), and a boy (Africa). The German Mother Holle also suggests the embodiment of a nature figure, as the act of shaking her feather quilt, or pillows, influences snowfall (A1135.2.1, "Snow from feathers or clothes of a witch"). Dwarfs are allied with nature so it is not surprising that in variants of "Strawberries in the Snow," the child sent out into the forest in winter to find fruit or flowers meets little men or dwarfs, the seasons, or the twelve months (Z122.3, "Twelve months as youths seated about fire"; Z122.4, "The four seasons personified").

The tests in AT 480 tales are generally simple deeds, requiring no magical intervention. These tests include willingness and competency in completing ordinary household chores, as in "Mother Holle" (G204, "Girl in service of witch"), compassion; as in a Haitian variant where the good girl willingly rubs an old woman's back that is covered with pieces of sharp glass ("Mother of the Water"); good manners; and obedience. The sharing of bread, a popular motif in folktales (Q42.1.1.1, "Reward for giving last loaf"), is the implicit test in "The Girl and the Hogs," a Mushkogen (American Indian) tale, in which the young girl shares her bread with old women. In the African "Anansi and His Son," the greedy father disobeys the directions not to pick vegetables that say "Don't eat me" and is bitten by snakes. His son, who obeys the instructions, returns successfully with food. In the African (Cameroon) "The Two Brothers," one boy cuts firewood for an old man, the other does not; the first learns how to get riches, the second gets nothing (Krug 1912, 113).

Steven Swann Jones argues that the structural symmetry of such tales emphasizes "the difference between successful and unsuccessful maturation" in an archetypal narrative ultimately about the kind girl's initiation into womanhood. Jones maintains that the "tale presents caricatured depictions of proper and improper socialization in order to encourage the child to follow the appropriate model" (1986, 153). Although such tales usually pertain to the maturation of girls, a Syrian tale, "The Good Apprentice and the Bad," provides an example of the proper and improper socialization of boys. Abu-Kheir, whose name signifies "Father of Good," is kind, generous, and enterprising, whereas Abu-Sharr, or "Father of Evil," is selfish and spiteful. However, this tale presents a twist to the idea of reward and punishment. Eavesdropping on three doves, Abu-Kheir acquires information that allows him to succeed. Abu-Sharr wishes to know the secret of Abu-Kheir's success, and the latter sends him to the place where he saw the doves, who are in fact afreets (demons or spirits). The afreets only arbitrarily punish Abu-Sharr because of the meaning of his name. Nevertheless, in the end, the good apprentice is rewarded with good fortune (Bushnaq, 1986).

HOSPITALITY REWARDED, MODEST CHOICE, POLITENESS REWARDED, AND ENCOUNTERS EN ROUTE

In tales closely related to AT 480, the virtue of extending hospitality is tested. In the Greek myth of Baucis and Philemon in Ovid's *Metamorphoses,* an elderly couple is rewarded for offering hospitality to strangers, who happen to be Zeus and his son Hermes (W1, "Hospitality is a virtue"; Q45, "Hospitality rewarded"). The inhospitable neighbors have their homes destroyed by a natural catastrophe (Q292, "Inhospitality punished"). The lesson here is that in being kind to human beings, you may find yourself being kind to gods and goddesses.

A second test is often inserted in this story, the selection of a large, medium-sized, or small container containing a gift (L211, "Modest choice: three caskets"; Q3, "Moderate request rewarded, immoderate punished"). Once again, the good person shows humility by selecting the smallest container, which is found to be filled with treasure, while the greedy person chooses the larger container, which is found to be filled with snakes or bees. Shakespeare uses this motif in *The Merchant of Venice.*

A related Irish variant has a man with a hunchback politely helping the fairies with a song, and he is rewarded by having his hump removed (Q41, "Politeness rewarded"; F344.1, "Fairies remove/replace hunchback's hump"; F331.3, "Mortal wins fairies' gratitude by joining in their singing"). The impolite man, who hopes to have his hump removed, instead is given the hump the fairies took from the good man, so he leaves with two humps (Q551.8, "Deformity as punishment"). In a Japanese variant, the men have wens on their faces, psychologically alluding to the Japanese precept, "saving face."

The good heroes or heroines show compassion to people, animals, or plants that they encounter on their journey and are subsequently rewarded. For example, in the African (Hausa) tale "Making Stew," the bad girls refuse to rub an old woman's back. The good girl does this task and is told the name of a young man. Later, when they visit a house, the bad girls are denied entrance because they do not know the man's name. The good girl, of course, passes the test. In another African (Congo) variant, "The String of Beads," the good girl strips off her garments and uses them to bind the wounds on an old woman's back (Q41.2, "Reward for cleansing loathsome person")

GOOD AND BAD NEIGHBORS AND GENEROSITY TO SUPER-NATURAL BEINGS AND ANIMALS REWARDED

Like tales about kind and unkind girls, those contrasting good and bad neighbors follow a symmetrical pattern. While good neighbors demonstrate generosity, kindness, and hospitality to animals and people, bad neighbors exhibit avarice and envy. In the Japanese story "The Old Man Who Made Flowers Bloom," an old woman finds a peach floating down the river and brings it home. The peach metamorphoses into a puppy, and the old woman and her husband care for it like a grandson. In return, the puppy brings the couple gold coins, igniting the neighbors' envy. The neighbors kill the puppy, which then transforms itself into other instruments of good fortune for the old woman and her husband (Seki 1963, 120–125). Whereas the bad neighbors in this story are punished only with defeat, in another Japanese tale the bad neighbors meet a different fate. In "The *Choja* Who Became a Monkey," Lord Iri and his wife, despite their poverty, welcome into their home a poor traveling priest, who is in fact the sun deity in disguise. When the rich, miserly neighbors of Lord Iri and his wife discover that the priest has granted them youth, the bad neighbors send for the same priest, but he transforms their family into monkeys and dogs (Seki 1963, 142–145). An Andalusian tale recounted by Juan Valera, "The Queen Mother," similarly opposes a good with a bad couple. The good couple, poor but generous, invite their friends over to celebrate a birthday. Trying to revive the kitchen fire, the good wife blows on it so hard she ends up passing wind. Embarrassed, she wishes the earth would swallow her up, and she suddenly is transported into a rich kingdom, where she is referred to as the queen mother and eventually rewarded with riches. Envious, her friend tries to duplicate the event, but is compensated for her ill will by a dunghill swarming with toads and snakes (Fedorchek, 2003). As in the case of the kind and unkind girls, stories about good and bad neighbors reinforce the values of socialization, specifically the values necessary to communal living.

Generosity on the part of a poor woman and her son to a saint, who appears as an old beggar monk, is rewarded in the Chinese tale "The Great Flood." The tale also integrates kindness to animals. During a flood, mother and son save ants, sparrows, and a wolf, and although the mother is killed by a wolf, the son is saved by the grateful animals and marries the daughter of an emperor (Eberhard 1965). In "The Man Who Cuts Down the Cinnamon Tree," a man tends an injured sparrow and is rewarded with a seed that produces a pumpkin filled with gold. An envious, cruel boy (J2415) throws a stone to injure a sparrow, then tends it, but instead of gold, his pumpkin is filled with bees. In another variant, a man steps out of the pumpkin and the boy and man both climb a vine to the moon, where the boy is forced to remain, trying to chop down a bejeweled tree that regenerates itself daily.

In "The Good Little Mouse," Marie-Catherine d'Aulnoy similarly combines kindness to animals with kindness to fairies. Imprisoned by an enemy king, a pregnant queen is given a mere three peas a day to eat. One day she invites a mouse to share her peas, and suddenly a table with partridges and jam appears. Because of her generosity, the mouse, who is in fact a fairy, eventually helps the queen save her daughter from the evil king (Zipes 1989).

When characters assist animals in distress, these animals often become the hero or heroine's helper. In Straparola's "Pietro the Fool" (1550), the hero spares the life of a tuna, who grants him his wishes (Zipes 2001). An Iraqi Cinderella, the heroine of "The Little Red Fish and the Clog of Gold," frees a catfish, who provides her with golden clogs and silk gowns to attend a bride's henna, a ceremony marking a bride's separation from her family upon her marriage (Bushnaq 1986). In d'Aulnoy's "Beauty with the Golden Hair," the hero Avenant saves a carp, a crow, and an owl, who assist him in finding a queen's ring, killing a giant, and obtaining magical water (Zipes 1989; see also d'Aulnoy 1997). In the Chinese tale, "The Gratitude of the Snake," a boy heals an injured snake, which later save his life (Eberhard 1965).

Anne E. Duggan and Ruth Stotter

See also: Otherworld Journeys.

REFERENCES

Bushnaq, Indea, trans. 1986. *Arab Folktales.* New York: Pantheon.

d'Aulnoy, Marie-Catherine, comtesse. 1997. *Contes I.* Intro. Jacques Barchilon; ed. Philippe Hourcade. Paris: Société des textes modernes.

Eberhard, Wolfram, ed. 1965. *Folktales of China.* Chicago: University of Chicago Press.

Fedorchek, Robert M., trans. 2003. "Juan Valera: 'The Queen Mother.'" *Marvels & Tales* 17 (2): 262–268.

Jones, Steven Swann. 1986. "Structural and Thematic Applications of the Comparative Method: A Case Study of 'The Kind and Unkind Girls.'" *Journal of Folklore Research* 23 (2–3): 147–161.

Kligman, Gail Ann. 1973. "The Tale of the Kind and Unkind Girl." MA thesis, University of California–Berkeley.

Krug, Adolph N. 1912. "Bulu Tales from Kamerun, West Africa." *Journal of American Folklore* 25 (96): 106–124.

Roberts, Warren E. 1994 [1958]. *The Tale of the Kind and Unkind Girls: AA-TH 480 and Related Tales.* Detroit: Wayne State University Press.

Róheim, Géza. 1953. "Dame Holle: Dream and Folk Tale." In *Explorations of Psychoanalysis,* ed. Robert Lindner, 84–94. New York: Julian Press.

———. 1992. *Fire in the Dragon and Other Psychoanalytic Essays on Folklore.* Ed. Alan Dundes. Princeton, NJ: Princeton University Press.

Seki, Keigo, ed. 1963. *Folktales of Japan.* Trans. Robert J. Adams. Chicago: University of Chicago Press.

Stotter, Ruth. 1998. *The Golden Axe: Versions from Around the World of the Classic Story "The Kind and Unkind Girl."* Stinson Beach, CA: Stotter Press.

Thompson, Stith. 1977. *The Folktale.* Berkeley: University of California Press.

von Franz, Marie-Louise. 1980. *The Psychological Meaning of Redemption Motifs in Fairy Tales.* Toronto: Inner City Books.

———. 1980 [1974]. *Shadow and Evil in Fairy Tales.* Dallas, TX: Spring Publications.

Zipes, Jack, trans. 1989. *Beauties, Beasts, and Enchantment: Classic French Fairy Tales.* New York: NAL.

———, ed. 2001. *The Great Fairy Tale Tradition: From Straparola and Basile to the Brothers Grimm.* New York: Norton.

❀ R ❀

Captives and Fugitives

Abductions

Motifs R10–R99

❁

Listed under Captives and Fugitives, motifs of kidnapping or abduction by supernatural creatures are numerous. Whether the abductors are gods, spirits, fairies, dwarfs, goblins, witches, or aliens from outer space, there are striking similarities. The seduced or captured abductee is always taken to another place, used or manipulated in some way, and, if released, returned in an altered form or with continuing aftereffects. Abductions by humans are also a part of folklore and literature, but Thompson did not include many motifs about human abductors in this chapter.

Perhaps the earliest forms of abduction are those associated with shamanism or priestly initiation rites, which may be compared to magical transformative journeys. Shamans, who gain power from their intercourse with the spirit world, are taken out of their bodies and into a spirit world where, in trance or semitrance, they are tested and tried, returning to the ordinary world with new powers and a new way of life. Abduction can thus be seen as a form of spirit or even demonic possession.

HELLISH ABDUCTIONS

An abduction motif that can be treated in an unusually humorous manner is R11.2, "Abduction by devil"; R11.2.1; "Devil carries off wicked people." An example is the Scots ballad "The Farmer's Curst Wife" (Child 1965, 278). The devil approaches a man plowing his fields and announces, "One of your family I must have now." When the devil says that he wants the farmer's wife, the man replies, "O welcome, good Satan, with all my heart! / I hope you and she will never more part." The devil hoists the wife on his back and runs down to hell. Of course, she is such a shrew that the devil ends up bringing her back to her husband, remarking, "I have been a tormentor the whole of my life, / But I ne'er was tormented so as with your wife" (Child 1965, 108, version A). This song was brought to the United States, where numerous variants were collected.

On the opposite end of the spectrum, one of the most famous and haunting images from Greek myth is the abduction to the underworld of the maiden Persephone, who is grabbed by Hades, lord of the dead, as she is gathering flowers in a meadow (R10.1, "Princess (maiden) abducted"). Another crucial abduction in Greek myth is that of Helen, wife of King Menelaus, by Paris, which is the cause of the Trojan War (some scholars including Thompson, characterize the act as an elopement rather than an abduction [R225, "Elopement"]).

Abduction of a maiden by a monster or an ogre (R11.1) is an important motif in several tale types (AT 301, 301A, 301B, 302, 311, 312). A representative tale, "Fitcher's Bird" ("Fitcher's Vogel," KHM 46; Type 311, *Rescue By the Sister*), was collected by the Grimms: "There was once a wizard who used to take the form of a poor man, and went to houses and begged, and caught pretty girls. No one knew whither he carried them, for they were never seen more" (*Grimms' Household Tales*). One day the wizard appeared at the home of three sisters. "He begged for a little food, and when the eldest daughter came out and was just reaching him a piece of bread, he did but touch her, and she was forced to jump into his basket. Thereupon he hurried away with long strides, and carried her away into a dark forest to his house, which stood in the midst of it." He tells the girl that she may go into any room in the house but one (C611, "Forbidden chamber"). When he leaves the house, she enters the room and finds "a great bloody basin . . . in the middle of the room, and therein lay human beings, dead and hewn to pieces, and hard by was a block of wood, and a gleaming axe lay upon it." For disobeying his command, she suffers the same fate as the others she had found, and the wizard goes back to her house and takes her middle sister, who also ends up in the basin, and then her youngest sister, who manages to outwit the wizard, restore her sisters (E30, "Resuscitation by arrangement of members. Parts of a dismembered corpse are brought together and resuscitation follows" [a particularly ancient motif in world mythology]), and effect their rescue and his demise.

An ancient example of Motif R11.1 ("Princess (maiden) abducted by monster (ogre)") is found in the *Ramayana* (the oldest Sanskrit text dates from between the second century BCE and the second century CE). Sita, wife of the god/prince Rama, is abducted by the demon Ravana, who keeps her captive on the island of Lanka for many years. With an army of monkeys, Rama is able to kill Ravana and rescue Sita. Doubting Sita's chastity despite her avowals, Ravana subjects her to an ordeal by fire (H221, "Ordeal by fire.

Suspected person must pass through or jump over fire to determine guilt or innocence"). Sita "called on the fire to protect her, and entered the blazing flame; but the god of Fire placed her in Rama's lap, assuring him that Sita had always been pure in thought as well as deed. Rama reinstated her, but when he doubted her again she disappeared forever back into the earth" (Doniger 2002, 105).

In some stories, it is the hero who abducts a princess, for example in *Faithful John* (AT 516). Versions of this story have been collected all over Europe as well as in Turkey, India, the Middle East, South America, and the West Indies. With the help of his faithful servant, a king abducts a princess after he has fallen helplessly in love with her portrait in a room of his father's castle that he was warned not to enter (C611, "Forbidden chamber"). Mozart's opera *The Abduction From the Seraglio* (1781) (based upon the libretto by Gottlieb Stephanie) features a hero abducting a princess from a Turkish harem, after she had been abducted by pirates and sold to a pasha (R12.1, "Maiden abducted by pirates (robbers)").

ABDUCTION BY ANIMALS

Abduction by all manner of animals occurs with great frequency in the world's folklore. The *Motif-Index* lists the following animal abductors: snake (R13.4.1), tiger (R13.1.4), wolf (R13.1.5), monkey (R13.1.7), rabbit (R13.1.8), leopard (R13.1.9). elephant (R13.1.10), fox (R13.1.11), and bird (R13.3). The motif of being carried off by a bird is particularly common. In the Grimms' tale of "Snow-White and Rose-Red" (KHM 161), the protagonists rescue a dwarf whom an eagle tries to abduct: "Now they noticed a large bird hovering in the air, flying slowly round and round above them; it sank lower and lower, and at last settled near a rock not far off. Directly afterwards they heard a loud, piteous cry. They ran up and saw with horror that the eagle had seized their old acquaintance the dwarf, and was going to carry him off" (*Grimms' Household Tales*). In "Fundevogel" ("Bird-foundling," KHM 51), a forester finds a child crying in the top of a tree, deposited there by a bird who had abducted it from its mother. A man is carried off to a cliff by a giant bird in a number of North American Indian tales (Thompson 1929, 318).

In Greek mythology, Ganymede is carried off to Mount Olympus by an eagle sent by Zeus, who had fallen in love with the youth when he saw him tending his flocks (R13.3.2, "Eagle carries off youth"). When Zeus falls in love with Europa, he changes himself into a bull and carries her on his back to Crete. In the Eskimo tale of "The Eagle and Whale Husbands," which is widespread from Greenland to Siberia, two girls are playing with the bones of an eagle and a whale, respectively, and each is carried off by that animal. The girl abducted

**Zeus changes himself into a bull (Motif D101, "Transformation: god to animal")
and carries Europa on his back to Crete (Motif R10.1, "Princess (maiden) abducted"). From *Hypnerotomachia Poliphili* (1499).**

by the eagle makes a string from the sinews of the little birds he brings her to eat
and she slides down from his nest and escapes; the girl held by the whale is
rescued by her two brothers who come for her in a boat (Thompson 1929, 160–
161). The latter's escape involves the obstacle flight (D672), in which she throws
objects behind as they flee in order to distract and slow down the pursuer.

A story from the Tahltan Indians of Canada tells how a woman whose
husband caught a killer whale cuts it up and then, as she puts her hands in
the water to wash away the blood, she is pulled underneath and taken to
the underwater kingdom of the killer whales. The husband enlists the aid
of a shark to help him rescue his wife (Thompson 1929, 162–163).

ABDUCTION BY FAIRIES

One of the most widespread categories of abduction is by fairies (F320, "Fairies carry people away to fairyland"). Tales of captives taken to fairyland are
especially prominent in the British Isles. Mortals, particularly attractive young
women or men, are detained in a subterranean otherworld, either because
they are enthralled by a fairy suitor, venture into a fairy hill, or are inveigled
into eating fairy food or drink (C211.1, "Tabu: eating in fairyland"). Infants
are most frequently stolen immediately after their birth and before baptism,
while their mothers are sometimes taken to serve as wet nurses to weak fairy
offspring. Sometimes human women are used to serve as midwives to fairy
females, for whom childbirth is notoriously difficult.

According to several of the Irish folklorists, young men are often kidnapped for their physical strength, to serve as bond-slaves and as participants in sports and faction-battles, since the elfin peoples are thought to be strong in brain but weak in brawn. However, medieval accounts of Thomas the Rhymer and similar figures suggest other, more typical motives. For example, Thomas is seduced and abducted by the beautiful Queen of Elfland, in part because of his poetic and musical skills and in part because she desires him. When returned to earth, he is an old man (time in fairyland differs from that on earth) but one with a special gift: he cannot tell a lie. More unvarnished and contemporary is the tale of John M'Namara, a man who spends "Twenty Years with the Good People." On a trip to Limerick to buy some leather for brogues, John, a shoemaker, vanishes. When he returns twenty years later, he announces to his wife and grown son that he cannot tell them where he has been, that he lacks the power to do so. Everyone knows that he has been with "the good people"—when they see the strange and beautiful shoes and boots he now can make (Knox 1917, 215–216). The fairies are also suspected of abducting the learned clergyman Robert Kirk, the seventeenth-century author of *The Secret Common-Wealth of Elves, Fauns, and Fairies,* holding him within a fairy hill, as punishment for revealing their secrets.

More frequently, though, the victims are young women taken to be brides of fairy kings and princes—though mortals think them vanished, tranced, asleep, or prematurely dead. Sometimes, by following elaborate rituals, their friends or lovers can reclaim them, but more often, they remain in the other world. An instance of the former pattern is the Scottish tale of the "Stolen Lady," in which a Highlander encountering a troop of fairies is suspicious about a bundle they carry. Making them exchange gifts with him, he discovers that the prize is a beautiful English lady, who lives with him for many years until found by her Saxon husband, who had thought her dead and buried (Keightley 1850, 391–392). In a similar story from Denmark, a smith rescues a woman from a troll and restores her and her newborn twins to her husband (Keightley 1850, 392).

Nursing mothers are also in demand to suckle fairy and half-breed babies, and are in special danger between childbirth and churching. Sometimes the abduction is intercepted, sometimes the victim is successfully restored (usually after a number of years, which she does not know had passed), but often the attempt at rescue fails. "The Lothian Farmer's Wife" is typical. Here, though the kidnapped wife repeatedly visits her children at night, telling them and her farmer husband how to rescue her, her spouse is not courageous enough to seize her from the trooping, noisy cavalcade of fairies (Briggs 1977, 62–63). However, mortal midwives to the fairies are almost always returned.

But it is babies and young and beautiful children that the fairies are most apt to steal. The thought is that such children are necessary to improve the fairy breed, since fairy women have much trouble in conceiving and in childbirth. Some people believed that since the fairies have to pay a tithe to the devil every seven years, they prefer to use human children as sacrifices rather than their own. Still others suggested that since the fairies' fate at Judgment Day is uncertain, they need mortals to stand up and plead for them. Whatever the reason, accounts of the theft of babies are widespread over the British Isles, France, Germany, and Scandinavia. Sometimes an aged fairy, feeble elf, wooden log or stock, or a "changeling" is substituted, but often the human child is simply taken (F321.1, "Changeling. Fairy steals child from cradle and leaves fairy substitute"). Numerous accounts of changelings and fairy thefts may be found in the works of the Victorian English folklorists, in the popular press, and especially in Irish prose and poetry, including that of William Butler Yeats (1969). The frequency and geographical spread of such kidnap accounts indicate a widespread cultural anxiety about the fate of young children. In cases where no changeling substitute is left, the human child is seldom restored; if it is returned, it is deformed, insane, or simply "changed."

ABDUCTION BY ALIENS

As traditional belief dwindled or was rationalized, kidnapping fairies from the otherworld became aliens from outer space who had much the same function and nature. The fairy-fascination subsided (though it did not die) in the 1920s, but before it was completely over the new kidnappers had appeared on the scene (F37§, "Inhabitants of another planet (extra-terrestrial) visit earth"). As early as 1895, Colonel H.G. Shaw of California reported to have been nearly abducted by a group of pale, thin, seven-foot-tall beings. The colonel believed that the aliens had come to earth to gather human specimens, but that he had escaped because he was too heavy for the fragile creatures to carry (Schnabel 1995, 10).

Multiple abduction cases and research about them really blossomed in the late 1950s and 1960s. Among the first of the many famous or notorious accounts was that of Antonio Villas-Boas, a Brazilian farm worker who insisted that in October 1957 he had been taken aboard a spaceship by short, gray-suited aliens and subjected to a series of physical tests. The culmination of his experience was his seduction-rape by a nude alien female and the aliens' harvesting of his sperm in order to improve their stock (Schnabel 1995, 22–23). In 1966, Barney and Betty Hill from New Hampshire were the victims of a similar experience. Experiencing a loss of time, both recollected under hypnosis that they had been abducted to a flying saucer and subjected to sexual experimentation.

Whitley Strieber's account of his own repeated abductions in *Communion*, his best seller of 1987, made both the imagery and the experience commonplace in American popular culture. Strieber's tale of repeated and terrifying kidnappings in which he was paralyzed, carried off by three-foot worker aliens, taken to a mysterious round chamber where his mind was read by larger alien leaders wielding wands and his body sexually probed by a large-eyed alien *femme fatale* piqued the interest of the American public.

Now very much a part of our popular culture, abduction accounts continue to stream in—supplemented by new alien phenomena such as "circles" and "signs." It is even possible to purchase UFO abduction insurance, as did the Heaven's Gate cultists.

Critics relate these stories to the near-death experience, contagious hysteria, or some real but peculiar experiences. Many think that it is linked to dissociative disorders or multiple personality disorders. In people who suffer from these disorders, the boundary between ordinary reality and an alternative state is easily crossed (Schnabel 1995, 122).

It is worth noting, however, how similar UFO abduction tales are to folkloric accounts of fairy kidnappings (Bullard 1989). Both involve a loss of time (F377, "Supernatural lapse of time in fairyland. Years seem days") as well as transport to another world. Both involve capture and examination, resulting in physical and mental change. Both focus on sexual and reproductive functions. Abduction reports often sound like rewrites of older supernatural encounters even to the presence of wands or rods (fairy wands), mysterious lights (fairy lights), the ability of aliens to paralyze (fairy-stroke), and descriptions of the circular, domed chambers to which abductees are taken (fairy hills). Interestingly, the appearance of the aliens, smaller than human, fragile in body, and marked by large hypnotic eyes, is like an updated version of the descriptions of "little people." Our old fears and fascinations are seemingly still with us; they have simply taken new, more technological and scientific forms.

Carole G. Silver

REFERENCES

Briggs, K.M. 1977. *A Dictionary of Fairies: Hobgoblins, Brownies, Bogies, and Other Supernatural Creatures*. Harmondsworth: Penguin.

Bullard, Thomas E. 1989. "UFO Abduction Reports: The Supernatural Kidnap Narrative Returns in Technological Guise." *Journal of American Folklore* 102, n. 404 (April–June): 147–170.

Child, Francis James. 1965 [1882–1898]. *The English and Scottish Popular Ballads*. Reprint: New York: Dover. Original ed. Houghton Mifflin.

Doniger, Wendy. 2002. "Ramayana." In *The Epic Voice*, ed. Alan D. Hodder and Robert E. Meagher. Westport, CT: Praeger.

Grimms' Household Tales. With the Authors' Notes. 1968 [1884]. Trans. Margaret Hunt. 2 vols. Reprint. Detroit: Singing Tree Press. Orig. ed. London: George Bell.

Keightley, Thomas. 1850. *The Fairy Mythology*. London: Bohn.

Knox, D. 1917. "Folk-Tales from County Limerick collected by Miss D. Knox." *Folk-Lore*: 28: 215–216.

Schnabel, Jim. 1995. *Dark White: Aliens, Abductions, and the UFO Obsession*. London: Penguin.

Silver, Carole G. 1999. *Strange and Secret Peoples: Fairies and Victorian Consciousness*. New York: Oxford University Press.

Strieber, Whitley. 1987. *Communion: A True Story, Encounters with the Unknown*. London: Arrow.

Thompson, Stith. 1929. *Tales of the North American Indians*. Cambridge: Harvard University Press.

Yeats, W.B. 1969. *Mythologies*. New York: Macmillan.

❀ S ❀

Unnatural Cruelty

Cruel Parents

Motif S10

❁

Kinder- und Hausmärchen (*Children's and Household Tales*), the title selected by the Grimm brothers for their famous collection, was well chosen, but although fairy tales may largely be about and for children, youngsters do not always fare well in these stories. Traditional collections are replete with accounts of innocent children who receive little but blows and scorn from the adults in their lives. These blameless heroes and heroines vindicate themselves as their stories unfold, and this vindication often includes retribution against the adults who tormented them at the beginning. Such stories have an obvious charm for children who feel that they too have been disciplined unfairly, a category that—at one time or another—could include almost everyone. The battered urchins who become kings and the overworked Cinderellas who become queens are appealing role models in a fantasy world, and the retribution episodes give youthful listeners a vicarious release of hostile feelings.

Earlier generations looked askance at "coddling" or "spoiling" a child. A switch stood in the corner of every kitchen, always visible and ready to correct a wayward child. Proverbial "wisdom" defends violence that today would be called abuse: "A father who spares the rod hates his son, but one who loves him keeps him in order" (Proverbs 13:24). And, as the following Dutch proverb suggests, if a parent beats a child, the child deserved it: "The child will tell that it has been whipped, but not why" (Jente 1947, no. 697).

The learning and proving process that parents put their children through can be cruel, "taught to the tune of the hickory stick," or worse. The Old Norse *Saga of the Volsungs* (1990) offers a case in point (ch. 6). Sigyn, doubting her two young sons' courage, stitches their shirt cuffs to their wrists. Crying out in pain, they fail this ordeal, and a second test as well, so Signy has them killed.

An even crueler test, documented in countless legends from northern Europe, is used to determine if a child who fails to grow and develop properly is a changeling, the offspring of fairies, who has been substituted for a human child. There is a benign test: to make the suspected changeling show surprise by doing something unusual, such as brewing beer in eggshells. But the more common method is to torture the child, and if it is a changeling, the fairy parents will rescue it, bringing back the stolen human child in the process. Thomas Crofton Croker, writing in 1825 and quoted here by William Butler Yeats (1983, 49), tells how parents who suspect their child might be a changeling are advised "to roast it alive on the griddle, or to burn its nose off with the red hot tongs, or to throw it out in the snow on the roadside" (F321.1.4). History has not recorded how many children, failing to meet their parents' expectations of growth and development, were subjected to such trials, but folkloric evidence suggests that it is not a small number.

A century ago, few would have questioned the parents' right to discipline their children however they saw fit or, in earlier epochs, to decide whether or not their offspring should live. Myths and legends are replete with accounts of heroes who as infants were abandoned and left to die of exposure (S301), but who were miraculously rescued. Romulus, Remus, and Oedipus are but three prominent examples. Fairy tales also reflect, if not an acceptance of, then at least a recognition of the reality of infanticide by abandonment. Thus, in Straparola's *The Facetious Nights* (3:4), when a childless couple decide to adopt a son, "they betook themselves to a certain spot where young children who had been cast off by their parents were often left, and, having seen there one who appeared to them more seemly and attractive than the rest, they took him home with them." Stories of the *Hansel and Gretel* type (AT 327A), built around the motif of children abandoned because of poverty (S321), are among the most widely distributed and popular of all international folktales.

History suggests that such tales are not merely products of delusional minds and literary fantasy. Belief in the natural right of parents to dispose of their children as they saw fit was apparently a significant obstacle that early Christian missionaries had to overcome in converting Europeans to the new faith. The account of the Christianization of Iceland (in the year 1000) contained in *Njal's Saga* (Hreinsson 1997, 3:1–220) illuminates the conflict. A Christian priest summarizes the compromise that led to the formal conversion: "This will be the foundation of our law," he said, "that all men in this land are to be Christians and believe in one God—Father, Son, and Holy Spirit—and give up all worship of false idols, the exposure of children, and the eating of horse meat. Three years' outlawry will be the penalty for open violations, but if these things are practiced in secret there shall be no punishment" (ch. 105)

Jacob Grimm, in his study of ancient laws, emphasizes that Germanic tribesmen claimed the right to abandon newborn children under numerous circumstances (1899, 1:628–635). Children with birth defects or other disabilities and those of questionable paternity were especially vulnerable. In this regard, children born from a multiple conception were particularly threatened. Not only did twins, and triplets place an additional burden on parents, but past generations also suspected that multiple births were caused by multiple sex partners, thus raising serious paternity questions (S314, "Twins (triplets) exposed").

Charles Perrault's "Little Thumb" (AT 327B), first published in 1697, offers a related example. An impoverished woodcutter and his wife have seven sons between the ages of seven and ten, for the mother, we are told, never had less than two at a time. But "their seven children inconvenienced them greatly," so they abandon the whole lot of them in the woods. However, the boys find shelter with an ogre, from whom the youngest brother steals a fortune, and they all return safely to their now joyful parents.

English folklore's most famous prolific breeder is the old woman who lived in a shoe. Iona and Peter Opie give a number of nursery rhymes about this woman and her brood, all of which depict violence against the children (1991, 434–435). The line "She whipped them all soundly and sent them to bed" is still familiar. A variant current in 1797 is even more drastic: "And she borrow'd a beetle [a heavy wooden pestle], and she knocked 'em all o' the head." A number of versions include the line "And when she went in, she found them all dead." The tone of these rhymes is disingenuously humorous, but playfulness notwithstanding, these rhymes are about the abuse, possibly fatal, of unwanted children.

Whatever was the rationalization for not accepting a child in ancient Europe, Jacob Grimm emphasizes that girls were more often abandoned than were boys (1899, 1:629; Motif S322.1.1, "Father who wanted son exposes (murders) daughter"). Patriarchal societies throughout the ages have placed a higher value on male than on female offspring. Gender-based infanticide is well documented both in fantasy tales and in believed legends. Thus the opening paragraph of the Italian tale "Wormwood" (Calvino 1980, no. 157; AT 882, *The Wager on the Wife's Chastity*) exhibits a matter-of-fact cruelty that seems quite natural in the medieval world of fairy tales: "Over and over it has been told that once upon a time there was a king and queen. Every time this queen had a baby, it was a girl. The king, who wanted a son, finally lost patience and said, 'If you have one more girl, I shall kill it.'"

Such fairy tales do not differ substantially from their ostensibly more credible counterparts, legends. The account of the birth of Helga the Fair, the leading female character in the Icelandic *Saga of Gunnlaug Serpent-Tongue* (Hreinsson 1997, 1: 305–333), offers a compelling example. At the beginning of the story, we read that her father, a powerful chieftain, was "wise, tolerant, and just in all things." His wisdom, tolerance, and justice notwithstanding, he instructs his pregnant wife, "You are soon going to have a baby. Now if you have a girl, it must be left out to die, but if it is a boy it will be brought up" (ch. 1). However, the episode has a happy ending. The woman does give birth to a girl, but cannot bring herself to abandon the child. Instead, she gives the infant to relatives to raise, telling her husband that his order has been carried out. Years later, the father meets his daughter, and, after learning the truth of her birth and rescue, accepts her lovingly.

In addition to gender-related and poverty-induced infanticide, there is also a large body of folklore describing human sacrifice (most often, children sold for this purpose by their own mothers) as a means of protecting vulnerable buildings (S261, "Foundation sacrifice"). If the folkloric record can be believed, this practice extended into the Christian era in Europe. Consider the following Baltic legend, quoted here in its entirety:

> When Christianity was introduced to Rügen, they wanted to build a church in Vilmnitz. However, the builders could not complete their task, because whatever they put up during the day was torn down again by the devil that night. Then they purchased a child, gave it a bread-roll in one hand, a light in the other, and set it in a cavity in the foundation, which they quickly mortared shut. Now the devil could no longer disrupt the building's progress. It is also said that a child was entombed in the church at Bergen under similar circumstances. (Haas 1903, no. 195)

Another ancient and widespread folktale depicting parental atrocity (but this time with a magical happy ending) is "The Girl without Hands" (AT 706, same title). The Grimms tell the story succinctly (KHM 31). A mysterious stranger offers to make an impoverished miller rich, in exchange for "that which is standing behind your house." The miller, thinking of his apple tree, agrees, but later he discovers that the stranger was the devil and that the item then standing behind his house was his own daughter. Because of her purity, the devil cannot take the girl, so he threatens the miller, offering to release him only if he will cut off his daughter's hands. Without hesitating, the father accepts the devil's bargain and chops off his daughter's hands (Motif S211, "Child sold (promised) to devil (ogre)"). He then offers to care for her the rest of her life, but she, unwilling to remain with the person who has thus abused her, sets forth alone. In fairy-tale fashion, she marries a king, who has silver hands made for her; then, with time, God causes her natural hands to grow back. Nothing more is said about the father who cut off his daughter's hands to save himself.

A child's mutilation by her own father is a vivid symbol of any unspeakable act. In some versions of this tale, the horrible deed is precipitated, not by a father's desperate effort to save himself, but by his unsuccessful attempts to seduce his daughter. In their commentary on the *Children's and Household Tales,* the Grimms relate another version of this tale in which the father, angered by his daughter's refusal to marry him, cuts off her hands and her breasts, then sends her into the world to fend for herself (1856, 3:57–58; Motif Q451.1, "Hands cut off as punishment").

Even more abhorrent to most humans than mutilation is the act of cannibalism, and more than a few folklore sources depict parents eating their own children, usually tricked into doing so by their spouses. An example from Norse mythology is found in *The Saga of the Volsungs.* Gudrun (known in *The Nibelungenlied* as Kriemhild) holds her husband Atli (known elsewhere as Attila the Hun) responsible for the death of her brothers. To extract revenge, she seizes her and Atli's two sons as they play by their beds, slits their throats, then serves their blood, mixed with wine, and their roasted hearts to their unsuspecting father (G61, "Relative's flesh eaten unwittingly").

"My mother killed me; my father ate me" are two lines from a folksong sung by Gretchen in Goethe's *Faust* (part 1, lines 4412–4420), written about 1774. Essentially the same song is an integral part of a folktale recorded in Low German by the painter Philipp Otto Runge and later incorporated into the Grimms' *Children's and Household Tales* under the title "The Juniper Tree" (KHM 47; AT 720, *My Mother Slew Me, My Father Ate Me*). The deed behind the song is terrifying. A boy's stepmother tricks him into leaning into a large chest with the promise of one of the apples inside. She then slams down the lid onto his neck, cutting off his head (Motif S121, "Murder by slamming down chest-lid"). To hide her crime, she cooks him in a stew, which she feeds to the boy's unwitting father. The boy appears in a new incarnation as a bird, singing repeatedly, "My mother killed me; my father ate me." This is, of course, a fairy tale, and by the story's end the cruel parent is dead, and the boy is restored to his human form.

Although the Grimms' version of this tale is an indictment of a stepmother's cruelty, not that of a natural parent, the quoted song—"My mother killed me; my father ate me," which is integral to most versions of the tale—suggests that in the story's earliest form it was a mother who committed the murder. Variants of Type 720 tales that do feature mothers as murderers occur in many countries, for example, Austria (Zingerle and Zingerle 1852, no. 12), England (Briggs 1970, 1: 476–477), Scotland (Chambers 1870, 49–51), and North America (Dorson 1967, no. 119). In at least one version, "The Dove" from the Ukraine, father and mother conspire together to kill and eat their son (Olesch 1980, no. 3).

Various motivations prompt these acts of cannibalistic cruelty. In the tales involving a stepmother, she is motivated by jealousy. In *The Saga of the Volsungs,* the mother kills her children to punish her husband. In "The Satin Frock" (Briggs 1970), the mother kills her daughter as punishment for getting her clean dress dirty, then cooks the girl in a stew to hide the body. In a number of tales, including "Eating the Baby" (Dorson 1967), a woman eats her husband's dinner while preparing it, then attempts to hide the theft by killing her child and substituting it for the stolen meat. Whatever the motivation behind these acts of murder and cannibalism, these tales reflect the worst fears of a child who perceives himself or herself as being unwanted. Whether the threats thus portrayed were real or only imagined, the wide distribution and longevity of type 720 tales suggest that they must have been very deeply felt.

Throughout the centuries, acts of horror sometimes have prompted, in addition to the expected feelings of disgust, a reaction of humor, perhaps as an expression of denial, by turning the event into a cruel joke. Such "sick jokes" are part of children's repertoires in many cultures, for example, a sketch collected in Ohio in the 1950s: "But Mommy, I don't want to go swimming."—"Shut up, brat, and get back in the bag" (Coffin and Cohen 1974, 42). The present writer recalls an even cruder joke from Idaho, also from the 1950s: "Mommy, Mommy, why am I running in circles?"—"Shut up, or I'll nail your other foot to the floor." Stories of cruel parents are not yet extinct.

D.L. Ashliman

See also: Abandoned or Murdered Children; Cannibalism.

REFERENCES

Briggs, Katherine M. 1970. *A Dictionary of British Folk-Tales in the English Language.* Part A, Folk Narratives. 2 vols. London: Routledge and Kegan Paul.

Calvino, Italo. 1980. *Italian Folktales.* Selected and retold by Italo Calvino. Trans. George Martin. New York: Harcourt, Crace, Jovanovich.

Chambers, Robert. 1870. *Popular Rhymes of Scotland.* New edition. London: W. and R. Chambers.

Coffin, Tristram Potter, and Hennig Cohen. 1974. *Folklore from the Working Folk of America.* Garden City, NY: Anchor Books.

Dorson, Richard M. 1967. *American Negro Folktales.* Greenwich, CT: Fawcett Publications.

Grimm, Jacob. 1899. *Deutsche Rechtsalterthümer.* 4th ed. 2 vols. Leipzig: Dietrich.

Grimm, Jacob, and Wilhelm Grimm. 1856. *Kinder- und Hausmärchen.* Vol. 3: Anmerkungen zu den einzelnen Märchen. Göttingen: Verlag der Dieterich'schen Buchhandlung.

Haas, Alfred. 1903. *Rügensche Sagen und Märchen.* Stettin: Johs. Burmeister's Buchhandlung.

Hreinsson, Viðar, ed. 1997. *The Complete Sagas of Icelanders.* 5 vols. Reykjavik: Leifur Eiríksson.

Jente, Richard. 1947. *Proverbia Communia: A Fifteenth Century Collection of Dutch Proverbs, Together with the Low German Version.* Bloomington: Indiana University Publications, Folklore Series.

Olesch, Reinhold. 1980. *Russische Volksmärchen*. Düsseldorf: Eugen Diederichs Verlag.

Opie, Iona, and Peter Opie. 1991. *The Oxford Dictionary of Nursery Rhymes*. Oxford: Oxford University Press.

The Saga of the Volsungs. 1990. Trans. Jesse L. Byock. Berkeley: University of California Press.

Straparola, Giovanni Francesco. 1898. *The Facetious Nights*. Trans. W.G. Waters. 4 vols. London: Privately printed for members of the Society of Bibliophiles. First published as *Le piacevoli notti*, 2 vols., 1550–1553.

Yeats, W.B., ed. 1983. *Fairy and Folk Tales of Ireland*. New York: Macmillan.

Zingerle, Iguaz Vinzenz, and Joseph Zingerle. 1852. *Kinder- und Hausmärchen, gesammelt durch die Brüder Zingerle*. Innsbruck: Wagner.

Cruel Spouses

Motif S60

❀

Cruel spouses, especially husbands, are a common fixture in international folktales, and domestic violence against a wife is seldom condemned. One of the rare folktales that criticizes a husband's arbitrary cruelty toward his wife, while at the same time depicting a woman more clever than her husband, is AT 888A, *The Wife Who Would Not Be Beaten,* from India (Bompas 1909, no. 28).

Told throughout the Indian subcontinent, this tale opens with the matter-of-fact sentence, "There was once a raja's son who announced that he would marry no woman who would not allow him to beat her every morning and evening." He finds a woman who agrees to this condition, but when he first raises a stick against her, she chides him, saying that because he has his wealth and position only through inheritance, he does not deserve to beat her until he has personally proven himself in the competitive world. Accepting her challenge, he sets out on a trading expedition, but forthwith loses all his goods, and his freedom as well, to a foreign raja. Learning of his fate, the wife wins back his freedom and his lost goods by engaging his new master in a rigged game of chance. After returning home, the newly freed husband takes up his old despotic habits, only to have his wife remind him of his recent servitude, and that she was the one who rescued him. Having learned this humiliating lesson, he gives up all ideas of beating his wife.

Historically, wife beating has not been considered cruelty, but simply sound family management, according—at least—to the folkloric record, which offers endless examples around the world. Folktale Type 670, *Animal Languages,* as represented by "The Bull and the Ass" from the *One Thousand and One Nights* (Burton 1885–1888, 1:16–23), graphically depicts this bias.

The tale opens when Allah grants a man the ability to understand the language of animals with the condition that, under penalty of death, he keep this gift a secret. One day, while eavesdropping on a humorous conversation between a bull and a donkey, the man laughs aloud. His wife wants to know what he finds so funny. He responds that it will cost him his life if he tells her, but she persists. He finally decides to give in to her wheedling; then, while making preparations for his death, he overhears a rooster bemoaning the situation with a dog. "I can control fifty wives," boasts the rooster, "but our master cannot manage one. He could solve his problem easily. He need only beat her until she dies or repents." The man takes heart from the rooster and beats his wife nearly senseless. She finally says, "I repent. With Allah as a witness, I will never again question you." Her parents and other members of the household rejoice, and thenceforth the husband and the wife live together the happiest of lives.

One must not assume that this cruel tale, a cornerstone of the *One Thousand and One Nights* frame story, marks a misogynistic bias found only in Arabic culture. Essentially the same story is found in the sacred *Jataka* tales of Buddhism (vd. 3, no. 386), and in numerous versions scattered throughout the Christian world. It is particularly revealing and sobering to discover this tale (and others similarly promoting wife beating) in English collections prepared specifically for children only three or four generations ago—for example, "The Snow, the Crow, and the Blood" (MacManus 1900, 153–174; AT 507A, *The Monster's Bride*) and "The Language of Beasts" (Lang 1903, 55–61; AT 670, *The Animal Languages*). In the first story, the hero marries the princess and breaks a blackthorn over her every day for ten days in order to dispossess her of the devil (D712.5, "Disenchantment by beating").

Although nineteenth- and early twentieth-century folktale publishers frequently apologized to their readers for any hints of vulgarity that might have slipped through the editing (and censorship) process, no such warnings were deemed necessary for stories promoting wife beating. For example, Andrew Lang's preface to *The Crimson Fairy Book* states specifically that the tales in his collection "are adapted to the needs of British children" (1903, v), but he shows no compunction for offering a story ("The Language of Beasts") that concludes: "As soon as the man understood this, he . . . seized a stick, and called his wife into the room, saying, 'Come, and I will tell you what you so much want to know'; and then he began to beat her with the stick, saying with each blow, 'It is that, wife, it is that!' And in this way he taught her never again to ask why he had laughed" (1903, 61).

A survey of novellas and jests from European medieval and Renaissance collections shows how deeply rooted this acceptance of wife beating is in the Western world, to say nothing of other regions. Boccaccio's *Decameron* (1972,

9:9; AT 910A, *Wise Through Experience*), Margaret of Navarre's *Heptameron* (sixteenth century) (1922, 5:46), and the anonymous *Hundred Tales* (1960, no. 97), to mention a few prominent examples, all contain stories that defend brutal corporal punishment of wives.

In the Boccaccio story (told by a woman), it is the biblical Solomon who offers the advice that leads to a wife's beating, thus suggesting that such behavior is divinely endorsed. Similarly, in the tales from the *One Thousand and One Nights* and the *Jataka* tales cited above, the beatings appear to be sanctioned, even ordered, by Allah and the future Buddha, respectively.

No part of the world seems free from such attitudes. Even the *Kalevala,* the Finnish national epic, instructs, ostensibly with divine authority, a young bridegroom how to chasten a recalcitrant bride—with a birch switch, behind closed doors, and taking care not to strike her in the face (1963, poem 24).

According to a traditional proverb, "Sauce to the goose is sauce to the gander," but folklore does not treat women and men at all alike when it comes to discipline. There are relatively few folktales about wives who physically abuse their husbands, two examples being "Mr. Vinegar" from England (Jacobs 1898, 28–30; AT 1009, 1415, 1653) and "Two Out of the Sack" from Russia (Afanasyev 1975, 321–324, AT 564).

Indeed, various public penalties evolved whose purpose was to quash such tendencies before they spread. In Germany, the guilty woman might be led through town riding backward on a donkey, holding its tail in her hands (Grimm 1899, 2: 318–319; Bächtold-Stäubli 1930, vol. 2, col. 1016–1017). A punishment even more graphically symbolic of the perceived danger was the ancient practice of roof removal. If it became known that a woman had beaten her husband, a procession of neighbors would advance on the guilty couple's house and with great ceremony dismantle its roof (Grimm 1899, 2: 319–322; Bächtold-Stäubli 1930, vol. 2, col. 115–116; Lyncker 1854, 231–233). This custom, which was known, if not actually practiced, for many centuries throughout Germany, served not only to put both husband and wife to public shame for a socially unacceptable reversal of roles, but also—symbolically at least—to release from the house the evil spirits that were causing the problem.

Mental cruelty may be a term invented by modern divorce lawyers, but it is an ancient concept, although, like corporal punishment, its marital use is often sanctioned by the folkloric record only when used by a husband to correct or to test a wife.

Two widespread folktale cycles offer dramatic examples: AT 887, *Griselda,* and AT 900–904, *The Shrewish Wife Is Reformed.* Each group has been immortalized by one or more classic authors, the former by Boccaccio (1972, 10:10), Petrarch (*De Obidentia ac fide uxoria mythologia*), and Chaucer ("The Clerk's Tale"); and the latter by Shakespeare (*The Taming of the Shrew*). In

Shakespeare's dramatization, the machinations used by Petruchio to transform his spirited wife Katharina into a conformable household Kate are too well known to require elucidation here. All of Petruchio's tricks, and many more of like kind, are found in folktales of types 900–904.

Griselda is less familiar today than is *The Taming of the Shrew,* although the basic plot is well represented in medieval and Renaissance ballads, chapbooks, and novellas throughout Europe. The story, in Boccaccio's version, begins with a certain marquis proposing marriage to a young woman named Griselda. In accepting his proposal, Griselda promises always to try to please him, never to be upset with anything he might say or do, and always to obey him. Shortly after the birth of their first child, a daughter, the marquis decides to test her promised patience. Claiming, for no specific reason, that she and her daughter are unworthy of their position, he demands that she surrender the newborn, ostensibly to be killed, and the wife dutifully and without complaint gives up the child. Later, Griselda gives birth to a son, and the marquis repeats his demand, taking this child away as well. Although Griselda believes that both children are dead, the father secretly has placed them in foster care.

Many years later, the marquis subjects Griselda to a final ordeal. Announcing his intentions to abandon her and to take a new wife, he orders her to make preparations for the wedding and for the new bride's arrival. All this Griselda does efficiently and without complaint, thus passing his last test of obedience and proving herself to be an ideal wife. As a reward, the husband restores to her her daughter (now twelve years of age) and her six-year-old son. The marquis's subjects congratulate him for his wisdom in designing and carrying out such a test, even though the trials to which he had subjected Griselda were considered extreme. The story thus has an ambiguous conclusion, the marquis being both praised and criticized in the same breath. Griselda, however, is unreservedly acclaimed for her wifely devotion.

In folklore and mythology, cruel husbands are rarely criticized, much less punished. A further case in point is the tale "The Son of Seven Mothers" from the Punjab (Steel 1894, no. 10; AT 462, *The Outcast Queens and the Ogress Queen*), with a very similar story also being told in Kashmir ("The Ogress-Queen," Knowles 1893, 42–50). In the Punjabi version, a king with seven wives falls in love with a bewitchingly beautiful young woman, who agrees to marry him only if he will prove his devotion to her by giving her the eyes of his other wives, all of whom are pregnant. He fulfills the young woman's wish, then throws his blinded wives into a dungeon, where they survive only by eating their babies as they are born.

Only one child survives, who is thus symbolically the son of seven mothers. He miraculously escapes and recovers the blinded women's eyes, restoring their sight. The king, now recognizing that he has married an ogress, has her put to death, brings the other seven wives back to the palace, and—the storyteller assures us—"everybody lived happily." Thus the temptress who seduced the husband into an unspeakably cruel act against his other wives is executed, but the man who actually performed the wicked deed is not so much as criticized.

This double standard of morality is nowhere more evident than in most cultures' attitudes toward extramarital relations, which for men typically are condoned, but for women almost universally are condemned. Punishments, as depicted in folklore, for women caught in adultery give new meaning to the legal term *cruel and unusual*. One such penalty often featured by medieval and Renaissance writers, including Boccaccio (1972, 4:9; AT 992, *The Eaten Heart*) and Margaret of Navarre (1922, 4:32; AT 992A, *The Adulteress's Penance*), is a husband forcing his adulterous wife to eat her lover's heart or to drink from his skull.

Another common punishment for adultery—at least in folklore—is physical mutilation. In a Danish example, recorded in the *Gesta Danorum* of Saxo Grammaticus (1894, book 2), the mistress of the legendary hero Hjalte asks her master how old a man she should marry, if she were to lose him. Hjalte considers her thoughts of marriage to another man to be proof of "the lecherousness of her soul." His response is to cut off her nose, thus making her unattractive to any future lover.

Similarly, in "The Weaver's Wife" from *The Panchatantra* (1964, 62–74), a man cuts off the nose of a woman who he mistakenly thinks is his unfaithful wife. Later, the victim expresses the fear that "he will do something worse next time, cut off ears and things."

Finally, halfway around the world, accounts of life among the North American Indians are replete with depictions of adulterous women being punished by having their faces mutilated (for example, Kinzie 1857, ch. 27; and Schultz 1907, ch. 10). Whether or not these accounts authentically reflect actual custom and behavior, they do promulgate a belief system that in the end creates its own reality.

D.L. Ashliman

REFERENCES

Afanas'ev [Afanasyev], Aleksandr. 1975. *Russian Fairy Tales*. New York: Pantheon.
Bächtold-Stäubli, Hanns. 1927–1942. *Handwörterbuch des deutschen Aberglaubens*. 10 vols. Berlin: Walter de Gruyter.
Boccaccio, Giovanni. 1972. *The Decameron*. Trans. G.H. McWilliam. Hammondsworth: Penguin.

Bompas, Cecil Henry. 1909. *Folklore of the Santal Parganas.* London: David Nutt.

Burton, Richard F., trans. 1885–1888. *The Book of the Thousand Nights and a Night: A Plain and Literal Translation of The Arabian Nights Entertainments.* 10 vols. plus 6 supplemental vols. Privately printed by the Burton Club.

Grimm, Jacob. 1899. *Deutsche Rechtsalterthümer.* 4th ed. 2 vols. Leipzig: Dietrich.

The Hundred Tales: Les Cent Nouvelles Nouvelles. 1960. Trans. Rossell Hope Robbins. New York: Crown.

Jacobs, Joseph. 1898. *English Fairy Tales.* 3rd ed. London: David Nutt.

The Jataka; or, Stories of the Buddha's Former Births. 1895–1913. Ed. E.B. Cowell. 6 vols. Cambridge: Cambridge University Press.

The Kalevala; or, Poems of the Kaleva District. 1963. Comp. Elias Lönnrot, trans. Francis Peabody Magoun Jr. Cambridge, MA: Harvard University Press.

Kinzie, Mrs. John H. [Juliette McGill Kinzie]. 1857. *Wau-Bun, the "Early Day" in the Northwest.* Chicago: D.B. Cooke.

Knowles, J. Hinton. 1893. *Folk-Tales of Kashmir.* London: Kegan Paul, Trench, Trübner.

Lang, Andrew. 1903. *The Crimson Fairy Book.* London: Longmans, Green.

Lyncker, Karl. 1854. *Deutsche Sagen und Sitten in hessischen Gauen.* Kassel: Verlag von Oswald Bertram.

MacManus, Seumas. 1900. *Donegal Fairy Stories.* New York: McClure, Phillips.

Margaret of Navarre. 1922. *The Heptameron of the Tales of Margaret, Queen of Navarre.* Trans. George Saintsbury. London: Privately printed for the Navarre Society Limited. First published 1558 under the title *Histoire des amans fortunez.* Published 1559 as *Heptaméréron des nouvelles.*

The Panchatantra. 1964. Trans. Arthur W. Ryder. Chicago: University of Chicago Press.

Saxo Grammaticus. 1894. *The First Nine Books of the Danish History of Saxo Grammaticus [Gesta Danorum].* Trans. Oliver Elton. London: David Nutt.

Schultz, James Willard. 1907. *My Life as an Indian: The Story of a Red Woman and a White Man in the Lodges of the Blackfeet.* New York: Doubleday, Page.

Steel, Flora Annie. 1894. *Tales of the Punjab: Told by the People.* London: Macmillan.

Abandoned or Murdered Children

Motifs S300–S399

❁

Child abandonment is a many-faceted concept within myth, folktale, and literature. In studying heroes in myth and literature, scholars have found that their lives have many points in common, including, in their infancy, abandonment or attempted murder by the father. Boswell attests to the prevalence of abandoned children "from Moses to *Tom Jones*" (Boswell 1988, 6).

However, abandonment can often lead to the death of the child. "Hansel and Gretel" (AT 327A), perhaps the most famous fairy tale centering on abandoned children, provides a rare instance of a happy ending with the return of the children and the prosperity of the reconstituted family, a group without a mother figure. Jack Zipes voices a concern that the Grimms' 1857 "Hansel and Gretel" actually rationalizes abandonment and abuse (Zipes 1997, 48). He observes that Wilhelm Grimm "went to great pains to explain and demonstrate why the father should be exculpated in the end" (50).

There are a number of motivations for abandoning a child. Exposing a child to avoid the fulfillment of a prophecy, as in the story of Oedipus in Greek mythology, is one scenario (M371; AT 930 or 931, depending on the emphasis). Sometimes children are killed as a sacrifice, to appease a god, as in Agamemnon's sacrifice of Iphigenia (S263.2), or as a foundation sacrifice to ensure the stability of a structure (S261). Sometimes children are abandoned or killed due to fear of social censure (T586.3, "Multiple births as indicator of sexual promiscuity"). Still other abandonments or murders are done as acts of revenge (S302) as in *Medea,* and even as acts of outright cruelty. These tales also intersect with Motif C867.1, "Tabu: abusing women or children."

Even if the child survives the ordeal of abandonment, as Oedipus does, the results are seldom happy. Abandonment is often associated with fear, jealousy, or dislike of the child or with deep poverty and looming hunger (S321) or the potential death of the adults in the family.

Tales of burying children alive in the foundations of buildings or bridges convey the sense that this is a terrible, though oddly necessary sacrifice of an innocent (S261, *The Höxter Ghost,* for example) that arises out of a superstition that the dead child will somehow guarantee the success and safety of the structure. The sacrificial object in some foundation stories is chosen at random—in one case because the child is alone and is thus a target of opportunity (one example is a German story, "The Secured Foundation Stone").

At the other end of the spectrum are children who are singled out because of their relationship to the adult who is about to harm them. Euripides' *Medea* is a case in point—the demise of no other children but Medea's own sons by Jason would cause him the pain she wishes to inflict as part of her revenge on him for marrying the princess and abandoning her. There are also cases of eliminating a child specifically because of her gender (Chinese—Western Yugur). The Mexican legend of "The Crying Woman" (*La Llorona*) tells of a woman who, like Medea, kills her own children out of anger when her lover (the children's father) betrays and abandons her. As Medea helps Jason steal the Golden Fleece from Colchis, so the woman helps Cortéz conquer Mexico; thus both women betray their countries. A key element in the Mexican tale that does not appear in Euripides' story is that La Llorona can be heard crying for and seeking her dead children.

The exceedingly cruel tale type, AT 720, *My Mother Slew Me, My Father Ate Me,* has many versions, including the Grimms' story "The Juniper Tree." In this tale, the stepmother kills the stepson, serves him up to his father, and tosses the child's bones away. His half-sister buries the bones, and the boy, who comes back initially as a bird, announces the stepmother's perfidy in his song (N271.4, "Murder discovered, knowledge of bird languages. Birds point out the murder"). The bird brings gifts to his father and sister, but brings a millstone for his murderer, thus crushing her to death. After her death, the murdered boy reappears as a boy and the new family gathers. Maria Tatar sees the tales of this type by the Grimms and Perrault ("Le Petit Poucet"; AT 327B, *Exchange of Caps*) as tales of development. "Development is thus traditionally defined in terms of growing away from the mother, who represents dependence and domesticity, and turning toward the father" (Tatar 1992, 226). In *The Folktale,* Thompson claims that "in many countries it is quite impossible to disentangle the two tales" of "Hansel and Gretel" and "Le Petit Poucet" (1946, 37). The child's capacity for independence prompts Lüthi to say, "children in fairy tales are by no means helpless; many of them free themselves by

Child abandonment (Motif S301) is a motif that occurs in myth, folktale, and literature. Heroes are often abandoned by their parents as infants and are found and raised by surrogates. From Geoffrey de Latour Landry, *Der Ritter vom Turn* (1493).

their own ability and cunning" (1976, 65). Another tale of abandonment in the literary fairy tale tradition, "Snow White" (AT 709; Motif S322.4.2, "Evil stepmother orders stepdaughter to be killed"), involves a child who seems unable to help herself, but survives anyway.

Even in cases when the children do not save themselves, the culprit is often revealed. A tale that has a key element of revealing the murder of the child is AT 780, *The Singing Bone*. The singing bones appear in stories by the Grimm brothers, and in tales from Italy, Russia, England, Nigeria, and Switzerland. Unlike the boy in AT 720, restoration of the dead child is not usually the outcome (the Russian story "The Silver Plate and the Transparent Apple" is an exception). Justice, however belatedly, comes to the murderers (Q211, "Murder punished"). The murder is usually the result of sibling treachery triggered by a parental promise of inheritance or some other prize for the one who finds a particular object. Jealousy because one sibling possesses an object the others desire can also be the motivation to murder.

Parents may get rid of a child born out of wedlock by exposing or abandoning it (S312, "Illegitimate child exposed"), but in some cases the dead child haunts the abandoner. In both a tale from Iceland and in George Eliot's novel *Adam Bede* (1859), a mother abandons her baby only to be haunted into a state of mental disarray. The Icelandic story tells of a mother who, after abandoning the child, is unhappy because she does not have the clothes to go to a party. At this shallow moment, the voice of her dead child sings to her and drives her mad. Eliot's Hetty Sorrel in *Adam Bede* gives birth to the illegitimate child of the local squire and tries to hide the event by abandoning the baby, but its cries follow her.

In the case of multiple births, which were unfortunately linked to suspicions that the woman had slept with multiple men (T586.3), we also see attempts to kill or abandon a child or children. In the Grimms' "As Many Children As There Are Days" (AT 762), a countess accuses a woman who gives birth to twins of promiscuity. The countess is then punished by giving birth to a child a day (Ashliman 1987, 155). A tale from the twelfth century *lais* of Marie de France, "Le Fresne," includes the same accusation about a woman who bears twins. As Boswell points out, the woman first thinks about killing one of the twins, but "her companions dissuade her from this, arguing that it would be a sin. Abandonment, however, was not" (Boswell 1988, 369). Most of a group of Sioux villagers in the story "The Bound Children" also have no objection to a mother who abandons her children. She leaves them so she can make an advantageous marriage with the chief's son. The majority view, however, does not find support in this tale. The woman's daughter throws filth in her mother's face, which transforms the coldhearted mother into a hag. The chief's son orders the children to be bound and abandoned when the camp moves on, but the old woman cuts their ropes and tells them where to find sustenance. In the end, the children save the villagers from the ravages of famine by supplying them with meat; however, the children give their abandoner only substandard fare and the old woman the best food, calling her grandmother. (S351.1, "Abandoned child cared for by grandmother (aunt, foster mother)").

Well-known literary examples of abandonment and child murder from Shakespeare and Homer highlight the trouble that comes from false accusations of infidelity (*The Winter's Tale*) and the lengths people go to in order to guarantee victory in war (*The Iliad*) and political power (*The Tempest*). In *The Winter's Tale,* Leontes, king of Sicily, thinks his queen, Hermione, has been unfaithful to him. His harsh treatment of her actually causes his son, Mamillius, to die of distress. Leontes orders that his newborn daughter, Perdita, be taken from his kingdom and abandoned. The man who abandons Perdita leaves articles with her that prove her nobility (S334, "Tokens of royalty (nobility) left with exposed child"). Miranda of *The Tempest* is set adrift with her father when her uncle seizes power. Politics and war lead to the cruel murders of prominent Trojan children in *The Iliad*. The Greeks throw the child Astyanax from a high wall and they kill Hecuba's daughter, Polyxena, on Achilles' grave.

Attempts to hold on to power also motivate both Herod in the Bible and Kamsa in the *Bhagavata Purana*. Herod commands that all recently born male babies be killed (S302.1, "All new-born male children slaughtered") as he seeks to destroy the child who, it is prophesied, will best him. Kamsa, in his attempt to kill Krishna, has both male and female babies killed. Both Jesus and Krishna escape, but the mass murder of children attests to the threat both Herod and Kamsa perceive should their nemeses survive. Though both tales link to the broader motif of avoiding foretold events, the element of slaughter distinguishes them as M375, "Slaughter of innocents to avoid fulfillment of prophecy."

Instead of being a potential joy, children in stories of abandonment or murder are problems or impediments for their guardians. Hunger and poverty, miseries in themselves, and superstitions can lead to abuse of the child. Children's fates are often tied to the fates and situations of their mothers, broader needs for political power, and fear of prophecies of the burgeoning power of the child. Those who survive their ordeal of abandonment appear to flourish and find happiness, and in some tales even murdered children are restored.

Susan M. Bernardo

See also: Cruel Parents; The Hero Cycle.

REFERENCES

Aarne, Antti. 1964. *The Types of Folktale: A Classification and Bibliography*. Trans. and ed. Stith Thompson. 2d revision. Helsinki: Suomalainen Tiedeakatemia.

Ashliman, D.L. 1987. *A Guide to Folktales in the English Language*. Bibliographies and Indexes in World Literature, 11. Westport, CT: Greenwood Press.

Boswell, John. 1988. *The Kindness of Strangers: The Abandonment of Children in Western Europe from Late Antiquity to the Renaissance*. Chicago: University of Chicago Press.

Eliot, George. 1996 [1859]. *Adam Bede*. Oxford, New York: Oxford University Press.

Lüthi, Max. 1976. *Once Upon a Time: On the Nature of Fairy Tales*. Bloomington: Indiana University Press.

Tatar, Maria. 1992. "Telling Differences: Parents vs. Children in *The Juniper Tree*." *Off with Their Heads: Fairy Tales and the Culture of Childhood*. Princeton, NJ: Princeton University Press.

Thompson, Stith. 1946. *The Folktale*. New York: Holt, Rinehart, and Winston.

Zipes, Jack. 1997. "The Rationalization of Abandonment and Abuse in Fairy Tales." *Happily Ever After: Fairy Tales, Children, and the Culture Industry*. New York and London: Routledge.

Persecuted Wife

Motifs S410–S451

❁

In literature and folklore, the motif of the persecuted wife generally plays out according to three principal types of narratives. In the first case, the heroine's persecution results from an unjust accusation of adultery by a male character whose advances she rebuffs. In the second, jealous female characters (sisters, mother-in-law, or friends) replace the heroine's child or children with animals, usually dogs, leading to her ostracism. Finally, the third type of narrative revolves around the husband testing his wife's endurance in particularly cruel ways, a story historically used as an exemplum of the perfect wife.

ALLEGED ADULTERY AND RESENTFUL MEN

Medieval tradition abounds in stories of wives unjustly accused of adultery. According to Roger M. Walker, the tale of Crescentia, more appropriately known as the "Conte de la femme chaste convoitée par son beau-frère" ("Tale of the chaste woman desired by her brother-in-law"), typically adheres to the following plotline: a husband goes on a trip and leaves his brother with his wife; the brother desires his sister-in-law, and she rejects him; the brother accuses his sister-in-law of adultery; the wife is condemned to be beaten and killed; she is rescued by a passerby, or flees; the heroine acquires healing powers; in the end, she is reconciled with her husband (1982, 2–3). The two main European sources for this tale type are the *Gesta Romanorum* and the *Chanson de Florence,* with the latter source providing a version of the story in which one of the husband's men proves the wife's accuser wrong, and it is the brother-in-law, not the wife, who is banished.

The story of Hildegard, Charlemagne's wife, comes out of the Crescentia tradition. In Jacob and Wilhelm Grimm's rendition, Charlemagne's stepbrother Taland attempts to seduce Hildegard during Charlemagne's absence, and she consequently imprisons him until her husband's return. However, Taland succeeds in convincing Charlemagne that it was Hildegard who tried to seduce him. Charlemagne orders his wife to be drowned, but Hildegard flees to Rome, where she learns the art of healing. Struck with leprosy and blindness, Taland goes to see the woman healer of Rome, without realizing that this woman is in fact Hildegard. After Taland agrees to confess, Hildegard heals him, she is reunited with Charlemagne, and Taland is banished (Grimm 1981, 2:64–66). The story of Geneviève or Genofeva of Brabant follows a similar plotline. While the count palatine Siegfried is on an expedition against the infidels, he entrusts his wife and castle to the care of his vassal Golo. Golo is filled with passion for Genofeva, but the countess repels his advances. Upon the count's return, Golo concocts the story that Genofeva committed adultery with the cook, who is the father of her child. Siegfried condemns to death wife and child, who end up taking refuge in a cave, where a doe nurses Genofeva's son. Eventually Siegfried discovers Golo's treachery, Genofeva and her son are reunited with the count, and a chapel dedicated to the Virgin Mary is built on the site where they had taken refuge (Grimm 1981, 3:165–168). Geneviève de Brabant's story circulated in Europe throughout the early modern period in chapbooks (Remy 1910), and by 1859 Offenbach brought the legend to the opera house in a comical version. It is notable that such stories emerged at the time of the crusades. With husbands away fighting the "infidels," the fidelity of wives and concern for the legitimacy of one's progeny were important concerns. Sanctified through their power to heal, exemplary characters like Crescentia, Hildegard, and Geneviève glorified the fidelity and even martyrdom of wives.

The Indian tale "Hanchi" represents a more secular version of the type. After leaving home to avoid her brother's incestuous desires and marrying the son of a wealthy man, Hanchi is pursued by the holy man Guruswami, her father-in-law's chief counselor. Although Hanchi outwits Guruswami on several occasions, the lecherous and spiteful man plants false evidence in Hanchi's room and declares to her father-in-law that he has surprised Hanchi with her lover. In order to force Hanchi to confess, her husband and his family beat and starve her, but to no avail. Finally, with the aid of an old woman, Hanchi clears her name, and her family asks her forgiveness (Ramanujan 1997, 74–79). Although "Hanchi" differs from its European counterparts in that the heroine does not become a saintly healer (in fact, Hanchi is more of a trickster character than a saint), it resembles Crescentia stories in that the false accuser is a person whom the husband trusts. All such tales emphasize the treachery and betrayal of the false accusation.

ANIMAL BIRTHS AND ENVIOUS WOMEN

In the second type of tale concerning the persecuted wife (AT 707, *The Three Golden Sons*), jealous women replace the wife's newborns with animals in order to incite the heroine's husband to repudiate, imprison, or kill her. Stories about the Swan Knight, a champion of unknown origin who wins a princess's hand, fused with a Germanic fairy tale about children who change into swans when their necklaces are removed (Remy 1910). This hybrid story became the model for European versions of the wife calumniated by the appearance of having given birth to animals. According to the Grimms' version of the medieval legend, Oriant, the son of King Pyrion and Queen Matabruna, marries Beatrix. In order to rid herself of a daughter-in-law of unknown birth, Matabruna plans to murder Beatrix's seven babies—all born with silver chains around their necks—and replace them with seven puppies. Believing his mother's accusations that Beatrix had intercourse with dogs, Oriant imprisons his wife. In the meantime, an old hermit raises the seven children. But Matabruna discovers that the children are alive and sends a hunter off to kill them. However, the hunter, not wishing to harm the children, removes their necklaces to bring back to the queen as proof of their death. The children turn into swans. In the end, one of Beatrix's sons, Helias, defends his mother's honor, the truth is revealed, and Matabruna is burned at the stake (Grimm 1981, 1:171–178).

In the sixteenth-century tale "Ancilotto, King of Provino," Straparola has the evil mother-in-law conspire with the heroine's two sisters. The heroine, Chiaretta, predicts that she will marry the king and have two sons and a daughter, born with golden necklaces and a star on their forehead, which indeed comes about. The two jealous sisters, Brunora and Lionella, both of whom married below their sister, replace the children with pups and throw the children into a chest, which they cast into the river. While Chiaretta is punished by having to do menial labor, the children are rescued and raised by a miller and his wife. Eventually, the children return to their father's court with a green bird, who reveals their true identity. The king's family is reunited, and the sisters and mother-in-law are thrown into a fire (Zipes 2001, 220–229). Marie-Catherine d'Aulnoy closely follows Straparola's version of the story in "Princess Belle-Etoile and Prince Cheri" (1998), but has the two younger sisters, Blondine and Brunette, suffer together when their eldest sister Roussette conspires with the mother-in-law to replace Blondine's three children and Brunette's son with puppies. D'Aulnoy notably makes the three sisters daughters of a dispossessed queen, providing them with a noble genealogy. Like Straparola's Chiaretta, Blondine predicts her children will be born with gold chains and a star on their forehead, and like her Italian counterpart, she is ostracized when her husband learns she gave birth to puppies. The story's resolution is also similar: the children return to their father's court with a green bird who reveals the truth, and the queen mother poisons herself (Zipes 2001, 229–263; d'Aulnoy 1998, 343–406).

In his 1717 collection of *Arabian Nights,* Antoine Galland includes a similar story, "The Jealous Sisters and Their Cadette." The youngest of three sisters marries a Persian sultan and predicts she will have a son with gold and silver hair, whose tears are pearls and whose smiles are rosebuds. Her jealous sisters replace her first son with a dead puppy, her second son with a kitten, and her third child, a daughter, with a mole. All three children are saved by the caretaker of the sultan's gardens. After the third birth, the sultan imprisons his wife next to a mosque with a window through which people spit upon and humiliate her. Again, the situation is resolved when the children return to court, and a talking bird reveals the truth (Zipes 2001, 270–302). The version related by the Brothers Grimm, entitled "The Three Little Birds" (1857), follows the general scheme of the other stories: the youngest sister of three marries a king, and she gives birth to a boy, whom the sisters substitute with a puppy; then she has a second son, again replaced with a puppy; and finally a daughter, who is switched with a kitten. The king imprisons his wife. A fisherman and his wife care for the children until they return to the king's court with the talking bird, who reveals everything. Their mother is released, and her sisters are burned to death (Zipes 2001, 302–305).

Most of the later versions retain the golden or silver chains present in the medieval story, although the chains only serve the function of establishing the true identity of the children and lose their magical powers to transform the children into swans. Also present from Straparola on is the talking bird, who reveals to the husband the truth about his wife and children. In all versions, the wife patiently endures her humiliating situation and forgives her husband for having punished her unjustly. Whereas stories regarding a wife unjustly persecuted for adultery are initiated by a male character's failure to seduce a virtuous wife, the stories in which the wife is persecuted for having given birth to animals are initiated by female characters who compete for status. While the queen mother fears for the status of her grandchildren and perhaps sees herself as her daughter-in-law's rival for her only son's affection, the sisters are jealous of a sister who marries above them and bears exceptional children, symbolized by the golden chains and the stars. Women's value in many societies was based on producing children, which the heroine does exceptionally well, making her the envy of her sisters.

Certain tales present variations on the theme of animal births and alleged adultery, while others emphasize the unreasonableness of the husband. In Marie de France's "Le Fresne," for instance, a woman gives birth to twins, and her envious neighbor announces that the woman therefore must have had intercourse with two men. Adultery is combined with the "monstrous" birth of twins. Despite the good woman's virtue, her husband begins to mistrust her, and he guards her as if she were in prison. Ironically, the neighbor herself becomes pregnant with twins (1986, 61–67). In "The Story of the Three Apples" from the *Arabian Nights,* a husband cuts his wife into nineteen pieces for having given an apple to her slave-lover, when in fact their son took one of the wife's apples, and a slave stole the apple from the son (Burton 1991, 271–278; Haddawy 1990, 150–157). In two Japanese tales, wives are repudiated for minor, insignificant offences. In "The Golden Eggplant," a woman married to a lord finds herself the object of her friends' jealousy. Rather than replace her child with a puppy, the envious friends put cornhusks in her husband's bed to make it sound as if the heroine broke wind before him. The lord immediately sends his pregnant wife away. Later the son confronts the father, who recognizes his hypocrisy and makes the boy his heir (Seki 1963, 173–175). In "The Bundles of Straw and the King's Son," a poor woman on her deathbed reveals to her son his true identity. She had been the wife of a king and one day exclaimed how magnificent she found a ship at sea, which caused people to stop their work and look at the ship. Her husband repudiated her because she led people to waste time. After relating the story, the mother dies, and the son finds his father, outwits him, and is declared king (Seki 1963, 175–179).

PATIENT WIVES AND CRUEL HUSBANDS

The third archetypal narrative of the persecuted wife is referred to somewhat problematically as The Patient Wife, whose best-known European heroine is Griselda (AT 887, same title). Whereas in the first two types of narratives the husband is merely the instrument by means of which the wife is persecuted by jealous men or women who manipulate him, in Griselda stories the husband himself carries out the persecution, arguably driven by his own insecurities and phantasms of control, but under the pretext of morality. "Griselda" first appeared in print in Boccaccio's *Decameron* (1349–1353). The story concerns Gualtieri, the marquis of Saluzzo, who is unenthusiastic about marrying but whose vassals entreat him to take a wife in order to have an heir. The marquis marries the daughter of a poor shepherd, who swears to comply with all his wishes. At court people marvel at the shepherdess's noble manners, and they find her admirable in conversation, virtuous, obedient, and devoted to her husband. Suddenly the marquis wishes to test his wife's patience, subjecting her to unusually harsh trials. After the birth of their daughter and their son, he makes Griselda believe that he has put them to death, when in fact he sends them to a kinswoman. Then the marquis repudiates Griselda, allegedly due to her low birth, and sends her back to her father with only a shift to cover her nudity. Years later, the marquis calls Griselda back to court, only to test her yet again. He tells her he wants her to prepare a new bride for life with him. Griselda stoically undergoes each trial without questioning her husband's wishes. The new bride turns out to be their daughter, whom he reunites with Griselda, finally revealing the truth. The narrator of the story carefully notes before relating it that he finds Gualtieri's actions remarkable for "their sense-less brutality" and clearly states that the marquis is not an exemplary husband, although he praises Griselda for her singular ability to endure such trials (Boccaccio 1995, 783–795).

While Boccaccio's tale is the earliest known written version of "Griselda," later written and oral versions grew out of Francis Petratrch's Latin transla-tion, "Griseldis" (1374), which served as the model for many European ren-ditions, evident in the wide use of the Latinized name (Golenistcheff-Koutouzoff 1933, 24–150). Significant versions of the tale include Philippe de Mézière's *Le Miroir des Dames Mariées, c'est assavoir de la merveilleuse pacience et bonté de Griseldis, Marquise de Saluce* (*The Mirror of Married Ladies, or the Marvelous Patience and Goodness of Griseldis, the Marquise of Saluce,* 1384–1389), the main conduit for the tale in France; Geoffrey Chaucer's "The Clerk's Tale" (1386–1400); Christine de Pizan's version, which appeared in *Le Livre de la Cité des Dames* (*The Book of the City of Ladies,* 1405); and Charles Perrault's "Griselidis," first published in 1691 and repub-lished in his *Contes en Vers* (*Verse Tales,* 1695). Compared to Boccaccio's version, Petrarch Christianizes the tale and exaggerates the exemplary virtue and obedience of Griseldis. He states, however, that his object is "not so much to encourage the married women of our day to imitate this wife's patience," but rather to urge his readers to emulate Griseldis's constancy in their submis-sion to God (Petrarch 1992, 2:668). That the relation between God and his flock is expressed in terms of wifely obedience to her husband (and Griseldis notably tends sheep) is not, however, unproblematic.

With Mézière's translation of "Griseldis" and despite Boccaccio and Petrarch's statements that Griseldis was not meant to be imitated, the tale regularly was published in books on marriage, books for the education of girls, and treatises on domestic economy and gastronomy in fourteenth- and fifteenth-century France (Golenistcheff-Koutouzoff 1933, 38–55). By the seventeenth century, the story of Griseldis was regarded as a tale told by mer-chants and villagers. Because the Latinized "Griselidis" had come to be asso-ciated with the lower classes, Perrault initially intended to name his heroine "Griselde" in the tradition of Boccaccio (Golenistcheff-Koutouzoff 1933, 149–150; Perrault 1981, 307). Perrault's revival of the tale among the upper classes cannot be separated from his critique of cultured aristocratic women, whom he viewed as uncontrollable and corrupt and to whom he opposed Griselidis, the "natural" and domesticated woman whose will is that of her husband (Duggan 2001, 151–153). Given the publishing history and wide diffusion of the tale, it clearly was being used as a pedagogical instrument to inculcate women of all classes with the notion that patiently obeying even cruel husbands can eventually lead to happiness, thus reaffirming the unconditional authority of the husband in the home.

While other types of narratives concerning the persecuted wife often include episodes probably influenced by Griselda tales (notably Marie de France's "Le Fresne" and d'Aulnoy's "Princess Belle-Etoile and Prince Cheri"), the tale itself was widely diffused in Europe and the Middle East. A Jewish Moroccan tale, "The Patient Wife," closely follows the archetypal tale. A father boasts about his daughter's patience and marries her to a wealthy merchant, who decides to put his wife's patience to the test. As in the European versions, the husband successively takes away the children (two boys and a girl), claiming he is sacrificing them to cure himself, but in fact has them well educated. And as in the European versions, the husband informs the wife that he is remarrying and wishes her to prepare the new bride, who is in fact the daughter. In the end, the husband rewards his father-in-law, marries his daughter to a rabbi, and lives happily ever after with his patient—or submissive—wife (Bar-Itzhak and Shenhar 1993, 25–39).

It is interesting to note that in tales about the persecuted wife, the husband's cruelty is often justified to some extent because it results from the manipulation of others or it causes the heroine to become an exemplum of wifely obedience. Whether motivated by an evil brother, mother, sister-in-law, or his wish to test the extent of his wife's endurance, the husband's responsibility for his wife's sufferings is diminished. This cannot be better demonstrated than in Jules Massenet's 1901 opera *Griselidis,* in which the heroine is put to the test not by her husband, but by the devil himself.

Anne E. Duggan

REFERENCES

Bar-Itzhak, Haya, and Aliza Shenhar. 1993. *Jewish Moroccan Folk Narratives from Israel.* Detroit: Wayne State University Press.

Boccaccio, Giovanni. 1995. *The Decameron.* Trans. and intro. G.H. McWilliam. New York: Penguin.

Burton, Richard F. 1991. *Arabian Nights: The Marvels and Wonders of The Thousand and One Nights,* ed. Jack Zipes. New York: Signet.

Chaucer, Geoffrey. 1992. *Canterbury Tales,* ed. A.C. Cawley. New York: Knopf.

d'Aulnoy, Marie-Catherine. 1998. *Contes II,* ed. Philippe Hourcade. Paris: Société des Textes Français Modernes.

Duggan, Anne E. 2001. "Nature and Culture in the Fairy Tale of Marie-Catherine d'Aulnoy." *Marvels & Tales* 15.2: 149–164.

Golenistcheff-Koutouzoff, Elie. 1933. *L'histoire de Griseldis en France au XIV et au XV siècle.* Paris: Droz.

Grimm, Jacob, and Wilhelm Grimm. 1981. *The German Legends of the Brothers Grimm.* Ed. and trans. Donald Ward. 2 vols. Philadelphia: ISHI.

Haddawy, Husain, trans. 1990. *The Arabian Nights.* New York: Norton.

Marie de France. 1986. *The Lais of Marie de France.* Trans. Glyn S. Burgess and Keith Busby. New York: Penguin.

Perrault, Charles. 1981. *Contes: Suivis du Miroir ou La métamorphose d'Orante, de La Peinture, poèrne, et du Labyrinthe de Versailles.* Ed. Jean-Pierre Collinet. Paris: Gallimard.

Petrarch, Francis. 1992 [1405]. *Letters of Old Age.* Trans. Aldo S. Bernardo, Saul Levin, and Reta A. Bernardo. 2 vols. Baltimore: Johns Hopkins University Press.

Pizan, Christine de. 1992. *La Cité des Dames.* Paris: Stock.

Ramanujan, A.K. 1997. *A Flowering Tree and Other Oral Tales from India.* Ed. Stuart Blackburn and Alan Dundes. Berkeley: University of California Press.

Remy, Arthur F.J. 1910. "Literary Legends." *The Catholic Encyclopedia.* Vol. 9, www.heiligen-gral.com/legends.htm.

Seki, Keigo, ed. 1963. *Folktales of Japan.* Trans. Robert J. Adams. Chicago: University of Chicago Press.

Walker, Roger M. 1982. "*La Chanson de Florence de Rome* and the International Folktale." *Fabula* 23 (1–2): 1–18.

Zipes, Jack, ed. 2001. *The Great Fairy Tale Tradition: From Straparola and Basile to the Brothers Grimm.* New York: Norton.

❀ T ❀

Sex

Conception and Birth

Motifs T500–T599

❊

"Where do babies come from?" is a question that has preoccupied children as well as adults since the beginning of time. Notions of how one might conceive are as vast and diverse as the human imagination. Many motifs on this subject are classified in the *Motif-Index* under Chapter T, Sex, which contains motifs on wooing, sexual relations, marriage, and the birth of children.

There is an extensive listing of "miraculous conceptions" (T510), and since extraordinary conceptions often precede the birth of extraordinary beings, many of these conceptions belong to stories about demigods and heroes and are cross-referenced under the entries "Birth and rearing of culture hero" (A511) and "Birth of culture hero" (A511.1).

A common example of miraculous conception is through eating (T511), including the consumption of various fruits, flowers, roots, and leaves. Also common is conception from a wish (T513), through a dream (T516), from sunlight (T521), moonlight (T521.1), and falling rain (T522). In his celebrated book *The Myth of the Birth of the Hero,* Otto Rank highlights the archetypal patterns underlying the birth of culture and religious heroes, from the Babylonian Sargon and Moses to the Norse hero Seigfried. Such narratives begin with a prophecy before or during pregnancy, warning that the child, generally of royal lineage, may endanger his father. At birth, the hero is cast into waters and miraculously saved, usually by animals or low-ranking characters, and eventually becomes a king or prophet (Rank 1964, 65). Although the birth of the hero typically concerns a male child, the *Chanson de Florence* provides an example of a female culture hero whose birth is prophesied to bring disaster (R. Walker 1982, 7).

MIRACULOUS CONCEPTIONS

One of the best-known miraculous conceptions is that of the Virgin Mary, who gave birth to Christ, son of God. A foundational myth of Christianity, the idea of a virgin becoming pregnant nevertheless has perplexed many, as Barbara Hanawalt contends in her discussion of medieval English folk songs (1980, 132–133). Poking fun at the notion of immaculate conception, Roberto Rossellini wrote and directed *The Miracle,* in which Anna Magnani stars as a simple peasant woman whom a man gets drunk and rapes. Unaware that a man has had sexual relations with her, Magnani's character believes she is a second Virgin Mary. Well before it was believed that Mary conceived miraculously of Christ, the Greeks and Romans were telling the story of Perseus, the son of Danaë, whom Zeus/Jupiter impregnated through a golden rain shower. In many different cultures and eras, apparently sterile women pray to God or the gods to become fertile, from the Judeo-Christian and Muslim stories about Sarah and Rachel, to the Nigerian tale of a woman who promises her first born to a god if he makes her fertile (B. Walker and W. Walker, 1980, 69–70). In seventeenth-century France, Louis XIV came to be known as "the God-given," for it was believed that his mother, Anne of Austria, was barren and that God finally granted her a child, who was to become one of France's greatest kings.

Praying to gods could be considered one form of conception from a wish. The western European fairy-tale tradition offers another common archetypal narrative of this type of impregnation, usually involving a lower-class male character who, out of anger and humiliation, wishes a princess to become pregnant. In Straparola's "Pietro the Fool" (1550), Luciana, daughter of King Luciano, becomes pregnant when Pietro wishes it so. Basile takes up the same theme in "Peruonto" (1634), in which the good-for-nothing hero similarly wishes Princess Vastolla to become pregnant. Marie-Catherine d'Aulnoy modifies the tale by focusing on the principal male character's ugliness and making him noble in "The Dolphin" (1698), whereas the Grimms combine lower rank with a hunched back to create their hero (see Zipes 2001).

Just as Zeus impregnates Danaë through rain, the Sun impregnates the mother of Wenebojo, the Chippewa culture hero, in a gust of wind. Conception from sunlight is a common theme in origin myths of Woodland, Plains, and Southwest Indians (see Barnouw 1977, 13–14). Folk traditions provide numerous examples of conception through contact with wind, rain, and sunlight. Impregnation can also occur by consuming everything from flowers to fish to plants. In the Nigerian tale "Three Wives and a Porridge," the porridge in question contains a remedy for sterility (B. Walker and W. Walker 1980). An Indian tale, "The Mother Who Married Her Own Son," includes an example of conception from bull's urine, while Chinese tale, "Why the Horns of Cattle

Are Curved," seems to combine the latter theme with conception from eating a vegetable: a woman eats a beet that floats down a stream and becomes pregnant with a girl; the father is a saintly ox who ate the leaves of the beet; it is this indirect contact that brings about the pregnancy (see Ramanujan 1997; Eberhard 1965).

CRAVINGS, BIRTHMARKS, AND BIRTHRIGHTS

As tales from Basile's "Petrosinella" (1634) and Charlotte-Rose de La Force's "Persinette" (1698) to Friedrich Schulz's "Rapunzel" (1790) and the Grimms' "Rapunzel" (1857) reveal, fairy-tale authors have been preoccupied by the idea of maternal cravings and their effect on the fetus or the fate of the baby. (Such concerns are also found in folk culture; see, for instance, Jalby 1971 [15–16] and Sébillot 1968, 1:4].) In Basile's tale, the pregnant Pascadozia craves the bed of parsley belonging to an ogress and fears that her baby will be born with parsley on its face if she does not yield to her desire. Although La Force transforms the ogress into a fairy, and the Grimms make her a sorceress, the narrative remains strikingly similar in all cases: the mother craves the forbidden parsley or rapunzel; she promises her unborn child to a supernatural creature; a daughter is born, locked in a tower, and becomes pregnant by a prince; the daughter goes through more trials and tribulations and, after much suffering, lives happily ever after. According to Holly Tucker, maternal cravings were deemed dangerous in folk and literary traditions, resulting, it was believed, in miscarriage or birthmarks. Cravings were associated with what was forbidden and, as Tucker contends, daughters of mothers who succumb to temptation in such tales are forced to redeem the sins of their mothers (Tucker 2000, 2003).

Birthmarks or other deformities signal the mother's sin. Golden chains and stars on foreheads, on the contrary, could be read as signs of a mother's virtue. Moreover, such objects and signs authenticate the children's noble birth at one point in the narrative of these stories. The legend of the Swan Knight is one of the earliest European versions of this type of tale. As the Grimms recount it, Oriant takes the beautiful and virtuous Beatrix as his queen. Beatrix has seven children, each of whom is born with a silver chain (1981, 2:171–178). Some tales have the heroine predict that her children will be born with necklaces or stars on their foreheads, as in Straparola's "Ancilotto, King of Provino" (1550), d'Aulnoy's "Princess Belle-Etoile and Prince Cheri" (1698), and Antoine Galland's "The Jealous Sisters and Their Cadette" (1717). In each story, the queen's jealous mother-in-law and/or sister(s) wish to destroy her babies, replace them with dogs, and accuse the heroine of having given birth to animals. After being unjustly punished, the queen finally is reunited with her children, in part thanks to the necklaces (Zipes 2001; see also Berlioz Brémond, and Velay-Vallantin 1989, 141–154).

Concerns about the process of pregnancy have also made their way into folk and fairy tales. Viewed in certain traditions in terms of sin, maternal cravings were believed to mark the fetus with the object of the mother's desire, manifest in the birthmark, whereas objects like gold chains around the necks of newborns usually signaled their true noble identity and eventual good fortune. As H.A. Rose has documented in the Punjab, good and bad fortune can also be determined by the day or date on which a baby is born (1907, 220–224). Although stories about multiple births and women giving birth to animals initially represent the situation as problematic, if not horrifying, their plotlines eventually lead to an unexpectedly happy or heroic resolution.

MALE PREGNANCY

When we think of conception and birth, we usually have women in mind. However, folk traditions also provide numerous examples of male pregnancy.

Surprisingly, the notion that a man could become pregnant is a motif in many different folk traditions (T578, "Pregnant man"). Often male pregnancy occurs by eating, as in the Scandinavian tale noted by Stith Thompson, in which a man catches a magic fish intended for his wife, eats it, and becomes pregnant with a girl, who is cut out of his knee (S. Thompson 1977, 123). In two Nigerian tales, a male becomes pregnant by eating porridge. In "The Man and the Fertility Porridge," a man goes to a diviner, who warns him not to eat the porridge, but the man stumbles, the porridge spills on his finger, he licks it, and eventually both he and his wife give birth. The hero of "The Tortoise and the Forbidden Porridge" meets a different fate. A male tortoise cannot resist the smell of the porridge he acquires from a diviner for his wife, eats it up, and dies from the pregnancy (B. Walker and W. Walker 1980).

Other tales about male pregnancy involve misdiagnosis or trickery. Roberto Zapperi has traced Italian stories about the pregnant man of Monreale to visual representations, in the Sicilian city's cathedral, of Christ healing a man with dropsy, who indeed appears to be with child. In the Italian tale "The Pregnant Priest," a priest has a peasant take a urine sample for him to the doctor. The peasant accidentally knocks over the bottle of urine and then asks a woman, who happens to be pregnant, to refill it. Fearing he is pregnant, the priest unsuccessfully seeks an abortion to avoid scandal, ends up throwing himself from a tree, falls over a hare's nest, and believes he has given birth to a rabbit (see Zapperi 1991). Richard Burton recorded a story from the *Arabian Nights,* "Tale of the Kadih Who Bore a Child," in which a wife takes vengeance on her avaricious husband by filling him up with beans. After the husband discharges, she pulls out a neighbor's newborn. Believing he has given birth, the husband flees to Damascus in shame, but eventually the couple are reconciled (Burton 1887). Although few examples exist of successful male pregnancy, Zapperi has pointed out that in medieval European iconography, Eve emerging from Adam's side represents a most powerful image of a man giving birth (Zapperi 1991, 3–32).

MULTIPLE AND OTHER EXTRAORDINARY BIRTHS

Tales in the tradition of the Swan Knight provide examples of stories in which multiple births are represented in a positive light. Sometimes, however, multiple births are viewed in negative terms. In Marie de France's twelfth-century tale "Le Fresne," a woman accuses her neighbor, who has just had twins, of having committed adultery. It was believed that a woman who gives birth to two children must have had sexual relations with two different men. Upon having twins herself, the woman regrets having made the accusation (1986). In other stories concerning the birth of five or more children, like "The Boy in the Fish Pond" and "The Birth of Aistulf," only the child who grasps the king's or his father's lance is spared (Grimm and Grimm 1981, 23, 38).

In stories like "Ancilotto" and "Princess Belle-Etoile," the queen is only led to believe that she gave birth to animals. Tales in the tradition of Straparola's "The Pig Prince" (1698), however, concern a queen—and in the case of the Grimms, a farmer's wife—who truly gives birth to an animal. D'Aulnoy's "The Wild Boar" (1698) and Henriette Julie de Murat's "The Pig King" (1699) closely follow Straparola's tale: a fairy capriciously wishes a queen to give birth to a pig, who can take human form only after marrying three times. In the Grimms' "Hans My Hedgehog" (1857), it is the farmer, angry he has no children, who wishes for a child, "even if it's a hedgehog" (Zipes 2001, 96). In the end, all the animals are transformed into handsome young men, usually after the animal skin is destroyed (see Zipes 2001; d'Aulnoy 1998).

Anne E. Duggan

See also: Hermaphroditism; The Hero Cycle; Monstrous Births.

REFERENCES

Arras, Jean d'. 1854. *Mélusine.* Ed. Charles Brunet. Paris: P. Jannet.
Barnouw, Victor. 1977. *Wisconsin Chippewa Myths and Tales and Their Relation to Chippewa Life.* Madison: University of Wisconsin Press.
Berlioz, Jacques, Claude Brémond, and Catherine Velay-Vallantin. 1989. *Formes médiévales du conte merveilleux.* Paris: Stock.

Burton, Richard F. 1887. "Tale of the Kadih Who Bore a Child." *Supplemental Nights to the Book of the Thousand Nights and a Night.* 6 vols. Benares: Kamashastra Society. 4:169–185.

d'Aulnoy, Marie-Catherine. 1998. *Contes II.* Ed. Philippe Hourcade. Paris: Société des Textes Français Modernes.

Eberhard, Wolfram. 1965. *Folktale of China.* Chicago: University of Chicago Press.

Grimm, Jacob, and Wilhelm Grimm. 1981. *The German Legends of the Brothers Grimm.* Ed. and trans. Donald Ward. 2 vols. Philadelphia: ISHI.

Hanawalt, Barbara A. 1980. "Conception Through Infancy in Medieval English Historical and Folklore Sources." *Folklore Forum* 13 (2–3): 127–157.

Jalby, Robert. 1971. *Le folklore du Languedoc: Ariège-Aude-Lauraguais-Tarn.* Paris: Maisonneuve et Larose.

Marie de France. 1986. *The Lais of Marie de France.* London: Penguin.

Ramanujan, A.K. 1997. *A Flowering Tree and Other Oral Tales from India.* Berkeley: University of California Press.

Rank, Otto. 1964. *The Myth of the Birth of the Hero and Other Writings.* Ed. Philip Freund. New York: Vintage.

Rose, H.A. 1907. "Hindu Birth Observances in the Punjab." *Journal of the Royal Anthropological Institute of Great Britain and Ireland* 37 (July–December): 220–236.

Sébillot, Paul-Yves. 1968. *Le Folklore de la Bretagne.* 2 vols. Paris: Maisonneuve et Larose.

Seki, Keigo, ed. 1963. *Folktales of Japan.* Trans. Robert J. Adams. Chicago: University of Chicago Press.

Thompson, Raymond H. 1974. "Gawain Against Arthur: The Impact of a Mythological Pattern upon Arthurian Tradition in Accounts of the Birth of Gawain." *Folklore* 85 (Summer): 113–121.

Thompson, Stith. 1977 [1946]. *The Folktale.* Berkeley: University of California Press.

Tucker, Holly. 2000. "Like Mother, like Daughter: Maternal Cravings and Birthmarks in the Fairy Tales of Mme d'Aulnoy and Mlle de la Force." In *The Mother in/and French Literature,* ed. Buford Norman. Atlanta: Rodopi.

———. 2003. *Pregnant Fictions: Childbirth and the Fairy Tale in Early Modern France.* Detroit: Wayne State University Press.

Walker, Barbara K., and Warren S. Walker, eds. 1980. *Nigerian Folk Tales.* Hamden, CT: Archon.

Walker, Roger M. 1982. "*La Chanson de Florence de Rome* and the International Folktale." *Fabula* 23 (1–2): 1–18.

Zapperi, Roberto. 1991. *The Pregnant Man.* Trans. Brian Williams. New York: Harwood.

Zipes, Jack, ed. 2001. *The Great Fairy Tale Tradition: From Straparola and Basile to the Brothers Grimm.* New York: Norton.

Monstrous Births

Motifs T550–T557

❀

Found under Chapter T, Sex, "Monstrous births" is a large cross-cultural heading that includes all deformed babies, such as those born as formless lumps of flesh (T551.1.1.), with two heads (T551.2), or without mouths (T551.6). It also includes hybrids such as babies born with limbs or heads of animals (T551.3–T551.3.4.2), those who are half human and half fish (T551.5), and those who are human and demon or alien blends (T556). Children who have unusual powers (T550.2), have adult characteristics (T551.13.2), or are abnormally large or small at birth (T553) are also classed as monstrous.

Seeing monstrous births as portents of divine will was a belief commonly shared in ancient, medieval, and early modern periods in Europe, Asia, and the Americas. Only after the scientific revolution in the West in the sixteenth and seventeenth centuries did the religious and moral interpretations of monstrous births come to be defined as "folk" or "popular," in contradistinction to the naturalized or medicalized "official" interpretations of birth defects or deformities (Smith 1980; Park and Daston 1981). Therefore, these folk narrative motifs outline moral universes, by definition, in their focus on the causes and effects, public or private, of women giving birth to monsters. Several examples follow.

AMERICAN INDIAN MYTHIC MONSTROUS BIRTHS

North American Indian origin myths are replete with monsters, which vary by tribe and region, such as the water monster Unktehi, the Great Rolling Head, and the giant Yeitso, cannibals all. Anthropologist Erminie Wheeler-Voegelin notes specific examples of births of monsters from the Jicarilla Apache:

> Birth of the monsters whom Killer-of-Enemies, Jicarilla Apache culture
> hero, kills before the Apache are created, is specifically accounted for by
> the Jicarilla Apache. Among the First People were women who misbe-
> haved, became pregnant, and give birth to a Giant Elk, a monster eagle, a
> kicking monster, the two running rocks, a monster rock (Flint Man), Big
> Owl, a giant fish—all of whom Killer-of-Enemies disposes of. (Wheeler-
> Voegelin 1972, 743)

In the beginning, the private indiscretions of First Women cause the monstrous births of cosmic beasts who must be overcome to establish cultural
order and harmony for the Apache.

For the Wintu, in a variant of "Rolling Head," a menstruating girl breaks a
taboo by following women into the woods to strip maple bark. Bark splinters
enter her finger, which bleeds without stopping. Sucking the blood causes the
girl to crave it, then to cannibalize herself and so give birth to herself as cannibalistic monster:

> So she ate her little finger, and then ate her whole hand. Then she devoured
> both her hands. Then she ate her leg, ate both her legs. Then she ate up her
> whole body. Then her head alone was left. It went rolling over the ground. . . .
> [S]he bounced up to the west across the river to the flat on the west, where she
> threw the people into her mouth. Without stopping, she turned the village
> upside down as she devoured them all. (Erdoes and Ortiz 1984, 210–211)

THE DEVIL BABY

In Judeo-Christian contexts, however, monstrous births do not cause community disasters so much as signal them, although these births too may have dire
public consequences. A biblical passage (1 Esdras 2: 4–8), noting signs and
portents, has often been quoted in this regard:

> The sunne shal suddenly shine againe in the night, and the moone thre times
> a day. Blood shal drop out of the wood, and the stone shal give his voyce. . . .
> There shalbe a confusion in many places, and the fyre shal oft breake forthe,
> and the wilde beastes shal change their places, and menstruous women shal
> beare monstres. (quoted in Park and Daston 1981, 25)

Perhaps Motif T556, "Woman Gives Birth to a Demon," is the most well-
known monstrous birth as sign within a Christian framework. In Europe and
England, demonic births as a result of intercourse with the Devil or a demon
or through witchcraft were, as noted, commonly believed in earlier times.
Alleged appearances of the Devil Baby in the New World occurred in 1637
and 1638. Anne Hutchinson, a pious Puritan who was labeled a religious heretic,

was brought to a civil trial in Boston in November 1637 for sedition; a church trial for heresy would follow. Hutchinson was, in addition to a preacher, a skilled midwife and mother of twelve children. She was apparently pregnant during her church trial, but either miscarried or had a tumor which she expelled. What is more certain is that her close friend and follower, Mary Dyer, had given birth to a premature, deformed infant in October 1637, and Hutchinson had been present at the birth. Writing many years later, Cotton Mather affirmed in *Magnalia Christi Americana* (1702) that Mary Dyer was

> delivered of as hideous a monster as perhaps the sun ever lookt upon. It had no head: the face was below upon the breast: the ears were like an ape's, and grew upon the shoulders. . . . it had on each foot three claws, with taleons like a fowl. . . . The midwife was one strongly suspected of witchcraft. (cited in Johnson 1995, 100–101)

The Jersey Devil, or Leeds Devil, is a Devil Baby legend associated with the southern New Jersey pine barrens. The legend, said to originate in 1740, involves Mother Leeds—a suspected witch or, in some versions, a woman who did not want another child, and cursed it, saying, "Let it be born a devil!"—who gave birth to what first appeared a normal baby. A description from 1896 continues:

> [It] soon took the shape of a dragon, with a snake-like body, a horse's head, a pig's feet and a bat's wings. This dreadful being increased in strength as it gained in size, until it succeeded the bulk and might of a grown man, when it fell on the assemblage [of people attending the birth], beating all the members of the party, including its own mother, with its long, forked, leathery tail. (Skinner 1896, 240).

The beast escaped, killing children and causing numerous agricultural disasters. For years afterward, the creature was blamed for many eerie noises and mysterious happenings that were seen as portents of disaster, shipwrecks, and wars (Perticaro n.d.). The Jersey Devil's "finest hour" seems to have come in 1909, when a flurry of sightings and descriptions was reported in newspapers in southern New Jersey and eastern Pennsylvania (Sullivan and McCloy 1974, 233–239). The creature is said to still live, apparently becoming immortal or at least having an extremely long life span. The Web site, The Jersey Devil of the Pine Barrens, relates sightings as late as the mid-1970s and notes that an episode of the popular television series *The X-Files* borrowed the legend for a story idea, however changing the beast into a savage woman (Perticaro n.d.).

Many alternative versions of the Jersey Devil's origins, shape, and escapades have been reported. The creature often takes the form of a hybrid beast, more like American Indian monsters than humanoid figures as in most other Devil Baby legends, although some of its features, such as cloven hoofs and a pointed tail, suggest a human/Devil blend.

Another famous version of the Devil Baby legend localized itself at Hull-House, a Chicago immigrant settlement house founded in 1889 by social reformer Jane Addams. The story began in 1914. Addams related the story in a number of publications, citing an "Italian version" and a "Jewish version" as follows:

> The Italian version, with a hundred variations, dealt with a pious Italian girl married to an atheist. Her husband in a rage had torn a holy picture from the bedroom wall saying that he would quite as soon have a devil in the house as such a thing, whereupon the devil incarnated himself in her coming child. As soon as the Devil Baby was born, he ran about the table shaking his finger in deep reproach at his father, who finally caught him and, in fear and trembling, brought him to Hull-House. . . . the Jewish version, again with variations, was to the effect that the father of six daughters had said before the birth of a seventh child that he would rather have a devil in the family than another girl, whereupon the Devil Baby promptly appeared." (Addams 1916, 3–4)

People came to Hull-House wanting (even demanding) to see the Devil Baby, which they had heard was housed there. Perhaps because of her feminist leanings, in the versions Addams relates, the mother is always seen as victim, not perpetrator, of the blasphemous act that leads to the Devil Baby's birth. It is interesting to note that Baughman has isolated a traditional motif implicating the mother of monsters (G303.25.21.1.1.5, "Blasphemous Mother Bears Monster Child") that is applicable to all the monstrous births discussed so far, but none directly blaming the father, as in Addams's published versions (Baughman 1966).

MONSTROUS BIRTHS AND HASTY WISHES

Mother Leeds's curses in the Jersey Devil legend and the father's curses in the account of the Devil Baby at Hull-House connect Motif T556, "Woman gives birth to a demon" with Motif C758.1, "Monster born because of hasty (inconsiderate) wish of parents." In the two examples that follow, childless couples each wish for a child with disastrous results.

In the medieval European legend of Robert the Devil (S223.0.1), a diabolical baby is born to a childless couple as a result of an appeal to the Devil to help in the child's conception (S211). Reputed to have been a historical figure, Robert the Devil was born, in some versions, with a full set of teeth

(T551.13.2) and wreaked havoc with his wet nurse, or even killed her. When he grew to maturity, he was saved from further evil by appealing to the Virgin Mary (Hibbard 1960, 49–57; Rudwin 1931, 179).

The story of Robert the Devil deviates from later Devil Baby legends in that no redemption is offered in the later versions. In the popular 1968 American horror film *Rosemary's Baby,* for example, Rosemary's maternal gaze at the end of the film implies that her demon child will live. And in the 1976 horror film *The Omen,* a couple whose own baby had been stillborn adopt a demonic child. The movie spawned two sequels, and in the third and last movie, the child, grown to maturity, attempts to prevent the Second Coming of Christ.

In the folktale "Mundig" told by Mrs. Marian Serabian and recorded in *One Hundred Armenian Folktales,* an old couple's hasty wish for children results in unusual births mitigated only by the world of fantasy. The old woman attracts a passing dervish, a holy man, and asks him what she should do to have a child. He tells her to get a handful of *sissair,* chickpeas, and sit on them and she will have a child. She does what the dervish suggests with these disturbing results:

> And sure enough! a whole bunch of babies, about as big as your thumb, were scattered all through the room! "Oh, what shall I do with all these little things?" the poor woman said, hitting her hands on her knees, pulling her hair and crying, "What shall I do with all these tiny things?" In the midst of all this, she remembered suddenly that she had to prepare her husband's lunch. So she hurriedly heated the oven and started to bake the bread. "I know what to do! I'll put all these babies in the oven right now and get rid of them." After she had baked the bread, she took all the babies and put them in the hot oven. Of course, they all died immediately. (Villa 1966, 235)

Although one baby, Mundig, escapes to live a while longer than his siblings, this tale exemplifies the dangers of entreating outsiders for help in conceiving a child.

EARLY DEATH OF MONSTROUS BABIES

Although Robert the Devil and other demonic children in American films live to be adults, most monstrous babies either die or are killed in infancy or early childhood, as indicated in the story of "Mundig." Various folk beliefs, showing a faint trace of the medicalized model of monstrous births in which severely deformed children are seen as not viable, suggest the moral inappropriateness of monsters living. Beliefs recorded among the Kosovo Rom, for example, report that a child born of a vampire father and a human mother will have no bones and will die shortly after birth (Wilson 1970). This belief is an example of a related motif, C101, "Sex tabu broken: Child born without bones."

In macabre variations of widespread Japanese legends about a ghostly mother feeding her living child, children are made monstrous because they are born posthumously in their mothers' coffins. In *Ghosts and the Japanese: Cultural Experience in Japanese Death Legends,* Iwasaka and Toelken present a story about an *Ubume* (the ghost of a mother who gave birth to her baby after she was buried):

> When they dug her up, they found not only that there wasn't any change in the color of her skin but also saw that she was clutching a little baby dressed in funeral clothes. This baby had a curved back, and had a rice cake in his hand and was licking it. Apparently the baby had been born after the woman's burial and had survived somehow. (1994, 64)

Iwasaka and Toelken note what might not be apparent to non-Japanese readers, that "the storyline itself may go back to an older (but residually persistent) idea that it is the baby who is the powerful and dangerous entity. The baby born in the grave, and thus unritualized as a newcomer . . . , is a potential danger to any passerby, to society, to the world." (1994, 64, 66)

Betty J. Belanus and Janet L. Langlois

See also: Bargain with Devil.

REFERENCES

Addams, Jane. 1916. *The Long Road of Women's Memory.* New York: Macmillan.
Baughman, Ernest. 1966. *Type and Motif Index of the Folktales of England and North America.* Folklore Series No. 20. The Hague: Mouton.
Booth, Sally S. 1975. *The Witches of Early America.* New York: Hastings House.
Dorson, Richard. 1950. *America Begins.* New York: Pantheon.
Erdoes, Richard, and Alfonso Ortiz, eds. 1984. *American Indian Myths and Legends.* New York: Pantheon.
Hibbard, Laura A. 1960. *Medieval Romance in England.* New York: Burt Franklin.
Iwasaka, Michiko, and Barre Toelken. 1994. *Ghosts and the Japanese: Cultural Experience in Japanese Death Legends.* Logan: Utah State University Press.
Johnson, Claudia Durst. 1995. *Understanding* The Scarlet Letter. Westport, CT: Greenwood.
Park, Katharine, and Lorraine J. Daston. 1981. "Unnatural Conceptions: The Study of Monsters in Sixteenth- and Seventeenth-Century France and England." *Past and Present* 92 (August 1981) 20–54.
Perticaro, Anthony. n.d. "The Jersey Devil of the Pine Barrens," www.strangemag.com/jerseydevil1.html.

Rudwin, Maximillian. 1931. *The Devil in Legend and Literature.* Chicago: Open Court Press.

Skinner, Charles M. 1896. *Myths and Legends of Our Own Land.* Vol. 1. Philadelphia: J.P. Lippincott.

Smith, Norman R. 1980. "Portent Lore and Medieval Popular Culture." *Journal of Popular Culture* 14: 47–59.

Sullivan, Jeremiah J., and James F. McCloy. 1974. "The Jersey Devil's Finest Hour." *New York Folklore Quarterly* 30 (3): 233–239.

Villa, Susie Hoogasian. 1966. *One Hundred Armenian Tales and Their Folkloric Relevance.* Detroit: Wayne State University.

Wheeler-Voegelin, Erminie. 1972 [1949]. "Monsters." In *Funk and Wagnalls Standard Dictionary of Folklore, Mythology, and Legend,* ed. Maria Leach and Jerome Fried, 743. New York: Funk and Wagnalls.

Wilson, Duncan. 1970. *Life and Times of Vuk Stefanovic Karadzic, 1787–1864: Literacy, Literature, and National Independence in Serbia.* Oxford: Clarendon Press.

Incest

Various Motifs in A (and T)

❀

In almost all cultures, incest is viewed as the ultimate tabu that, according to Claude Lévi-Strauss, is at the foundation of human culture itself. While it is often portrayed in terms of shame and horror, incest can be viewed positively when it constitutes the foundational myth of a particular culture, and it is extremely common in creation myths around the world. Usually, incest between gods is a divine marriage, but incest between mortals is profane. This duality is reflected in the classification of incest motifs in the *Motif-Index:* incest between various family members who are gods or demigods occurs under A, Mythological Motifs, such as A164.1, "Brother-sister marriage of the gods," and A164.1.1, "Mother-son marriage of the gods." Incest between mortals is classified under section T, Sex, with the incest motif (T410) located under Illicit Sexual Relations (T400).

Incest has been the subject of intensive scrutiny and theorizing by anthropologists, and there are varying ideas on why the tabu, which is virtually universal, arose. Known exceptions to the incest tabu involved marriages between royal family members in Hawaii, the Inca Empire, Central Africa, and Egypt, where ritual incest was an expression of sacred kingship. In general, those societies in which incest was condoned have myths that take a neutral view of incest.

BROTHERS AND SISTERS

A number of creation myths resort to incestuous peopling of the earth for purely pragmatic reasons. If the first humans were few in number, possibly only two, then their offspring had no choice but to mate with siblings. A myth from the Kabyl people of North Africa tells that the first humans were a man and a woman who had fifty children, half boys and half girls. When mature, they married (A1552.3, "Brother-sister marriage of children of first parents"), and thus the entire human race has descended from twenty-five brother-sister unions (Frobenius and Fox 1937, 49–57).

The first book of Moses (Genesis 4:1–17) implies a similar beginning. Although only two of Adam and Eve's first children are named, there must have been more, for Cain, after killing his brother Abel, lay with Abel's wife and had a son. The Bible does not identify this unnamed woman as Cain's sister, but at least two folktales (Sheykh-Zada 1886, 395; Hanauer 1935, 240–241) specifically state that each brother had a twin sister. God directed each one to marry the other's twin, but Cain, perceiving his own twin sister to be more beautiful, rejected God's order, thus bringing about the conflict that ultimately led to the fratricide.

Famously, in Egyptian mythology, Osiris marries his sister Isis, and brother-sister marriages among the Egyptian pharaohs were not uncommon, with the practice existing among commoners as well. Marriage between brother and sister serves as the foundational myth of the Inca: Inti, the sun god, marries his sister, the moon goddess Mama Quilla. Their children, Maco Capac and his sister and wife Mama Occlo (or Oello), are sent to earth to found Inca society (Vega 1961, 3–8).

The Aborigines of Australia have a myth from northeastern Arnhem Land that recounts how, during the "dreamtime," a brother and two sisters (the Djanggawul) wandered over the earth creating plants, animals, and the ancestors of the Aborigines—the sisters were constantly being impregnated by their brother (Poignant 1967, 130–131).

An account from the Indian *Brihadaranyaka-Upanishad* tells of an androgynous and incestuous pairing that is viewed more equivocally. In the beginning was self, in the shape of a person. He said, "I am," but felt no pleasure. Wishing for a second being, he caused himself to separate into two pieces, and thus were born husband and wife. He approached her, but she said, "How can he embrace me, having produced me from himself? I shall hide." She then became a cow, but he became a bull and united with her, and thus cows were born. She became a mare, and he a stallion, and thus horses were born. She became a ewe, and he a ram, and thus sheep were born. In like manner he created everything that exists in pairs, down to the ants (*Upanishads* 1897, vol. 2, Adhyaya 1, Brahmana 4, stanzas 1–4). Another incestuous encounter occurs in the dialog from the *Rig Veda* (10:10) between Yama, the first son of the sun, and his twin sister Yami. Here, in alternating stanzas, we hear Yama's pleas for intimacy and his sister's polite but firm refusals. In the end, he resigns himself to finding another woman. This is an unusual example in myth of the incest tabu enforced.

In the Norse creation myth, the giant Ymir produces a man and a woman from beneath his arm, and one of his legs begets a son with the other leg. This is the beginning of the frost ogres. Moreoever, many of the gods have a heritage marked by incest. The earth is Odin's daughter and his wife as well, and by her he has his first son, Thor (Snorri 1954, 33–34, 37). An episode from Norse mythology as recorded in the *Saga of the Volsungs* (1990, ch. 7) is an example of incest condoned in a royal family. Signy, a princess of the Volsung dynasty, is unhappy with the cowardly sons produced by her exogamous marriage, so she seduces her brother Sigmund (T415) and conceives by him a son named Sinfjotli, who with time proves to be a champion worthy of the Volsung name and blood.

Creation myths often include accounts of catastrophic floods, resulting in the necessity of repopulating the earth with only a few potential parents, and sometimes they are brother and sister (A1006.2, "New race from incest after world calamity"). In Ovid's account of a Greek flood myth (1981, book I), the only survivors are a son and a daughter of Prometheus, Deucalion and Pyrrha (although they have different mothers). They repeople the earth, but not through sexual procreation. Instead, they throw stones behind them, and the stones grow into men and women. Classical mythology, of course, does not shy away from tales of incestuous relations. Zeus was the oldest son of the Titan brother and sister, Cronus and Rhea (Apollodorus 1975, 1:4; A112.1, "God from incestuous union"), and Adonis was the product of Smyrna's seduction of her father (Apollodorus 1975, 3:183–184; A112.11, "God from father-daughter incest"), to mention but two of many instances.

In a flood myth of the Miao people of China (Werner 1922, 406–408) A-Zie and his sister (for whom no name is given) are the sole survivors of a great deluge. The brother wishes the sister to become his wife, but she objects. Finally she agrees to a test (H300, "Tests connected with marriage"). Each will roll a millstone from opposite hills into a valley, and if they come to rest, one lying atop the other, she will marry him. The test is carried out, but A-Zie rushes to the valley floor and sets one millstone atop the other before his sister arrives. Still reluctant, the sister proposes a second trial. This time they will throw knives into the valley, and if both land inside a single sheath she will marry him. Again A-Zie arrives there first and places both knives in one sheath. Brother and sister marry and have a child, but it is born without arms or legs. A-Zie kills the misshapen baby and cuts it to pieces. The next day the pieces have become men and woman, and thus the earth is repopulated.

One account of the genealogy of the North American Chippewa culture hero Winabogo entails sister-brother incest, also not viewed in neutral or positive terms. In "The Incest of Wenebojo's Grandparents," a sister sleeps with her brother at night without his knowledge. When the brother discovers he has been having intercourse with his sister, he is ashamed and sends his sister through a hole in the earth to punish her. When the sister comes out the other side, she must promise a turtle the daughter she carries. Wenebojo is the son of the daughter and the turtle (Barnouw 1977, 73–74).

The folktale "Kora and His Sister," from India (Bompas 1909, no. 50), appears to be an etiological tale explaining the origin of the tabu against brother-sister marriages. A young man named Kora declares that he will marry the woman who picks a certain flower, and his own sister (whose name is not given) picks the flower. Insistent on carrying out his declaration, Kora pursues his sister, who flees from his advances. After much privation, the sister seems to accept her fate and lies down by Kora's side, only to cut her own throat. Seeing that she has killed herself, he too cuts his throat. Their blood flows in opposite directions, and when they are cremated, the smoke from their bodies rises in two separate columns. Seeing that neither the blood nor the smoke will mingle (F1075), those present conclude, "It is plain that the marriage of brother and sister is wrong," and from that time forth such marriages have been discontinued (A1552.1, "Why brothers and sisters do not marry").

The generic title of Type 313E* tales, *The Girl Flees from a Brother Who Wants to Marry Her,* summarizes a group of stories especially well represented in eastern Europe. An example is the Russian tale "Prince Danila Govorila" (Afanasyev 1975, 351–356).

FATHERS AND DAUGHTERS

Many variants of Type 706 folktales, *The Maiden Without Hands,* told throughout the world depict a girl mutilated by her father (or sometimes a brother) after she refuses his sexual advances. For examples see the Grimms' commentary to their "The Girl without Hands" (KHM 31; 1980, 3:69–72). Type 706B folktales depict a woman beset by unwanted sexual advances, most frequently from a brother (T415.1). She responds by mutilating herself, then giving the amputated parts (usually hands or breasts) to her tormentor (S11.1). The best-known example of this tale is "The Girl with the Maimed Hands" from *The Pentamerone* of Basile (1932, 3:2).

A similar plot is also widely known among the indigenous people of the North American Arctic, but here as a solar myth. In one version, first collected in the nineteenth century, a brother seduces his sister under cover of darkness. Discovering who her partner was, the sister cuts off her breasts and throws them at him, then runs off into the night carrying a lighted torch. He picks up another torch and follows her, but stumbles, putting out his light. Then a windstorm lifts them both into the sky. The sister becomes the sun and the brother the moon. She stays away from him as best she can, coming out only when he is not present (Erdoes and Ortiz 1984, 161–162). In a twentieth-century version (Millman 1987, 21), the incestuous seduction takes place between the moon and the sun, with no humans mentioned. The end results are the same, with the female sun's self-mutilation and her constant flight from her brother: "And still he pursues his sister, even today, to get her for his mate. But she is faster and always keeps well ahead of him. Thus, owing to the moon's lust, does night follow day."

Many stories about father-daughter incest find ways to diminish the father's guilt, while others eliminate his culpability altogether. In the Old Testament story of Lot and his daughters, Lot's daughters get their father drunk before seducing him. Although this story as well as the story of Isaac and Rebecca condones incestuous marriage, later in the Bible incest is prohibited (Leviticus 18, 20). In the Greek tale of Myrrha, the heroine with the help of her old nurse tricks her way into her father's bed. When her father discovers her identity, he tries to kill her; she flees and later gives birth to Adonis (Ovid 1981, 233–238). In both stories, the fathers are alleviated of all guilt, clearly having been seduced by the daughters.

The most widespread international folktale depicting attempted incest is Type 510B, *The Father Who Wanted to Marry His Daughter,* a close relative of the Cinderella tales. The Grimm brothers' "All-Kinds-of-Fur" (KHM 65) is exemplary. A dying queen extracts a promise from her husband that should he remarry, his new wife will be as beautiful as the queen. Although such a demand may be a ruse on the part of the wife, who in fact does not wish for her husband to remarry, it also legitimates the husband's desire for their daughter, since she is the only person to meet this requirement. The father proposes marriage to his daughter (T411.1), and to gain time, she requests dresses patterned after the moon, the stars, and the sun, and also a coat made of every kind of fur, all of which the king supplies. His daughter escapes by smearing her face with soot, wrapping herself in the fur garb, and running into the woods. Another king finds her there, and she becomes his kitchen servant, suffering many indignities. With time, however, the young king discovers her true beauty, and they marry. That the daughter is placed in abject situations and moves from her father to her husband suggests that it is the daughter who has undergone a process of penitence and substituted one object of desire for another, not the father, who in most versions drops out of sight and is not mentioned again after the daughter makes her escape (the exception being Straparola's "Tebaldo," where the father is quartered in the end). Modern retellings often highlight the problematic side of such tales. Robin McKinley's *Deerskin* (1993), for instance, rewrites the story precisely in order bring out the violence and paternal culpability absent from so many versions (see also Rutledge 2001).

In the various renditions of these archetypal stories, the father is depicted as being more or less culpable. Perhaps one of the oldest versions of such stories, *Apollonius of Tyre,* a Greek work that was translated into Latin and made its way into the *Gesta Romanorum* (*Deeds of the Romans,* late thirteenth century), tells the story of King Antiochus, who falls in love with his own daughter and rapes her. In this story, the father is represented in unambiguously criminal terms and eventually is struck dead by the gods. In *Belle Hélène de Constantinople* (thirteenth–fourteenth century), however, the culpability of the father is lessened because the pope approves of his plan to marry his daughter and because he eventually is reconciled with Hélène (Zipes 2001, 26–27). Although Hélène loses a hand over the course of the story, it is because of her mother-in-law's machinations, not her father's criminal behavior. In Philippe de Rémi's *La manekine* (ca. 1270), the heroine mutilates herself in order to avoid marrying her father, for a king of Hungary cannot marry a disfigured woman. Much like Joie of *La manekine,* the heroine of Basile's "Penta the Handless" (1634) has a slave cut off her hands, for the king of Pietrasecca, her brother, who wishes to marry her, finds her hands particularly attractive (Zipes 2001, 512–518; Basile, ca.1958, 190–198).

MOTHERS AND SONS

The most famous story of mother-son incest is that of Oedipus, told in bits and pieces by many ancient writers. Sophocles made the story the subject of one of the greatest Greek tragedies, *Oedipus Rex.* Many versions begin with an oracle before the birth of the hero that announces the tragedy to come, and, taking heed of such warnings, the usually noble mother exposes or abandons her child. However, the child is raised by a peasant family and survives to adulthood. The fact that the hero is abandoned as a child makes plausible the failure of both son and mother to recognize each other, and they marry. Although in many versions the son kills his father before marrying his mother, the episode of father-son rivalry is not an essential element of the story, as Slavic and Indian versions confirm (see Krauss 1984, 11–13; and Ramanujan 1997, 111–113). Usually, after the marriage, mother and son discover the truth about their relationship, which results in tragedy. Sophocles's Oedipus tears out his eyes and Jocasta commits suicide.

The basic plot, having made its way into world folklore, is found in different setting in folktales from many nations (AT 931, *Oedipus*). One of the most intriguing is the apocryphal account of Judas Iscariot as recorded in *The Golden Legend* (1900, vol. 3). This biography of Judas almost exactly parallels that of Oedipus. On the night of his conception, Judas's mother dreams that her child will destroy their people. Acting on this dream, she and her husband set the child adrift in a basket shortly after his birth. A distant queen discovers the baby and raises him as her own. After growing to adulthood, he enters the service of Pilate, the provost of Jerusalem. One day, when the two of them are passing the garden of Judas's natural father (who, of course, is not known to him), Pilate expresses a desire for some of the fruit that grows there. Judas jumps over the wall to satisfy his master's whims. He is accosted by his father and kills him in the ensuing struggle. Pilate's reaction to the altercation is to seize the dead man's goods and to give his widow to Judas in marriage. Judas thus unwittingly marries his own mother, adding incest to the list of sins he will later commit.

Thompson says, "The [Oedipus] story seems to be particularly popular among the Finns and has been collected several times in Hungary and Romania, and sporadically in Lithuania, Lapland, and from the Cape Verde Islanders in Massachusetts" (1977, 141). In an Albanian version, the son ends up killing himself, his wife/mother, and their son (Hasluck 1984, 6–7). However, not all such narratives end tragically. In an Oceanic version, after the son kills his father, he and his mother live together happily ever after (Lessa 1984, 57–60).

It is notable that few tales exist concerning same-sex incest. F.E. Williams (1984) did record a story from Papua New Guinea, in which a father sodomizes his son. However, his motivations are not explicitly sexual: the father wishes to help his son grow. The tale also offers an example of mother-son incest, which differs from those discussed above in that the father ends up killing his son and is reunited with his wife.

BROADER DEFINITIONS OF INCEST

Although the proscription against incest usually lessens as kinship distance from the nuclear family increases, in many traditions incest is defined broadly to extend beyond the nuclear family. Both the Bible (Leviticus 18:6–18, 20:17–21; Deuteronomy 27:20–23) and the Koran (4:22–23) prohibit sexual intercourse not only with blood relatives, but also with specified in-laws and step- and foster relatives. These Old Testament definitions carried over into Christianity, as evidenced in Paul's first letter to the Corinthians (5:1–2), in which he expresses indignation that a Christian had married his own widowed stepmother.

In Shakespeare's *Hamlet* (1:5), Claudius's marriage with his murdered brother's widow is labeled "incestuous." In the earliest record of the legendary story upon which Shakespeare based his play, the *Gesta Danorum* of Saxo Grammaticus (1894, book 3), we read that the murderer "took the wife of the brother he had butchered, capping unnatural murder with incest." Hamlet's own incestuous feelings for his mother are a subtext of the play, his rivalry with his father displaced onto his uncle.

Otto Rank has argued that stories like Hamlet and those classified as the Lustful Stepmother could be read in terms of the transference of the relations constitutive of the mother-son incest narrative from immediate family members to more distant ones. Mother-son incest often is transformed into a son's love for his stepmother, as in the various renditions of Don Carlos, the most famous being the play of that name by Friedrich Schiller (1787), or a stepmother's love for her stepson. Perhaps the most famous lustful stepmother is Phaedra, whose desire for her stepson Hippolytus is figured in particularly monstrous terms. Phaedra's mother, Pasiphaë, had had sexual relations with a bull and gave birth to Phaedra's half-brother, the Minotaur. By association with her mother, Phaedra's sexuality thus is identified with transgression, even aberration, which is emphasized in Jean Racine's 1677 play, *Phèdre* (1995). Emile Zola returned to the theme of Phaedra in his 1872 novel *La Cureé* (*The Kill*, 1990). Situating the story within a bourgeois family during the Second Empire, he makes of Renée's incestuous desire for her stepson a sign of general social decadence.

Incest can also be treated in a comical way, as in the Ozark tale "Jack and His Family," in which a brother tells his sister she is "lots better than Maw," to which the sister replies, "that's what Paw always says"; and the story of the boy who calls off his wedding because his fiancée is a virgin for, as his father remarks, if she "ain't good enough for her own kinfolks, she ain't good enough for us, neither!" (Randolph 1986, 18–20, 80–81).

D.L. Ashliman and Anne E. Duggan

See also: Sister and Brother.

REFERENCES

Afanas'ev, Aleksandr N. 1975. *Russian Fairy Tales.* New York: Pantheon.

Apollodorus. 1975. *The Library of Greek Mythology.* Trans. Keith Aldrich. Lawrence, KS: Coronado Press.

Aulnoy, Marie-Catherine d'. 1994 [1690] *L'Histoire d'Hypolite, comte de Duglas.* Ed. Shirley Day Jones. Somerset: Castle Cary Press.

———. 1998. "La Princesse Belle Etoile et le Prince Chéri." *Contes II.* Ed. Philippe Hourcade, 343–406. Paris: Société des Textes Français Modernes.

Barnouw, Victor. 1977. *Wisconsin Chippewa Myths and Tales and Their Relation to Chippewa Life.* Madison: University of Wisconsin Press.

Basile, Giambattista. 1932. *The Pentamerone.* Tran. from the Italian of Benedetto Croce. Ed. N.M. Penzer. 2 vols. New York: Dutton. First published 1634–1636 as *Lo Cunto de li Cunti.*

Bernard, Catherine. 1979 [1687]. *Les Malheurs de l'amour. Première nouvelle: Eléonor d'Yvrée.* Intro. René Godenne. Geneva: Slatkine.

Bompas, Cecil Henry. 1909. *Hawaiian Mythology.* Honolulu: University of Hawaii Press.

Bushnaq, Inea, trans. 1986. *Arab Folktales.* New York: Pantheon.

Edmunds, Lowell, and Alan Dundes. 1984. *Oedipus: A Folklore Casebook.* New York: Garland.

Erdoes, Richard, and Alfonso Ortiz. 1984. *American Indian Myths and Legends.* New York: Pantheon.

Frobenius, Leo, and Douglas C. Fox. 1937. *African Genesis.* New York: Stackpole Sons.

The Golden Legend, or Lives of the Saints [Legenda aurea]. 1900. Comp. Jacobus de Voragine 1275. Trans. William Caxton 1483. Ed. F.S. Ellis. London: Temple Classics. First published in Latin 1470.

Graffigny, Françoise de. 1993. *Lettres d'une Péruvienne.* Intro. Joan DeJean and Nancy K. Miller. New York: MLA.

Grant, Michael. 1962. *Myths of the Greeks and Romans.* New York: New American Library.

Grimm, Jacob, and Wilhelm Grimm. 1980. *Kinder- und Hausmarchen* [KHM], Ed. Heinz Rolleke, 3 vols. Stuttgart: Reclam. Based on the edition of 1857.

Hanauer, J.E. 1935 [1907]. *Folk-Lore of the Holy Land: Moslem, Christian, and Jewish.* London: Sheldon Press.

Hasluck, Margaret. 1984. "Oedipus Rex in Albania." In *Oedipus: A Folklore Casebook,* ed. Lowell Edmunds and Alan Dundes, 3–9. New York: Garland.

Krauss, Friedrich S. 1984. "The Oedipus Legend in South Slavic Folk Tradition." In *Oedipus: A Folklore Casebook,* Lowell Edmunds and Alan Dundes, 10–22. New York: Garland.

Lessa, William A. 1984. "Oedipus-type Tales in Oceania." In *Oedipus: A Folklore Casebook,* Lowell Edmunds and Alan Dundes, 56–75. New York: Garland.

Lévi-Strauss, Claude. 1949. *Les structures élémentaires de la parenté.* Paris: Presses universitaires de France.

McKinley, Robin. 1993. *Deerskin.* New York: Ace.

Millman, Lawrence. 1987. *A Kayak Full of Ghosts: Eskimo Tales.* Santa Barbara, CA: Capra Press.

Ovid. 1981. *Metamorphoses.* New York: Penguin.

Perrault, Charles. 1981. *Contes.* Ed. Jean-Pierre Collinet. Paris: Gallimard.

Poignant, Roslyn. 1967. *Oceanic Mythology: The Myths of Polynesia, Micronesia, Melanesia, Australia.* London: Paul Hamlyn.

Racine, Jean. 1995. *Phèdre.* Paris: Gallimard.

Ramanujan, A.K. 1997. *A Flowering Tree and Other Oral Tales from India.* Ed. Stuart Blackburn and Alan Dundes. Berkeley: University of California Press.

Randolph, Vance. 1986. *Pissing in the Snow and Other Ozark Folktales.* Chicago: University of Illinois Press.

Rank, Otto. 1992 [1912]. *The Incest Theme in Literature and Legend: Fundamentals of a Psychology of Literary Creation.* Trans. Gregory C. Richter. Baltimore: Johns Hopkins University Press.

Rutledge, Amelia A. 2001. "Robin McKinley's *Deerskin:* Challenging Narcissisms." *Marvels & Tales* 15 (2): 168–182.

The Saga of the Volsungs. 1990. Trans. Jesse L. Byock. Berkeley: University of California Press.

Saxo Grammaticus. 1894. *The First Nine Books of the Danish History of Saxo Grammaticus [Gesta Danorum].* Trans. Oliver Elton. London: David Nutt.

Scudéry, Madeleine de. 1973 [1660]. *Clélie, Histoire Romaine.* 10 vols. Geneva: Slatkine.

Sheykh-Zada. 1886. *The History of the Forty Vezirs; or, The Story of the Forty Morns and Eves.* Trans. E.J.W. Gibb. London: George Redway.

Snorri Sturluson. 1954. *The Prose Edda of Snorri Sturluson: Tales from Norse Mythology.* Trans. Jean I. Young. Berkeley: University of California Press.

Thompson, Stith. 1977 [1946]. *The Folktale.* Berkeley: University of California Press. Orig. ed: New York, Holt, Rinehard and Winston.

The Upanishads. 1897. Trans. F. Max Müller. 2 vols. in 1. New York: Christian Literature.

Vega, Garcilaso de la. 1961. *The Royal Commentaries of the Inca.* Trans. Maria Jolas. New York: Orion.

Werner, E.T.C. 1922. *Myths and Legends of China.* London: George G. Harrap.

Williams, F.E. 1984. "Oedipus in Papuan Folklore." In Oedipus: A Folklore Casebook, Lowell Edmunds and Alan Dundes, 43–46. New York: Garland.

Zipes, Jack, ed. 2001. *The Great Fairy Tale Tradition: From Straparola and Basile to the Brothers Grimm.* New York: Norton.

Zola, Emile. 1990 [1872]. *La Curée.* Paris: Gallimard.

❀ U ❀

Nature of Life

Justice and Injustice

Motif U10 and Various Motifs

❀

Social psychologists point to the importance of a belief in justice as a motivating factor for the individual. Melvin Lerner writes, "People want to and have to believe they live in a just world so that they can go about their daily lives with a sense of trust, hope, and confidence in their future" (1980, 14). Moreover, Lerner observes, ordinary people value justice so highly that under certain circumstances they are willing to make exceptional investments in pursuit of it. In fact, he finds through meta-analysis of a series of experiments, "it is clear that people value justice more than profit, and at times more than their own lives" (175). Movement toward social equality has rested largely on a series of extensions of the expectation of just treatment to members of different groups, followed by each group's struggle to achieve such treatment.

Motifs dealing with justice and injustice fall under Chapter U, The Nature of Life. In *The Folktale,* Thompson begins a discussion of justice by remarking how the majority of folktales concern the contrast between evil deeds of malevolent persons and the commendable activity of the heroes or heroines, and "in such conflicts good shall eventually triumph and wickedness receive a fitting punishment" (Thompson 1977, 130). However, the location in the *Motif-Index* of justice and injustice under Life's Inequalities (U0–U99) is an indicator of the tenor of this topic in regard to formal or judicial justice. Here tales focus on the unfairness of life, exposing unjust judgments, disproportionate punishments, favoritism, and hypocrisy. Related motifs may be found under Q, Rewards and Punishments, but those under U are, as Thompson notes, "of a homiletic tendency. A tale is told with the sole purpose of showing the nature of life. 'Thus goes the world' is the text of such tales" (Intro., *Motif-Index*).

There are cross-references to various supernatural indicators of unjust decisions (D1318.1.1, "Stone bursts as a sign of unjust judgment"; D1318.2.1, "Laughing fish reveals unjust judgment"; and T575.1.1.3, "Child in mother's womb reveals unjust judgment"). One cluster of motifs (U11) centers on "small trespasses punished; large crimes condoned"—for example, U11.1, "Ass punished for stealing mouthful of grass; lion and wolf forgiven for eating sheep," and U11.1.1.2, "Penitent in confession worries about little sins and belittles the big ones." Elsewhere in this group such unjust outcomes are connected explicitly to social power and connections, as when a lion holding court and listening to the sins of other animals forgives all the powerful animals but punishes the meek (U11.1.1.1), and when he who steals much is called king, while he who steals little is called robber (U11.2)

The U15 complex concerns laughter as an appropriate response to rampant injustice, recalling physicist Niels Bohr's comment that there are some things so serious you just have to laugh at them. U18 presents a filial response to parental experience of injustice ("the fathers have eaten sour grapes and the children's teeth are set on edge"). Another cluster, U21 ("Justice depends on the point of view"), contains tales of hypocrisy in which characters commit the same acts for which they have condemned others. In one way or another, nearly all of the motifs Thompson cites here serve to assure victims of injustice that they are not alone. The stories imply further that the corruption of society is so pervasive that to be a victim of injustice may be taken as a sign of moral superiority.

POETIC JUSTICE

In folklore, on those occasions when justice is realized, it tends to be of the poetic sort rather than the judicial. Such examples of justice are cross-referenced under "Murder Will Out," (N271), which is found under Chance and Fate.

Singing Bones and Talking Birds

A very popular motif is E632, "Reincarnation as musical instrument. A musical instrument made from the bones of a murdered person, or from a tree growing from the grave, speaks and tells of the crime." It is also a tale type (AT 780, *The Singing Bone*). Thompson says that stories concerning murders revealed by some reincarnation of the victim are to be found in all parts of the world (1977, vol. 1:136). The motif is very common, for example, in central Africa. Often the story concerns the murder of one sister by another sister, or one brother by another brother. "Sometimes a harp is made from various parts of the body, or a flute from a bone, or some other instrument from a tree which has grown over the murdered person's grave. The musical instrument is played in public and sings out the accusation of the murder" (Thompson 1977, vol. 1:136). Child collected numerous examples of the ballad "The Twa Sisters" (Child 10) (also known as "The Cruel Sister") from England, Scotland, Wales, and Ireland and found versions in many other parts of Europe, particularly Scandinavia. The ballad was remarkably popular: over 120 versions were collected in the United States and Canada among descendants of early British settlers.

The Princess Who Murdered Her Child (AT 781) is a related story, which also shows versions in Africa. A man who can understand birds hears one in a tree above him say "The bones lie under the tree," and a murder is solved (B131.1, "Bird reveals murder"; N271.4, "Murder discovered through knowledge of bird languages. Birds point out the murder"). The Grimms include a version of AT 720, *My Mother Slew Me, My Father Ate Me,* as "The Juniper Tree." The story in its original form was not thought suitable for children so versions included in children's collections were considerably sanitized. A stepmother murders her husband's son, cooks him, and serves him to his father, who unknowingly eats the meal with great relish. The woman's daughter gathers up the boy's bones in a silk handkerchief and puts them under a juniper tree. A bird arises from the bones and sings the story of his murder (E613.0.1, "Reincarnation of murdered child as bird"). He eventually causes the death of his murderer and is then reincarnated again in his true form, and he, his stepsister, and his father live happily together without the evil stepmother. Child cites a popular tale about an innkeeper and his wife killing one of their guests for his money, burning the body, and using the ashes to make a dish, which speaks and denounces the murderers (1965, 126). Thompson lists Motif E633 ("Bones made into dish. These speak"). He lists an example from Japan.

THE JOKE OF JUSTICE

There is a widespread tradition of humorous tales concerning ineffectual judges meting out sentences that are unjust but follow a sort of logic. The following is an example from Yiddish tradition:

> A great calamity befell Chelm one day. The town cobbler murdered one of his customers. So he was brought before the judge, who sentenced him to die by hanging. When the verdict was read a townsman arose and cried out, "If Your Honor pleases—you have sentenced to death the town cobbler! He's the only one we've got. If you hang him who will mend our shoes?"

"Who? Who?" cried all the people of Chelm with one voice. The judge nodded in agreement and reconsidered his verdict. "Good people of Chelm," he said, "what you say is true. Since we have only one cobbler it would be a great wrong against the community to let him die. As there are two roofers in the town, let one of them be hanged instead!" (Ausubel 1948, 337)

THE BELL OF JUSTICE

In this example of AT 207C (*Animals Ring Bell and Demand Justice*) from *Cento novelle antiche (The Hundred Old Tales*), an Italian collection compiled at the end of the thirteenth century and published in 1525, a horse procures justice for himself.

> In the days of King John of Acre [or Atri] a bell was hung for anyone to ring who had received a great wrong, whereupon the king would call together the wise men appointed for this purpose, in order that justice might be done.
>
> It happened that the bell had lasted a long time and the rope had wasted, so that a vine clung to it.
>
> Now it befell that a knight of Acre had a noble charger which had grown old, so that it had lost its worth, and the knight, to avoid the expense of its keep, let it wander about. The famished horse tugged at the vine to eat it. As it tugged, the bell rang.
>
> The judges assembled, and understood the petition of the horse who, it seemed, asked for justice. They sentenced that the knight whom the horse had served when it was young, should feed it now that it was old. The king commanded him to do so under grave penalties. (Ashliman 1996–2004)

RELIGIOUS FOLKLORE

Direct redress, however, is not the only means of preserving confidence in ultimate justice. If justice cannot be had now, there may still be hope that it will come eventually. A promise that temporal injustice will be recompensed in an afterlife, so that the "last shall be first," is a central feature of many religious belief systems. A related motif is Doomsday (A1002). Motifs that profess belief in pervasive injustice in life may be seen as a secondary response to a need for predictability in life. If everything that happens is likely to be unjust, then at least one can avoid further disappointments and take cold comfort in having expected as much.

Religious folklore also includes a set of tales that emphasize the limitations of human observation in discerning divine justice (AT 759, *God's Justice Vindicated*). In these stories, "From his seat in the heavens, God looks down and bestows his blessings on the righteous and metes out stern justice on all trespassers of the Divine Will. The ways of the Almighty often seem dark, but a real insight into his activities will always show perfect justice" (Thompson 1977, 130). Terrence Leslie Hansen cites a narrative from Argentina in which a foolish man sees two drunk and sleepy travelers misplace their money. Two other men find and take it. Meanwhile, the first pair stops and questions another pair of men who have not seen the money. Finding this response unsatisfactory, they beat one of them and kill the other. Based upon what he has just seen, the observer concludes that "the Lord is unjust." God appears and explains that the first men were thieves, the second were deserving poor, and that the dead man was a murderer who had so far gone unpunished. It is now apparent to the observer that "the Lord is just" (Hansen 1957, 88). Thompson remarks that a version of this type, "The Angel and the Hermit," was a very popular exemplum used by medieval priests (1977, 130). On a larger scale, the inscrutability of divine justice, and hence the need for faith, is central to the biblical story of the tribulations of Job.

In literature, the preoccupation with justice may show up in unlikely places, as in the episode of Don Quijote (1615) in which the knight encounters the famous bandit Roque Guinart. Guinart tells Don Quijote that after each robbery all the bandits are required to place whatever they have stolen in a communal pile from which he distributes equal shares. If he were not to do so, Roque explains, there would be no living with his men. When Sancho observes epigrammatically that justice is so good that even thieves find it necessary, the men take offense and only Roque's intervention prevents them from beating the squire (Cervantes Saavedra 1968, 980–981). The focus on social justice and/or injustice has been especially notable in the picaresque novel, which viewed the world through the lens of the young orphan who lived by his wits; in realism, which demonstrated the increasing influence of photography in its detailed portraits of the destitute and desperate, and in the testimonial social justice literatures that have arisen in response to particular instances of injustice: abolitionist narratives, for instance, narratives of the Holocaust, and accounts of civil wars in African and Latin America.

Kimberly A. Nance and Jane Garry

See also: Doomsday; Good and Evil; Origins of Inequality

REFERENCES

Ashliman, D.L. 1996–2004. *Folklore and Mythology Electronic Texts,* www.pitt.edu/~dash/folktexts.html.
Ausubel, Nathan. 1948. *A Treasury of Jewish Folklore.* New York: Crown Publishers.

Cervantes Saavedra, Miguel de. 1968. *Don Quijote.* Barcelona: Juventud.

Child, Francis James. 1965 [1882–1898]. *The English and Scottish Popular Ballads.* 5 vols. New York: Dover. Orig. ed., Houghton Mifflin.

Hansen, Terrence Leslie. 1957. *The Types of the Folktale in Cuba, Puerto Rico, the Dominican Republic, and Spanish South America.* Berkeley: University of California Press.

Lerner, Melvin. 1980. *The Belief in a Just World.* New York: Plenum.

Thompson, Stith. 1977 [1946]. *The Folktale.* Berkeley: University of California Press.

❀ Z ❀

Miscellaneous

The Double

❀

The double, at its most basic, is a duplicate of an individual or a part of a divided individual. Numerous versions of this complicated archetypal figure are found in dreams, mythologies, rituals of primitive peoples, ancient and medieval alchemists' narratives, folklore, and literature (including drama, poetry, stories and novels, and the scripts of radio, television, and film). A.E. Crawley suggests that the sources of the double, as a term, are the "mathematical ideas of multiplication and division," the "main connotation of the term" being the doppelgänger (the double-goer), visible or invisible, material or spiritual (1920, 853). The double-goer is variously designated: the Other, the alter ego, and the second self, among other names.

The source of the double as a phenomenon of duplication may be the "twin-cult," versions of which were discovered by anthropologists in primitive cultures in Africa, Asia, Europe, and the Americas, according to James Rendel Harris. Probably based on superstitious fears regarding the births of twins, the twin myth apparently evolved into the twin figures of mythology. For example, Romulus and Remus, their mother killed, are set adrift in a hollow oak trunk on the Tiber and saved, eventually, by a wolf and a woodpecker; eighteen twins sail aboard the *Argo* from Thessaly to Colchis, seeking the Golden Fleece; Jason, the captain of the *Argo,* is himself one of the twins, although his brother Triptolemus has remained ashore to farm the land. The stages in the evolution of the twin tabus were as follows: (1) the mother and the twins were killed; (2) one twin was killed; (3) the mother and the twins were banished to a twin-town; and (4) the twins were revered as children of the sky god of thunder and/or lightning—as benefactors, protectors, builders (Harris 1913, xxiii–xxiv, 226, 229, 412).

The second stage of the twin tabu may have evolved into the concept of the mortal/immortal pairs (Harris 1913, 217). For example, it might have been eventually decided that one of the twins had been fathered by a human, the other by a god, a decision that may have generated those pairs in mythology that include one twin (or brother, or friend) who lives or succeeds, while the other dies or disappears. In the *Thousand and One Nights,* the evil Qasim and the good Ali Baba are brothers. Qasim learns from his brother about the cavern of riches, goes there, and is murdered by the forty thieves. Ali Baba survives, a wealthy man, into old age. In the Sumerian epic of Gilgamesh, when the primitive Enkidu dies, the civilized Gilgamesh, feeling that a part of him has died with Enkidu, sets out to seek immortality. As the animal is lost, the search for the angel begins; as the material body loses its power, the search for a spiritual self intensifies.

The source of the double as a concept of division is located by Freud in the idea of an immortal soul, an idea rising, according to Freud, from infantile narcissism or primitive superstition. When some impression revives in the psyches of civilized adults those infantile complexes or primitive beliefs, the double no longer appears to be an assurance of immortality, but rather appears as an "uncanny harbinger of death" ("The 'Uncanny'"). Freud notwithstanding, peoples around the world believe that the "soul" is an invisible duplicate of each individual's body, constitutes the life of that body, is separated from that body at death, and afterward becomes visible only on rare occasions, when it is called a "ghost." This almost universal belief is found in all primitive societies and all ancient cultures. For example, in the Egypt of antiquity, the soul, the *ka,* was conceived of as a miniature duplicate of the person whose soul it was.

The source of the double as a concept of division was located, by Carl Jung, much further back than the infantile or primitive. Jung placed that source at the lowest depths of the collective unconscious, the level of the instinctual—or, even deeper, at that level where the World is "chemical substances." The psyche is, simply, the World (Jung 1959a, 21–22, 173). Consciousness, Jung claimed, is a "recent acquisition" and is therefore menaced by various dangers, one danger being a dissociation of consciousness, or a splitting in the psyche, which results in a loss of identity (Jung 1964, 6–7). Many primitive societies regarded an individual's shadow, reflection (as in water), or portrait as the individual's soul, or at least a vital part of the individual, that must be carefully protected (Frazer 1981, 141, 148). Divisibility of personality is suggested throughout Jung's writings on archetypes, "primordial types," "universal images," "patterns of instinctual behavior," which we project into the external world (Jung 1959a, 5, 44, 59).

Numerous archetypes exist, but it is the shadow, and the anima or animus, that "have the most frequent and the most disturbing influence on the ego," and the most accessible of these, and the easiest to experience, is the shadow, for its nature can "in large measure be inferred from the contents of the personal unconscious—from a dream, for instance" (Jung 1959b, 8). The shadow is "a sort of second personality" to the primary or ego personality (Jung 1959a, 262). Odin and Loki, at the beginning of time, exchange vows of friendship, becoming blood brothers, but Loki grows malicious, ultimately bringing on the twilight of the gods, in which Odin, and Loki himself, are destroyed. In Mary Shelley's *Frankenstein, or The Modern Prometheus* (1818), the "creature" murders the brother, best friend, and bride of his creator, Dr. Frankenstein, who also dies, as does the "monster" himself. In the film *King Kong* (1933), a gigantic gorilla threatens human accomplishment, symbolized by the Empire State Building; the monster climbs the building, is shot dead by men in airplanes, and falls to the street below. The shadow can be positive, as well as negative. An animal in a fairy tale represents a shadow self, but the animal may help the hero or heroine in some essential way.

Another important doubling by division in mythology and literature is that of the male/female pair Jung called the "divine syzygy"—the god and goddess of mythology, like Apollo the sun god and his twin, Artemis the moon goddess. Or the king and queen in alchemists' symbolic descriptions of the *opus:* the "king" descends into the "waters" and is there wed to the "queen"; the two die, and an androgynous "child" ascends from their death. Jung related the "divine" pair to the anima and animus archetypes, the double configuration evolving into the modern concept of male consciousness and the female unconscious (Jung 1959a, 59, 173, 175–76). Jung adds two archetypes to the divine couple, Wise Old Man and Chthonic Mother, to form a quaternion, a scheme of the self (Jung 1959b, 21–22, 242). This configuration, applied to narratives, is often a familial one in which four characters are paternal, maternal, fraternal, and sororal types. King Cepheus is helpless when Queen Cassiopeia offends Poseidon, who sends a monster to harass the country. Cepheus's daughter Andromeda is offered as a sacrifice to the monster, but Perseus arrives, slays the monster, and marries Andromeda.

A quaternion may comprise two pairs of male/female couples, a "higher" and a "lower." Jung discusses a Grimm tale in which a hero and a princess are riding horses. Jung interprets the animals as the shadow selves, the "lower" selves, of the royal pair. At the end of the tale, the horses are transformed into a second hero and a second princess (Jung 1959a, 243–254). In Nathaniel Hawthorne's novel *The Marble Faun* (1860), two American art students in Rome, Kenyon and Hilda, meet Donatello, an innocent with a "wild, forest nature," and Miriam, a mysterious dark lady. Miriam is being stalked and harassed by a man who is likened to a reptile; Donatello kills the man, with Miriam's approval. Donatello's moral sense is born, he has committed a sin and feels remorse, he has become human. He willingly enters a dungeon in a "sepulchral fortress" to pay for his crime. Miriam is seen by Kenyon and Hilda at a distance, lifting her hands toward them in a blessing and farewell, before disappearing.

Doublings other than self and shadow, and male and female, exist, of course. The good/evil opposition is one important example. The scapegoat may be considered the evil double of the entire tribe from which it is driven. The "ills" are expelled from the people or the village when they are "loaded" on the scapegoat (Frazer 1981, 182). During their annual spring festival, the American Mandan Indians appointed one man to paint his face black and frighten the women, acting the part of the Devil until the tribe chased him out of the village (Frazer 1981, 183–184). Frazer wrote his influential work at the end of the nineteenth century. Early in the twentieth century, doubled characters in literary works began to appear. In Edgar Allan Poe's "William Wilson" (1839), two men, one good and one evil, share the same name. In Robert Louis Stevenson's tale "The Strange Case of Dr. Jekyll and Mr. Hyde" (1886), Jekyll and his other self, Hyde, are described as "polar twins." In Oscar Wilde's *The Picture of Dorian Gray* (1890), Dorian remains young and beautiful while the Dorian in his portrait grows old and hideous, a "misshapen shadow," as a result of years of crimes, cruelties, and corruption.

Doubleness is indicated in characters in fiction similarly to the way it is indicated in mythology and fairy tales—where the characterization is spontaneous, of course. The use of the reflection, as in water or a mirroring device of any kind, is common. Snow-White, the good princess, lies asleep in the glass coffin, while the evil queen gazes into her wonderful looking glass, the reflection suggested by the mirror and the coffin made of glass pointing to the double identity of queen and princess. In the film *The Woman in the Window* (1945), a man gazes at a portrait of a woman in a gallery window, sees her reflection in the window glass, and turns to find the living woman standing beside him. Other indications of doubleness are physical resemblance, disguises, impersonations, and effigies such as portraits, photographs, and statues. In the Pygmalion and Galatea tale in Ovid's *Metamorphoses,* Venus turns the statue executed by the sculptor Pygmalion into the living woman, Galatea.

Regarding doubling as duplication, at the end of the twentieth century the biological phenomenon of the vanishing twin was discovered through the use of fetoscopy and the ultrasound technique. It was found that a high percentage of twin gestations diagnosed earlier than ten weeks are delivered as singletons, one twin having disappeared or, at least, having degenerated into formless tissue. Hillel Schwartz discusses this new appearance of the "twin-cult," as well as other aspects of twinship, in *The Culture of the Copy* (1996). Schwartz also discusses such related topics as dummies and dolls, puppets and parrots, forgeries, facsimiles, and déjà vu. In regard to doubling by division, the divided personalities of living persons began to be studied toward the end of the nineteenth century. Psychologists call the condition multiple (or dual) personality, or "alternating personality," as William James does, citing several well-documented cases (James 1891, X, (3) b.).

A certain sense of division, however, is not necessarily pathological. Some of the most admired authors seem obsessed with doubleness: Shakespeare, Dickens, Faulkner, and numerous others. Samuel Clemens's sense of division was such that for his pen name he chose "Mark Twain," a phrase used by steamboat pilots that means "two fathoms deep." (Clemens/Twain was a boat pilot on the Mississippi for several years.) Indeed, we all of us have two "minds" in our heads, left brain and right brain, each with abilities the other brain does not have. René Girard suggests that the "elementary phenomena" of weeping and laughing may be behind the process of catharsis, which begins with an expulsion and ends with a sense of reconciliation (1988, 123–24). Ultimately, the sources of doubling may be as elementary as the positive and negative charges in the atom.

Joan Peternel

REFERENCES

Crawley, A.E. 1920. "Doubles." In *Encyclopedia of Religion and Ethics,* ed. James Hastings, 853–860. New York: Scribner.

Frazer, Sir James. 1981 [1890]. *The Golden Bough.* 2 vols. in 1. New York: Random House.

Freud, Sigmund. 1953–1974. "The 'Uncanny,'" Vol. 17; "Some Character-Types Met with in Psycho-Analytic Work," Vol. 14, *Standard Edition of the Complete Psychological Works of Sigmund Freud.* Ed. James Strahey. 24 vols. London: Hogarth.

Girard, René. 1988. *To Double Business Bound: Essays on Literature, Mimesis, Anthropology.* Baltimore: Johns Hopkins University Press.

Harris, James Rendel. 1913. *Boanerges.* Cambridge: Cambridge University Press.

James, William. 1891. *The Principles of Psychology.* New York: Holt, Rinehart, and Winston.

Jung, Carl. 1959a. *The Archetypes and the Collective Unconscious.* Vol. 9, I of *The Collected Works of C.G. Jung.* Princeton, NJ: Princeton University Press.

———. 1959b. *Aion: Researches into the Phenomenology of the Self.* Vol. 9, II of *The Collected Works of C.G. Jung.* Princeton, NJ: Princeton University Press.

———. 1964. "Approaching the Unconscious." *Man and His Symbols.* Ed. Carl Jung, Marie-Louise von Franz, and John Freeman. New York: Dell.

Schwartz, Hillel. 1996. *The Culture of the Copy: Striking Likenesses, Unreasonable Facsimiles.* New York: Zone Books.

Good and Evil

Various Motifs

❀

The concept of good versus evil is often seen as an archetypal struggle, especially in mythology. El-Shamy cites good versus evil as an abstraction that is an archetype (El-Shamy 1997, 38). Jung includes it in a list of recurrent contrasts, along with spirit/body, east/west, living/dead, masculine/feminine, sun/moon, and so on, examples of the *coniuntio oppositorum,* or union of opposites (Jung 1970, 3).

While evil has been a philosophical and ethical concern throughout time, it is beyond the scope of this article to discuss the concept in depth, but two definitions may be noted: "evil is simply the difference between the way one wishes the world to be and the way the world is" (Weidhorn 1988, 470) and "evil appears antithetical to the reverence for life, antagonistic to the development of human potential, and opposed to divine or temporal principles of order" (Daemmrich and Daemmrich 1987, 101).

Virtually every culture has had a god or gods who personify evil, or destructive forces, and often they are in direct opposition to a counterpart who is creative and life-giving. As a few examples, there is Gaunab "the Destroyer, the supreme god of evil, with whom all evil omens (eclipses, meteors, whirlwinds) are associated [and who] causes illness and death and is the opponent of Tsuni-Goab" (Hottentots, South Africa); Zambi-a-n'bi, "the god and author of all evil, as opposed to Zambi, or Nsambi, the good deity" (the Bafioti, Gabon); Apophis, or Apep, "serpent demon personifying evil in conflict with Ra, the sun god" (Egyptians) (all quoted in Leach 1992).

MYTHOLOGY

The creation myths of many cultures address the problem of evil and how it came into the world. The section of mythological motifs in the *Motif-Index* contains a number of motifs illustrating the struggle between good and evil, for example, Motif A50, "Conflict of good and evil creators"; A106, "Opposition of good and evil gods"; A106.2, "Revolt of evil angels against god"; A107, "Gods of darkness and light: Darkness thought of as evil, light as good"; and A525, "Origin of good and bad culture heroes."

The opposition between good and evil is the essence of the double, or doppelgänger, an archetype found in mythology and literature. Good and evil are often personified in mythology as twins. For example, in the ancient Persian (Iranian) religion of Zoroastrianism, Ahura Mazda, "Lord Wisdom," the supreme god, fathered twins, Spenta Mainyu, "Holy Spirit," and Angra Mainyu, god of lies and darkness. The struggles between these two gods are told in the hymns of the *Avesta,* the holy book of the Zoroastrians, dating from the second millennium BCE (Knappert 1993, 19). The genealogy changes somewhat in later sources, when Zurvan ("Time") becomes the father of the twins Ormazd (Ahura Mazda) and Ahriman (Angra Mainyu). After alternate periods of ruling the world, Ormazd (the principle of good) ultimately defeats Ahriman.

In Hinduism there are a number of representations of the conflict between good and evil. One important one is the conflict in which Indra, the supreme being, slays Vrtra, identified with drought and darkness, the story of which is told in the *Rig Veda,* the oldest collection of Vedic hymns, dating to at least 1500 BCE (Klostermaier 1998, 207).

In the ancient Greek pantheon, the gods and goddesses were not monolithically good or bad. In a paper on "The Problem of Evil in Mythology," Karl Kerényi singles out the Greek god Hermes and the Norse god Loki as "primordial rogues" (1967, 3–17), not quite the embodiments of evil, but tending in that direction. Loki and Hermes are, coincidentally, two of only a few examples of the trickster figure in European tradition. Esther Clinton, in her article on the trickster on page 472 in this volume, notes that when Christianity takes hold in areas where their stories are told, tricksters are often equated with the devil, an unequivocally evil character.

The supreme god, Zeus, gives both good and bad fortune to mortals. Homer writes in the *Iliad,* "There are two urns that stand on the door-sill of Zeus. They are unlike for the gifts they bestow: an urn of evils, an urn of blessings" (24, 527–528). Zeus distributes some of the contents of these two urns to each mortal, whose life will contain sorrow and happiness in proportion to how much Zeus gives from each urn.

One explanation for how illness and other evils originated is seen in Hesiod's *Works and Days* (seventh century BCE). In retribution for Prometheus having stolen fire and given it to mortals, Zeus says, "I will give men as the price for fire an evil thing in which they may all be glad of heart while they embrace their own destruction"(11, 58–59). Zeus has Hephaestos fashion a beautiful woman, Pandora, whom he sends to earth, and she opens the lid of a jar from which escape all the evils that are now in the world (C321, "Tabu: Looking into box (Pandora)).

The Old Testament is explicit that one god is responsible for both good and evil, and that one god, Yahweh, is the only god. He says, "I form the light, and create darkness: I make peace, and create evil" (Isaiah 45:7) The Old Testament addresses the problem of a world in which God allows suffering, injustice, and death, especially in the Book of Job. As Widengren remarks, "The cause of all Job's sufferings is that God has given him—not his person but everything he possesses—into the hands of Satan. Thus on the one hand Satan is a source of the evil that strikes Job, but on the other he is one of the sons of God, wholly obedient to God, and can act only with Yahweh's approval" (1967, 23–24). However, Gordon demonstrates that "the myth of the dualistic battle [between forces of good and evil] was deeply entrenched in Canaan from pre-Hebraic times" and "was absorbed by the Hebrews along with the language, literature, and lore of Canaan from the very start of Hebrew history in Canaan" (1961, 201).

Among the Onondaga of the Iroquoian tribes in the American Northeast, there is a story of how good and evil people came into the world, again involving twins. The daughter of the first woman gave birth to two sons, the first males on earth. One was born the normal way and the other from her armpit. The armpit child, who would engender evil people, killed his mother and blamed it on his brother (Leeming and Leeming 1995, 216–217).

In the world view of the Hopi of the American Southwest, evil is personified by a crow who "had a power to influence those who did not possess strong hearts. He could project sickness into their bodies and evil thoughts into their hearts, and caused some of them to steal and gossip. . . . Good people were thus turned into evil under the influence of the crow, but the old people told them that there was a good power in the world striving to overcome evil" (Talayesva 1974, 431).

The frost giant Ymir (or Imir) is the source of creation in Icelandic myth. As Leeming and Leeming remark, "He is an unusual source because he is seen as evil. This is in keeping with the strangely pessimistic view of life contained in Norse myths" (1995, 97–98).

In the *Watunna,* the creation cycle of the Makiritare, or Yekuana, people of the Orinoco River in Venezuela, a spirit messenger named Seruhe buries his own placenta "which gives birth to an ugly human called Kahu (also called Odosha). He is evil and jealous of Wandi [a combination of god, hero, and shaman in Heaven who orders the earth]. Because of Kahu/Odosha there is hunger and sickness and war. He teaches people to kill." He is also served by a hairy dwarf whom he created. (Jackson 1994, 607).

FOLKTALES AND LITERATURE

In folktales, scholars have stressed the simplistic polarity of good and evil on the level of both plot and character. For example, "Most folktales hinge on the struggle between good and evil" (von Franz 1967, 85); "The characters in the stories are . . . either altogether good or altogether bad, and there is no evolution of character" (Opie and Opie 1980, 18); "Within the hero himself we find no psychological conflicts" (von Franz 1967, 85). The characters are not only starkly good or evil, but also courageous or cowardly, jealous or innocent, kind or unkind, self-sacrificing or greedy, self-effacing or arrogant. In many folktales, the personification of evil is often a "wicked stepmother," an ogre, a witch, a troll, or other such character who must be defeated in order for the hero or heroine to triumph and a happy ending to be achieved. Evil is almost always punished, or at least driven away by the hero with the help of a supernatural character (von Franz 1967, 85). A very widespread European folktale is "The Dragon Slayer" (AT 300), in which the hero rescues a princess from a wicked dragon. The story of the hero slaying the dragon or other monster derives from ancient myth. One of the most common medieval iconographic symbols of good vanquishing evil in Europe is Saint George, the Christian saint, killing the dragon.

Like folklore, the literature of Europe in the Middle Ages had for the most part a sharply drawn dichotomy between good and evil. The didactic genre of the exemplum drew clear contrasts, and epic narrative and poetry often employed the good versus evil contrast. For example, Weidhorn writes that in *Beowulf* (ca. eighth century), evil is an external agency, in the form of the monster Grendel, and in *Chanson de Roland* (ca. 1100), it is human, but "black and white, we and they" (1988, 475). In much literature of the medieval period, evil is simply personified as Satan, the devil.

The literary treatment of evil begins to evolve in the late eighteenth and early nineteenth centuries. Daemmrich and Daemmrich (1987), noting that in Gothic literature "the fundamental contrast pattern of good and evil either diminishes or vanishes," mention such works as Matthew Gregory Lewis's *Tales of Terror* (1801) and Charles Robert Maturin's *The Fatal Revenge* (1807). The Marquis de Sade's writings probe depravity; in *Justine* (1791) he claims that God is evil and the source of the protagonist's sufferings. Baudelaire published a collection of poems meditating on evil, *Les Fleurs du Mal* (1857), in which evil triumphs over good. The ambiguous nature of evil is explored in the works of Nathaniel Hawthorne. For example, in the short story "Young Goodman Brown," (1835) set in Puritan Massachusetts, a young man leaves home one evening for an "evil purpose." After keeping his appointment with a man in the forest who appears to be the devil, Goodman Brown decides he would prefer to turn back, saying, "My father never went into the woods on such an errand, nor his father before him. We have been a race of honest men and good Christians since the days of the martyrs" (1946, 167). His mysterious companion says that, on the contrary, he is well acquainted with Brown's family: "I helped your grandfather, the constable, when he lashed the Quaker woman so smartly through the streets of Salem; and it was I that brought your father a pitch-pine knot, kindled at my own hearth, to set fire to an Indian village, in King Philip's war" (168). Goodman Brown then sees all the most pious people of the village, including the minister and the deacon, traveling to the meeting place in the forest. The realization that seemingly good people do evil (especially in the name of religion) turns Goodman Brown into "a stern, a sad, a darkly meditative, a distrustful, if not a desperate man" (1946, 178).

Characters become more realistic and psychologically complex through the nineteenth century. Dostoyevsky writes in *The Brothers Karamazov* (1880), that good and evil are monstrously mixed up in man: "Man is broad, too broad, indeed. I'd have him narrower . . . god and the devil are fighting there and the battlefield is the heart of man" (Dostoyevsky 1955, 127). Stevenson's *The Strange Case of Dr. Jekyll and Mr. Hyde* (1886) explores how good and evil coexist in one man: Dr. Jekyll creates a potion that isolates the evil tendencies in his personality, allowing a completely malevolent character, Mr. Hyde, to emerge. As Massey comments about Bram Stoker's *Dracula* (1897), "Repeatedly, we are told that the source of evil is the good. It is not, in fact, a matter of the good being infected by the evil, though that is the superficial form which the process takes. Evil is inherent in good" (1976, 99).

Society—man's creation—comes under scrutiny, and the evil it contains is explored. Some writers have focused on the industrial revolution (Blake, Dickens) and some on social injustice (Hugo, Zola) as sources of evil. Ironically, Huxley's *Brave New World* (1932) depicts a society based on pleasure where "everyone has all needs promptly attended to in a society that, stratified and orderly, is built on creature comforts, labor saving devices, instant gratification, and evasion of painful truths like death and solitariness. Yet it is so dehumanized thereby that a heresy springs up in favor of old evils like suffering and tragedy" (Weidhorn 1988, 484).

Whether in folklore or elite literature, evil is a powerful force that drives plot and character. Daemmrich and Daemmrich state that "works that introduce evil as a causative agent (temptation, inspiration) . . . project through the mental anguish of the figures a polar vision of good and evil commanding intellectual reflection concerning the essence of a desirable existence" (1987, 101).

Jane Garry

See also: The Double; Fight of the Gods and Giants; Trickster.

REFERENCES

Daemmrich, Horst S., and Ingrid Daemmrich. 1987. *Themes and Motifs in Western Literature: A Handbook.* Tubingen: A. Francke.

Dostoyevsky, Fyodor. 1955. *The Brothers Karamazov.* Trans. Constance Garnett. New York: Vintage.

El-Shamy, Hasan. 1997. "Archetype." In *Folklore: An Encyclopedia,* ed. Thomas Green, 37–38. Santa Barbara, CA: ABC-CLIO.

Gordon, Cyrus H. 1961. "Canaanite Mythology." In *Mythologies of the Ancient World,* ed. Samuel Noah Kramer. Chicago: Quadrangle.

Hawthorne, Nathaniel. 1946. *Hawthorne's Short Stories,* ed. and intro. Newton Arvin, 165–179 ("Young Goodman Brown"). New York: Vintage.

Jung, C.G. 1970. *Four Archetypes.* Trans. R.F.C. Hull Princeton: Princeton University Press.

Jackson, Guida M. 1994. *Encyclopedia of Traditional Epics.* Santa Barbara, CA: ABC-CLIO.

Kerényi, Karl. 1967. "The Problem of Evil in Mythology." In *Studies in Jungian Thought: Evil,* ed. James Hillman. Evanston, IL: Northwestern University Press.

Klostermaier, Klaus. 1998. *A Concise Encyclopedia of Hinduism.* Oxford: One World Publications.

Knappert, Jan. 1993. *Encyclopedia of Middle Eastern Mythology and Religion.* Shaftsbury, Dorset, and Rockport, MA: Element.

Leach, Marjorie. 1992. *Guide to the Gods.* Santa Barbara, CA: ABC-CLIO.

Leeming, David, and Margaret Leeming. 1995. *Encyclopedia of Creation Myths.* New York: Oxford University Press.

Massey, Irving. 1976. *The Gaping Pig.* Berkeley: University of California Press.

Opie, Iona, and Peter Opie. 1980. *The Classic Fairy Tales.* New York: Oxford University Press.

Talayesva, Don C. 1974 [1942]. *Sun Chief: The Autobiography of a Hopi Indian.* New Haven, CT: Yale University Press.

von Franz, Marie-Louise. 1967. "The Problem of Evil in Fairy Tales." In *Studies in Jungian Thought: Evil,* ed. James Hillman. Evanston, IL: Northwestern University Press.

Weidhorn, Manfred. 1988. "Evil." In *Dictionary of Literary Themes and Motifs,* ed. Jean-Charles Seigneuret, 470–485. Westport, CT: Greenwood Press.

Widengren, Geo. 1967. "The Principle of Evil in the Eastern Religions." In *Studies in Jungian Thought: Evil,* ed. James Hillman. Evanston, IL: Northwestern University Press.

Trees

Various Motifs

❁

THE WORLD TREE AND THE TREE OF LIFE

Trees have had an important place and meaning in world cultures throughout time. A source of food, fuel, and shelter, trees are also symbolic of eternal life (the evergreen) or cyclical rebirth as they lose their leaves and sprout new ones every year (deciduous trees). The world tree, often regarded as the world axis, is a universal symbol. It is imagined to have roots that reach down to the underworld and branches that reach to heaven (A652.1, "Tree to heaven;" A652, "World-tree. Tree extending from lowest to highest world"). Trees, generally, can be seen as connecting the three primary realms: the underworld (through the roots), the earth (the trunk), and heaven (the top and upper branches).

Examples of the world tree include Yggdrasil, the mighty ash tree of the Norse, and Ceiba or Yaxche of the Mayans (Biedermann 2002, 55). Of Yggdrasil the Prose Edda states, "its branches spread out over the whole world and reach up over heaven" (Leeming and Leeming 1995, 296). The world tree is also found in Malaysia, Polynesia, China, Japan, Egypt, North America, and India. In Arabic-speaking lands, the stars were thought to be the fruits on a world tree (Philpot 1897, 115–119). The Assyrians depicted the tree of life as the date tree, and since they artificially pollinated their date trees to produce a greater amount of fruit, the trees were also a symbol of conception.

In addition to the world tree, a celestial tree figures in the cosmologic myth of the Seneca of New York State (A652.3, "Tree in upper world"). The celestial tree is "so tall that not one of the beings . . . could see its top. On its branches flowers and fruit hung all the year round. The beings who lived on the island used to come to the tree and eat the fruit and smell the sweet perfume of the flowers." Later, the tree is pulled up, and the sky mother falls through the hole in the sky to earth. She has two twins, dark and light. As there is yet no sun, the light twin creates a tree of light, "a great tree having at its topmost branch a great ball of light . . . [which] brought forth flowers from every branch" (Parker 1912, 610)

In the Hebrew Garden of Eden, there are two special trees among many: "And out of the ground made the Lord God to grow every tree that is pleasant to the sight, and good for food; the tree of life also in the midst of the garden, and the tree of knowledge of good and evil" (Genesis 2:9; Motif C621, "Forbidden tree. Fruit of all trees may be eaten, except one"; C621.1, "Tree of knowledge forbidden"). In Revelation 2:7, it is said, "To him that overcometh will I give to eat of the tree of life, which is in the midst of the paradise of God."

Stories of a great deluge are found in many cultures, and there are numerous stories of people surviving the deluge by clinging to a tree (A1021.0.4, "Deluge: Escape on floating tree"; A1023, "Escape from deluge on tree") or sheltering in a hollow trunk (A1021.0.5, "Deluge: escape in hollow tree trunk"). These stories are known from Indian, American Indian (Paiute, Plains Cree, Catawba, Ackawoi, Seneca), Latin American (Caingang, Cuayaki, Maina), and Korean sources.

There is a more general motif, R311, "Tree refuge" in which animals or people climb trees to escape from danger or pursuers. Such tales are found around the world, including China, North and South America, Japan, and Africa.

PEOPLE FROM TREES

In the Norse *Prose Edda,* the gods come upon two trees which they fashion into the first man and woman, from whom all humans descended. The Mixtec of Mexico also believed that the first people were born from trees (Leeming and Leeming 1995, 195).

TREE WORSHIP

Many gods are associated with specific trees in various cultures. It would be impossible to list them all, but a representative sample follows. Illustrations in the Egyptian *Book of the Dead* portray the soul of a dead person traveling to the other world, stopping at a sycamore tree along the way and reaching out to receive what is offered by the goddess Nut, who stands within the tree: "O, sycamore of the Goddess Nut, let there be given to me the water which is in thee" (Philpot 1897, 25–26). In *The Epic of Gilgamesh* (standard version, seventh century BCE), Gilgamesh and Enkidu marvel at the great cedar forest:

> They stood at the edge of the forest,
> They gazed at the height of the cedars,
> . . .
> They saw the cedar mountain, dwelling of the gods, sacred to
> The goddess Irnina.
> On the slopes of that mountain, the cedar bears its abundance,
> Agreeable is its shade, full of pleasures. (1995, 5:1–8)

Gilgamesh and Enkidu cut down the great forest and go on to commit other infractions, and as punishment the gods decree that one of them (Enkidu) must die.

In the Aegean world, trees were a central part of religion from at least the Bronze Age (ca. 3000–ca. 1100 BCE), as we know from illustrations such as Dionysus before a tree sanctuary and Hermes sitting in a great tree on vases and other objects (Hornblower and Spawford 2003). In classical times, certain gods became identified with specific trees. Athena was associated with the olive, Apollo with the laurel, Artemis with the myrtle. The oak tree was sacred to the mighty Zeus. Priests, and later priestesses, interpreted the god's pronouncements by listening to the rustling of the leaves (D1311.4, "Oracular tree"). Among the Ancient Greek nymphs, or lesser female divinities of nature, the dryads or hamadryads were the nymphs of trees who lived within them (Smith 1958, 202). Among the Romans, Silvanus was the god of the countryside, associated primarily with forests. Rumina, the goddess of nurture, had a sanctuary in the Roman Forum, near which stood a sacred fig-tree (Hornblower and Spawford 2003).

Amerarat is the spirit of immortality and guardian of all plants and trees in the Zoroastrian religion (Rose 1998, 11). Aerico in Albanian folklore is a negative spirit who resides in an old cherry tree. Askafroa is the well-known tree spirit of Nordic and Teutonic folklore and is also known as the Eschenfrau; Bitaboh is believed to be the tree spirit of the Niam Niam people of Gabon; likewise, Co-Tinh and Co-Hon of Vietnamese folklore (Rose 1998, 3, 22, 41, 72). Benign tree spirits include Bariaua of the Melanasian culture and Bisan, the Malaysian camphor-guardian spirit. Frau Wachholder is the female goblin of the juniper tree known in Scandinavian folklore as Hylde-Moer (Rose 1998, 35, 41, 98).

In southern to central Europe, especially "among the Celts of Gaul the Druids esteemed nothing more sacred than mistletoe and the oak on which it grew" (Frazer 1960, 184–185). In the version of the ballad "Glasgerion" (Child 67) printed in Percy's *Reliques* (1765), the eponymous hero swears an oath "by oake and ashe and thorne," which Child suggests is a relic of high antiquity (Child 1965, 2:137).

In Islamic hagiography, trees are believed to shelter the saints. Similarly, saints can come out of tree ashes and saints may grow trees (Gölpinarli 1958, 25, 36, 52).

In other tales, the soul of a man is kept within a tree; when the tree dies, the human being dies. This motif is known as the external soul (E710; AT 303), as in an ancient Egyptian story called "Tale of the Two Brothers." In this story, a man leaves his heart in the flower of an acacia tree and dies when the tree is cut down. Sometimes, however, the action is reversed and a tree will sicken or die as a person does.

In Shakespeare's *The Tempest* (1610–1611), the magician Prospero has rescued the spirit Ariel from inside "a cloven pine" where he was imprisoned by the witch Sycorax, and warns him, "If thou more murmur'st, I will rend an oak / And peg thee in his knotty entrails till / Thou has howled away twelve winters" (1.2. 274–276; Q435, "Magic imprisonment in cleft tree").

MAGIC TREE

Magic trees of all sorts figure in many tales from cultures all over the world, including Danish, Irish, German, Persian, Chinese, Indonesian, Latin American (Quiché), North American (numerous), and African (Zulu, Upoto). In Greek myth, the Hesperides, daughters of Night, have a garden at the western edge of the world. In the garden is a tree with golden apples guarded by a dragon. Heracles's penultimate labor is to fetch these apples, which he tricks Atlas into doing for him. Sometimes magic trees talk (D1610.2, "Speaking tree"): among North American Indian tales, a common motif is D1313.4, "Blinded trickster directed by trees." In the Cinderella cycle of tales, some feature a magic tree from which the heroine alone can pluck fruit (H31.12, "Only one man is able to pluck fruits from tree"). This motif, along with D1648.1.2, "Tree (forest) bows down to holy person (saint)," is exemplified in the ballad "The Cherry Tree Carol" (Child 54), on which the tallest boughs of a cherry tree bend down so that Mary alone may pluck cherries. Child states that it is derived from the Pseudo-Matthew's gospel and that the original story tells of a palm tree; in English versions the tree is a cherry tree and in versions from Catalan and Provençal it is an apple tree (Child 1965, 2:1).

Magic trees figure in the Grimms' tale "The Old Woman in the Wood" (KHM 23; AT 442, *The Old Man in the Forest*). A girl, left alone in the forest, sits beneath a tree and weeps. A white dove flies to her and drops a golden key in her hand, telling her it fits the lock on a great tree nearby, and if she opens it, she will find food. The dove also gives her keys to two other trees, one having clothing inside and the other containing a bed. (F562.2, "Residence in a tree"). Thus, the girl has food, clothing, and shelter provided by the trees. The tale also contains the motif of a man transformed into a tree

(D215, "Transformation: Man to tree"). After a time, the dove asks the girl to go to the house of an old woman and bring back a certain ring, and when she does,

> she leant against a tree and determined to wait for the dove, and, as she thus stood, it seemed just as if the tree was soft and pliant, and was letting its branches down. And suddenly the branches twined around her, and were two arms, and when she looked round, the tree was a handsome man, who embraced and kissed her heartily, and said, "Thou hast delivered me from the power of the old woman, who is a wicked witch. She had changed me into a tree, and every day for two hours I was a white dove. (1968)

Other tales that contain the motif of residence in a tree are Types 450 (*Little Brother and Little Sister;* KHM 11), 706, (The *Maiden Without Hands;* KHM 31) and 710 (*Our Lady's Child;* KHM 3). Type 468, *The Princess on the Sky-Tree,* tells of a tree which reaches the sky and a princess living in its branches. These stories also contain the motif of a king or prince finding a maiden in the woods or actually inside a tree (N711.1). In India we find tales with the motif "Hollow tree as residence for hero" (F811.10.1).

In tales involving supernatural tasks (AT 460–462), the hero is sent on a quest by a king in order to thwart the prophecy that the penniless boy will marry the king's daughter. In the course of his quest, the boy is asked a number of questions, including "Why does not a certain tree flourish?" (H1292.2, "Question (propounded on quest): Why does not a certain tree flourish?"). The answer is either that gold is hidden under it or a serpent is under its roots. In addition to European variants, these tale types are found in China and Japan.

TRANSFORMATION INTO A TREE

Numerous examples of dead lovers whose relationship is thwarted in life, but from whose graves arise plants or trees that twine together (E631, "Reincarnation in plant (tree) growing from grave") occur in Chinese, Papuan, North American Indian (Zuñi, Kato), Latin American (Amazon), African (Kaffir, Ekoi), Indian, Indonesian, Polynesian (Easter Island, Marquesas, Hawaii), and European sources.

Child lists Scandinavian versions of the Scottish ballad "Kemp Owyne" (Child 34) in which a maid transformed into a tree by her stepmother is freed upon being kissed by a man (Child 1965, 1:307).

An unusual example of transformation into a tree is the motif Q338.1, "Request for immortality punished by transformation into tree." Thompson gives numerous examples in his *Tales of North American Indians* (1929, 276).

One of the best-known transformation myths tells of the Greek nymph

"Suddenly the branches twined round her and turned into two arms." The girl has freed the prince from the spell of a witch who had changed him into a tree (Motif D215, "Transformation: man to tree"). From *Little Brother and Little Sister, and Other Tales, by the Brothers Grimm,* illustrated by Arthur Rackham (1917).

Daphne, who, while running away to escape Apollo's importunities, calls upon her father, the river god Peneus, who turns her into a laurel tree (D215.1, "Transformation: man (woman) to laurel"). Throughout the world, there are stories of people being turned into specific trees: ash (D215.3), linden (D215.4), apple (D215.5), mulberry (D215.6), almond (D215.7), mango (D215.8).

The motif of a man transformed into a tree appears in Virgil's *Aeneid* (19 BCE; 3:27–42), Ariosto's *Orlando Furioso* (1516; 6:26–53), and Spenser's *The Faerie Queene* (1596; Book I, ii). In these examples the protagonist of each story discovers that the tree is a transformed man by breaking a bough; it bleeds or the tree cries out.

OTHER LITERARY TREATMENTS OF TREES

In literature the forest often plays an important symbolic role. It is a mysterious, hidden place where magic or sensuality can prevail and where one can be free of the prying eyes of the court or village. The scenes set in the Forest of Arden in Shakespeare's *As You Like It* (written about 1598) immediately come to mind in this context. The forest is also seen as immutable and eternal. Macbeth, in Shakespeare's play of that name (1605–1606), is assured by the witches' apparition that he shall rule until "Great Birnam Wood to high Dunsinane Hill / Shall come against him." Macbeth muses: "That will never be./ Who can impress the forest, bid the tree/ Unfix his earth-bound root?" (4.1:93–96)

In Hawthorne's novel *The Scarlet Letter* (1850), the forest is a refuge where the pariah Hester Prynne can be at one with nature and where she and the minister Dimmesdale can speak frankly of their past and future.

A tree that bears witness to an unlawful love scene is rent by a strike of lightning in Charlotte Brontë's *Jane Eyre* (1847). The Byronic Mr. Rochester asks Jane to marry him in the garden near a great chestnut tree. Not knowing that he cannot legally marry since he is already wed, she assents, and a violent storm comes up. "Before I left my bed in the morning, little Adele came running in to tell me that the great horse-chestnut at the bottom of the orchard had been struck by lightning in the night, and half of it split away" (ch. 23).

Jane Garry and Hande A. Birkalan

REFERENCES

Biedermann, Hans. 2002. *Knaurus Lexikon der Symbole.* München: Droemer Knaur Verlag.

Birkalan, Hande A. 2000. "Geleneksel Türk Sanatı, Kadın ve Yaratıcılık: Nurten Sahin." *Folklor/ Edebiyat* 21: 47–54.

Boratav, Pertev Naili, and Wolfram Eberhard. 1953. *Typen der Türkischen Voksmärchen.* Wiesbaden: Franz Steiner Verlag GbmH.

Brückner, Wolfgang. 1996, "Lebensbaum." In *Enzyklopädie des Märchens,* Band 8:820–824. New York: Walter De Gruyter.

Child, Francis James. 1965 [1882–1898]. *The English and Scottish Popular Ballads.* 5 vols. New York: Dover. Original ed., Houghton Mifflin.

Dixon-Kennedy, Mike. 1997. *European Myth and Legend: An A–Z of People and Places.* Blanford: London.

El-Shamy, Hasan M. 1999. *Tales Arab Women Tell.* Bloomington: Indiana University Press.

Frazer, Sir James. 1960. *The Golden Bough.* New York: Macmillan.

George, Andrew, trans. 1999. *The Epic of Gilgamesh.* London: Penguin.

Gölpınarli, Abdülbaki. 1958. *Menakıb-ı Hacı Bektaş-ı Veli.* Istanbul: Inkılap Kıtabevı.

Grimms' Household Tales. With the Authors' Notes. 1968 [1884]. Trans. Margaret Hunt. 2 vols. Reprint. Detroit: Singing Tree Press. Original ed., London: George Bell.

Hornblower, Simon, and Antony Spawford, eds. 2003. *Oxford Classical Dictionary.* New York: Oxford University Press.

Kunos, Ignácz. 1896. *Turkish Fairy Tales and Folk Tales.* Trans. R. Nisbet Bain. London: Lawrence and Bullen.

Leeming, David, and Margaret Leeming. 1995. *Dictionary of Creation Myths.* New York: Oxford University Press.

Parker, Arthur C. 1912. "Certain Iroquois Tree Myths and Symbols." *American Anthropologist,* n.s., 14 (4): 608–620.

Philpot, J.H. 1897. *The Sacred Tree; or, The Tree in Religion and Myth.* London: Macmillan.

Rose, Carol. 1998. "Spirits Associated with Woods, Trees, and Wood." In *Spirits, Faries, Gnomes, and Goblins: An Encyclopedia of the Little People.* Santa Barbara, CA: ABC-CLIO.

Smith, Sir William. 1958. *Smaller Classical Dictionary.* Rev. ed. New York: Dutton.

Thompson, Stith, ed. 1929. *Tales of the North American Indians.* Bloomington: Indiana University Press.

The Trickster

Various Motifs

❀

The term *trickster,* when used by social scientists, refers to more than simply a deceptive character. Tricksters are destroyers and creators, heroes and villains, often even both male and female (Motif K309§, "Trickster character composed of opposites"; Turner 1972). Many trickster figures, such as Coyote and Maui, are demiurges or culture heroes who provide human beings with necessities such as the sun (usually Motifs A728, "Sun caught in snare," or A1411, "Theft of light"); fire (A1415, "Theft of fire"); and tools for procuring food, such as fishing nets (A1457.3, "Origin of net for fishing") and fish hooks (A1457.1, "Origin of fish hook"). Maui even acts as earth diver (A812, "Earth-diver"), thereby creating the land, in some Oceanic traditions. Although the trickster does things that benefit people, he—most tricksters are male, but see "Female trickster" (Motif J1129§)—is also an impulsive, selfish, even grotesque character who steals food, tricks women into sex, and casually profanes sacred rituals. This duality of character has troubled both scholars and those who tell and hear trickster tales (Radin 1956, 147).

THE TRICKSTER IN THE *MOTIF-INDEX*

Although the trickster is an important concept in *The Motif-Index of Folk Literature,* there is no specific trickster motif. Instead, there are many motifs that describe either who the trickster is or what he does.

Examples of motifs describing who the trickster is include "God as dupe or trickster" (A177.1); "Culture hero as dupe or trickster" (A521); and "Coyote as trickster" (J1117.1). Note that trickster and dupe are equated in two of these motifs; the trickster may be clever, but he also pays for his mischief by often playing the dupe to others' deceptions. Examples of motifs that describe what the trickster does include "Trickster puts on buffalo skull; gets head caught" (J2131.5.1) and "Animals killed by trickster's breaking wind" (F981.3). Both of these examples highlight trickster's role as deceptive fool over his role as creator or culture hero.

The *Motif-Index* was compiled before Paul Radin wrote his important study *The Trickster* and therefore presents a fairly one-dimensional view of the trickster; in fact, when one looks up "trickster" in the index to the *Motif-Index,* one encounters the phrase "Trickster, see also clever person" (817). Although the trickster can be clever, the terms are not truly synonymous. In addition, while the *Motif-Index* admits that some tricksters have animal aspects, these are not generally focused on. Many of the trickster motifs, such as "Trickster masks as doctor and punishes his cheaters" (K1825.1.3), clearly refer to human tricksters.

However, tricksters are usually associated with an animal of some type, and later scholars such as Radin have tended to emphasize the trickster's animal aspects. Among the Native Americans, Coyote (J1117.2, "Coyote as trickster"), Hare, Raven, and Spider are the primary trickster animals. Claude Lévi-Strauss points out that trickster animals are usually carrion eaters and suggests that they therefore mediate between carnivores and herbivores (Lévi-Strauss 1963). This is interesting and serves to remind us that tricksters (and the animals with which they are associated) refuse to fit into standard categories. However, not all trickster animals are carrion eaters; while coyotes and ravens do eat carrion (although not exclusively), spiders and hares do not. Clearly, Lévi-Strauss's observation does not apply to all tricksters or to all trickster animals.

Thompson's only motifs that specify particular animals as tricksters are "Coyote as trickster" (J1117.2) and "Jackal as trickster" (J1117.1), although new motifs specify "Fox as trickster" (J1117.1.1§), "Ass as trickster" (J1117.2§), "Camel as trickster" (J1117.3§), and "Hedgehog [porcupine] as trickster" (J1117.4§). Since Stith Thompson included tales from the northwest coast raven cycle in his *Tales of the North American Indians,* we would expect the *Motif-Index* to include at least "Raven as trickster," but the closest we come is "Raven as culture hero" (A522.2.2).

The trickster's sexual and bodily-based escapades are also inadequately described in the *Motif-Index,* which is notoriously prudish. For example, Wakdjunkaga catches and kills some ducks and, worn out from his exertions, decides to take a nap. He asks his anus to keep watch to make sure no one steals his ducks, but when thieves come it is only able to pass gas. The thieves, undeterred, make off with the trickster's ducks (Radin 1956, 16–17). The

Motif-Index presents this motif as "Buttocks as magic watcher" (D1317.1), which rather sanitizes the story (and diminishes the humor). The trickster's sexual adventures are similarly sanitized; consider "In darkness of night Trickster instead of her chosen lover elopes with girl" (T92.4.3). Although technically accurate (the trickster does accompany the girl instead of the person she intended to elope with), it is misleading; the term *elope* minimizes the deception and arrogance the trickster uses to essentially kidnap the girl. Later motif indexes (such as Hasan El-Shamy's) have been more open about the trickster's bodily and sexual adventures.

Tricksters primarily occur in belief tales such as myths (it is sometimes difficult to distinguish between myth and legend in Native American tales), so Aarne and Thompson's *Types of the Folktale,* which categorizes Märchen and other fictitious folktales, includes few tales that could be considered true trickster tales. There are some Aarne-Thompson tale types that use the term *trickster* (see, for example, Type 1358, *Trickster Surprises Adulteress and Lover*) but in cases like this *trickster* means simply deceptive or clever person. There are, however, many trickster tale types defined in Remedios S. Wycoco's "The Types of North-American Indian Tales (1951)".

THE TRICKSTER'S PSYCHOLOGICAL AND SOCIAL SIGNIFICANCE

Jung and others equate the trickster with the collective shadow, the dark part of a people's (as opposed to an individual's) psyche. Jung describes the shadow as the basest and most animal-like part of the human psyche and believes that it consists of those feelings of guilt and fear that mature individuals repress (Jung 1956). The collective shadow reflects a specific culture's tabus, guilt, and anxieties. Liliane Frey-Rohn notes that a collective shadow figure can be either good or evil (1967, 176), much like the trickster himself. Jung also equates the shadow with a base, animal nature, again like the trickster. This interpretation fits with Radin's belief that the trickster is a primal figure (Radin 1956, xxiii).

Telling and listening to trickster tales therefore serves various social functions. First, telling a trickster tale or enjoying one is a safe outlet for criticizing one's culture and the sacred (Radin 1956, 151ff). It is also cathartic to hear about someone breaking the social taboos that one must obey; in this sense, trickster tales are functionally similar to carnivals (Jung 1956). But these tales are not only subversive; the cultural norms and taboos that the trickster breaks are specifically stated in these tales, so the trickster's punishment reminds the listener of the consequences of breaking taboos. Finally, trickster tales are quite humorous and are generally enjoyed by both the teller and the audience (Radin 1956, xxiv).

THE TRICKSTER AMONG NATIVE NORTH AMERICANS

Radin's *The Trickster* contains a Winnebago tale about the trickster Wakdjunkaga. Wakdjunkaga violates many tabus. First, he decides to go on the warpath, an option not open to the chief of the upper phratrie. (Radin 1956, 114). Then, he ignores his sacred feast and has sex with multiple women, acts that are forbidden to someone about to go on the warpath (116). Finally, Wakdjunkaga avoids his entire responsibility to his tribe and, wandering off on his own, has various typical trickster encounters (described at length in *The Trickster*). Radin analyzes this tale according to its social context and then compares Wakdjunkaga to other Native American tricksters such as Coyote and Raven.

Coyote is the best-known Native American trickster, and tales are told about him by Native tribes located in the American West and Midwest. Coyote is more godlike than many trickster figures; in some traditions, he is instrumental in shaping the land by sending out another being as "Earth diver" (A812). But, in true trickster form, Coyote also often acts as marplot (A60, "Marplot at creation"), interfering with Creator's plans (as in J2186, "Trickster's false creations fail him. A trickster creates man from his excrements"). It is significant that Coyote shapes man out of his excrements; trickster tales often focus on disgusting bodily-based humor, involving trickster's excrements or phallus. There are many tales involving Coyote's appetites, both for food and for sex (Thompson 1946, 319ff).

Among the northwest coast tribes such as the Tlingit, the trickster is Raven. Raven transforms himself into a hemlock needle so that he can both impregnate a chief's wife and be born as her son (T511, "Conception from eating or drinking"). As a baby, he cries and cries until his parents let him play with the box that contains the sun (A721, "Sun kept in a box"), which he eventually steals to place in the sky. This is helpful for his people because it brings light and warmth (Thompson 1929, 19–22). But by choosing to turn himself into an ephemeral hemlock needle instead of something more durable, Raven also brings death to his people (A1335ff, "Origin of death"). Here we see Raven as both a creative and a destructive force in human lives.

THE TRICKSTER IN AFRICA AND THE CARIBBEAN

The Dahomey trickster Legba (along with his Yoruban cognates Elegbara and Eshu) was brought to the Caribbean by African slaves and eventually became important in Haitian and New Orleans voodoo (Leach and Fried 1949,

"Legba"). Eshu teaches human beings how to do Ifa divination, thereby mediating between the divine world and the human world (Hyde 1998, 108ff). Eshu brings cosmic information to humans and, in return, takes the human sacrifice that accompanies Ifa divination back to the gods. Of course, Eshu takes a portion of that sacrifice for himself. But within this system Eshu's goals are subversive; he seeks to mislead people and even to refocus fate for his own designs. Eshu may be a mediator between humans and gods, but he is a self-interested and treacherous one.

Tales about Anansi, the other main African trickster, were also brought to the Caribbean and the new world by African slaves. Anansi is associated with the spider, as is the Native American Inktomi (one of the Siouan tricksters). Tricksters are probably associated with spiders because spiders appear to be clever and treacherous by spinning webs to catch their prey without having to fight. Spiders, like tricksters, are also good at hiding. Anansi tales began in West Africa, but are now a staple in the Caribbean, Surinam, and Curaçao (Leach and Fried 1949, "Anansi" and "Anansesem"). In the Gullah islands he is called Aunt Nancy (clearly etymologically related to Anansi). Anansi does such positive things as steal the sun for mankind, but most of the tales told about him focus on his cleverness and his ability to get out of difficult or dangerous situations.

THE TRICKSTER IN OCEANIA

Maui is the trickster in Polynesia and parts of Melanesia. Born after his mother's unusual conception (T510, "Miraculous conception"), Maui is clearly more than human and less than divine (at the end of the Maui cycle, he actually dies). Maui is credited with fishing up the earth (at great cost to himself: he uses his own blood and the jawbone of an ancestor), snaring the sun, and stealing fire. Maui is fairly benevolent to human beings and generally saves his tricks for the divine world. He even tries to make man immortal, but dies in the attempt (Leach and Fried 1949, "Maui").

THE TRICKSTER IN JAPAN

In Shinto mythology, the trickster Susa-nö-o is the brother of the sun goddess, Amaterasu. He is associated with storms and blamed when rice paddies are damaged or destroyed; he even defecates under his sister's throne (Hyde 1998, 178). But he also helps people; he brings food to human beings by killing the food-goddess, from whose body come rice and grains. Lewis Hyde points out that this myth serves to remind us that life and death are interconnected (179).

THE TRICKSTER IN CHINA

Monkey, the hero of the sixteenth-century Chinese epic that bears his name (Waley 1943, 2, 6) is the primary Chinese trickster. The story relates how Monkey accompanies Tripitaka (a historical person who lived in the seventh century CE), Pigsy (a constantly hungry buffoon), and Sandy on a pilgrimage to India (Waley 1943, 6). On the way they have various ribald, humorous, and sometimes dangerous adventures. In typical trickster fashion, Monkey often extricates them from trouble through cleverness and trickery.

THE TRICKSTER IN INDIA

The Hindu god Krishna, one of the avatars of Vishnu, is most often cited as the Indian trickster. Krishna is a primary character in the Indian epic *The Mahabharata*. Krishna is nicknamed "the butter eater" because, as a child, he refuses to eat the food his mother prepares for him and, after she leaves the house, he steals and eats the butter. There are two primary trickster ideas operating here: first, the desire for food, and second, the refusal to do what one is supposed to do. If Krishna were simply hungry, he could eat the food his mother offers, but, as a trickster, he prefers to eat the rich food he wants on his own terms. As an adult, Krishna is associated with warfare and with dishonesty, but he does save human beings from a flood sent by the angry god Indra (Leach and Fried 1949, "Krishna"). Generally Krishna is more mischievous than dangerous, although he can be both.

THE TRICKSTER IN EUROPE

Some scholars argue that pure trickster figures occur only in Native American tales, African and Caribbean tales, and Oceanic tales, seeing the typical trickster as more human than divine (Makarius 1993). Other scholars would admit that Monkey fits the trickster paradigm, but would resist including Krishna and Susa-nö-o because they are essentially divine beings. Also, Krishna and Susa-nö-o's animal aspects are unimportant (if they are present at all). There is even more controversy about the main suggested tricksters from Europe.

The ancient Greeks had two primary trickster figures: Hermes and Prometheus, and some scholars see trickster elements in Odysseus. Hermes seems to fit the pattern better than Prometheus. Hermes is a charming figure who, in the "Hymn to Hermes," first steals from Apollo and then convinces him to support Hermes's bid for divinity. Hermes is also the god of luck, thieves, and fertility. Hermes is not divine in the same sense that Apollo or

Zeus are; instead, he acts as mediator between humans and the gods (as tricksters often do). But after he is granted divine recognition, Hermes becomes a representative of the Olympian establishment. Once his special status has been acknowledged, he no longer behaves as a subversive trickster; instead, he does what the other gods, particularly Zeus, want him to do (Leach and Fried 1949, "Hermes"). Motifs associated with Hermes include L301, "Hermes distributes wit," and A1461.2, "Origin of lyre. Hermes makes it from a tortoise."

Prometheus is more problematic. He helps mankind by stealing fire for them (A1415, "Theft of fire"), but, like Raven, he also brings death. His creation of Pandora unleashes further ravages upon mankind (F34, "Pandora sent as temptress"; C321, "Tabu: Looking into box. Pandora"). Ultimately, Prometheus's theft of fire so angers Zeus that he chains Prometheus to a mountain. Tricksters may often seem to deserve such eternal punishment, but only two trickster figures actually suffer it: Prometheus and his Norse cognate, Loki.

The Norse god Loki is half giant (giants are the eternal enemies of the Norse gods) and half brother to Odin, the Norse high god. In his creative aspect, Loki helps to create human beings. Loki also has the ability to change his shape, or shapeshift (a frequent trickster motif), becoming a seal, a salmon, and even a mare. As a mare he bears Sleipnir, Odin's eight-legged horse (T465.2, "Foal born of Loki and mythical stallion"). But then Loki takes a darker turn, orchestrating the murder of Balder, the only pure god (K863, "Balder's death"). As punishment for this murder, Loki is bound so that snakes drip poison in his face (Q501.3, "Serpent above Loki continually drops venom in his face"). His patient wife, Sigyn, catches the poison in a bowl, but when she must empty the bowl the poison hits his face, making him writhe in pain and causing earthquakes (A1145, "Earthquakes from movements of subterranean monster"). Loki's binding recalls Prometheus's punishment, and in fact some Indo-European scholars believe that Loki is directly related to Prometheus (Simek 1993, 195). Unlike Prometheus, Loki eventually gets free and leads the giants against the gods at Ragnarok, the cosmic battle at the end of the world (A1070, "Fettered monster's escape at end of world"; A1082.1, "Battle of gods and giants at end of world"). Tales of Loki's evil and binding are clearly influenced by the later Christian identification of Loki and the Devil (tricksters, perhaps because of their profane character, are often equated with the Devil if their original culture is converted to Christianity). In Loki's case, it is unclear how much of his evil was rewritten by Christians and how much was part of pagan Norse tradition.

THE TRICKSTER IN POPULAR CULTURE

Jung wrote that "[t]he trickster is a collective shadow figure, an epitome of all the inferior traits of character in individuals. And since the individual shadow is never absent as a component of personality, the collective figure can construct itself out of it continually. Not always, of course, as a mythological figure" (Jung 1956, 209). So we find the trickster in modern literature and television.

In the 1960s, Hugo and Nebula award-winning science fiction writer Roger Zelazny wrote an intriguing short story, called "Love Is an Imaginary Number," that equated Prometheus and Loki. The best-selling fantasy novel *American Gods,* by Neil Gaiman (2001), includes several trickster figures (often working at cross-purposes), including Anansi, Whiskey Jack (etymologically related to Wakdjunkaga), and Loki. Television also offers many examples of tricksters. Bugs Bunny is perhaps the best example; he is a rabbit (or hare, one of the major Native American trickster animals) with considerable appetites (he is usually pictured with a carrot in his mouth, and he is willing to go to great lengths to find a woman) who often dresses as a woman, is very clever, and, at the same time, keeps getting himself into tight spots. Wily E. Coyote, with his elaborate (but ultimately unsuccessful) plans to catch the roadrunner in the Roadrunner cartoons, represents the trickster as irrepressible dupe. Many American children and adults enjoy these cartoons without ever realizing that they are seeing into the mythic realm of the trickster.

Esther Clinton

REFERENCES

Aarne, Antti, and Stith Thompson. 1964. *The Types of the Folktale: A Classification and Bibliography.* Helsinki: Suomalainen Tiedeakatemia.

El-Shamy, Hasan. 1995. *Folk Traditions of the Arab World: A Guide to Motif Classification.* 2 vols. Bloomington: Indiana University Press.

Frey-Rohn, Liliane. 1967. "Evil from the Psychological Point of View." In *Evil: Studies in Jungian Thought,* ed. Curatorium of the C.G. Jung Institute. Trans. Ralph Manheim and Hildegard Nagel. Evanston, IL: Northwestern University Press.

Gaiman, Neil. 2001. *American Gods.* New York: Harper Collins.

Hyde, Lewis. 1998. *Trickster Makes This World: Mischief, Myth, and Art.* New York: Farrar, Straus and Giroux.

Jung, C.G. 1956. "On the Psychology of the Trickster Figure." In *The Trickster: A Study in American Indian Mythology,* ed. Paul Radin. New York: Schoeken Books.

Kerényi, Karl. 1956. "The Trickster in Relation to Greek Mythology." In *The Trickster: A Study in American Indian Mythology,* ed. Paul Radin. New York: Schoeken Books.

Leach, Maria, and Jerome Fried, eds. 1949. *Standard Dictionary of Folklore, Mythology, and Legend.* San Francisco: Funk and Wagnalls.

Lévi-Strauss, Claude. 1963. *Structural Anthropology.* Trans. Claire Jacobson. 2 vols. New York: Basic Books.

Makarius, Laura. 1993. "The Myth of the Trickster: The Necessary Breaker of Taboos." In *Mythical Trickster Figures: Contours, Contexts, and Criticisms,* ed. William J. Hynes and William C. Doty. Tuscaloosa: University of Alabama Press.

Radin, Paul. 1956. *The Trickster: A Study in American Indian Mythology.* New York: Schocken Books.

Simek, Rudolf. 1993. *Dictionary of Northern Mythology.* Trans. Angela Hall. Cambridge; Rochester, NY: D.S. Brewer.

Thompson, Stith. 1929. *Tales of the North American Indians.* Bloomington: Indiana University Press.

————. 1946. *The Folktale.* Berkeley: University of California Press.

Turner, Victor. 1972. "Myth and Symbol." In *International Encyclopedia of the Social Sciences.* ed. David Sills. New York: Macmillan and the Free Press.

Waley, Arthur, trans. 1943. *Monkey: Folk Novel of China by Wu Ch'eng En.* New York: John Day.

Wycoco, Remedios S. 1951. "The Types of North-American Indian Tales." PhD diss., Indiana University.

Zelazny, Roger. 2001. "Love Is an Imaginary Number." *The Doors of His Face, the Lamps of His Mouth.* New York: ibooks.

Union of Opposites, or Coniunctio Oppositorum

Various Motifs

Coniunctio oppositorum (hence, *coniunctio*) is a term C.G. Jung used to designate "union of opposites" (Jung 1970, 167). Jung's own writings about the *coniunctio* were inspired largely by his copious researches into alchemy, a medieval school of speculative chemistry concerned with fusions and separation of different substances (including the possibility of liberating gold from base metals). His writings about alchemy illustrate one of the perennial problems of defining archetypes and motifs—specifically, that archetypes and motifs can be defined at different levels of abstraction. In his great synthesis about alchemy, *Mysterium Coniunctionis,* Jung sometimes speaks as if the general pattern of the *coniunctio*—the "union of opposites"—is itself an archetype.

> What the union of opposites really "means" transcends human imagination. Therefore the worldly-wise can dismiss such a "fantasy" without further ado. . . . But that doesn't help us much, for we are dealing with an eternal image, an archetype, from which man can turn away his mind for a time but never permanently. (Jung 1970, 167)

At other moments, however, Jung speaks of *coniunctio* as a general psychic pattern or structure, as if reserving the term *archetype* for more specific images or motifs, such as hermaphroditism. Finally, Jung sometimes provides lists of recurrent contrasts that he treats less as archetypes in themselves than as ingredients or associations typically drawn into specific motifs of *coniunctio*.

However, we do not yet know enough to resolve the dilemmas posed by different orders of abstraction in defining archetypes. Emphasizing only the more general notion of *coniunctio* could leave us lost in abstraction, while emphasizing only specific motifs could blind us to the possibility of a deeper metaphysics of *coniunctio*—which is Jung's big point. The best course for the present would seem to be to allow both possibilities, even though it implies the necessity of defining archetypes at very different levels of generality.

Although Thompson's *Motif-Index* does not assign an independent motif for the general theme of "opposites," numerous examples of the occurrence of the theme in the folk traditions of various national groups are found in that work. Among such motifs are "Opposition of good and evil gods" (A106); "Earlier universe opposite of present. Everything in the earlier world was the reverse of the present world" (A633); "Opposite of present. Everything on the earth—courses of rivers, height of mountains, human reproduction, etc.—are at first the reverse of the present condition" (A855).

Another term denoting opposites that frequently recurs in Thompson's *Motif-Index* is *contrasts*. Thus, we find such motifs as "Two brothers as contrasts" (P251.5.4); "Peasant and his wife in hut near castle (palace) as contrasts to king and queen" (P411.1.1); "Wealth and poverty" (U60); "Justice and injustice" (U10); and "Contrasting qualities found in otherworld garden" (F162.1.2).

A critical facet of the concept of opposites is the perceived inherent interconnectedness or union between opposites (Motif U20§). This union constitutes a new affective entity that is greater than mere elaboration of either component. For Jung, the "union of opposites" designates a general pattern found in many myths as well as other human mental products such as rituals, social structures, and philosophical and sociological treatises. In most general terms, *coniunctio* refers to the idea that opposites attract and combine to make up wholes greater than the sum of the opposing parts. But the connotations of *coniunctio* as used by Jung and other scholars are frequently even stronger than this: *coniunctio* sometimes implies, for example, that any given entity contains within itself its own opposite. It is interesting to note that while some myths do seem to assume that entities can contain their own opposites, other, more pragmatically inclined branches of folk wisdom insist on an antithetical principle—a discreteness of essences. For example, proverbs that tell us that we should not or cannot squeeze blood from turnips, make silk purses from sow's ears, or make mountains from molehills seem to discourage thinking in terms of possible radical interpenetration of contrastive substances (Motif J2219.3§, "Foolishness of seeking an object (service) at an illogical source" (El-Shamy 2004).

Jung provides a list of opposites at the very opening of *Mysterium Coniunctionis:* cold/warm, upper/lower, spirit/body, heaven/earth, fire/water, bright/dark, active/passive, volatile/solid, precious/common, good/evil, open/hidden, east/west, living/dead, masculine/feminine, sun/moon. These opposites are expressed in such motifs as "Material of which angels are created (fire, water, and snow)" (A52.3), from Jewish traditions; "Conflict of good and evil creators" (A50), from Jewish, Hindu, and Persian traditions; and "Opposition of good and evil gods" (A106), from Hindu, Mexican Indian, South American Indian, and Jewish traditions. Also, other major motif divisions with numerous submotifs reflect oppositions, as in the cases of "Nature of the upper world" (A660) and "Nature of the lower world" (A670); "Sweet and bitter fountain in otherworld garden" (F162.1.2.1); "Objects on one side of palisade in otherworld garden black, on other white" (F162.1.2.3); and "Soul leaves or enters the body" (E720) from Irish myths (Cross 1952).

Similarly, the notion that good and evil, truth and falsehood, and so on, are interdependent opposites is reported as part of the emergence of early religious systems. In ancient Egypt, for example, mythical accounts such as "The Blinding of Truth by Falsehood" illustrate this point. According to this allegorical narrative dating back to the New Kingdom, Dynasties 18–20 (1554–1085 BC), Truth is presented as a male who is blinded by the gods at his brother Falsehood's instigation. At the end of the story, Truth is rescued and vindicated by his son, and Falsehood is punished—but *not* destroyed. Referring to this text and other similar narratives, Egyptologist Edward F. Wente concludes:

> In none of these myths or stories is the antagonist totally annihilated, but rather a resolution is effected so that a harmonious situation is achieved with the elimination of further strife. Such a resolution of conflicting opposites is typically Egyptian and reflects the application of the principle of *Maat,* which embraces the concepts of balance and harmony as well as truth. (Wente 1972, 127)

This principle has been designated as Motif A1100.1§, "Balance and harmony as well as truth': The *Maat-* (*Mayat*)-principle of world order"; Type 613B§, *Council of Judges (Gods) Rules in Error (The Judgment of the Ennead): The Lost Or Damaged Item* (El-Shamy 1995, 2004).

In Semitic religions, good and evil, truth and falsehood, the holy and the profane, are depicted in the concepts of God and Satan. It is virtually impossible to think of one without recalling the other. This mentifact is characteristic of the patterns of thinking of the typical believer. According to sacred religious dogma, God is eternal while Satan has existed as the embodiment of evil since his fall from grace and will continue to exist until the end of time (i.e., semi-eternally).

CONIUNCTIO IN LITERATURE AND THEATER

A literary verse in the *Arabian Nights* illustrates this archetypal trait of "union of opposites." As translated from the Arabic by Richard Burton the verse reads: "Two contraries and both occur in opposite charm. / And charm so contraired by contrast lovelier show" (Burton 1894, 4:20). An alternate translation by El-Shamy reads: "Two opposites were united in diversity of glamour / An entity's beauty would be manifested [only] by its opposite" (*Alf laylah wa laylah* 2:143). The motifs here are U103§, "Contrasts are drawn to each other ('Opposites attract')," and U103.0.1§, "The beauty of an entity (object) is brought out by its opposite" (El-Shamy 2004).

In a more intricate context, Shakespeare's *A Midsummer Night's Dream* (written about 1595) may be seen as incorporating the *coniunctio* principle. The play, set in "a wood outside Athens," is a comedy in which forest spirits meddle in the love affairs of humans, and the setting itself is a player in the comedy. As Katherine B. Perrault in a recent study notes, "The symbolism of the *coniunctio* is in essence a transcendent, ideal view of the world. In *Midsummer,* it marries the natural with the spiritual (as well as pagan [i.e., Dionysian rites] and Christian [i.e., marriage rites]), integrating the physical microcosm and macrocosm, as well as the inner and outer psyche in a tenuous, synergistic balance of opposites" (Perrault 2003). Thus, we see several of Jung's pairs of united opposites animating the play's physical setting as well as its main protagonists from the two opposite worlds: humans and spirits (cf. AT 480, discussed below).

CONIUNCTIO IN FOLKLORE

In a North African folktale, a virtuous wife comments on the attractiveness of a black object on a white one (dark henna on her white hand). Her statement triggers suspicion and jealousy in her husband, who accuses her of infidelity with a black lover and punishes her. This theme is designated as Motifs U103.1§, "Black and white attract (each other)"; U103.1.1§, "A female's casual remark that 'black on white' looks pleasing causes accusation of (interracial) unchastity" (El-Shamy 2004). With reference to this theme, folktales (and elite literature) are replete with situations in which a crazed husband murders or disfigures his wife because of her involvement with a black paramour—for example, AT 1511, *The Faithless Queen* (Wife prefers loathsome paramour).

Another example of the interdependence of opposites may be found in the many tales in which kindness and unkindness are contrasted (Motif Q2, "Kind and unkind"; AT 480, *The Spinning Women by the Spring. The Kind and Unkind*

Girls). An important variation on this tale-type depicting sibling rivalry among stepsisters presents a "balanced view toward various objects in one's environment . . . ; thus things that are typically viewed as evil are still accorded some positive value" (El-Shamy 1995, 255–262). The tale type also highlights the role such a realization of "balance" between opposites plays in the process of individuation. According to an oral text from the Western Desert of Egypt, a woman sends her own daughter, whom she pampers, and her stepdaughter, whom she maltreats, on an errand to acquire a household utensil from the ogress. The encounter with *coniunctio* occurs when the persecuted stepdaughter (the heroine) plays the role of mediator between conflicting pairs. The tale goes as follows:

> She went down the road to the house of Mother Ogress. On her way she saw two date palm trees, a male and a female, quarreling: the female would say [narrator speaks in a tone denoting contention], "I am the female. I bear fruit!" Then the male would retort, "No, I am the male. I am better!" When they saw her, they asked her, "Who is better, I, the female, or he, the male?" She replied [narrator speaks in a conciliatory tone], "You are the female; you yield fruit that is good for us, and he is the male that yields pollen that we use to make you bear fruit. You can't do without him, and he would be worthless without you!" When the two palm trees heard that they said to her [in a tone denoting contentment], "Go, May God make our length in your hair and not in your legs!" So her hair became long.
>
> After a while she met two birds—a [white] she-dove and a raven—quarreling; the she-dove would say, "I am better than you are!" and the raven would say, "No! I am better than you are!" She said to them, "You, she-dove, are good, and he, the raven, is also good! White is fine, like milk; black is also fine; without the black [pupils] of the eye, we would not be able to see! You, [she-dove] give us baby chicks to eat, and you [raven] clean up the place [by eating rats and dead animals]. So, you are good and he is good." The she-dove said to her, "Go. May God make my whiteness in your face, not in your hair!" And the raven said, "Go. May God make my blackness in your hair, not in your face!" [Thus, her face became white and her hair black].
>
> She continued [going] down the road. She met two—a rose and a bee arguing. The rose would say, "I am better!" and the bee would retort, "No, I am better." She said to them, "You, the rose, are red and fragrant, and you, the bee, give us sweet honey!" The rose said to her, "May God make my redness in your cheeks and not in your eyes!" And the bee said, "May God make my honey ['s sweetness] in your mouth [words], and my sting not in your tongue!"
>
> Then she came to two threshing grounds; one was a sesame threshing ground, while the other was . . . . safflower! They also were quarreling. She reconciled the two of them. The sesame and the safflower said to her, "Take

some [sesame] from me," "Take some of my safflower oil." [She uses these objects later to appease the ogress.]

That was it, of course, she became beautiful, with long black hair, white complexion, black eyes, rosy cheeks and a honey-dripping tongue.

[She also marries the prince and moves away from her cruel stepmother.]

(El-Shamy 1999, 257–258)

By contrast, the pampered daughter fails to comprehend the merits of opposites and sees things in a limited way: either good or evil. She is punished for her social and spiritual immaturity, remaining unwed and attached to her mother. Consequently, it may be argued, the girl who recognizes the merits of the "union of opposites" undergoes the process of individuation successfully: she achieves beauty, recognition, and other social and personal rewards accorded prominent individuals. Conversely, her stepsister fails to be individuated and remains a burdensome dependent on her mother.

From this perspective, the key motifs in this account are U280§, "Balance between merits and demerits, advantages and disadvantages, good and evil"; U280.1§, "Everything found to have merit"; U281.2§, "Merits and demerits of gender (female, male)"; U281.1§, "Merits and demerits of color (black, white)"; and J1030.1§, "Maturity (growing up, independence, 'individuation') gained by leaving home" (El-Shamy 1995; 1999, 257–258).

CONCLUSION

In considering explanations of why the *coniunctio* pattern exists, one confronts a difference of emphasis between traditional religious accounts and those of modern secular thinkers. The religious traditions in which the symbolism of *coniunctio* figure prominently tend to offer top-down explanations: *coniunctio* patterns in the details of human life are seen as particular manifestations or emanations of those patterns as they exist in the character of the demiurge or as the deepest principles of the cosmos as a whole (for example, when the demiurge is of dual nature or perhaps a twin deity). Modern secular thinkers, by contrast, tend to offer a bottom-up approach, seeing the *coniunctio* patterns found in traditional, mythic cosmologies as projections of concrete human experiences.

For example, because human bodies are approximately symmetrical in form, perhaps we project this immediate experience of dualism—or, more precisely, of dualism within unity—onto the cosmos as a whole (see especially Hertz 1978). The Durkheimian school of sociology has particularly enlivened this theme of cosmological projection: in addition to Hertz's arguments about the body, Durkheim and Mauss (1972) focus on the cosmological projection of social structures based on paired moieties (see also Ortiz 1969), while gender dualism figures importantly in Mauss's (1967) analysis of the ways in which gender oppositions in ritual and economic exchange shape social custom and cosmological speculation.

Moreover, in psychoanalytic literature on ambivalence, in the structuralist focus on oppositions and their mediation, and in Marxist interest in Hegelian metaphysics, one encounters statements as much imbued with the idea of the union of opposites as anything found in traditional mythology—for example, the claim of Marx and Engels (1970, 131): "Production is thus at the same time consumption, and consumption is at the same time production. Each is simultaneously its opposite." The fervent archetypalist thus might regard it as ultimately arbitrary, even though practically necessary, to limit the study of the *coniunctio* theme to traditional folk narratives.

These seemingly esoteric Marxian and similar theses are not unique to elite academic circles. They do have older counterparts in folk cultures based on folkloric behavior. As argued: "There are indications that such psychological (and sociological) concepts . . . do appear in folk expressions as a matter of *empirical observation,* and that they can be of significant classificatory (indexing) usefulness" (El-Shamy 1995, xiii–xiv; emphasis added). A folk truism from Egypt reveals that the folk view consumption and production as constituting a "union of opposites": "Were it not for breakage, kilns (pottery-making) would not exist" (designated as Motif P775.3.0.1§ under the economic institution of "Consumption: an economic necessity" (P775.3§).

Hasan El-Shamy and Gregory Schrempp

See also: Good and Evil; Hermaphroditism; Individuation.

REFERENCES

Aarne, Antti, and Stith Thompson. 1964. *The Types of the Folktale: A Classification and Bibliography.* FFC, no. 184. Helsinki: Suomalainen Tiedeakatemia.

Alf laylah wa laylah. n.d. 4 vols. Cairo: Maktabat al-Jumhûriyyah al-¿Arabiyyah.

Burton, Richard F., ed. and trans. 1894. *Arabian Nights: The Book of the Thousand Nights and a Night.* London: H.S. Nichols.

Cross, Tom P. 1952. *Motif-Index of Early Irish Literature.* Bloomington: Indiana University Press.

Durkheim, Émile H., and Marcel Mauss. 1972. *Primitive Classification.* Chicago: University of Chicago Press.

El-Shamy, Hasan. 1980. *Folktales of Egypt: Collected, Translated and Annotated with Middle Eastern and African Parallels.* Chicago: University of Chicago Press.

———. 1995. *Folk Traditions of the Arab World: A Guide to Motif Classification.* 2 vols. Bloomington: Indiana University Press.

———, ed. and trans. 1999. *Tales Arab Women Tell, and the Behavioral Patterns They Portray.* Bloomington: Indiana University Press.

———. 2004. *Types of the Folktale in the Arab World: A Demographically Oriented Type-Index.* Bloomington: Indiana University Press.

Hertz, R. 1978. "The Pre-eminence of the Right Hand." In *Right and Left,* ed. R. Needham, Chicago: University of Chicago Press.

Jung, C.G. 1970. *Mysterium Coniunctionis: An Inquiry into the Separation and Synthesis of Psychic Opposites in Alchemy.* Trans. R.F.C. Hull. Princeton, NJ: Princeton University Press.

Marx, K., and F. Engels. 1970. *The German Ideology.* London: Lawrence & Wishart.

Mauss, M. 1967. *The Gift.* New York: W.W. Norton.

Ortiz, A. 1969. *The Tewa World.* Chicago: University of Chicago Press.

Perrault, Katherine B. 2003. "Astronomy, Alchemy, and Archetypes: An Integrated View of Shakespeare's *A Midsummer Night's Dream,*" www.cgjungpage.org/content/view/367/0/1/5.

Simpson, William Kelly, ed. 1972. *The Literature of Ancient Egypt.* New Haven, CT: Yale University Press.

Wente, Edward F. 1972. "The Blinding of Truth by Falsehood." In *The Literature of Ancient Egypt,* ed. W.K. Simpson, 127–132. New Haven, CT: Yale University Press.

Water

Various Motifs

❀

The vast role of water in the world's stories is reflected in the very large number of motifs devoted to it. These motifs are found throughout various chapters of the *Motif-Index.*

The symbolism of water is ambivalent: on the one hand, it animates and creates; on the other hand, it functions as a symbol of destruction (E82, "Water of life and death. One water kills, the other restores to life"). While water is perceived as the source of life on earth and necessary for its sustenance, it is also where the sun sets down in order to give warmth during the night to the realm of the dead. A common motif in the journey to the underworld is the crossing of a body of water. In Greek myth, the dead are ferried across the river Styx to reach Hades. The gods sometimes take oaths by the river Styx, pouring out the water from a cup as they do. Wayland Hand notes that the idea of the dead crossing a river or a body of water is perceived as a safe way to keep them from coming back to plague the living (Hand 1983, 7).

In *Gilgamesh,* originally a Sumerian story and reworked over 2,000 years, the hero undertakes a journey to the otherworld, actually an earthly paradise at the confluence of two rivers, which involves crossing a body of water—"the waters of death"—with the help of a boatman. Gilgamesh is warned by the possibly divine tavern keeper Siduri that "none from the beginning of days has been able to cross the sea. . . . / Painful is the crossing, troublesome the road, / And everywhere the waters of death stream across its face" (10.2.24–25).

Beautiful rivers, fountains, and streams are prominent fixtures in descriptions of earthly paradises. Four rivers flow from the Garden of Eden. The Old Testament prophet Isaiah speaks of the need to bring water to the barren lands

Beautiful rivers, fountains, and streams are prominent fixtures in descriptions of earthly paradises. From *Hypnerotomachia Poliphili* (1499).

of Israel: "I will open rivers in high places, and fountains in the midst of the valleys: I will make the wilderness a pool of water, and the dry land springs of water" 41:18–20.

CREATION MYTHS

Creation myths universally describe how various bodies of water came into being. In the Mythological Motifs section of the *Motif-Index,* under Cosmogony and Cosmology, Creation of the Earth, there is a section devoted to water features, A910–949. What we now know as scientific fact—that life started in the oceans—the ancients seemed to know intuitively. The Greeks considered Oceanus—water—as the great cosmic power through which all life grows, represented in mythology as a benign old god. Oceanus is a primal river encircling the globe, giving rise to all other rivers.

Creation myths of cultures around the globe contain a story of a deluge as a world calamity (A1010, "Deluge. Inundation of whole world or section"). The myths of many cultures have gods and goddesses devoted to water realms, for example A421, "Sea-god"; A427.1, "Goddesses of springs and wells"; A421.1, "Sea-goddess." Both the Greeks and the Romans attributed a prophetic power to springs, such as the ancient one at Delphi. In Norse mythology, the spring of Mimir at the base of Yggdrasil, the world tree, is an example of holy water. (Lindahl, McNamara, and Lindow 2000, 2:1029).

THE WATER OF LIFE

Water of life (E80, "Water of Life. Resuscitation by water") is a well-known motif around the world. The water, generally believed to be found in a far-off lake, spring, or well, has the power to restore youth. The search for this water is a motif in numerous stories (H1321.1, "Quest for healing water"), and the tale type in which it occurs is AT 551, *The Sons on a Quest for a Wonderful Remedy for Their Father.* In the version which the Grimms collected, "The Water of Life" (*Das Wasser des Lebens,* KHM 97), a sick king can be cured only by the water of life, and his three sons set out one at a time to find it. The story encompasses the motif of the kind and unkind (Q2), since the two older brothers are rude to a dwarf along the way, who then enchants them, but the youngest son is kind to him, and the dwarf directs him to the water. After a series of adventures, the youngest brother obtains the water of life, cures his father, and marries an enchanted princess.

In the Babylonian tradition, the goddess Ishtar descends to the underworld, searching for Tammuz in order to restore him with the water of life. However, she, too, has to be given fresh living water before her ascent to the upper world (Van der Toorn et al. 1999, 867).

In folktales, people often enter a lower world through a hole, spring, or cavern (F92), or a well (F93.0.2.1). In the Grimms' tale "Frau Holle" (AT 480, *The Spinners by the Well*), a mistreated stepdaughter who is made to spin every day by a well drops her shuttle in when she is washing her blood from it, and "in the sorrow of her heart she jumped into the well to get the shuttle. She lost her senses; and when she awoke and came to herself again, she was in a lovely meadow where the sun was shining and many thousands of flowers were growing" (*Grimms' Household Tales* 1968, 79).

An analogous tale told by the Chaga of Africa also has the motif of entering the underworld through water. A girl, in despair of her parents' anger, jumps into a pool. She too sinks down until she comes to the underworld.

There are magic wells (D926), magic springs (D927), and magic fountains (D925) in folklore throughout the world. Wells may also be the portal to fairyland (F212.1, "Fairyland entered through well") or provide a channel of communication between the world of the living and the world of the dead. Mysterious helpers and the shades of the departed may be met at wells. In the Chinese tale "Husband and Wife in This Life and the Life to Come," a man who sets out to find his dead wife is told he must wait for her by a well (Eberhard 1965, 31). In another Chinese tale, "The Water Mother," a poor woman is compelled to work day and night and fetch water several times a day from a distant well. She sits down at the edge of the well and speaks aloud about throwing herself down into it. "Suddenly an old white-haired woman appeared, who motioned her back, saying, "Why do you want to die?" The old woman gives her a magic wand and tells her that all she need do to have water is strike the pail once, and only once, with the rod, and never tell anyone else about it" (Eberhard 1965, 112–113).

IN LITERATURE

The historical and belief legend of Alexander is rich in motifs related to water. El-Shamy notes these motifs as the following: D1338.1.2, "Water of youth"; H1376.7, "Quest for immortality"; H1321.3, "Quest for the water of youth." An example is the legend of Iskendername, in the Ottoman court literature. El-Shamy notes that this legend shows similarities to the Babylonian epic *Gilgamesh*, including the "hero's invincibility, his search for immortality, the discovery of precious stones in the dark part of the earth, the plant (or water) of immortality, the acquisition of the plant (or water) of immortality by an animal or person who was not originally interested in it, and the hero's inevitable death and the perpetual life of the creature who got the plant or water" (El-Shamy 1980, 272).

In the *hikaye* (oral tale performance) tradition in Anatolia (Turkey), the quest for the water of life motif appears in the *Köroğlu* epic from the fifteenth century. Köroğlu (son of the blind) is a victorious bandit who rebels against the feudal authority. Köroğlu's horse drinks from a spring, which happens to be the fountain of youth. Once the fountain of youth is not a secret anymore, it disappears (Boratav 1984, 68–69). Köroğlu's father describes such a fountain and recites a chapter from the Qur'an, and then one star from the east and one from the west conjoin. Köroğlu sets off in that direction in order to find the fountain and get the curing water to open the eyes of the old blind man (D1505.5, "Magic water restores sight") (Boratav 1984, 81).

Plunging the sick into water (E80.1, "Resuscitation by bathing") has been a widely known cultural practice in the world in order to obtain a kind of a blessing or cure from water. In Islam, too, the ritual washing is also a symbolically purifying ritual. For ablution, where water is missing (in the desert), one may use clean sand instead. In a ritual reminiscent of the symbolic value of baptism in Christianity, the bodies of the deceased are washed according to religious rules in both Islam and Judaism, in order to cleanse the dead from their sins. In ancient Greece, "in the so-called 'Orphic' texts . . . the soul is 'parched with thirst' and wants to drink the water of Memory; in the eschatological myths of Plato and Virgil, the souls drink the water of Oblivion" (Hornblower and Spawford 2003).

Hande A. Birkalan and Jane Garry

REFERENCES

Aarne, Antti, and Stith Thompson. 1964 [1961]. *The Types of the Folktale: A Classification and Bibliography.* Helsinki: Suomalainen Tiedeakatemia.

Asad, Muhammad. 1980. *The Message of the Koran.* Gibraltar: Dar Al-Andalus.

Boratav, Pertev Naili. 1984 [1931]. *Köroğlu.* Istanbul: Adam Yayinlari.

Boratav, Pertev Naili, and Wolfram Eberhard. 1953. *Typen der Türkischer Volksmärchen.* Wiesbaden: Franz Steiner Verlag GmbH.

Chauvin, Victor. 1902. *Bibliographie des ouvrages arabes ou relatifs aux arabes, publiés dans l'Europe chrétienne de 1810 à 1885, 5:6.* Liège: H. Vaillant-Carmanne.

Eberhard, Wolfram. 1965. *Folktales of China.* Chicago: University of Chicago Press.

El-Shamy, Hasan M., ed. 1980. *Folktales of Egypt.* Chicago: University of Chicago Press.

Epic of Gilgamesh, 2001. Trans. and ed. Benjamin R. Foster. *The Sumerian Gilgamesh Poems* trans. Douglas Frayne. *The Hittite Gilgamesh* trans. Gary Beckman. New York: W.W. Norton.

Gölpınârli, Abdülbaki. 1958. *Menakıb-ı Hacı Bektaş-ı Veli.* Istanbul: Inkılap Kıtabevı.

Gray, John. 1985 [1982]. *Near Eastern Mythology.* Rev. ed. New York: P. Bedrick Books.

Grimms' Household Tales. With the Authors' Notes. 1968 [1884] Trans. Margaret Hunt. 2 vols. Detroit: Singing Tree Press. Original ed., London: George Bell.

Hand, Wayland. 1983. *Boundaries, Portals, and Other Magical Spots in Folklore.* London: Folklore Society.

Hornblower, Simon, and Antony Spawford, eds. 2003. *Oxford Classical Dictionary.* New York: Oxford University Press.

Jones, Allison. 1995. *Larousse Dictionary of World Folklore.* New York: Larousse.

Leach, Maria, and Jerome Fried, eds. 1949. *Funk and Wagnalls Standard Dictionary of Folklore, Mythology, and Legend.* New York: Funk and Wagnalls.

Lindahl, Carl, John McNamara, and John Lindow, eds. 2000. *Medieval Folklore: An Encyclopedia of Myths, Legends, Tales, Beliefs, and Customs.* Santa Barbara, CA: ABC-CLIO.

Nigg, Joe. 1995. *Wonder Beasts: Tales and Lore of the Phoenix, the Griffin, the Unicorn, and the Dragon.* Englewood, CO: Libraries Unlimited.

Özkirimli, Atilla. 1987 [1982]. "Ab-i Hayat." In *Türk edebiyati ansiklopedisi,* 5:1, 23. 4th ed. Istanbul: Cem Yayinevi.

Toorn, Karel van der, et al. 1999. *Dictionary of Deities and Demons in the Bible.* Brill: Leiden.

Index